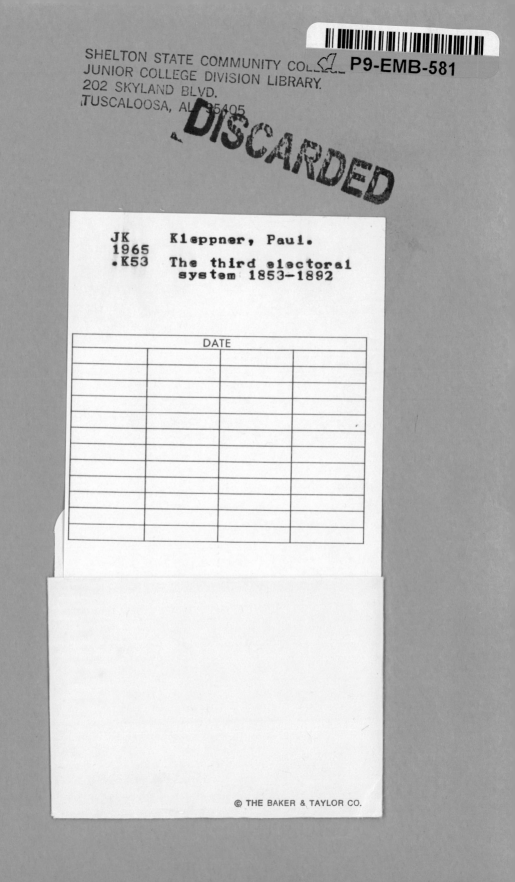

JK
1965
.K53

Kleppner, Paul.

The third electoral
system 1853-1892

DATE		

The Third Electoral System, 1853–1892

The Third Electoral System, 1853–1892

Parties, Voters, and Political Cultures

by Paul Kleppner

The University of North Carolina Press / Chapel Hill

Library of Congress Cataloging in Publication Data

Kleppner, Paul.
  The third electoral system, 1853–1892.

  Bibliography: p.
  Includes index.
  1. Elections—United States—History.   2. Voting—
United States—History.   3. United States—Politics and
government—19th century.   I. Title.
JK1965.K53   324'.2   78-7949
ISBN 0-8078-1328-1

Both the initial research and the publication of this work were made possible
in part through grants from the National Endowment of the Humanities, a
federal agency whose mission is to award grants to support education, scholar-
ship, media programming, libraries, and museums, in order to bring the
results of cultural activities to a broad, general public.

For my mother

Contents

Maps

Tables

Preface

This book constitutes the second installment of my continuing effort to analyze the social bases of American mass political behavior. The first was a monograph that analyzed the political realignment of 1893–96 in the Midwest—especially in the states of Michigan, Ohio, and Wisconsin.[1] Future works will explore the social bases of partisanship and participation during the fourth party system, the social and political preconditions of minor-party voting, and the impact of realigning sequences on both recruitment of elites and subsequent transformations in policy.

The present book presents a description and analysis of mass voting behavior over the course of this nation's third electoral era (1853–92). In part, the research was designed to fill a gap in knowledge to which I had drawn attention earlier.[2]

Historians have devoted considerable attention to the story of late nineteenth-century politics. Yet their studies typically have not included careful and detailed explorations of the patterns of mass voting behavior. And even less intellectual energy has been expended to analyze the social and attitudinal bases of that behavior. These omissions are especially curious for at least two reasons. First, officeholding, and therefore the capacity of elites to shape policy directly, depended ultimately on electoral success. Second, the era was marked by high levels of participation by citizens in electoral politics. Although late nineteenth-century party battles may appear vacuous and vapid to most historians, to most involved contemporaries election results mattered. And high voter turnout provides stark evidence of that broadly diffused sense of concern and involvement.

Yet despite its inherent substantive and theoretical potential, until the past decade or so political historians have not paid much attention to analyses of voting behavior. Widespread commitment to a "letristic method" accounts for that neglect, for that method, no less than any other, predetermines the types of evidence that will be examined and,

1. Paul Kleppner, *The Cross of Culture*.
2. Kleppner, *Cross of Culture*, p. 7.

therefore, the range of descriptive and analytical questions that can be posed.[3] Those who apotheosize such a method and abjure the use of relevant quantitative evidence are compelled either to treat incidentally or to ignore entirely some areas of research. Unhappily, exclusive reliance on a letristic method, in my judgment, has produced a political history preoccupied with themes that at best are systemically tangential. At the same time it has deflected investigative attention away from the important questions that bear on the essence both of the operation of the political process and of the nature of past society.

An analysis of voting behavior combined with the use of relevant letristic evidence enables historians to address systemically critical questions. Which census categories—e.g., farmers, laborers, Germans, Irish, Baptists, Catholics, etc.—*behaved* politically as social groups? Which sets of political and social conditions enhanced, and which eroded, the political cohesiveness of a group? How, if at all, did the political culture of a group attain partisan bearings? How did party auras begin to resonate emotionally with the dispositions of a social group? In what ways did the character of its support groups influence the practices and policies of a party? How did parties tailor their auras, and their policy stances, to accommodate new support groups? And especially, how did they do that when the political cultures of the new and the old support groups involved irreconcilable expectations?

Posing questions of this order draws attention to the extrapartisan sources of party combat and to the ways in which social group antagonisms structured party cleavages. Such questions illuminate the dimly lighted aspects of the dynamic interrelations between the electoral system and the larger social environment. And this book is concerned with questions of this order.

The focus of this book is on mass electoral politics, the party in the electorate. The objective is to describe and then to analyze the social bases of mass partisan support. Other aspects or categories of party activity will be treated but always from the perspective of the ways in which they were related to this central concern. That does not mean that I assume, even implicitly, that analyses of the party in office and the party as organization are unimportant enterprises. I recognize that the fundamentals of logic require that any effort to reconstruct a multi-

3. The quoted term is from Eric E. Lampard, "Two Cheers for Quantitative History," p. 13. As the notes in this book should make clear, a combination of methods is required to broaden the scope of the evidence examined and, therefore, the range of the questions that can be posed. Thus, the term *quantitative history*, even when it is not employed pejoratively, is something of a misnomer. It is especially misleading when used to imply a mutually exclusive dichotomy between the use of quantitative and letristic evidence.

dimensional historical reality must begin by distinguishing among its components. And the logic of research design requires that any study select and specify only particular aspects of complex realities.[4] Mass electoral behavior is the aspect selected and specified here both because it is a fundamental ingredient of party action and because better than any other single aspect of political activity it provides insight into the most neglected dimension of the past—mass cognitions.

Both the underlying approach and organizational framework of this book are analytic rather than narrative. The conceptions that inform my analysis of mass voting behavior, and the assumptions involved, are explicitly outlined in chapter one. The concept of a party system, or electoral era, provides the organizing and integrating framework for the study. That overarching conception is delineated and is applied to nineteenth-century electoral data in chapter two. In turn, that empirical description rivets attention on the parameters and systemically significant properties of the third electoral era and thereby establishes the analytical agenda for the rest of the book.

This use of the party-system conception represents something of a departure from traditional historical practice. Conventionally, for example, historians have divided the 1853–92 time sequence into two, and sometimes three, discrete and bounded segments. By partitioning American electoral history into time periods set off by critical realignments, massive transformations in the shape of the electoral universe, the party-system approach provides a conceptual unity and a theoretical richness that chronological sequencing and qualitative periodization lack.[5] Moreover, using the empirically delineated properties of the system as focal points enables the analysis to penetrate beyond tangential themes to questions demonstrably pertinent to an understanding of the electoral system.

Analyzing mass voting behavior over a forty-year period, and in a nation of continental size, necessarily involved making some tactical decisions. First, I have not attempted to deal here with contests for local offices—e.g., mayor, city council, county officers. However, I have examined and have analyzed the data for literally hundreds of such contests. Discussions of those data would have appreciably increased the length of this book without any corresponding increment in analytical reward. Second, the geographic scope of my analysis of group-voting behavior is designedly uneven. The sparsely settled West and the states of the former Confederacy receive less attention than those in other

4. Lee Benson, *The Concept of Jacksonian Democracy*, p. 123.
5. For indications of that theoretical richness, see Walter Dean Burnham, *Critical Elections and the Mainsprings of American Politics*, pp. 1–13.

areas of the country. The voting patterns exhibited by the West and the Confederacy have not been wholly neglected. They have, for example, been compared with the patterns displayed by other regions, and their relation to the larger systemic pattern has been made clear. However, I have not attempted the same analysis of voting behavior and political cultures in these regions as I have in those in which 73.0 percent of the nation's voters resided in 1890. To have attempted that task for the West would have required recovering large quantities of prestatehood data.[6] And to move beyond a description of the racial polarities that underlay the former Confederacy's systemically asymmetric political behavior would have required extensive recovery of subcounty voting and demographic data. Both enterprises might have been eminently worthwhile, but neither was presently practical. Nor was it likely that the analytical payoff would have justified the incremental investment of time and energy. That is especially so in the case of the former Confederate states, since I have presented an analysis of the political behavior of southern-stock groups in comparable contexts, the states of Maryland and Missouri.[7]

Beyond the West and the Confederate South, I have examined voting and demographic data by counties for all states from New England through the West North Central area over at least whatever portion of the 1848–92 span each was in the Union. And I have examined subcounty data for all voting units in fifteen of these states over the same time period, or for whatever part of it those data were reasonably available.[8] I have framed analyses of data at these levels of aggregation within the larger contexts of state, regional, and national patterns. In this way the small patterns evident in detailed case studies are woven into the larger overview of the electoral system. Through this approach it is possible to remain sensitive to the enormously significant ways in which geopolitical and historical contexts conditioned mass political behavior and to

6. Prior to 1880 only four western states—California, Colorado, Nevada, and Oregon were in the Union. Between 1889 and 1892, four more western states—Idaho, Montana, Washington, and Wyoming—were admitted. In addition North Dakota and South Dakota were admitted as part of the West North Central region. Collectively, the eight western states held 6.1 percent of the nation's voting-age population in 1890.

7. See the relevant sections of Chapters 4 and 5.

8. County-level voting and demographic data are from the Historical Data Archives, Inter-University Consortium for Political and Social Research, University of Michigan. All subcounty data were analyzed for fifteen states: Connecticut, Maine, Massachusetts, New Hampshire, Rhode Island, Vermont, New Jersey, Pennsylvania, Michigan, Ohio, Wisconsin, Iowa, Minnesota, Missouri, and Maryland. In addition I have examined subcounty data for most of New York's counties and all of its cities and for scattered counties in Illinois and Indiana. For more specific information concerning the sources of subcounty data, see the bibliography; for the time segments for which subcounty voting data are available, see Walter Dean Burnham, *Sources of Historical Election Data*.

integrate these specifics into a coherent understanding of the electoral dynamics of the third party system.

Of course, this book does not represent the first scholarly effort to analyze nineteenth-century voting behavior, though it is the first to do that for a series of states in more than a single region of the country. As a "voting study" focused on the second half of the nineteenth century, it necessarily covers some previously trod ground. To sharpen comparisons and to highlight differences in essence or emphasis, it is useful to ask explicitly: what's new in this? Perception is a selective phenomenon. Ultimately, then, what is seen to be new will depend somewhat on the reader's angle of view.

For those who view history as "the story" of the past and who are interested primarily in the details of nineteenth-century politics, this work will fill some of the glaring gaps by broadening the range and enhancing the credibility of what is known. For instance, most of the earlier voting studies have dealt with states in the Midwest. Commentators have wondered whether the voting patterns of social groups there were similar elsewhere. Now they need no longer wonder. This book compares the political behavior of social groups, party coalitions, and party characters across regional contexts. It also treats in detail matters that I glossed over in my earlier study of midwestern politics. Thus, it analyzes the impact of the Civil War on party coalitions and on the problems of Republican party formation and Democratic party redevelopment. It describes the political impact of the depression of the 1870s and combines that with a comparative assessment of the role played by the reenergized temperance movement of that decade. It analyzes the "Farmer" parties of the 1870s and their role in the rejuvenation of the Democracy. And it compares those parties and their social bases of support with the Farmer-Labor parties of the 1880s and early 1890s. Finally, it treats some groups of voters that I had neglected earlier—e.g., Danish immigrants and northern-stock and southern-stock natives.

This examination of the behavior of a wider variety of social groups than earlier, and in contexts beyond the Midwest, has led me to reformulate my explanation of the observed central tendency. As presented here, my conception of a pietistic-ritualistic continuum now takes into account the separate dimensions of religiosity and distinguishes among groups according to the ways in which these dimensions were tied together in human belief systems. Thus, centrally important to understanding differences in the social and political outlooks of religious groups is not a simple belief-vs.-behavior dichotomy but the distinguishable ways in which belief, which is central to all religious thought, was linked with other dimensions of "being religious." This conception, unlike the earlier one, makes it possible to integrate into the analytical framework the distinctive behaviors of evangelical pietists and salvationist pietists as well as the differences in political culture between categories of ritualists, e.g., between Catholics and German Lutherans.

However, not all historians are primarily interested in ''the story'' of nineteenth-century politics. Correctly, they see little value in detail piled upon detail or incident upon incident. Their concern, and my own, is not with the study of the past for its own sake but with the ways in which historical analysis can contribute to the development of social theory.

This is, and always has been, a relatively vast and heterogeneous society. Although those conditions complicate the development of descriptive generalizations, they also provide opportunities to enhance our knowledge of the dynamics of social-group behavior. We can take advantage of the heterogeneity of the society, explore contextual distinctions, and pose analytically significant questions concerning the conditions requisite to specified types of social-group behaviors. Once we answer such questions of enough groups across a sufficient variety of contexts and conditions, then we will be able to begin to develop a meaningful social theory that will account for distinctive modes of social-group consciousness.

In my judgment, analysis that aims at that end is the proper objective of historical practice. For that reason I have been concerned with exploring social-group behavior in a wide variety of contexts and conditions. And for that reason I have emphasized such matters as, for example, a comparison of Yankee political cohesiveness in the Midwest with that in New England and contextual as well as political-generational differences among subgroups of German Lutherans. Thus, if the reader's concern be with the eventual development of at least middle-range social-science theory, then the exploration of contextual and conditional distinctions in social-group behavior is new here.

Acknowledgments

Transforming a general idea for research into a book is a complex undertaking that requires assistance at each of its stages. This particular enterprise benefited from unusually generous assistance in a variety of forms. It is more a pleasure than a duty to acknowledge here those who have contributed to its fruition.

A National Endowment for the Humanities Fellowship for Younger Humanists and an appointment as visiting research associate in the American Studies Program at The Smithsonian Institution gave me the time and access to sources necessary for the research. A sabbatical leave from Northern Illinois University provided the time for writing. To be able to devote one's time exclusively to research and writing is something of a luxury. To have three years freed from all other academic responsibilities is an extraordinary luxury that merits proportionate gratitude. So, too, does the sustained research support provided by the Council of Academic Deans, Northern Illinois University. That took the form of several summer grants and a series of research grants that always guaranteed adequate funds for travel, photocopying, and hiring research assistants. The Department of History, Northern Illinois University, provided financial support over a four-year period for coding the large quantities of subcounty data that were used in the analysis, and a research grant from the American Philosophical Society enabled me to collect and code the Boston and Massachusetts data.

To researchers who expend time and encounter frustration attending to the tasks involved in cleaning data files and processing routine jobs, the advantages that allegedly inhere in using a computer may seem chimerical. I was spared much of that drudgery by the services of extremely competent and dependable research assistants. Three of these, all of whom were at the time graduate students at Northern Illinois University, must be singled out: Curtiss M. Trout, Departments of Mathematics and Computer Science; Eugene Maczek, Departments of Political Science and Mathematics; and Stephen C. Baker, Department of Political Science. Through their expertise, their never failing dependability, their

[xxi]

willingness to do more than expected, and their good humor, they contributed in creative and valuable ways.

Others also gave generously of their time and intellectual resources. As my department chairman for several years, Emory G. Evans was actively supportive of my commitment, even when that entailed my prolonged absence from campus, and he was always understanding and patient. His successor, J. Carroll Moody, has been equally so. Wilcomb E. Washburn was always willing to listen to my ideas and to pose perceptive questions. Merrill D. Peterson, Jiri Nehnevasja, and the late John L. Shover offered encouragement and support when they were most needed. Walter Dean Burnham, Ronald P. Formisano, Samuel P. Hays, Richard Jensen, Robert Kelley, Daniel Mazmanian, and Otto Olsen took the time and trouble to read the entire manuscript and to offer insightful suggestions that improved its quality. Edward L. Mantler, Enoch Pratt Free Library, Baltimore, was extremely helpful in securing photocopies of much of the subcounty data that I have used for Maryland.

In its final stage the manuscript benefited from the attention given to it by The University of North Carolina Press. If my experience is any guide, the Press's outstanding reputation for professionalism and superior editorial and production work is well merited. Besides, Malcolm L. Call, editor-in-chief, and Mrs. Gwen Duffey, managing editor, were always pleasant and thoughtful. And to Katherine M. Vansant fell the task of transforming my Ciceronian sentences into readable prose. Whatever grace of expression appears on these pages is due more to her efforts than to mine.

The Third Electoral System, 1853–1892

A Prologue to the Analysis of Past Politics

Political history is often sterile stuff, a collection of names, titles, and events beaded on a chronological string. Yet a time perspective can yield an awareness of dimensions of the political system that otherwise escape detection. The wars of domestic politics, like those between nations, are not events of a moment but extend through the years.

V. O. Key, Jr.

The analysis of past politics is replete with potential pitfalls and unique analytical opportunities. Conceived as a series of recurring, but individually unique, developments "beaded on a chronological string," political history produces analytically "sterile stuff." More broadly conceived, political analysis enables us to move beyond idiosyncratic happenings and to penetrate the relation between society and political system.

Traditional research strategies have encumbered that sort of analytical penetration. They have focused instead on exciting events, colorful personalities, and the dramaturgy of political notables. Pertinent evidence has often been skillfully blended to produce graceful, and even elegant, narratives. Yet for all of their informational value and analytical insights, these subordinate conceptual unity to chronological sequencing. Their central preoccupation has been telling the "story."

The ways that events unfolded and the roles that particular elites played are neither unimportant nor irrelevant to an understanding of past politics, but they do not constitute the beginning, the middle, and the end of political history. Yet traditional research strategies typically have focused on these aspects of past politics to the virtual exclusion of mass electoral behavior. Most political narratives, of course, refer to elections and to their results, but those references occupy a distinctly secondary role. Far less attention and fewer pages of monographs are devoted to them than to elite machinations.[1] And the interpretive frameworks use the categories and terms of understanding peculiar to the elites. The result is a political history only tangentially concerned with mass behavior, and then only as refracted through the mental eyes of political notables.[2]

Approaches of this genre constrain the analytical potentialities of political history and at best provide a socially jaundiced view of the past. To obviate these limitations, one must broaden the conceptual framework and apply it within the context of a different type of research strategy. We need to treat mass electoral behavior, not as a coincidental afterthought, but as the primordial building block of the electoral system. And that treatment must begin, not with elite descriptions of how the masses reacted, but with an examination of *observable voting behavior*. This study was designed to apply such an approach to an analysis of late nineteenth-century electoral behavior.

The essential nature of political action during what Mark Twain dubbed "The Gilded Age" has not been an object of heated dispute among most historical analysts. Despite some shifts in emphasis and ostensibly fresh interpretations, accounts of late nineteenth-century party battles generally continue to be conceived within older frames of reference and analytical categories. The "persuasive rhetoric" of Lord Bryce and James Ford Rhodes, on the one hand, and that of Charles Beard and Matthew Josephson, on the other, continues to exercise a "tyranny" over current conceptions.[3] These analyses differ in their particulars and underlying values, but their legacy is a shared and still dominating motif: the politics of the Gilded Age were dull and sterile; they were evasive of

1. H. Wayne Morgan, *From Hayes to McKinley*, devotes pp. 57–117 to discussing the preelection-day events in 1880; he confines his analysis of the outcome and references to the group bases of politics to pp. 118–21. That relative allocation of space and analytical concern is a common feature of historical accounts of past politics.

2. The term *political notables* is a designedly ambiguous one; as a matter of stylistic convention, it will be employed here synonymously with the term *political elites*. Neither term, however, is meant here to imply that those so designated exercised decision-making power, that they influenced those who did, or that they necessarily were at the same time economic and/or social elites. In other words, I am here simply using these terms to refer to that group of prominent contemporary figures who have been regularly quoted and cited by historians as sources of information concerning late nineteenth-century politics.

3. Thomas C. Cochran, "The 'Presidential Synthesis' in American History," p. 374, observes that "history probably suffers more than any other discipline from the tyranny of persuasive rhetoric." The rhetorically persuasive works that have shaped interpretations of late nineteenth-century politics are James Bryce, *The American Commonwealth*, vol. 2; James Ford Rhodes, *History of the United States from Hayes to McKinley, 1876–1896*; Charles A. Beard and Mary R. Beard, *The Rise of American Civilization*, especially 2:285–343; Charles A. Beard, *The American Party Battle*, pp. 76–93; Matthew Josephson, *The Robber Barons*; idem, *The Politicos, 1856–1896*.

the "real" issues of the era, the questions arising from the massive economic and social transformations that were the hallmarks of nineteenth-century America.

There are distinguishable elements of credibility in that view. American electoral politics have never been organized exclusively around social-class polarities. Questions of political economy have not always and everywhere in the electoral past mobilized mass constituencies and determined election outcomes. Nor, for that matter, has most electoral behavior been issue oriented. Yet even granting these elements of credibility does not enhance the explanative power of the larger view, for that view ultimately relies on the a priori assumption that political action lacking such characteristics must necessarily and inherently be evasive and irrelevant. That assumption, in turn, makes the analyst's norms the criteria against which the rationality of past behavior is to be assessed. Analyses conceived within this framework reveal little of the attitudes and values of those uncounted millions who were the involved participants. Yet they do provide considerable insight into the shared values and a priori assumptions that have shaped most historical descriptions of past politics. Although it is not appropriate here to digress into an extended conceptual critique of those formulations, it is useful to draw attention to some of their essential and common elements.

First, they reveal a shared but implicit commitment to the *desirability* and to the operation of a liberal-rational model of public-opinion formation. That view posits a political system composed of "an atomized collection of individuals, each more or less informed about public issues and possessing views about them. This preconception produces a picture of social conflict organized along issue alignments as individuals independently form their opinions." Applied to mass electoral behavior, the model explains voting decisions as the result of a process in which men ponder the logical relations between their own political wants or goals and the alternative policy stances of the contending parties. The ideal political universe is thus presumed to be one disproportionately populated by active, informed, and issue-oriented citizens.[4]

Second, and because it is both a logical corollary and requisite condition of the liberal-rational model, most historical descriptions reflect consensual agreement on the proper role of political parties. Political

4. The quotation is from V. O. Key, Jr., *Public Opinion and American Democracy*, p. 60. Key here characterizes what he calls "classical treatments of public opinion"; it is my judgment that this description can be used to categorize the public-opinion model that historians have employed. For specification and discussion of the conditions for issue-oriented voting, see Angus Campbell et al., *The American Voter*, pp. 169–87.

parties should articulate unequivocal stances on issues and shape these into distinctive and logically constrained programmatic packages; they should function as instruments of policy articulation and integration. Only by performing in this way would political parties provide issue-conscious citizens with partisan alternatives that were consonant with unambiguous policy distinctions. And only then would elections constitute the "outcomes in particular," the series of referenda or policy that the liberal-rational model assumes they should be.[5]

Whenever concrete party behaviors fail to conform to these desiderata, the analytical judgments are harsh. On the one hand, when historians have perceived that parties failed to present distinctive policy alternatives, they have often internalized and reiterated the complaints of the nineteenth-century political notables that party politics were devoid of "live issues."[6] That assessment, however, relies directly on the normative assumption that the exclusive nature of party is programmatic; and that assumption, in turn, is a deduction from the liberal-rational model of public-opinion formation and not one derived from observation and analysis of past behavior. On the other hand, that same model produces an even more astringent assault on appeals to party loyalty. Nothing more directly undermines the model, after all, than a "standing decision." Frequently echoing and invariably citing the political notables, historians regularly denigrate party loyalty and wistfully allude to the voter "who wished to follow his own conscience."[7] Reflecting and perhaps sharing in the antiparty animus of the political elites, analysts regularly devote more energy to a normative critique of party loyalty and the mechanisms sustaining it than to an understanding of either its social origins or of the role of party as a reference symbol.

Finally, traditional descriptions of past politics offer evidence of a broad diffusion among historical analysts of the assumption that social-class distinctions are, or ought to be, the invariable substructural linch-pins of political behavior.[8] Other types of social-group differences are

5. Theodore J. Lowi, "Party, Policy, and Constitution in America," pp. 238–76, uses the phrase (p. 263) and perceptively analyzes American electoral politics as representing "outcomes in general" that have imparted shape to large clusters of public policy.

6. See, for example, John A. Garraty, *The New Commonwealth, 1877–1890*, p. 240; and the claim by John M. Dobson, *Politics in the Gilded Age*, p.43, that the lack of issues produced a "political scene that closely resembled that seldom-achieved hypothetical situation in which all other things *were* equal." Emphasis in the original.

7. The quotation is from Dobson, *Politics in the Gilded Age*, p. 43. For the attitudes of the political notables toward "party spirit," see John G. Sproat, "*The Best Men*," pp. 60–66. And for an example of a historian's internalizing the notables' view of party, see Geoffrey Blodgett, *The Gentle Reformers*, p. 40.

8. Sometimes this results from confusing the concept of economic interest group with social class, as in Morgan, *Hayes to McKinley*, pp. 120, 318. At other times it

portrayed either as temporary distractions or as superstructural images of these underlying realities. Thus, if mass politics are seen as failing to pivot on what the analyst regards as the "real" (i.e., substructural) distinctions, it follows axiomatically that the prevailing bases of cleavage must be evasive or derivative. That conclusion, of course, is nothing more than a deduction from the starting premise. It is, moreover, a deduction with starkly elitist implications, for ultimately it hinges on the analyst's projecting his own values on past men and arguing implicitly that *they* should have perceived the public concerns to which those values are addressed as the most important ones.

I do not mean to suggest that most historians consciously intend to interpret the past in terms of their own values but only that their norms and implicit assumptions shape their research strategies and often, perhaps unconsciously, influence their receptivity to evidence that reinforces their preconceptions. Those research strategies aim at an objective reconstruction of specified aspects of past experience. The tactical means to that end entail careful and painstaking examinations of traditional sources, such as correspondence, diaries, newspapers, and public utterances. These types of sources, if construed literally, provide researchers ample grist for their issue-oriented mills.

Political notables such as George William Curtiss, E. L. Godkin, and Carl Schurz—as well as "radical" elites such as Eugene Debs, Ignatius Donnelly, and Robert Schilling—were active, well informed, and articulate. Theirs were political worlds of principles and policy, information and issues. They frequently and cogently articulated their concern with specific matters such as tariffs, civil service, and currency expansion or monopolies, wages, and labor organization. Moreover, they linked these separate ideas into a larger frame of reference. They had knowledge, not only of specific, but of interstitial information that enabled them to discern what went together and why it did, for in their political belief systems discrete ideas were glued together, or were psychologically constrained, by "a few crowning postures." Those crowning postures provided judgmental yardsticks with which to measure and make sense of a wide range of information. To describe and analyze their political values is to glimpse the type of belief system characteristic of those *at one level* of the political structure.[9]

However, we cannot assume that the linkages that characterized

---

reflects the simple, though deceptively phrased, economic determinism called for by James R. Green, "Behavioralism and Class Analysis," p. 98, and given more detailed expression by David Montgomery, *Beyond Equality*. For a critique of the logic underlying these approaches, see Lee Benson, *Turner and Beard*, and especially pp. 151–60.

9. For the concept of belief system, see Philip E. Converse, "The Nature of Belief Systems in Mass Publics," pp. 206–61. And for an understanding of the properties and

belief systems at that level extended to all other levels of the political structure. To interpret mass behavior through a reconstruction of elite belief systems is to present a typology of past political concerns that mirrors only the thinking and issue-oriented focus of relatively small, self-conscious, and self-enclosed groups of "abnormal citizens."[10] To project elite cognitions to the mass public requires assuming that most nineteenth-century contemporaries possessed the same levels of awareness and involvement, concrete and interstitial information, as the political notables. It implicitly assumes that most voters perceived their political worlds in the same ways, and in the same terms, as the political elites. That assumption ignores the enormous differences in kind between mass and elite cognitions. Most people generally lack the levels of contextual information that are common among the elite. As a consequence, mass belief systems are more loosely constrained, they encompass a narrower range of relevant ideas, and the character of those elements central to the mass systems is typically less generic or abstract than in elite belief systems.

To point out these distinctions is not to claim that only elites have opinions or beliefs, or even that elite belief systems are qualitatively superior to those of nonelites. It is rather to assert that analysts must aim at reconstructing the belief systems of a wide variety of groupings within the social and political structures and that in so doing we should not automatically assume "that whatever beliefs 'go together' in the visible political world (as judged from the attitudes of elites and the most articulate spectators) must naturally go together in the same way among [the] mass public."[11]

If elite cognitions cannot be assumed to be wholly reflective of mass opinions, how then do we reach beyond politics "at the top"?[12]

---

organization of belief-disbelief systems, see Milton Rokeach, *The Open and Closed Mind*, pp. 31–70.

10. The characterization is from Cochran, " 'Presidential Synthesis,' " p. 376.

11. Converse, "Nature of Belief Systems," p. 230. This should not be construed to imply that mass belief systems are illogical and, therefore, inferior to elite belief systems. Logical systems are only a subclass, a special type, of psychological system; see Rokeach, *Open and Closed Mind*, pp. 33–35. Converse's essay has sparked considerable research on the separate but related questions of issue constraint in mass belief systems and issue-oriented voting. For analyses that point to increased levels of both after the 1950s, see Gerald M. Pomper, "From Confusion to Clarity," pp. 415–28; Norman Nie and Kristi Andersen, "Mass Belief Systems Revisited," pp. 540–91. And for a superbly conceived analysis of the problem of issue voting, see Michael Margolis, "From Confusion to Confusion," pp. 31–43. It is worth noticing that even at its increased level mass attitudinal consistency across issue domains remains quite weak in an absolute sense, and as Margolis demonstrates, it falls significantly short of the requisite criteria for issue-oriented voting.

12. The expression is from Morgan, *Hayes to McKinley*, p. vi.

How do we determine what public questions mattered to most citizens, what touched their daily lives and energized their commitments? It is useful to tackle that conundrum by presenting an outline of the conceptions and research strategy that underlie this book, as well as an explicit statement of its assumptions.

Studies of mass politics must begin with observations of mass behavior. How a group voted—whether Democrat or Republican, how strongly, and under what conditions—can be resolved, not by deduction or inference, but only by thorough, systematic analysis of the relevant empirical data. For purposes of this study, that has required the collection, processing, and statistical analysis of large quantities of county and minor civil-division voting and demographic data over an extended temporal sequence. Through such an approach it is possible to describe the regular patterns of a social group's partisanship and to notice breaks in those patterns.

Of course, it is considerably easier to assert that studies of mass voting behavior should begin with descriptive statements of the central tendencies of group partisanship than it is to arrive at those statements. To provide credible descriptive statements requires avoiding deterministic models in which both the research design and the conclusions are simply deductions from a priori assumptions. It is not the substantive nature of the conclusions but the logic of the research design that indicates employing a deterministic approach. To avoid that pitfall, research designs must test the effects of a variety of potential determinants of voting behavior. This study has made use of a wide variety of economic, ethnic, and religious indicators in order to describe group voting behavior. These have been employed in a number of statistical ways, ranging from simple cross-tabulations to select units or groups of units for illustrative purposes, to multiple-regression models to assess the relative simultaneous contributions of distinctive types of variables. I have also tested for the impact of contextual effects, demographic as well as political, and for observable differences dependent on levels of aggregation. Although most of the negative findings are not presented in statistical detail, the descriptions provided derived from a multivariate data analysis.

Systematic observation and description of social-group behavior is the requisite first step. That constitutes the only credible basis for insight into the beliefs, attitudes, and values of a group. *Only from behavior* can these be inferred.[13] And it is equally important to emphasize that *they can only be inferred*. Arrays of statistical data do not demonstrate,

13. Rokeach, *Open and Closed Mind*, p. 32; idem, *Beliefs, Attitudes, and Values*, p. 2.

nor even address, the problems of human motivation. Why people responded politically as they did cannot be demonstrated statistically. Analytical and factual questions are of different logical orders and accordingly require different designs of proof. *How* a group voted is a factual question *requiring* an empirical response. *Why* it voted that way involves an analytical question that can be posed meaningfully only after the factual one has been answered empirically.

To move beyond statistical aggregates and penetrate human motivation, the researcher must search extensively through the society to identify group antagonisms and conflicts and determine which of these became sources of party combat. The past political world must be reconstructed in terms of its *political subcultures. Culture*, or any specified aspect thereof, is one of those vague conditioning concepts, or catchwords, whose rhetorical value becomes perishable in practical applications.[14] To be of analytical use, the involved sequence must be specified in more detail and must be linked with an explicit conception of political party.

Involvement with a group shapes members' beliefs, attitudes, and values; it imparts a perspective to assist them in organizing their perceptual fields.[15] This group-anchored perspective is something of a screen, or filter, through which the members process and compare external stimuli. Technically, that process is called cognitive interaction, and through it a response, or behavior, is shaped. The collective behavioral manifestation of that shared, internalized, group-imparted perspective is designated by the term *group subculture*. In turn, *political culture* is the political aspect of that group subculture: "a historical system of widespread, fundamental, behavioral, political values . . . classified into subsystems of identity, symbol, rule, and belief." A group's political culture consists of its politically relevant purposive desires, cognitions, and expressive symbols. It refers to the internalized expectations in terms of which the political roles of the group's members are defined and through which their regularized patterns of political behavior come into being.[16]

14. On the role of catchwords in the social sciences, see J. P. Nettl, *Political Mobilization*, pp. 42–53.

15. My understanding of the psychological processes involved owes a great deal to three works by Milton Rokeach. In addition to the volumes cited in notes 9 and 13, above, see *The Nature of Human Values*.

16. The quotation is from Donald J. Devine, *The Political Culture of the United States*, pp. 14–18; the following two sentences are adaptations of the definition of political culture given by Harry Eckstein, "A Perspective on Comparative Politics, Past and Present," p. 26. For the formulation that has directly shaped my thinking about the concept of political culture, see Ronald P. Formisano, "Deferential-Participant Politics," pp. 473–87.

Political subcultures are not created by political parties. The causal flow is in the opposite direction. Party oppositions and alliances are formed from antagonistic relations between (or among) group political cultures. Yet not every social-group conflict translates into party distinctions. It is not enough to point to the existence of conflict and then assert its relevance to party struggle. Historical explanations cannot rely on reference to the wondrous workings of some unspecified process of political immanence. Some conflicts may have no relevance to the political system; others may generate demands on the system through channels other than party, e.g., through pressure groups and bureaucracies. And even among those conflicts that are expressed through party, some will be more intense than others because they involve ideas more central to the belief systems of the combatants.

When antagonistic political cultures *do* generate party oppositions, attachment to the group comes to involve a set of political orientations that includes a partisan proclivity. Initially, of course, the reasons for the party attachment are "alive" in the members' minds. As memories fade, as membership turns over, the situation- or object-specific reasons become, in the neutral sense of the word, stereotypes, "the subtlest and most pervasive of all influences," the "pictures" in the mind through which the members of the group impart order to their political worlds. In time, through habituated and group-anchored partisan response, the party as institution itself becomes a reference group.[17] Thus, "political party," as a social grouping, can be thought of as a very special case of the much more general group-influence phenomenon. It is a special case of the phenomenon, not simply because its political salience in any electoral situation is exceedingly high and unidirectional, but because individuals come to psychological membership in it through the intermediary of involvements with other social groups. The influence of a group leads members to identification with a party, and the latter serves as a kind of "self-steering mechanism" that guides and shapes responses to new political stimuli.[18]

Political parties, of course, are not only reference groups or symbols; they are also concrete and complex entities. That quality of dynamic complexity has eluded traditional historical analysis of party

17. The quotation is from Walter Lippman, *Public Opinion*, pp. 59–60. On the concept of party as a reference group, see Robert E. Lane, *Political Life*, pp. 299–300. And see the perceptive comments on the party name as "an 'image' that shades imperceptibly into the voluntary realization of its meaning" in Graham Wallas, *Human Nature in Politics*, p. 104.

18. See the discussion of "Secondary Groups, the Political Party, and the Influence Process," in Campbell et al., *The American Voter*, pp. 327–31; also see Converse, "Nature of Belief Systems," pp. 229–30, 234–35, 239–41.

struggles. Those accounts generally avoid an explicit conception of party and rely instead on working definitions deduced from implicit theories of political system. Given some conception of political system, analysts can readily infer that certain functions ought to be performed, and they search for the concrete institutions that carry out those requisite functions. Thus political parties emerge largely by indirection and deduction. This approach perpetuates misconceptions that becloud the analysis of past politics. It encourages analysts to view parties as somehow detached from their sociopolitical contexts, as "reforming missionaries from some far-off places" set loose in the political system to impart order and coherence to it.[19] Second, it underlies the view of parties as the exclusive structures through which contending and competing social demands are articulated and aggregated. Conceiving this intermediary role of party as an invariant given deflects analytical attention both from analogous roles played by other durable structures within the political system and from the ways in which party's role may have changed across time. Third, by not explicitly designating the meaning of the term *party*, analysts readily blur the distinctions among different types of party activity and thus fail to recognize that each involves particular cognitions and behaviors. Fourth, concentration on the functions of party leads researchers to a common descriptive metaphor: the party as electoral machine.[20] Concealed beneath that literary device, combat among parties in traditional accounts has been emptied a priori of its social, cultural, and ideological content. It is one thing to think of parties as, inter alia, mobilizing agencies but quite another to present them as sufficient causes of that mobilization. Exaggeration of the electoral-machine metaphor does the latter and thus precludes analysis of the extrapartisan sources of party struggle.

If parties and their activities are proper objects of analysis, then we must provide explicit conceptions of what those terms designate. A *political party* may be defined as a specialized institution within the boundaries of the political system that, through its dual capacity both to articulate and to aggregate interests, provides direct links between the decision makers and large numbers of interest groups outside the bound-

19. Frank J. Sorauf, "Political Parties and Political Analysis," pp. 48–55; the quotation is on p. 49. For perceptive discussion of the analytical need to view parties as intervening, dependent, and independent variables, see David E. Apter, *The Politics of Modernization*, pp. 181–82.

20. Bryce, *American Commonwealth*, 2:76–153; Henry Jones Ford, *The Rise and Growth of American Politics*, pp. 141–49, 294–310; Dobson, *Politics in the Gilded Age*, pp. 51–52. The view of party as electoral machine typically assumes hierarchical organization with the flow of authority running from the top downward. For an extensive refutation of the notion that late nineteenth-century parties were organized and controlled from the top down, see Robert D. Marcus, *Grand Old Party*.

aries of the political system.[21] The definition remains incomplete, however, until we indicate the specific ways in which political party may be distinguished from other institutions assigned to the same genus.

Party differs from other specialized political institutions that both articulate and aggregate interests (e.g., the bureaucracy) in that it alone selects candidates and contests elections, attempts to organize elected governmental decision makers, and attempts to win converts or recruits. Analogous to these three clusters of distinguishing activities, party alone among the specialized political institutions is characterized by a distinctive tripartite pattern of organization. As Frank Sorauf has suggested, we can think of party as being composed of three elements or sectors. First the organization proper, which ''has an internal life of its own''—the party officials, the hyperpolitical activists, ''the purposeful, organized, initiating vanguard of the party.'' Second the party in office, whether executive or legislative, which includes the caucuses, floor leaders, whips, and patronage networks—those who ''have captured the symbols of the party and speak for it in public authority.'' Third the party in the electorate—the ''least stable, least active, least involved, and least well organized'' sector; those who attach themselves to the party either through habituated support at the polls or through self-identification; those who ''are 'of' the party'' because it is for them ''a symbol that provides cues and order to the political cosmos.''[22] Party, of course, is no *one* of these elements but all in interaction: ''Party exists when activists, officials, and voters interact and when they consciously identify with a common name and symbols.''[23]

This tripartite structure is party's telling characteristic, for unlike other specialized political institutions the object of party's mobilizing efforts—its clientele—is not external to it. Rather, party includes its own clientele, as well as a tangible political organization and sets of officeholders. Thus, party's ''membership'' encompasses the widest possible range of involvement and commitment. It is at once a ''well-defined, voluntary political organization and an open, public rally of loyalists.''[24] By its activists and officeholders party may well be seen as

21. For this dual capacity of party, see Gabriel A. Almond and G. Bingham Powell, Jr., *Comparative Politics*, pp. 100–104. For an explicit conception of political system and the necessity of delineating the boundaries of that system, see Lee Benson, ''Political Power and Political Elites,'' pp. 282–87.

22. For the activities of party and the discussion of its tripartite structure from which the quotations have been taken, see Sorauf, ''Political Parties and Political Analysis,'' pp. 46, 36–38, respectively; for the description of party officeholders, see Frank J. Sorauf, *Party Politics in America*, p. 11.

23. Formisano, ''Deferential-Participant Politics,'' p. 475.

24. The discussion is based on Sorauf, *Party Politics*, pp. 10–12; the quotation is on p. 12.

a programmatic instrument, but by its mass supporters it is only necessary that it be perceived as an object of habitual loyalty, a reference symbol. However, since party's activity within all three categories of membership is goal oriented and since the goals depend ultimately on electoral victories, the party must act to attain the goals of its activists, its officeholders, and its clientele.[25] Indeed, in arguing from cleavages over policy among political elites to partisan distinctions among social groups within the mass electorate, historians have implicitly assumed an absolute identity of goals among all three sectors of party. There is neither reason nor need to make as sweeping an assumption.

Nor need we assume that the relations of dominance and subordinance among the sectors are invariant across time or space. There is no standard mix, no predetermined proportions and intensities among the elements, that we need accept either as a sine qua non or as a criterion. We should expect different mixes, different patterns of relations across both time and space. Description and analysis of these patterned relational distinctions, at all levels of governmental action and within varied sociopolitical contexts, and of their permutations across time are prerequisite for understanding the development of the political system.

Yet just as the presence of party requires interaction among its three sectors, so that implies the existence of *some* relation among them. If that relation need not be one of programmatic congruence, it must at least be one of psychological rapport. That is, I assume, as a minimal condition, that the three elements are "glued" together through a shared "common latent value continuum."[26] Analysis that tries to reconstruct the essence of those shared values is crucial to probing beyond politics "at the top." Understanding the nature of the psychological bridges that linked a party's officeholders and activists with its loyal followers enables us to penetrate the political worlds of those who composed the mass electorate, for in the nature of that rapport between a party's character and the dispositions of its constituent groups are clues to the concerns and emotions that permeated the latter, energized their commitments, and transformed social-group antagonisms into party oppositions.[27]

25. Goal orientation, of course, does not automatically presuppose an exclusive focus on the allocation of tangible resources. Furthermore, it is important to emphasize that party loyalists may, under specified conditions, see party as more than a reference symbol; they may be as programmatically oriented as activists and officeholders. In saying that they must *at least* see party as a reference symbol, I mean only to draw attention to the minimal necessary condition.

26. The quoted phrase is from Murray Edelman, *The Symbolic Uses of Politics*, p. 155. Also see Paul F. Lazarsfeld and Neil W. Henry, *Latent Structure Analysis*, pp. 15–44; Robert E. Lane, *Political Ideology*, pp. 10–11; Robert E. Lane, *Political Thinking and Consciousness*.

27. For works that develop the concept of political character, see Robert E. Lane,

Analysts of past politics cannot recapture that shared bond of psychological rapport in the same ways as political scientists and sociologists do with modern parties and voters. We do not enjoy the luxury of being able to administer a structured questionnaire to a past electorate to inquire into its perceptions and motivations. Instead, we must use the materials that are available, knowing and acknowledging that they are at best crude and imprecise surrogates for modern instruments that measure public opinion. Historical sources—elite sources, such as newspapers, speeches, and party platforms—allow us to probe mass opinion only inferentially, and then only if we move beyond their manifest content and search for the evocative code words and symbols, the emotions and values with which rhetoricians knew their listeners or readers to be already imbued.[28] When congruent with systematic description of observable behaviors, that analysis enables historians to posit sets of structured inferences concerning which public matters resonated emotionally with group political characters and, thus, about *why* groups voted as they did.

This is the conceptual framework that underlies the research strategy of this book. That strategy involves two assumptions that have only been implied thus far. First, I assume that a number of social variables as experienced and internalized by individuals are equally capable of shaping their voting decisions and partisan commitments. Second, I assume that for most citizens the experiencing and internalizing are group processes, that the "cleavages that involve mass publics are [shaped] in terms . . . of loyalties to competing groups."[29] The concrete result of applying such a strategy to an analysis of past politics differs from the products of traditional political history. It depicts party combat in terms of antagonistic political cultures; it views elections as integral parts of a larger and ongoing social process.

"Political Character and Political Analysis," pp. 115–25; Ronald P. Formisano, "Political Character, Antipartyism, and the Second Party System," pp. 685–88. Also see David Riesman, Nathan Glazer, and Reuel Denny, *The Lonely Crowd.*

28. Ronald P. Formisano, *The Birth of Mass Political Parties*, p. 13.

29. Key, *Public Opinion*, p. 60.

2

The Third Electoral System:
An Empirical Perspective

To this day many of our comrades still do not understand that they must attend to the quantitative aspect of things—the basic statistics, the main percentages and the quantitative limits that determine the qualities of things. They have no "figures" in their heads and as a result cannot help making mistakes. . . . In all mass movements we must make a basic investigation and analysis of the number of active supporters, opponents and neutrals and must not decide problems subjectively and without basis.

Mao Tse-tung (1949)

Periodization is both a tool and an objective of historical analysis. By demarcating a specified period of time and assigning a particular label to it, historians mean to denote that it has certain qualities or characteristics setting it apart from other periods of time. And the assigned label suggests the nature of those qualities—for example, the Era of Good Feelings, The Gilded Age, The Progressive Era. These semantic tags are employed as shorthand surrogates for concepts; each concept, in turn, refers "either to a class of phenomena or to certain aspects or characteristics that a range of phenomena have in common."[1] That is, the concepts integrate and thus impart analytical unity to a variety of discrete occurrences whose aggregate quality is posited to differ from that of the occurrences in other specified periods of time. Often, however, historical periodization proceeds "subjectively and without basis." Researchers tend to ignore the fact that concepts are logical abstractions that refer to underlying empirical phenomena. They regularly write of ages, epochs, and eras without first attending "to the quantitative aspect of things."

To avoid that mistake, one must begin with an overview of "the quantitative limits." Within a nation of continental proportions, even

1. Social Science Research Council, Report of the Committee on Historiography, *The Social Sciences in Historical Study*, pp. 89–95; the quotation is on p. 91.

such a summary review of "the basic statistics" of a time segment of the voting universe requires more than a national perspective. To implant the "figures" in our heads, we must examine longitudinally and cross-sectionally the relevant data at the national, regional, and state levels.[2] And tactically it is useful first to clarify the integrating framework and then to structure the empirical inquiry to bring into focus several important qualities of the late nineteenth-century party system.

Electoral Systems and Realigning Sequences

Elections are recurring events reflecting underlying and ongoing socio-political processes. To abstract that dimension of similarity, however, does not imply that all elections are precisely similar. Some differ from others in behaviorally and systemically significant ways.

Empirical studies of the American electoral universe point to two broad categories of elections that differ from each other in *kind* and not merely in degree. Some elections primarily maintain the electoral system. The outcomes of these elections reflect some mixture of traditional party identifications and short-term, or *surge*, factors associated with current events or particular candidates. The relative importance of these long- and short-term components may vary, and on the basis of their valences in any particular mixture, we can distinguish three subtypes of elections. In *maintaining elections* the prevailing coalitional structure continues to dominate with only marginal changes from the earlier pattern. In such elections existing partisan loyalties are the primary attitude influences that shape voting decisions. In *deviating elections*, short-term attitude influences produce an outcome that differs significantly from the normal distribution of party loyalties. In these elections immediate events or personalities deflect party loyalties and produce an outcome that is inconsistent with the underlying balance of partisan attachments. In counterdeviating, or *reinstating*, elections the normal patterns reassert themselves following the expiration of the deviation-producing surge factors. However, none of these subtypes of elections drastically or permanently alters the coalitional bases of mass politics. The "standing

2. By the term *longitudinal*, I refer to a statistical measure calculated over time. For example, the Democratic longitudinal mean for the presidential contests between 1836 and 1848 would be the sum of the Democratic percentage in each of the elections divided by the number of elections. The term *cross-sectional* refers to a statistical measure for a single time calculated across the smaller subunits of some larger entity: for example, the Republican mean strength in the nation calculated by states or a party's mean strength in a state calculated by counties.

decision'' that structures the basic division of party loyalties among the mass electorate remains essentially intact.[3]

However, in some elections that ''standing decision'' is overturned. These are *realigning*, or critical, elections. Occurring relatively infrequently, such elections have distinct characteristics that set them apart from electoral system–maintaining elections. Realigning elections involve a large-scale and durable reshuffling of the coalitional bases of party voting support that extends to all levels of partisan elections. They evidence abnormally high levels of intensity—which is reflected in the process of selecting a candidate, unusually sharp issue polarization, and higher-than-normal levels of voter participation. Because they constitute a broadly diffused negation of the earlier ''standing decision,'' such elections change the shape of the voting universe.

Sequences of realigning elections are infrequent occurrences, but they are not random happenings. Integrally related to the essentially constituent nature of American parties, they emerge directly from the dynamics of that function. That is, realignments ''arise from emergent tensions in society which, not adequately controlled by the organization or outputs of party politics as usual, escalate to a flash point.'' When such tensions are felt intensely and diffused broadly among the mass public, they shatter the existing coalitional structure of mass politics by providing new bases for electoral mobilization. In turn, that produces significant ''transformations in large clusters of policy'' as well as alterations in the roles played by institutional elites. Realigning sequences, then, ''are involved with redefinitions of the universe of voters, political parties, and the broad boundaries of the politically possible.''[4] Their cyclical recurrence allows us to describe the predominant rhythm of mass partisan politics over the past two centuries as one of long periods of electoral stability punctuated by infrequent, short, and intense bursts of electoral reorganization. Each burst of electoral reorganization has produced a discrete party system. Each party system has shared common elements with the others, but each has also displayed its own ''characteristic patterns of voting behavior, of elite and institutional relationships,

3. The formulation in this and the following paragraphs borrows heavily from Walter Dean Burnham, ''The United States,'' pp. 664–69. For the original effort to elaborate the conceptual framework for classification of presidential elections, see Angus Campbell et al., *The American Voter*, pp. 531–38; for another effort at classification, see Gerald M. Pomper, *Elections in America*, pp. 99–125.
4. For the conception of critical realignment, see Walter Dean Burnham, *Critical Elections and the Mainsprings of American Politics*, pp. 1–10; the quotations are on p. 10. Burnham's conception builds on the seminal work of V. O. Key, Jr., ''A Theory of Critical Elections,'' pp. 1–18. On the meaning of realignment, also see James L. Sundquist, *Dynamics of the Party System*, pp. 1–38.

and of broad system-dominant decisions."[5] Viewed across time, American electoral politics have witnessed no fewer than five national party systems.

The first party system, from 1789 to about 1820, was marked by an experimental, hesitant, sometimes nonpurposive, and never fully successful groping toward the creation of durable partisan structures. It might more properly be termed a *preparty* party system. The second party system, from 1828 to the realignment of the 1850s, grew from a host of local political alignments; it was characterized, inter alia, by a fully nationwide two-party competition. The third party system, or the Civil War party system, from 1853 to 1892, emerged from the collapse of one of the major parties, the breakdown of nationwide partisan competition, and the reorientation of both the party system and its policies along explicitly sectional lines. The fourth party system, from 1893 to about 1932, emerged from the incapacity of the third system to accommodate the emergent demands of the cash-crop agrarians of the South and the West coupled with the onset of an urban-industrial depression in early 1893. Unlike the other party systems, this one was characterized by the absence of viable partisan competition both at the national level and in a majority of the states. It was marked, too, by a steep decline in the high rates of voter mobilization that had been a hallmark of the third electoral era. Finally, the fifth party system, or the New Deal party system, resulted from the depression and realignment of the 1930s. It was marked by the gradual emergence of two-party competition in areas where that had not existed for decades and by the addition of class cleavage to the traditional mixture of voting alignments.

This terse overview of the nation's party systems draws attention to two features of American electoral politics. First, we can usefully and meaningfully periodize American electoral history in terms of a succession of discrete party systems. In doing that, however, it is essential to bear in mind that the term *party system* refers to voting systems or electoral-politics systems and does not relate to organizational structures. More specifically, the term *party system*, or *electoral era*, designates a set of maintaining, deviating, and reinstating elections bounded by realigning sequences.[6] Expressed in the terms appropriate to the analogous conception of a *voting cycle*, we can describe each electoral era as involving a stable (or equilibrium) phase bounded by fluctuation phases.[7]

5. Walter Dean Burnham, "Party Systems and the Political Process," p. 289; the analysis on pp. 289–304 provides the basis for my characterization of the party systems.
6. Thomas P. Jahnige. "Critical Elections and Social Change," p. 468; Burnham, *Critical Elections*, p. 11.
7. For the concept of a voting cycle, see Lee Benson, *The Concept of Jacksonian*

Second, since party systems can be demarcated by realigning sequences and since realigning elections, by transforming the basic shape of the electoral universe, differ in kind from other types of elections, we can both time the emergence of each party system and describe its structure empirically.

However, in employing the party-system conception as a periodizing and integrating tool, we should not expect each discrete party system to be a pure type. Transformations in the contours of empirical data seem invariably more abrupt and sharper in their outlines than underlying transformations in political culture. Thus, we should expect each electoral era to exhibit mixtures of the old and the new, to be marked by syntheses of mixed forms and practices, cognitions and behaviors. Only by being attuned to the possibility of such mixtures, and the need to analyze the valences of their components, can we take into account the temporally and spatially uneven development of the electoral system.

Contours of the Third Electoral System

The transition from the second to the third electoral era entailed more than a simple substitution of the Republicans for the Whigs as the major opposition to the Democrats. It involved as well a change in the balance between the contending major parties and a shift in their regional sources of support. Longitudinal measures of partisan strength and balance provide convenient ways of summarizing these dimensions of the transition. Table 2.1 presents the mean strength of each of the major parties over the sequences of presidential elections from 1836 to 1852 and from 1856 to 1892 and the arithmetic difference between those means within each time segment.[8]

At the national level the swing appears to have been a mild one. The minuscule Whig lead that prevailed over the last five presidential elections of the second electoral era was transformed into a larger, but still mild, Republican lead. However, underlying that marginal national transformation were enormous sectional swings. Those shifts in partisan balance within regions, when aggregated to the national level, tended to counterbalance each other. The Midatlantic and East North Central areas

---

Democracy, pp. 125–31; Paul Kleppner, *The Cross of Culture*, pp. 8–17; Charles Sellers, "The Equilibrium Cycle in Two-Party Politics," pp. 16–38.

8. The 1836–52 span demarcates most of the stable phase of the second party system. Over the longer 1828–52 segment, the Democracy held a partisan lead at the national level of 4.1 percentage points. The shorter span has been used as the point of comparison here to avoid distortions arising from the unevenly diffused surge factors

TABLE 2.1 *Longitudinal Measures of Partisan Strength, 1836–1852 and 1856–1892* [9]

	Partisan Means				Partisan Leads	
	1836–52		1856–92		1836–52	1856–92
	Dem	Whig	Dem	Repub		
U.S.	48.0	48.2	45.3	47.2	0.2W	1.9R
New England	44.5	47.1	38.1	58.4	2.6W	20.3R
Midatlantic	47.5	48.1	45.4	49.6	0.6W	4.2R
East N. Cent.	48.0	47.4	45.5	51.1	0.6D	5.6R
West N. Cent.	56.0*	42.5	40.4	49.5	13.5D	9.1R
Confederacy	50.7	48.6	51.1	31.2	2.1D	19.9D
Border	45.5	54.3	50.5	34.4	8.8W	16.1D
West	-†	-	42.9	46.5	-	3.6R
Deep South	51.9	46.5	54.9	27.9	5.4D	27.0D
Outer South	50.0	49.8	48.7	33.3	0.2D	15.4D

*Includes only Missouri through 1844 and Iowa and Missouri through 1852.
†Only California was in the Union through 1852.

---

associated with Andrew Jackson's candidacy. For a good illustration of the operation of those factors in one state, see Roger D. Petersen, "The Reaction to a Heterogeneous Society," pp. 85–93.

9. The sectional categorization used here generally parallels the nineteenth-century census regions, except that the area designated as the "Confederacy" includes those eleven states that shared the common experience of secession. The division of the Confederacy into two subregions involves categorizing as "Deep South" the states of Alabama, Georgia, Louisiana, Mississippi, and South Carolina, and as "outer South" the states of Arkansas, Florida, North Carolina, Tennessee, Texas, and Virginia. The border area includes Maryland, Kentucky, and after 1863 West Virginia. To avoid misunderstanding, I have listed the states included within each of the other regions. *New England*: Connecticut, Maine, Massachusetts, New Hampshire, Rhode Island, and Vermont. *Midatlantic*: Delaware, New Jersey, New York, and Pennsylvania. *East North Central*: Illinois, Indiana, Michigan, Ohio, and Wisconsin. *West North Central*: Iowa, Kansas, Minnesota, Missouri, Nebraska, North Dakota, and South Dakota. *Mountain*: Colorado, Idaho, Montana, Nevada, and Wyoming. *Pacific*: California, Oregon, Washington. For some purposes I will employ a sectional categorization that aggregates these areas into four larger regions. In that categorization the *North* includes New England and the Midatlantic regions; the *Midwest* includes the East North Central and West North Central areas; the *South* encompasses both the Confederate and border regions; and the *West* includes the Mountain and Pacific areas. Since the Mountain and Pacific states were sparsely populated during most of the third electoral era—and particularly during its first phase—I will in some tables use the category *West* along with the six smaller regions.

swung sharply to the Republicans and provided that party with partisan leads that pale only in comparison with the level of Republican dominance in New England. In these areas the relatively tight partisan balance of the second party system gave way to much wider Republican leads. Countermovement in two other regions somewhat balanced these anti-Democratic swings. The Democrats opened a wide lead in the eleven-state Confederacy and converted the border region from its earlier Whig attachment.[10]

This two-way movement across the regions of the country gave the third party system a shape reflective of sectional polarities that were unknown during the second electoral era. We can explore that suggestion and develop additional insights into the structure of the third electoral system by examining the Democratic percentage of the total presidential vote and its associated measures of central tendency and dispersion for separate elections over a span of time encompassing all of the third and parts of the second and fourth party systems (see Table 2.2).

The data afford two views of the third electoral system. First, an election-by-election inspection of the level of Democratic percentage strength reveals the changes in that party's political fortunes across time. The Democracy reached its nineteenth-century low point with its sectional split in 1860. Despite its apparently rapid resurgence in 1864 and 1868, Democratic strength remained somewhat artificially depressed through its postwar nadir in 1872. Over the twenty years after 1872, however, Democratic strength was obviously and rather consistently higher than it had been in the elections from 1856 to 1872. By implication, the data simultaneously point to the rather precarious national position occupied by the major anti-Democratic party. The Republicans won the presidency in 1860, but they polled only 39.7 percent of the total vote cast. The subsequent secession of eleven southern states reduced the size of the electoral universe, postwar Reconstruction measures changed the character of the southern electorate, and the Republicans polled majorities of the total vote in the 1864, 1868, and 1872 presidential elections. However, the party was unable to replicate that feat in any subsequent election, presidential or congressional, prior to 1896. In fact, in the sequence of presidential elections from 1876 to 1892, the Republicans were weaker than the Whigs had been over the sequence from 1836 to 1852.[11] Yet declining Republican strength did not translate

10. The shifts in the West and West North Central areas were due to the admission of new states and not to the changed behaviors of old ones.
11. That was the case whether looked at in absolute or relative terms. In the 1866–92 sequence the Republican mean was 47.0 percent, and the Democratic mean was 48.4 percent; the Democratic partisan lead was thus 1.4 percentage points. For the earlier Whig absolute and relative strength, see Table 2.1.

TABLE 2.2   *Distribution of the Democratic Presidential Vote*

| | | Measures of Central Tendency | | | |
| | | By States | | By Sections | |
Year	Dem %	Mean	σ^2	Mean	σ^2
1848	42.4	45.4	92.33	44.4	40.91
1852	50.8	52.7	61.46	51.1	12.39
1856	45.6	48.1	127.46	46.1	53.33
1860*	29.4	23.8	266.66	27.2	137.89
1864	44.8	42.1	100.60	43.0	46.71
1868	47.2	45.8	133.40	47.8	76.51
1872	43.8	42.1	76.21	43.4	17.05
1876	50.9	50.4	95.84	50.1	33.91
1880	48.2	48.9	99.40	47.8	34.9S
1884	48.5	49.2	95.64	47.6	29.44
1888	48.6	50.2	133.40	47.4	36.79
1892	46.0	41.8	468.28	41.0	197.16
1896†	46.7	51.6	318.97	48.6	224.14
1900†	45.5	49.0	204.63	46.1	54.98

*Douglas Democrat only.
†The Utah vote has been excluded from these calculations.

automatically into surging Democratic majorities. In the presidential contests between 1880 and 1892, neither party was able to command the voting allegiance of as much as 50.0 percent of the total participating electorate.

The measures of central tendency and dispersion provide another dimension of information and a better view of the shape of the party system. The variance data (σ^2) require some preliminary clarification. *Variance* is a measure of dispersion about the mean of a distribution. Each item in a series is subtracted from the mean of the series and each remainder is squared; those products are summed and then divided by the number of items in the series. That quotient, the variance of the distribution, indicates the average squared deviation of the individual items from their own mean. The higher the variance, the greater the average (squared) distance of the dispersion of the items around the mean of the series. Applied to cross-sectional election data, low variances indicate relatively even distributions of support for a party across the reporting units. In comparison, increases in variance indicate some mixture of very high and very low levels of support across the units in the series.[12]

An examination over time of the means and variances presented in Table 2.2 points to a sectional rupture of the partisan distributions as a prime factor underlying the collapse of the second party system. That sectional disruption occurred in two distinct stages. In the first stage the sectionally based Republican party was substituted for the nationally oriented Whig party as the major anti-Democratic opposition. The systemic impact of that substitution is dramatically evident in the sharp increase in variance (and decrease in mean percentage) for the major anti-Democratic party between 1852 and 1856. The Whig vote in 1852, whether calculated by states or by sections, was one of the most uniformly distributed in American electoral history. In contrast, the Republican votes in 1856 and 1860 were among the most unevenly distributed.[13] This upsurge of variance mirrored the Republican party's nonexistence below the Mason-Dixon line coupled with its preponderant strength in New England. Although the variance of the Democratic distribution by states more than doubled over the interval from 1852 to 1856, the even sharper increase in its variance by sections provides evidence of the underlying strains that shortly thereafter tore the party (and the nation) asunder. The nearly fivefold increase in the variance of the Democratic distribution by sections reflected the party's collapse in New England combined with marginal increments in its level of voting support in the states that later formed the Confederacy. The second stage of this process of sectional polarization came between 1856 and 1860. It is apparent in the sharp reductions in the Democratic mean figures and in yet another more than doubling of the variance both by states and by sections. The collapse of the Douglas Democrats in the Confederate and border regions underlay these changes.

With the violent disruption of the Union and postwar legal changes in the character of the voting universe, the variances of each of the partisan distributions were reduced, only to begin slow but uneven increases

---

12. The square root of the variance is the standard deviation (σ) of the distribution. The description in the text oversimplifies the matter somewhat. These are measures of dispersion around a particular mean. When the two (or more) series being compared are measured in different units, or when their means are widely disparate, comparisons of the relevant standard deviations and variances can be misleading. In those instances a measure of relative dispersion, the coefficient of variability (V), is needed. That is calculated by dividing the standard deviation of the distribution by its mean and multiplying by 100 to convert to a percentage.

13. The 1852 Whig mean by states was 42.3 percent, with $\sigma^2 = 41.86$; by regions, $\bar{M} = 44.5$, with $\sigma^2 = 7.30$. The Republican 1856 mean by states was 26.2 percent, with $\sigma^2 = 725.76$; and by regions, $\bar{M} = 26.8$ percent, with $\sigma^2 = 465.30$. In 1860 the Republican mean by states was 32.1 percent, with $\sigma^2 = 765.07$; and by regions, $\bar{M} = 22.9$ percent, with $\sigma^2 = 527.85$.

from their shared 1872 lows. From that point forward (with the exception of 1884) the variances increased from one election to the next through 1892. The sharp upturn in the measures of Democratic variance in 1892 resulted from the party's virtual collapse in the Mountain states and its sharp drop in the West North Central area. The Republican distribution became less homogeneous across time, as that party's efforts to develop a southern base collapsed and as its strength remained relatively intact (at least through 1888) in the Mountain states. As with the Democratic distribution Republican variance surged upward in 1892, marking the beginnings of the sharp North-and-East vs. South-and-West political polarization that reached its dramatic climax (though by no means its termination) in 1896.

Each of these angles of view provides insight into the structure of the third party system. Viewed across time, the Democratic percentages suggest something of a transition (if not transformation) in electoral state at some point between 1872 and 1876. It is at least clear that from 1876 through 1892 the Democrats drew consistently higher levels of voting support and that there was less election-to-election fluctuation in the amount of that support than during the period from 1856 through 1872.[14] Viewed cross-sectionally (by states and by geographic regions), the data point to immense imbalances in the geographic distributions of party strength: sectional polarities of a nature and magnitude that distinguish the third from the second party system. That succession of party systems involved the post-1852 collapse of *national* parties and their displacement by parties that drew disproportionate support from one or more sections of the country.

Although the variance data bring into focus the sectional polarities underlying late nineteenth-century party oppositions they also draw attention to another significant feature of the third party system. The Democrats tended to gain strength over time in those parts of the country in which they had initially been weak. Although the Democratic regional mean in 1868 was nearly identical with that of 1888, the variance of the regional distribution had been reduced by more than half over the intervening twenty years.[15] And the pattern is a relatively consistent one. Excluding the 1872 and 1892 deviating elections, higher means and lower variances characterize the post-1876 Democratic distributions when compared with those of the sequence from 1856 to 1868. And again, as

14. For the 1856–72 and 1876–92 Democratic longitudinal means and variances, see Table 2.5.

15. With exactly the same variance in the two years, the mean by states had increased by 4.4 percentage points.

with the percentage strength data, 1876 seems to stand out as something of a turning point.

Phases of the Third Electoral System

Any electoral era consists of a set of electoral system–maintaining elections bounded by realigning sequences. Yet it is necessary to isolate the breakpoint between the realigning and maintaining sequences. Then we can divide the system into its behaviorally distinct parts and describe the empirical "qualities" of each.

To address this problem, one must shift the angle of view from cross-sectional to longitudinal comparisons. Although a number of distinct ways exist to do that, each involves calculating a statistical measure for one sequence of adjacent elections and comparing that with a similar measure for the next sequence. For example, Walter Dean Burnham has statistically compared the first five of a sequence of ten successive presidential elections with the second five to "identify 'cutting points' of transition between one system of electoral politics and another."[16] Using presidential data at the national level, Burnham found an unusually sharp cutting point associated with the midpoint 1874, separating the 1856–72 presidential sequence from the 1876–92 sequence. We can follow Burnham's lead, but with two modifications. First, we will evaluate longitudinal means based on sequences of five biennial elections. Second, the evaluation will be executed at the national and regional levels. Specifically, that procedure involved calculating a longitudinal mean for every possible five-election sequence of biennial elections for the nation and for three regions from 1848 to 1904.[17] Second, I used a t test for differences between means to compare each mean with that for the next sequence to determine whether the observed difference was greater than that in their standard deviations would lead us to expect. Leaving aside the breaks in the series associated with the realignments of the 1850s and 1890s, the array in Table 2.3 indicates the peak values of t and the midpoints separating the two sets of five-election sequences with which each is associated.

16. Burnham, *Critical Elections*, pp. 12–16; the quotation is on p. 13. Burnham used discontinuity coefficients and t tests to evaluate differences between longitudinal means.

17. The sparsely populated West has been included in the national figures but has not been presented as a separate region here. I have also fit a regression line to each time series; the patterns of the residuals show breaks in the series at the same points as the t values.

TABLE 2.3   *Longitudinal Discontinuity: Peak t Values*

	Democratic		Republican	
	Midpnt	*t* value	Midpnt	*t* value
Nation	1873	4.302	1873	4.543
North	1873	2.708	1875	2.956
Midwest	1881	2.726	1873	4.010
South	1877	2.735	1877	3.468

The critical values of *t* for *df* = 8,

	Two-tailed test	One-tailed test
.05	2.306	1.860
.01	3.355	2.896

The midpoints and the biennial sequences with which
each is associated:

Midpoint	Biennial sequence
1873	1864–72/1874–82
1875	1866–74/1876–84
1877	1868–76/1878–86
1881	1872–80/1882–90

The national *t* values are higher than those within any of the regions, and they show a between-party uniformity that is present in only
one region, the South. Their association with midpoint 1873 provides
evidence that nationally we can subdivide the third party system into
a realigning sequence from 1856 to 1872 and a stable phase from 1874
to 1892.

Five of the six regional *t* peaks occur in association with a midpoint
in the 1870s. In the South the break in the series occurs for both parties
in the same year, and that midpoint sets the post-Reconstruction elections off from the Reconstruction-era contests. Beyond that region three
of the four *t* peaks come in association with midpoints 1873 and 1875.
In the North the Democratic *t* value associated with midpoint 1873
marks an abrupt break in that party's series; the three immediately

preceding midpoints (1867, 1869, and 1871) have a mean t value of 1.302, and midpoint 1871 shows a t of only 0.933, the lowest in the series to that point. On the other hand, although the Republican t peaks at midpoint 1875, it had a high t value (2.903) at midpoint 1873 and continued to show a high t associated with midpoint 1878 (2.851). The sudden surge in the Democratic t value reflects the party's gains in the 1874 election and its failure to gain much additional strength after that. Yet on the Republican side the picture is one of step-by-step losses, beginning in 1874 and continuing through the 1878 election. This obvious noncongruence both in time and quantity between Republican losses and Democratic gains points to a role played in the process by minor parties.

The most glaring anomaly occurs in the Midwest. There Democratic t values remain low throughout the 1870s, never exceeding 0.951 from midpoint 1865 through midpoint 1879 and surging only at midpoint 1881. The Republican t peaks at midpoint 1873 and continues to show high t values at the next two midpoints.[18] In this region, as in the North, minor parties played a role in producing this incongruence, but in the Midwest those parties were both stronger and more persistent than they were in the North.

The data array brings into focus another characteristic of American electoral politics. The parts are not simple microcosms of the whole; the sectional patterns are not reflections of some larger national pattern. To the contrary, the national resultant is best conceived as a vector of its regional patterns.[19] That observation again draws attention both to the uneven temporal and spatial development of party systems and to the fact that any single benchmark year will fail to capture regional variations. Yet even with this limitation in mind, one can use the national cutting points to distinguish between the realigning and system-maintaining sequences of an electoral era.

Of course, we cannot simply assume that the 1873 cutting point separated two phases of the same electoral system. We need to inquire more precisely into the nature of the electoral behavior implied by that break in the series. Specifically, we need to distinguish between changes of the type associated with the phenomenon of critical realignment and those involved with transitions from realigning to stable phases.

Realigning sequences transform the shape of the voting universe. They produce a new electoral system that differs significantly and sys-

18. For the Republican series these are the relevant t values: 1875 = 2.652; 1877 = 2.651; and 1879 = 1.128.
19. If the data were disaggregated to the state level, it would be equally apt to observe that each regional resultant was a vector of the patterns of the states within it.

tematically from the old. We would expect, therefore, a comparison of prerealignment with postrealignment sequences to display sharp breakpoints, much like those exhibited by the national data in Table 2.3.[20] Yet even a cursory knowledge of the unprecedented events of the 1860s— secession, Civil War, Reconstruction, and the former Confederate states' readmission—and of their impact on the electoral and political systems mandates a more precise inquiry. Intuitively, it seems plausible that, following as they did the realignment of the 1850s, the military and political convulsions of the 1860s caused an extraordinary level of partisan fluctuation and that the effect of the change in the mid-1870s was not still another realignment but the restoration of the pretrauma partisan structure. It is plausible that the elections of the mid-1870s constituted a *reinstating* sequence.

To distinguish empirically between realigning and reinstating effects, we can pursue two distinct though analogous modes of reasoning. If the changes in the 1870s involved a transformation in the shape of the electoral universe, then elections after that point would exhibit low correlations with the realignment of the 1850s. Conversely, if the elections after the mid-1870s show high levels of association with the realignment of the 1850s, we would have some indication that the shifts of the 1870s had a reinstating effect. We can test for the presence of such effects by correlating each biennial election from 1860 through 1892 with the 1856 distribution. We can then calculate and compare the means of the squared correlation coefficients across specified time segments. Panel A of Table 2.4 presents the results of such operations.[21]

The first indication that the voting shifts of the 1870s did not transform the shape of the electoral universe lies in the fact that for the country and for two of its regions, the 1856 vote explains nearly 50.0 percent of the variances of the subsequent distributions. Since critical realignments produce upheavals of seismic proportions, we would expect correlations of a much lower magnitude than those for the United States, the North, and the Midwest. The 1856/1860–92 mean r^2 for the South more nearly satisfies the anticipated empirical effects of realigning sequences.

For the country as a whole, the partisan swings of the 1870s give clear-cut evidence of a reinstating effect. The post-1872 sequences show a higher mean r^2 with 1856 than does the sequence from 1860 to 1872.

20. Burnham, *Critical Elections*, p. 17, is somewhat ambivalent about whether the 1874 break evidenced a realignment. Yet in his later essay, ''The United States,'' Table 4, p. 666, Burnham classifies the 1876 election as a reinstating one.
21. The squared correlation coefficient (r^2) is the coefficient of determination, which can be interpreted as the proportion of the total variance of the dependent variable that is explained by the independent variable.

TABLE 2.4   *Realignment or Reinstatement? Democratic Distributions*

A. *Mean Coefficients of Determination*

	U.S.	North	Midwest	South
1856/1860–92	.456	.478	.493	.165
1856/1860–72	.385	.532	.421	.236
1856/1874–88	.534	.452	.545	.150
1856/1874–92	.514	.442	.540	.130
1876/1878–88	.554	.769	.585	.063
1876/1878–92	.520	.756	.619	.060

B. *Time-Series Partials*

	1856/1880 · 1860–76 (5th-order partial)	1856/1880 (zero-order r)
U.S.	+.693	+.821
Iowa	+.276	+.192
Maine	+.248	+.663
Massachusetts	+.078	+.633
Maryland	−.511	−.429
Missouri	−.031	−.212
Wisconsin	+.012	+.691

Although the increment in r^2 is not overpowering—14.9 percentage points at its peak—it is of analytical importance. We normally expect some erosion from one election to the next in the tightness of fit between two distributions, and we expect that this erosion between pairs of elections is additive across time; so in the normal course of events, the longer the span of time between elections, the lower the anticipated correlation. Yet at the national level these normal expectations have been reversed. Instead of weaker correlations as time intervened, and therefore lower levels of r^2, elections in the second segment of the third party system show a tighter fit with the beginnings of that system than those in its first segment.

The same correlational pattern and reinstating effect are evident in the data for the Midwest. However, those for the North and the South exhibit different patterns that imply distinct behavioral phenomena. The

North best mirrors that nearly step-by-step erosion that we typically anticipate in time-series election correlations. Better at least than the other regions, it evidences a tendency toward partisan decay that was additive over time. In the South the change in system state was not a matter of erosion but of abrupt transformation followed by continued oscillation of a magnitude not characteristic of the other parts of the country. Although the outlines of the Democracy's resurgence and dominance were in place within the South by the mid-1870s, subsequent shifts represented continuing stages in a temporally extended process of electoral-universe transformation.[22]

The time-series partials (Panel B, Table 2.4) allow us to inquire into the nature of the electoral behavior of the mid-1870s, both at a different level of aggregation and from a somewhat distinct logical perspective. Forces act over time to decay or erode any set of structured relations. Therefore, we regularly anticipate that distributions of party strength (by counties within states) will not remain unchanged from one election to the next. For instance, some proportion of voters will respond to the short-term forces that characterize any election and will defect from their regular party loyalty. Yet if party loyalty is strong, we expect the likelihood of a second defection to be weaker and that of a third weaker still. This election-by-election defection constitutes a sort of random background "noise" and reduces the size of the correlation between election pairs. It is precisely for this reason that the size of the correlation typically decreases as the interval between elections increases. Yet if the defection is random, we should find some nonzero partial whose magnitude is a positive function of the existence of an underlying trend toward continuity, a "homing" tendency. Where the partial disappears, or is negative, we can say that any apparent relationship in the zero-order correlation between the two elections has been transmitted completely through the intervening measured states.[23]

In the case in point, the presence of a positive fifth-order partial between the 1856 and 1880 distributions indicates that the oscillation of the 1870s produced a distribution that evidenced such a homing tendency. The partials reflect the reinstating effects of those shifts for the nation (by states) and for four of the states. Although the size of the homing tendency varied, the electoral behavior of these states in the mid-1870s did not create a new electoral universe but reinstated the one formed by

22. Notice especially the mean r^2 between 1876/1878–88 and 1876/1878–92 for the South, and compare those with the corresponding measures for the other regions.

23. We should also expect that the size of the partial will decline as we move to progressively higher-order partials. The logic here follows Philip E. Converse, "Survey Research and the Decoding of Patterns in Ecological Data," pp. 474–81.

the prewar realignment. The opposite was the case in Maryland and Missouri. The fluctuations of the 1870s in these states offer no evidence of a homing tendency toward the 1856 distributions. The realigning sequences that shaped their late nineteenth-century voting universes came after the 1856 election.

Taken together, the data in Tables 2.3 and 2.4 make clear that the shifts of the mid-1870s did not produce the sort of uniform change in electoral state that is associated with critical realignments. With the exception of the South, the overall effect of those shifts was reinstating. The data also make it possible to distinguish the two distinct phases of the third electoral era. Viewed nationally, the realigning phase of that system began as early as the off-year elections of 1853 and continued through the 1872 election. The successive upheavals associated with secession, the war, and its aftermath upset—from this perspective—the ''crispness'' that we associate with realigning sequences. Normally, realigning sequences are brief and are marked by intense bursts of electoral reorganization. The realignment of the 1850s satisfied these criteria in the North and the Midwest, but the South remained sui generis. The action of southern elites in proffering their own partisan alternative in 1860 and the subsequent secession of eleven states had the national effect of extending the duration of the realigning sequence. Only with the reintegration of the former Confederacy into the national polity did the fluctuation phase, or realigning sequence, of the third party system end and its stable, or equilibrium, phase begin. The rebound of Democratic strength in 1874 reflects the beginnings of that reintegration, coupled with the nonsouthern gains of the party that came from the effects of the nation's first urban-industrial depression.

Realigning and stable phases of party systems exhibit analytically important distinctions in electoral behavior. If for the third party system we use the 1873 cutting point to demarcate those phases, then the next step must be to inquire into the nature of the behavioral distinctions.

Electoral Stability and Partisan Competitiveness

Compared with those of the realigning sequence, elections during the equilibrium phase of the third electoral system displayed higher levels of Democratic strength, less longitudinal fluctuation in party percentages, and higher levels of partisan competitiveness. Although these qualities are obviously not unrelated to each other, it is useful to disentangle them descriptively. One can begin by observing the differences in Democratic longitudinal means and variances for the electoral system as a whole and for each of its phases (see Table 2.5).

The Democracy's mean strength during the stable phase of the third party system was generally higher than it had been during the realigning sequence.[24] More importantly, the variances of the Democratic longitudinal means were considerably smaller than they had been during the phase from 1856 to 1872. Although the party's strength displayed some election-to-election fluctuation during both of the specified post-1874 sequences, the range of that fluctuation was much narrower than it had been earlier.

Even if the data are disaggregated to the state level, these hallmarks of the third party system's stable phase persist. If we compare the longitudinal means from 1856 to 1872 with those for the sequence from 1876

TABLE 2.5   *Longitudinal Measures of Democratic Strength*

	Biennial Sequence	Mean	σ^2
Nation	1856–92	47.6	26.85
	1856–72	45.3	41.45
	1874–88	50.2	1.54
	1874–92	49.6	9.52
North	1856–92	42.3	11.90
	1856–72	39.2	24.52
	1874–88	44.8	2.46
	1874–92	45.1	2.17
Midwest	1856–92	42.7	12.25
	1856–72	43.4	12.86
	1874–88	43.1	2.53
	1874–92	42.0	12.68
South	1856–92	55.6	138.39
	1856–72	47.3	375.31
	1874–88	60.7	16.42
	1874–92	61.4	15.85

24. The Midwest is an ostensible exception to that generalization, but there both major parties registered lower longitudinal means for the stable phase, and the Democratic decline was less severe than the Republican. I have presented longitudinal means for both the 1874–88 and 1874–92 sequences since the final two biennial elections of the third party system displayed "unusual" features; for a discussion of those, see Chapter 8.

through 1892, the Democracy registered gains in twenty-seven states and lost strength in only nine.[25] Although not every state showed lower variance about the Democratic longitudinal mean, the fluctuation was considerably less than had existed during the realigning sequence. The data in Table 2.6 provide a somewhat panoramic view.[26] The comparative stability of the equilibrium phase of the third party system with both its realigning sequence and with the fourth and fifth party systems is apparent. During the sequence from 1876 to 1892, states with fully two-thirds of the nation's population showed standard deviations of 4.9 percentage points or less, and only 16.7 percent of the population lived in states where the Democratic longitudinal means had standard deviations of more than 7.4 percentage points.

Increased and stabilized levels of Democratic voting support underlay the narrow partisan balance that prevailed during the stable phase of the third party system. Indeed, that electoral sequence frequently, and with at least superficial accuracy, has been characterized as an era of "no decision." From the national perspective it was indeed a period during which neither major party regularly commanded the support of a

TABLE 2.6   *Standard Deviations of the Democratic Vote by Period and Percentage of Population by State*

σ	Period and Percentage of Total Population			
	1856–72*	1876–92*	1896–1928†	1932–48†
0.0– 2.4	2.7	27.7	0.0	7.6
2.5– 4.9	48.0	39.1	23.4	46.0
5.0– 7.4	18.6	16.3	45.5	23.0
7.5– 9.9	15.2	6.7	20.9	13.8
10.0–14.9	15.3	10.0	8.7	2.8
15.0+	0.0	0.0	1.4	6.8

*Based on biennial election sequences.
†Based on presidential sequences.

25. Because it did not conduct statewide popular elections prior to 1860, South Carolina has been excluded from this summary. The Republican 1876–92 mean was greater than its 1856–72 strength in only three states; it was lower in thirty-three.

26. The data below for the fourth and fifth party systems are from Burnham, "The United States," Table 8, p. 679. These data are not wholly comparable to those presented for the third party system. The latter are derived from biennial election sequences, and since off-year elections regularly involve more "background noise" than those in presidential years, the data for 1856–92 are conservative when compared with the standard deviations for exclusively presidential sequences. That fact, of course, makes the differences between the third system and those that followed even more striking.

majority of the voters. The Republicans elected their candidate in three of the era's five presidential contests, but twice (1876 and 1888) the winning Republican polled fewer popular votes than the losing Democrat. Only in 1880 did the Republicans secure a plurality of the national vote, and then it was the less-than-landslide margin of 9,457 votes of the over 9.2 million votes cast. Nor did the Democrats do considerably better. They secured a majority of the total popular vote in 1876 (exactly 50.0 percent), but by 1892 their share of the presidential vote was 1.2 percentage points *below* the level they had polled in the 1868 election. Even if we measure relative partisan strengths in terms of the two-party vote—a less exacting indication—it still shows that neither party was able to attain dominance. The Democracy did poll over 50.0 percent of the two-party vote in four of the five presidential elections (and 49.9 percent in 1880), but the party's 51.7 percent in 1892 was only 0.2 percentage points higher than in 1876 and 6.1 percentage points *lower* than in 1856.

The contrast in partisan dominance between the realigning and stable phases of the third system becomes apparent from an examination of the outcomes of elections to the U.S. House of Representatives.[27] In the Thirty-fifth through the Forty-third Congresses (the elections of 1856 through 1872), the Republicans controlled the House seven of nine times; they held over 70.0 percent of the membership in the Thirty-ninth through Forty-first Houses (elected 1864 to 1868). However, in the ten Houses of the Forty-fourth through the Fifty-first Congresses (the elections of 1874 through 1892), the Republicans had a majority only twice; the apex of their strength was 51.1 percent of the membership of the Fifty-first House (elected 1888). The Democrats did better. They organized the House eight of ten times during the stable phase; they elected over 70.0 percent of the membership to the Fifty-second House (elected 1890) and over 60.0 percent of the membership of the Forty-eighth and Fifty-third Houses (elected 1882 and 1892, respectively). Yet the Democracy's success in electing candidates to the House did not signal an underlying popular majority for the party. Of the total vote cast in the House elections between 1876 and 1892, the Democrats never rose above the 51.9 percent that they polled in 1890, and only four other times did they receive as much as 50.0 percent of the total vote.[28]

Thus, the postrealignment phase of the third electoral system was

27. U.S., Bureau of the Census, *Historical Statistics of the United States, Colonial Times to 1957*, pp. 691–92.

28. The 51.8 percent that the party polled in the 1876 congressional election was its second highest during the period. Using the two-party vote only, the Democrats were over 50.0 percent in each of these nine elections, and their apex was 55.4 percent in 1890. The data are conveniently reported in Burnham, ''The United States,'' pp. 676–77.

one in which election outcomes, when aggregated to the national level, were exceedingly close; in which neither party commanded a regular, or normal, majority; and in which neither party was able to open much partisan lead over its major opposition. Elections viewed from the national level displayed extraordinarily high levels of partisan competitiveness with a very distinct and geographic skew. The data in Table 2.7 bring several aspects of this competitive structure into focus.

The stable phase of the system displayed more competitiveness than its realigning phase. At the national level the moderate Republican

TABLE 2.7   *Partisan Competitiveness during the Third Electoral Era*

A. *Shift in Party Competitiveness*

	Partisan Lead		Net Shift in Competitiveness
	1856–72	1876–92	1856–72/1876–92
U.S.	5.0R	1.4D	+ 3.6
New England	29.6R	11.0R	+18.6
Midatlantic	7.0R	1.4R	+ 5.6
East N. Cent.	8.2R	2.9R	+ 5.3
West N. Cent.	7.5R	10.6R	− 3.1
Confederacy	15.7D	23.2D	− 7.5
Border	21.3D	10.7D	+10.6
West	0.9R	6.4R	− 5.5
Deep South	17.0D	34.8D	−17.8
Outer South	12.5D	17.6D	− 5.1

B. *Competitiveness by Percentage of States and of Population by States*

Partisan Lead Categories	% of States		% of Population	
	1856–72	1876–92	1856–72	1876–92
20.0%+D	5.5	21.6	5.7	17.6
10–19.9D	5.5	16.2	5.8	15.2
5– 9.9D	19.1	5.4	14.0	3.9
0– 4.9D	5.5	10.8	5.7	17.2
0– 4.9R	13.8	16.2	30.7	26.6
5– 9.9R	19.4	13.5	18.1	10.9
10–19.9R	8.3	13.5	7.1	7.9
20.0%+R	22.2	2.7	12.7	0.5

lead from 1856 to 1872 was converted into an even narrower Democratic lead. Leaving aside the West and West North Central areas, whose partisan leads were more reflective of the post-1856 admission of new states than of the changed behavior of old ones, four of the remaining five areas exhibited positive net shifts in competitiveness.[29] The New England and border areas showed the sharpest increases in competitiveness, with the Republicans losing strength in the former area and gaining in the latter. Yet although New England became more competitive, and by the end of the stable phase was no longer a bastion of Yankee Republicanism, throughout that phase it remained the party's strongest area of popular support. The border area became more competitive but continued throughout to be regularly Democratic. The amount of competitive shift was less in the Midatlantic and East North Central states, but its effect was more telling. Over the course of the stable phase, the Republicans were able to cling to only fragile leads in these two populous regions. The former Confederacy represented the extreme case of declining partisan competition, though within that region the decline among the states of the outer South was much less steep than among the five states of the Deep South.

Some sense of the geographic skewness of the competitive structure of the equilibrium phase emerges from the data in Panel B of Table 2.7.[30] The proportions of states and of population that fell into the most competitive categories, those in which neither party held a partisan lead of more than 4.9 percentage points, increased. During the realigning sequence those two categories contained 19.3 percent of the states and 36.4 percent of the total population; that increased during the stable phase to 27.0 percent of the states and 43.8 percent of the population. Even more significant, however, were the changes within the most partisan categories, those in which either party held a partisan lead of 10.0 percentage points or more. Across the sequence from 1856 to 1872, those four categories contained 41.5 percent of the states and 31.3 percent of the population, but over the stable phase the respective proportions increased to 54.0 percent and 41.2 percent. These increases reflected the growing number of one-party or modified one-party Democratic states. From the realigning to the stable phases, the proportions of states and of population within those two Democratic categories increased, respectively, by 26.8 and 21.3 percentage points.

An enumeration of the states in the two pairs of most partisan

29. In the West North Central area, Kansas, Minnesota, Nebraska, North Dakota, and South Dakota were admitted after 1856, as were Colorado, Idaho, Montana, Nevada, Oregon, Washington, and Wyoming in the West.

30. Both the partisan lead categories in Panel B and the corresponding qualitative descriptions of partisan status used in the discussion have been borrowed from Burnham, "The United States," p. 673.

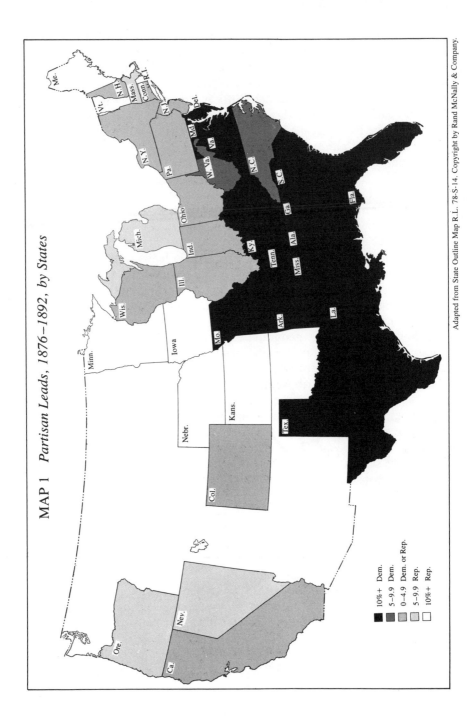

MAP 1 *Partisan Leads, 1876–1892, by States*

Adapted from State Outline Map R.L. 78-S-14. Copyright by Rand McNally & Company.

10%+ Dem.
5–9.9 Dem.
0–4.9 Dem. or Rep.
5–9.9 Rep.
10%+ Rep.

categories again highlights the sectionalism that pervaded the third electoral era (see Map 1). From 1876 to 1892, the Republicans held a mean lead of 10.0 percentage points or more in only six states: Maine, Rhode Island, and Vermont in New England and Kansas, Minnesota, and Nebraska in the West North Central region. The fourteen states in which the Democracy commanded a lead of at least 10.0 percentage points included all five states of the Deep South; all of the states of the outer South except North Carolina; and Delaware, Kentucky, Maryland, and Missouri.[31]

Although strong sectional polarities were evident throughout the third electoral era, comparison of the partisan leads for the two phases suggests that they were stronger during the system's realigning sequence than during its stable phase. Sectional polarities played a causal role in the dynamics of the realigning sequence, but as time elapsed and conditions as well as population composition changed, they seem to have become less critical in all but one region, the former Confederacy. The unique experience of that eleven-state region intensified the commitment of most of its (white) voters to the anti-Republican party, and after 1876 the Confederacy became both less competitive and more politically homogeneous internally.[32] Although the behavioral forces at work there affected both subparts of the region, especially the states of the Deep South, they did not extend as uniformly to the border region. That area became more competitive.[33] The New England, Midatlantic, and East North Central regions also moved toward greater partisan competition and increased levels of internal political heterogeneity. That movement, of course, was neither so rapid nor so extinguishing that it failed to leave residual traces of the sectional cleavage that had partially underlain the genesis of the third party system. Yet the direction of the movement, the opposite of that required to support a hypothesis of increasing sectionalism, suggests some waning in the partisan significance of the old polarities.

The extended period of national political equilibrium was produced by the growth of disproportionate Democratic strength in the former Confederacy, combined with declining Republican dominance in that party's pre-1872 areas of strength. As those Republican declines—

31. West Virginia and North Carolina both fell into the 5–9.9 percent D category.
32. That is, on the average there was less dispersion of the Democratic vote around its mean after 1876 than in that year or earlier. The observation in the text pertains to trends in partisan movement and does not mean to imply that the process through which the Confederacy became almost irretrievably Democratic had been completed.
33. That resulted from counterbalancing movement. West Virginia swung to the Democrats, and Kentucky was one of only nine states in which the Democratic 1876–92 mean was lower than the party's 1856–72 strength.

especially in the New England, Midatlantic, and East North Central regions—were temporally extended, they had the effect of reducing the party to a minority of the 1892 vote in every region of the nation except New England.[34] The gradual decline of Republican strength in the North and part of the Midwest, as well as the fact that Democratic gains in these areas were not proportionate to Republican losses, calls attention to another feature of stable phases of voting cycles—secular trends.

Secular Trends and the Third Electoral System

Critical realignment involves short and intense bursts of electoral reorganization that produce large-scale coalitional adjustments. Yet viewed over time, and in the aggregate, large numbers of voters may apparently shift their partisan allegiances without the intrusion of the intense coalition-shuffling effects typically associated with realigning sequences. That process, *secular realignment*, entails a cross-party movement of voters that extends over several elections and is independent of the unique factors influencing the vote at individual elections. It involves slight election-to-election shifts in the same direction, which tend to become cumulative across time.[35]

Secular realignment, however, is best thought of as a particular subtype of a broader category of secular change. Not all such trends necessarily involve the realignment of voter groups. We can distinguish two other types of slight and unidirectional shifts that tend to produce additive effects when viewed longitudinally: changes in population composition and the emergence of minor parties. Although neither of these phenomena involved systemic voter-group realignment, each made a contribution to the partisan structure of the third era's equilibrium phase. The data in Table 2.8 provide an overview of that contribution.[36]

Between 1850 and 1890 the country's population increased by

34. The Republicans received 52.0 percent of the total vote in New England in 1892; their second strongest area was the Midatlantic area, in which they polled 47.9 percent. The Republicans received less than 50.0 percent in every region except New England, but they still held an 1892 lead over the Democracy in every region except the East North Central, the Confederate, and border areas.

35. The definition of secular realignment is from V. O. Key, Jr., "Secular Realignment and the Party System," pp. 198–210.

36. The "% Foreign Voters" is a shorthand label for the proportion of total males twenty-one years of age and over who were either foreign born or native born of foreign-born parents. The "% Manufacturing" is the proportion of the labor force engaged in manufacturing occupations and comes from Harvey S. Perloff et al., *Regions, Resources and Economic Growth*, Appendix Table A–6, p. 632. The "% Urban" is from U.S., Bureau of the Census, *1970 Census of Population*, Table 18, pp. 1-62–1-71. The data as

TABLE 2.8   *Indicators of Secular Change*

A. *Minor-Party Voting and Population Characteristics by Regions*

	$\overline{M}$ Minor Party		Population Characteristics, 1890		
	1876–88	1876–92	% Frgn Voters	% Mfg	% Urban
U.S.	2.8	4.4	37.7	24.3	35.1
New England	2.8	2.8	44.7	47.8	61.6
Midatlantic	2.0	2.4	50.7	36.6	57.8
E. N. Cent.	3.3	3.8	48.1	25.0	37.9
W. N. Cent.	4.8	8.3	44.9	16.4	25.8
Confederacy	1.9	4.9	7.2	9.6	12.8
Border	1.8	2.6	17.4	19.3	25.4
West	1.6	6.9	44.2	21.7	37.0
Deep South	0.6	4.6	5.6	8.1	12.7
Outer South	2.7	5.1	8.4	10.9	12.9

B. *Shifts in Competitiveness 1856–72 to 1876–92 by Demographic and Partisan Categories*

	Means by States				
Net Shift	% Foreign Voters	% Mfg	% Urban	% Repub 1856–72	% Minor Pty 1876–92
+5.0 or more (*N* = 15)	40.5	31.8	37.1	58.5	6.1
−5.0 or more (*N* = 10)	10.4	12.2	17.9	47.9	4.8

168.3 percent, and the ethnic, economic, and residential composition of that population also changed drastically. It would not be realistic to suppose that changes of such an order were without reverberating effect on partisan politics—especially since the 1890 data reveal immense unevenness in the geographic distribution of at least three potentially

reported and used here have been adjusted to constitute a substantially consistent series based on the pre-1950 census definition of urban population—i.e., all people living in incorporated places of 2,500 or more.

relevant characteristics of the population. For example, it is suggestive to notice that the two most strongly Democratic regions of the nation—the Confederacy and border—also had the lowest proportions of foreign-stock voters among their electorates and were among the least industrial and least urban sections. Moreover, the states within these regions were by and large moving in a sharply anticompetitive direction over the phase from 1876 to 1892.[37] Such findings square with the long-standing, but frequently only implied, description of the late nineteenth-century Democracy as a party of territorial defense, a "southern party," or a party defending an amorphously conceived preindustrial culture. Surely it was, but two dimensions of the data question the analytical sufficiency of those characterizations.

First, the nation's second great "colonial" outpost, the West North Central region, became both less competitive and more Republican. Thus, the two great semicolonial regions of the nation, the Confederacy and the West North Central area, both became politically less competitive and more internally homogeneous but moved in *opposite* partisan directions. Although the cash-crop agrarians of these regions surely harbored resentments and animosities against the nation's urban-industrial metropole, these were not yet expressed as party oppositions. Instead, they remained cleavages that crosscut the dominating social fissures of the third electoral era.

Nor did the urban-industrial imperium become either more Republican or more politically homogeneous during the equilibrium phase. Those states that showed the sharpest net increases in competitiveness (i.e., moved in a pro-Democratic direction) were precisely the *most* foreign, the *most* industrial, and the *most* urban ones. With only minor exceptions they were states in the North and Midwest, and their increasing competitiveness was clearly related to long-term changes in the composition of their populations.[38] Higher levels of industrialization and urbanization in these units did not produce increased levels of Republican support but underlay the small though cumulatively important shifts to the Democrats that are apparent at the aggregate level.

The data in Table 2.8 bring into view another secular trend of some

37. Eight of the ten states in the −5.0 category (Panel B) were former Confederate states; Delaware and Missouri were the other two. Only Kentucky (+5.55) and West Virginia (+6.56) were in the category of states showing the sharpest competitive shifts. Kentucky's increased competition came from Democratic losses and West Virginia's from increases in the Democratic longitudinal mean.

38. Only three of the states in the +5.0 category had 1876–92 Democratic means that were below the party's strength across the 1856–72 sequence: Kentucky, Michigan, and Nebraska. The three states that were not either in the North or Midwest: Kentucky, West Virginia, and California.

analytical importance. Minor parties, which had been virtually nonexistent during the third system's realigning sequence, played important, though regionally uneven, roles during its stable phase. The relative importance of minor parties in increasing partisan competitiveness is evident from the size of the longitudinal minor-party means from 1876 to 1888 as well as those from 1876 to 1892, which were greater than the Republican mean partisan lead in the populous Middle Atlantic and East North Central regions. Over all, Republicans mean losses from the realigning to the stable phases of the third party system exceeded Democratic gains in twenty-three states; in seven more both of the major parties lost mean strength. Comparison of the longitudinal strength of the minor parties across the states within each of the extreme-shift categories succinctly, if only suggestively, summarizes the case.

Although we can descriptively isolate two distinct species of secular trends, it is important to recognize that they may intersect analytically. Given the essentially constituent nature of electoral politics and the lines of cleavage in the third electoral era, demographic changes may have induced tensions that could not be accommodated within the prevailing party system. With their emergent demands not being adequately aggregated by the existing parties, the affected groups may have resorted to partisan mobilization beyond the bounds of the dominant two-party system. Such a hypothesis may help to account for the relatively high levels of minor-party voting that marked post-1876 politics in the West North Central region—as well as the sudden upturn in such voting there, in the Confederacy, and in the West associated with the Populists' advent in 1892. Minor-party voting in these regions during the equilibrium phase may have presaged the colonial-metropole polarity that shaped the fourth party system. In the New England, Midatlantic, and East North Central regions minor-party voting was of a somewhat different character. Yet it still may have resulted from a similar process involving different groups and different types of emergent tensions.[39] Whatever the particulars of the cases, it is clear that both dynamic, but geographically uneven, changes in the demographic structure of the society and the emergence of minor parties played important roles during the stable phase of the third electoral era.

39. See Burnham's perceptive discussion of minor-party movements as proto-realignment phenomena in *Critical Elections*, pp. 27–31. It seems equally plausible that new tensions arising from shifts in population may be aggregated by one or another (or both) of the parties; that in turn may alienate some proportions of their old supporters. Such minor parties (e.g., the Prohibitionists) would not satisfy the criteria for classification as protorealignment movements. Yet they are important both as behavioral phenomena and as tangible factors influencing the outcomes of particular elections.

Voter Mobilization and the Third Electoral System

One feature of the postwar electoral system especially distinguishes it
from subsequent party systems. The stable phase of the third electoral
era was a period of extraordinarily high levels of voter participation (see
Table 2.9).[40] In every region of the country except the sparsely settled
West, electoral participation was high, whether judged by our own late
twentieth-century norms or by those of the fourth party system.[41] In
every region except the former Confederacy, the trend over time was
toward increasing levels of voter participation. And even within that
region sharp differences in longitudinal means and regression-line trends
existed between the states of the Deep South and those of the outer
South. Only among the former had the steep turnout-rate decay already
set in.

Shifting to the state level and assigning the units to categories based
on their turnout means from 1876 through 1892 provides a general sense
of the *extensiveness* of voter mobilization. Fully 69.4 percent of the
potential voters lived in states that regularly had turnout rates of 65.0
percent or better, and 83.1 percent were in states in which the normal
turnout rates were at least 60.0 percent. Moreover, there was a clear,
though not perfectly direct, relationship between turnout and competitiveness. Generally, the more competitive the state, the higher the turnout mean. Yet there are a sufficient number of deviant cases within each
of the categories to cause one to be wary of suggesting that turnout was
high solely because competitiveness was. States such as Kansas and
Missouri had atypically wide partisan leads (16.3R and 13.4D, respectively) but longitudinal turnout rates of 70.0 to 79.9 percent. Yet California, with a very narrow gap between the parties (0.3R), fell into the
50.0 to 59.9 percent category—as did South Carolina, with the strongest
partisan lead (51.2D) in the nation.

By disaggregating the data, we can examine the distribution of
turnout by counties within states as well as its relationship to two social-

40. The turnout figures here, and throughout, have been based on the total number
of males twenty-one years of age and over as reported in decennial census years, with
linear interpolation for noncensus years but without any effort to adjust for state-by-state
variations in voter-eligibility requirements. When compared with Burnham's figures,
mine are consistently *lower*, but the *pattern* over time is the same. In other words, using
total males twenty-one and over as the denominator will produce turnout estimates that
are consistently conservative. For a convenient array of Burnham's data, see Burnham,
"The United States," p. 677.
41. On these matters see Walter Dean Burnham, "The Changing Shape of the
American Political Universe," pp. 7–28; Burnham, *Critical Elections*, pp. 18–21,
71–91.

TABLE 2.9 *Longitudinal Measures of Voter Mobilization*

A. *Presidential Turnout, 1876–92*

	Mean	σ^2	Net % Shift (on regr line)
U.S.	71.1	11.03	+ 2.57
New England	61.1	19.80	+ 6.97
Midatlantic	73.4	19.71	+ 3.40
East N. Cent.	80.6	19.45	+ 6.39
West N. Cent.	73.2	24.54	+20.36
Confederacy	63.8	22.66	−25.92
Border	75.8	24.70	+23.26
West	51.8	38.16	+45.10
Deep South	55.3	142.98	−51.96
Outer South	70.8	17.52	+ 9.88

B. *Turnout Categories by Percentage of States, Potential Voters, and Mean Competitiveness*

Turnout $\bar{M}$ 1876–92	% States	% 1890 Males 21+	$\bar{M}$ Competitiveness 1876–92*
80.0% and over	8.1	11.1	3.5
70.0–79.9	21.6	22.1	7.7
65.0–69.9	24.3	36.2	10.0
60.0–64.9	21.6	13.7	22.4
50.0–59.9	13.5	10.5	21.9
under 49.9%	10.8	6.3	36.5

*This is a mean of the partisan lead by states, irrespective of party.

structural variables (see Table 2.10).[42] Apart from the states of the Deep South, the typical trend at the state level was toward increased rates of

42. The "% Urban" is the proportion of the county's population living in places of 2,500 or more. The figure has been calculated for each census year from the data reporting population by minor civil divisions, and linear interpolations have been used for noncensus years. The "Average Value of Farm Products" is the total cash value of farm products divided by the number of farms. The cash value of farm products is given in census reports in current dollars; I transformed that measure into one adjusted for changes in the purchasing power of dollars. And, again, linear interpolations have been used for noncensus years.

TABLE 2.10   *Cross-Sectional Measures of Voter Mobilization*

A. *Turnout by Counties*

	1876		1888		1892	
	Mean	σ^2	Mean	σ^2	Mean	σ^2
Iowa	79.3	120.1	82.3	34.1	83.2	30.3
Maryland	84.5	104.0	86.0	118.1	80.0	60.6
Massachusetts	54.9	54.5	56.8	29.3	58.2	20.3
Minnesota	66.4	479.5	83.0	308.4	78.0	240.2
Missouri	80.5	101.4	86.1	68.7	82.0	67.7
New Jersey	83.5	64.7	81.8	64.0	79.7	50.3
Wisconsin	84.2	143.3	84.0	243.5	77.4	75.2

B. *Turnout Social Indicators: Mean r^2 1870–92*

	% Urban	Average Value Farm Products
Iowa	.074	.036
Maryland	.199	.072*
Massachusetts	.095	.073
Minnesota	.047	.019
Missouri	.124	.031
New Jersey	.236	.097
Wisconsin	.025*	.048*

*The mean of the zero-order correlations is *positive*.

voter participation.[43] Moreover, as a comparison of the 1886 and 1888 means and variances indicates, the increased 1888 turnout means reflected a more even distribution in each state (except Wisconsin) than had been the case earlier. Thus, not only was turnout higher, but it was generally spread more evenly across voting units. That suggests that the high rates of participation during the third electoral era affected most social groups and none disproportionately.

Although we are accustomed in the late twentieth century to expect

43. This observation derives from the net percentage shifts along the 1870–92 turnout regression line. Only New Jersey shows a negative shift, a minuscule −1.4 percent. New Jersey was a strongly competitive state; its 1876–92 Democratic partisan lead was only 2.1 percentage points.

strong and positive relationships between turnout rates, on the one hand, and urbanization and wealth or status indicators, on the other, that was not the nineteenth-century case.[44] Contemporary urban elites may have believed that "urban machines" exaggerated their strength by encouraging their supporters to "vote early and often," but the factual bases for those claims is shaky at best. Only in New Jersey was there a relationship of any appreciable magnitude between urbanism and turnout, and that explained only 23.6 percent of the variance in turnout. And there, as in five of the other states, high levels of urbanization were negatively associated with high turnout rates. On the whole, nonurban voting units exhibited turnout rates that consistently were at least equal to urban turnout rates and that often were considerably higher. And it was not merely the richer farmers who participated. In no case was there a consistently strong relationship between high average values of farm products and high rates of turnout, and in two of the states the patterned relationship was negative. Whatever the underlying social dynamics of partisan commitments, they were at least intensely enough felt to move most voters to participate in elections.

This overview of the basic statistics of the third party system has been designed to bring into focus several of its more significant qualities and draw attention to the distinctions between that era's realigning and stable phases, to its regional polarities, to its geographically skewed competitiveness, and to the operation of secular trends. Taken collectively and within the context of a research strategy aimed at exploring the social-group bases of mass partisan coalitions, these qualities provide both a loose analytical agenda and an organizing framework for this study.

44. For some of the contemporary norms, see Campbell et al., *American Voter*, pp. 304–16; Lester Milbraith, *Political Participation*, pp. 42, 116–17; Sidney Verba and Norman H. Nie, *Participation in America*, pp. 339–41.

3

From Equilibrium to Realignment: Shaping the Third Electoral System

A Yankee is a Yankee over the globe, and you might know him if you meet him on the mountains of the moon in five minutes by his nationality. We love and honor him for it, whenever it is not carried by a blinding prejudice.

Western Monthly Magazine
(Cincinnati, June 1828)

Few Yankees were loved by others. Their distinctive "nationality" typically was carried by a "blinding prejudice," for the Yankee was not only conscious of "being a New England man," he was also convinced that Yankees collectively "brought in themselves the germs of every quality essential to national greatness."[1] And their "blinding prejudice" was fused with a nearly inexhaustible energy for minding the business of others. Yankees helped their neighbors, even when those neighbors resisted that assistance, for their determination to correct wrongs, to extirpate sin, to refashion others in the Yankee image, was fueled by moral imperatives. It was their divinely mandated task "to produce in the nation a more homogeneous character."[2] Yankee behavior in pursuit of that goal, and the reactions to it, created the dual and intersecting fault lines of the third party system.

The Shaping of the Third Electoral System

If we conceive critical realignment as a systemic and durable change in the distribution of partisan loyalties, then on qualitative grounds alone the upheaval of the 1850s should qualify. The political events of that

1. Richard Lyle Power, *Planting Corn Belt Culture*, pp. 45–46.
2. The quotation is from Lyman Beecher, *The Reformer* 1 (October 1820): 236–37, quoted in Power, *Corn Belt Culture*, p. 6.

decade were without parallel, before or since. The disintegration of a major national party, the Whigs; the sudden success of a party whose roots were in a secret society, the Know-Nothings; the rise of a sectionally based major anti-Democratic party, the Republicans; and the 1860 fissure of the remaining national party, the Democrats, pointed to a reorganization of the coalitional bases of mass parties. And if nothing else, the decision by eleven states to secede rather than to accept the outcome of the 1860 election was a sign that the high levels of intensity typically associated with realigning sequences characterized the politics of the late 1850s.

Longitudinal studies of mass political behavior have empirically documented the partisan realignment. Using separate and statistically independent measures, researchers have described the systemic reshuffling of partisan coalitions.[3] From the national perspective, realigning fluctuation began as early as the off-year elections of 1853–54, extended through the war and immediate postwar years, and terminated with the reinstating sequence of 1873–76. The latter sequence marked the end of the realigning phase of the third electoral system and the beginning of its stable phase.

Unprecedented developments produce seemingly peculiar data arrays; the political events of the 1850s were no exception (see Table 3.1). Although the data bring into focus both the uniform wartime fluctuations (compare for both parties 1860/1864 and 1864/1868) as well as the reinstating character of the 1876 election, they also highlight considerable temporal dissimilarity in the process of realigning change in the two distributions.

Sharp breakage occurred in the distribution of the major anti-Democratic opposition between 1852 and 1856, and the emerging Republican distribution bore scant resemblance to that of the earlier Whig party. That statistical discontinuity reflected the peculiarly sectional character of Republican strength, in contrast to the nationwide polling power of the Whigs. The Democratic distribution changed little between 1852 and 1856 but was dramatically transformed over the subsequent pair of elections. However, Democratic strength declined between 1852 and 1856, and the shape of its distribution changed.[4] These facts imply

3. Walter Dean Burnham, *Critical Elections and the Mainsprings of American Politics*, pp. 15–19, 34–40; James L. Sundquist, *Dynamics of the Party System*, pp. 39–91; Gerald M. Pomper, *Elections in America*, pp. 113–15, 267–69. For detailed studies of the realignment of the 1850s, see Ronald P. Formisano, *The Birth of Mass Political Parties*; Michael Fitzgibbon Holt, *Forging a Majority*; Roger D. Petersen, "The Reaction to a Heterogeneous Society."

4. The variance of the Democratic distribution, both by states and by regions, was greater in 1856 than it had been in 1852, and the Democratic mean percentages were lower. See Table 2.1.

TABLE 3.1   *Major-Party Autocorrelations: The U.S.*
             by States

Election Pair	Dem $r =$	Whig/Repub $r =$
1848/1852	.781	.603
1852/1856	.814	.038
1856/1860	−.513	.968
1860/1864	.082	.193
1864/1868	.779	.779
1848/1868	.350	−.309
1852/1868	.479	−.032
1856/1868	.535	.633
1848/1876	.606	−.031
1856/1876	.803	.788

considerably less continuity than we might otherwise surmise from the high autocorrelation. The party's North-vs.-South rupture produced the dramatic discontinuity between its 1856 and 1860 distributions.[5] After realigning fluctuation had ended, however, the Democratic distribution displayed greater continuity with its prerealignment counterpart than did that of its major opposition.

A massive transformation in the shape of the electoral universe occurred in the 1850s and 1860s. Yet that realignment occurred in separate stages, and it involved distinct behavioral phenomena. When aggregated to the national level, where regional crosscurrents tend to cancel out statistically, the picture seems more mixed and indicative of greater continuity than the underlying social realities support. We can best explore these distinctions in the realigning process by shifting the level of aggregation to the state and by making use of other descriptive dimensions.

If we examine the amount and the amplitude of change in conjunction with the timing of the reorganization of electoral coalitions, we can describe two distinct patterns of shift among the nonslave states. Table

5. The Douglas Democrats polled only 9.5 percent of the total vote in the thirteen states of the greater South (eleven Confederate and two border), compared with the Democratic strength of 56.1 percent in 1856. In the eleven-state Confederate area, Douglas in 1860 polled 8.4 percent compared with 58.1 percent Democratic in 1856. In 1860, 91.3 percent of the eleven-state vote went to the Constitutional Unionists and Southern Democrats, and 89.9 percent of the vote in the thirteen-state area went to those two parties.

3.2 presents the partisan autocorrelations for states displaying each of these patterns.[6]

The belt of middle states ranged westward from New Jersey through Iowa and included New York, Pennsylvania, Ohio, Michigan, Indiana, Illinois, and Wisconsin. In these states the type of patterned and severe fluctuation in county-party percentages that we associate with realignment began in the off-year elections of 1853–54 and ceased by about 1864. However, in most instances the shape of the emerging realignment was visible as early as 1856. Oscillation after 1856 involved the expiration of the Whigs, the demise of the Know-Nothings, the split of the anti-Republican vote in 1860, and the deviating election of 1862.[7]

On the Democratic side the realigned distributions displayed remarkably strong continuity with their prerealignment counterparts. Although Democratic percentage strength in these states was sharply reduced, the geographic base of the party's support remained essentially intact. Breakage was far more evident on the anti-Democratic side. Although the Republicans had inherited nearly intact the geographic base of the old Whig party, the new party also recruited nearly all the former Free-Soil voters and a strong majority of those who had earlier cast Know-Nothing ballots.[8]

TABLE 3.2 *Patterns of Fluctuation: Partisan Autocorrelations, States by Counties*

	Democrat				Whig/Republican			
	1852/ 1856	1852/ 1864	1856/ 1864	1848/ 1864	1852/ 1856	1852/ 1864	1856/ 1864	1848/ 1864
Middle Belt:								
New Jersey	.895	.760	.874	.566	.126	.666	.096	.691
Wisconsin	.702	.728	.774	.602	.481	.431	.769	.466
New England:								
Massachusetts	.942	.694	.831	.629	.478	.408	.705	.324
Vermont	.887	.844	.863	.778	.450	.353	.869	.390

6. There was a third distinctive pattern and that was characteristic of the slave states. See Chapter 4 for a discussion of those developments.

7. Compared with the 1856–92 regression-line trend, 1862 was a deviating election. In the East North Central states, the Democratic percentage in 1862 was 11.3 percent above regression-line trend and 11.6 percent above trend in the Midatlantic states.

8. The 1856/1864 Republican autocorrelation in New Jersey seems low and anoma-

The relatively high 1852/1864 (as well as the 1848/1864) autocorrelations point to the extremely narrow amplitude of severe shift in these states. If we define *severe shift* as a loss of ten percentage points or more between the Democratic 1836–52 longitudinal mean and its 1860–76 mean, then 181 counties, or 33.9 percent of the total counties in these states, were involved.[9] For the most part these sharp anti-Democratic breaks were geographically concentrated in clusters of counties whose populations were predominantly from New England or New York. There was some counterbalancing movement toward the Democrats, though of much more modest proportions. In all, 72 counties, 13.5 percent of the total, exhibited Democratic gains of five percentage points or more across the two sets of longitudinal sequences. And for the most part, these were counties of German or Catholic concentration.[10]

In these middle-belt states, then, were sharp departures from past voting patterns. Begun during the 1850s, they were stabilized by about 1864. Yet the realignment was of an exceedingly narrow geographic breadth, involving only about one-third of the counties. And these geographically confined breaks were partially offset by modest pro-Democratic movement in slightly more than one-tenth of the counties. This two-way movement benefited the Republicans primarily because the units moving away from the Democracy cast a larger proportion of the total vote than those moving in the opposite direction.

The six New England states displayed a different pattern. The political upheaval of the 1850s converted that region, which had been a competitive and politically mixed one, into a bastion of Republicanism. As it had in the middle-belt states, realigning fluctuation began with the 1853–54 elections. However, in New England more extensively than elsewhere, the processes that culminated in the reorganization of elec-

lous. That was due to the 1856 split of the anti-Democratic vote at the presidential level; the Republicans received 28.5 percent, and the Know-Nothings 24.2 percent. At the gubernatorial level the anti-Democrats fused. Using the 1856 fusion vote for governor yields the following correlations: with Republican president 1856 = .008; with Know-Nothing president 1856 = .618; with Republican president 1864 = .899. For regression estimates of cross-party voter movement in Illinois, Indiana, Michigan, and Ohio, see Ray Myles Shortridge, ''Voting Patterns in the American Midwest, 1840–1872.'' See John Lockwood Hammond, Jr., ''The Revivalist Political Ethos,'' pp. 200–201, for analogous regression estimates for Ohio and New York, and pp. 194, 197, 199 for a multiple-regression analysis of the Republican vote in these two states.

9. The raw data for the counties of a number of northern states are given in Petersen, ''Reaction to a Heterogeneous Society,'' pp. 272–78. I have reaggregated and reanalyzed these data and have used the comparable data for other states reported in the appropriate editions of *The Tribune [Whig] Almanac and Political Register* and Walter Dean Burnham, *Presidential Ballots, 1836–1892.*

10. For an illustration see Burnham's data for Pennsylvania in *Critical Elections*, p. 37. For more information on the social nature of the swings, see Table 3.3.

toral coalitions had begun in the 1840s with the emergence of the Liberty and Free-Soil parties.[11] As early as 1848, 19.7 percent of the region's total vote had been cast beyond the bounds of the two-party system. The Free-Soil movement was extensive: in 1848 only 45.3 percent of the counties in the region registered a majority for any party, and in 1852 that rose to only 53.1 percent of the total counties. Yet by 1856, 93.9 percent of the region's counties returned a partisan majority, and the Republicans carried 89.3 percent of all of the counties in New England.[12] Indeed, by 1856 the basic contours of the realigned distributions were in place. Oscillation after 1856 owed much more to the split of the anti-Republican vote in 1860 than it did to the expiration of the Know-Nothings. And as in the New Jersey–Iowa belt, 1862 was a deviating election in New England—though in the opposite direction, with the Democratic vote remaining 13.1 percent below regression-line trend. The relatively forlorn status of the Democracy as an organization is well captured by the 1862 developments in four states. In Massachusetts the party abandoned its name and formed an ad hoc popular-front party, the People's party, to oppose the Republicans. In Maine and New Hampshire the party split, fielding both a regular and a Union Democratic ticket. And the Rhode Island Democrats were too enfeebled even to field a gubernatorial candidate.

As in the middle-belt states the realigned Democratic distribution showed greater continuity with its pre-1856 pattern than did the Whig/Republican side. The Democrats came through the realignment with their geographic base essentially intact, though with their strength quite markedly reduced, but the anti-Democratic forces experienced considerably greater discontinuity.[13] New England's Republicans were not simply the old Whigs rechristened. The Republicans had inherited most of the Whig geographic base, which was combined with virtually all of the 1852 Free-Soil voters and, except in Massachusetts and Connecticut, the preponderant majority of the earlier Know-Nothing voters.[14]

In these respects the political behavior of the New England states resembled that of states like Pennsylvania and New Jersey. Yet there was

11. The same processes were at work in the Yankee counties in the middle-belt states, but since these were a relatively small number of each state's total counties, the impact at the state level was less dramatic but no less significant electorally and behaviorally.

12. In 1848 the Whigs carried 22.5 percent of the total counties and 21.8 percent in 1852.

13. New Hampshire was an exception to the generalization.

14. Regression estimates of the subsequent partisan behavior of Know-Nothing voters point to Maine and Massachusetts as examples of antipodal cases. In both states those 1856 Know-Nothing voters who participated in the 1864 election were unanimously Republican. However, the interparty flow of voters in Massachusetts was much

a distinction—a "distinction with a difference." The amplitude of the shift was immensely greater in the New England region than in the middle-belt states. Fully 75.0 percent of New England's counties registered severe Democratic losses of ten percentage points or more, and only 4.6 percent returned Democratic gains of at least five percentage points. We can summarize this distinction directly: in each of the middle-belt states the Democratic mean (by counties) declined between 1852 and 1856, and the variance of the distribution of county percentages about the mean increased. This empirically points either to a bipolar, or two-way, movement of voting units or to very large swings concentrated in a relatively small number of voting units. Yet although all of the states in New England registered sharp declines in Democratic mean strength, only in Connecticut and Massachusetts was there any indication of either of these possibilities. And in these two states the increases in variance were considerably more muted than in the New Jersey–Iowa belt. The other four New England states registered declining Democratic means accompanied by sharp declines in variance. That empirical pattern reflected a regional reaction—that is, a sharp diminution in the partisan distance among social groups.[15]

The realignment of the New England states, then, shared some characteristics with that of the middle-belt states. In both categories realignment began with the off-year 1853–54 elections, the distributions stabilized by about 1864, and greater discontinuity was apparent on the anti-Democratic side than in the Democracy's geographic base of support. In the states of both areas, the Free-Soil vote moved virtually intact into the Republican column, as did most of the Whig base and a majority of the Know-Nothing support. In New England, however, the

---

more complex than that finding suggests. There slightly more than one-third of the 1854 Know-Nothing voters had cast Democratic ballots in 1852. Across both the 1854–55 and 1855–56 pairs of elections, there was voter movement from the Know-Nothing ranks to the Democrats: 14.6 percent of the 1854 Know-Nothings voted Democratic in 1855, and 16.6 percent of the 1855 Know-Nothings cast Democratic ballots in 1856. Since all of the 1856 Democrats who balloted again in 1864 voted Democratic, the 1864 Democracy in Massachusetts contained an appreciable number of voters who had earlier been Know-Nothings. In both states, however, virtually all of the 1852 Free-Soil voters moved to the Republican ranks by 1856. For the region as a whole, about one-fifth of the 1852 Free-Soil vote originally came from the Democratic ranks. For detailed data on the Massachusetts case, see Kevin Sweeney, "Rum, Romanism, Representation, and Reform," pp. 116–37; Dale Baum, "The Political Realignment of the 1850s."

15. For a discussion of sectional reactions, see Lee Benson, "Research Problems in American Political Historiography," pp. 164–65. None of Connecticut's counties registered Democratic declines of −10.0 percentage points, and one (New Haven) increased in Democratic strength by at least +5.0 percentage points. In Massachusetts 86.0 percent of the counties registered severe Democratic losses and only Suffolk County (Boston) showed a gain of at least +5.0 percentage points.

consolidation of former minor-party supporters, especially the former Know-Nothings, was much further advanced by 1856 than it was in most of the middle-belt states.[16] Yet setting New England apart was not just the timing of the consolidation of the anti-Democrats but the enormous amplitude of the shift.

This brief overview of the shaping of the third party system focused on changes in the distributions of county-party percentages and distinctions in the processes of that change between two categories of states. We can add another dimension to the description, and simultaneously provide a convenient bridge to analyze the social dynamics of the realignment, by examining the partisan percentages over time within several groups of counties (Table 3.3).

TABLE 3.3 *Partisan Strength by Types of Counties, 1848–1892*[17]

A. *Yankee-Stock Counties: Percent Whig/Republican of Total Vote*

	Yankee (N = 65)	Rest of States	Entire States
1848	39.1	47.3	46.1
1852	39.8	44.8	44.1
1854	53.1	48.5	49.1
1856	65.2	39.1	42.9
1860	65.8	51.4	53.4
1862	61.1	46.8	48.8
1864	63.9	51.9	53.5
1876	58.6	49.1	50.2
1892	52.8	46.7	47.4

16. Only 5.7 percent of the total New England vote in 1856 went to minor parties, compared with 20.3 percent in the Midatlantic states and 11.0 percent in the Midwest. Massachusetts was an exception to the generalization among the New England states, and Michigan was an exception among the middle-belt states.

17. The counties so categorized had at least 10.0 percent of their 1870 population of the designated stock, and no other single out-of-state population stock comprised as much as 5.0 percent of the total. The categorization is consistent with those employed by John H. Fenton, *Midwest Politics*; V. O. Key, Jr., *American State Politics*; Frank Munger, "Two-Party Politics in the State of Indiana."

TABLE 3.3, *continued*

B. *Southern-Stock Counties: Percent Democratic of Total Vote*

	Illinois (N = 10)	Indiana (N = 8)
1848	64.2	53.4
1852	66.3	58.6
1854	92.4	52.2
1856	72.8	58.8
1860*	73.1	54.6
1862	78.7	55.9
1864	57.6	52.6
1876	51.5	54.8
1892	49.4	50.8

C. *German Counties: Percent Democratic of Total Vote*

	Illinois (N = 4)	Indiana (N = 6)	Wisconsin (N = 10)
1848	62.8	50.7	49.7
1852	72.4	57.5	59.6
1854	76.9	53.3	41.4
1856	48.5	60.5	53.2
1860*	53.5	54.1	55.4
1862	54.6	64.0	63.8
1864	48.1	59.9	64.0
1876	55.2	59.6	63.2
1892	52.3	58.8	63.0

*Sum of Douglas and Breckinridge vote.

The debt that the emerging Republican majorities in Illinois, Indiana, Iowa, New York, Ohio, Pennsylvania, and Wisconsin owed to their Yankee-stock counties, as well as the marginal nature of the swing, is evident.[18] The tidal wave of Republican voting that had engulfed New England swept westward along a very narrow and selective trail, the New England–New York diaspora. Within this relatively small string of counties, sharp anti-Democratic voter movement took place among vot-

18. Compare with Burnham's discussion of Pennsylvania in *Critical Elections*, pp. 35–38.

ers. And from the majorities that the anti-Democratic coalition received in these counties, it forged its electoral success.[19] Just as New England evidenced a strong and regionally oriented (that is, antisouthern) voter movement, so did its outposts in the wilderness—New York's Burned-Over District and its Pennsylvania extension, Ohio's Western Reserve, and the less-renowned areas of Yankee settlement in Indiana, Iowa, Wisconsin, and the northern tiers of counties in Illinois.

More remarkable, perhaps, than the simple flourishing of nascent Republicanism in these Yankee outposts was their coming to their partisan attachment through the same route as did their regional homeland. Within the Yankee counties outside of New England, Free-Soilism had taken root. In 1848 these sixty-five counties gave 30.1 percent of their total vote to the Free-Soil party and in 1852, 14.2 percent.[20] By 1856 these Yankee–Free-Soil strongholds found natural refuge in the Republican party (65.2 percent); only a relatively small proportion of their vote (5.6 percent) went to the Know-Nothings. Yankee-stock areas were not unattracted by nativism, but the congruence of their antisouthern and antiimmigrant (especially anti-Catholic) attitudes produced a reasonably rapid consolidation of voting support against the Democracy, the party of the South *and* of the (Catholic and German Lutheran) immigrants.

In 1856 the Native American party polled 15.8 percent of the total vote of the non-Yankee counties in these states.[21] These had been the areas most resistant to Free-Soilism (3.9 percent of their 1852 vote) and the areas least susceptible to inroads by the early Republican party— they gave the Republicans only 39.1 percent of their 1856 vote, though by 1860 and 1864 even these non-Yankee areas had swung marginally Republican, giving that coalition 51.4 percent and 51.9 percent, respectively, of their total vote. Thereafter they rebounded somewhat; so the Democrats in and after 1876 normally secured a plurality of the total vote cast outside the Yankee counties.

Some southern-stock voters formed an important element of the Democracy's coalitional base. In the face of the increasing salience of sectional identifications, Illinois's southern-stock counties swung sharply anti-Republican in 1856 and 1860 and then waned in their Democratic support as the Republicans draped themselves in the symbols of patriotism and the Union. Though registering consistently and markedly lower

19. The Yankee counties comprised only 11.5 percent of the total counties in these states and collectively cast 16.3 percent of their total 1860 vote.

20. For a multiple-regression demonstration of Yankee support for Free-Soil, see Hammond, "Revivalist Political Ethos," pp. 153, 178, 182.

21. For example, in Wisconsin the 1848 Free-Soil correlated with the 1856 Know-Nothing vote at −.405, and the 1852 Free-Soil distribution with the Know-Nothing vote at −.324.

levels of Democratic support, Indiana's southern-stock areas followed a pattern similar to those in Illinois.[22]

If this contrast between the political movement of the Yankee and southern-stock counties brings one cleavage line of the third electoral system into focus, an examination of the behavior of the German counties draws attention to the second. The Democrats retained their voting support in these areas.[23] Just as in New England, where the only considerable countertrend was in two counties with larger-than-average (for that region) foreign-stock elements; so among some groups of immigrant voters elsewhere, the Democrats continued to poll a majority.[24]

By combining the broadly drawn inferences from these data with the knowledge that the emergence of the third party system involved sectional polarities of a nature and magnitude unknown to the second party system, we can describe the global bases of political cleavage rather succinctly. The partisan cleavage of the third electoral era involved ethnocultural conflict along two separate, but partially intersecting, dimensions. The first entailed a value-and-interest conflict between Yankee moralist subculture and white southern subculture.[25] The second, in the northern states and especially in the middle-belt states, involved a religious-value conflict between pietistic and antipietistic subcultures.

Analytically, we can think of two separate dimensions of party oppositions. Yet we need to be cognizant of their being interwoven. Yankee moralist subculture formed the larger part—and in forming the Republican party, the more dynamic part—of an ethnoculturally more inclusive pietistic subculture. And antipietistic subculture encompassed traditional white southern subculture as well as nonsouthern subcultures whose shared sense of cohesiveness was formed or materially sharpened in battle with pietistic subculture.[26] These two broad subcultures overlapped geographically. That some states, especially those of the Midwest, received streams of population from both the South and from New England brought into contact, and into conflict, bearers of divergent subcultures. That party divisions followed the broad outlines of these (and other) streams of the population is merely another way of observing that partisanship originated in subcultural conflict.

22. The 1876 election was an obvious exception. For variations in southern-stock voting behavior, see the data for Missouri in Table 4.3.
23. The German counties in Pennsylvania behaved politically in the same way as those in Illinois and Indiana, but those in Iowa did not.
24. The observation pertains, of course, to areas outside the South and states that behaved politically like southern states.
25. Walter Dean Burnham, "The United States," pp. 667–68.
26. Southern pietism differed in kind from the Yankee variety. For a more precise delineation of the politically relevant distinctions, see Chapter 5.

The driving force of that conflict, and of the fault lines of the third electoral era, was "Yankee-cultural imperialism."[27] Yankees channeled their seemingly boundless energy into the God-given mission of eradicating sin, making "holy" their world, and—in less euphemistic terms —devoting themselves tirelessly to minding the business of others. As that sense of "being a New England man" entailed these commitments, so it also came to involve a psychological affinity for the Republican party, the Yankee-fashioned engine of God's will.

Broadly framed generalizations normally demand qualification, and this instance is no exception. Most Yankee-stock voters had been anti-Democrats before the mid-1850s; not all Yankees became Republicans after that point, nor did every non-Yankee vote for the Democracy. It would be erroneous to assume that all Republican voters were moved exclusively or equally by any single impulse. Instead, historians must identify all potentially relevant political subcultures and search for the nexus between each and its partisan proclivity. Ultimate resolution of the complex motivation underlying the realignment of the 1850s will require microcosmic analysis, along with more sophisticated understanding of the effect of social and political environments on attitude formation. We can at least examine the broad outlines of the social origins of the third party system.

The Social Dynamics of Realignment

It is a standby of American political history that the realignment of the 1850s resulted from a paroxysm of moral anguish arising from the passage of the Kansas-Nebraska Act of 1854. By explicitly repealing the Missouri Compromise of 1820 and opening the Nebraska Territory to the possibility of slavery, the Kansas-Nebraska Act allegedly aroused the moral outrage of the North. This pervasive anti-Nebraska sentiment spawned a variety of local groupings—composed of former Whigs, Free-Soilers, abolitionists, and disgruntled northern Democrats—dedicated to opposing the extension of slavery. Some of these groupings adopted the name *Republican* and called for the creation of a new political party focusing on nonextension. Thus, "before the end of the summer of 1854, the emergent party had its name and its basic principle."[28]

27. The phrase is from Power, *Corn Belt Culture*; see Chapter 1, "The Cultural Imperialism of the Yankees," pp. 5–25.

28. John M. Blum et al., *The National Experience*, p. 308. A later edition (1973) eliminates the phrase, but the causal sequence remains the same. The quotation from the textbook has been used because it is a succinct statement of a broadly accepted causal sequence. For examples of other works that employ the *essential* elements of that causal

Even as a capsulized statement of the complex processes involved, that standby explanation misleads more than it enlightens. At the very least it misleads by implying a direct, singular focus that belies reality. Neither the realignment nor the birth of the Republican party occurred as immediately or with as narrow an appeal. Instead, a series of blows shattered the second party system and created a new social pattern of partisanship.

The Whig-Democratic polarity of the second electoral era revolved around a fundamental value conflict over the nature of man, of society, and of government's role. The party of moral order and positive government (the Whigs) pitted itself against that of laissez-faire ethics and passive government (the Democrats). The Whigs sought moral integration of the community through enforced conformity to Anglo-Protestant norms. Resistance to such encroachments, an acceptance of cultural pluralism, bound together the otherwise disparate groups that composed the anti-Whig coalition. Conflicts between political subcultures committed to these contending value systems structured partisan controversy.

Yet that structure was not identical in all locales, nor did each social group behave in precisely the same political way in all social contexts. The Democracy's coalition was not the same in Maine as in Michigan, nor was either precisely replicated in Illinois. And Maine's Yankee Baptists were not as intensely anti-Democratic in the 1840s as Michigan's. Two general principles help account for these anomalies. First, party builders had to fashion the raw materials at hand into enduring coalitions. As demographic patterns varied, so did party practices and characters. Second, social-group characteristics never automatically produced political consciousness. These characteristics became politically salient only when *party* alternatives tended to parallel distinctions in social attributes. And *how* that parallelism emerged becomes the central question for historical political analysis. Critical and commonly shared experiences that initially shaped a group's partisanship were important to the formation of its enduring attachments. Through such experiences particular social outlooks were created, internalized, and imbued with a partisan salience that persisted long after the events themselves had faded into memory. With these principles in mind, we can describe the pattern of social partisanship during the second electoral era.

Whig-Democratic political distinctions did not involve simple native-immigrant polarities. Neither native nor immigrant groups re-

---

explanation, see Eric Foner, *Free Soil, Free Labor, Free Men*, pp. 126–27, 155, 163–64; George H. Mayer, *The Republican Party, 1854–1966*, pp. 25–27; Hans L. Trefousse, "The Republican Party, 1854–1864," pp. 1144–46.

sponded to political stimuli as cohesive voting blocs. Most post-1790 immigrant groups supported the Democrats. Irish Catholics were the most strongly and consistently Democratic of the newer immigrant groups. And among the German Catholics, French and French Canadian Catholics, the New Dutch, Norwegians, German Lutherans, and German Reformed, the Democracy received strong, though contextually varying, support. Yet everywhere and despite immense internal cultural distinctions, the New British group—English, Scots, Welsh, and Protestant Irish—were politically cohesive and strongly anti-Democratic.[29]

Even more than the immigrants, native groups displayed diverse voting patterns. Indeed, some of the most interesting and sharpest political cleavage occurred between different groups of natives.[30] From the coast of Maine through the fertile prairies of the Midwest, Whiggery drew disproportionate support among Yankee Presbyterian and Congregational voters. Both at its mass base and in its leadership, the Whig party was unmistakably a Yankee-Presbyterian-Congregational party. Apparently that fact, coupled with the effect of the battles over disestablishment in the New England states, led Yankee Baptists, Methodists, Unitarians, and Universalists to oppose the Whigs. And when footloose Yankees moved westward, they carried with them both these hostilities and the partisanship that they had produced.

The West was a wilderness to be saved for God and New England civilization. As the Yankees came into contact and conflict with other groups, the shared sense of being above all else a New England man frequently eroded old hostilities and created the bases for new ones. Thus, Yankee qua Yankee voting behavior was more cohesive in New York, Michigan, Illinois, and other parts of the wilderness than in any New England state. In Michigan, for example, despite the clear Yankee Presbyterian character of the Whig party, Yankee Baptists were strong anti-Democratic voters. And in all contexts of the wilderness, Yankees served as powerful negative referents to a variety of other social groups. Conflicts between migrant Yankees and native Yorkers in New York

29. This description of the social bases of partisanship during the second electoral era draws heavily on the insights and analysis, and in some instances my own reanalysis, of data in several works: Lee Benson, *The Concept of Jacksonian Democracy*; Formisano, *Birth of Mass Parties*; Holt, *Forging a Majority*; Alexandra McCoy, "Political Affiliations of American Economic Elites"; Petersen, "Reaction to a Heterogeneous Society"; William Gerald Shade, *Banks or No Banks*.

30. Benson, *Concept of Jacksonian Democracy*, pp. 165–85, and Formisano, *Birth of Mass Parties*, pp. 165–94, correctly observe that some of the more interesting political conflicts occurred between different groups of immigrants. That view is not mutually exclusive with the one advanced here. Benson and Formisano aimed at correcting the older interpretation that viewed ethnocultural conflict solely in terms of native-vs.-immigrant groups.

impelled the latter to support the Democracy, and both groups carried these partisan results westward. The settlement of the Old Northwest by people from the upper South and from New England (often via New York) brought together divergent subcultures. In states such as Illinois, Indiana, and Ohio, upland southerners, viewed pejoratively by Yankees as a "heterogeneous mass," resisted the encroachments of the Yankee life-style by voting Democratic. Yet in other contexts, where migrating Yankees did not encounter new and hostile groups, they often clung to the partisan identifications originally honed during the crises over disestablishment in their native states. In the Pennsylvania counties adjacent to New York's Burned-Over District, for example, some Yankee Baptist and Methodist communities voted nearly unanimously Democratic as late as the early 1850s.[31]

The crisis over disestablishment, the battle against the Yankee Congregationalist standing order, had partisanized conflict among religious groups in New England. Very likely, the violent battle over extending the franchise in Rhode Island in the early 1840s had reinforced that partisanship by imbuing it with status-group connotations.[32] In other parts of the North, especially in the Midwest, constitution making had served as a critical partisanizing experience. Questions such as extending the franchise to aliens, supporting public school systems, and adopting free banking laws elicited responses consonant with subcultural values. Elections of delegates to the constitutional conventions and the ensuing referenda on the documents themselves provided opportunities for mass expressions of those values. Such issues and occasions did not create the conflicts among social groups; those had long existed. Yet mobilization of the mass electorate projected them into the public arena. And the interests, the passions, and the aspirations thus unleashed among the mass electorate tended thereafter to fix both the style and substance of politics.

This partisan structure began to shake in the 1840s and crumbled in the 1850s. It required a series of shocks to lead most voters to a new interpretation of political reality and thence to a new party system. Abolitionism turned antislavery, unleashed temperance and sabbatarian enthusiasm, resurgent antipopery, and pervasive antipartyism—all bound together symbolically in broad antisouthernism—convulsed the political

31. On the concept of *wilderness* in the Yankee belief system, see Edward A. Tiryakian, "Neither Marx or Durkheim . . . Perhaps Weber," pp. 19–24; for the pejorative connotations of the term *heterogeneous*, see Power, *Corn Belt Culture*, p. 35.

32. It had that effect substantively in Rhode Island and perhaps symbolically elsewhere. For indications of the relation between the disestablishment struggles and partisan oppositions, see William G. McLoughlin, *New England Dissent, 1630–1833*, 2:831, 840–41, 875–80.

universe and ultimately coalesced to transform it.[33] From that transformation emerged a new pattern of partisanship. In its broad outlines the social structure of partisanship during the third electoral era involved a union of native and immigrant pietistic religious groups in *party* opposition to antipietistic groups.

The attitudinal transformation that underlay the reshaping of the electoral universe began well before the 1850s. Its roots were in the revivals of the 1820s and 1830s, for Charles Grandison Finney, by preaching a new understanding of the nature of man, transformed the world views of those who experienced the revivals and internalized their ethos.[34] The revivalists emphasized free will and the agency of man in conversion. By an act of will, man could achieve harmony with God and thus salvation. Moreover, as the use of the revivals to promote conversions implied, man had the power to save others. These two tenets gave shape to the abolitionist movement.

If every man were made by God a free moral agent, then enslaving any man denied him his own moral responsibility. Slavery, therefore, was evil, not because it was inconsistent with human liberty, but because its lack of liberty was inconsistent with free will. Of course, Finney and his followers were not the first to posit that slavery was wrong. But they gave "the demand for temporal freedom a compelling urgency" that it had lacked earlier, for to them "slavery was not only wrong, but sinful."[35]

The belief in free will also implied that man had the ability to do good. In turn, this yielded an emphasis on moral obligation. The Christian had to show that he was converted by displaying "an habitual disposition to obey the requirements of God . . . [which] gives a right direction to all our conduct."[36] God required that the converted prefer his glory to their own private interests. Those who had experienced a change of heart and its consequent change of conduct would work for the good of others. Commitment to a voluntary, but active and eventually aggressive, benevolence became to the revivalist an integral aspect of salvation. As it did, the revivals provided the already existing benevolent empire—that cluster of interlocking mission, tract, Sunday school, and education societies—with new members, new motives, and new

33. For a brilliant delineation of the psychological linkages, see Formisano, *Birth of Mass Parties*, pp. 217–77.

34. My analysis here draws heavily from Hammond, "Revivalist Political Ethos," especially pp. 115–223. For other useful analyses see Whitney R. Cross, *The Burned-Over District*; Timothy L. Smith, *Revivalism and Social Reform*.

35. John L. Hammond, "Revival Religion and Anti-Slavery Politics," p. 184.

36. Charles Grandison Finney, *Sermons on Important Subjects*, p. 62.

resources and thereby transformed them into organizational expressions of the new social movement. This ever-expanding web of benevolent enterprises provided the revivalists with their organizational base for the extermination of sin. They also became involved in pressure-group politics. The petition campaigns of the General Union for Promoting the Observance of the Christian Sabbath and the United States Temperance Union first brought home the message: "Political action was another way of doing the work of the Lord."[37] And the failure of the petition campaigns taught yet another lesson: pressure-group activity was not enough; it was necessary to mobilize masses of voters to do the Lord's work.

The revivalist impulse also brought to politics the spirit of the religious enthusiast, the believer who is convinced that he is in the right. Just as Finney viewed opposition to the revivals as "the devil's most successful means of destroying souls," the revivalists regarded resistance to their benevolent activities as equally sinful. Transferred to political action, such a disposition endowed politics with a right-vs.-wrong, with-us-or-against-us attitude. Where the pragmatic, accommodating temperament of the coalition-building politician aimed at compromise between contending views, the religious enthusiast moralized political questions, bestowed on them an all-or-nothing quality, and thereby escalated political tension.[38]

The revivals and the disposition that they inculcated spread beyond the Presbyterian-Congregational church. The acceptance or rejection of the New Measures was a focal point of controversy and cause of schism among all Protestant denominations during the 1830s and 1840s.[39] And as the revivalist movement spread, a larger support clientele was created for potential political mobilization.

Of course, as has been brilliantly documented for Michigan, the attitudes thus forged were not without partisan salience during the second electoral era. The revivalist impulse, for example, was the engine that drove Anti-Masonry. And there the Blessed Spirit contributed to a moralization of politics and a consequent hardening of party lines, as well as to the evangelical antipartyism that became a hallmark of Whiggery. In that and other ethnoculturally heterogeneous environments, this moral legacy gave the Whigs a stridently antiforeign aura that drove all but the New British groups into the ranks of the Democracy.[40] New

37. Clifford S. Griffin, *Their Brothers' Keepers*, p. 134.
38. Charles Grandison Finney, *Lectures on Revivals of Religion*, pp. 14–15. On the disposition of the religious enthusiast, see Ronald Knox, *Enthusiasm*, pp. 17–19.
39. Robert Baird, *Religion in America*; Smith, *Revivalism and Social Reform*, pp. 45–62.
40. Formisano, *Birth of Mass Parties*, pp. 60–80.

England's Blessed Spirit infested Whiggery less exclusively than Michigan's, and from Maine to Connecticut, the Democracy evidenced a moralistic tone and aura unlike that of its midwestern counterparts. However, Democratic moralism always seemed to reflect a kind of secular ethos of "public regardingness" rather than one of evangelical temper.[41] Yet just as its social coalition differed from that of the party in the Midwest and Midatlantic areas, so the New England Democracy's character was distinct. Here, too, was a potential support clientele—attached to the Democrats by tradition—that could be broken off and united into a new coalition should critical events lead appreciable numbers of voters to a new interpretation of political reality. And these were in the offing.

In the 1840s and 1850s a series of developments unleashed preexisting attitudes and cumulatively channeled them into new partisan directions. Although we can sort out the developments and attitudes descriptively, it is crucial to remember that they coexisted in time and often in individuals. They did not flow separately through the political universe in neatly demarcated compartments but "permeated one another with emotional resonance."[42]

The first was political antislavery. The moral conviction that slavery was sin led some abolitionists to political action. Beginning with pressure-group activities—the petition campaigns of the 1830s and inquiry into the party nominees' positions on slavery—they moved, with a reluctance and suspicion born of the evangelicals' distaste for party, to the organization of the Liberty party in 1840 and then of the Free-Soil party in 1848. Liberty and Free-Soil probably won few new converts to antislavery, but as political parties they had other effects. The Liberty party attracted voting support among Yankee-stock voters, especially those who had been influenced by the revivals, and thus eroded their attachments to Whiggery. The Free-Soil party broadened that base. Free-Soil was more pragmatic and compromising, less overtly a religious crusade than the Liberty party had been. It still appealed primarily to Yankee-stock voters, but not as exclusively as the Liberty party had to Yankees of revivalist disposition. And even more significantly, in some contexts the Free-Soil party began to attract support from among former Democrats. In New York, for instance, some 40 percent of the 1844 Democrats switched to Free-Soil voting by 1848, and in some New England locales former Democrats cast perhaps as much as 20 percent

41. Compare the Whig and Republican antiparty attitudes in *Boston Daily Advertiser*, 11 November 1844, and *Boston Evening Transcript*, 30 August 1860, with the Democratic expressions in *Boston Post*, 7 November 1848, 10 October 1860.

42. Ronald P. Formisano, "To the Editor," p. 188.

of the 1848 Free-Soil vote.[43] Yet the Liberty and Free-Soil parties did more than weaken the attachments of some voters to the old parties. They played critical roles in conditioning mass opinion in the North. They injected antisouthernism into mass politics by alerting northern opinion to the aggrandizements of the Slave Power, the growing and aggressive arrogance of the South and its control over national politics. From the congressional gag rule, to Tyler's veto of the bank bill, to the war with Mexico and Texas annexation, to the prosouthern stance of the Polk administration in its opposition to internal improvements and advocacy of lower tariffs, Liberty party men especially, and Free-Soilers only somewhat less, sounded the alarm to northern men that the "southern Slave Power" was aggressively on the march.

Probably only the already converted read Liberty party tracts, attended their meetings, heard their speeches, and voted for their candidates. Merely raising such themes, however, required responses by both major parties. To avoid defections by supporters who shared the evangelical temperament of the antislaveryites, the Whigs responded with an antisouthernism as strong in tone as the Liberty party's. The Democratic stance came more slowly, was more a response of tactics than conviction, and never evidenced the heat of the Whig and Liberty charges. To undercut the Liberty and Free-Soil appeal, the rhetoric of both major parties stained them with "niggerism." And *abolition*, in both Whig and Democratic rhetoric, became an emotionally charged code word symbolic of black equality or, in the pejorative epithets of the day, of "niggerism" and "racial amalgamation."[44]

The second development that shook the old party structure was the rekindling of temperance and sabbatarian zeal. Again the churches led the charge. When religious groups defined intemperance and Sabbath desecration as sin, they viewed their elimination as nonnegotiable. And as they sought to exterminate sin, that nonnegotiable demand became a political objective. Moral suasion gave way, slowly and agonizingly at first, to pressure-group politics: church-based temperance and sabbatarian groups inundated state, town, and city legislators with petitions

43. Hammond, "Revivalist Political Ethos," pp. 153, 156, 178, 180, 182. For Massachusetts Sweeney estimates that 17 percent of the 1847 Democrats voted Free-Soil in 1848; Sweeney, "Rum, Romanism, Representation, and Reform," Table I, p. 118. For other indications of Free-Soil proclivities among Democrats, see *Boston Post*, 19 October 1848; Richard A. Hebert, *Modern Maine*, 1:199; James Duane Squares, *The Granite State of the United States*, 1:211–12; Walter Hill Crockett, *Vermont*, 3:378–79, 425.

44. On the diffusion of antisouthernism, see Merton L. Dillon, *The Abolitionists*, pp. 87–88, 103, 106, 142–43, 199–202; Thomas E. Powell, *The Democratic Party of the State of Ohio*, 1:105–108; Cross, *Burned-Over District*, p. 277. For the use of antiblack rhetoric, see Ronald P. Formisano, "The Edge of Caste," pp. 19–41.

and memorials. The move to total prohibition and mass mobilization followed. And try as they would, party politicians could not suppress this reenergized zeal nor prevent it from fracturing party lines.

Whig support groups, more than Democratic ones, shared the dispositions of the temperance and sabbatarian crusaders. In the 1830s and 1840s the Whigs had frequently been identified with support for those causes. In locales where this was the case, renewed temperance and sabbatarian enthusiasm probably reactivated and reinforced existing social-group polarities and partisan identifications. In other areas, however, Whiggery had grown pragmatic and had begun to play down the more overtly aggressive aspects of its moral character to win votes among the country's increasing number of "adopted citizens." And in some locales the religious groups spearheading the temperance and sabbatarian drives —especially the Baptists and Methodists—were Democrats. Under such conditions mass-mobilization efforts aimed at evoking a yes-or-no response on temperance had the potential for causing "a derangement of parties."[45]

And so it did. Statewide referenda on general prohibitory laws (Maine Laws) in the early and mid-1850s from Maine through Iowa, as well as an uncounted number of local-option and liquor-license referenda, fragmented party coalitions. Both state and community general elections in which prohibition or its enforcement became the focal point accelerated the pace of partisan "derangement."

In New England, where the prohibition agitation had begun, the Democracy's social base seemed to have been most disturbed. There, two years before Douglas conceived the Kansas-Nebraska Act, Democratic spokesmen pointed correctly to "the ultra temperance feeling *in all parties*" and prayed that the issue might "be shorn of party struggle." That prayer was an implicit realization that temperance zeal had infected some normally Democratic voter groups. The impact of that infection may be inferred from the way in which the party's spokesmen changed their public postures. Though always more halting and equivocal than midwestern Democrats, they shifted from a "keep-it-out-of-politics" plea to an eventual condemnation of the measure.[46]

45. The quotation is from [Neal Dow], *The Reminiscences of Neal Dow, Recollections of Eighty Years*, p. 440. Also see Hebert, *Modern Maine*, 1:190–91; *Boston Post*, 8 November 1852, 14 December 1852.

46. Respectively, the quotations are from *Boston Post*, 10 November 1852, emphasis added; the address of New Hampshire's Democratic governor to the 1852 legislature, quoted in Dudley P. Frasier, "The Antecedents and Formation of the Republican Party in New Hampshire," p. 32. Also see Griffin, *Their Brothers' Keepers*, pp. 151, 223–26. For some of the differences in Democratic postures on temperance even within New England, see Crockett, *Vermont*, 3:413–14; Charles Stickney, *Know-Nothingism*

The increased immigration of the late 1840s had been one of the factors propelling temperance and sabbatarian zeal. The arrival of hordes of new immigrants, especially Irish Catholics, created a renascent anti-popery and imbued that with partisan salience. Anti-Catholic attitudes were not new to American society in the 1850s. They had been displayed rhetorically, politically, and violently well before that decade. Yet they had not earlier given rise to a mass-based political party, the Know-Nothing (or American) party, whose purpose was declared to be "Anti-Romanism, Anti-Bedinism, Anti-Pope's Toeism, Anti-Nunneryism, Anti-Winking Virginism, Anti-Jesuitism, and Anti-the-Whole-Sacer-dotal-Hierarchism with all its humbugging mummeries. Know Nothing-ism is for light, liberty, education and absolute freedom of conscience."[47] Stripped to its essentials, this Know-Nothing self-description was a crudely expressed listing of native Protestant objections to Catholicism. Its focus was a perception of Catholicism as aggressively subversive of American values. The events of the late 1840s and early 1850s, at least as filtered through the perceptual screens of native Protestants, resonated with their preconceptions and converted the latter into self-fulfilling prophecies.

On several fronts Catholics seemed to assault traditional native Protestant values. The effort to force lay boards of trustees to vest control of church property in the clergy was seen as an attempt to extend the power of an overbearing, arrogant, and foreign hierarchy. That battle was protracted and acrimonious, and even more importantly it was publicized by both the secular and non-Catholic religious press. If the attempt to extend clerical ownership was not itself seen as subversive of American practice, the importation in 1853 of a papal nuncio, Msgr. Gaetano Bedini, to arbitrate the controversies in Buffalo and Philadelphia was evidence of direct intervention by the pope in American affairs. Bedini's subsequent tour of Catholic centers in the United States stirred violence and further fueled the antipopish fires.[48]

To many native Protestants, it seemed that Catholics, controlled as

---

in Rhode Island, p. 7; Carroll John Noonan, *Nativism in Connecticut, 1829–1860*, pp. 152–54.

47. The self-description is from the *Know-Nothing Almanac of 1855*, quoted in Laurence Frederick Schmeckebier, *History of the Know-Nothing Party in Maryland*, p. 11. Also see Ray Allen Billington, *The Protestant Crusade, 1800–1860*.

48. On the trusteeism controversy see Joseph L. J. Kirlin, *Catholicity in Philadelphia*, pp. 268–74; Francis E. Tourscher, ed., *Diary and Visitation Record of the Rt. Rev. Francis Patrick Kenrick, 1830–1851*, pp. 45–51; Frederick J. Zwierlein, *The Life and Letters of Bishop McQuaid*, 1:53–65. On Bedini's visit see Sr. Evangeline Thomas, *Nativism in the Old Northwest, 1850–60*, pp. 119–23; James F. Connelly, *The Visit of Archbishop Gaetano Bedini to the United States of America*, pp. 95–111, and pp. 193–287 for Archbishop Bedini's report to Cardinal Fransoni.

they were by a foreign monarch, waged open war on hallowed institutions and practices. Catholics demanded an end to Bible reading in the public schools. Worse yet, in Maryland, New York, Ohio, and Pennsylvania they initiated legislative efforts to secure public money for the support of the parochial schools in which their "foreign" doctrines were taught.[49] Nor did native Protestants see this merely as some vague or transitory peril. Catholics had "been taught to idolize the Pope of Rome as an incarnate God . . . and [had been] trained in the unrepublican habit of passive obedience and non-resistance to a foreign *Hierarch* [*sic*] who claims the right to think for them."[50] That Catholics were not free to think for themselves—not free to do right—but were ruled by the "despotic power" of "the Romish priesthood" posed a threat to civil as well as religious liberty.[51] That threat was perceived all the more clearly as a result of the political activity of Catholic voters. Chief among these activities was their support, especially that of the highly visible and assertive Irish, for the Democracy.

As early as the 1830s, some evangelical spokesmen had called for the creation of a Christian party to oppose the Catholics. A stark and pervasive perception of the Catholic threat made it possible in the early 1850s to translate that old suggestion into reality. What the anti-Catholic zealots had been proclaiming for two decades seemed to some to be coming to fruition. In response large numbers of native Protestants were mobilized by a political vehicle dedicated to antipopery—the Know-Nothing party. In the North it was beyond doubt a "No-Popery party." And its appeal harnessed a long-smoldering anti-Catholicism to partisan ends.[52] Most significantly, as early as the spring elections of 1854 and in

49. Alfred G. Stritch, "Political Nativism in Cincinnati, 1830–1860," pp. 258–64; Harold M. Helfman, "The Cincinnati 'Bible War,' 1869–70," pp. 369–70; Schmeckebier, *Know-Nothing Party in Maryland*, pp. 15–16; Douglas Bowers, "Ideology and Political Parties in Maryland, 1851–1856," pp. 203–205. For an explicit statement of the homogenizing function that the public schools were intended to carry out, see *Boston Evening Transcript*, 4 September 1860.

50. George Robertson, *The American Party*, p. 2.

51. The quoted phrases are from Charles Beecher, ed., *Autobiography, Correspondence, Etc., of Lyman Beecher*, 2:335; *Proceedings of the Convention of the General Synod of the Evangelical Lutheran Church in the United States, 1853*, p. 42. For similar expressions of anti-Catholic attitudes, see *Annual Report of the American Baptist Home Mission Society, 1848*, p. 49; *Minutes of the [Presbyterian] Synod of Philadelphia, 1843*, p. 17; *Minutes of the Annual Session of the Wisconsin Baptist State Convention, 1855*, p. 13; and Alexander Blaikie, *A History of Presbyterianism in New England*, p. 334.

52. The Rev. Ezra Stiles Ely issued the call for a "Christian party in politics" in 1827; see Joseph L. Blau, "The Christian Party in Politics," pp. 18–35. On the anti-Catholic character of Know-Nothingism in the North, see Billington, *Protestant Crusade*, p. 386; Noonan, *Nativism in Connecticut*, pp. 164–65; Humphrey J. Desmond, *The Know-Nothing Party*, p. 10.

a wide range of localities throughout the North, it cut sharply into Democratic strength among native Protestant voters, especially in those communities in which Methodists and Baptists had remained Democrats.

These developments—a political antislavery that taught the lessons of antisouthernism, an unleashed temperance and sabbatarian zeal, and a driving antipopery—shook the old political structure. They had their origins and exhibited their initial effects before "Bleeding Kansas" became a focus of public concern. These tensions created potential support clienteles for party builders. And the latter, aware of the sentiments and emotions with which their constituents were imbued, wove them together in symbolic ways to fashion mass coalitions. Two themes, antipartyism and antisouthernism, emerged as common ingredients of that symbolism.[53]

A revulsion against the "Spirit of Party," against the structured divisiveness that it implied, and against the ethos of loyalty to its norms had long and diverse roots in the political culture. In the 1850s antislavery groups, temperance and sabbatarian advocates, and antipopish men shared that animus. As they saw it, the "demands of a reckless, all absorbing party spirit," a spirit more concerned with "the preservation of party" than "the maintenance of principle," repeatedly frustrated their efforts at moral reform.[54] To act beyond the bounds of party, to do what was right regardless of party dictates, was no new experience to them. Rhetoric emphasizing the nexus between "party spirit" and the sundry evils of the day reflected and activated their energies while enlisting their voting support, as could a political symbolism that addressed itself to the theme of antisouthernism. That theme spoke of Slaveocracy's political power—of its capacity to dictate to the North and to obstruct pronorthern legislation, such as tariffs and rivers and harbors bills. It alluded to southern domination over the Democratic party as well as over other "party men" who subjugated themselves to the commands of these southern slave masters. And perhaps above all else, it spoke of the aristocratic, overbearing, and "alarming pretension" of the "aggressive spirit of the slave power," of that "sectional despotism" by which "both parties were enthralled."[55] In this context the "anti" theme exhibited its positive side and became as well a defense of the northern spirit of egalitarianism.

53. My intellectual debt here and in the analysis that follows is to Formisano, *Birth of Mass Parties*, pp. 56–80, 207, 213, 269–70, 279–81; idem, "Political Character, Antipartyism, and the Second Party System," pp. 683–709.

54. *Boston Daily Advertiser*, 11 November 1844; [Dow], *Reminiscences of Neal Dow*, pp. 446–49. And for the increasingly widespread diffusion of antiparty attitudes in the 1850s, see Michael Fitzgibbon Holt, "The Politics of Impatience," pp. 316–17.

55. *Boston Evening Transcript*, 7 November 1860, 6 September 1860; *Boston Post*, 2 August 1860, quoting Republican Congressman Anson Burlingame.

Antisouthern themes and the code words they employed had broad emotional significance. They were articulated to and for groups whose political outlooks had been conditioned by involvement in antislavery, temperance-sabbatarian, and/or anti-Catholic crusades. Code words such as *slavery*, the *slave power*, and their various synonyms were designed to resonate emotionally with preexisting attitudes, to convey a sense of psychological linkage between the political characters of the groups holding such attitudes and that of the political leaders articulating them. To such groups *slavery* referred emotionally to more than the South's "peculiar institution," for whatever restrained man's liberty was antithetical to the operation of his free will—his right to do right. Salvation for man, and for society, was possible only through an act of free will; whatever restrained man's liberty jeopardized his, and society's, salvation. Moreover, God commanded that the "saved" exalt His glory and work for the salvation of others. To break the chains that bound the free will of others—whether the bondage of the black man to his white owner or of the immigrant to the pope or of any man to Demon Rum or to the Spirit of Party—was nothing less than God's dictate. It was *his* nonnegotiable demand, for each and all of these forms of bondage were sinful obstacles to God's work.[56]

This symbolic unity reflected shared dispositions that had earlier been evident in the overlapping leadership and membership among antislavery, temperance, and anti-Catholic groupings. Not every antislavery man was also necessarily anti-Catholic, nor was every anti-Catholic invariably a supporter of temperance, nor were all equally repulsed by the "Spirit of Party" and the "Slave Power." Yet there was broad value-system and attitudinal congruence, and the antiparty and antisouthern themes became the least common denominators expressing that shared psychological rapport.

The convergence of these emotional streams shattered the old structure of partisanship and created a new one. The new pattern was not the product of a spontaneous outpouring of moral anguish over the Kansas-Nebraska question. That agitation crystallized a variety of smoldering resentments, and it provided opportunity for party builders to refine their symbolic appeals and again to escalate the levels of political tension. However, it was not a single-principled party that emerged from that agitation by midsummer of 1854. In fact, it was not even a *party*. It was a broad, loosely structured popular-front coalition that can best be

56. For examples of such sentiments, see *Minutes of the New Jersey Annual Conference of the Methodist Episcopal Church, 1854*, pp. 18–19; *Minutes of the Annual Meeting of the Maine Baptist Convention, 1860*, p. 9; Henry Crocker, *History of the Baptists in Vermont*, p. 111; *Minutes of the General Assembly of the Presbyterian Church [New School] in the United States of America, 1852*, pp. 181–82.

designated an *anti-Democratic grouping*. It was a coalition that in most localities eschewed the name *Republican*, and used instead labels such as *Fusion*, *Independent*, or *People's*. It was, in other words, an antiparty popular front, an ad hoc coalition of groups united by their shared opposition to *Democracy* and all that that label symbolized.

The mechanics and tempo by which this popular-front grouping began to develop into a political party varied from locality to locality. In some places (Michigan) cooperative arrangements were worked out as early as 1854, with Know-Nothings supporting "Anti-Nebraska" men rather than offering their own slates. In other locales (western New York) cooperation was not effected until after the 1854 election. In still others (Pennsylvania) the cooperative negotiations were even more protracted. And in all places the mechanics of party building interacted with the necessity of developing a mass coalition. A view of the changing shape of that mass constituency can provide insight into both the process of Republican party formation and the character of the emerging party.

In its initial incarnation in 1854, the anti-Democratic popular front attracted the support of the bulk of former Whig voters and virtually all of the old Free-Soilers. Where the Know-Nothings "cooperated," it also attracted the votes of native Protestants who had earlier been Democrats. By 1856, a year after the American party had experienced its North-vs.-South rupture, Know-Nothing cooperation was more extensive, and throughout the North more native Protestant former Democrats moved into the anti-Democratic coalition. At the same time the anti-popish image of the new grouping enabled it to begin to carve out slender beachheads among anti-Whig foreign Protestant voters, especially among some of the Dutch and Norwegians in the Midwest and the more pietistic German groups throughout the North. Yet the rancid aura of Know-Nothingism, to say nothing of its still separate existence in some locales, inhibited the movement of foreign voters and that of some older-stock groups, such as the Scotch-Irish Presbyterians, who were repelled by secretiveness. Through 1856, then, the anti-Democratic coalition succeeded in uniting virtually all the Free-Soilers, the bulk of the former Whigs, and probably more than half of those Yankee Protestants who had been Democrats earlier. Since Whiggery and Free-Soil had both drawn heavily for their support on Yankee-Protestant subculture, the anti-Democratic popular front was more clearly a Yankee-Protestant party than Whiggery had ever been.[57]

Between 1856 and 1860 the popular front began to develop into a

57. For indications of the cross-party movement of voters, see the regression estimates in Shortridge, "Voting Patterns in the American Midwest," pp. 75–77, 82–83, 108–109. In 1856 in the Midwest there was still considerable support for the Know-

political party. And as it did it acquired "a survival-urge that dictated pragmatism and eclecticism in acquiring votes." These impulses required conscious and calculated efforts to consolidate existing mass support and to attract the votes of more former Democrats, even foreign-born Democrats. That involved pushing prominent former Democrats to the front as nominees for office, toning down the repugnant aura of Know-Nothingism by tacitly merging antipopery into the rhetoric of antisouthernism, and identifying "Catholicism with 'party,' Democracy, and slavocracy."[58] This pragmatic, vote-garnering orientation induced restiveness among the Know-Nothings, but it paid dividends in votes by 1860.

That year in their national platform the builders of the anti-Democratic coalition were emboldened enough to call themselves the Republican party.[59] And they were eclectic enough to stand foursquare against "any change" in the naturalization laws or any state legislation that "abridged or impaired" the rights of immigrants. Thus they gave their local stalwarts at least a talking point to counter the visible presence of Know-Nothings within their ranks. Yet they were pragmatic enough to avoid the nomination of a candidate repugnant to the antipopish men. At the state level Republicans frequently preferred to rely on their standing image rather than run the risk of policy pronouncements that might alienate one or the other of the elements of the coalition. Pragmatism and eclecticism produced small, but behaviorally and electorally significant, gains. Formerly Democratic Baptist and Methodist voters, as German pietists and rationalists and Dutch and Norwegian pietists, continued their motion toward the Republicans. And the anti-Democrats also made slight gains among German Lutheran voters. For instance, in fifteen virtually homogeneous German Lutheran towns in Wisconsin, Republican strength increased by 3.1 percentage points between 1856 and 1860. In similar units in Michigan, Democratic strength in 1860 was 7.8 percentage points below its 1852 level. Throughout Pennsylvania, especially in urban contexts, the Democrats drew lower levels of support among German Lutheran voters than they had in either 1854 or 1856.[60]

Nothings among southern-stock former Whig voters; see Hammond, "Revivalist Political Ethos," pp. 194, 199–200, 208.

58. The quoted phrases are from Formisano, *Birth of Mass Parties*, pp. 266, 310.

59. Compare the preambles of the 1856 and 1860 national platforms, in Kirk H. Porter and Donald Bruce Johnson, comps., *National Party Platforms, 1840–1968*, pp. 27, 31–32. At the state level the Republicans usually did not call themselves a party until after 1856; for an example, see Joseph P. Smith, ed., *History of the Republican Party in Ohio*, 1:33.

60. See the data in Petersen, "Reaction to a Heterogeneous Society," pp. 123, 174; William A. Gudelunas, Jr., "Before the Molly Maguires," pp. 70, 79, 85, 88, 92,

The voter movement in the late 1850s was not unidirectional. Not at all remarkably, some southern-stock groups resisted the Republican surge. Most southern-stock voters who had earlier been Whigs probably voted for Lincoln in 1860, though considerably lower proportions of them had voted for Fremont in 1856. Yet more southern-stock voters voted against Lincoln in 1860 than had voted anti-Whig earlier. More remarkably, the highest-status religious group, the Episcopalians, were not active participants in the Republican tide. Episcopalians, voters and elites, were less Republican in 1860 than they had been Whig in 1856 or earlier. And, of course, as they resisted antipopery, Catholic voter groups of all ethnic backgrounds and across all status levels cohered even more solidly in the ranks of the Democracy than they had earlier.[61]

Describing the direction of voter-group movement over time is not the same thing as describing the social-group coalition of a party at any given time. These two dimensions of description and subsequent analysis need always to be disentangled. Thus, former Democrats—Yankee Protestant Methodists and Baptists as well as pietistic Norwegian, Dutch, and Germans, along with quite small numbers of German Lutherans— were by 1860 "in motion" toward the Republicans. Yet except for the Yankee Protestants and Norwegians the Democrats still retained majority support among these politically mobile groups. Even among the Yankee Protestants, especially the Methodists, there were instances of persisting majority support for the Democracy. And if Episcopalians and some southern-stock voters were less Republican than they had been Whig, not in all locales did a majority of them vote for the Democrats.

Secession, War, and Party Development

Party development and coalition shuffling did not terminate with Lincoln's election in 1860. Indeed, shortly after his inauguration both parties entered a new phase in which the motion was accelerated. The secession of eleven southern states, the firing on Fort Sumter, and the calling of northern men to arms altered the context of political action. The crusade and political movement aimed at destroying that hydra-headed monster slavery became a war to preserve the Union. In an

---

96; Holt, *Forging a Majority*, pp. 367–68; Formisano, *Birth of Mass Parties*, pp. 144, 183, 301, 313, 315; Joseph Schafer, *Four Wisconsin Counties*, pp. 146, 388, 390, 392–93, 395–96.

61. McCoy, "Political Affiliations of American Economic Elites," pp. 129–30, 137–38, 140; Petersen, "Reaction to a Heterogeneous Society," pp. 118–19, 167; Formisano, *Birth of Mass Parties*, pp. 140, 183; Holt, *Forging a Majority*, pp. 326, 354, 365–66.

atmosphere overheated by decades of moralistic rhetoric and a political culture permeated by strong strains of antipartyism, actions that otherwise might have been viewed as oppositional politics were equated with aid to the rebellion. The us-against-them, right-vs.-wrong moralism that had penetrated politics readily transmuted dissent into "treason" and political opponents into "copperheads." Proximate events were viewed within the ultimate context of loyalty to the country. And wartime events, Democratic behaviors, and the Republicans' self-created aura all reverberated with emotional resonance and bestowed new legitimacy on anti-Democratic voting.

Writing a decade or more after the North's victory, county and local historians frequently described the social atmosphere of the war with oblique euphemisms such as "feeling ran high" or "a period of intense excitement." Antagonisms too bitter and persisting to be ignored underlay such references. Throughout the northern states church congregations and social clubs were split, "neighbors and families were divided, and discussions often ended in violence." With the administration's resort to the draft to supply manpower for the Union armies, the scope of that violence was extended and its levels were raised. In virtually every state were outbreaks of violent resistance, ranging from the physical destruction of the draft-enrollment lists, to the wounding of scores of draft officials, to the killing of some thirty-eight others. [62]

These emotions burst into party channels and intensified partisanship. For some voter groups they both reflected and reinforced prewar party attachments. For others they provided continuing impetus to their prewar motion away from the Democracy. For at least one group the war constituted a "critical experience" that deflected the direction of its prewar partisan movement. And for both major parties the war created existential crises and new auras. For the Democrats the crisis centered on maintaining the antebellum party—on keeping alive the interaction and identification with common symbols among officials, activists, and voters that are necessary for a party's existence. For the Republicans the

62. For examples of oblique allusion to the social conflict, see Louis Falge, ed., *History of Manitowoc County, Wisconsin*, 1:354; *History of Green County, Wisconsin*, pp. 1056, 1105. For indication of the intensity of the conflict and its effects on social relations, see Edward P. Brand, *Illinois Baptists*, p. 83; Arthur Charles Cole, *The Era of the Civil War in Illinois*, pp. 307, 423–24; Hebert, *Modern Maine*, 1:214–15; Marion Ramsey Furness, "Childhood Recollections of Old St. Paul," p. 122; Joseph Calvin Evers, *The History of the Southern Illinois Conference of the Methodist Church*, pp. 136–37, 186–87; William W. Sweet, *The Methodist Episcopal Church and the Civil War*, pp. 81–82; Joseph H. Creighton, *Life and Times of Joseph H. Creighton, A.M. of the Ohio Conference*, pp. 162–63; *Minutes of the General Assembly of the United Presbyterian Church of North America, 1865*, p. 84. On the violence engendered by the draft, see Robert E. Sterling, "Civil War Draft Resistance in the Middle West."

crisis lay in *forging* that requisite interaction and symbolic unity.

Elections during the war and Reconstruction were marked by considerable fluctuation in partisan support, as well as by unusual patterns of voter movement into and from the electoral universe. Table 3.4 provides a broad overview of both of these features and draws attention to the peculiar swing-counterswing rhythm that marked the period.[63] The Republican victory in 1860 was followed by the immediate resurgence of the Democrats in 1862; that rebound was cut short by strong countermovement to the Republicans over the 1863 to 1866 elections; and that, in turn, was followed by another Democratic resurgence in 1867. Each of these elections might be analyzed individually and intensively, but for present purposes it is more critical to focus on the broader contours of voter movement and party development.

The Republicans were a remarkably disparate coalition. The heterogeneity of Republicanism was unmistakable: former Liberty party men and Free-Soilers, Whigs, Democrats, and Know-Nothings; pietistic Yankee Protestants, anti-Yankee but pietistic Norwegian, Dutch, and German sectarians; small numbers of German Lutherans and nearly all of their natural enemies, the German rationalists. This motley mixture was held together by a powerful anti-Democratic animus that sublimated the potential tensions existing among its subgroups. Yet not for long could those who had been commanded by God "to do right" be stilled nor their energy turned to the more pragmatic tasks of party and coalition building. As Yankee cultural imperialism burst forth, the anti-Democratic coalition experienced ceaseless unease.

It is important to realize the central position that pietistic Yankee Protestants occupied within the anti-Democratic coalition. In New England as well as in the counties where they had settled throughout the middle-belt states, their strong swing against the Democrats had underpinned the coalition's initial electoral success. And they remained crucial cial sources of its mass voting support. Their political conversion had produced a set of relatively safe congressional constituencies. In a period of fluctuating levels of support for the party and consequently high turnover among public officials, those regularly returned from safe constituencies tended to play disproportionately important roles as public spokesmen for the party. Finally, pietistic Yankee Protestants continued

63. The drop-off calculation (Panel B) is a measure of the customary pattern of decline in the total vote between presidential and succeeding off-year elections. The figures presented are reciprocals of the percentage of the presidential-year vote that was cast in the next off-year election. If the Democratic vote in the two elections had been the same, drop-off would be zero; if the size of the off-year vote cast for the party was *larger* than its vote in the presidential year, then drop-off would be *negative*. See Walter Dean Burnham, "The Changing Shape of the American Political Universe," p. 9.

TABLE 3.4   *Partisan Support by Regions, 1860–1872*

A. *Percent Republican of Total Vote*

	New Eng.	Midatl.	East N. Cent.	Three Regions
1860	61.8	53.7	52.7	54.5
1862	60.4	48.7	48.7	50.4
1863	58.7	51.8	56.2	54.5
1864	63.4	50.6	55.2	54.5
1866	64.3	51.0	55.6	54.7
1867	56.7	47.5	52.1	50.6
1868	63.8	50.3	54.5	54.0
1870	58.6	48.8	52.2	51.5
1872	65.0	56.5	55.7	57.3

B. *Drop-off in Size of Vote (as %)*

1860–62				
Dem	14.3	0.1	10.4	6.6
Repub	19.2	18.2	23.6	20.6
1864–66				
Dem	19.1	−0.1	−1.8	1.5
Repub	16.0	−1.8	−3.6	0.6
1868–70				
Dem	9.5	9.8	15.6	12.3
Repub	27.6	15.3	23.2	20.8

to operate as a pressure group. Through their religious conferences and benevolent societies they unleashed their zeal in the form of petitions and memorials to state and national lawmakers.[64] As officeholders, probably as activists, and certainly as voters and lobbyists, pietistic Yankee Protestants powerfully and indelibly shaped the tone and character of the Republican party. And when they moved to Republicanism, they carried with them an important feature of their political culture— antiparty values. Their religious values prized above all free will, the

64. On the emergence of a set of safe congressional seats, David Donald, "The Republican Party, 1864–1876," pp. 1284–85. For examples of Yankee pietistic attitudes toward the war, see *Minutes of the Maine Annual Conference of the Methodist Episcopal Church, 1861*, p. 18; *Minutes of the Wisconsin Annual Session of the Baptist State Convention, 1861*, p. 9; *Minutes of the New Jersey Annual Conference of the Methodist Episcopal Church, 1862*, pp. 16–17; *Minutes of the Annual Meeting of the General*

"right to do right." They accepted Republicanism, not as a party, but as an antiparty crusade for righteousness. They would be bound by principle, by right, and never by "the lash of the party drill master."[65] Such voters, critically important as they were to the anti-Democratic coalition, were precisely those most resistant to the norms of party loyalty.

Yankee antipartyism also made it difficult for party builders to institutionalize requisite interaction among officials, activists, and voters —to exercise what Yankees deprecated as "party discipline." Those with antiparty values opposed efforts aimed at imparting centralized shape and direction to the coalition. At every turn they sought to minimize the opportunities for party managers to exert their influence and potentially enhance their authority. The party met in national conventions and nominated candidates for national office, for the federalized structure of the American political system required no less. Unlike the Democrats, however, Republicans' calls for such conventions did not permit delegates to be selected by state conclaves or at-large elections. Neither would those who held antiparty values allow the national convention to adopt rules requiring state delegations to vote as a unit, nor would they require the presidential nominee to attain more than a simple majority of the delegates' votes. Any of these moves would have enhanced the potential for the "wire pullers" to exert a type and degree of party discipline abhorrent to those who believed that "the great principles of the Republican organization demand that each man shall have his vote himself and not be bound by some party or power that is behind him."[66]

Association of New Hampshire [Congregational Churches], 1862, pp. 11–12; Minutes of the General Assembly of the Presbyterian Church [New School], 1863, p. 287; Minutes of the Vermont Annual Conference of the Methodist Episcopal Church, 1864, p. 39; The Rev. W. H. Eaton, Historical Sketch of Massachusetts Baptist Missionary Society and Convention, 1802–1902, pp. 90–91; Crocker, Baptists in Vermont, pp. 474–78.

65. Marshalltown (Iowa) Times, 7 March 1872, quoted in Mildred Throne, "The Liberal Republican Party in Iowa, 1872," pp. 131–32.

66. The remark was made by a Kansas delegate to the 1876 Republican National Convention. The quotation and the items of information here are from Donald, "Republican Party," p. 1285. However, Donald's interpretation emphasizes the importance of localism and does not adequately explore the roots of the articulated values. For evidence of the persisting opposition among Republicans to the unit rule and indications of the antiparty values reflected in that opposition, see the resolution of the New Hampshire Republican party and the letter of a New York Republican convention delegate on the subject in Appletons' Annual Cyclopaedia and Register of Important Events of the Year 1880, pp. 558, 575. And contrast these attitudes with the ones articulated by the Democrats in Connecticut, Kentucky, Louisiana, Minnesota, and New York, ibid., pp. 197, 421–22, 484, 525–26, 574. It is revealing of the nature of Pennsylvania's parties that the Republicans accepted the unit rule and the Democrats rejected it; see ibid., pp. 616–18.

Despite their election of a president and their control of Congress, the Republicans at the opening of the Civil War occupied a precarious political position. Beyond the New England region were few states in which the Republican label was a rallying symbol enlisting strong majority support. Indeed, in as pivotal a state as Pennsylvania even in 1860, the "party" had been only a "loose aggregation" of old Whigs, Know-Nothings, antislavery Democrats, and radical Republicans "united under the flag of the People's party."[67] Even where the Republican label had been used in 1860, there remained traces of the distinct emotional streams that had converged to produce the original anti-Democratic popular front. Thus, the task confronting Republican party builders during the post-1860 years, especially in the Middle Atlantic and East North Central states, was not one of retaining normal majority support, but of developing it. To extend the party's coalition while not permitting value conflicts among its constituent groups to fragment it required delicate orchestration.

Of course, the problem was an extension of the one that the party builders had faced after 1856. To build a party required developing psychological rapport among officials, activists, and voters; to build a successful party mandated increasing the number of habituated voters. That required, as it had earlier, heavy infusions of pragmatism and eclecticism. In 1861 the North was at war: "feeling ran high." To channel that feeling to partisan advantage, to broaden the party's mass base, Republican strategists offered a massive dose of "no-partyism."

It only seems paradoxical that the Republicans employed no-party themes to develop partisan strength, for they purposively directed the no-partyism at drawing partisan lines to their own advantage. As Republican party builders argued repeatedly that they knew "no party in . . . [their] present troubles," they intended both to redefine the basis of party cleavage and to project new auras to the major-party contenders. The erosion of old partisan loyalties—the ones that the Democrats were consciously attempting to reactivate—gave Republicans occasion to assist voters in coming to a new interpretation of political reality. Borrowing a line from the 1860 Democratic presidential nominee, Stephen A. Douglas, Republican party builders proclaimed righteously, "There can be no neutrals in this war—*only patriots—or traitors.*"[68] Throughout

67. [Alexander] K. McClure, *Old Time Notes of Pennsylvania*, 1:403, 500. McClure was the 1860 state chairman of the People's party.

68. The line is from Douglas's "Address to Democrats," 1 May 1861, quoted in Sterling, "Civil War Draft Resistance," p. 32, emphasis in the original. For an elaborate exposition of Republican antipartyism, see the pamphlet published and circulated as campaign material, *No Party Now but All for Our Country*. For an example of Republican

the North by late 1861, that theme dominated Republican rhetoric, and as it did, proximate events were placed into ultimate contexts. Qualified acceptance of the administration's war aims or criticism of the conduct of the war, placed in the ultimate context of loyalty to the nation, became the northern counterpart to southern rebellion, for "a conditional Union man is an unconditional traitor." And within the ultimate patriot-traitor context even "those who . . . talk of the right of *habeas corpus* sympathize with the rebels."[69]

Tactically, Republican party builders implemented their strategy through two related moves. First, they recruited prominent Democrats, the so-called War Democrats, and thrust them to the fore as nominees for office and even as party managers. Second, and more important, they tacitly recognized the impotence of the Republican label as a rallying symbol and instead styled themselves the "Union party." That change in the party's designation was of immense symbolic significance. Where necessary (as in Pennsylvania) it allowed the party to continue to operate as an anti-Democratic popular front; and everywhere it permitted the party to identify itself with the cause of the Union, to put itself on the patriot side of a mutually exclusive patriot-traitor dichotomy.[70]

Coalition building requires that political parties "take the roles of publics whose support they need." A party leader must design his acts, speeches, and postures to make "those behaviors significant symbols, evoking common meaning for his audience and for himself and so shaping his further actions as to reassure his public and in this sense 'represent' them."[71] The wartime acts, speeches, and postures of the Republicans—summed and symbolized in their "no-party-but-country" appeals and in the Union label—aimed at "representing" two sets of groupings.

---

fears that the Democrats would successfully reactivate antebellum partisan loyalties, see Bion Bradbury to I. Washburn, 27 July 1861, in Gaillard Hunt, comp., *Israel, Elihu, and Cadwallader Washburn*, pp. 99–100.

69. Respectively, the quotations are from Israel Washburn's 1861 address to the Maine legislature, Hunt, comp., *Washburns*, p. 103; and *Illinois Staats-Zeitung*, 19 April 1862, quoted in Cole, *Era of the Civil War in Illinois*, pp. 300–301. For examples of the increasingly extensive use of the theme by Republicans, see DeAlva Stanwood Alexander, *A Political History of the State of New York*, 3:46; Charles Moore, *History of Michigan*, 1:423. The concept of the relation between proximate events and ultimate contexts is borrowed from Clifford Geertz, who applies it to the role of religious ritual in "Religion as a Cultural System," p. 28.

70. For Pennsylvania see McClure, *Old Times Notes*, 1:251, 340–45, 403, 496–502, 526–32; for the decision by James G. Blaine, the Republican state chairman in Maine, to drop the Republican label, see Hebert, *Modern Maine*, 1:217. Donald, "Republican Party," p. 1287, exaggerates the frequency with which *Republican* was used as the party's official designation during the war years.

71. Murray Edelman, *The Symbolic Uses of Politics*, p. 188.

First, Republican no-partyism resonated with the antiparty values of pietistic Yankee Protestants. To them the war had been caused by parties; it was evidence that the nation had "been betrayed by corrupt politicians, who for party, have . . . brought ruin upon the best government in the world by sacrificing *truth* and *right* to expediency." Yet they also saw the war as "a golden opportunity," for it was "God's method for purifying—and thus blessing and saving—the nation." However, "salvation" would be possible only when all citizens recognized that their "allegiance to God" required "rising above all questions of party politics"; opposing the "organized opposition to President Lincoln and his administration [that] is . . . giving aid and comfort to our enemies"; and offering instead their "loyalty, unreserved and unconditional" to the Union cause.[72] And throughout the 1860s their conference meetings and benevolent societies bombarded state and national lawmakers with petitions and resolutions praying for legal action to enforce their conception of the right: the constitutional prohibition of slavery, the enfranchisement of the freedmen, the congressional version of Reconstruction, the impeachment of Andrew Johnson, and the demand that the "fruits of the war" not be lost by allowing the traitors to return "to the places of political power."[73] Republican acts, postures, and— above all—no-party symbolism were aimed at reactivating and reinforcing the partisan proclivity of this group. No-partyism reminded pietistic Yankee Protestants that Republicanism was no mere party but was still *their* uncompromising, crusading vehicle for God and country.

Second, Republican no-partyism sought to evoke "common meanings" from other Protestant groups that had earlier been Democratic. It appealed here less to evangelical, and more to secular, strains of patriotism. It offered a new context within which to define partisanship, a

72. For the quoted phrases see *Minutes of the Session of the New England Annual Conference of the Methodist Episcopal Church, 1864*, p. 23, first emphasis added; *Minutes of the Providence Annual Conference of the Methodist Episcopal Church, 1863*, pp. 24–25; ibid., *1864*, p. 29; *Minutes of the Annual Session of the [Presbyterian] Synod of Pennsylvania, 1861*, p. 13; *Minutes of the Maine Annual Conference of the Methodist Episcopal Church, 1864*, p. 24; *Minutes of the Annual Meeting of the General Association of New Hampshire [Congregational Churches], 1861*, pp. 8–9; *Minutes of the General Convention of Congregational Ministers and Churches in Vermont, 1863*, pp. 12–13. These and similar sentiments abounded in the conference journals during the war and Reconstruction.

73. *Minutes of the Maine Annual Conference of the Methodist Episcopal Church, 1867*, pp. 20–22. For other examples of these sentiments, see *Minutes of the National Council of the Congregational Churches of the United States of America, 1871*, p. 43; *Minutes of the Providence Annual Conference of the Methodist Episcopal Church, 1867*, p. 21; *Minutes of the Session of the New England Annual Conference of the Methodist Episcopal Church, 1868*, pp. 33–34; *Minutes of the New Jersey Annual Conference of the Methodist Episcopal Church, 1866*, pp. 26–27; *Minutes of the Anniversary of the Ohio Baptist Convention, 1866*, pp. 13–14.

context that pitted the party of "patriotism" against the party of "rebellion." And at the grass-roots level Republican party organizers worked to shape a "Protestant party" by merging patriotism with a continuing and accelerating attack on the pope and his American coreligionists. If additional fuels were needed for the antipopery fires, they pointed to the tepid support of (if not outright opposition to) the Union cause offered by the Catholic press.[74] Thus, by depicting theirs as a movement for the Union, of patriotism, of opposition both to rebellion and Catholics, Republicans sought to present themselves as a "nonparty" meriting support from Protestant Democrats who had earlier been repelled by the association of the Republican party with the Whigs, with the "nigger-loving" Abolitionists, or with the Know-Nothings' disreputable secrecy and nativism. Pragmatic Republican party builders played down these old associations. In their wartime state platforms they avoided stands on issues and public postures on questions—such as tariffs, banks, temperance—that might be reminiscent of the cultural values that had structured antebellum party loyalties. Instead, they frequently called down the blessings of the old Democratic patron saints, especially those of Andrew Jackson. And they used the Union label, with its no-party and patriotic implications, to socialize voters into the practice of casting ballots for anti-Democrats.

Republican no-party and patriot-or-traitor themes, combined with recruitment of the War Democrats, created a literal existential crisis for the Democracy. It had lost some of its prewar officials and activists; its patron saints and symbols had been usurped; in many locales its county organizations had been fractured. Everywhere it had to defend its loyalty. It had become an opposition party in a context not supportive of oppositional politics, a context in which opposition had become treason.

The prewar leaders who had remained with the Democracy were cognizant of the party's problems, including the withdrawal of the War Democrats. On the one hand, the movement of prominent Democrats into the Union ranks gave public credence to the Republican claims that theirs was not a party but a movement for the country. On the other, and more significantly, their withdrawal meant that the roles of the Democratic party's public spokesmen would be occupied by many who were prosouthern (though not necessarily prosecession) and who stridently condemned the war effort.[75] Such behavior eventually reinforced the Republican claim of treason.

74. Robert H. Lord, John E. Sexton, and Edward T. Harrington, *History of the Archdiocese of Boston*, 2:704–18. For evidence on the continuing partisan salience of antipopery, see Gudelunas, "Before the Molly Maguires"; Douglas V. Shaw, "The Making of an Immigrant Community."
75. For information on the War Democrats, see Cole, *Era of the Civil War in*

That did not occur immediately. The off-year elections of 1862 marked the low point in the political fortunes of the "party of patriotism." All over the Union, even in New England where Democratic unity was rent by opposing "war" and "peace" candidates, disproportionate drop-off in the size of the Republican vote reduced the party's strength. As the data in Tables 3.4 and 3.5 show, the size of the drop-off in the Republican vote exceeded that of the Democrats in all subregions and in three of the four social areas. However, the loss of over 20,000 votes in the German areas and 50,000 in the Yankee counties proved devastating. Yet the peril was short-lived; the Republicans rebounded in the state elections of 1863 and extended those gains in the following presidential-election year. That Republican resurgence resulted from an ability to rally their supporters in German and Yankee counties and to poll new voting support in the southern-stock areas. In the latter counties the total Republican vote in 1864 was 7,000 above 1860 and almost 10,-000 higher than 1862; they gained an additional 8,400 votes in 1866.[76]

What turned the tide? The acts, speeches, and postures of the Democrats were mainly responsible. In 1863 Democratic state platforms offered even starker denunciations of the war than they had earlier, and typically they called for an immediate end to hostilities. In state legislatures Democrats in an almost cohesive voting bloc had opposed measures to allow the soldier in the field to vote. All through the months of 1863 and 1864, there had been a literally uncounted number of local, county, and regional meetings of citizens, presided over and addressed by prominent Democrats, at which resolutions opposing continuation of the war and calling for immediate peace had been passed. And to a war-wearied populace those demands, just as the battle seemed to turn in favor of the North, smacked of a missed opportunity to savor the "fruits of victory." As if these were not enough to taint the Democracy's image, a new and more extensive outbreak of violent resistance to the

---

Illinois, pp. 260–62, 279; Albert Bushnell Hart, ed., *Commonwealth History of Massachusetts*, 4:588–89; McClure, *Old Time Notes*, 1:143–44. It is important to notice, however, that the War Democrats were more prominent than they were numerous. That they quickly were moved into visible roles within the anti-Democratic coalition represented a tactical effort to attract mass support among normally Democratic voters. However, the effort should not be mistaken for evidence that the mass movement was of comparable proportions; see Sundquist, *Dynamics of the Party System*, pp. 73–74. For an example of the use of the War Democrats in anti-Democratic rhetoric, see *Boston Daily Advertiser*, 27 October 1864.

76. Between 1862 and 1864 the Republicans almost doubled the size of their vote in Scandinavian areas, but in the latter year that brought them only a total of slightly more than 8,000 votes. Although the 1864 Republican percentage in the German areas remained below its 1860 level, the raw vote was only 1,800 below its 1860 level. The Democratic vote in the German counties was 14,000 above the 1860 total. Between 1864 and 1866 the Democrats gained 6,000 votes in the southern-stock counties.

TABLE 3.5   *Partisan Support by Types of Counties, 1860–1872*

A. *Percent Democratic of Total Vote*

	Yankee (N = 71)	Southern Stock (N = 18)	German (N = 43)	Scandinavian (N = 33)
1860*	34.1	69.8	50.6	35.0
1862	38.4	64.7	57.8	45.0
1864	36.0	54.6	55.0	31.8
1866	35.7	51.2	52.3	26.8
1868	36.3	54.8	52.2	27.5
1870	39.7	54.6	55.0	30.1
1872	35.7	50.7	50.6	28.0

B. *Drop-off in Size of Vote (as %)*

	Yankee	Southern Stock	German	Scandinavian
1860–62				
Dem	5.1	38.0	0.4	10.6
Repub	21.6	22.0	25.8	39.1
1864–66				
Dem	0.8	−25.3	7.0	11.7
Repub	−0.4	−43.4	−3.8	−12.5
1868–70				
Dem	10.5	0.7	21.2	25.6
Repub	22.7	−0.2	29.6	34.5

*Unlike Table 3.3, the percent Democratic for 1860 given here is the sum of the Douglas, Bell, and Breckinridge vote, and counties in Minnesota have been used in the Yankee, German, and Scandinavian categories.

draft began in the summer of 1863. Democratic leaders certainly did not organize that, but in the Midwest it burst out "in counties where the climate of opinion was largely shaped by Democratic editors and politicians." And elsewhere, as in Boston and New York, Democratic support groups, especially the Irish, were most often and most publicly identified with the violence.[77]

77. Sterling, "Civil War Draft Resistance," p. 249. For Irish involvement see Adrian Cook, *The Armies of the Streets*, pp. 52, 55–58, 189, 194; McClure, *Old Time Notes*, 1:81–82; Justin Windsor, ed., *The Memorial History of Boston, Including Suffolk County, Massachusetts, 1630–1880*, 3:268–71. For examples of some of the Democratic

Taken collectively, events confirmed for many the often-repeated Republican claim that the northern Democracy was in league with the disunionists of the South and was no less guilty than they of treason. In the context of the developments of 1863–64, Republican denunciations of traitors, calls to patriotic duty, and appeals to no-partyism were more likely than earlier to evoke common meanings for both Republican party leaders and the publics whose support they needed. That enabled the party of the Union to rally its supporters in Yankee, German, and Scandinavian areas and to enlist new support in the southern-stock counties.[78]

Viewed over time, the behavior of the southern-stock counties was highly revealing. They had been soft spots for the Democrats in 1862. The enormous drop-off in the size of the Democratic vote indicated a group squeezed between conflicting loyalties. Southern kin-group connections; the upland southerner's traditional antipathy to slavery as an institution of the tidewater aristocracy; intense antagonism to blacks; traditional support for the Democracy as the anti-Yankee party; revulsion over the antisouthernism of the Republicans; and that party's obvious association with "black abolitionism," Yankee cultural imperialism, and old-line Whiggery mixed to exert enormous cross-pressures. The movement into the Union ranks by prominent prewar Democratic county leaders in southern-stock areas, such as John A. Logan in Illinois, only added to those cross-pressures.

The cross-pressures that result from conflicting values and attachments do not always result in nonvoting. They lead the voter to withdraw from the political field only when he perceives reasons to avoid both alternatives. The 1860–62 drop-off data strongly indicate such a reaction among voters in southern-stock areas. Their initial response was avoidance, a disproportionate degree of nonvoting and especially of non-Democratic voting, as that party polled 11,296 fewer votes than it had two years earlier. When the voter is strongly attracted to both alternatives, however, he is more likely to remain in the field, to consider both actively, and to make a final choice.[79] Voters in these counties did return to the political field between 1862 and 1864, and Republican candidates

---

anti-war activities, see Charles A. Church, *History of the Republican Party in Illinois, 1854–1912*, p. 91; Cole, *Era of the Civil War in Illinois*, pp. 299–300, 320–21; Benjamin F. Gue, *History of Iowa From the Earliest Times to the Beginning of the Twentieth Century*, 2:84–89, 123–24; Squires, *Granite State*, 1:399–400; Lynwood G. Downs, "The Soldier Vote and Minnesota Politics, 1862–65," p. 191.

78. V. Jacque Voegeli, *Free But Not Equal*, pp. 84, 127–28, 131; McClure, *Old Time Notes*, 2:60; Crocket, *Vermont*, 3:568–69; William F. Zornow, "Clement L. Vallandingham and the Democratic Party in 1864," pp. 36–37.

79. Ithiel de Sola Pool, Robert P. Abelson, and Samuel L. Popkin, *Candidates, Issues, and Strategies*, pp. 76–78.

were the beneficiaries. In the interim between elections, both parties stepped up their activities and rhetoric. The Republicans emphasized their no-party and patriotic appeals. The Democrats, to reactivate the old psychological rapport that had long existed between the party and upland southerners, reenergized their themes of negrophobia. Democratic rhetoric gave renewed emphasis to the Republican connections with "nigger equality" and demanded that this remain "a white man's government."[80] Against the backdrop of conditions in 1864, Republican patriotism proved the more effective rallying cry, and the Union the more potent symbol. The Republican aura, and that that they had projected to the Democracy, gave new legitimacy to anti-Democratic voting.

Democratic party leaders were not unaware of the potential vote-winning significance of the patriot-vs.-traitor themes and of the Union label.[81] Nor were they unaware of the ways in which party behaviors and external events had interacted by 1864 to endow them with greater emotional significance and partisan salience. The growing importance that they attributed to them, as well as to their own party-maintaining strategy, can best be inferred from the changing ways in which they responded. From the beginning of the war, the Democracy had taken pains to avow its loyalty. Its state platforms in 1861 and 1862 had criticized the conduct of the war but had done so in ways designed to reactivate the commitments of the party's antebellum supporters. Repeated appeals to "liberty loving citizens," denunciations of the "fanatics" and "abolitionists" who had brought on the war, condemnation of the "despotic exertion of power" evidenced in the suppression of dissent within the North had immense symbolic (as well as substantive) meaning. They involved code words embodying the values, the emotional and psychological perspectives, of the party's constituent groups. They were used in wartime rhetoric by Democratic leaders in an effort to indicate the continuing resonance between the political characters of those groups and that of the party. The aim was to reconstruct the party around the antebellum lines of subcultural conflict.[82] With that same

80. The attitudes and references were common; for examples and discussion see Jasper W. Cross, "The Civil War Comes to 'Egypt,'" pp. 160–69; Voegeli, *Free But Not Equal*, pp. 52–64, 151–52. Also see the suggestive comments by Elihu Washburn to Mrs. Washburn, 11 September 1864, in Hunt, comp., *Washburns*, p. 231; John Sherman to W. T. Sherman, 18 December 1864, in Rachael Sherman Thorndike, ed., *The Sherman Letters*, pp. 240–41.

81. For a succinct statement of what the Union label symbolized to the War Democrat, see the address by Robert J. Breckinridge of Kentucky to the 1864 Union Republican National Convention, quoted in Smith, ed., *Republican Party in Ohio*, 1:173.

82. For the use of such code words by the Democrats in antebellum rhetoric, see Thomas J. McCormack, ed., *Memoirs of Gustave Koerner, 1809–1896*, 2:9; Val Björnson, *The History of Minnesota*, 1:151–52; John D. Denison, *Iowa Democracy*, 1:127–

objective in view, and unlike the wartime Republicans, Democratic state platforms offered public postures on those prewar questions reminiscent of the cultural values that had structured the old party coalitions.

In 1864 the old code words, themes, and patron saints were still used, of course, but in a different and revealing context. Although earlier the Democrats had emphasized criticism of the war and the administration conducting it, in 1864 they concentrated on defending their own patriotism. Maine's Democrats, for instance, at the beginning of their platform declared that their party "is and ever has been the true Union party of the country." The rhetoric of the Massachusetts Democracy emphasized the theme that to vote for the party was "to rally round the Flag." Atypically, Ohio's Democrats offered a remarkably terse platform; even more atypically it contained only a single note of criticism. It concentrated instead on emphasizing the party's traditional devotion to the Constitution and invoked the blessings of the triune god of the antebellum Democracy—Jefferson, Madison, and Jackson. Assembling in mid-June 1864 to select their delegates to the party's national convention, Illinois's Democrats enacted a resolution declaring the war a failure and demanding its immediate end. By the time of their state nominating convention in July, they had had second thoughts. To avoid having to offer any posture on the divisive war-peace question, they took the unprecedented tack of endorsing no state platform.[83]

Such acts and shifts in rhetorical emphasis, intensified efforts to identify themselves with the cause of loyalty, suggest that Democratic leaders perceived the nature of the cross-pressures that were operating on their support groups by 1863–64. The stress that they placed on defending their own loyalty and the ways in which they cloaked that in the old code words and party symbols suggest that they perceived the aura of treason to be eroding the commitment of their normal supporters. They feared that the publics whose support they needed were coming to a new understanding of partisan distinctions. To prevent that, to reactivate the latent loyalties of their constituent groups, Democratic rhetoricians lowered their levels of criticism and increased the levels of their defensive assertions.

28, 140–41. Shade, *Banks or No Banks*, pp. 131, 143, 172–73, indicates the ways in which the code words expressed the political characters of the party's constituent groups. And for their use in a pre-1864 Democratic wartime platform, see the 1862 platform in *Ohio Platforms of the Republican and Democratic Parties from 1855–1881, Inclusive*, pp. 17–18.

83. *Appletons' Annual Cyclopaedia, 1864*, pp. 494, 510; *Ohio Platforms*, pp. 23–24. On Illinois see Walter A. Townsend, *Illinois Democracy*, 1:122; Cole, *Era of the Civil War in Illinois*, p. 322. For the Democracy's themes in Massachusetts, see especially the *Boston Post* editorials of 7, 8 November 1864.

None of this implies, of course, that the Democratic party collapsed after 1861 or even after the tide of battle had begun to turn in mid-1863. To the contrary—as a party in the electorate, as a rallying symbol to large numbers of voters, Democracy proved remarkably resilient. Even in 1864 the party ran spirited and strong campaigns; everywhere observers were impressed with the fact that "the party meetings were well attended" and the election "earnestly contested." Only after Lincoln's reelection and the final victory of the North did contemporaries begin to speak of the party's demoralization. "A feeling of hopelessness to party success" was reported among the party activists at Illinois's state convention in 1866. And a year earlier, in Iowa's state election, the party had not been able to field its own gubernatorial candidate but instead had endorsed one put forward by a convention of returning soldiers. [84]

Those returning soldiers, whose patriotism one would think to have been unassailable, revealingly chose to designate themselves the "Union Anti-Negro Suffrage party." That they felt it necessary symbolically to link their announced opposition to black suffrage with an overt affirmation of their continuing patriotism provides us with a good clue to the ways in which distinguishable ideas had been tied together in mass belief systems. It suggests that the returning soldiers perceived that the black suffrage question would become another litmus test of loyalty to the Union party. And that, in turn, points to another stage in party development.

The question of black political equality was to contemporaries, and has been to historians, a complex and anguishing one. [85] It was, first of all, part of a larger set of measures associated with the Reconstruction of the southern states. The motives and values that underlay the contending policy subcultures that battled over Reconstruction have yet to be credibly sorted out and evaluated systematically. Moreover, both the Fourteenth and Fifteenth Amendments were "Reconstruction" measures that were not confined in their social implications to the former rebel states. And the battle over the Fifteenth Amendment, which all contemporaries recognized as one over black suffrage, was fought in several political

84. The quotations are from McClure, *Old Time Notes*, 2:155; Townsend, *Illinois Democracy*, 1:127–28. For the Iowa contests, see Gue, *History of Iowa*, 2:122, 3:2–4; Denison, *Iowa Democracy*, 1:219–21. For reports of demoralization among Democratic activists in New England, see Hebert, *Modern Maine*, 1:230; Crockett, *Vermont*, 3:614–15.

85. John H. Cox and LaWanda Cox, "Negro Suffrage and Republican Politics," pp. 303–30, is the best historical survey. For more recent works, see Willis F. Dunbar and William G. Shade, "The Black Man Gains the Vote," pp. 42–57; Robert R. Dykstra and Harlan Hahn, "Northern Voters and Negro Suffrage," pp. 205–12; Phyllis F. Field, "Republicans and Black Suffrage in New York State," pp. 136–47; Formisano, "Edge of Caste," pp. 19–41.

arenas: in Congress, in state legislatures, and among the mass public, which voted on black-suffrage referenda or for candidates representing public postures on the question. It is well beyond the parameters of my current research design to disentangle the complex motivations involved in those tripartite battles. However, several simple observations are pertinent.

First, Reconstruction symbolized in mass opinion a fruits-of-the-war syndrome, a kind of postwar twist on the prewar antisouthernism that had energized political battles. However, it was an antisouthernism intensified by the war experience. Second, these fruits-of-the-war themes (the "bloody shirt") became effective rhetorical expressions articulating and reinforcing the psychological rapport between Republican party leaders and voters. Third, black suffrage apparently became linked in mass belief systems with this fruits-of-the-war antisouthernism. In the late 1860s these cumulative linkages made ratification of the Fifteenth Amendment possible by transforming it into a clear-cut partisan issue. In the longer run they represented another critical stage in party development.

Black suffrage was not a new question in the late 1860s. It had been agitated in some states for as long as two decades. And well prior to 1860 it had acquired traces of partisan overtones: Democrats—both officeholders in state legislatures and mass voters—tended to oppose black suffrage (or other questions dealing with blacks, such as their right to migrate to and reside in particular midwestern states) more heavily than Whigs. The early demand of evangelical abolitionists, and later of the Liberty party men, for black equality—often social as well as political equality—had earned them the contemptuous sobriquet *Black Abolitionist*. And both Whigs and Democrats, though appealing to different support groups, had used *abolitionist* as a code word for black equality and racial amalgamation. As contemporary politicians were well aware, there simply was no large reservoir of mass support in the North for black political equality. Wherever and whenever voters were given the opportunity to express their views in referenda, they regularly delivered large majorities against black suffrage and for black exclusion.[86]

However, none of this prewar agitation had transformed black suffrage into a symbol of partisan loyalty. Although Democratic leaders

86. Tom LeRoy McLaughlin, "Popular Reactions to the Idea of Negro Equality in Twelve Non-Slaveholding States, 1846–1869," Table 1, p. 37, provides a review of voting on black-rights referenda. Prior to 1867 only Wisconsin (in 1849) gave a majority for black suffrage but reversed that in 1857 and reaffirmed the reversal as late as 1865. In all 63.0 percent of the total ballots cast in these twenty-two referenda between 1849 and 1869 were cast against black rights. For examples of the other matters referred to in this and the following paragraph, see Dillon, *Abolitionists*, pp. 237–39; Björnson, *His-*

and voters were more antiblack than Whig leaders and voters, both sets of leaders and voters opposed black political equality. That each party could and did use black-rights issues against the other indicates that each perceived that the support groups of the other would be repelled by such an identification and that neither feared that its own constituent groups would be offended by its use of such themes.

By the late 1860s the situation had been drastically altered, in part as a result of the acts, speeches, and postures of Republican leaders. It was not that most Republican spokesmen anxiously championed the cause of blacks. During the war years they had recognized (probably because they had internalized) the racist attitudes of most northern whites and had attempted to undercut the Democracy's strenuous efforts to make black issues into tests of partisanship. In the early postwar years, however, the necessity of dealing with the question of the civil status of the freedmen, the continuing softness of support for the party in large areas throughout the North, the perceived likelihood of Democratic strength in the former rebel states, plus other elements, changed the context within which Republican leaders assessed questions of black political equality.

Their subsequent changed behavior did not spring from any single impulse but from a variety of motives—made all the more complex because analytically distinguishable impulses often interacted with one another even in the same person, and both their weights and valences changed over time. Some Republican leaders were driven as they had been earlier by a strongly felt humanitarianism. To them it was not a matter of how many voters would be won or lost by such a posture. It was a moral question: "The Republican party is strong enough to dare to do right and cannot afford to shirk a duty. . . . Let the Republican party have the courage to do justice."[87] To other party leaders it was a response to support-group pressures. The Yankee Protestant pressure groups continued to demand, as a minimum, political equality for blacks both in the North and South. And their support for black suffrage was not confined to verbal declarations. By 1865 five of the six northern states that allowed blacks to vote were New England states; and, as the data in Table 3.6 show, voters in Yankee counties beyond the New England area were the only ones offering strong support for black-suffrage

tory of Minnesota, 1:376–77; Church, *Republican Party in Illinois*, p. 36; Formisano, "Edge of Caste," pp. 30–33; George H. Porter, *Ohio Politics during the Civil War Period*, p. 34; David C. Shilling, "Relation of Southern Ohio to the South during the Decade Preceding the Civil War," pp. 8–10.

87. Hiram Price at the Iowa Republican State Convention, 14 June 1865, quoted in Gue, *History of Iowa*, 3:1–2. For a similar attitude on the part of Governor Palmer of Illinois, see D. W. Lusk, *Eighty Years of Illinois: Politics and Politicians*, p. 105.

referenda.[88] Perhaps other Republican leaders were moved by nothing more complex than a vengeful antisouthernism. And certainly some were motivated by the prospect of republicanizing the South through the votes of the freedmen.[89]

TABLE 3.6 *Voting on Black-Suffrage Referenda**

%	Yankee	Rest of States	Total States
For	58.9	44.5	46.9
Against	41.0	55.4	53.0

*The referenda were in Wisconsin, 1865; Ohio, 1867; Minnesota, 1868; and New York, 1869. For the Yankee counties in these states, $N = 36$.

Whatever the mixture of motives and however that mixture changed, it was clear to contemporaries that Republican, at least more than Democrat, represented black suffrage. In legislatures throughout the North and Midwest, for example, voting for ratification of the Fourteenth Amendment, and even more so the Fifteenth, became an acid test of Republican party loyalty: Democratic legislators united in cohesive opposition.[90] It was true that Republican state platforms did not "rejoice" (before 1870 at least) in the prospect of black political equality, but neither did they pledge themselves to the preservation of an exclusively "white man's

88. The data on the black suffrage referenda are from *Tribune Almanac, 1866*, p. 57; ibid., *1868*, p. 45; ibid., *1869*, p. 74; ibid., *1870*, p. 53. By 1865 only Connecticut among the New England states had failed to enact some form of black suffrage. New York was the sixth state, but its black-suffrage provision was a qualified one. For examples of the resolutions by religious conferences on black-equality questions, see *The Annual Anniversary of the Boston North Baptist Association, 1865*, pp. 9–10; *Minutes of the Maine Annual Conference of the Methodist Episcopal Church, 1866*, p. 25; *Minutes of the Annual Meeting of the Maine Baptist Convention, 1865*, p. 6; *Minutes of the Session of the New England Annual Conference of the Methodist Episcopal Church, 1862*, p. 24; *Minutes of the General Assembly of the United Presbyterian Church of North America, 1865*, pp. 78–79.

89. William Gillette, *The Right to Vote*, argues that some moderate Republicans supported the Fifteenth Amendment to increase the size of the party's voting clientele in the North. With a soft base of mass support, black voters would enhance Republican chances. The argument, however, ignores the fact that Republicans were well aware of the fact that they stood to lose more white voters over the question than they could possibly have gained from the enfranchisement of blacks. And Republican leaders did not have to guess, nor even be very perceptive; the referenda indicated white attitudes.

90. When the Democrats won control of the New Jersey and Ohio legislatures in the 1867 elections, they revoked the earlier Republican-engineered ratification of the Fourteenth Amendment; see Lawrence Grossman, "The Democratic Party and the Negro," p. 14. For indications of the party-cued voting on these and other black-rights

government.'' Democratic platforms, except in the New England states, made these commitments and used these code words.[91]

Historians' assessments of Republican attitudes on the black-suffrage question have invariably noticed that the party "did not hew a straight line."[92] In some locales it was supportive, in others lukewarm and evasive, in still others openly hostile. However, political rhetoric should never be construed literally; instead it must be searched "for the emotions and values appealed to because the rhetorician [knew] that his readers or listeners [were] already imbued with them."[93] Certainly Democratic rhetoric—the code words used, the linkages made—left no doubt that the party's leaders sought to evoke common meanings between themselves and groups antagonistic to blacks. Nor does the mildness of Republican public statements leave any doubt that they recognized the immense unpopularity of black political equality and sought to avoid its potentially coalition-destroying impact. The officials and activists who crafted Republican rhetoric recognized that antiblack themes might resonate emotionally with the political characters of many of their own support groups. Yet pietistic Yankee Protestants, a voting and pressure group important to the party, demanded such action and gave it their voting support. To respond to this group ran the risk of alienating other publics whose support the party needed. Failure to respond ran the risk of lost votes among a group whose mass support had been critical and whose antipartyism had long made it resistant to mere party norms.

The rhetorical solution to this dilemma was to present measures favoring black political equality as fruits-of-the-war, antisouthern, antirebel measures. It was portrayed in Republican rhetoric as a measure designed to secure what "has been accomplished by the war," because

---

issues in the state legislatures, see Porter, *Ohio Politics*, pp. 201–202; Powell, *Democratic Party of Ohio*, 1:175–79; Dunbar and Shade, "Black Man Gains the Vote," pp. 47, 51–52; Kenneth Larry Tomlinson, "Indiana Republicans and the Negro Suffrage Issue, 1865–1867," pp. 57–67, 219; Church, *Republican Party in Illinois*, pp. 100–101; Hobart Pillsbury, *New Hampshire*, 2:553, 561; Hebert, *Modern Maine*, 1:220.

91. For example, see the Illinois and Michigan Democratic state platforms, in *Appletons' Annual Cyclopaedia, 1868*, pp. 350, 369. The sentiment was a common one in Democratic state platforms and conspicuous by its absence from Republican platforms. Typically, the Republicans remained silent or used the code word *impartial suffrage*. It is significant that with the exception of Connecticut, which in 1865 had voted 55.0 percent against black suffrage, no 1868 Democratic state platform in New England attacked extension of the franchise to blacks.

92. Voegeli, *Free But Not Equal*, p. 127. His reference is to 1863, but it could have been applied to any point prior to 1868, at least.

93. Formisano, *Birth of Mass Parties*, p. 13; for stylistic reasons only, I have shifted the verb tenses in the sentence.

this tapped ideas central to the belief systems of the party's constituent groups. And it was presented in contexts laden with emotionally denotative code words—*southern fanatics, spirit of rebellion, patriotism, secessionists*—because these had become the symbols of psychological linkage between the behavior of the party's leaders and the values of its voters. Most critically, by 1868 Republican rhetoric linked *opposition* to black suffrage with the treason-stained Democracy, with Democratic efforts to "resuscitate the rebellion," and with that party's continuing allegiance to the southern rebels.[94]

Republican leaders knew, and the state referenda continued to inform them, that there was little mass support for black suffrage. Normally one expects that a party's rhetoric will identify itself only with those public postures that it knows to be popular and will tag its opposition with those that it knows to be unpopular. Ostensibly, Republican rhetoric defied these expectations. Yet the Republican leaders' rhetorically identifying the Democracy with a position that they knew to be popular suggests that the publics whose support the Republicans needed did not perceive that issue in isolation but as part of a larger cluster of ideas. It had become inextricably bound together in their belief systems with an antisouthernism seared into consciousness by the war experience, with patriotism and opposition to treason, and with hostility to the party of treason.

This final linkage—that the opponents of black suffrage were the Democrats—is the most critical. It provided the direct cue to behavior; and as it reverberated with Democratic acts, speeches, and postures, it transformed black suffrage into a test of party loyalty—not just among officials and activists, but among the mass electorate as well.[95] And by making the question a partisan one, the Republicans channeled mass opinion to carry into law a measure for which there was very little popular support.

94. These types of linkages and code words were common; but for example see the 1868 Ohio Union Republican platform, in *Ohio Platforms*, pp. 33–34; the Republican platforms in Maine and Massachusetts, in *Appletons' Annual Cyclopaedia, 1868*, pp. 444, 460.

95. Field's New York data show that in 1860 the Republican vote correlated with support for that year's black suffrage referendum at .78, but in 1869 the corresponding correlation was .89; "Republicans and Black Suffrage," pp. 141, 146. The 1846 vote for black suffrage in New York correlated with the Whig percentage at only .31. Ohio's Republican vote correlated with the 1867 vote for black suffrage at .97. For the 1846 New York and 1867 Ohio data, see Hammond, "Revivalist Political Ethos," p. 156. In Iowa support for black suffrage correlated with the Republican vote at .92; see Dykstra and Hahn, "Northern Voters and Negro Suffrage," p. 208. Also see the correlations by minor civil divisions for eighteen Michigan counties, in Formisano, "Edge of Caste," p. 31.

"Fruits-of-the-war" antisouthernism had a larger behavioral significance as well. It solidified Republican as a party in the electorate. A party exists when its activists, officials, and voters interact and when they consciously identify with a common name and symbols. A party develops voting clienteles, exists as a "party in the electorate," when the party as an institution has become a positive reference group inducing habituated loyalty and when its symbols have become positive reference symbols providing cues to the political cosmos.[96] *Republican* as a party in the electorate developed more slowly and more circumspectly than Republican as a corps of officeholders and a band of hyperpolitical activists. It evolved through distinct stages. Before the war emerged a broad and heterogeneously motivated congeries of social groups that cohered as an anti-Democratic popular front. During the war and continuing through 1866, activists broadened that front and accustomed the social groups that composed it to anti-Democratic voting practices through the use of Union and patriotic symbols. Finally, in 1868 and 1870 Republican party builders began to use *Democracy* as a negative reference symbol and *Republican* as its positive, and patriotic, counterpart.

The leaders who hone a party's rhetoric point with pride to their own accomplishments and symbols and decry the acts and symbols of the opposition only when they perceive such usages to have attained partisan salience among their constituent groups. Through 1866 Republican party builders expended their energies in keeping the Republican symbol out of view and using the Union label and patriotism to make it easier for those who had earlier identified with *Democracy* to vote against that party.[97] Their platforms and campaign speeches condemned those in the North who aided the rebels in the South—a reading of their rhetoric makes clear *whom* they meant—but the symbol *Democracy* had not been used pejoratively. On the contrary, they had regularly recited the litany of Democratic patron saints; and as late as 1867, Ohio's Unionists had explicitly used the symbol positively to legitimize their own commitment to "impartial manhood suffrage." By 1868 in Ohio and elsewhere, Republican party builders felt sufficiently self-assertive to use *Democracy* and *Democratic party* as emotionally powerful negative reference symbols. And in that same year they began extensively to use

96. Ronald P. Formisano, "Deferential-Participant Politics," p. 475; Frank J. Sorauf, "Political Parties and Political Analysis," pp. 37–38.
97. Murat Halstead, editor of the Cincinnati *Commercial*, wrote to Salmon P. Chase, 24 August 1863, explicitly advising that type of rhetoric and symbolism; quoted in Porter, *Ohio Politics*, p. 180.

Republican as a positive symbol—the frequency of which increased sharply in most locales by 1870.[98]

When they used these reference symbols, Republican party builders endowed each with distinctive character traits. "The present Democratic party" aided the rebellion; "Democracy" stands for "a restoration of treason"; a "Democratic party" electoral victory would imperil "the fruits of the late bloody and obstinate struggle." The Republican party had crushed the "wanton and wicked rebellion"; it had "stood 'like a wall of fire'" against the rebel states; and Republican electioneering represented nothing less than "continuing their great contest against the political action which culminated in open rebellion."[99]

Such linkages testify to the aura that Republicans projected to Democracy, to the political character of Republican as a positive reference symbol, and to the nature of the psychological rapport that bound together its activists, officials, and voters. They testify as well to the emotional intensity, to the right-vs.-wrong moralism, that anchored those party identifications. Commitments formed in the crucible of emotional and moral intensity were not readily abandoned, and through the 1870s and 1880s—and even beyond in some locales—rhetoric speaking to those searing experiences was still capable of reactivating latent loyalties.[100]

Over the course of the 1860s, that emotional and moral intensity solidified and habituated Republican party voting among native and immigrant pietistic groups. In the social atmosphere of those decades, Republican party builders had been able to project auras of southernism and treason to their opposition and patriotism and morality to themselves. The right-vs.-wrong, us-against-them moralism of the 1840s and 1850s had been kept alive, had been rechannelled in the early 1860s into the patriot-vs.-traitor dichotomy, and by the late 1860s had been translated into Republican-vs.-Democratic partisan identifications.

Yet by the end of the 1860s, the balance of political identifications was only mildly tilted toward the "party of patriotism" and of "great

98. The observation derives from an analysis of all of the Republican state platforms for 1868 and 1870, in *Appletons' Annual Cyclopaedia, 1868;* ibid., *1870.* For the 1867 references in the Ohio platform, see Republican Union platform in *Ohio Platforms*, p. 31.

99. Respectively, the quotations are from the 1868 Republican platforms in Pennsylvania, Nebraska, and Illinois; in *Appletons' Annual Cyclopaedia, 1868*, pp. 620, 532, 350.

100. The code word *copperhead* was still in frequent usage in Republican symbolism into the 1890s; see the references in Throne, "Liberal Republican Party in Iowa," p. 129; Arthur C. Millspaugh, *Party Organization and Machinery in Michigan since 1890*, p. 15.

moral ideas.'' With the readmission of the former Confederate states, with the completion of the war-interrupted realignment there and in the border states, and with the post-1872 resurgence of the Democracy in the North and the Midwest, even that precarious margin evaporated. When it did the third party system stabilized into an era of political equilibrium.

4

From Realignment to Equilibrium: Stabilizing the Third Electoral System

For I believe, on my conscience, that on the continued ascendency of [the Union] party, depends the safety of this great nation. If impartial suffrage is excluded in the rebel States, then every one of them is sure to send a solid rebel representative delegation to Congress, and cast a solid rebel electoral vote. They, with their kindred copperheads of the North, would always elect the President and control Congress.

Thaddeus Stevens (1867)

Stevens was not prescient, but he could count. He was aware by 1867 of the softness of Republican voting strength in electorally critical states of the North.[1] He was aware, too, that Republican antisouthernism and Yankee pietism would not naturally translate into voting strength among former Confederates. And most importantly, he was aware of the impact that the readmission of the seceded states would have on the arithmetic of American politics.

In 1860 the eleven states that a year later united to form the Confederate States of America contained 27.9 percent of the country's total population; they had cast 18.2 percent of the nation's popular vote and 29.0 percent of its electoral vote. The region was entitled to elect one-third of the full Senate membership, as well as 25.2 percent of the House. Indeed, Republican control in the Thirty-seventh Congress (elected in 1860) was assured only with the withdrawal of the southerners and was secured throughout the war years by their continued absence coupled with abnormally strong Republican delegations from the loyal slave states. Although growth in population, the admission of new states, and subsequent decennial reapportionments of congressional districts

1. The Stevens quotation is from *Appletons' Annual Cyclopaedia and Register of Important Events of the Year, 1867*, p. 207. Nor was Stevens a voice in the wilderness; other Republicans recognized the same danger. See James G. Blaine, *Twenty Years of Congress*, 2:408; Kenneth Larry Tomlinson, "Indiana Republicans and the Negro Suffrage Issue, 1865–1867," pp. 9–13.

slightly shrank the South's share of these measures of political influence, throughout the remainder of the nineteenth century the former Confederate states accounted for about one-fourth of the membership of each branch of the Congress and of the nation's electoral vote. And the three border states accounted for roughly an additional 6.0 percent of each of these measures. As Stevens and other Republican leaders recognized, the revitalization of the Democracy in these two areas combined with the electoral support of "their kindred copperheads of the North" imperiled future Republican national hegemony.

By the mid-1870s what Stevens had seen, and had feared, as a potential danger to "the safety of this great nation" had become a reality. The most obvious indicators of the Democratic resurgence were the 50.9 percent of the total national vote polled by the party's presidential nominee in 1876 and the 52.2 percent of the House elections won by its candidates.

Two distinct sets of electoral changes underlay these simple indicators. Each of these involved a resurgence of Democratic voting strength, each was evident before 1876, and each was geographically and behaviorally distinct from the other. The first involved completing the realignment in those states where its course had been interrupted by the war; and the second, occurring in other parts of the country, centered primarily on the surge in Democratic voting strength associated with the depression of the 1870s. The intersection of the two produced the systemic equilibrium, the era of "no decision," that typified the American political universe during the final two decades of the third electoral era.

The Politics of "Redemption"

In 1860 slavery was a legal institution in fifteen states. Eleven of these seceded from the Union. Four slave states—Delaware, Kentucky, Maryland, and Missouri—remained in the Union; they were joined by the fifty counties that had seceded from Virginia and had become the state of West Virginia in June 1863. The political development of each of these sixteen states was either interrupted or materially distorted by the breakup of the Union, and in each case its subsequent course was shaped by the war and its aftermath. The particulars varied from state to state, of course; but we can describe two broad patterns. The first of these pertains to the states that left the Union: they shared both the effects of losing the war and, with the exception of Tennessee, military reconstruction. The second describes the political behavior of the slave states that remained in the Union and did not experience pre-1870 black enfranchisement.[2] To a large extent the differences between the two categories relate to accidents of timing, rather than to essential distinctions in behavioral responses. Yet secession and military occupation were extraordinary experiences, either of which would provide ample qualitative grounds for the categorization.

The national resurgence of the Democrats by the mid-1870s was due in part to their revival in the former slave states. The reincarnation of Democracy in these states did not instantaneously follow the end of hostilities, nor did it entail a simple restoration of prewar political divisions. Within both categories of states, the temporally extended process reflected considerable discontinuity with the lines of antebellum political cleavage. And in both, the war and postwar years constituted politically critical experiences that redefined the meaning of partisan identifications.

Historical narratives have regularly associated "Redemption" of the former Confederacy with the end of Reconstruction, the return of "white man's rule," and the emergence of the Democrats as the predominant party in the electorate. They have also typically summed these characteristics and have used the term *Solid South* to designate both the region's unswerving political fealty to the Democratic party and the emergence there of a one-party political system. However, that region's unique political system did not immediately emerge with the final withdrawal of federal troops. As J. Morgan Kousser has indicated, its coming into being was an extended process, involving passage from an active, competitive system in the 1880s to the "enforced tranquility" of the early twentieth century. Central to that transformation were varied statutory and constitutional enactments that disfranchised black voters plus the institution of the direct statewide Democratic white primary. Together such measures insured a politics reflective of, and responsive to, the interests of the upper and middle socioeconomic strata. The legalized contraction of the southern electorate eliminated the normal political avenues through which lower-strata groups might have articulated their economic interests. "Progressivism" in Dixie (and elsewhere as well) involved an enforced constriction of electoral participation as an indispensable means to the stabilization of society "in the interests of the local established powers."[3]

Late nineteenth-century politics in the old Confederacy differed *in kind* from this postdisfranchisement political universe. The predisfran-

2. Though it did not exist as a state prior to 1863, West Virginia has been included in this category.
3. J. Morgan Kousser, *The Shaping of Southern Politics*, pp. 225, 230. In the book Kousser has substituted the phrase *mandatory tranquility* for the expression that he had employed in his dissertation. For more on the interpretation of stabilization, see Raymond H. Pulley, *Old Virginia Restored*.

chisement electoral system was marked by relatively high rates of voter participation—on the whole, an average of 63.8 percent of southern adult males voted in elections during the 1880s—as well as by viable, if sporadic, political competition. It was characterized, too, by quite narrow differences in participation rates by white and black voters; in the 1880s black participation averaged 60.7 percent, compared to 69.7 percent for white adult males.[4] Postdisfranchisement southern politics displayed the opposites of these characteristics: sharply reduced overall rates of participation, strong margins of victory for the Democrats, and wide differences between white and black voter turnout.

The electoral characteristics that have properly been associated with the term *Solid South* have been incorrectly applied to post-Reconstruction politics in Dixie. The Solid South was produced by disfranchisement, not by the Compromise of 1877. The resurgence of Democratic strength that came with the end of Reconstruction should best be seen as a stage in the region's onward march toward a politics exclusive of lower-status interests.[5] That resurgence, in turn, resulted from the interaction of shared group values and the experiences of the preceding two decades.

No less than the rest of the nation, the states that were to secede by 1861 were affected by the political tumult of the mid-1850s. The vituperative rhetoric of the congressional struggle over the adoption of the Missouri Compromise of 1820 did not engender the violent mass reaction that its repeal did a generation later. This points to the intervening development of an expanded and heightened political consciousness in the South as well as in the North. It also points to the emergence among southerners of an antinorthern counterpart to the antisouthernism of Liberty, Free-Soil, Whig, and Republican adherents.[6] Increasing political unity, evidence of a sectional response, seems to have characterized both sides of the Mason-Dixon line.

Although our knowledge of the voter movement within the South during the 1850s is sorely deficient, the data in Table 4.1 offer some intriguing suggestions. The partisan autocorrelations for adjacent presidential elections between 1848 and 1856 indicate a two-step erosion of party coalitions. The first, between 1848 and 1852, had greater impact

4. These are unweighted means calculated from data in Kousser, *Shaping of Southern Politics*, pp. 27–28; also see ibid., pp. 224–37, especially Figure 8.1, p. 225, for the postdisfranchisement political universe.

5. That does not mean, however, that we can resort to a principle of immanent causation to explain the developments.

6. Walter Dean Burnham, "Party Systems and the Political Process," p. 283. There are intimations of the growing diffusion of antinorthern attitudes scattered throughout William Barney, *The Road to Secession*.

TABLE 4.1 *Partisan Change in the Confederate States*

A. *Partisan Distributions (by States)*

	Democrat			Anti-Democrat		
	%	$\overline{M}$	σ^2	%	$\overline{M}$	σ^2
1848	49.1	50.4	62.25	50.8	49.5	62.25
1852	55.1	58.8	52.85	42.5	39.4	68.39
1856	58.1	58.9	26.52	41.8*	40.9	24.12
1860D	8.4†	7.7	27.24	40.3‡	38.5	45.38
1860BR	50.9§	53.3	81.76			
1860D + BR	59.3	61.2	46.01			
1870	51.0	50.1	66.94	48.9	49.8	66.94
1872	46.4	45.4	75.30	53.4	53.9	84.08
1876	59.5	59.0	63.94	40.4	40.8	63.94

B. *Partisan Autocorrelations (by States)*

Elec. Pair	Democrat	Anti-Democrat
1848/1852	.747	.611
1852/1856	.757	.697*
1856/1860D	−.255†	.672‡
1856/1860BR	.445§	
1856/1860D + BR	.673	
1848/1870	.088	−.794
1852/1870	−.063	−.433
1856/1870	−.104	−.160
1860D + BR/1870	−.690	−.690
1870/1872	.748	−.085
1870/1876	.692	−.168

*Know-Nothing Vote 1856.
†Douglas Democrat 1860.
‡Constitutional Union Vote 1860.
§Breckinridge Democrat 1860.

on the Whig than on the Democratic distribution. And although neither change severely disrupted the Democratic distribution, that party's auto-correlations for each pair of elections were only moderately high.[7]

Between 1848 and 1856 the region experienced a two-staged net shift of 9.0 percentage points in favor of the Democrats, and 6.0 percentage points of that came between 1848 and 1852. In 1848 the two major parties each carried five of the ten states in which popular elections had been held, in 1852 the Democrats carried nine of these, and by 1856 they carried all ten. Not only did Democratic strength in the region as a whole increase, but also by 1856 it was much more evenly distributed than it had been earlier. This increasing political homogeneity within the region did not yet mean the extinction of political opposition. The Know-Nothings in 1856 and the Constitutional Unionists in 1860 essentially inherited Whiggery's 1852 geographic base. However, it did mean that their legacy was a degree of anti-Democratic voting that had shrunk below its 1848 level and was still eroding.

Gradual but cumulative changes in the geographic and social bases of party support seem to have occurred in the South during the 1850s. These both predated, and were a major cause of, the dissolution of southern Whiggery. The shifts involved strong Democratic gains in areas and among social groups that had been traditionally Whig. Mississippi's parties prior to the 1850s, for example, exhibited clear evidence of economic polarization. The Democracy's strength was in counties with small-sized farms, low proportions of slaves, and relatively low levels of cotton production. Whiggery drew its support from the prosperous, cotton-producing, slave-belt counties. After 1848 the old political structure began to shake; the 1848 Democratic vote by counties explained only 29.1 percent of the variance of the 1852 Democratic vote.[8] A unidirectional movement of voters underlay the break in the partisan distributions. In areas where the Democrats had been strong, they retained that support, and they began to cut into the Whig coalition in areas of that party's normal strength. That process continued through the 1860 presidential election. In Louisiana Whiggery held on through the 1852 election, but thereafter the pattern of shift was similar to Mississippi. Among the sharpest Democratic gains in 1856 were those registered in the traditionally Whig southern Louisiana Planter and Bayou parishes,

7. Democrat 1848/1852, $r^2 = .556$; 1852/1856, $r^2 = .573$. In other regions of the country, the 1848/1852 Whig autocorrelations were larger than the Democratic autocorrelations. In other words, the shifts in the South depressed the magnitude of the 1848/1852 Whig autocorrelation at the national level; see Table 3.1.

8. In contrast, Democrat 1844/1848, $r^2 = .774$. For the data and discussion see Hugh Brady, "Voting, Class, and Demography in Ante-Bellum Mississippi."

and Democracy also picked up new support in areas of its own traditional strength.[9]

In these states, and probably elsewhere in the region, geographic bases of support were not exchanged; rather, the differences in group voting behavior narrowed. Such movement, of course, was implied by the sharp reduction in the variance of the distribution of the Democratic vote (by states) between 1848 and 1856 and by Democratic gains in Whig strongholds. This evidence, along with the fact that the vote distributions of 1856 and 1860 and the changes in percentage strength after 1848 did not correlate strongly with any of the customary social predictors, points to the growing political salience of regional consciousness.[10] It points as well to the southern Democratic party as a critical intermediary between the heightened sense of "being a southern man" and its eventual policy consequence, secession.

Against this background the postwar efforts by Republicans to build a party in the former Confederacy must be seen, for to many southerners, even before Reconstruction, *Republican* had become a powerful negative reference symbol denoting a party that they perceived as "hideous, revolting, loathesome, a menace not only to the Union of these States, but to Society, to Liberty and to Law."[11]

Yet we should not blithely assume linear continuity between the prewar and postwar electoral systems of these states. The partisan auto-correlations are statistical artifacts that overdraw the continuity at the mass base of Dixie politics.[12] The war and Reconstruction drastically changed the composition of the southern electorate. The disfranchisement of supporters of the Confederacy and the enfranchisement of blacks, inaugurated by the military reconstruction acts of Congress in 1867, permanently altered the course of southern political development. In the short run the Republicans were the beneficiaries. With proven or alleged Confederate sympathizers denied access to the polls and with

9. Democratic gains in 1856, compared with mean 1836–52 strength and when correlated with that mean, generate an $r^2 = .002$; the relevant data are in Perry H. Howard, *Political Tendencies in Louisiana*, p. 427; also see his discussion of antebellum Louisiana politics, pp. 59–103.

10. In Mississippi the 1840–52 change in Democratic strength had its strongest association with 1840 cotton production, and that produced a weak $r^2 = .151$. For Alabama data and for data on the relation of party to the vote for secession, see Thomas B. Alexander et al., "The Basis for Alabama's Ante-Bellum Two Party System," pp. 243–76.

11. The *Augusta Chronicle & Sentinel*, quoted in Barney, *Road to Secession*, p. 138. The argument in the text is simply another way of saying that the process through which *Republican* came to be a negative reference symbol was a critical proximate cause of secession and war.

12. On the Democratic side 1852/1876, $r = .655$; and 1852/1884, $r = .827$.

the newly enfranchised freedmen giving overwhelming support to the party of the Great Emancipator, Grant in 1868 carried six of the eight readmitted Confederate states, and the Republicans elected 89.2 percent of the region's congressional delegation. However, as the data in Table 4.1 suggest, the Democracy's resurgence began as early as 1870, when the party elected 53.8 percent of the region's members of Congress. That rebound was deflected by the disastrous Greeley candidacy in 1872, but in 1874 and 1876 the Democrats carried all the former Confederate states except Florida, Louisiana, and South Carolina. And by 1878 all eleven were in the Democratic camp, however tenuously in particular instances.[13]

The Democracy that surged forth in the Confederacy in the 1870s was not the old Jacksonian Democratic party resuscitated. Certainly, it shared most of the geographic mass base and policy stances of the antebellum party.[14] However, values shared by most white southerners, especially a sense of regional self-consciousness that had become inseparable from a potent antipathy to blacks, had initially been given partisan salience by the prewar experiences and then had been reinforced by the war and the "ordeal" of Reconstruction. This led to a redevelopment of the Democratic party in the South, evident among activists and officeholders in the presence of prewar Whigs in the Democratic lists. At the party's mass base it was evident in white voting support garnered in the formerly Whig black-belt counties. And symbolically it was evident in the party's substitution of the name *Conservative* for its own time-hallowed rallying symbol.[15]

Although Democracy might not have risen phoenixlike from the ashes of war, *Republican*, *Radical*, and their local variations continued to serve as sufficiently powerful negative reference symbols. That prewar sense of Republican as a "hideous, revolting, loathesome" party since 1860 had acquired concrete referents: military rule, enforced black political participation, black elected officials and party activists. As Republican thus came to symbolize "black rule," anti-Republican—at first

13. In 1874 the Democrats elected 79.1 percent of the congressional delegation; they did not drop below that percentage through 1892. Between 1874 and 1892 the mean proportion Democratic of the congressional delegation was 88.9 percent.

14. The similarity in disposition was most apparent in the strong distrust of legislatures that was evident in the Redeemer constitutions; compare C. Vann Woodward, *Origins of the New South, 1877–1913*, pp. 65–66, with William Gerald Shade, *Banks or No Banks*, pp. 117–20.

15. Woodward, *Origins of New South*, pp. 2–3; Alwyn Barr, *Reconstruction to Reform*, pp. 8–9. In reporting the results of the 1871 state elections, *The Tribune Almanac and Political Register, 1872*, p. 76, offered this observation on Virginia: "Elected a Legislature in 1871, which is preponderantly Conservative, which means Democratic in Virginia."

as Conservative and only later as Democracy—came to represent "white man's government." The consequence was a permanent alienation of most white southerners from the Republican party—an alienation that over time acquired the psychological force of a regional tradition.[16] That alienation produced a pattern of partisan support marked by levels of racial polarization unknown in other parts of the country. For example, for the 1880 election Kousser has estimated that on the average 52.0 percent of the adult white males and 20.7 percent of the adult black males in the eleven-state region supported the Democrats and 10.9 percent of the whites and 44.5 percent of the blacks voted Republican.[17] To put it more directly, of those within each category who did vote, the Democrats outpolled the Republicans by over four to one among whites; they were outpolled by the Republicans among blacks by better than two to one.

This does not mean that there was insignificant white opposition to Democratic rule. By itself the fact that an average of 34.7 percent of the adult whites did not vote in 1880 indicated a potential reservoir of anti-Democratic support. Yet for the most part, that white opposition could not effectively be rallied under the symbol *Republican*. Instead, it coalesced in a series of separately named "parties," none of which had sufficient durability to develop the bonds of psychological attachment necessary to sustain a sense of partisan identification among a mass clientele. This incapacity to develop an opposition party in the electorate, one that could cut across the black-white polarity, prevented the emergence of a competitive *party* system. Yet at the same time, the combination of sporadically mobilized anti-Democratic voting among lower-status white groups with that of normally Republican support groups, though typically under some non-Republican party banner, was responsible for the active political competition of the 1880s.

There were, however, two geographic and social sources of normal Republican voting support in the post-Reconstruction Confederacy: the

16. Vincent P. DeSantis, *Republicans Face the Southern Question*, pp. 25, 58; Paul Buck, *Road to Reunion*, pp. 69–70. See General J. B. Gordon's explanation of why *Republican* was for him a negative reference symbol, quoted in James Ford Rhodes, *History of the United States from the Compromise of 1850 to the Final Restoration of Home Rule at the South in 1877*, 6:186–88; also see David Montgomery, *Beyond Equality*, pp. 51–52.

17. These are unweighted means calculated from data in Kousser, *Shaping of Southern Politics*, p. 15. The racial polarization that marked postbellum southern politics was unknown elsewhere until the 1960s; see Walter Dean Burnham, *Critical Elections and the Mainsprings of American Politics*, pp. 152–61. It was true that black voters in the North were strongly Republican, but polarization involves the behavior of two groups; whites were not as exclusively anti-Republican in the North as they were in the South.

black-belt and mountain counties. In these areas Republican was a viable political party: its officeholders, activists, and mass supporters interacted and psychologically identified with common sets of symbols. The basis of that unity was different in each area. Among blacks Republican was the party of emancipation and legal enfranchisement; among mountain-county whites it was the party of opposition to their long-standing antagonists, the lowland gentry—the "elegant, smooth mannered, oily tongued bondholders, bond speculators, banks and members of financial boards."[18] The white-vs.-black polarity that characterized politics elsewhere in the former Confederacy was less relevant among whites in the mountain counties simply because there were relatively few blacks there. Without the perceived threat of a black-dominated county government, the mountaineers' antagonism to blacks did not shape their partisan attachment. Instead, their strong sense of identity as a group, shaped by their physical isolation and given political salience by their prewar struggles against the gentry, had been reinforced by secession and war and by the increasingly potent postwar identification of the Democracy with the lowland whites.[19] Yet even when they acted in tandem, these two types of areas did not contain enough voters (in most states) to sustain a competitive Republican opposition.

The electoral systems of the loyal slave states had not been suspended by secession and war; yet they were materially distorted by the effects of those developments. In some of them pitched battles for territory were waged between Union and Confederate armies; the recruiters for those contending forces also competed for manpower. In most there were periodic guerrilla incursions—resulting in forced civilian evacuations; the breakdown of normal governmental, commercial, and financial activities; and the imposition of varied forms of Union military rule. War-induced chaos, proscriptive measures aimed at eradicating anti-Unionist activities, and migration by Confederate sympathizers to enlist in the ranks of Lee's armies distorted the political systems of these states during the war and immediate postwar years. That distortion took the form of abnormally high levels of anti-Democratic voting. Although no state ever precisely replicates the political behavior of any other, an examination of the relevant data for two states, Maryland and Missouri,

18. Martin Gary, Edgefield County, South Carolina, quoted in Woodward, *Origins of New South*, p. 76.
19. Gordon Bartlett McKinney, "Mountain Republicanism, 1876–1900"; and V. O. Key, Jr., *Southern Politics in State and Nation*, pp. 277–97. For insights into the subculture of the white mountaineers, see Berton H. Kaplan, *Blue Ridge*, pp. 19–69, 105–22; W. D. Weatherford and Earl D. C. Brewer, *Life and Religion in Southern Appalachia*, pp. 1–32, 66–163; Harry K. Schwarzweller, James S. Brown, and J. J. Mangalam, *Mountain Families in Transition*, pp. 3–72.

provides insight into the broad pattern that underlay the Democratic re-surgence in the Unionist slave states.

Over the course of the second party system, Maryland had been a politically competitive state, showing a narrow but regular Whig ma-jority, and Missouri had been a modified one-party Democratic state. The distributions of county-party percentages in both states began to give signs of change by the mid-1850s (see Table 4.2). In Maryland the breakage centered around the rise of the American party and its dis-placement of the Whigs as the state's major anti-Democratic party. The Know-Nothings particularly disrupted Democratic strength in Baltimore City and county and in Harford and Howard counties. At the same time the rise of a stridently anti-Catholic party as the major Democratic opposition produced surging Democratic majorities in several former Whig strongholds, especially in heavily Catholic Charles and St. Mary's counties on the western shore south of Baltimore City.[20] These very large, two-way swings, concentrated in a relatively small number of voting units, generated the crisp break apparent in the 1852/1856 auto-correlations for both the Democrats and their major opposition.

However, as the data in Table 4.2 indicate, the 1856 distributions bore only minimal resemblance to those that characterized Maryland politics by 1864 and later.[21] The 1856 break was followed by the 1860 split of the Democracy; that, in turn, was only a mild prelude to the war-induced disruption of the state's electoral system. Fluctuation in the county-party percentages continued in Maryland throughout the war and immediate postwar years. By 1866 the Democrats were able to poll 59.3 percent of the vote and regained control of the state. Yet neither the shape of the partisan distributions in that year, nor in 1867 and 1868, much resembled the stable pattern that characterized the state's third

20. Between 1852 and 1856 the Democrats gained 23.5 percentage points in Charles County and 41.7 in St. Mary's. For the anti-Catholic animus of Maryland's Know-Nothings, see Sr. Mary St. Patrick McConville, *Political Nativism in the State of Maryland*; Laurence Frederick Schmeckebier, *History of the Know-Nothing Party in Maryland*, p. 53; Douglas Bowers, "Ideology and Political Parties in Maryland, 1851–1856," pp. 211, 213–14; Benjamin Tuska, *Know-Nothingism in Baltimore, 1854–1860*, pp. 3, 7.

21. Nor do the 1859 or 1860 southern Democratic distributions show much stronger relationships. Jean H. Baker, *The Politics of Continuity*, p. xiv, argues that 1859 was a realigning election in Maryland and that there was continuity from that point through 1868. However, she has incorrectly interpreted the zero-order correlations that she gives in footnote 58, p. 131 and footnote 85, p. 164. Those data show the following Demo-cratic coefficients of determination: 1859/1864, $r^2 = .405$; 1861/1866, $r^2 = .315$; and 1863/1866, $r^2 = .385$. The measures testify to the continuation of realigning fluctuation and not to postrealignment stability. Moreover, the autocorrelations with the post-1868 distributions are consistently either negative or, at their strongest, positive and trivial—e.g., southern Democrat 1860/1876, $r = .038$.

TABLE 4.2   *Political Transformation: Maryland and Missouri*

A. *Democratic Distributions (by Counties)*

| | Maryland | | | Missouri | | |
	%	$\overline{M}$	σ^2	%	$\overline{M}$	σ^2
1848	47.7	44.9	29.57	55.0	59.8	161.29
1852	53.2	48.7	29.08	56.1	60.1	156.25
1856	45.0	49.5	85.75	54.5	59.8	174.24
1860BR*	45.6	46.0	80.50	18.9	25.9	275.56
1860D†	6.3	6.6	35.21	35.5	34.3	156.25
1868	67.2	74.0	215.98	41.1	42.9	396.01
1870	57.0	55.1	29.97	62.5	58.5	320.04
1872	50.3	47.8	27.35	55.4	56.0	216.09
1876	56.0	54.7	31.81	57.7	58.5	210.25

B. *Democratic Autocorrelations (by Counties)*

Elec. Pair	Maryland	Missouri
1848/1852	.841	.909
1852/1856	−.499	.709
1856/1860BR*	.586	.568
1856/1860D†	.309	−.040
1848/1864	−.831	−.338
1852/1864	−.688	−.313
1856/1864	.291	−.444
1848/1870	.307	−.269
1852/1870	.363	−.253
1856/1870	−.154	−.249
1868/1870	−.195	.709
1870/1872	.748	.660
1870/1876	.718	.730
1872/1876	.863	.933
1876/1888	.727	.932

*Breckinridge Democrat 1860.
†Douglas Democrat 1860.

party system. Maryland's partisan distributions stabilized and its third party system emerged only by 1870. And when it did, the state's electoral system was marked by a moderately strong but regular Democratic edge.[22]

The shape of Maryland's third party system was remarkable in the extent to which its geographic base reflected discontinuity with that of the second party system. No single prewar partisan distribution (from 1848 forward), including that of the 1860 election, accounted for more than 13.2 percent of the variance of either the Democratic or Republican distributions of 1870.[23] The shifts in political geography stand out when we compare the mean strength by counties for biennial elections over the 1848–52 period with those over the 1876–92 sequence. During the later period the Democrats gained an average of 7.4 percentage points in the counties of the southwestern shore and 4.4 percentage points on the eastern shore; they lost an insignificant 0.5 percentage points in the northwestern-shore counties. Democratic percentage strength was about as evenly distributed across the state's counties during the third party system as it had been during the second. The former Whig strongholds of the southwestern and eastern shores were after 1870 centers of Democratic voting strength; and with the exception of Baltimore City, anti-Democratic strength was greater among the northwestern-shore counties than it had been earlier.[24]

The transition from the second to the third electoral era in Maryland, then, involved something of an interparty exchange of geographic bases of support. However, the absolute amounts of shift involved were relatively small, and with a single exception neither party regularly polled as much as 60.0 percent of a county's vote.[25] Missouri's transition entailed a similar interparty exchange of geographic bases, but one whose amount and amplitude of shift were considerably severer than

22. Calculated across biennial elections, Democratic strength exhibited the following longitudinal means and variances: 1836–52, $\bar{M} = 48.1$, with $\sigma^2 = 6.89$; 1856–68, $\bar{M} = 53.1$, with $\sigma^2 = 63.32$; 1870–88, $\bar{M} = 54.3$, with $\sigma^2 = 8.72$; 1870–92, $\bar{M} = 54.2$, with $\sigma^2 = 7.38$. These data again illustrate that realigning fluctuation persisted across the full 1856–68 sequence.

23. That derives from the .363 autocorrelation of the 1870 Democratic and Republican distributions with, respectively, the 1852 Democratic and Whig percentages.

24. At first glance the conclusion may appear inconsistent with recorded levels of Republican strength in the old Whig counties, but the Republican strength came largely from prewar nonvoters, the enfranchised freedmen.

25. The exception was Wicomico, an eastern shore county, whose 1876–92 Democratic mean was 60.2 percent. Comparing the 1848–52 mean with the 1876–92 mean, only two counties, Worcester on the eastern shore and Montgomery on the southwestern shore, registered Democratic gains of 10.0 percentage points or more. And no county registered Democratic losses of −10.0 or more, although the decline in Allegany was −9.5 percentage points.

Maryland's. If we compare the 1848–56 mean Democratic percentage for each county with the 1868–92 mean, 44.9 percent of Missouri's counties exhibited losses of 10.0 percentage points or more, and 22.0 percent displayed gains of at least 5.0 percentage points.

As they had in Maryland, Missouri's county-party percentages also began to oscillate in the 1850s, but that owed more to Democratic factionalism than to an interparty shuffling of coalitional bases of support.[26] As it had in Maryland, the American party in 1856 displaced the Whigs as Missouri's major anti-Democratic party; in doing so, it inherited the bulk of the Whig mass base and attracted supporters from the Benton wing of the Democratic party. Even more clearly than in Maryland, however, Missouri's 1856 partisan distributions did not survive intact through the war years. The oscillation of the 1850s was mild compared to the political disruption of the 1860s.

That political upheaval began with the three-way split of the anti-Republican presidential vote in 1860. And neither the distribution of the Douglas Democratic vote nor that of the Breckinridge Democrats nor that of the Constitutional Union party nor any combination of these showed a very strong relation with the 1852 or 1856 Democratic presidential vote. After 1860 the Civil War raged in Missouri on the battlefield and in the political arena. Its disruptive effect was indicated by the 7.9 percent of the state's counties that made no presidential returns in 1864; 2.6 percent failed to do so even in 1868. Yet even eliminating these cases, the party distributions after 1860 displayed extraordinarily high levels of volatility. The strongest correlations between any possible 1860/1862 or 1862/1864 election pair explained less than 20.0 percent of the variance.[27] Partisan fluctuation continued between 1864 and 1868 but at a more reduced level than between 1860 and 1864. In fact, by 1864 the outlines of the realigned distributions began to emerge.[28] They became more clearly visible in the 1868 and 1870 elections, and by 1872 the shape of Missouri's third party system was firmly in place.

26. The 1850 factional struggle, for example, did not disturb the 1848 to 1852 Democratic continuity; 1848/1850 Benton Democrat, $r = .343$; 1848/1850 anti-Benton Democrat, $r = .139$; but 1848/1852, $r = .909$. For a useful examination of antebellum Missouri politics, see John Vollmer Mering, *The Whig Party in Missouri*.

27. On the anti-Democratic side the strongest was Emancipation 1862/Union 1864, $r^2 = .165$; on the Democratic side, Constitutional Union 1860/Democrat 1862, $r^2 = .050$.

28. Although Democratic strength in Missouri remained considerably depressed in 1864, the partisan autocorrelations increased to the point of explaining at least a third of the variance of subsequent distributions. And the Democratic interoffice correlations showed the tight fit that we customarily expect when voting selections are party cued. The following Democratic coefficients of determination illustrate: 1862/1864, $r^2 = .043$; 1864/1866, $r^2 = .628$; 1864/1876, $r^2 = .374$; 1868/1876, $r^2 = .581$.

In Missouri the realignment represented an even sharper break with the prewar distributions than it had in Maryland. Large portions of the prewar coalitions of each of the major parties were broken off and were exchanged. As a result the 1852/1872 partisan autocorrelations were negative, and the interparty correlations were positive.[29] The postwar Democrats inherited the majority of the anti-Benton Democratic base and most of the 1860 Breckinridge Democrats, along with significant accretions from both the 1852 Whigs and the 1856 Know-Nothings.

Missouri's realignment resulted from a severe two-way swing of socially distinct voting units, which is depicted in Table 4.3. The geographically compact cluster of counties in the southwestern quadrant of the state, the western Ozark or Tennessee-stock counties, which had been strongholds of the antebellum Democracy, swung sharply and consistently away from that party (see Map 2). Moving in the same anti-Democratic direction, though less sharply and with less consistency, were two additional strings of counties: one in the northern third of the

TABLE 4.3   *Percent Democratic by Types of Counties: Missouri*

Year	Tenn $(N = 9)$	Yankee $(N = 9)$	German $(N = 6)$	Tenn-Ky $(N = 11)$	Ky-Va $(N = 12)$	Total State
1848	71.3	56.6	63.1	59.8	48.1	54.9
1852	68.3	57.3	65.4	63.2	47.8	56.2
1856	45.2	59.3	60.4	68.9	46.3	54.5
1860*	57.8	59.5	51.1	64.6	51.3	54.4
1864	11.6	11.3	25.8	36.9	52.9	29.9
1868	30.0	28.1	38.7	70.1	53.4	43.0
1870†	44.4	47.7	75.2	74.6	67.8	62.5
1872‡	43.8	43.6	44.2	72.7	66.4	55.4
1876	45.9	45.8	50.3	77.5	68.3	57.7

$\overline{M}$ Shift in % Democrat, $\overline{M}$ 1848–56/$\overline{M}$ 1868–92

−31.7	−17.4	−22.3	+7.4	+14.5	−1.5

*Douglas and Breckinridge Democrat 1860.
†Bolter (or Liberal Republican) 1870.
‡Liberal Republican 1872.

29. Democrat 1852/1872, $r = -.321$; but Whig 1852/Democrat 1872, $r = +.321$. The same pattern exists on the Republican side and persists whether one examines 1852/1868, 1856/1868, or 1856/1872.

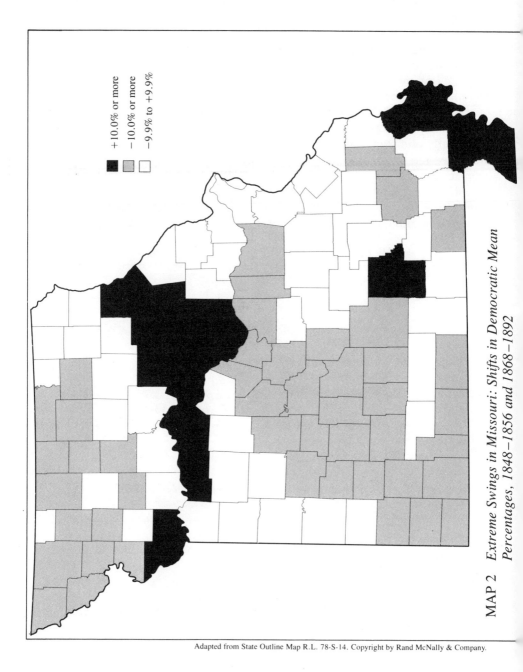

MAP 2 *Extreme Swings in Missouri: Shifts in Democratic Mean
Percentages, 1848–1856 and 1868–1892*

Legend:
- ■ +10.0% or more
- ▨ −10.0% or more
- □ −9.9% to +9.9%

state, the "Yankee" counties, and one in the central part of the state, extending from the Mississippi to the Ozarks, the German counties.[30] While these formerly Democratic counties moved away from the postwar Democracy, the counties in the southeastern quadrant (the Tennessee-Kentucky–stock counties in the eastern Ozarks and the cotton-growing lowlands) became even more Democratic than they had been prior to 1860. And a string of old Whig counties, the "Little Dixie" counties settled by migrants from Kentucky and Virginia, swung sharply and consistently to the Democracy. This rotation of the geographic mass bases of the prewar parties did not much alter the partisan balance of the state. Missouri remained after 1870, as it had been before the war, a normally and regularly Democratic state.[31] Yet the war did change the social composition of Missouri's partisan coalitions and thereby transformed the character of its electoral system.

The contours of the third electoral era in the loyal slave states were forged in the war and its related experiences. Taken collectively, and for most citizens, the developments of those years created a new fault line of partisanship. They gave new partisan salience to preexisting group values and by doing so redefined the meaning of partisan identifications and transformed the quality of party combat. It was not merely that some of these states shifted from Whig to Democrat, as Maryland had; in all of them the renascent Democracy was not the antebellum Democracy but a redeveloped party whose social coalition and political character had been permanently altered by its war-related experiences.

It should not be astounding that the war experiences had an enduring effect on the partisan structures of these states. For all contemporary Americans, of course, the Civil War was figuratively one between fellow citizens; but for the residents of the loyal slave states it was literally "a war between fellow citizens and neighbors, and sometimes it was between kinsmen—even brothers."[32] Their own locales were literal battlefields, subjected to the ravages of infrequent pitched conflict and continuing guerrilla warfare. Under such conditions few could, or did, remain neutral. In areas where Unionist sentiment predominated, some

30. The term *Yankee* here and elsewhere in reference to Missouri counties designates areas settled by northern-stock population groups, mostly from Ohio. See John H. Fenton, *Politics in the Border States*, pp. 4, 9–11, and figures 1, 2, 3, 20, for outlines of the state's areas of settlement.

31. Calculated across biennial elections, Democratic strength displayed the following longitudinal means and variances: 1836–52, $\bar{M} = 56.9$, with $\sigma^2 = 2.71$; 1856–68, $\bar{M} = 43.3$, with $\sigma^2 = 82.25$; 1870–88, $\bar{M} = 55.3$, with $\sigma^2 = 9.95$; 1870–92, $\bar{M} = 54.7$, with $\sigma^2 = 10.86$.

32. Return I. Holcombe, who had spent several years traveling across Missouri's counties gathering material for local histories, quoted in *St. Louis Globe Democrat* in 1891, in Walter B. Stevens, *Centennial History of Missouri, 1820–1921*, 1:792.

Confederate sympathizers "were shot, others hanged without court or jury, their homes burned and their property stolen." And similar forms of instant neighborhood justice were meted out to Unionist sympathizers in predominantly Confederate locales.[33] Finding more rebel than loyal sympathizers in these states, Union military commanders, to facilitate waging the war, resorted to suppression of dissent. Martial law—accompanied by loyalty-oath requirements, arbitrary arrests and imprisonment, suspension of habeas corpus, suppression of newspapers, the closing of churches and private clubs, and the seemingly ubiquitous presence of federal troops—fueled the fires of bitterness. In such an atmosphere it was no great wonder that "friendships were dissolved, the ties of blood severed, and an invisible but well-understood line divided the people." Neither was it surprising that fully three decades after the war "the tradition survives and still continues to be a factor, silent, but not without influence, in the politics of the State."[34] Nor is it much of a mystery how that "well-understood line" divided the people in a partisan way—how, that is, Democracy eventually represented opposition to the war and to the war-related acts of the pro-Union state governments. And as it did that, it mobilized within its ranks, not only die-hard Confederate supporters, but large numbers of antebellum Whigs, many of whom had been pro-Union.

Even more so than in the other Union states, the Democratic party in the loyal slave states faced a crisis of existence during the war years. Several factors contributed to that crisis. First, many Democratic office-holders and activists had been publicly identified with states' rights prior to secession; they continued to resist the federal efforts to coerce the seceded states even after April 1861. Perhaps not all were as adamant and outspoken as Governor Claiborne Fox Jackson, who replied to Lincoln's request that Missouri supply its quota of federal troops by denouncing the requisition as "illegal, unconstitutional and revolutionary in all its objects, inhuman and diabolical, and cannot be complied with. Not one man will the State of Missouri furnish to carry on such an unholy crusade."[35] Yet even in the absence of such acerbic rhetoric, the standing image of the Democracy was that of a party supportive of states' rights

33. William Rufus Jackson, *Missouri Democracy*, 1:734; the discussion refers to Pulaski County, but also see the developments in Audrain, Greene, Mercer, and Livingston counties, 1:543–45, 619, 690, 990. For further indications see John Rothensteiner, *History of the Archdiocese of St. Louis*, 2:211; John J. O'Shea, *The Two Kenricks*, pp. 295–301.

34. Mayor George William Brown of Baltimore, quoted in Matthew Page Andrews, *Tercentenary History of Maryland*, 1:846.

35. Claiborne Fox Jackson to Simon Cameron, 17 April 1861, quoted in Jackson, *Missouri Democracy*, 1:152.

and antagonistic to the sectionalized Republican party that was prosecuting the war effort. Second, some prominent Democratic officeholders and activists, and even more members of the party in the electorate, left the loyal slave states to join the Confederate armies, or at least to live behind the Confederate lines. Such movement both reinforced the standing image of the Democracy as prorebel and reduced the size of the potential voting clientele that such an image might mobilize on its behalf.[36] Finally, and most critically, the crisis-induced atmosphere in these states simply did not support any form of oppositional politics. Opposition to the war, or to the home-front measures that it had made necessary, was tantamount to treason. Unless those "party lines which have heretofore unhappily divided us" were obliterated, it would not be possible "to present an unbroken front in the preservation and defense of . . . our firesides."[37]

Tarred with the image of treason, and with the ranks of its officeholders, activists, and supporters depleted, the Democratic party in Maryland and Missouri was both demoralized and disorganized during the early years of the war. In Maryland, for example, in 1861 the Democrats merged with the new States' Rights organization and eschewed the use of their own time-hallowed rallying symbol. From 1861 to 1864 no state-level Democratic party existed in Maryland. Missouri's state-level Democracy, which had disintegrated by mid-1861, was not revived effectively until early 1867.[38] Such developments created political vacuums that enabled the anti-Democrats to secure political control.

In Missouri, more than the Democratic party had disintegrated. By July 1861 the state's duly elected civil government had also collapsed. The Democratic governor and most of the Democratic legislators had fled the state. Civilian authority was then assumed by a hastily reconvened and moderately pro-Union state convention, whose members declared the offices held by those who had fled to be vacant and appointed successors to fill them.[39] In October and November 1861 the state convention introduced the test oath into Missouri politics. It required all

36. Nathan H. Parker, *The Missouri Hand-Book*, p. 44; Baker, *Politics of Continuity*, pp. 71–73, 90–91.
37. Resolution adopted by a Baltimore mass meeting, 19 April 1861, quoted in Andrews, *Tercentenary History of Maryland*, 1:837. See also Baker, *Politics of Continuity*, p. 113; Parker, *Missouri Hand-Book*, pp. 26–27.
38. In Maryland the Democracy was kept alive at the county level, however. On the Maryland developments see Baker, *Politics of Continuity*, pp. 67, 115–18, 121; Charles B. Clark, "Politics in Maryland during the Civil War," p. 378. And for the reorganization of the Democracy in Missouri, see William E. Parrish, *A History of Missouri*, pp. 239–40.
39. Stevens, *Centennial History of Missouri*, 1:817–40; Parrish, *History of Missouri*, pp. 1–29.

civil officials to take an oath of allegiance to both the state and federal governments. As guerrilla warfare increased during the winter of 1861, the provost martial general extended the test oath to anyone suspected of disloyalty. The enforcement of even these relatively mild loyalty-oath requirements disfranchised large numbers of otherwise eligible voters in the 1864 gubernatorial election and in the elections of delegates to a new state convention.[40]

Missouri's constitutional convention of 1864–65, dominated by the state's most prominent "radical," Charles Drake, passed an emancipation ordinance and new fundamental law for the state. The new state constitution included an "iron-clad oath" aimed at permanent disfranchisement of Confederate supporters. Taking the oath required that an individual swear that he was innocent of some eighty-six specified acts of alleged disloyalty against Missouri and the Union. The oath was to be used to determine voter eligibility; to ensure its application, the new constitution empowered the legislature to enact a system of biennial voter registration. Pursuant to that authority, the legislature in 1865 passed a registry bill providing for a supervisor of registration for each county. The supervisor, appointed by the governor for the 1866 election and thereafter to be elected by each county, was to determine the validity of the test oath; his decisions were appealable to a board composed of him and his assistants.

The particulars and the chronology differed somewhat in Maryland, but the essentials of the approach remained the same. Once in power the Unionists sought to perpetuate that dominance through a constitutionally sanctioned test oath and voter-registration law. The aim, as in Missouri, was to disfranchise the rebels and to secure continued Unionist political control among an electorate shrunken in size through the constitutional disqualification of a large segment of the political opposition.[41]

With the potential electorate thus conveniently reduced in size, the Unionist regimes of these states might have appeared to have been firmly in control. Yet the extremely narrow margins by which both Maryland's 1864 constitution and Missouri's 1865 document were approved by the electorate pointed rather to the tenuousness of their control.[42] Not all of those who had opposed secession and who had been

40. The 1864 Union candidate for governor polled 70.3 percent of the total vote; that compares with the 52.9 percent that the three anti-Democratic candidates collectively polled in 1860 against Claiborne Fox Jackson, who received 47.0 percent. Lincoln in 1864 received 69.7 percent, compared with 10.3 percent in 1860. The combined Douglas-Breckinridge percentage in 1860 was 54.4 percent.

41. Baker, *Politics of Continuity*, pp. 104–109, 135–36, 145.

42. In both states the soldier vote, which was disproportionately in favor of the new constitutions, secured their ratification. See ibid., p. 109; William George Paul, "The Shadow of Equality," pp. 53–54; Parrish, *History of Missouri*, p. 128.

caught up in that ground swell of patriotism that marked the early years of the war were willing to see the slaves emancipated and large numbers of whites disfranchised. And even more ominous were the continuing factional quarrels within the ranks of the Unionists that brought into stark focus the issue that ultimately shattered their coalition: what should be the future political status of the freedman?

The test oath, emancipation, and black suffrage became linked in mass belief systems, and in mutual interaction they resuscitated and redeveloped the Democracy (as well as its opposition) in Maryland and Missouri. In neither state had most Unionists sought to connect themselves with the black-rights question. Yet in both states Unionists had supported, and Democratic spokesmen had opposed, emancipation. And in both states only among Unionists, and then only among a minority of them, was there any public support for black enfranchisement. Even more clearly, in both states Unionists sponsored, and Democrats vehemently resisted, the test oaths and registry laws that disfranchised whites. Through the consistent acts, speeches, and postures of its spokesmen, then, Democracy ultimately represented those who opposed the coerced contraction of the white electorate as well as the extension of the franchise to the former slaves. Its often repeated affirmation of the sanctity of "white man's rule" was both a tactic to mobilize voters and an articulation of the psychological rapport that bound together the officeholders, activists, and voters of the new Democratic party.

The process through which the contending parties became reference symbols to large and persisting elements of the electorate was both quicker and more direct in Maryland than it was in Missouri. In the former state the schism within Unionist ranks over the emancipation issue was apparent as early as 1862–63. It produced an open rupture in the 1863 election, with the Conservative Unionists both stigmatizing the Unconditionals with emotionally loaded code words—"'abolitionists, radicals, and 'niggerlovers' ''—and cooperating with old-line Democrats.[43] Given encouragement by the Unionist split and a sense of necessity by the impending revision of the state's constitution, the Democrats revived their state organization in early 1864. And in that year the Democracy unveiled its new image, that of a "white man's party formed on the single issue of opposition to abolitionism. Too long already has the Negro been pushed forward and the white man thrust back."[44] The results of the fall elections of that year gave some portent of the emerging shape of Maryland's new party system. Among the antebellum

43. The information is in Baker, *Politics of Continuity*, pp. 84–87, but she imperceptively treats the use of such code words as "political billingsgate" (p. 86).
44. *Maryland Union*, 3 March 1864, quoted in ibid., p. 128.

Whig counties on the eastern and southwestern shores, the Democrats polled means of 59.3 percent and 82.9 percent, respectively; but they secured a mean of only 40.6 percent on the northwestern shore.[45]

Aware of their increasingly precarious political hold, the Unconditional Unionists by late 1865 denounced the suggestions of Republicans in Congress that black suffrage be imposed on the South. Yet when the Democrats swept the 1866 elections and began preparations for a rewriting of the state's constitution, Maryland's Unionists appealed to their congressional compatriots. As they did, their dependence on the congressional Republican party increased; by early 1867 they had adopted the label *Republican Union party*. Their state convention that year espoused black enfranchisement and endorsed the "radical" program of southern Reconstruction.[46] Probably because they incorrectly anticipated overt congressional intervention if the General Assembly failed to enact black suffrage, Maryland's Republicans seated black delegates at their May 1867 state convention and appointed five blacks from Baltimore and several from rural districts to their State Central Committee.[47] Such Republican acts and postures merely reinforced the image that the Democrats were projecting to them—an image of Republican as the "abolition" party, an epithet that in Maryland "came to mean support of Negro equality."[48]

Only with the ratification of the Fifteenth Amendment did black political equality become a reality. Black votes, cast for the first time in the 1870 elections, reduced the size of the Democratic margins in the counties on the eastern and southwestern shores, and the Democrats made marginal gains among white voters in four northwestern-shore counties. With the Democratic-supported elimination of the iron-clad oath secured by the constitution of 1867 and with the Republican-supported enfranchisement of blacks, Maryland's third party system took

45. The 1846 results were a portent of the emerging party oppositions in a very particular sense. Only whites were voters, and the Democrats received strong white support in areas where they had been weak prior to the war. In other words, the Democratic 1868/1870 autocorrelation, $r = -.195$, resulted not from shifts of white voters, but from enfranchisement of blacks. The difference between the Democracy's 1864 state percentage (44.9 percent) and its mean percentage by counties (61.8 percent) conveys a sense of the polarity that was emerging. The partisan pattern reflected the condition that one delegate to Maryland's 1864 constitutional convention described: "Sir, the State of Maryland has been sectionalized, . . . the northern and western counties . . . are wantonly waging an aggressive war upon the institutions of Southern Maryland." Quoted in Charles L. Wagandt, "Election by Sword and Ballot," p. 143.

46. Baker, *Politics of Continuity*, pp. 176–77; Paul, "Shadow of Equality," p. 73.

47. When Congress failed to intervene, the Republicans backed off and excluded blacks from the 1868 to 1870 ward meetings and conventions; ibid., pp. 85–88.

48. Baker, *Politics of Continuity*, p. 86. And also see T[homas] J. C. Williams and Folger McKinsey, *History of Frederick County, Maryland*, 1:296.

firm shape by 1870. From that point through (at least) 1892, Republican voting strength was confined to black voters, who were concentrated in the counties on the eastern and southwestern shore and in Baltimore City, and among pockets of white voters in the western counties of Allegany, Frederick, Garrett, and Washington.[49] And although Maryland's Democrats rarely resorted to the racist rhetoric of their Confederate counterparts, they thereafter relied on their standing image to guarantee that theirs remained as much a "white man's party" as it was in Dixie.

Developments in Missouri were somewhat more protracted than in Maryland. Missouri's state-level Democratic party did not revive until 1867, and it did not emerge as the dominant party in the electorate until after 1872. Yet the essentials of the process were the same. The Democrats organized opposition to the Drake Constitution and its test oaths and registry act; they identified the Unionists with the depredations of the war, with emancipation, with black equality, and—most tellingly—with support for the 1868 black-suffrage referendum.[50] And as in Maryland, they seized on Unionist factional quarrels, made common though covert cause with the self-styled "Liberal Republicans" in the 1870 gubernatorial election, and swept the "radicals" from control of the state government. The Democratic legislature in 1871 liberalized the already unevenly enforced registry law; and in 1874 the Democrats, without Liberal Republican cooperative arrangements and with former Confederates openly participating in party affairs, elected a governor.[51]

The restructured Democracy of Missouri continued to draw strong support, as it had before the war, from among the white voters of the southeastern counties. More significantly, however, it drew strong support among the white voters in the prosperous rural counties of Little Dixie. Voters in these two groups of counties had felt most severely the effects of the test oath. And with the enforcement of that requirement relaxed somewhat after the 1870 enfranchisement of blacks, these voters went to the polls in virtually unprecedented numbers and gave disproportionate support to the Democrats.[52] And not just antebellum Demo-

49. On black voting behavior after the 1870s, see Paul, "Shadow of Equality"; Margaret Law Callcott, *The Negro in Maryland Politics, 1870–1912*; Deborah Raab, "A Study of Voting Behavior in Maryland, 1875–1890"; Margaret M. Moore, "Voting Behavior Analysis, 1880–1892."

50. The Republican state platform endorsed black suffrage in 1868; Parrish, *History of Missouri*, pp. 244–45.

51. The voters also gave majority support to a referendum calling for a new constitutional convention. The delegates to the convention were elected in January 1875, and the new constitution was approved on 30 October 1875.

52. The size of the Democratic vote in the "Little Dixie" counties (Kentucky-Virginia stock) increased by 81.3 percent between 1868 and 1870; it increased by 84.9

crats, but Whigs, "many of whom were slave owners and suffered along with the others, identified themselves with the Democratic party, and their progeny followed in the footsteps of their forbears."[53] To voters who had shared a common experience of political ostracism, the Democracy, which had partaken of the same experience, became a natural haven. That party's opposition to "the damnable Draconian Code" and to black suffrage resonated with their value systems and provided an unmistakable partisan cue.[54] The increasingly visible presence of ex-Confederates among the party's county-level officials and activists further reinforced the psychological bonds uniting these strata of the party with their supporters in the electorate. As a rallying symbol, *Democracy* in Missouri evoked memories of the "Lost Cause" and thus solidified a partisan structure forged in the white heat of civil conflict.

For the very reasons that *Democracy* became a positive reference symbol to these groups of voters, it acquired powerful negative reference qualities for other Missourians. As the former slave-owning planters shifted to the Democracy, their natural enemies, the East Tennessee–stock mountaineers of the Ozarks, gave the majority of their votes to the anti-Democrats.[55] And so, too, did the state's "Yankee-stock" counties, whose post-1860 voting behavior paralleled that of similar units in the middle-belt states. Indeed, in these areas for better than a quarter of a century after the Civil War, "it required men of strong convictions . . . and fearless hearts to support the Democratic ticket."[56]

The revival of a redeveloped Democratic party in the former slave states was one-half of the party's national rebound in the mid-1870s. That the rejuvenation of Democracy there was combined with surging levels of mass support in other parts of the country accounted for the systemic equilibrium and close electoral balance that marked the remaining two decades of the third electoral era.

---

percent in the southeastern counties. For the state as a whole, the size of the Democratic vote increased by 59.0 percent, and the Republican vote declined by 28.2 percent.

53. Jackson, *Missouri Democracy*, 1:558; also see 1:182, 192, 545, 739, 747.

54. Ibid., p. 739.

55. For indications that most of the Tennesseans in these areas were from East Tennessee, see James Fernando Ellis, *The Influence of Environment on the Settlement of Missouri*, pp. 89–97; Stevens, *Centennial History of Missouri*, 1:517–40. East Tennesseans in Missouri were behaving politically just as their kinfolk back in East Tennessee; see J. Morgan Kousser, "Post-Reconstruction Suffrage Restrictions in Tennessee," pp. 655–83. It was also significant that there were very low proportions of blacks in the Ozark counties.

56. Jackson, *Missouri Democracy*, 1:690, discussing Mercer County.

The Politics of Depression

On 18 September 1873 one of the country's leading and ostensibly most stable investment houses, Jay Cooke & Company, closed its doors. The next day another nineteen financial institutions suspended activity, and stock prices plummeted. The exchange was seized with frenzy: "Men rushed wildly about in the drenching rain gesticulating and screeching commands which no one understood."[57] The following days witnessed additional financial failures and runs on a number of banks. To combat the frenzy, Wall Street's bankers, brokers, and financiers closed the New York Stock Exchange during the following week. They, and the nation, were in the midst of a financial panic.

The Panic of 1873 was more than a Wall Street crisis. It quickly broadened into the nation's longest, and one of its most severe, deflationary periods of the nineteenth century. Even the reopening of the stock exchange on 30 September and the mid-October resumption of business by several of the financial houses that had suspended earlier failed to allay the commercial and industrial downturn. By the end of 1873, iron mills, cotton mills, rail mills, and most other types of manufacturing establishments had cut prices, had laid off workers, and had reduced the wages paid those who still held their jobs. Financial panic had given way to industrial depression.

The depression struck the economy like "a thunderbolt from a clear sky."[58] The growth of the economy in the North had been sluggish during the Civil War years but had accelerated sharply after 1866. That resurgence was abruptly interrupted by the economic downturn that began in September 1873. The seeming suddenness with which "good times" turned to "hard times" probably helps to account for part of the incomprehension with which contemporaries reacted. Yet two other dimensions of the downturn also helped to shape that response.

The depression of the 1870s was both lengthy and severe. Its contraction phase lasted sixty-five months, nearly twice as long as the two contraction phases of the depression of the 1890s and twenty months longer than that of the Great Depression of the 1930s.[59] For over five

57. *New York World*, 18 and 19 September 1873, quoted in Herbert George Gutman, "Social and Economic Structure and Depression," p. 1; see ibid., pp. 1–30 for a succinct and useful description of the panic and early depression.

58. Rhodes, *History of the United States*, 7:41–43.

59. Arthur F. Burns and Wesley C. Mitchell, *Measuring Business Cycles*, Table 16, p. 78. The 1893–94 and 1895–97 contraction phases of the depression of the 1890s lasted a total of thirty-five months, and the 1929–33 contraction phase spanned forty-five months.

uninterrupted years and without any large-scale efforts to create public employment or to augment the incomes of the unemployed, the nation endured the downward economic spiral. And that downturn was not one of insignificant proportions. Most of the relevant economic indicators underscore the severity of the hard times of the 1870s. For example, between 1872 and 1873 the rate of business failures jumped by 29.6 percent; and for the 1873–78 depression years as a whole the rate of 129.3 failures (per 10,000 business concerns) was 63.7 percent greater than the 1870–72 average rate. The average of only 10.6 bank suspensions per year during the first three years of the 1870s increased to 70.7 per year over the next six years.[60] Even more critical for an assessment of the political impact of the depression was its effect on both employment and the real earnings of workers. Unemployment had averaged 4.1 percent from 1870 to 1872 and had reached its low point of 2.3 percent in the latter year. In 1873 the unemployment rate more than doubled, reaching 4.8 percent; and it averaged 10.7 percent over the next five years of the depression. From their predepression high point in 1872 to their depression low point in 1877, the real earnings of all workers dropped by 15.8 percent, and those of employed workers fell by 6.7 percent.[61]

The entrepreneurial response to the hard times was to cut output and costs. The resulting layoffs and reductions in wages hardened the feelings between workers and entrepreneurs. Although some labor spokesmen publicly counseled their followers to "accept the situation for the time being," the rank and file often ignored that advice and rejected the manufacturers' proposed reductions.[62] The ensuing strikes and lockouts increased and spread across most trades and industries, and

60. The calculations are based on data in U.S., Bureau of the Census, *Historical Statistics of the United States, Colonial Times to 1957*, pp. 570, 636. For other views of the depression, see Rendigs Fels, "American Business Cycles, 1865–79," pp. 325–49; Samuel Rezneck, "Distress, Relief, and Discontent in the United States during the Depression of 1873–78," pp. 494–512; O. V. Wells, "The Depression of 1873–79," pp. 237–51.

61. The data for the calculations are in Jeffrey G. Williamson, *Late Nineteenth-Century American Development*, Table C.5, p. 304. For a review of local efforts to provide relief to the unemployed, see Leah Hannah Feder, *Unemployment Relief in Periods of Depression*, pp. 37–70.

62. *Workingman's Advocate*, December 1873, January 1874, quoted in Gutman, "Social and Economic Structure," p. 25. Similar editorial advice was offered by *Printers' Labor Tribune*, 25 November 1873. Yet it also carried reports of rank-and-file rejection of that counsel, especially among workers in the iron trades and mining; for examples, see *National Labor Tribune*, 10, 24 January 1874. In early January 1874 the *Printers' Labor Tribune* changed its masthead to *Weekly Labor Tribune*, and by mid-January to *National Labor Tribune*.

by the late spring of 1874 *Iron Age* aptly described relations between workers and employers as being close to "guerilla warfare."[63]

The effects of the depression were not confined to the manufacturing sector of the economy; agricultural producers suffered as well. The depression years, especially 1874 to 1876, were marked by declines in wheat and corn prices that exceeded the rate of secular-trend decline. Those years also witnessed a renewal of the deteriorating trend in the farmer's position in the market, a trend that had been mildly reversed by the economic resurgence of the immediate postwar years.[64] The economic condition of agriculture in the early 1870s was further affected by ongoing improvements in transportation facilities, by the dry growing seasons of 1873 and 1874, and by a locust plague in parts of the West North Central states. Such factors, as well as differences in type and degree of specialized production, produced a somewhat more variable impact from the depression in agricultural than in nonagricultural areas.[65]

However, focus on any single set of events sometimes produces unwitting exaggeration. Surely the depression of the 1870s was severe, and surely its effects extended to most groups in the society. Yet the economic indicators were more mixed and more equivocal than during the nation's other industrial depressions. For instance, during the contraction phases of the depressions of the 1870s, the 1890s, and the 1930s, all of the indices of prices and financial activity declined. Yet although 94.0 percent of the indices of commercial and industrial activity fell off in the 1890s, and all of them in the 1930s, only 50.0 percent of them declined during the 1873–79 contraction phase.[66] The behavior

63. "Making War upon Capital," *Iron Age*, 26 May 1874, p. 14, quoted in Gutman, "Social and Economic Structure," p. 29. Ibid., pp. 19–30, provides an excellent description of employer-worker relations. No systematic strike data are available, but see the reports on individual strikes over the 1873–76 years in U.S., Commissioner of Labor, *Third Annual Report of the Commissioner of Labor, 1887*, pp. 1059–67.

64. It was highly significant that even with that postwar resurgence prices remained below their 1860–61 levels, as did the farmer's relative market position. For example, relative wheat prices—that is, wholesale wheat prices divided by the wholesale price index for all commodities—show the following means by time segments: 1860–61, $\bar{M} = 1.61$; 1862–65, $\bar{M} = 1.18$; 1866–68, $\bar{M} = 1.38$; 1874–76, $\bar{M} = 1.16$; 1874–79, $\bar{M} = 1.32$; 1877–79, $\bar{M} = 1.44$. The data for the calculations are in Bureau of the Census, *Historical Statistics*, pp. 115, 123–24; also see Williamson, *Nineteenth-Century American Development*, pp. 150–51. When regressed on time, wheat and corn prices both exhibit strong 1866–1900 secular declines.

65. On conditions in the West North Central States, see Wells, "Depression of 1873–79," p. 242; *Report of the Iowa State Agricultural Society for the Year 1874*, p. 5. The year 1874 was described as a year of "general prosperity among farmers" in *Annual Report of the Secretary of the Maine Board of Agriculture for the Year 1874*, p. xiv; but it was referred to as a year of hard times in *Annual Report of the New Jersey State Board of Agriculture, 1874*, p. 5.

66. Burns and Mitchell, *Measuring Business Cycles*, Table 24, p. 103; for the indices used see ibid., Table 22, p. 101.

of indices of manufacturing output was one critical area in which the depression of the 1870s differed from subsequent ones. The drop in manufacturing output from predepression peak to depression trough was 9.6 percent in the 1870s, compared to 13.9 percent in the 1890s and 48.3 percent in the 1930s. In both the 1890s and 1930s, the level of manufacturing output in the final year of the contraction phase remained below that at its beginning—by 6.4 percent in the 1890s and 37.9 percent in the 1930s. However, the index of manufacturing output in 1878 was 3.2 percent *higher* than it had been in 1872.[67] Even more arresting, the real earnings of employed workers *increased* from the 1870–72 average of $392.33 to an 1873–78 average of $398.50. The total increase, 1.5 percent, was certainly not great, and it fell below the average per annum rate of increase of 2.1 percent after 1879. Yet it contrasted sharply with the 3.2 percent *decline* in real earnings experienced by employed workers during the contraction phase of the 1890s.[68] That contrast resulted partially from the sharp decline in the cost of living during the hard times of the 1870s. Cost-of-living indices exhibited long-term and fairly steep secular declines from 1866 to the end of the century. However, during the depression of the 1870s, the decline was 5.4 percent steeper than the secular trend; whereas during the contraction phase of the 1890s, it was 2.0 percent less than the secular trend.[69]

Contemporaries, of course, did not perceive events within a context that compared them with what would happen in the 1890s and 1930s. Nor were they preoccupied with examining the movement of the relevant indices of economic activity. They reacted instead to the real world of the mid-1870s, as they perceived that world. And central to those perceptions, for most citizens, must have been the almost daily news of financial closings, layoffs at factories, reductions in wages, strikes, and marches for "bread and jobs." To the psychological impact of an economywide and persisting depression did the Commissioner of Labor refer when he later reported that "like all other depressions, there was

67. Although 1878 was the last full year of the depression, it did drag into part of 1879. If we compare 1879 with 1872, the levels of manufacturing output show an increase of 16.1 percent. The calculations use Frickey's indices of production for manufacture for both the 1870s and 1890s and the Federal Reserve Board index of manufactures for the 1930s; both are reported in Bureau of the Census, *Historical Statistics*, p. 409.

68. The calculations are based on data in Williamson, *Nineteenth-Century American Development*, Table C.5, p. 304.

69. For the regression on time, I used the Burgess cost-of-living index, which displays a steep rate of secular decline from 1866 to 1900; $b = -1.065$, and $r^2 = .742$. It does not matter whether one uses the Burgess index or the New York Federal Reserve Bank cost-of-living index; for the time segment indicated the correlation between the two yields an $r^2 = .958$. Both indices are in Bureau of the Census, *Historical Statistics*, p. 127.

much apprehension to be added to reality.'' And as reality was compounded by apprehension, the effects of the depression permeated the body politic ''as dyspepsia does the human system, partly by cutting off the supply of vital force, but much more by keeping its victim in constant thought about his ailments.''[70]

Yet the political effects of the ''economic dyspepsia'' were comparatively and surprisingly mild, for unlike those of the 1890s and 1930s, the industrial depression of the 1870s did not transform the shape of the voting universe. Partially that may have been because the severest effects of the depression were less widespread than they were in the later downturns. Yet it was also powerful testimony to the intensity of prevailing partisan identifications. Forged as they had been in a then recent realignment, such commitments were not facilely abandoned by most voters. To cross party lines was nearly as unthinkable as changing one's religion or doffing the Union blue to put on the Confederate gray. Not even an industrial depression could produce that effect.

If the depression of the 1870s did not fundamentally alter the shape of the electoral universe, it markedly changed the competitive parameters of the party system, and it did so by reinstating, or restoring, the normal structure of partisan distributions. The balance of partisan strength had been distorted first by the patriotism-rooted surge factors operating during the war years and subsequently by the extraordinary depression of Democratic turnout that underlay the Republican landslide in 1872. The effects of the 1872–74 and 1874–76 shifts were counterdeviating; they restored the Democratic vote to its normal size and normal proportion. That restoration did not involve as much massive cross-party movement as the reactivation of latent Democratic proclivities among voters who had been repelled either by the party's aura of ''treason,'' or by its disastrous nomination of Horace Greeley, or by both.

The association of the Democracy's resurgence with the impact of the depression was reasonably clear. The initial indicator of that was the size and distribution of the Democratic gains in the 1874 congressional election. The Democracy elected 57.8 percent of the Forty-fourth House, and that included 51.2 percent of the congressmen from states beyond the old Confederacy. The party's impressive gains in percentage strength extended to every region and to all but two of twenty-one states. Those gains produced nine new congressional seats in New England, twenty each in the Midatlantic and East North Central regions, six in the West North Central states, and one in the West. Moreover, the Democracy's

70. Respectively, the quotations are from U.S., Commissioner of Labor, *First Annual Report of the Commissioner of Labor, 1886*, pp. 63–64; *Printers' Labor Tribune*, 25 November 1873.

percentage-point gains were more evenly distributed across regions than they had been, for example, between 1868 and 1870. Although the size of the Democratic 1872–74 mean gain was twice as large as the 1868–70 gain, its variance was less than half that of the earlier shift.[71] Both the geographic extent and shape of the Democratic resurgence indicated the operation of systemwide, and not merely localized, influences. Further confirmation lay in the Democrats' scoring their sharpest gains in the more heavily industrialized states, precisely the ones most severely impacted by the depression. In the eight states in which the proportion of the labor force engaged in industrial activities exceeded that in agriculture, the Democrats registered mean 1872–74 gains of 9.6 percentage points; that contrasts to an average 4.5 percentage-point gain in the twelve states in which the agricultural labor force was relatively larger than the industrial sector.[72] Moreover, in the industrial states a correlation of the net 1872–74/1874–76 shift with the same measure of industrialism explained 32.6 percent of the variance of the shift, but within the nonindustrial category it accounted for only 2.3 percent of the variance. We can explore these leads further by shifting the level of aggregation and examining the relevant data below the regional and state levels. Table 4.4 presents an array of data for three states.[73]

The data draw attention to several important dimensions of the shift. First, the Democrats gained strength in outstate as well as urban-industrial areas. That is, the political impact of the depression cut across rural-urban lines. Second, in these states (and most, but *not* all, others) the size of the 1872–74 Democratic gains was larger in urban-industrial than in rural areas. Third, and most significant, the Democracy's gains in percentage strength reflected sharp increases in the size of its vote (compared with 1872), combined with generally smaller decreases (ex-

71. For the 1868–70 shifts $\bar{M} = 2.8$, with $\sigma^2 = 6.38$; but for the 1872–74 shifts $\bar{M} = 5.6$, with $\sigma^2 = 2.87$.

72. Though it otherwise qualified empirically, Rhode Island has been excluded from the industrial category because of its unique franchise restriction and because there were no formal Democratic nominations in 1874. For these calculations states have been categorized as "industrial" if the combined proportion of the 1880 labor force engaged in manufacturing and mining exceeded that engaged in agriculture. Similar results were obtained using the 1870 labor-force data. For the data used see Harvey S. Perloff et al., *Regions, Resources, and Economic Growth*, Appendix Tables A-1, 2, 3, and 6, pp. 622, 624, 626, 632.

73. The "Urban-Industrial" areas of Illinois included Cook County (Chicago) and the major coal-mining counties—Bureau, Grundy, LaSalle, Macoupin, and St. Clair. The Massachusetts cities used were Fall River, New Bedford, Lawrence, Lynn, Newburyport, Cambridge, Lowell, Boston, and Worcester. And the New Jersey cities used were Camden, Newark, Jersey City, Hoboken, Trenton, Paterson, and Elizabeth. The "Outstate" vote used in the table is the total state vote minus the vote cast in the designated urban-industrial areas.

TABLE 4.4   *Democratic Reinstatement: Urban-Industrial and Outstate Areas, 1868–1876*

A. *Democratic Percent of Total Vote*

	Urban-Indus	Outstate	Total State
Illinois			
1868	42.0	44.6	44.1
1872	40.3	43.6	42.9
1874*	54.7	54.0	54.1
1876	50.9	45.6	46.7
Massachusetts			
1868	37.7	27.3	30.3
1872	36.3	28.3	30.7
1874	58.0	48.7	51.8
1876	49.2	38.1	41.9
New Jersey			
1868	52.4	50.2	50.8
1872	45.3	45.5	45.4
1874	53.9	53.4	53.6
1876	52.7	52.8	52.8

B. *Drop-off in Size of Vote, 1872–74 (as %)*

Illinois			
Dem	−26.3	−2.6	−6.8
Repub	29.5	31.4	30.9
Massachusetts			
Dem	−74.1	−56.3	−62.6
Repub	28.0	34.9	33.1
New Jersey			
Dem	−30.5	−25.7	−27.2
Repub	7.8	8.5	8.3

*Two-Party Contest for Superintendent of Public Instruction.

cept in Illinois) in the size of the Republican vote. And again, the Democratic gains in voters were sharpest in the urban-industrial areas.

Not all states behaved in similar fashion. In some the Democracy's 1872–74 gains in rural areas exceeded those in urban-industrial areas. Yet even within such states a closer examination of the relevant minor civil-division data gives evidence that the comparative political response was analogous to that of states such as Illinois, Massachusetts, and New Jersey. Data for three representative coal-mining counties in Ohio and Pennsylvania (see Table 4.5) illustrate the point.[74] In each of these counties, the Democrats registered sharper 1872–74 gains in the mining than in the nonmining units, and in each instance the gains mirrored increases in the size of the Democratic vote, contrasted to its shrinkage in nonmining units. The Democrats gained strength in the mining units because they attracted new votes, but their percentage-point gains in the nonmining units came from the fact that the size of their vote did not drop off as sharply as it did on the Republican side.

One final indicator that the factors primarily underlying the shifts were not localized was the relatively uniform way in which the shape of the Democratic distribution changed between 1872 (or 1868 for that matter) and 1876. Whether that distribution was examined by counties within states, by minor civil divisions within counties, or by wards within cities, the linkage among the relevant measures was apparent: the size of the Democratic vote and the party's percentage strength increased, the Democratic mean percentage increased, and the variance about that mean in most instances decreased sharply.[75] The relatively uniform movement of these measures—despite obvious and enormous variations from state to state, county to county, and city to city in such elements as political-system contexts, party-organization strength, and candidate attractiveness—is immensely impressive. And it strongly indicates that the observed political response was one shaped *primarily* by the systemwide influences set in motion by the hard times of the 1870s.[76]

74. For more detailed discussion of the voting behavior in these and other Ohio coal-mining counties, see Paul Kleppner, *The Cross of Culture*, pp. 28–31; for Schuylkill County see the data in William A. Gudelunas, Jr., "Before the Molly Maguires," pp. 59, 61, 70, 79, 83, 88, 96, 103.

75. I have examined the distributions for states by counties for all states from New England through the West North Central area; for counties by minor civil divisions for New Jersey, New York, Pennsylvania, Ohio, Michigan, Wisconsin, Connecticut, Maine, Massachusetts, New Hampshire, Vermont, Maryland; for scattered counties in Illinois, Indiana, Iowa, and Minnesota; by wards for Boston, Chicago, Baltimore, St. Louis, Minneapolis, St. Paul; and for all cities in New Hampshire, New Jersey, New York, Pennsylvania, Ohio, Michigan, and Wisconsin.

76. For contemporary assessments of the political impact of the depression, see R. B. Hayes to Carl Schurz, 3 November 1876, in Frederic Bancroft, ed., *Speeches,*

TABLE 4.5   *Coal-Mining Communities: Democratic Percentage Strength*

	Belmont County (Ohio)		Perry County (Ohio)		Schuylkill County (Pa.)	
	Mining	Nonmining	Mining	Nonmining	Mining	Nonmining
1868	48.7	50.2	50.4	54.8	49.1	58.3
1872	44.5	46.5	49.8	54.9	47.1	58.6
1874	49.1	47.5	63.8	62.6	51.6	61.6
1876	49.3	50.8	53.4	59.9	51.3	60.4

Drop-off in Size of Vote, 1872–74 (as %)						
Dem	−6.9	8.1	−11.5	10.2	−1.5	7.4
Repub	13.9	12.8	37.8	34.1	15.4	18.4

However, the operative word in that sentence, as in most generalizations concerning mass voting behavior, is *primarily*, for voting behavior, no less than any other aspect of human behavior, is complex. That is especially the case when two or more factors potentially relevant to partisanship appear simultaneously. Such a set of circumstances occurred in the early years of the depression of the 1870s. The roles of two behaviorally distinct types of factors other than the depression need to be considered. First, several of the midwestern states were engulfed in 1873 and 1874 by antirailroad agitation. That ground swell produced variously named "Farmer" parties, whose rhetoric focused on the evil practices of monopolies in general, and of railroad monopolies in particular. Second, in the Midwest and elsewhere was a renewed outpouring of temperance zeal. The precise demands of the "cold-water" crusaders were different from one state to the next, but they shared a common goal, legislative action to restrict the liquor traffic.

The Farmer parties have attracted the most analytical attention. Typically, they have been depicted as representing one stage in an ex-

---

Correspondence, and Political Papers of Carl Schurz, 3:339; Hayes to Col. A. T. Wikoff, 20 September 1875, in Charles R. Williams, ed., *Diary and Letters of Rutherford Birchard Hayes*, 3:293; Blaine, *Twenty Years of Congress*, 2:549; William Dana Orcutt, *Burrows of Michigan and the Republican Party*, 1:160; John Sherman, *Recollections of Forty Years*, 1:505–506.

tended process of agrarian radicalization.[77] This stage, which coincided with the spreading popularity of the Grange, has been portrayed as one in which farmers rose in holy fury to secure enactment of state laws putting an end to the abusive rate-setting practices of the railroads. Discovering that pressure-group activity alone was insufficient, they organized political parties to mobilize voters in support of favorably disposed candidates. Appearing as "Reform" in Wisconsin, as "Anti-Monopoly" in Iowa and Minnesota, as "Independent Reform" in Illinois, as "Independent" in Indiana, and as an uncounted number of county-level titles, these organizations sprang up in 1873 and 1874. It seems plausible that their appearance might have played a formative role in shaping the Democratic resurgence in these states.

In fact, that resurgence was also evident in states in which no such organizations appeared, as well as those in which the Farmer parties allied themselves with the anti-Democrats. Although a number of important analytical questions need to be posed concerning these Farmer parties, we need to inquire here only into the roles that such parties played in the Democratic resurgence in the states in which they did appear.[78] The data in Table 4.6 make that possible.

There was some continuity between the 1874 Farmers' vote and earlier Democratic distributions. That was to be expected in light of the leadership and state-ticket fusions that were worked out. Some Democratic leaders eagerly sought that fusion. It seemed to them one way to overcome the stigma of copperheadism and to aid the party's recovery from the sharp reverses that it had experienced in 1872. To these old-line Democratic leaders fusion was thought to be a way to revive the party's prerealignment constituency. They inaccurately assumed that antimonopoly rhetoric, with railroads as the object of attack, would be reminiscent of the party's antebellum battles against the banking monopoly and would resonate with the political characters of its old support groups. Yet both that rhetoric and the impetus for the fusions were shaped principally by the Liberal Republican elements that had earlier infiltrated the party's leadership. The result was a party aura and a vote distribution remarkable more for their discontinuity than for their continuity with the earlier Democracy. Nor did that discontinuity imply a

77. Fred Emory Haynes, *Social Politics in the United States*, pp. 153–54. And the same view has found its way into more recent and more sophisticated analyses; see Daniel A. Mazmanian, *Third Parties in Presidential Elections*, pp. 49–51. The term *Farmer* has been designed solely for stylistic convenience to designate all of the variously named parties. The use of the label does not imply any a priori assumptions concerning the social base or character of any of those parties.

78. See Chapter 7 for an analysis of the relation of these parties to later spasms of "agrarian radicalism."

TABLE 4.6   *Role of 1874 Farmer Parties: Coefficients of*
Determination (r^2) with Democratic Distributions

Elec. Pair	Iowa	Illinois	Wisconsin
1868/1874	.537	.129	.198
1874/1876	.603	.270	.236
1868/1876	.682	.799	.839
1868/1888	.367	.790	.609
1874/1888	.372	.207	.304
1876/1888	.646	.841	.824

permanent reshaping of the electoral universes of these states; further discontinuity was also the most striking characteristic of the comparisons of the 1874 distribution with subsequent Democratic distributions.[79]

Anti-Monopoly in Iowa, Independent Reform in Illinois, and Reform in Wisconsin induced voting patterns that crosscut the prevailing lines of party cleavage. Most likely, they were patterns that were not anchored in identifications with social groups, and quite clearly, they proved to be ephemeral. Whatever the underlying behavioral influences, they simply were not strong enough to produce persisting alterations in the structure of partisanship.

Of more enduring significance was another public outburst of the fulsome zeal of the temperance movement. During the war and immediate postwar years temperance supporters had neither lost nor sublimated their interest in abolishing the evils of the liquor traffic. At the grass roots, and especially in their church-based temperance societies, they kept alive the "great and holy cause." If enthusiasm for temperance appeared to have waned, it was only because their simultaneous involvement in the antislavery cause and the inherent drama of the war have overshadowed the cold-water crusade in the eyes of later analysts. Also,

79. Iowa only appears to give evidence of greater continuity between Democracy and Anti-Monopoly. That resulted from the coincidence of Anti-Monopoly's appeal in the river counties with the Democracy's normal strength there. In fact the 1874 Anti-Monopoly strength explains only 5.6 percent of the variance of the net 1872–74/1874–76 shifts in the state, whereas a measure of traditional Democratic strength (the 1860 vote for Douglas) explains 47.1 percent of the variance. And Iowa, unlike Illinois and Wisconsin, experienced considerable change in the shape of its partisan distributions between 1876 and 1892. For an analysis of that change and its relation to persisting prohibition agitation, see Chapter 8.

the objects of their continuing pressure-group activities were less dramatic than had been the mass-mobilizing "holy crusades" for state prohibitory laws in the 1850s. With such laws in place in twelve non-slave states, temperance supporters turned their attention thereafter to enforcement, and especially to legislation creating a state constabulary (or state police force).[80]

Although the temperance crusaders never lost their enthusiasm, the developments of the 1860s dampened their optimism and set the stage for a postwar spasm of organizational activity. Several developments were of particular importance. Some of the hard-won prohibitory laws were struck down by state courts or were rendered impotent by state legislative action. The Internal Revenue Act of 1862, by requiring payment of a license fee, seemed to give the implicit blessings of the national government to the liquor traffic. And since the license fee was to be set by congressional decision, it stimulated those engaged in the liquor traffic to organize for pressure-group activity. To the temperance crusaders the United States Brewers Association, formed in November 1862, was more than a single-interest economic grouping; it was an unholy alliance of those engaged in a sinful business to pervert the political process. They responded to the challenge of the "Beer Congress," to its attack on "the menacing attitude of Temperance and Sabbatarian Fanatics," by exhorting "the friends of temperance . . . to secure righteous political action for the advancement of the cause."[81]

Yet what constituted "righteous political action"? To that question temperance zealots never gave a unanimous response. The temperance movement was never a unitary one. It was a grass-roots movement, organized from the bottom up; so it lacked the cohesiveness typical of movements organized from the top down. State and national temperance organizations could at best coordinate, suggest, implore, but not dictate to their constituent groups. Besides, those involved actively in the movement were animated by commitment to principle, precisely the type of mind set that resisted any attempt to dictate to their consciences. Participants in the movement agreed that the liquor traffic was evil and that it was nothing less than God's will that it should be eradicated. And they agreed on the necessity for "righteous political action" to advance the cause, as long as the forms of that action remained unspecified. When they were made concrete, however, fissures appeared.

80. D. Leigh Colvin, *Prohibition in the United States*, pp. 47–48.
81. *Proceedings of the Sixth National Temperance Convention, 1868*, pp. 65–66; for the resolution of the Seventh Convention of the United States Brewers Association, 1867, see Colvin, *Prohibition in the United States*, p. 57. For more details on these matters, see Paul Kleppner, "The Greenback and Prohibition Parties," pp. 1568–71; also see the analysis of the Prohibition party in Chapter 7.

Did "righteous political action" entail only working for measures to facilitate moral suasion, measures such as temperance instruction in the public schools? Or did it necessarily involve support of coercive legislation? What form, then, should that legislation take? Was it adequate to support local-option, or high-license, measures; or should no compromise short of total prohibition be accepted? What energy should be expended on allied causes? Should they work for woman's suffrage, believing as they did that the female vote was an untapped reservoir of support for temperance? What of immigration restriction? Certainly the zealots perceived the immigrants, especially the Irish and Germans, to be major contributors to the growing intemperance that they perceived to exist. And, too, there was the matter of purifying the electoral process, for surely only the intrusion of corrupting elements accounted for the frequent electoral reversals of God's will. Finally, did "political" action imply "partisan" action? And, if so, did that "partisan" action mean support of a distinct, narrowly focused party, or support of major-party candidates sympathetic to the cause?

These and similar questions posed irresolvable dilemmas for a movement that could not decree unity, a movement composed of members whose norms exalted the "free will to do right." The fact that temperance crusaders chose distinct paths to righteousness in different locales, has deflected analytical focus and has minimized the behavioral significance of the movement. Historical analysts regularly seek to isolate the common and concrete elements that bind a movement together. They typically inquire into what specific measures, beyond platitudes, a movement's supporters espoused. It is difficult to find such common and concrete elements among temperance crusaders who in one locale condemned local option and in another supported it. Yet within the context of a federated political system there is no reason, save inaccurate a priori assumption, to expect such unity. Nor is failing to find it, especially among activists whose norms mitigated against enforced uniformity, adequate demonstration that the movement was too inchoate to be of enduring behavioral significance. The lack of tactical consensus may complicate description and analysis, but it does not make that any the less necessary.

The absence of a common set of tactics, especially on the related questions of making the movement partisan and single-issue voting, had always been a source of tension among temperance supporters. By the late 1860s, the levels of that tension had increased. The drink traffic was growing, liquor-imbibing immigrants continued to pour into the country, and the enemies of God's will were better organized than earlier. Moreover, those enemies and their immigrant allies could count on the unwavering support of the Democratic party, for the "Rumocracy" was everywhere perceived by temperance crusaders to be the avowed enemy of "true piety"—a party that wouldn't "support for office anyone who . . . [would] vote to control the Sabbath-day or sale of liquors."[82]

Although they perceived a continued and growing psychological rapport between Rumocracy and the liquor traffic, some temperance supporters questioned the political character of the party of "great moral ideas," the Republicans. The prewar temperance crusaders had allied themselves with the Republican party; but by the late 1860s they had discovered that the requirements of pragmatic party building sometimes, and in some locales, conflicted with their righteous demands. Sensitive to the growing size of the Irish and German voting population, some Republican leaders sought to avoid antagonizing them. That meant assisting them to redefine the meaning of their partisanship by, at least, toning down the divisive cultural questions that had driven them initially into the lists of Democracy. However, to do that, as the temperance crusaders saw it, was to pander to the "saloon vote," to compromise principle for mere votes. Some temperance crusaders began to question the sincerity of the party's commitment to righteousness. Those questions increased in intensity and frequency when the party in 1872 approved a national platform voicing disapproval of laws "for the purpose of removing evils, by interference with rights not surrendered by the people to either the state or national government." Although ambiguously phrased, the plank, authored by the editor of the *Illinois Staats Zeitung*, was perceived by temperance supporters as an effort "to appease the liquor vote."[83] God's own holy cause had been betrayed.

The increased organizational, propagandistic, and political activity for temperance that marked the late 1860s and early 1870s was driven by a combined sense of urgency and betrayal. The need for action was urgent, because the problem was sin and the problem was growing daily. The great reform had been betrayed by the political party to which it had been entrusted. Yet the response of the temperance activists was ambivalent as always. Some insisted on the creation of their own distinct partisan organization, the Prohibition party. Others redoubled their efforts to work within the Republican party and to secure pledges—and

82. *Proceedings of the Sixth National Temperance Convention, 1868*, pp. 26, 64. Although the perception of the Democracy was generally an accurate one, in some locales there remained considerable sentiment for temperance (though not necessarily for prohibition) among Democratic voters.

83. It was the sixteenth plank of the 1872 Republican national platform; see Kirk H. Porter and Donald Bruce Johnson, comps., *National Party Platforms, 1840–68*, pp. 47–48. The plank was authored by Herman Raster. For the prohibitionist perception of the plank and the quotation, see Colvin, *Prohibition in the United States*, p. 96.

acts—affirming the reciprocal nature of the alliance. Although both approaches redounded to the electoral disadvantage of the Republicans, the second is of immediate interest here.[84]

The postwar spate of temperance activity in a number of forms was addressed to a variety of specific objectives. In states where some form of prohibitory law was already in effect—such as Connecticut, Iowa, Kansas, Maine, Massachusetts, Michigan, Nebraska, New Hampshire, and Vermont—temperance advocates worked, sometimes unsuccessfully, to resist repeal; to add wine, cider, and beer to the list of intoxicants; to strengthen the civil-damages provisions; and/or to establish state police forces to guarantee better enforcement of the law in hostile localities. And in Rhode Island in 1874, they secured the reenactment of the prohibitory law that had been repealed in 1863. In other states the temperance forces worked for the passage of local-option legislation. They secured such measures in California and Pennsylvania, but in New York they found the legislature unable to override the veto of a Republican governor. In Indiana and Wisconsin they supported the high and restrictive license laws that were enacted by those legislatures. They persuaded the West Virginia legislature to increase sharply the civil-damage provisions of that state's license law. And in Ohio they mobilized their mass base to resist a state referendum that would have repealed section eighteen of the state's 1851 constitution and thereby would have given the legislature the authority to license the sale of liquor in the state.[85]

This public agitation for temperance legislation was combined with the highly visible 1873–74 Women's Prayer Crusade against demon rum, the resulting formation of the Women's Christian Temperance Union, and the accelerated membership drives of the Independent Order of Good Templars and other temperance organizations, as well as with the continuing fusillade of petitions from the church societies. All of this increased public awareness, especially since it was all reported and discussed extensively in both the partisan and religious press. And this reminded social groups that one party or another better represented their subcultural values.

84. For the spirited debate over which set of tactics to pursue, see *Proceedings of the Seventh National Temperance Convention, 1873*, pp. 46–61; for an earlier debate over the question of single-issue voting, see *Proceedings of the Fifth National Temperance Convention, 1865*, pp. 78–79.

85. For an overview of the legal provisions, see *The Cyclopaedia of Temperance and Prohibition*, pp. 275–360. The details of the 1870–76 state actions can be followed in *Appletons' Annual Cyclopaedia*. It is tempting to argue a connection between temperance activity and the hard times of the 1870s. However, the renewed temperance activity began well before September 1873, and most of the actions referred to also came before that date.

Most Republican activists and officeholders in the early 1870s did not identify themselves with the prohibitory cause. Only in Connecticut and Massachusetts in 1873—and in Indiana, Kansas, Maine, Nebraska, New Hampshire, and Ohio in 1874—did the Republicans explicitly present themselves as "the party of temperance."[86] Yet in no state did they overtly oppose the objectives of the reformers, and in no state did the Democracy support them. However, it was less the current pronouncements than the standing images of the parties that shaped mass responses. And on that score there could be no doubt that *Republican* resonated with the political characters of the groups supporting temperance, just as *Democracy* had developed time- and battle-honored bonds of psychological rapport with those opposing it.[87] In the political context of the 1870s, the heightened salience of the temperance question reactivated the latent loyalties of numerous Democrats who earlier—and especially in 1872—had drifted away from the party. It did that by drawing to the forefront of their consciousness the image of Democracy as the "party of personal liberty" and of the old Democracy as the party that had identified itself with antebellum opposition both to the Know-Nothings and to the prohibitory laws of the 1850s and had supported alien suffrage. And it reminded them, too, that the pietistic crusaders continued to pose threats to their cherished values and attendant lifestyles.

The partisan outcome of the renewed temperance agitation was immediately apparent. Even before the panic and depression had struck, the Democrats registered gains in the spring elections of 1873.[88] In New Hampshire's March gubernatorial election the Democrats ran 1.2 per-

86. The platforms are in *Appletons' Annual Cyclopaedia, 1873,* pp. 238, 474; ibid., *1874,* pp. 414, 436–37, 513–14, 586, 595–96, 668. The endorsements were as unequivocal as platform planks ever were; in context their object of appeal is unmistakable. It is interesting to notice that only in Iowa did the Farmer party declare its opposition to legislation that interfered with "personal liberty," and then only after having voted down at its state convention a more explicit statement calling for repeal of the state's prohibitory law. In Indiana the Farmer party declared in favor of restricting the liquor traffic, and the Democrats opposed that state's new restrictive licensing law. And in Illinois, before fusing, the Democratic state convention announced its opposition to all "sumptuary laws"; the Farmer party remained silent on the subject. For all of these matters, see ibid., pp. 402–404, 412–15, 418–19; John D. Denison, *Iowa Democracy,* 1:249.

87. The standing images were clear and well recognized by contemporaries; see *Cyclopaedia of Temperance and Prohibition,* pp. 148–53, for the Democracy's image, and pp. 585–95 for that of the Republicans. Also see the discussions in *Proceedings of the Sixth National Temperance Convention, 1868,* p. 56; *Proceedings of the Seventh National Temperance Convention, 1873,* pp. 46–61; *Proceedings of the Eighth National Temperance Convention, 1875,* pp. 47–62.

88. In some locales it was not temperance, but other moral questions, that served this purpose. For instance, Oregon's state election was held on the first Monday of June

centage points above their 1872 level and 4.5 percentage points stronger in Connecticut's April election. Both states in the interim had been convulsed by temperance agitation. In New Hampshire that had focused on efforts to substitute a licensing statute for the state's prohibitory law, and it had led the temperance forces to reenergize their organizations and to form a State Temperance Union to coordinate the activities of the town and county temperance unions, the church societies, and the local "reform" clubs. Connecticut's storm over temperance had been precipitated by the implicit repeal of the state's prohibitory law in 1872. Charging the Republicans with "treachery," Connecticut's temperance supporters put their own candidate into the gubernatorial lists in 1873. And to minimize defections, the Republican activists countered with a commitment to support "such further legislation as shall be required" to eradicate the liquor traffic.[89] The outcome was much the same in Maine's early September gubernatorial contest. A series of demands for more rigid enforcement of the prohibitory law, and especially the elimination of "cider tippling"; the formation of local Temperance Reform Clubs; Republican commitment to the cause of stronger enforcement, "especially in the cities and larger villages"; and a declared Democratic advocacy of "the greatest individual liberty" combined to produce a Democratic gain of 8.2 percentage points between 1872 and 1873.[90]

In other states the 1873 elections were held after the panic had begun, though before it had broadened and the worst effects of the depression had been felt. Yet even in these states the heightened salience of cultural identifications played roles in shaping the partisan outcomes. In Pennsylvania, for example, the 1872 local-option law, under which sixty-six counties had voted no license, was a focal point of controversy.

1873, and the 1872–73 swing to the Democrats was an enormous 18.8 percentage points. The focal point of the election was the Democracy's anti-Mormon crusade, one in which they identified an incumbent Republican senator as a member of the Mormon faith; see *Appletons' Annual Cyclopaedia, 1873*, pp. 618–19.

89. Colvin, *Prohibition in the United States*, p. 101; the Connecticut Republican platform, in *Appletons' Annual Cyclopaedia, 1873*, p. 238.

90. The demands for temperance were made explicit in the resolutions of the State Temperance Convention, 16 January 1873; the Republican commitment comes from Governor Nelson Dingley's message to the legislature; and the Democratic opposition from the party's state platform; all in *Appletons' Annual Cyclopaedia, 1873*, pp. 458–60. Also see Ernest Hurst Cherrington, ed., *Standard Encyclopedia of the Alcohol Problem*, 4:1661; Richard A. Hebert, *Modern Maine*, 1:237. In all three states Democratic strength in 1873 was greater than in either 1868 or 1872; except in Maine it was higher than it had been in 1870. It is also important to notice that the Democracy's position on temperance in northern New England was still more equivocal than in the East North Central or Midatlantic states. That obviously reflected the fact that in the former states the Democrats still clung to relatively large numbers of native-stock voting supporters.

And the Democracy, pledging itself to oppose "all interference by law with the private affairs . . . of men," gained 8.0 percentage points in the state's German counties. Ohio's case was considerably more mixed. There support *for* temperance (though not necessarily statutory prohibition) had long characterized the state's southern-stock voting areas, which were also Democratic. Without the hated Greeley at the top of the ticket, the Democrats in 1873 restored their percentages in these voting areas, as they did in most other areas of the state. Yet they registered their smallest gains among the counties of the Western Reserve, the only cluster of counties that had disproportionately opposed the license referendum in August 1873.[91]

The panic, the Graham Liquor Law, and an antirailroad reform movement were all elements present in Wisconsin's 1873 election contest. The Democratic-Reform ticket carried the state with 55.2 percent of the total vote, 10.3 percentage points above the Democracy's 1872 strength. Although sorting out the valences of coinciding developments is always perplexing, several facts stand out to assist in the process for Wisconsin's voting behavior in 1873 and 1874. First, the 1872 liquor law, whose provisions for enforcement were tightened by the Republican legislature in 1873, was far more salient in the 1873 election than in 1874, when it had already been repealed. Second, both the standing images and the current pronouncements of the parties left no doubt that Democracy better represented antitemperance values.[92] Third, Democratic gains, both absolute and proportionate, were most noticeable in German communities. In the state's German counties the Democrats gained 11.0 percentage points; and in a subset of fifteen heavily German Lutheran towns, the 1873 Democratic mean was 82.7 percent, compared with 75.2 percent in 1872 and 83.7 percent in 1870. On the other hand, the Democracy's proportionate increases in Scandinavian and native counties and towns were generally much smaller and resulted from dis-

91. Pennsylvania's 1883 Democratic platform is in *Appletons' Annual Cyclopaedia, 1873*, pp. 634–35. Ohio's Western Reserve counties, excluding urban Cuyahoga County (Cleveland), voted 55.9 percent against license, but the rest of the state voted only 48.9 percent against. For discussion of the Ohio developments, see Clifford H. Moore, "Ohio in National Politics, 1865–1896," pp. 289–90; Kleppner, *Cross of Culture*, pp. 112–14; John Lockwood Hammond, Jr., "The Revivalist Political Ethos," pp. 262–65, for the long-term sources of temperance support in Ohio. Ohio's state election was the second Tuesday of October and Pennsylvania's the Tuesday after the first Monday in November.
92. The Republicans were silent, and the Democrat-Reform fusion condemned "all enactments which usurp to the State jurisdiction over private conscience." For the party platforms see *Appletons' Annual Cyclopaedia, 1873*, pp. 774–75; see ibid., p. 776 for the platform of the American Constitutional Union, which had been organized by Germans in Milwaukee in August 1873 to coordinate the state-level fight against the liquor law. For more information see Kleppner, *Cross of Culture*, pp. 114–15.

proportionate Republican drop-off. Finally, in 1874, when the salience of the temperance question had receded somewhat, the Democrats registered absolute and proportionate gains in Yankee and Scandinavian counties but saw both their percentage and number of voters fall off in the German counties.[93] Indeed, within this context both the wholly anomalous character of the 1874 election and the role that the prohibition question played in restoring normal Democratic strength in Wisconsin become apparent. That two different sets of factors were at work in 1873 and 1874 is evident from the fact that the Democratic-Reform distributions for the two adjacent elections showed an r^2 of only .255. Yet the 1873 distribution, not that of 1874, more nearly approximated the shape of the subsequent Democratic vote; for the 1873/1876 distributions r^2 was .721, and the 1874/1876 exhibited an r^2 of .236.[94]

What occurred in Wisconsin between the 1872/1873 and 1873/1874 elections was atypical in the magnitude and direction of its swing. In most states the Democrats did not lose strength between 1873 and 1874 but continued to gain.[95] However, given the fact that the panic had not developed into depression overnight, it is significant that in the eleven states that held state elections in both years the mean 1872–73 Democratic gains were 6.5 percentage points, compared with an 1873–74 mean gain of only 1.2 percentage points. That is, most of the Democratic gains in these states had been registered before the panic deepened into depression. And with the exception of Minnesota, they came on the heels of renewed and heightened agitation for temperance.

This does not suggest that the complexities of voting behavior in the early 1870s can be reduced to a single and succinctly stated cause —temperance. Nor does it ignore the systemic implications of the depression. Although it is considerably more difficult to pin down, the geographic extensiveness of the temperance agitation made it nearly

93. In the Scandinavian counties between 1872 and 1874, Democratic strength increased by 14.6 percentage points, and the Democratic drop-off was an astounding −145.9 percent; in the Yankee counties the gain was 12.3 percentage points, and drop-off was −51.4 percent. The German counties had been 61.1 percent Democratic in 1872 and 72.1 percent in 1873; they fell to 60.9 percent in 1874. The 1872–74 Democratic drop-off in the German counties was 4.5 percent. *Negative* drop-off figures indicate that the size of the vote in the second election was larger than in the first election.

94. And the same was true over the longer term: 1873/1888, r^2 = .597; 1874/1888, r^2 = .304. Although Ohio's interyear Democratic autocorrelations were typically stronger than Wisconsin's, or those of any other East North Central state, the same pattern was evident there: 1873/1876, r^2 = .958; 1874/1876, r^2 = .884; 1876/1888, r^2 = .926; 1873/1888, r^2 = .887; 1874/1888, r^2 = .826.

95. The Democrats polled 55.2 percent of Wisconsin's total vote in 1873 but only 50.1 percent in 1874. Iowa and Minnesota were the only other states in which the Democrats lost strength between 1873 and 1874; respectively, those declines were 1.5 and 1.6 percentage points.

systemwide as well. Instead it suggests that the two causes interacted with each other. For some groups that interaction was reinforcing, but for others it had a cross-pressuring effect. That two potentially powerful causes interacted and exerted cross-pressures on some voter groups, pulling them in opposite directions, helps significantly to account for the fact that the depression of the 1870s did not change the shape of the electoral universe.

It also helps to explain the particular shape that the 1872–76 shifts did take, for by 1874 not only temperance agitation, but the effects of the depression as well, had cut into Republican voting support. The data in Table 4.7 once again point to the systemwide nature of the political response to the hard times. Between 1872 and 1874 the Democrats gained percentage strength, and the absolute size of their vote increased in virtually all types of social areas.[96] Yet in fact it was a systemwide swing with a revealing, if mild, coloration. The sharpest Democratic gains came in the German counties, where both sets of current events interacted and reinforced each other. And by 1876 the level of Democratic support in the German counties remained further above the pre-1874 levels than in any of the other social areas. Certainly, the difference in the comparative sizes of the percentage-point shifts was not great: e.g., the 1868–76 shift in the German counties was +3.6 percentage points and +3.5 in the Yankee counties. However, two other indicators were of greater magnitude. First, most obviously in the German counties were the Democrats successful in widening the gap between themselves and the Republicans. In 1872 the difference between the percentages of the two major parties had been a mere 1.3 percentage points; by 1876 it was 12.4 percentage points. Second, between 1872 and 1876 the absolute size of the Democratic vote in the German areas increased by 49.6 percent; that was fully 30.0 percentage points larger than the increase of the Republican vote in the same counties and nearly 15.0 percentage points larger than the increase in the Democracy's total vote in any of the other social areas.[97] These indicators point unmistakably to a Democratic resurgence that was especially strong in social areas in which both the depression and the temperance movement pulled voters in the same direction. And the phenomenon was not confined to these German counties. It recurred in other states—for example, in Massachusetts and New

96. The 1872–74 decline in the size of the Democratic vote in the southern-stock counties of Illinois and Indiana resulted from the three-way contest in Illinois. The Republican vote and percentage strength also declined, by more than the Democracy's. In 1872 the Democratic partisan lead was 9.3 percentage points; that increased to 14.2 in 1874 and was 12.4 by 1876.

97. The same comparative pattern persists whether one uses 1868 or 1870 for the comparisons with 1876.

TABLE 4.7   *Partisan Strength by Types of Counties, 1868–1876*

A. *Percent Democratic of Total Vote*

	Yankee (N = 71)	Southern Stock (N = 18)	German (N = 43)	Scandinavian (N = 33)
1868	36.3	54.8	52.2	27.5
1870	39.7	54.6	55.0	30.1
1872	35.7	50.7	50.6	28.0
1874	40.3	52.3	57.6	33.6
1876	39.8	53.3	55.8	26.5

B. *Drop-off in Size of Vote (as %)*

1868–70				
Dem	10.5	0.7	21.2	10.5
Repub	22.7	−0.2	29.6	22.7
1872–74				
Dem	−4.2	16.1	−5.8	−4.2
Repub	19.5	36.9	21.4	19.5

Jersey—among Catholic voters, irrespective of ethnicity and regardless of residential context.[98]

The shifts of the mid-1870s reinvigorated the Democracy. Everywhere Democratic officeholders and activists had been demoralized by the electoral disaster in 1872. The enormous depression of Democratic turnout in that year had led some to question Democracy's viability as a party in the electorate. In some locales even the party's activists were willing to write its obituary. However, the news of Democracy's death was greatly exaggerated, for everywhere between 1873 and 1876 the party in the electorate was revitalized, and its officials and activists were consequently infused with "a new vigor." By 1876 "the enthusiasms of the earlier [antebellum] years were again in evidence."[99]

98. That can most readily be seen in the increased magnitude of the second-order partial correlation of percent Democratic with percent Catholic, controlled by percent rural and percent employed in manufacturing activities. In Massachusetts, for example, the size of the partial increased from .658 in 1868 to .812 in 1876; in New Jersey the increase was from .294 to .601.

99. The quotation is from Walter A. Townsend, *Illinois Democracy*, 1:137. For

The voting shifts in the early 1870s, then, reactivated the latent loyalties of relatively large numbers of "normally" Democratic voters, who had either drifted away from the party in 1872 or earlier, or who had never been socialized into the practice of Democratic voting. Yet by and large, they were members of social groups whose political characters were consonant with Democracy's. The combined impact of hard times and threats of temperance legislation transformed that latent consonance into active voting support. As it was, and as the Democrats gained strength throughout the North and Midwest, the third party system stabilized into that much maligned "era of no decision."

Political combat during the stable phase of the third electoral era reflected intense and irreconcilable distinctions among social groups. These antagonistic political subcultures did not spring to life in response to partisan rhetoric. Rather, the rhetoric expressed the emotional and psychological perspectives of each party's constituent groups. And this underlying conflict between political subcultures structured party controversy. Thus to understand the nature of party oppositions during the late nineteenth century, and the subcultural conflict that they reflected, we need to describe more precisely the stable pattern of social-group partisanship. Then we can proceed to inquire more fully into the nature of the bonds of psychological rapport between political parties and political subcultures.

---

similar observations see A[lexander] K. McClure, *Old Time Notes of Pennsylvania*, 2:353–55; Joseph P. Smith, ed., *History of the Republican Party in Ohio*, 1:330; *Boston Post*, 10 April 1874. For a good account of the earlier willingness of the party's leaders to abandon permanently its name and organization, see *Dubuque Herald*, 13 August 1873.

5

Political Confessionalism:
The Ethnoreligious Roots of Partisanship

Men make their own history, but they do not make it just as they please; they do not make it under circumstances chosen by themselves, but under circumstances directly encountered, given, and transmitted from the past. The tradition of all the dead generations weighs like a nightmare on the brain of the living.

Karl Marx (1869)

Marx probably would have characterized the American electoral universe as a sequence of recurring nightmares. Its long-term stability, sporadically punctuated by brief bursts of electoral reorganization, evidenced the weight of the "tradition of all the dead generations." That systemic stability, in turn, resulted from the fact that the voters who comprised the system voted under circumstances "encountered, given, and transmitted from the past." Their orientations were shaped by those "dead generations" as well as by their own past experiences and were channeled by the standing images of the contending parties. To understand their voting behavior at any time requires a *historical* explanation.

Modern social scientists implicitly recognize this need when they refer to the differences between long-term and short-term forces as distinguishable components of the election outcomes. Indeed, the short-term component, the circumstances unique to a given election, becomes "notable primarily because it lacks continuity with the past."[1] Yet our capacity to notice and evaluate that *dis*continuity depends on an adequate description and explanation of the underlying bases for partisan continuity. And that necessitates an understanding of the way group partisanship was established and was sustained. Indeed, understanding the "normal," or regular, pattern of partisanship that characterized an electoral era is more important to historical political analysis than describing its fluctuations.

1. Philip E. Converse, "The Concept of a Normal Vote," p. 15.

Nineteenth-century American partisanship was not rooted in economic distinctions. Neither gradations in wealth nor perceived differences in status nor shared orientations toward the work experience were at the core of partisan commitments. Partisan identifications mirrored irreconcilably conflicting values emanating from divergent ethnic and religious subcultures. And nineteenth-century political parties were not aggregations of individuals professing the same political doctrines but coalitions of social groups sharing similar ethnocultural values.[2] Once we realize that the "tradition of all the dead generations" shaped those values, and the partisanship that they structured, then the seemingly epiphenomenal quality of American electoral behavior becomes more comprehensible.

Patterns of Partisanship

Contemporary politicians sometimes referred to an "immigrant vote." When they did, however, they must have had concrete referents in mind, for neither native-stock nor immigrant voters uniformly coalesced into homogeneous voting blocs. If they had, the task of describing and analyzing group voting behavior would be immensely simplified. Instead, it is necessary to subdivide each of these broad categories and to specify the partisan proclivities of a variety of discrete ethnocultural groupings.

One County / DeKalb County, Illinois, was surely not a microcosm of the nation, nor of the Midwest for that matter. It was more heavily native-stock, Anglo-Protestant, and rural than Illinois, the Midwest, or the United States. It may well have been precisely these atypical characteristics that made it attractive for a field survey of party identifications.[3] Whatever the reasons, it was one of those relatively few midwestern

2. It is relevant to point out that the conclusion derives from multiple-regression analysis employing a variety of economic and ethnoreligious indicators. Whether executed by counties within states or by minor civil divisions within counties (or subsets of counties), the results consistently demonstrated the much greater importance of ethnoreligious variables to an explanation of major-party voting. To conserve space, the discussion that follows will not present a labored demonstration of these negative findings. However, where relevant, as in the unique set of conditions that shaped political cultures in Rhode Island, I will draw attention to the ways in which the two types of identifications interacted to reinforce each other. For the analysis of the Rhode Island developments, see Chapter 8, and see Chapter 7 for analysis of the role played by economic identifications in explaining Farmer-Labor party voting.

3. The data are reported in *Voters and Tax-Payers of DeKalb County, Illinois*. For analyses of comparable field surveys of late nineteenth-century partisan identifications,

counties for which individual data were collected and published. Those data identify the place of birth, age, occupation, religion, and party preference of each of the county's voters. Collected in 1875–76 and sampled, processed, and analyzed a century later, the data provide us with a rare glimpse at individual rates of partisanship (see Table 5.1).[4]

Several caveats should be made explicit before considering the data. First, Illinois had a Farmer party in the field in 1874, and that party designated itself "Independent Reform"; so we cannot simply assume that an identification as "Independent" meant that the individual perceived himself as a *political independent* in the commonly accepted sense of that term. It may only have meant that the respondent had voted for, and continued to identify with, the Farmer party.[5] Second, one should be cautious concerning the relatively high incidence of responses suggesting the absence of any formalized religious involvement. These responses were disproportionately concentrated among native-stock voters; also, a number of active clergymen indicated "no religion." Some respondents may have felt that such an important matter was simply none of the business of the interviewer. In any case, both aggregate data and individual church records indicate that far less than 42.7 percent of the county's adult population was without church affiliation.[6] Finally,

---

see Richard J. Jensen, *The Winning of the Midwest*, pp. 60–62, 309–15; Melvyn Alan Hammarberg, "The Indiana Voter." The counties on which Jensen and Hammarberg report shared DeKalb's disproportionately native-stock, Anglo-Protestant, and rural characteristics.

4. The data were sampled and processed by Robert L. Schroeder. For a demonstration of the absence of any meaningful pattern of partisanship by economic groupings, see his "The Challenge to Republican Supremacy in DeKalb County, 1874–1896." I have reanalyzed Schroeder's data. The 20.0 percent systematic sample that was drawn produced a total $N = 1328$, but 210 individuals did not disclose a place of birth; so for purposes of Table 5.1, the usable sample was reduced to $N = 1118$.

5. That assumption would be especially tenuous in Indiana where the Farmer party in 1874 officially designated itself as "Independent"; see *Appletons' Annual Cyclopaedia and Register of Important Events of the Year, 1874*, p. 413. Hammarberg's analysis of individual data from nine Indiana counties, reported in "The Indiana Voter," pushes the meaning of the Independent response much further than that state's political context in the mid-1870s justifies. Moreover, the way in which he operationalizes the concept of "group norms *vis a vis* a party" (see pp. 50–56) assumes an ordering of human responses that is at variance with what one would anticipate from reference-group theory.

6. The proportion reported is based on the total sample size of 1328. An additional twenty-seven of the "no religion" respondents could be identified as formal church members from contemporary accounts of church activities. However, since I made no systematic effort to track down the "no religion" group, I have not reclassified these twenty-seven. Neither church membership nor even an expressed denominational preference are necessary preconditions for religious belonging. "Clearly membership is not coterminous with religious feeling or personal commitment, nor is it a prerequisite." N. J. Demerath III, *Social Class in American Protestantism*, p. 10. Moreover, statistics

TABLE 5.1 *Partisan Affiliation by Ethnoreligious Groups: DeKalb County,*
Illinois, 1876

	N		% Repub	% Ind	% Dem
Native Groups					
Baptist	47		80.8	17.0	2.1
Congregational	18		83.3	5.5	11.1
Episcopal	8		25.0	50.0	25.0
Methodist	86		74.4	17.4	8.1
Presbyterian	31		80.6	9.6	9.6
Catholic	16		18.7	25.0	56.2
Protestant	89		61.7	19.1	19.1
No Religion	463		67.6	15.7	16.8
Total Natives	758		67.9	16.3	15.6
Immigrant Groups					
German	46		41.3	17.3	41.3
Catholic		(8)	0.0	37.5	62.5
Lutheran		(23)	56.5	17.3	26.0
No Religion		(15)	40.0	6.6	53.3
Swedish	61		85.2	9.8	4.9
Lutheran		(31)	87.0	9.6	3.2
No Religion		(30)	83.3	10.0	6.6
Norwegian Lutheran	17		76.4	23.5	0.0
British	76		48.6	31.5	19.7
Denominational		(17)	52.9	17.6	29.4
No Religion		(59)	47.4	35.5	16.9
Irish	91		13.1	12.0	74.7
Catholic		(45)	4.4	8.8	86.6
Meth/Presby		(9)	88.8	11.1	0.0
No Religion		(37)	5.4	16.2	78.3
Other					
Protestant	54		50.0	20.3	29.6
No Religion	15		53.3	40.0	6.6
Total Foreign	360		46.7	19.4	33.8
Total Sample	1118		61.1	17.3	21.5

the data are not presented here as prototypical. They are given in order to examine the patterns of a single county, to provide some baseline for comparisons, to suggest some clues for further inquiry, and to give a concrete sense of both the direction and structure of that inquiry.

The patterns of the data in Table 5.1 are sufficiently clear that they require no extended discussion, merely some minor clarification and underscoring. DeKalb County's native-stock voters, other than those who were Episcopalians or Catholics, exhibited a remarkable measure of political cohesiveness. Even those without a declared religious preference, as well as those who failed to record a denominational preference, were strongly Republican. That these were overwhelmingly Yankee-stock voters helps to account for their partisan response.[7]

More interesting and revealing divisions occurred among the county's foreign-born voters. The Norwegian and Swedish Lutherans, despite their economic subordinance to the Yankees and their articulated consciousness of that difference in status, joined their Yankee enemies in the Republican coalition. And they were joined there by those Irish who declared a preference for one or the other of the Protestant denominations.[8] As a group the German-born divided evenly between the two major parties, but that division concealed significant differences within the group. The German Catholics were Democrats, the General Council Lutherans were mildly Republican, and those without a religious preference displayed a slight Democratic cast. In light of other research findings, the British (English, Scots, and Welsh) were the most anomalous group.[9] In DeKalb County they were a relatively large group but one that failed to display any disproportionate division in its partisan preference. It may have been behaviorally significant that, unlike any of the

---

on church membership consistently understate the number of people who have a religious preference: see Jensen, *Winning the Midwest*, pp. 85–97; H[enry] K. Carroll, *The Religious Forces of the United States*, pp. xxxiv–xxxvi; Rockwell C. Smith, "Church Affiliation as Social Differentiator in Rural Wisconsin."

7. Notice, for example, the rates of Republican cohesiveness among the old stock (and presumably Yankee-stock) voters in Geneseo, Illinois, and among the Congregationalists and Methodists in Rock Island and Logan counties, Illinois, reported in Jensen, *Winning the Midwest*, pp. 61–62; contrast these with the relatively lower levels of political cohesiveness among the native-stock voters in the nine Indiana counties examined in Hammarberg, "The Indiana Voter," p. 116. For evidence of a shared Yankee background and continuing Yankee self-consciousness among the native stock of DeKalb County, see Kermit A. Lambert, "Yankees in the Cornfield."

8. The Swedes without religion were quite likely also Lutherans, since there was no history of Swedish sectarians in the county. Of the Irish with "no religion," nineteen of the twenty-nine who were Democrats lived in DeKalb City and very probably constituted the core of the Roman Catholic congregation there.

9. For the strong Republicanism of the British groups, see William A. Gudelunas, Jr., "Before the Molly Maguires"; Ronald P. Formisano, *The Birth of Mass Political*

other foreign-born groups, the British were distributed across every township in the county; nowhere did they constitute a solid core of settlement. In any case, only the Episcopalians and those without declared religious preference among the British were Democrats; the declared Methodists and Presbyterians were unanimously Republican.

DeKalb County's voters provided several instructive clues to the shape of the larger electoral universe. First, there was a clear-cut Catholic–non-Catholic dimension to their political preferences. The only group among the native stock to exhibit any preference for the Democrats were the Catholics. And foreign-born Catholics, whether Irish or German, were even more strongly Democratic. Second, the difference in the degree of Democratic support between native and foreign-born Catholics may indicate a dimension of native-immigrant tension that exerted cross-pressures on native Catholics. That same sort of cross-pressure may account for the unexpectedly low levels of Republican voting among subgroups of the British immigrants. Third, the voting behavior of the German group was obviously not a simple ethnic response. Its internal divisions suggest the need to examine religious variations within the group. Fourth, those Lutheran immigrant groups from pietistic backgrounds, Swedes and Norwegians, were just as strongly Republican as the native denominationals; so, too, were the Irish and English Methodists and Presbyterians. Whatever native-immigrant tensions existed, some common bond between these immigrant groups and the native denominationals transcended those antagonisms. Finally, despite differences in denominational attachments, the sense of "being a New England man" evoked strong political cohesiveness among native-stock voters.

Catholic Voters / Separate streams of immigration created an ethnoculturally heterogeneous Roman Catholicism in the United States. Catholic immigrants from Ireland, Germany, Holland, Belgium, Poland, Bohemia, and Canada (as well as other countries) came into social contact in the United States as they never had in Europe. The result was a seemingly endless series of conflicts over the language to be used in the non-Latin portions of the liturgy, in the schools, and in the host of church-related societies and sodalities that typified the Catholic parish. There were conflicts, too, over the legitimacy of peculiarly national and local religious customs—such as the feast days of national and village

---

Parties, pp. 308–10; Paul Kleppner, *The Cross of Culture*, pp. 53–55. However, Hammarberg in another native-stock environment shows the English-born to have been 25.0 percent Republican, 46.9 percent Independent, and 29.0 percent Democrat. Hammarberg, "The Indiana Voter," Table 4.5, p. 118.

patron saints, religious processions, and festivals.[10] All of these conflicts were of immense social importance for the evolution of Roman Catholicism in the United States. Yet with one significant exception none of them was relevant to the nineteenth-century partisanship of Roman Catholic voters.

With the exception of the French Canadians, Catholic voters regardless of ethnicity were strong Democrats (see Table 5.2).[11] Germans and Irish might have quarreled within the church, and both probably sneered at Bohemians, but all three groups were united in voting support of the Democracy; so, too, were other, but smaller-sized, groups of Catholic voters—Belgians, Dutch, Old French, and Poles.[12] Even where they lived in proximity, tensions among ethnic groups did not shatter the

10. For information on such matters, see Jay Dolan, "Immigrants in the City," pp. 354–68; Colman J. Barry, *The Catholic Church and German Americans*, pp. 17–19, 192–93, 250–76; Philip Gleason, *The Conservative Reformers*, pp. 21, 24–25. Diocesan and parish histories frequently mention ethnic tensions among Catholics; for examples, see George Paré, *The Catholic Church in Detroit, 1701–1888*, p. 483; Hugh J. Nolan, *The Most Reverend Francis Patrick Kenrick Third Bishop of Philadelphia*, pp. 141, 190; James W. Smyth, *History of the Catholic Church in Woonsocket [Rhode Island] and Vicinity*, pp. 118–19.

11. The time span for the longitudinal means in Panel A varies across states with the availability of minor civil-division voting data. For Iowa it was calculated for the elections of 1875, 1881, 1882, 1885, 1887, 1888; for Minnesota, 1886, 1888; and for Wisconsin, all 1876–88 state elections. The terminal year 1888 was used here to avoid the inflation of the Democratic percentage that would have resulted from inclusion of the 1890–92 sequence. The regression estimates in Panel B (and elsewhere in this study) required three steps. First, it was necessary to make a regression estimate of the number of potential voters within each ethnic and religious category. Second, using those calculations, and with all data percentagized by the total number of potential voters, estimates were calculated of the partisan proportions for each category. Finally, those proportions were translated into the major-party division of the vote among those who cast ballots. If, for example, among the potential Irish voters actually casting ballots, the Democrats outpolled the Republicans by four to one, the two-party division became 80.0 percent Democrat to 20.0 percent Republican. An estimate was calculated for every major office—president, Congress, governor—for each election year, and the means presented here were then calculated over the 1876–88 span. For Maryland and New Hampshire, where the only uniformly available demographic data for subcounty units were from the 1870 and 1880 census manuscripts, the longitudinal means were calculated over the 1876–84 span. All estimates were derived from areally weighted data, and the value of the independent variable was adjusted from year to year by linear interpolation between adjacent sets of demographic data. For details on regression estimates, see Leo A. Goodman, "Some Alternatives to Ecological Correlation." pp. 610–25; Eric A. Hanushek, John E. Jackson, and John F. Kain, "Model Specification, Use of Aggregate Data, and the Ecological Correlation Fallacy," pp. 89–107; Allan J. Lichtman, "Correlation, Regression, and the Ecological Fallacy," pp. 417–34; E. Terrence Jones, "Using Ecological Regression," pp. 593–96; John Lockwood Hammond, Jr., "The Revivalist Political Ethos," Appendix IV, pp. 327–38.

12. So, too, were other, but smaller-sized, Catholic voter groups, such as the Belgians, Dutch, Old French, Bohemians, and Poles. For information on these groups, see Kleppner, *Cross of Culture*, pp. 59–61, 66–69; Albert Charles Edward Parker, "Empire Stalemate," pp. 130–32.

TABLE 5.2 *Catholic Voting Behavior*

A. *Mean Percent Democratic (of Total Vote) in Catholic Voting Units*

	Iowa (N)	Minnesota (N)	Wisconsin (N)
Bohemian	73.3 (7)	82.4 (4)	69.7 (7)
Irish	73.5 (13)	83.9 (10)	73.2 (8)
German	84.7 (8)	83.2 (27)	76.1 (20)
Mixed Ethnic	74.5 (9)	-	69.4 (24)

B. *Mean 1876–88 Estimates: Percent Democratic of Two-Party Vote*

	Catholic	Irish	French Canadian
Iowa	67.9	74.8	N.C.
Maryland*	52.5	60.8	N.C.
Massachusetts†	N.C.	84.2	49.2
Minnesota	77.5	74.5	N.C.
Missouri	60.2	61.9	N.C.
New Hampshire†	54.4	57.9	47.8
New Jersey*	58.1	87.6	N.C.
Rhode Island†	56.1	85.6	42.1
Wisconsin	78.0	67.5	N.C.

*Catholic estimates calculated by counties; Irish estimates by minor civil divisions, excluding cities.
†Calculated by minor civil divisions, excluding cities.
(N.C. indicates that the estimates were not calculated.)

shared bond of Catholicism nor reduce its partisan salience. A sense of religious unity preceded and gave rise to this manifest partisan unity. As Cincinnati's German Catholics had proclaimed at a mass meeting in 1872: "We are Catholics, and only then are we Germans."[13]

That sentiment both oversimplified and exaggerated the case. Ethnic tensions within the Roman Catholic church could have been relevant to partisanship. And that possibility was recognized by some political leaders who spoke more wistfully than realistically of channeling those conflicts into anti-Democratic voting behavior. That tactic was success-

13. The meeting was held to protest the Kulturkampf; the resolution is quoted in G. A. Dobbert, "German-Americans Between New and Old Fatherland, 1870–1914," pp. 666–67. Also see Ernest Bruncken, "How Germans Became Americans," p. 111.

ful, however, only among the French Canadians, and even then it was successful only in the eastern states.[14]

In New York and in the New England states, French Canadians confronted their Irish coreligionists. More than other Catholic immigrant groups, both the French and the Irish had developed a sense of group-consciousness before coming to the United States. That had emerged in the Irish from centuries of conflict with the Protestant English and in the French Canadians from generations of struggle with Protestant English-speaking Canadians. And for both groups the essence of that group-consciousness was a syncretism of religious and ethnic values that culminated "in a 'sanctification' of ethnicity and the 'ethnization' of religion."[15] French Canadians regarded preservation of their language as essential to the preservation of their faith: "Loss of language meant loss of faith, and loss of faith meant loss of eternity." The French language was to them a kind of "mystical bond" that served as the "guardian of faith."[16] The Irish, of course, placed no such value on the use of the French language, nor did they share the French Canadian commitment to parochial schools as an institutionalized means of maintaining that language. To the Irish the French Canadians were "foreigners" who were clannish and slow to accept "American" (i.e., Irish) ways; and the Irish "were not averse to violence by way of showing their distaste for the newcomers."[17]

One of the Irish ways that the French Canadians were slow to adopt was the practice of voting for Democrats. The visible presence of the Irish in the lists of the Democracy virtually guaranteed a negative reaction by the French Canadians. Yet they were in New England, "the land

14. In the Midwest the French Canadians were Democrats; see Kleppner, *Cross of Culture*, pp. 56–58; Formisano, *Birth of Mass Parties*, pp. 172–79, for the Old French and conflicts with Yankees. On the French Canadians in the Northeast, see Donald B. Cole, *Immigrant City*, pp. 149–50; Richard P. Harmond, "Tradition and Change in the Gilded Age," pp. 165–69, 260; Philip Thomas Silva, Jr., "The Spindle City," pp. 135–38, 144–46, 165–69, 205, 232, 344–65, 434–47, 727–29; David B. Walker, *Politics and Ethnocentrism*; Parker, "Empire Stalemate," pp. 124–29.

15. Harold J. Abramson, *Ethnic Diversity in Catholic America*, p. 132. For useful background and insights, see for the Irish, Kathleen Hughes, *The Church in Early Irish Society*, and Emmet Larkin, "Church and State in Ireland in the Nineteenth Century," pp. 294–306; for the French Canadians, Mason Wade, *The French Canadians, 1760– 1967*, especially vol. 1, and Stanley Lieberson, *Language and Ethnic Relations in Canada*.

16. Joshua Fishman, *Language Loyalty in the United States*, pp. 254–55; Abramson, *Ethnic Diversity*, p. 134.

17. Jacques Ducharme, *The Shadow of the Trees*, p. 25; and Thomas T. McAvoy, *The Great Crisis in American Catholic History, 1895–1900*, p. 62. Irish disdain for "foreign" Catholics was not confined to the French Canadians; see Francis E. Tourscher, ed., *Diary and Visitation Record of the Rt. Rev. Francis Patrick Kenrick, 1830– 1851*, pp. 179–80; John Tracy Ellis, *The Life of James Cardinal Gibbons*, 1:333.

of the Puritan, to whom Frenchmen and Papists were an abomination.''
When their religion was assaulted, as it was in Massachusetts in the late
1880s, French Canadians, despite the Irish, gave majorities of their vote
to the Democracy.[18]

Although the Irish and French Canadians arrived in America with a
clear sense of group-consciousness, other Catholic immigrant groups
honed that consciousness on these shores. The result was less a sense of
being a Belgian, a German, or a Bohemian and more a consciousness of
being a *Catholic* Belgian, a *Catholic* German, or a *Catholic* Bohemian.
Sometimes a syncretic fusion of religion and nationality analogous to
that transplanted by the Irish and French Canadians resulted. And always these groups complained of the ever assertive Irish hierarchy.
They resented and resisted Irish clerical domination, especially that of
the so-called liberal, or Americanizing, Irish prelates.[19] Yet always the
greater enemy was the anti-Catholic native or immigrant group. When
that battle was joined, and despite their resentment of the Irish, these
groups offered disproportionate support to the ''Catholic'' party, the
Democracy. And support of the ''Protestant'' party, the Republicans, by
''Americanizing'' Irish bishops, and especially Archbishop John Ireland, merely reinforced that proclivity.

Not all Catholic groups were equally strong Democrats, of course.
In the Midwest, where the Irish were less numerous than in the East and
less visibly dominant in the local and county Democratic organizations,
there were only minimal differences in their degrees of partisanship,
though even there the Irish Catholics were the most consistent in their
strong Democratic support. In the eastern states the Irish were clearly the
most strongly Democratic of the Catholic groups. At the other extreme
—as the Maryland, New Jersey, Rhode Island, and DeKalb County data
suggest—it was likely that native-stock Catholics were the least Democratic of the Catholic voter groups.[20] And everywhere, East and Midwest, urban Irish Catholics were even more strongly Democratic than

18. Ducharme, *Shadow of the Trees*, p. 8. The Massachusetts battle focused on the
parochial schools and was linked with a prohibition struggle; see Chapter 8.
19. The ''Americanizing'' Irish prelates were called ''Clerical Know-Nothings''
by non-Irish prelates; see Ellis, *Life of Gibbons*, 1:331–42, 549–52, 658–89, 2:24–25.
On the development of group consciousness by immigrants, see Victor R. Greene, ''For
God and Country,'' pp. 446–60; Abramson, *Ethnic Diversity*, pp. 143–44; Fishman,
Language Loyalty, p. 27.
20. For other indications of the partisan salience of this type of ethnocultural
distinction among Catholics, see Lee Benson, *The Concept of Jacksonian Democracy*,
pp. 187–91; Thomas T. McAvoy, ''The Formation of the Catholic Minority in the
United States, 1820–1860,'' pp. 13–34. Parker, ''Empire Stalemate,'' Table VI-1, p.
195, shows that Yorker Catholic units had an 1876 Republican mean of 49.1 percent,
Yankee Catholic units 53.9 percent, but Irish Catholic units 36.2 percent.

rural Irish Catholics. In Baltimore, for example, they regularly gave about 95.9 percent of their two-party vote to the Democrats; in Boston, 96.8 percent; in New Hampshire, 85.0 percent; in Minnesota, 91.4 percent; in New Jersey, 96.7 percent; and in Rhode Island's cities they were virtually unanimous in their commitment to the Democracy.[21] So strong and virtually unswerving was the Irish Catholic support for the Democrats that it appeared to some political observers that " 'Irish-Catholic-Democrat' [was] a single concept.' "[22]

German Voters / No observer would have made a similar claim about German voting behavior. Yet nineteenth-century politicians of both major parties frequently referred to "our Germans," "German Republicans," and our "German friends."[23] Such references were to particular subgroups of the Germans and indicated contemporary politicans' implicit recognition that German immigrants did not constitute a cohesive voting bloc.

Who were the "German friends" of each of the major political parties? With the exception of the German Catholics, who were consistently and strongly Democratic, that question cannot be answered simply and unqualifiedly. To begin to answer it, we first must distinguish among the major non-Catholic creedal subgroups of the Germans: Lutherans, Calvinists (Reformed), and Sectarians (United Brethren, Evangelical Association, Baptists, Methodists, and the "Peace Germans"—Mennonites, Moravians, and Amish). Second, within each group we then need to take into account both the experiences of the group at the point of its involvement in American electoral politics and the nature of the socio-

21. These are longitudinal means of regression estimates calculated over the same time spans as indicated in note 11. Since no single city in the four states indicated had a sufficient number of wards to provide reasonably stable estimates, the calculations were executed across all wards of the largest cities within those states. For Rhode Island the cities were Newport, Providence, and Woonsocket; for New Hampshire, Keene, Manchester, Nashua, Concord, Portsmouth, and Dover; for Minnesota, Minneapolis, St. Paul, Duluth, Shakopee, St. Cloud, and Winona; for New Jersey, Camden, Trenton, Hoboken, Jersey City, Newark, Paterson, and Elizabeth. In making these estimates and in dealing with the size of the Irish Catholic group in general, I have assumed that 85.0 percent of the Irish born were Catholics. That is, of course, an extremely conservative assumption.

22. The quotation is in Edward M. Levine, *The Irish and Irish Politicians*, p. 109.

23. Rutherford B. Hayes to S. Birchard, 23 April 1872, in Charles R. Williams, ed., *Diary and Letters of Rutherford Birchard Hayes*, 3:211; Joseph Benson Foraker, *Notes of a Busy Life*, 1:106; Grover Cleveland to Joseph L. Haberstro, 14 July 1884, in Allan Nevins, ed., *Letters of Grover Cleveland, 1850–1908*, p. 36. And some imperceptive Yankee elites did accept the notion of a "German vote" and incorrectly viewed Carl Schurz as "its holder"; see Charles Francis Adams, Jr. to Schurz, 16 July 1875, in Frederic Bancroft, ed., *Speeches, Correspondence and Political Papers of Carl Schurz*, 3:156–57.

political context within which it continued to live. Finally, for the German Lutherans we need to be aware of the sharp intragroup distinctions in their views of confessional Lutheranism. These differences, which can be traced initially to the historical evolution of Lutheranism in the various provinces of Germany, found expression, although an admittedly imperfect one, in attachment to separate Lutheran synods in the United States. Once alerted to such distinctions among non-Catholic Germans, we can begin to describe the central tendencies of their voting behavior and to specify at least some of the conditions that underlay its variations.

German Lutheran voters tended to support the Democratic party.[24] That innocuous description conceals an enormous range in the degree of their Democratic partisanship. The data in Table 5.3 highlight two dimensions of that variation. First, the greater the degree of confessionalism among German Lutherans, the more heavily Democratic they tended to be. At least that was so in Wisconsin, where the hyperconfes-

TABLE 5.3   *German Lutheran Units: Percent Democrat of Total Vote*

	Confessional	(N)	Less Confessional	(N)	All Units
Iowa	69.7	(13)	56.3	(7)	64.9
Minnesota	73.0	(11)	57.7	(17)	63.7
Wisconsin	64.7	(20)	58.5	(18)	61.7
Missouri	74.8	(9)	23.8	(11)	46.7

sionalists of the Wisconsin Synod gave greater support to the Democracy than did the Missouri Synod Lutherans, and in Iowa and Minnesota, where the Missouri Synod Lutherans were stronger Democrats than other less confessional German Lutherans. Yet that was not the case in Missouri, where all the units were formally linked with the Missouri Synod and where one set was about as strongly Democratic as the other was anti-Democratic.

The split in German Lutheran voting behavior in Missouri was sharper than in Iowa, Minnesota, or Wisconsin. It was neither the character of the German Lutheran group, nor the quality and intensity of its

24. For supportive evidence in states other than those discussed, see Formisano, *Birth of Mass Parties*, pp. 298–303; Frederick C. Luebke, *Immigrants and Politics*, pp. 71–116, 122–50; Louise E. Rickard, "The Impact of Populism on Electoral Patterns in Kansas, 1880–1900," pp. 21–33.

commitment to confessional Lutheranism, but the sociopolitical context within which these voters shaped their partisan orientations that differed in Missouri. The character of late nineteenth-century political combat there differed from that of Iowa, Minnesota, and Wisconsin, and *it also differed* from the character of Missouri's antebellum political battles. Neither ethnoreligious values, nor any other set of values, are automatically salient to partisan identifications. Rather, they acquire that salience only as they interact with particular sociopolitical contexts. And to account at any time for a group's continuing commitment to a party, we need to be cognizant, not only of the context as it then exists, but of the ways in which the group's values shaped its initial partisanship. That original partisanship, if perceived by the group to be linked to the defense of cherished values, would not readily be abandoned. Forged during cultural combat, it tended to become an integral part of the group's political subculture, of its orientation to the electoral system; so it was with one subgroup of Missouri's German Lutherans.

The strongly Democratic German Lutheran units in Missouri were populated by the Old Lutheran emigrants from Saxony and their descendants. The Saxon Lutherans who came to Missouri in the late 1830s had emigrated to escape what they viewed as the increasingly Calvinist orientation of the Lutheran church in their home province. As their Old Lutheran counterparts from Pomerania and Brandenburg who had come to Wisconsin to escape the union of the Reformed and Lutheran churches, these Saxon emigrants fled ''Sodom and Gommorah'' to ''save their souls, to live their faith, to establish true public worship, and to have a truly Christian school for their children.''[25] Those objectives had early brought them into collision with native Protestant, especially Yankee, efforts to create a culturally homogeneous society; had exposed them to ''American emotional Christianity's'' moralizing crusades aimed largely at ''uplifting'' and changing their behavior; and had led them to resist those efforts by supporting the anti-Yankee party, the Democrats. In contrast, the heavily Republican German Lutheran units in Missouri were populated by more recent arrivals who had not shared the social and political experiences of the Old Lutheran generation. Nor in Missouri, at least, was there anything in their Lutheranism that impelled them to support a Democracy that was stigmatized as the ''party of treason'' for upholding the Confederacy.

25. The quotations, respectively, are from Walter O. Forster, *Zion on the Mississippi*, p. 1; C. F. W. Walther quoted in August C. Stellhorn, *Schools of the Lutheran Church–Missouri Synod*, p. 41. On the background of the Wisconsin Old Lutherans, see Kleppner, *Cross of Culture*, pp. 44–45. And for the cultural distinctiveness of the Old Lutherans, even among other German Lutherans, see Fishman, *Language Loyalty*, pp. 206–52.

The partisan perseverance of Missouri's Old Lutherans was not entirely atypical. In other parts of the country, and even among those whose creedal orientations might otherwise have been expected to lead them to anti-Democratic voting, German Lutheran groups socialized into Democratic partisanship during the second party system tended to retain that partisan orientation during the course of the third party system. Surely, in particular cases, contexts, and elections, they reduced their levels of Democratic voting support. However, the earlier native-vs.-immigrant, and particularly what German Lutherans had seen as Yankee-vs.-German, conflicts had firmly cemented the general direction of that partisanship. Within such groups, to be a Democrat was to continue to defend one's faith and one's Germanness (and the two can be separated only analytically); and that was a role that members of the group were expected to fulfill.

Pennsylvania's German Lutheran communities were a good illustration. Many of them had been swept by the "New Measures" of the 1830s.[26] And even more of them had willingly united with German Calvinists to form "union" churches—the very sort of creedal admixture that had driven the hyperconfessionals who later constituted the Missouri and Wisconsin synods to emigrate from Germany. The midwestern Lutherans had consciously rejected affiliation with these eastern Lutherans and had stridently condemned the latter's version of the confession as "un-Lutheran." Yet despite practicing a Lutheranism that appeared "watered down" to the hyperconfessionals, Pennsylvania's General Council Lutheran units continued to vote strongly Democratic during the third party system, as they had during the second. Their average 69.3 percent Democratic vote was not materially different from the level of partisan support tendered the party by their more doctrinally pristine brethren to the west.[27]

In New York the Old Palatine Germanic Lutherans, even those

26. On the strains of pietism in Pennsylvania German Lutherandom, see Johannis Jacob Mol, "Theology and Americanization," pp. 136–217; Ellis B. Burgess, *History of the Pittsburgh Synod of the General Synod of the Evangelical Lutheran Church*, pp. 60, 89–95, 98–107, 113–14. On both the Pennsylvania and Maryland Lutherans, see John G. Morris, *Life Reminiscences of an Old Lutheran Minister*, pp. 94–96, 117–18; and G. H. Gerberding, *Life and Letters of W. A. Passavant, D.D.*, pp. 49–53, 61, 81–85. For the Maryland Lutherans in particular, see Abdel Ross Wentz, *History of the Evangelical Lutheran Synod of Maryland of the United Lutheran Church in America*. And the attitudes were apparent in a variety of discussions and resolutions that can be followed in *Minutes of the Annual Convention of the General Council of the Evangelical Lutheran Church in America, 1867–92*; *Proceedings of the Annual Convention of the General Synod of the Evangelical Lutheran Church in the United States, 1850–92*; *Minutes of the Annual Convention of the German Evangelical Lutheran Ministerium of Pennsylvania and Adjacent States, 1848–92*.

27. The proportion is the 1876–88 Democratic mean strength, and $N = 43$.

affiliated with the highly pietistic Franckean and Hartwick synods, clung tenaciously to their old voting habits and continued to offer moderate majorities to the Democrats.[28] The German Lutherans in Frederick and Washington counties, in Maryland, were connected with the General Synod, the haven for the most pietistic of the German Lutheran groups. Even the General Council Lutherans attacked the un-Lutheran confessionalism of the General Synod. Yet these German Lutherans (along with their Reformed brethren) remained a bastion of Lutheran voting support in the otherwise generally hostile Republican environment of western Maryland (see Table 5.4). Their Democratic commitment had

TABLE 5.4   *Group Voting Behavior: Frederick and Washington Counties, Maryland*

	(N)	$\overline{M}$ % Dem 1876–88
German Lutheran and Reformed	(8)	57.8
German Sectarian	(8)	37.7
Native Methodist	(5)	37.1

been formed well before the 1850s, had been reinforced by the Know-Nothing crusade, and had been sustained by continuing local-option battles.

However, even the time-hallowed Democratic partisanship of German Lutheran voters began to waver under one powerful condition. German Lutherans were not the friends of the "Catholic party." And where the Democracy took on that aura, where it was the party of the German and Irish Catholics, German Lutherans took the latter as negative referents and reduced their levels of Democratic voting support. In Wisconsin, for example, strongly German, but mixed Catholic and Lutheran, towns averaged only 59.5 percent Democratic, far below what one would have expected on the basis of the voting behavior of their separate enclaves. Despite the fact that both Missouri's Old Lutherans and its German Catholics were strong Democrats in their own "island

28. Parker, "Empire Stalemate," Table V-1, p. 155, shows an 1874–92 Democratic mean of 51.7 percent in Franckean Synod units; 54.4 percent in Hartwick, New York, and New Jersey Synod units; and only 46.4 percent in the more confessional Missouri and Joint Ohio Synod units. Also see Samuel T. McSeveney, *The Politics of Depression*, pp. 117, 201, 210, for other indications of persisting Democratic support among the Old Palatine Germans.

communities,'' the units averaged only 49.2 percent Democratic where they lived together.[29] The phenomenon did not depend on geographic proximity, of course; but it was very likely heightened by it. The fact that it was also helps account for lower levels of German Lutheran Democratic voting in those urban areas where Irish and German Catholics dominated the party. In urban contexts such as Baltimore (see Table 5.5), German Lutherans seemed consistently to have been less Democratic than either of the Catholic groupings and less so even than comparable rural Lutheran groups.[30]

Just as German Lutheran voting behavior varied, not only with the degree of their commitment to confessional Lutheranism, but also with their sociopolitical contexts and political-generational experiences, so did the responses of the two remaining creedal subgroups of the non-Catholic Germans: the Calvinists and the Sectarians. German Reformed voters were neither as numerous nor as conveniently isolated as German Lutherans, but the scanty evidence available does suggest that they tended to be moderately Democratic. Their Sectarian fellow Germans, especially the United Brethren and Evangelical Association, tended more frequently than other German subgroups to be strong anti-Democrats. Their values inclined them to support "moral" measures, such as temperance and Sunday closing; and their past experiences impelled them to oppose their Lutheran and Catholic fellow countrymen. Yet when they perceived that the challenge was to their "Germanness," then they responded in kind—and with Democratic voting.[31]

Scandinavian Lutheran Voters / Scandinavians were a heterogeneous lot. Their national and provincial origins, religious orientations, and political-generational experiences probably all interacted to shape their partisanship.

Scandinavians immigrated from Norway, Sweden, and Denmark. However, immigration from each of these countries was much more disproportionately a post-1865 phenomenon than that from Ireland and

29. German Catholic districts in Missouri had an 1880–88 Democratic mean of 73.2 percent, $N = 22$.

30. Among Baltimore's German Lutherans 33.2 percent were affiliated with the strongly confessional Synodical Conference. That was a much higher percentage of ritualistic German Lutherans than in Frederick and Washington counties. For evidence of similar reactions by German Lutherans in other urban contexts, see Gudelunas, "Before the Molly Maguires," pp. 76, 85–86, 91–92; Parker, "Empire Stalemate," pp. 133–36 and data in Tables IV-9 and IV-10, pp. 122, 123; Paul Kleppner, "Lincoln and the Immigrant Vote," pp. 176–95.

31. Kleppner, *Cross of Culture*, pp. 49–51; Parker, "Empire Stalemate," pp. 183–84 and data in Tables V-6 and VI-5, pp. 186, 203. And notice the voting levels of the German Sectarians in Maryland, in Table 5.4.

TABLE 5.5 *Group Voting Behavior: Baltimore City, Maryland*

Ward Type	(N)	$\overline{M}$ % Dem 1876–84	$\overline{M}$ % Dem 1876–88
Irish	(2)	74.3	72.1
German Catholic	(2)	67.1	66.7
German Lutheran	(3)	52.3	51.2

Germany. With the exception of a subgroup of the Danes, it was overwhelmingly a migration of rural, preindustrial people.[32] For all three nationalities the migration of family units and groups produced separate communities in America, distinguished one from the other not only by nation but as well by province of origin. In these communities the dialect and the dress, the dances and the songs, the folktales and the traditions of the home district were kept alive. The "thought life" of the inhabitants of these settlements was not generically Norwegian, Swedish, or Danish but was specifically that of their home provinces and communities: "Our social life was lived among men and women of our own race."[33]

Yet despite enormous distinctions within each of the groups—of such magnitude, for example, that Norwegians who spoke one dialect might not understand those who spoke another—and despite some mutual antipathy between Norwegians and Swedes, both responded to their political worlds with remarkable cohesiveness. In their "island communities" in Iowa, Minnesota, and Wisconsin—as well as in Nebraska, New York, and probably elsewhere—Norwegian and Swedish voters were strong Republicans (see Table 5.6).[34] Yet their commitment to Republicanism did not depend on their physical and psychological isolation. Even where they lived in strongly native-stock environments—as in DeKalb and Henry counties, Illinois—both groups retained their partisan faith.[35] For the Swedes in Illinois we can find further confirma-

32. Carlton C. Qualey, "Some National Groups in Minnesota," p. 26; Emmer Engberg, ed., *Centennial Essays*, p. 111; Odin W. Anderson, "The Attitudes of the Norwegian Lutheran Church towards Social and Economic Problems," p. 12; Ruth G. Sanding, "The Norwegian Element in the Early History of Wisconsin," pp. 3–4.

33. Laurence M. Larson, *The Log Book of a Young Immigrant*, p. 100; G. Everett Arden, ed., *The Journals of Eric Norelius*, pp. 5–6; A. E. Strand, ed., *A History of the Swedish-Americans of Minnesota*, 1:271.

34. For New York see Parker, "Empire Stalemate," Table IV-1, p. 87, pp. 139–41; for Nebraska see Luebke, *Immigrants and Politics*, pp. 102, 150.

35. See Table 5.1 for the DeKalb County data; for Geneseo, Henry County, Illi-

TABLE 5.6   *Scandinavian Lutheran Voting Behavior: Percent Democratic of Total Vote*

	Iowa (*N*)	Minnesota (*N*)	Wisconsin (*N*)
Norwegian Lutheran	15.4 (25)	19.5 (28)	18.5 (20)
Swedish Lutheran	21.2 (7)	13.7 (31)	12.7 (14)
Danish Lutheran	45.1 (4)	37.4 (6)	33.9 (8)

tion in an unusual survey compiled in 1879. Of the Swedish Lutherans who responded to the biographical inquiry, 88.4 percent indicated an identification with the Republican party, and only 2.5 percent called themselves Democrats.[36]

The Republicanism of the Norwegians and Swedes cut across provincial distinctions within each of the groups. It also cut across their shared and expressed antipathy to Republican-voting Yankees. These Scandinavian immigrants, the ones who came after 1865 as well as the earlier arrivals, no doubt experienced Yankee scorn and ridicule. That contemptuousness was exemplified in one of the more common, and more charitable, of the Yankees' references to them as "wooden shoe people."[37] Nor was there any doubt that Norwegians and Swedes were cognizant and resentful of the obvious economic dominance of the Yankees, as well as their self-assumed aura of moral superiority. The former they attributed to Yankee cunning, a quality that they pejoratively defined as the capacity "to get the better of you in a bargain"; the latter they ridiculed as evidencing "an almost pharisaical severity" on the part of those whom they condemned as "whited sepulchres."[38] Yet

nois, see Jensen, *Winning the Midwest*, p. 61. The Swedish Methodists in Geneseo were 100.0 percent Republican, and the Lutherans 98.5 percent Republican.

36. The rest were Independents (4.8 percent) or Greenbackers (4.1 percent). Of those not indicating a religious preference, 53.7 percent were Republicans, 6.2 percent were Democrats, 23.7 percent were Independents, and 16.2 percent were Greenbackers. The survey was probably an economically biased one. If so it offers confirmation that Swedish Lutheran Republicanism did not vary much with intragroup status levels, since these respondents were about as anti-Democratic as those in DeKalb and Henry counties. The data were compiled by C. F. Peterson and published in 1880 in *Svensharna i Illinois*; they are conveniently summarized in Oliver A. Linder, "The Story of Illinois and the Swedish People within Its Borders," 1:50.

37. George M. Stephenson, "Sidelights on the History of the Swedes in the St. Croix Valley," p. 397.

38. Theodore C. Blegen, ed., *Land of Their Choice*, pp. 315, 272–73.

neither glib definition nor moral deprecation could obliterate the stark and perceived reality:

> We had known just the rock slopes of Norway,
> Gave the Yankees the best of the land;
>
> . . . .
> We would work for the Yankees a time;
> We would labor and slave to our utmost,
> Were so willing 'twas almost a crime.[39]

Perceived status-group subordinance, interacting with the virulent antiforeignism of the Yankee Whigs, combined during the second party system to produce moderately Democratic voting among some of the earlier Norwegian immigrants. And residual traces of that earlier hostility and the partisanship that it had produced survived into the third electoral era.[40] The realignment of the 1850s, however, had redefined the meaning of partisanship. And among those Norwegian and Swedish Lutherans who were socialized into political behavior after the 1850s, as well as among a majority of those who had been earlier, Republican party voting became the norm. To the "dry" party, the "party of great moral ideas," these voters gave their political fealty; that party's aura was consonant with their pietistic political characters.[41] And the more pietistic the subgroup, the more heavily Republican its voting behavior. Thus, the hyperpietistic Haugean Norwegians in Iowa, Minnesota, and Wisconsin averaged better than 15.0 percentage points stronger in their Republican voting than the somewhat more ritualistic members of the Norwegian Church in America.[42]

Although Lutheran Swedes and Norwegians were unmistakably and powerfully Republican, Danish Lutheran voters displayed a marked partisan ambivalence. In each context they were clearly less strongly Republican than either the Norwegians or Swedes; and, in what were admittedly rare instances, some Danish units actually returned Democratic majorities. Lack of religious cohesiveness inhibited the development of partisan unity among the Danes.

39. "Korlejdes Dae Gjek" ("How Things Have Gone"), a pioneer folk ballad that first appeared in print in 1878 "appears to have been the most popular of all songs written in this country in a Norwegian rural dialect"; for the translation and evaluation see Einar Haugen, "A Norwegian-American Pioneer Ballad," pp. 1–19.

40. For an indication see the data in Jensen, *Winning the Midwest*, Table 13, p. 144.

41. Larson, *Log Book*, pp. 112, 164, 233, 246; Rasmus B. Anderson, *Life Story*, p. 377; Strand, ed., *Swedish-Americans of Minnesota*, 1:308–309.

42. For earlier evidence and explanation see Kleppner, *Cross of Culture*, pp. 51–52, 84–88. The observation here is based on a comparison of the unweighted 1876–88 means of regression estimates for both groups.

Most Danes who came to the United States in the nineteenth century were Lutherans, but that label told very little about Danish religious outlooks. More so than Norwegian and Swedish Lutheranism, Danish Lutheranism had been sectarianized and fragmented. The developments that culminated in separate Danish Lutheran churches in America began in Denmark, but there they had remained as incipient sects within the formal structure of the established Lutheran church. The conflicts revolved around questions such as the primacy of the Bible as opposed to that of the church and its sacraments, the role of lay preachers, and the nature and importance of conversion and sanctification. From such developments three distinct strains of Danish Lutheranism emerged, and each of the practicing groups claimed adherence to the traditional confessions of the faith and the exclusive right to be called "good Lutherans."

The first strain reflected the formalism and orthodoxy of the established Danish Lutheran church, and most of its small number of immigrant adherents seem to have been absorbed by the Norwegian-Danish Conference of the Norwegian Church in America. More important among the emigrating Danes were the other two strains: the Grundtvigian and the Inner Mission. Grundtvigianism began in early nineteenth-century Denmark as a movement against the rationalism and "exegetical popery" of the established church. Its followers accepted the Scriptures as the basis for faith but rejected the established church's singular reliance on them. Instead, they viewed the church as the "living word" of God and united scriptural belief with an emphasis on individual rebirth through baptism. An integral part of their religious renewal, and opposition to the established church, focused on the maintenance of the Danish language and support of the folk high-school movement that had begun among the peasants. The Inner Mission movement owed its origins to the Grundtvigian movement. Although it had been enormously influenced by Grundtvig's views on individual rebirth, it rejected "den kirkelige anskuelse" (the churchly view)—the emphasis on sacraments and the church. It emphasized instead repentance, personal faith, and a decisive rejection of the world. In Denmark the movement was kept alive as an incipient sect by the self-styled "godly gatherings" of pious lay people.

Neither Grundtvigianism nor the Inner Mission movement became separate churches in Denmark. Yet each ultimately made its impress on the established orthodoxy; so by the end of the nineteenth century, the Danish Lutheran church was less rationalist, and more pietist, than it had been in the beginning of the century. In the United States the two strains developed into separate churches. The Grundtvigian strain was imbedded in the Danish Evangelical Lutheran church, and the Inner

Mission spirit in the United Evangelical Lutheran church. The latter was far more pietistic than the former; and among the Grundtvigians, and not the Inner Mission people, "it became a generally accepted belief" that the Danish language and the Danish community "were so closely interlinked that the one could not exist without the other." [43]

In the United States the two groups existed in powerfully antagonistic relation to each other. As early as 1877, each had founded a religious paper to carry on a defense of its version of "the true Lutheran faith" against the assaults of the other. [44] Continuing conflicts among the adherents of the contending strains produced frequent fissures of church congregations. Both battled against the smaller number of Danes who became Baptists, and the Grundtvigians especially attacked the Norwegian pastors and the "Americanizing" proclivities of the Norwegians. [45]

Contention of this type and intensity, carried on among people living in island communities, restrained the development of a Danish political cohesiveness comparable to that that characterized both Norwegian and Swedish Lutherans. And although the evidence is scanty, the Grundtvigians were likely the more Democratic of the two major religious subgroups of the Danes. [46] In any case, it seems probable that the wide variations in Danish Lutheran voting behavior were products of the ongoing and bitter religious controversies.

Other Non-Catholic Immigrant Voters / We can round out this description of immigrant-group voting behavior by examining that of two additional groups: the Protestant New British and the Dutch Calvinists.

Protestant New British is a composite designed to include the English, Scottish, Scotch-Irish, Welsh, and English Canadian immigrants. To use the term as a label to designate a convenient categorization does not imply an a priori assumption that its components were culturally homogeneous. There were, of course, immense cultural differences among these designated streams of immigrants. For that matter, there were significant cultural differences *within* each of them. Scottish highlanders differed from Scottish lowlanders; although Cornwall was officially only an English county, its inhabitants retained their own vernacu-

43. Paul C. Nyholm, *The Americanization of the Danish Lutheran Churches in America*, p. 223.
44. John M. Jensen, *The United Evangelical Lutheran Church*, pp. 66–67.
45. Thomas P. Christensen, "Danish Settlement in Minnesota," pp. 364, 366–67, 373, 379; Nyholm, *Americanization of Danish Lutheran Churches*, pp. 81–90.
46. For example, in Minnesota two Danish communities in Lincoln County were more Grundtvigian than most other Danish communities, and the Democrats polled a mean of 41.5 percent of their votes in 1888. In one of the towns, Marshfield, they secured more than 50.0 percent of the vote in both 1886 and 1888.

lar, and in America Cornish immigrants "consistently considered and referred to themselves as Cornishmen, not Englishmen."[47] Thus, the relevant question is not *whether* such distinctions existed among the subgroups of the Protestant New British, but whether they had partisan salience. Did the identifiable components of the Protestant New British respond in a politically cohesive fashion?[48]

For several of the subgroups, the answer is both clear and unequivocal: Scots, Scotch-Irish, Welsh, and Cornish were everywhere and consistently strong Republicans. In New York, for example, Scots towns were even more heavily Republican than Yankee towns, and the Welsh and Scotch-Irish did not lag far behind in their dedication to Republican voting. In the Midwest, Welsh and Cornish units, whether in farming or mining environments, were always strongly Republican. Pennsylvania's Scotch-Irish Presbyterian units averaged only 30.5 percent Democratic (even slightly lower than New York's 34.4 percent) and were consistently among the lowest-ranking Democratic units in their counties. And among the mining districts of "bloody" Schuylkill County, Pennsylvania, Welsh and English miners continued the religious wars against their Irish Catholic coworkers; the Catholic miners were Democrats, but the Welsh and English units gave the Democracy an average of only 37.5 percent of their 1876–88 votes.[49]

Despite cultural distinctions among these subgroups, as well as those within some of them, their political behavior, regardless of sociopolitical context, was marked by a consistent and strong anti-Democratic orientation. Each of these subgroups technically differed from the others in formal denominational affiliation, and each valued highly its own church. Those churches, separated though they were by language and polity, shared a strongly moralist religious outlook. Everywhere contemporaries described these immigrants as being "deeply religious,"

47. George Fiedler, *Mineral Point*, p. 161. On the differences within and among the various ethnocultural subgroups of the Protestant New British, see Rowland T. Berthoff, *British Immigrants in Industrial America, 1790–1950*, pp. 1–5.

48. That is, of course, the relevant question for any ethnoreligious category. One can always point to differences that exist *within* any designated category of people; those distinctions may be, for some purposes at least, highly important. Yet ultimately one needs to ask: did they influence behavior? And, more specifically, did they influence voting behavior? To answer that requires, at a minimum, *observation* of voting behavior. Thus, whether any category or element within it reacted in a politically cohesive way (i.e., gave evidence of constituting a group in the social and psychological senses of the term) is a matter in the first instance for empirical inquiry.

49. Parker, "Empire Stalemate," Tables IV-1, IV-5, pp. 87, 114; McSeveney, *Politics of Depression*, pp. 30, 95, 117, 158; Kleppner, *Cross of Culture*, pp. 53–55; Roger D. Petersen, "The Reaction to a Heterogeneous Society," Tables 37, 38, pp. 161, 163; Gudelunas, "Before the Molly Maguires," p. 23, 88, 104. I have used the units identified in the latter two works and calculated the relevant partisan percentages.

strict observers of the Sabbath, and total abstainers.[50] And everywhere, of course, that description distorted reality, for among the Cornish and Welsh especially there was an element that "belonged to the old fighting, hard-drinking school."[51] This neither minimizes their piety nor undervalues their religious involvement but draws attention to the two separate sources of their Republicanism. Those within the groups who were strong temperance and sabbatarian supporters could readily embrace Republicanism for those reasons. Yet even those who were not— like the Welsh miners of Schuylkill County who had learned "to drink beer like water, to get as drunk as tinkers"—could identify their Republicanism with opposition to Catholics, especially to Irish Catholics.[52]

Among the remaining components of the Protestant New British, the English and the English Canadians, the case is more ambiguous. New York's "New English" seem to have been strongly Republican, as they were in some locales of the Midwest where they were clustered near Irish Catholics.[53] Yet there were interesting and suggestive exceptions. Le Mars was an English colony in northwestern Iowa, and it was a "whiskey town" with fifteen saloons, including the fashionable House of Lords. Its Englishmen were nominally Episcopalians, but an even larger proportion of them appear to have been unchurched. In either case, the moral tone of the community was not that of quiet piety but one in which the "gentlemen's sons [the young Englishmen]" were reputed to have "a superabundance of animal spirits, and . . . [to] go in for what constitutes a 'good time,' with little regard to what people generally may think of their actions." The local Yankees, especially the Methodists, were scandalized by those actions. Antagonisms between the two groups threatened to produce what one local newspaper termed a "War between the Races."[54] Unlike Welsh and Scottish communities (in Iowa and elsewhere), Le Mars was not a stronghold of Republicanism. The Englishmen there supported the anti-Yankee Democracy, and

50. Fiedler, *Mineral Point*, pp. 162–63; James A. Bryden, "The Scots in Wisconsin," p. 156; William Bebb to Griffith Owen, 10 October 1850, in Alan Conway, ed., *The Welsh in America*, p. 91. And on the Welsh also see Daniel Jenkins Williams, *One Hundred Years of Welsh Calvinistic Methodism in America*; Edward George Hartmann, *Americans from Wales*, pp. 101–26.

51. James Fisher, "Michigan's Cornish People," p. 384; Berthoff, *British Immigrants*, pp. 146–47.

52. The quotation is in ibid., p. 146.

53. Parker, "Empire Stalemate," Table IV-1, p. 87, pp. 109–10; McSeveney, *Politics of Depression*, pp. 30, 95; and Kleppner, *Cross of Culture*, pp. 56–68.

54. Jacob Van Der Zee, *The British in Iowa*; the quotations are on pp. 214, 212, 211, respectively; for a description of the community, its mores, its reaction to prohibition, and its politics, see pp. 109–12, 210–15. Also see Jensen, *Winning the Midwest*, p. 79. Le Mars is in Plymouth County, northwestern Iowa.

their Democratic voting increased at the end of the 1880s when Republicans became identified with that state's crusade for prohibition.[55]

In other sociopolitical contexts dominated by native-stock voters, the English tended to divide between the major parties. In nine native-stock Indiana counties only 25.0 percent of the English identified with the Republicans, and 29.0 percent with the Democrats. And any strong Republican leaning was also absent among DeKalb County's Episcopalian English or those without a declared religious affiliation.[56] In contexts where *Democrat* was not synonymous with "Irish Catholic," native-vs.-immigrant tensions seem to have led Englishmen, especially nonpietistic Episcopalians, to higher levels of Democratic voting than in other sociopolitical contexts.

Analogous conditions influenced the voting behavior of English Canadians. Everywhere English Canadians were Republican, but the degree of their Republicanism varied with the extent to which they perceived the Democracy as the "Catholic party." Thus, in rural New Hampshire, where Democracy still retained much of its older (second party system) Yankee tone and character, English Canadians were about 10.0 percentage points more Democratic than in outstate Massachusetts, where the Democrats were more clearly perceived as the party of Irish Catholics.

Dutch Calvinists were only slightly more unitary a category than the Protestant New British. They shared a common language, a common homeland, and a common commitment to the "Reformed" religion; but there were considerable differences among the subgroups of the Dutch Reformed. The Old Dutch of New York and New Jersey, who had emigrated prior to 1790, had transplanted the established Calvinism of the Netherlands. Theirs was a rather formal Calvinism in which evangelistic fervor had been supplanted by codes of religious behavior. In the Netherlands the formal orthodoxy and growing rationalist spirit of the established church precipitated a secession in the early 1830s. The "New Light" Seceders were intense pietists who rejected formalism and advocated a code of puritanical conduct. The Seceding Calvinists emigrated to the United States in the 1840s and established outposts of the Dutch Reformed faith in Iowa, Michigan, Wisconsin, and elsewhere. Both groups of the Old and New Dutch were Calvinists, and both laid claim to the title *Dutch Reformed*. Yet there was a difference. Though both

55. The Democratic 1889–91 mean was 6.0 percentage points higher than the 1887 Democratic percentage.
56. Hammarberg's "English" category includes Welsh, Scots, and Canadian born; see Hammarberg, "The Indiana Voter," Table 4.5, p. 118. For DeKalb County the basic data are in Table 5.1, and the conclusion here is based on a retabulation of only that subpart of the "British" category that was from England.

groups contained strains of pietism, the New Dutch were more intensely pietist than their eastern brethren.[57] A Dutch Reformed minister from New York who visited the Holland settlement in Michigan in 1849 reported, with only slightly concealed amazement, that the Michigan Dutch were "praying and converted persons. Their religious habits are very strict and devout. They do all things with prayer and praise. They sing and pray in the morning, after their dinner, and after their supper. They pray when they meet for business. At a bee work they pray. . . . The appearance and tone of piety is purer and higher than any thing I have ever seen, and seemed like the primitive Christians."[58]

The Seceders would have agreed that the tone of their piety was much more pristine than that of the eastern churches. Except for some of their leaders—especially Albertus Christiaan Van Raalte, the "pope" of the Michigan Dutch—they scorned the Americanized and watered-down version of the faith that was practiced by the Reformed Protestant Dutch Church of New York. They rejected abandonment of the Dutch language and insisted on a strict and severe observance of the Sabbath. And when Michigan's "Pope and his cardinals" pushed too hard for a union with the New York church, the more traditional Calvinists seceded once more and formed the True Christian Reformed Church.[59]

The Michigan schism pitted the pietist assimilationists, Van Raalte and his group, against the True Christian Reformed, who insisted on rigid preservation of the Dutch language, condemned secret societies, and opposed any union or cooperation with non-Calvinist religious bodies. The Van Raalte group exaggerated the similarities between their own brand of Dutch Calvinism and that of the New Yorkers. True, the latter condemned the rampant rationalism of the state church in the Netherlands, but they were not as pietistic as the Van Raalte group. To the ultrapietism of the "Pope and his cardinals," the True Christian Reformed reacted negatively. They were antirationalist but more committed to the traditional forms and practices of the Dutch Reformed faith and to the maintenance of the Dutch language than was the Van Raalte group. Succinctly summarized, the True Christian Reformed group was

57. For the development of pietism among the Old Dutch, see Mol, "Theology and Americanization," pp. 32–58.

58. Report of Rev. Isaac N. Wyckoff to Reformed Protestant Dutch Church, New York, May 1849, quoted in Albert Hyma, *Albertus C. Van Raalte and His Dutch Settlements in the United States*, p. 199.

59. For the phrase *Pope and his cardinals* see Engbertus Van der Veen, "Life Reminiscences," in Henry S. Lucas, ed., *Dutch Immigrant Memoirs and Related Writings*, 1:512. And on the secession of the True Christian Reformed, see Hyma, *Van Raalte*, pp. 207–219; Henry Jacob Ryskamp, "The Dutch in Western Michigan," pp. 24–40, 136–44; Henry Beets, *The Christian Reformed Church*, pp. 56–63; Marian M. Schoolland, *The Story of Van Raalte*, pp. 101–102.

more pietistic than the New York Old Dutch but less so than the Van Raalte group and the bulk of the Seceders who had established colonies in Iowa and Wisconsin.[60]

Differences in religious outlooks, in sociopolitical contexts, and in historical experiences all explain the variations in Dutch Calvinist voting behavior. New York's Old Dutch were moderately Democratic, and slightly more so where they lived near Yankees. That level of Democratic voting support, however, was considerably less than they had given to the Democracy during the second electoral era.[61] The Old Dutch had experienced the invasion of the Empire State by "restless" Yankees; they had also experienced the resulting Yankee disdain. They defended their ethnoreligious identity by voting for the anti-Yankee party. However, the changing context of political behavior, in which the Democracy became identified as the Catholic party, cross-pressured their partisanship. The character of New York's Republican party resonated with their own restrained pietism and strong anti-Catholicism and led many of the Old Dutch to the practice of anti-Democratic voting.

Early in their political life cycle Michigan's New Dutch had been strong Democrats. As late as 1856, all of their centers of population had returned Democratic majorities. As their brethren to the East, they had reacted politically to the antiforeignism of Michigan's Yankee-Presbyterian Whigs, especially to the "contempt" with which they had treated the Dutch immigrants.[62] Yet even more than those of New York's Old Dutch, the religious value system of the core of Michigan's Seceders was consonant with the moral character of that state's Republican party. Slowly and haltingly at first, and then more decisively as Democracy was stained with both "treason" and Roman Catholicism's assault on

60. The New York group designated itself the Reformed Protestant Dutch, and a schism within that group in 1824 led to the creation of a True Reformed Church there. Those who seceded from the Van Raalte group in Michigan called themselves both the Christian Reformed and the True Christian Reformed. In the early 1880s continuing tension over Masonry led to another breakoff from the Reformed Protestant Dutch, and this group along with the True Reformed then joined with the True Christian Reformed. On these developments, see Paul Honigsheim, "Religion and Assimilation of the Dutch in Michigan," p. 56.

61. For the New York Dutch partisanship during the second party system, see Benson, *Concept of Jacksonian Democracy*, pp. 181–82, 185. Parker, "Empire Stalemate," Table IV-1, p. 87, shows that the Old Dutch towns were only marginally Democratic. Their 1874–92 mean Democratic percentage was 51.4 percent; but where the Old Dutch lived in a Yankee context, the Democratic mean was slightly higher, 53.8 percent. The single New Dutch town in New York registered a mean of 17.2 percent Democratic. New Jersey's Old Dutch were also mildly Democratic; see McSeveney, *Politics of Depression*, pp. 58–59.

62. Van Raalte spoke of that contempt and warned his compatriots of it; see his letter to Paul Den Bleyker, 9 January 1851, in Hyma, *Van Raalte*, p. 182.

the free "public schools," they moved to Republicanism.[63] During the stable phase of the third electoral era, Michigan's pietistic Dutch averaged only 33.9 percent Democratic. Yet those units in which the True Reformed were more numerous were 6.8 percentage points more strongly Democratic. And Wisconsin's pietistic Dutch Calvinists gave the Democrats an average vote of 26.5 percent.

Iowa's Dutch units appear to have behaved in a manner similar to those in Michigan and Wisconsin. They returned an average Democratic vote of 30.2 percent in the 1875 and 1881 elections. However, that mean vote concealed a sharp distinction. The Pella colony in Marion County was strongly Democratic; the Sioux County Dutch were about as strongly Republican. Iowa's Pella colony had been settled by the same type of Dutch Seceders as those who had settled in Michigan and Wisconsin. If qualitative accounts are reasonably accurate, a stronger proportion of Pella's settlers came from urban and skilled-craftsmen backgrounds than the preponderantly peasant stock that had gone to western Michigan.[64] Whether it was that difference, or antagonism between the arriving Dutch and the Democratic-voting native stock then in Lake Prairie township, Pella's Dutch entered the voting universe as Whigs.[65] Agitation for temperance, Whiggery's support of the 1855 prohibitory law, and the associated flurry of Know-Nothing activity drove the Dutch to the Democracy. Lake Prairie township voted 65.1 percent Democratic in 1854, 88.9 percent against prohibition in 1855, and 70.3 percent Democratic in the 1856 presidential election. From that point through at least 1892, the Pella Dutch were steadfast Democrats. Their adherence to the Democracy remained unaffected by the pro-Republican entreaties of the colony's guiding spirit, Henry Peter Scholte. Continuing and intensified agitation over prohibition sustained that partisanship. (They voted 71.4 percent against the 1882 prohibitory amendment.) Pella's Dutch were not intemperate, but they had linked the agitation for prohibition during the 1850s with the Know-Nothing movement. And thereafter they continued to perceive prohibition as an anti-immigrant measure. Since they identified the Republicans with support

63. Aleida J. Pieters, *A Dutch Settlement in Michigan*, p. 109; Formisano, *Birth of Mass Parties*, p. 308.

64. Jacob Van Der Zee, *The Hollanders of Iowa*, pp. 68–69; Albertus C. Van Raalte to Dr. J. Garretson, 1852, in Hyma, *Van Raalte*, pp. 158–59; Henry S. Lucas, "The Beginnings of Dutch Immigration to Western Michigan, 1846," p. 647; Ryskamp, "Dutch in Western Michigan," pp. 8–19.

65. That was in 1852, and Lake Prairie Township was 60.1 percent Whig in that year. In 1851, when only the native stock had voted, the township had been 82.0 percent Democratic. The data are from Robert P. Swierenga, "The Ethnic Voter and the First Lincoln Election," pp. 134–35.

of prohibition, Democratic voting was their attempt " 'to kick would-be despots and exclusivists into the abyss of political oblivion.' "[66]

The Sioux County settlements were colonized from Pella in the early 1870s, and from their beginning these Dutch townships were strongly Republican. That county had been Republican before the Dutch arrived, but it was improbable that the Dutch simply abandoned their old partisanship to blend into their new political environment.[67] The explanation more likely lay in the combined effect of two other factors. First, reputedly at least, the settlers who left Pella to settle in Sioux County were "young married men just starting out in life." Possibly, such men had not yet been socialized into the practice of Democratic voting; at least, they had had fewer occasions to engage in that practice. The partisan identification of these "young" settlers might on that account have been weaker than those of the older inhabitants of the Pella community. Second, not all of the Sioux County Dutch came from Pella. The new settlements yearly attracted Dutch migrants from Michigan, Minnesota, Wisconsin, and the Netherlands.[68] These settlers had not shared the Pella experience; they had not made the linkages among prohibition, Know-Nothingism, and Republican voting that were part of the political culture of the Pella Dutch. The new settlements opposed prohibitory laws, to be sure; Holland township voted 83.0 percent and West Branch township voted 100.0 percent against the 1882 prohibitory amendment. And when prohibition became a salient factor, there were marginal but temporary increases in their anti-Republican voting levels. Yet for these new arrivals the critical link between antiprohibition voting and Democratic support was lacking, because the intervening link between Know-Nothingism and the Republican party had not been a part of their political-generational experience.

Native Protestant Voters / If DeKalb County, Illinois, had been all the world, there would be little partisan variation to take into account among the native Protestant voter groups. However, that county was something less than a microcosm of the larger electoral universe. There were ana-

66. *Pella Gazette*, 1856, quoted in Van Der Zee, *Hollanders*, p. 225; for details on these matters, see pp. 220–31. Through 1892 the lowest Democratic vote in Lake Prairie Township was 63.5 percent in 1881. The city of Pella was organized by 1887; from that election through 1892, all three wards were Democratic, and the lowest Democratic vote was the 54.6 percent returned in ward one in 1888.

67. Sioux County voted 54.5 percent Republican in 1868 and 59.6 percent in 1870. The "blend" theory is especially unlikely in view of the fact that the Pella Dutch continued to vote heavily Democratic despite the fact that Marion county gave the Republicans a majority in every election between 1864 and 1876.

68. Van Der Zee, *Hollanders*, pp. 141, 155, 161, 169.

lytically important distinctions in the voting behavior of native-stock groups, on which we can begin to focus by examining three sets of individual data (see Table 5.7).[69]

TABLE 5.7   *Republican Percentage of Two-Party Identifications*

	DeKalb Co., Illinois	Henry, Logan, & Rock Island Cos., Illinois	Nine Cos., Indiana
Baptist	97.4	64.9	51.4*
Congregational	88.2	91.4	-
Disciples	-	71.8	63.3
Methodist	90.1	78.1	69.2
Presbyterian	89.2	60.8	87.4

*Mission Baptists only.

All of these groups were Republican.[70] Within the two contexts other than DeKalb County, there was considerable partisan variation from one denomination to the other; and within each denomination there was variation from one context to the other. These variations underscore the importance of sociopolitical contexts to voting behavior, but they also draw attention to three additional factors. First, they suggest the need to examine native-stock Protestant voters by discrete ethnocultural groups. Contrary to customary and casual usage, terms such as *native stock* and *old stock* are best thought of as composites that need to be further subdivided into their distinct ethnocultural components. Second, the variations show that denominational labels are only crude indicators of religious beliefs. It is well known, for example, that within any denomination—or within any single congregation, for that matter—some individuals are more involved, more religious, than others. Yet some-

69. The data for Henry, Logan, and Rock Island counties are given separately in Jensen, *Winning the Midwest*, Tables 3, 4, pp. 61–62; I have reaggregated the data from these tables. The Hammarberg data are in "The Indiana Voter," Tables 4.6, 4.7, pp. 119, 121; I have repercentagized his data, as well as the original DeKalb County data (see Table 5.1), to compare both with Jensen's percentages, which were calculated on the basis of the two-party division.

70. The Mission Baptists in the nine Indiana counties were obviously the least Republican of the groups examined in Table 5.7. In these counties the Regular Baptists and "Baptists" (without further identification) were Democrats, the Regular Baptists rather strongly so—83.3 percent. I have used the Mission Baptists here since they correspond more closely in religious outlook to the Baptists in the other two samples. It was certain, for example, that the Regular Baptists in central Indiana were originally the Anti-Mission Baptist group.

times overlooked are the multiple religious beliefs and practices that may exist within some denominations. These differences may reflect earlier conflicts and schisms, formally smoothed over but still alive within particular subgroups of the denomination. That is especially likely to be the case within those denominations—e.g., the Baptists—whose formal governance not merely allowed but virtually apotheosized local congregational autonomy. Third, not all native religious groups, nor all subgroups within some denominations, were equally pietistic. Some were much more so than others. With these considerations in mind, we can begin the task of unraveling the puzzling problems of native Protestant voting behavior.

DeKalb County's native Protestant voters were politically cohesive because they were largely of Yankee stock. Their religious outlooks and ethnocultural identities reinforced each other. This was also the case in the rest of the Yankee zone of culture beyond New England. Regardless of denominational affiliation or sociopolitical context, Yankee-stock voters were consistently more Republican than non-Yankee native Protestant voters, even when the latter were of the same denomination as the Yankees.

The contrasts between Yankees and Yorkers in New York State were probably typical of the differences that existed throughout the midatlantic and midwestern states. Albert Parker's rich New York data point to two important observations. First, the Republican voting support of both Yankee and Yorker units varied almost monotonically with the degree of pietism of their principal denominations. Second, within each denominational category Yankee units were more heavily Republican than native non-Yankee units. For example, in 1876 Yankee Baptist units were 62.0 percent Republican, and the Yorker Baptist towns gave the Republicans 48.8 percent of their collective vote. Yankee Methodist towns were 60.6 percent Republican, and Yorker Methodists 52.8 percent; Yankee Presbyterian-Congregational units were 57.1 percent Republican, and similar Yorker units 49.0 percent: The same types of differences in degree of Republicanism between Yankees and Yorkers also pertained in Pennsylvania, Michigan, and other parts of the Midwest.[71] Yet it is also important to remember that Yorker units were more Republican during the third party system than they had been during the second. However, this pro-Republican movement among the Yorkers left voting distance between them and Yankee units.

71. Parker, "Empire Stalemate," Tables IV-1, VI-1, VI-2; pp. 98, 195, 197; Petersen, "Reaction to a Heterogeneous Society," Tables 32, 34, 37, pp. 147, 150, 161; Formisano, *Birth of Mass Parties*, pp. 168–69; Kleppner, *Cross of Culture*, pp. 61–64. For comparisons with the second party system, see Benson, *Concept of Jacksonian Democracy*, pp. 177–79, 181–85.

Ethnocultural and religious values played different roles in shaping the partisanship of each of these groups. Yankee ethnocultural and religious values interacted and reinforced each other to produce higher levels of political cohesiveness than among other native groups. For the Yorkers, however, ethnocultural and religious values were in conflict. Earlier Yankee-Yorker battles had probably created Yorker ethnocultural-group consciousness in the first place. In defense of their values and life-styles, Yorkers had resisted the abrasive encroachments of Yankee "civilization." An integral part of the resulting Yorker political culture was its anti-Yankee voting, which did not fade quickly. However, as anti-Yankee Democrat became associated with support for Catholics, immorality, and treason (and these were not separable items in contemporary belief systems), Yorker party identification was cross-pressured. The ultimate resolution of that cross-pressure produced a swing of Yorker voters to the Republicans, the pattern of which was revealing. Not all Yorkers resolved the tension between ethnocultural and religious values through increased Republican voting, but that was chosen by the more pietistic of the Yorker religious subgroups. As a result, the partisan and pro-Democratic cohesiveness that had characterized Yorker voting during the second electoral era was lacking during the third, and the ethnocultural group split about evenly between the two major parties. The distinguishing element of that partisan division lay in the religious outlooks of the Yorker subgroups: the more pietistic the religious perspective, the more Republican its partisanship.

Southern-stock voters who lived beyond the physical (though probably not the psychological) confines of Dixie constituted yet another distinguishable native ethnocultural group. Here, however, considerable caution has to be exercised in delineating the group. It was not a simple matter of place of birth. Many of those who lived in the Midwest and who reported their place of birth in 1870 or 1880 (or their father's place of birth in the latter year) as one of the Confederate states were in reality descendants of eighteenth-century migrants to the South. Streams of population—Palatine German, English, Scots, Scotch-Irish, Quakers—had flowed, usually from Pennsylvania, through the Valley of Virginia into the South. In the nineteenth century some of these groups were seized by a renewed wanderlust. The incidence of that rekindled urge to migrate was not random. Groups whose values were antipathetic to slavery were impelled, sometimes by external physical means, to renew the trek. Those Quakers whose quiet pietism and relentless opposition to slavery had led their slave-owning neighbors to drive them from the Carolinas are the best known of these groups. Yet some of the Palatine Germans—especially those who were United Brethren, Evangelical

Association, or pietistic Lutheran—and even incipient New Light Presbyterians were also "invited" to leave. The historical experiences of these groups set them apart from their coreligionists who had not experienced southern "hospitality"; those experiences usually made them more intensely antislavery, antisouthern, and Republican. Yet those experiences did not make them part of a southern-stock ethnocultural grouping. In fact, their position outside of that grouping caused their enforced hegira.

If place of birth is not an adequate indicator, what can be used operationally to distinguish a southern-stock ethnocultural grouping? Two elements must be used in combination: place of birth *along with* religious connection. For example, there were enormous differences between the values and attitudes of northern and southern Methodists or northern and southern Baptists. Those differences did not *arise* from the fact that the churches had split into sectional branches prior to 1860. To the contrary—the cultural differences predated the religious divisions, and the latter occurred when it became no longer possible to mute, or contain, those conflicts between value systems.

Southern-stock religious groups—with the notable exception of the Christians, or Disciples of Christ—were strongly Democratic (see Table 5.8). The North-South, Union-Confederate conflicts that underlay Missouri politics had their counterpart in the political polarization of the state's religious groups. Similar conflicts had shaped the structure of Maryland's third party system, but they were not reflected in such stark religious-group polarities. The southern-stock religious groups there were sharply Democratic, and the southern Baptists were more strongly so than Missouri's group; but Methodists and Presbyterians who were connected with the northern church bodies were also slightly Democratic. The differences mirror reactions to sociopolitical contexts. Maryland's northern-stock Methodists were strongly Republican in the western counties of the state, where there were relatively few blacks. In those areas they behaved politically just like northern Methodists in Michigan or New York.[72] However, when these northern-connected Methodists lived in the southern or eastern-shore counties of the state, where there were large concentrations of blacks, they voted strongly antiblack and Democratic. In all likelihood this was also true of the state's northern Presbyterian voters. Missouri's northern-stock religious groups were largely clustered in the counties of the northern third and

72. See Table 5.4, and note that the native Methodist units in western Maryland were Methodist Episcopal–North. Most of Maryland's Methodist and Presbyterian churches had retained formal connections with the northern wings of their respective church organizations.

TABLE 5.8 *Northern vs. Southern Religious-Group Voting*

A. *Missouri Voting Districts: Percent Democratic of Total Vote*

	$\overline{M}$ % Dem 1880–88	(N)
Northern Methodist	39.0	(27)
Southern Meth and Bapt	72.3	(41)

B. *Mean 1876–88 Estimates: Percent Democratic of Two-Party Vote*

	Maryland	Missouri
Baptist - South	93.9	68.9
Meth - North	50.8	2.0
Meth - South	72.0	97.4
Presby - North	51.1	1.0
Presby - South	67.9	71.0

southwestern quadrants of the state, and most of the southern Baptists who supported the Republicans were concentrated in the latter area. In neither of those areas were there appreciable concentrations of blacks; so their religious-group values were not impacted by the perceived possibility of black-controlled local governments.

Of course, neither Maryland's nor Missouri's southern-stock religious groups voted as they did *because* of their religious values. Other factors and experiences shaped their partisanship. Yet given the well-known revivalistic orientations of those groups, one might have expected their religious values to lead them to the national party of morality and thus reduce their levels of Democratic voting support. One might expect that, however, only if one thoroughly misunderstood the pietism of southern-stock religious groups and ignored the historical evolution of their religious traditions. Nothing in their religious value systems would have inclined them to support the Republicans. They remained steadfast Democrats, then, because they were regionally self-conscious, anti-black, and unmoved by the specific tenor of Republican morality.

One final and large-sized southern-stock religious group, the Disciples of Christ, seems enigmatic. In Missouri they were Democrats, averaging about 60.5 percent of their vote for that party over the 1876–

88 elections. Yet in Iowa they were just as strongly Republican (62.9 percent) over the same time. And they were even more strongly Republican in Logan and Rock Island counties in Illinois (71.8 percent) and in Hendricks County, Indiana (73.6 percent). Yet in other central Indiana counties they appear to have been less strongly Republican (56.3 percent) than in Hendricks, and in parts of western Michigan and southern Ohio, they were Democrats.[73]

Only a part of the dilemma disappears if we admit the past tendency to exaggerate the southern-stock composition of the Disciples. Subgroups of the denomination were not southern at all. In New York, for instance, Yankee Disciple units voted 58.8 percent Republican. The cultural and attitudinal differences between northern-stock and southern-stock groups within the denomination underlay much of the internal discord that the Disciples experienced. In Indiana those differences may help account for the fact that the southern-born Disciples were 20.0 percentage points more Democratic than the northern-born members of the denomination. Yet even with that, the southern-born Disciples remained marginally Republican.[74] It may have been that the reputedly undenominational character of the group, its claims to practice a nineteenth-century version of ecumenism, coupled with its predominantly pietistic value system, made even large proportions of its southern-stock subgroup more malleable politically than other southern-stock religious groups. It may have been better able than the others, at least in the absence of factors that heightened ethnocultural-group identity, to close ranks with other pietists in the political pursuit of common moral goals.

Not just ethnocultural-group distinctions, but denominational heterogeneity, degree of pietism, the historical experiences of the group, and sociopolitical contexts were also considerations (and not entirely separable ones) relevant to native Protestant voting behavior. The Baptists, perhaps, represent the classic case of internal denominational variety. Even the narrower term *Regular Baptist (North)* did not designate a

73. For Logan, Rock Island, and Hendricks counties see Jensen, *Winning the Midwest*, pp. 60, 62. For the nine central Indiana counties, which include Hendricks, see Hammarberg, "The Indiana Voter," Table 4.7, p. 121; Table 2.1, p. 34, indicates that the subsample from Hendricks County represented 12.69 percent of the total N. For Michigan and Ohio see Kleppner, *Cross of Culture*, pp. 64–65.

74. The vote for the Yankee Disciple units is the 1876 mean; see Parker, "Empire Stalemate," Table VI-1, p. 87, and also see Table V-1, p. 155, which shows that all "Christian" units within the state had a Republican 1860–92 mean of 54.2 percent. For the Indiana data see Hammarberg, "The Indiana Voter," Table 4.13, p. 127; notice that although more Democratic than the northern-born, the southern-stock Disciples were still only 44.0 percent Democratic and 50.4 percent Republican. And for the roots of discord within the group, see David Edwin Harrell, Jr., "The Sectional Origins of the Churches of Christ," pp. 261–77, especially pp. 262–63.

grouping unified in its religious beliefs and practices. For example, in Illinois and Indiana many of the local congregations classified as Regular Baptist (North) had their spiritual and psychological roots in the older Anti-Mission tradition of the Baptist faith. They were severe predestinarians, strict Calvinists who opposed missions, evangelism, and those "damned Yankees" who supported both. Yet that same term, *Regular Baptist (North)*, in the New England states (and elsewhere) designated groupings that were largely pietistic. And the distinction was not just an East-West one, for even in the eastern states there were separate congregations of Anti-Mission Baptists whose distinctive identities and orientations were blurred by the label *Regular Baptist (North)*. If the political differences that existed between the two subtypes in central Indiana pertained elsewhere, then that blurring concealed attitudinal distinctions of great behavioral significance. The Regular Baptists (North) in central Indiana were strong Democrats (83.3 percent), and the Mission Baptists displayed a mild Republican cast.[75]

That does not mean that the most pietistic among the Baptists (or among the subgroups of the other denominations) should be assumed everywhere to have been strongly anti-Democratic *and to about the same degree*. To be sure, in northern states Baptists, Congregationalists, Methodists, and Presbyterians were Republican. The state-to-state (and even locality-to-locality) differences in the degrees of their Republicanism reflected distinctions in ethnocultural-group composition and intradenominational variations in religious beliefs, but they also provided evidence of the roles played by historical experiences and sociopolitical contexts in shaping partisanship, for native Protestant voters, no less than immigrant voters, had reached their partisan identifications "under circumstances directly encountered, given, and transmitted from the past." A single and simple paired comparison can illustrate the point. New Hampshire's Yankee Methodists were less Republican (by 13.3 percentage points) than Iowa's Methodists. The inner sense of "being a Methodist" did not differ from one place to the other. The

75. Hammarberg, "The Indiana Voter," Table 4.7, p. 121. The southern born among the Regular Baptists were 87.9 percent Democratic; see Table 4.12, p. 126. Among the Mission Baptists, 48.8 percent identified with the Republicans and 46.3 percent with the Democrats; if the Independents are excluded, the two-party division was 51.4 percent Republican. On the Anti-Mission Baptists in general, see William Warren Sweet, *Religion on the American Frontier, the Baptists, 1783–1830*, pp. 58–76; but Sweet incorrectly describes the movement as a frontier response. For the Anti-Mission character of some groups of Regular Baptists (North) in Illinois and Indiana, see Edward P. Brand, *Illinois Baptists*, pp. 68–69; on their role in one of Hammarberg's Indiana counties, see Jensen, *Winning the Midwest*, pp. 66–67, and Table 2, p. 60. For examples of eastern Anti-Missionism, see Norman H. Maring, *The Baptists in New Jersey*, pp. 132–40.

groups had different politically relevant experiences and lived in different sociopolitical contexts.

It was possible that the migration westward was not religiously random. Much of the Yankee westward movement was group migration, and was designed to establish outposts of Yankee civilization in the wilderness. Much of it, undertaken in response to pleas "to save the West" for Christianity, constituted the "Great Offensive" of the "evangelical united front" to save the area from the evils of infidelity and popery.[76] If the willingness to migrate was an indicator of religious commitment, then those who settled the West were likely among the more intensely pietistic of their religious groups. In any case, those Yankees who did migrate underwent a set of experiences that their compatriots in the East did not share. Early, frequently, and acrimoniously, they battled with hostile groups—German Lutherans, German and Irish Catholics, and upland southerners—who resisted the "uplifting" efforts of these Yankee civilizers. Those conflicts probably sharpened their sense of "being New England men," and their persistence throughout the nineteenth century underlay the group's political cohesiveness.

In New Hampshire, on the other hand, the "tradition of all the dead generations" continued to weigh on the present in a different way. Until passage of its 1819 Toleration Act, New Hampshire had continued its long-established practice of authorizing the towns to maintain Protestant ministers. The effect was to focus conflict over support for churches and ministries on the town meetings. Even the Toleration Act, which ostensibly ended the town support of an established religion, did not immediately terminate the strife. There were some towns with contracts covering the next twenty years or more; other towns ignored the legal change; and there were questions over the distribution of the trust funds for supporting the churches that had been accumulated over the years.[77] All of these battles kept memories of the struggle for disestablishment alive and politically salient. The Toleration Act had not separated church and state in New Hampshire; it had in fact implicitly supported the conception that New Hampshire was a Protestant commonwealth. It had left untouched the sentiment of Article VI of the 1784 Declaration of the Rights of the People of New Hampshire, which avowed that "morality and piety, rightly grounded on evangelical principles, will give the best and greatest security to Government."[78] And it did not touch the consti-

76. Formisano, *Birth of Mass Parties*, p. 103; Charles I. Foster, *An Errand of Mercy*. Lyman Beecher's *A Plea for the West* is only the best-known statement of what was a general theme among Yankee Protestants; see Bernard A. Weisberger, *They Gathered at the River*, pp. 10–12.

77. Charles B. Kinney, Jr., *Church and State*, pp. 107–13, 126.

78. Quoted in Kinney, *Church and State*, p. 123; also see William G. McLoughlin, *New England Dissent, 1630–1833*, 2:910.

tutional requirement that all public officials be professed Protestants. Both Article VI and the religious test for officeholding were focal points of continuing conflict. Resolutions to modify both were hotly debated during the 1851 constitutional convention and were rejected by the state's voters in the ensuing referendum. Abolition of the religious test was finally and narrowly approved in an 1876 referendum, but Article VI remained intact well beyond the end of the nineteenth century. And at the same time that they accepted the elimination of the religious test, 84.4 percent of New Hampshire's voters approved a constitutional amendment to prohibit the use of public funds for support "of the schools or institutions of any religious sect or denomination." That amendment, however, was not just another step on the road to church-state separation in New Hampshire. As its proponents were quick to underscore, it was aimed at Roman Catholics. It was designed there, as it had been in twenty-two other states, to prevent the appropriation of tax funds for the support of "sectarian" (i.e., Catholic) education or custodial institutions.[79]

Yet the religious test and the constitutional approbation of a "piety . . . grounded on evangelical principles" had not originally been Catholic-Protestant issues. They had been questions that pitted one set of native Protestants against another, for the term *Protestant*, as construed by the established order, had not included "dissenter groups"—e.g., Baptists, Methodists, Episcopalians. Those groups mobilized politically to resist that exclusion. These cultural conflicts had underlain the party oppositions of New Hampshire's second party system. Only as the state's Catholic population increased and, as it appeared to native Protestants, became more assertive were the old battles fought within a new context. The old rhetoric and symbols acquired new meanings. Although earlier they had resonated with the political characters of the dissenter groups, they came slowly to be perceived by those same groups as defensive of Catholic aggressions. The dissenter groups had never advocated a libertarian separation of church and state; they had demanded a "Christian" state. By that each meant a commonwealth in which its own brand of evangelicalism would prevail.[80] Whatever those particular species of evangelicalism, they shared a common enemy, popery.

This change in context, and consequent shift in belief-system linkages, did not occur quickly. There had been traces of antipopery and

79. Kinney, *Church and State*, pp. 129–39. On the 1850s see *The Whig Charge of Intolerance against the New Hampshire Democracy and Gen. Franklin Pierce*, especially the analysis of the vote by towns on the proposal to abolish the religious test for officeholding, pp. 13–14.
80. McLoughlin, *New England Dissent*, 2:1270.

nativism in New Hampshire in the 1850s, but the sharp Catholic and Lutheran vs. Yankee Protestant conflicts that raged in other places had not been replicated there. Indeed, the realignment of the 1850s was milder in New Hampshire than in the other New England states. Thus, well into the third electoral era New Hampshire's Yankee Methodists (and other Yankee religious groups) displayed stronger residual traces of the partisanship of the second electoral era than was the case in the Midwest. And the psychological distance between the political characters of the state's major parties was generally smaller than in the midwestern states. There the Democracy was not as early the party of immigrants and Catholics, as it was in Iowa, but it longer retained its moralist and Yankee tone.

Black voters, the final native Protestant group to be considered here, exhibited none of the sort of variations displayed by other native voting groups. As the data in Table 5.9 indicate, the black-white polarities that Kousser has described for Dixie pertained in Maryland as well.[81] Blacks were largely connected with Methodist and Baptist religious bodies, and some were Catholics in Maryland's southern counties. Their voting behavior, however, seems unrelated to religious-group distinctions. Racial self-consciousness probably led black voters everywhere to cast a majority of their ballots for the party of the Great Emancipator.

Political Confessionalism

By definition, variations and exceptions are departures from some regular pattern; they are notable and explicable only in light of the normal. Detailed overviews of group voting behavior (as all microanalytic explorations) are sometimes prone to concentrate too heavily on "the weave of small patterns" and too lightly on the larger framework from which these derived analytic meaning and significance.[82] It is useful here to view the broad contours of the distribution of partisan strength among groups. Table 5.10 presents the relevant data.[83]

81. Registration data for voting units are reported by race from 1884 through at least 1892 in *The Baltimore Sun Almanac*. For 1876–82 I have assumed that the racial character of the units was about what it was when first reported. Means of regression estimates for all voting units in the counties of the eastern shore and the southwestern shore show that over the 1884–88 sequence blacks voted 58.9 percent Republican. Estimates over the 1876–88 sequence in Missouri (by counties) indicate that blacks voted 55.4 percent Republican in that state; in New Jersey, estimates calculated by minor civil divisions put the Republican proportion at 63.7 percent.

82. The phrase is from Sam B. Warner, Jr., *Streetcar Suburbs*, Chapter 5. Warner's study is an excellent example of one that sensitively delineates the dynamic interplay between smaller and larger patterns.

83. For the basic steps involved in the calculation of the estimates for each group

TABLE 5.9   *Black vs. White Voting Behavior: Maryland, 1876–1888*

County	$\overline{M}$ % Dem, 1876–88			
	White Units *(N)*		Black Units *(N)*	
Anne Arundel	65.2	(2)	39.8	(2)
Dorchester	56.1	(2)	33.7	(2)
Prince Georges	62.6	(4)	39.1	(4)
Totals	61.6	(8)	38.7	(8)

The data point powerfully to the formative roles played by religious and ethnocultural values in shaping the partisan structure of the third electoral era. In that, they support a series of recently executed case studies that individually point in the same direction. Collectively these works have underscored the nexus between distinctive clusters of religious values and partisan selections. Although differing somewhat in terminology, they emphasize the distinction between a syndrome of religious values that can be labeled *pietistic* and one that can be designated *ritualistic*.[84]

Our own late twentieth-century perspectives sometimes make it difficult for us to comprehend the formative role that religion played in an earlier society. Yet even current data point to the continuing role of religious values, independent of class relations or status-group distinctions, in shaping nonreligious (secular) attitudes and behavior. For example, the pioneering voting behavior study in Erie County, Ohio, in 1940 discovered that the observed relation between religion and voting intention was not a spurious one that could be accounted for by mutual interrelations with economic status. Instead, on each level of socioeconomic status, "religious affiliation plays an important role in deter-

---

for each election year, see note 11. Using those calculations, I obtained the estimates in Table 5.10 through the following further steps: a) the 1876–88 longitudinal mean of the estimates for each group was calculated; b) each group was weighted by its size relative to the total size of that group in all of the states for which estimates were calculated; c) the weighted sum of the estimates for each group was calculated across all specified states; d) to mitigate impressions of spurious accuracy, each weighted sum was rounded off to the nearest figure evenly divisible by five. The estimates were calculated for Illinois, Iowa, Maryland, Massachusetts, Michigan, Minnesota, Missouri, New Hampshire, New Jersey, Ohio, Rhode Island, and Wisconsin.

84. Benson, *Concept of Jacksonian Democracy*, pp. 198–207; Formisano, *Birth of Mass Parties*, pp. 102–27; Jensen, *Winning the Midwest*, pp. 58–88; Kleppner, *Cross of Culture*, pp. 69–91.

TABLE 5.10   *The Nonsouthern Electoral Universe: Estimates of Partisan Strength by Ethnoreligious Groups*

	% Dem	% Repub
"Immigrants"		
Irish Catholics	80.0	20.0
All Catholics	70.0	30.0
Confessional German Lutherans	65.0	35.0
German Reformed	60.0	40.0
French Canadian Catholics	50.0	50.0
Less Confessional German Lutherans	45.0	55.0
English Canadians	40.0	60.0
British Stock	35.0	65.0
German Sectarians	30.0	70.0
Norwegian Lutherans*	20.0	80.0
Swedish Lutherans	15.0	85.0
Haugean Norwegians†	5.0	95.0
"Natives"		
Northern Stock		
Quakers	5.0	95.0
Free Will Baptists	20.0	80.0
Congregational	25.0	75.0
Methodists	25.0	75.0
Regular Baptists	35.0	65.0
Blacks	40.0	60.0
Presbyterians	40.0	60.0
Episcopalians	45.0	55.0
Southern Stock		
Disciples	50.0	50.0
Presbyterians	70.0	30.0
Baptists	75.0	25.0
Methodists	90.0	10.0

*Norwegian Church in America (Norwegian Synod).
†Hauges Synod and United Norwegian Church.

mining political affiliation.'' On each level Catholics were more strongly Democratic than non-Catholics.[85]

There was nothing uniquely ''in the air'' in 1940 to have elicited such a result.[86] However, voters never approach their current voting decision with blank minds but with ''internalized expectations'' in terms of which they have defined their political roles and patterned their political behavior.[87] These expectations are products of complex and historical social conditioning. Thus, what the time-specific Erie County study, and others, have captured and described is not some new phenomenon but the remaining traces of long-standing political-cultural distinctions among ethnoreligious groups. That such differences have persisted is inferentially powerful testimony both to their original intensity and to the fact that credible explanations of human behavior must be *historical* explanations.

To begin the task of explaining the relation between religion and partisanship in the late nineteenth century, we need to define some commonly used terms. Religion comprises a system of symbols, beliefs, values, and practices focused on questions of ultimate meaning—i.e., on matters pertaining to the nature, meaning, and purpose of reality. And religion can be distinguished from secular ideologies, which may sometimes function as religions, by its ontological first premise—the relation between the natural and the supernatural, the human and the sacred. Religion, then, involves a rationale for existence, a view of the world, a perspective for the organization of experience; it is a cognitive framework constituting a matrix within which the human actor perceives his environment.[88]

Religion is not the human actor's only perspective. Individuals par-

85. Paul F. Lazarsfeld, Bernard Berelson, and Hazel Gaudet, *The People's Choice*, pp. 21–25; the quotation is on p. 22. For some examples of other studies showing a persisting relation between religious outlooks and secular behavior, see J. Milton Yinger, *The Scientific Study of Religion*, pp. 408–56; Andrew M. Greeley, *The Denominational Society*; idem, *Ethnicity in the United States*; Gerhard Lenski, *The Religious Factor*; Lawrence L. Kersten, *The Lutheran Ethic*; W. Widick Schroeder and Victor Obenhaus, *Religion in American Culture*; Jeffrey K. Hadden, *The Gathering Storm in the Churches*; Merton P. Strommen et al., *A Study of Generations*; Michael Parenti, ''Political Values and Religious Cultures''; Milton Rokeach, ''Value Systems in Religion'' and ''Religious Values and Social Compassion.''

86. As there was, in contrast, in 1960, and which had the effect for some voters of increasing the salience of the Catholic-Protestant cleavage; see Philip E. Converse, ''Religion and Politics,'' pp. 96–124.

87. Thus, in part, has Harry Eckstein defined political culture in ''A Perspective on Comparative Politics,'' p. 26.

88. Charles Y. Glock and Rodney Stark, *Religion and Society in Tension* pp. 3–6; Tamotsu Shibutani, ''Reference Groups as Perspectives,'' pp. 103–13; Milton Rokeach, *The Open and Closed Mind*, pp. 31–70. Also see Philip E. Converse, ''The Nature of Belief Systems in Mass Publics,'' pp. 206–61.

ticipate in a variety of social worlds, and from each of these they derive a perspective.[89] Most of these are partial or fragmentary and provide "interpretation" for only limited segments of people's total experience. Since such perspectives do not overlap, they are highly compatible and can exist in nearly any combination. One can be at the same time, for instance, a carpenter, a parent, and a tennis player and can shift with facility from one perspective to the next because each is limited to a particular sphere of activity and all are mutually compatible. Yet some perspectives address themselves to reality in general, not to specific activities; they become all-embracing world views. Religion is precisely such a perspective. It penetrates all the partial and fragmentary social worlds in which men participate; it organizes and defines how they perceive and relate to society in general. Alternative perspectives of this order obviously cannot be accommodated; one *cannot* simultaneously be a Roman Catholic and a Methodist.[90]

What does it mean "to be" a Methodist, or a Catholic? What, in general, is the meaning of religious commitment? Religiosity is not a unitary attribute but a multidimensional quality. It involves a set of five core dimensions: belief, knowledge, practice, experience, and consequences. Accepting the truth of some set of supernatural tenets, knowing something about the tenets and traditions of the faith, practicing acts of worship and devotion, experiencing religious emotion, perceiving and acting out the secular consequences of the other dimensions constitute *being religious*. And *all* religious groups, or denominations in American parlance, expect their adherents to manifest their religiousness along *all* five dimensions. That, in fact, is the critical point. We cannot distinguish one religious denomination from another in terms of the presence or absence of any of these expectations, for all denominations expect and prescribe involvement on all five dimensions. What differs are the emphases that denominations give to each of these dimensions of involvement and the types of linkages that they make among them.[91]

89. The term is from Shibutani, "Reference Groups as Perspectives," pp. 108–10.

90. Glock and Stark, *Religion and Society in Tension*, pp. 5–6; Peter L. Berger, *Invitation to Sociology*, p. 51. In fact I do not assume a priori that religion penetrates all social worlds but only that it has the capacity for so doing. The extent of its penetration is precisely the proper object of empirical inquiry.

91. For contemporary research showing relatively low levels of interrelation among these dimensions, see Rodney Stark and Charles Y. Glock, *American Piety*, pp. 174–82; Kersten, *Lutheran Ethic*, pp. 52–53. Sociologists of religion now conceive them as relatively separate ways of being religious. We should not, however, assume that that was always the case; the contemporary data may again simply reflect residual traces of earlier and stronger levels of interconnection. Quite apart from that is the more important matter of the types of linkages among these dimensions prescribed by particular religious belief systems. My use of the term *denomination* in this paragraph and elsewhere is a convenient labeling device; it is not intended to exclude *sects*.

Although a mechanistic weighting is impossible, and probably inappropriate, we can delineate two broad categories of emphases and linkages. Faith, or belief, is at the heart of all theologies, and all religions are concerned with the salvation of souls. Yet the way that belief was conceived, and the linkages that were emphasized between it and the other dimensions of religiousness, produced quite distinct prescriptions for salvation. For one cluster of denominations—here broadly termed *pietist*—the emphasis flowed from belief to experience and consequences; and for another cluster—termed *ritualist* here—the emphasis was on belief as linked with knowledge and practice.

To that central question of religious concern—how is a man to save his soul?—the two sets of groups gave different responses. For the pietist the route to salvation did not lie in the rote learning of creedal confessions nor in regularized ritual practices; it lay in experiencing the change of heart that came from being "born again," from the direct confrontation between God and man. It was an active, emotional, and fervent faith, which emphasized the experience of individual regeneration. It was as well a personal, individualized faith—which emphasized the continuing effects of that change of heart, an "habitual disposition" to behave rightly. Right conduct to the pietist was not merely an option but a necessary consequence of salvation. To ritualists, on the other hand, salvation was imparted, not through individual emotional experience, but by the grace of God through the mediation of the church and the sacraments it administered. The road to salvation, then, lay in visible membership in the church and adherence to its creeds and practices. This was a passive, nonemotional perspective, which emphasized acceptance of the traditional confessions and practice of the ordained rituals. Ritualistic churches expected their adherents to lead good moral lives; they spoke of "good works" in the theological sense, but they never made the sort of axiomatic linkage between these and salvation that was the essence of the pietist's imperative to right behavior.[92]

This is not to claim that the varieties of religious experience were so uniform that they can simply be dichotomized into two mutually exclusive types. Pietistic and ritualistic perspectives should not be seen as "either-or" attributes but as qualities that were "more-or-less" characteristic of the respective denominations. Moreover, since the descrip-

---

92. Roman Catholic theology more so than German Lutheran spoke of "good works" in the context of guides to behavior, but Roman Catholic theology distinguished between *precepts* (those rules of life necessary to attain salvation) and *counsels* (those rules of life above the minimum necessary for salvation). The counsels most nearly accorded with the pietist conception of correct Christian behavior, but in Catholic theological terms (and in the German Lutheran, although less explicitly) these were meritorious to the individual only if done from a supernatural motive.

tions here should be construed as ideal types demarcating opposing poles of an underlying continuum or scale, it is useful to draw explicit attention to some critical distinctions within each of these perspectives. Although Quakers, Mennonites, northern Methodists, and southern Baptists were all pietists, surely the differences among some of them were of kind and not merely of degree. Consideration of some of these differences can help us distinguish several subtypes of pietists.

For example, Quakers differed from northern Methodists in two respects. First, there was a difference in style; the Quakers were not devotees of revivalistic religion. Second, Quakers had an ambivalent attitude toward involvement in the world. Quaker quietism, that distinctive blend of perfectionism and mysticism that recognized the Inner Light as the sole basis for religious authority, involved a principled rejection of worldly activities. Yet men who were in the world, especially as they became affluent, found it increasingly difficult not to be of the world. The discord and schism that beset the Friends from the 1820s had their roots in this persisting tension between religious ideals and worldly practices. By the second half of the nineteenth century, most Quaker groups, however uneasily, had resolved that tension in favor of involvement. Although their style of religious practice remained distinctly antirevivalist, in essentials of outlook they shared values with pietists who practiced revivals.[93]

The Quaker problem was not unique to that group. The religious perspectives of some other groups included a withdrawal from the affairs of a fallen and depraved world. For example, the Mennonites differed from other pietists not only in their antirevivalism and their ethnocultural backgrounds, but far more importantly in their radical rejection of the world. That withdrawal often took the extreme form of exhorting the faithful to avoid even such weak indicators of worldly involvement as voting. Far more interesting and important, however, were the much larger groups of southern pietists—Baptists, Methodists, and Presbyterians. These were all strongly committed to revivalism, and in all other external indicators they apparently resembled the northern pietistic groups. Yet the similarities were those of accidents, and the difference one of essence.

The southerners were a different brand and breed of pietist. Their religious perspectives did not include a central belief of the northern

93. Robert W. Doherty, *The Hicksite Separation.* That is, by the second half of the nineteenth century, the Quaker perspective shared by and large that that was essential to what I define as ''evangelical pietism'' although, of course, Quakers were not ''evangelicals'' in the popular sense of that term, i.e., they were not committed to revivalistic emotionalism.

evangelical pietists—the capacity of the individual through an act of will to save himself. In their view man was depraved, incapable of saving himself, and totally dependent on the mercy of God for forgiveness. Central to salvation was conversion, through which and at the moment of which man "passed from death unto life." Yet for the southern pietists the assurance of salvation lay in the experience of conversion itself and not (as with the evangelical pietists) in the good works that necessarily followed. To the southern pietist salvation was an act, a transaction between God and the individual, that was separable from the life that followed. Those who had been born again were expected to practice Christian morality, to behave rightly in their own lives, and to work and pray for the conversion of others. Yet these expectations were never connected with any imperative to transform their culture in the name of Christ. They did not deprecate the world about them; they simply saw religious life as something to be carried on in a separate compartment. Their focus was not the moral integration of the community but the salvation of the individual. And they perceived the church as having no responsibility at any level other than that of the individual. They were *salvationist pietists* whose religious outlook was dominated by the vertical man-to-God relation and who saw no direct line from these personally relevant vertical imperatives to their horizontal, man-to-man, relations.[94]

The behaviorally significant difference between evangelical pietists and salvationist pietists lay in the belief system linkages that they made between man-to-God and man-to-man (or man-to-world) relations. To the salvationists these were two distinct compartments; to the evangelicals they were one. The salvationists would save the world by saving individuals; the evangelicals went beyond that to a divinely commanded, and therefore *necessary*, commitment to sanctify the world about them. Evangelical pietists were as concerned as the salvationists with individual regeneration and with individual reform as a means of uplifting the community. However, unlike the salvationists this was not the totality of their concern, for the man who had saved himself by a free act of will had a correlative moral responsibility to "do good" for others. It was the divine commission of those who had been born again to see to it that all men behaved rightly; it was the mandate of the "saved" to "make holy" their society. This goal, the moral integration of the community, distinguished the evangelical from the salvationist pietist.

94. The label is from Samuel S. Hill, Jr., *Southern Churches in Crisis*, p. 96. Also see Dickson D. Bruce, Jr., *And They All Sang Hallelujah*; James D. Davidson, "Religious Belief as a Dependent Variable." For the persisting relevance of such orientations, see Lowell D. Streiker and Gerald S. Strober, *Religion and the New Majority*.

The evangelical perspective encompassed a necessary link between man-to-God and man-to-man relations, and the salvationists compartmentalized the two. The evangelical pietist's commitment to the creation of the moral society had direct behavioral and eventual partisan significance.[95]

A similar sort of distinction can be made within the ritualistic category, though in the nineteenth-century context it was less uniformly relevant to partisanship than among pietists. In their compartmentalization of the sacred from the secular, all ritualistic groups were closer to the perspective of the salvationist than to that of the evangelical pietist. Yet the German Lutheran perspective, especially that of the more confessional groups, differed somewhat from that of Catholics (even German Catholics).[96] For the German Lutheran the separation of the spiritual from the temporal was sharper and more complete than for the Catholic. The "two worlds" of the German Lutheran had no overlapping areas, and the church divorced itself from the contamination of the secular. The good Lutheran was expected to lead a proper Christian life, but this consequential dimension of religious commitment focused exclusively on individual moral conduct. German Lutheranism did not direct its practitioners to build the kingdom of God in this world, for any effort to externalize religion and translate its imperatives into secular rules and regulations only debased it. The Catholic perspective, on the other hand, saw no *necessary* separation between the church and the world. The Catholic historical tradition reinforced its theological outlook that the secular arm might serve as an instrument of God's will. Yet the Catholic perspective was far from the oneness of all human activity that was the hallmark of evangelical pietism, for Catholics sharply distinguished between those human acts that related to man's eternal welfare and those that did not. The former, summed in creedal belief and ritual practice, were essential to God's redeeming grace. With these supernatural rights no secular authority might interfere; neither might secular

95. The difference reflects something of the tension within "pietism" between moral order and moral freedom that William G. McLoughlin delineates in "Pietism and the American Character," pp. 163–67. For the continuing importance of these distinctions, compare the data for the southern Baptists with those for the northern Methodists and Congregationalists in Glock and Stark, *Religion and Society in Tension*, pp. 95–96, 98, 106. These measures correspond rather neatly with the items that compose Davidson's indices of Vertical and Horizontal Belief in "Religious Belief," p. 82.

96. On the Lutherans, see Kersten, *Lutheran Ethic*; on the Lutherans and Catholics, see Smith, "Church Affiliation as Social Differentiator"; Luther B. Otto, "Catholic and Lutheran Political Cultures in Medium-Sized Wisconsin Cities." The distinction was more salient to political attitudes in the later twentieth century, and that can be seen in the differences between German Lutherans and Catholics on welfare questions; see Smith, "Church Affiliation as Social Differentiator," pp. 90–91; Otto, "Catholic and Lutheran Political Cultures," pp. 92–94.

authority redefine and extend what God required of man for salvation.

For both pietists and ritualists these religiously rooted attitudes toward the secular had the most political relevance. Their conceptions and specific definitions of the nexus between the man-to-God relation, which is the essence of any religious involvement, and the man-to-man relation were integral parts of their political cultures. Their religious perspectives gave substance to their internalized expectations, defined their political roles, and eventually shaped their habituated partisan behavior.

No religious denomination was ever, of course, a pure ideal type; and the perspectives delineated here cut across denominational boundaries. Yet even so, the congruence between religious and political central tendencies was unmistakable: the immigrant and native religious denominations that shared most fully the perspective of evangelical pietism were also the most strongly Republican groups. And the religious groups that were either predominantly ritualistic or salvationist pietistic were the most heavily Democratic. The relations were neither monotonic nor wholly uniform; nor should we expect them to have been, for even the political species of human behavior is complex and not amenable to monistic explanation. Surely, for instance, there were ethnocultural factors at work, operating independently (as far as they can be separated) in some instances to reinforce the religious impulses and in others to cross-pressure them.

Moreover, religious perspectives had only *potential* sociopolitical relevance. Neither religious outlooks nor any other types of outlooks immanently transformed themselves into partisan identifications. They became salient only as their holders perceived consonance between those perspectives and party acts, speeches, and postures. And as party behaviors began to evoke common meanings for party officeholders and activists as well as for the mass adherents of religious groups, party began to represent those religious perspectives. As it did, identifying with a specific party then itself became part of those internalized expectations that composed the group's political culture. And nineteenth-century political parties became the uniquely American analogues of "political churches."

The psychological processes through which *party* became a positive reference symbol were not simple, but complex—not frozen in time, but extended over time. The way these processes had been initiated in the 1850s (and some earlier), reinforced in the 1860s, and reactivated in the early 1870s has already been indicated. However, it is useful here to delineate the nature of the linkages between political cultures and political parties more explicitly in order to draw attention to the types of public questions that reinforced and heightened their salience.

Critical to the dynamic was the evangelical pietist's conception of the community as a morally integrated whole. When all men had been born again, the moral oneness of the community would be assured and all would behave rightly because they shared a common religious outlook. "To spread holiness," to create that Christian commonwealth by bringing all men to Christ, was the divinely ordered duty of the "saved." Their mandate was "to transform the world into the image of Christ." Evangelization of the sinner was the most reliable means to that end, but more earthly techniques were also part of the arsenal of the regenerate. If those who were mired in sin and infidelity resisted Christ's love, then at least they had to be compelled to obey his command to behave rightly, for above all else God's law had to be obeyed; all men had to be holy. Sin was an obstacle to individual and social sanctification, to the transformation of the nation into "Immanuel's land—a mountain of holiness and a habitation of righteousness." And the duty of the government, no less than that of the individual, was to eradicate sin.[97]

To resort to using the compulsive power of government to purge their society of sin was to the evangelical pietist merely the natural consequence of "the divinity of our civil mission."[98] This legalized elimination of sin would not convert the sinner, but it would be pleasing to God in its own right and would at least create a moral atmosphere more conducive to the individual "change of heart" that ultimately would produce the morally integrated community.

The progression from conversion to social responsibility to legal coercion of the unregenerate was a divinely dictated one for religious enthusiasts who were convinced of the righteousness of their beliefs. They saw themselves engaged in an unceasing battle with the forces of satanic perdition. They never doubted the outcome of that battle, for

> right is right, since God is God,
> And right the day must win;
> To doubt would be disloyalty,
> To falter would be sin.

97. Respectively, the quotations are from *Minutes of the Ohio Annual Conference of the Methodist Episcopal Church, 1875*, p. 228; *Minutes of the Annual Meeting of the Maine Baptist Missionary Convention, 1890*, p. 13; *Minutes of the Rhode Island Congregational Conference, 1872*, p. 40. My reconstruction of the attitudes of religious groups is based on wide reading in conference journals, periodicals, and denominational histories. Unless otherwise indicated, only direct quotations will be footnoted, and the sequencing of references within each note will parallel that of the quoted phrases.

98. *Minutes of the Providence Annual Conference of the Methodist Episcopal Church, 1863*, p. 30.

And in such a conflict "an aggressive spirit should pervade all God's people." They should not fear to be vocal and "to bear onward the blood-stained banner of the Crucified." They should not tremble in quiet but should "believe in agitation! There is POWER in it! It keeps the question alive."[99] Nor should they be dissuaded by false arguments that they imperiled the liberties of others, for the freedom to transgress God's law was only subversive of true liberty: "Liberty is not license; *it is the right to do right.*"[100]

Evangelical pietists did not fail to be aggressive, nor to agitate, against what they perceived as the major sins of their day. Chief among these were Sabbath breaking, demon rum, and popery. Nor were they reticent to inform their practitioners of their moral responsibility to combat these forces of evil. It was "the duty of all Christian men to vote as they pray." And they were not contented with vague, unstructured entreaties but frequently made explicit reference to particular legislation, to the moral qualities of candidates, and—less often—to the moral value of an identified political party.[101] Their declarations offered concrete guides to voting behavior, not merely abstract prescriptions for morality, for these religious enthusiasts did not see two worlds, the sacred and the secular, but only one; and from this view of the essential

99. *Minutes of the Session of the New England Annual Conference of the Methodist Episcopal Church, 1879,* p. 22; *Minutes of the Annual Meeting of the General Association [of Congregational Churches] of New Hampshire, 1872,* p. 33; *Proceedings of the Anniversary of the Rhode Island Baptist State Convention, 1856,* p. 17; *Minutes of the Session of the New Hampshire Annual Conference of the Methodist Episcopal Church, 1877,* p. 17, emphasis in original.

100. *Minutes of the Session of the New England Southern Annual Conference of the Methodist Episcopal Church, 1883,* pp. 60–61, emphasis added. For similar views on the "true" nature of liberty, see *Minutes of the Annual Meeting of the General Association [of Congregational Churches] of New Hampshire, 1870,* p. 19; *Minutes of the Anniversary of the Philadelphia Baptist Association, 1873,* pp. 26–30; *Minutes of the Annual Session of the Wisconsin Baptist State Convention, 1876,* p. 35; and *Minutes of the Annual Meeting of the Maine Baptist Missionary Convention, 1891,* p. 14.

101. The quotation is in *Minutes of the Maine Annual Conference of the Methodist Episcopal Church, 1869,* p. 10. For some examples of the explicit linkages, see *Proceedings of the Maine Free Baptist Association at Their Annual Meeting, 1892,* p. 11; *Minutes of the Annual Meeting of the Maine Baptist Missionary Convention, 1885,* p. 10; *Minutes of the Anniversary of the Philadelphia Baptist Association, 1882,* p. 32; *Minutes of the Annual Meeting of the General Conference of the Congregational Churches in Maine, 1884,* pp. 11–12; *Minutes of the General Association [of Congregational Churches] of New York, 1866,* pp. 26–28; *Minutes of the National Council of the Congregational Churches of the United States of America: Annual Session, 1886,* pp. 47–53; *Minutes of the New Hampshire Annual Conference of the Methodist Episcopal Church, 1884,* p. 31; *Minutes of the Minnesota Annual Conference of the Methodist Episcopal Church, 1882,* pp. 53–55; *Minutes of the Annual Session of the Northwest Iowa Conference of the Methodist Episcopal Church, 1884,* pp. 32–33; *Minutes of the General Assembly of the United Presbyterian Church of North America, 1863,* p. 8; *Minutes of the General Assembly of the Cumberland Presbyterian Church, 1881,* p. 16.

oneness of all activity, they deduced that "in his relations to political parties . . . each man is as directly responsible to God as for any [other] acts." Party was no more to be conceived as a neutral agency than government itself; rather, "Christians should use party to do good. . . . [E]very Christian should . . . make his ballot effective for righteousness, and temperance, and humanity."[102]

Immigrant evangelical pietists, no less than natives, shared a religious commitment to use their votes to purge their world of sin. Ethnoculturally, these were a diverse lot—from Denmark, Germany, Holland, northern Ireland, Norway, Scotland, Sweden, and Wales. They brought with them their distinctive forms of religious practice, as well as their own languages. Some of those forms appeared distinctly liturgical to native evangelicals; and most of the immigrant pietists—the Swedish Lutherans, for example—eschewed ultra-emotional revival meetings and substituted the catechism for the "anxious bench."[103] If their pietism was less noisy than the native variety, it was no less enthusiastic and no less aimed at sanctifying their society. And native pietists recognized the consonance of belief systems. Ever critical of the immigration that brought with it "Lutheran formalism [or] Romish superstition," they welcomed immigrant evangelicals, and especially the Norwegians and Swedes. These they described as a "religious people," committed to "Bible doctrines," "morality," and "temperance"; they were immigrants who "make good Christians and good citizens."[104]

Despite the fact that these immigrant pietists maintained their own island communities, their own religious forms, and their own languages, native evangelicals perceived them as rapid assimilators: "They at once upon arrival become Americans."[105] The perception arose from the

102. *Minutes of the Session of the New England Annual Conference of the Methodist Episcopal Church, 1878*, p. 26; *Minutes of the National Council of the Congregational Churches of the United States of America: Annual Session, 1892*, pp. 90–91. For a similar view of evangelical pietists, see McLoughlin, "Pietism and American Character," pp. 168–69. It is important to notice the differences between the ways in which the denominations communicated norms in the nineteenth century compared with the twentieth century. Glock and Stark, *Religion and Society in Tension*, pp. 183–84, point out that twentieth-century churches use a level of abstraction that makes it unlikely that most practitioners would see the connections between their everyday activities and the denomination's moral guides. That was unmistakably *not* the nineteenth-century case.

103. Engberg, ed., *Centennial Essays*, p. 79. There were exceptions; the Haugean Norwegians, for instance, were strongly revivalistic.

104. *Annual Report of the American Baptist Home Mission Society, 1885*, p. 16; ibid., *1879*, p. 19; ibid., *1883*, p. 19; ibid., *1881*, p. 22. Also see *Annual Report of the American Home Missionary Society, 1886*, pp. 58–59; *Minutes of the Annual Meeting of the General Conference of the Congregational Churches in Maine, 1871*, p. 24; *Minutes of the Annual Session of the West Wisconsin Conference of the Methodist Episcopal Church, 1883*, pp. 259–60.

105. *Minutes of the Annual Session of the Wisconsin Baptist State Convention, 1891*, p. 29.

immigrant pietists' right behavior. They supported temperance; they opposed Catholics; they hallowed the Sabbath; and generally at least, they supported the public schools. This was not simply conformity to Anglo-Protestant norms but a reflection of their own internalized religious values.

Not all immigrant pietists defined *sin* to include the same specific acts as the native evangelicals. Probably the Norwegians and Swedes were consistently closest to the native pietist's conception of right behavior. These groups did not bring with them to the United States the highly formal and secularly detached state-church traditions of their native lands. Instead, they transplanted a Lutheranism that had earlier been shaped by pietistic revivals. Since many of the immigrants had themselves been pietistic dissenters within the state churches, the church organizations they created in America reflected that pietism. Their list of sinful acts was virtually identical with that of the native pietists; and as the natives, they saw it to be "the duty of the Christian voter" to cast his vote to eliminate sin, especially the sins of imbibing demon rum and desecrating the Sabbath.[106] Such voters rejected "the whiskey party" and supported instead the party of morality.[107]

Other immigrant pietists were more equivocal and less vehement in constructing their catalogues of sinful practices. Members of the Norwegian Church in America, Dutch Calvinists, and German Sectarians urged their members to practice temperance, and the latter two eventually called for legal prohibition; but none of them exhibited the same single-mindedness—"fanaticism," contemporaries termed it—as the other native and immigrant pietists.[108] And the pietistic German Lutheran groups, especially the constituent members of the General Synod, in many contexts were cross-pressured between their ethnocultural and religious identities. The latter led them to extremely strong positions on Sabbath keeping and temperance. Yet as Germans they were concerned with the maintenance of the German language—for its literary and cultural value and not for its connections with faith—and antagonistic to the anti-Christian secret societies. Secretiveness, as exemplified by the Know-Nothings-turned-Republican, and the nativist attack on the

106. A[lvin] D. Mattson, *Polity of the Augustana Lutheran Church*, pp. 433–35, quoting an 1880 Augustana Synod resolution. Also see Larson, *Log Book*, pp. 56–59.

107. Ibid., pp. 142–43; Arlow W. Andersen, *The Salt of the Earth*, p. 110.

108. The Norwegian Synod, or Norwegian Church in America, which was more ritualistic than the two Haugean groupings of Norwegians, had not condemned slavery as a sin in the 1850s; see O. N. Nelson, ed., *History of Scandinavians and Successful Scandinavians in the United States*, 1:184–86. Also see Parker, "Empire Stalemate," p. 205; United Brethren in Christ, Wisconsin Annual Conference Records, 1890, State Historical Society of Wisconsin, microfilm, reel 2, pp. 43–44.

German language in the 1850s apparently inhibited the swing of these groups to the party of morality.[109]

Ritualistic religious groups and salvationist pietists were no less religious than the evangelical pietists, but they were religious in a different way. These groups saw the world as sinful but did not see it as their role to purify it. Paramount was the salvation of the individual soul, not the spiritual transformation of the society. Personal redemption for the salvationist pietist resulted from miraculous spiritual regeneration, and for the ritualist it was the result of creedal conformity. There were also differences of degree within the ritualistic category.

Protestant Episcopalians were largely urban and associated with the fashionable life-style of the upper class. Theirs was not a religion of "mere sensation and emotion," and they frequently found it necessary to defend their "high church ritualism" from Congregationalists and other pietistic groups.[110] Partially, that was because Episcopalians avoided religious crusades. They called for a better Sabbath observance but explicitly denied the pietistic view and argued that Sabbath keeping was "not of divine creation." And they rejected the position of the "extreme prohibitionists" and supported high-license measures as a means of "practical temperance reform." To evangelical pietists the liquor traffic was sin, and any form of licensing that allowed sin to persist was "an agreement with hell and a covenant with death."[111]

Confessional German Lutherans emphasized faith and doctrinal orthodoxy. Men were saved by believing, by knowing, and by practicing the faith. The belief systems of these hyperritualists produced several dispositions that were relevant to politics. First, these people compartmentalized their lives into the sacred and the profane. Not everything that man did bore on his salvation, and consequently not everything had to be seen in moralistic terms. And God told man what was sinful. Thus, German Lutherans never defined as sin many of those actions that the

109. For the attitudes of these groups, see Harry J. Kreider, *History of the United Lutheran Synod of New York and New England*, p. 107; *Minutes of the Annual Meeting of the Evangelical Lutheran Synod of East Pennsylvania, 1853*, pp. 13–14; ibid., *1854*, p. 21; *Proceedings of the Annual Convention of the General Synod of the Evangelical Lutheran Church in the United States, 1853*, p. 47; ibid., *1855*, p. 11; ibid., *1864*, pp. 43–46; ibid., *1877*, pp. 44–47.

110. *The Churchman* (New York), 2 July 1892, 1 July 1876; also see *Journal of the Proceedings of the Annual Convention of the [Protestant Episcopal] Diocese of Massachusetts, 1878*, p. 49. Most Episcopalians, of course, were not upper class. The image delineated here is that that the more pietistic groups often used to criticize the Episcopalians.

111. *The Churchman* (New York), 3 July 1892; Rt. Rev. W. E. Armitage, "The German Sunday," pp. 62–71; *The Church Times* (Delavan, Wis.), April 1896; *The Churchman*, 20 March, 30 January 1886; *Minutes of the Session of the New England Southern Annual Conference of the Methodist Episcopal Church, 1886*, p. 61.

pietists had come to see as nonnegotiable—e.g., drinking and Sabbath breaking. Moreover, they bitterly resisted the efforts by "self-appointed or false prophets" to extend the list of sinful activities, to "make sin what God made not sin."[112] Second, confessional German Lutherans sought an institutionalized means to transmit their faith to succeeding generations. Since allowing children to receive "instruction in schools without religion or with a false religion" was not biblical, they committed themselves to a system of parochial schools. In this way they sought to preserve and transmit their faith to their children; their parochial schools became "the chief means for our preservation and our continuation."[113] Third, they sought to preserve and continue, not just Lutheranism, but the German language as well. And to confessional German Lutherans the two were inseparable. To them the language question was not simply a cultural and literary matter but one integrally and inextricably linked with their faith.[114]

Catholic theological perspectives, more than confessional German Lutheran, had room for the preaching of social ethics. Yet Catholics never became reformers in the evangelical sense, because the two groups held different definitions of sin. To the Catholic, drinking in itself was no sin, although excessive drinking might be. It might be desirable to encourage individuals to abstain, but it was surely no violation of God's law should they fail to do so. To the evangelical pietist drinking was sinful; God demanded the liquor traffic be destroyed. Not even those Irish prelates who consciously conformed to Anglo-Protestant norms and worked to "Americanize" the Catholic immigrant went that far. They encouraged temperate behavior and worked with the Catholic Total Abstinence Union but were always careful to draw the line between "legal restriction of the liquor traffic" and total prohibition. Try as they otherwise might to behave as respectable Anglo-Protestants, they never jumped aboard prohibition's water wagon.[115]

One behavioral act that Catholics did come to regard as sinful was failing to provide their children with a Catholic education. The original commitment by Catholics to their own school system in America was

112. C. F. W. Walther to Rev. E. J. M. Wege, 29 July 1844, describing the Methodists, in Carl S. Meyer, ed., *Letters of C. F. W. Walther*, pp. 63–69; Heinrich H. Maurer, "Studies in the Sociology of Religion," pp. 55–57.

113. C. F. W. Walther to Rev. E. W. Kaehler, 14 April 1876, in Meyer, ed., *Letters of Walther*, pp. 116–17; Walther in *Der Lutheraner*, 15 February 1873, in ibid., p. 22. Also see Stellhorn, *Schools of the Lutheran Church*.

114. Fishman, *Language Loyalty*, p. 227.

115. The quotation is from an 1884 resolution of the Catholic Total Abstinence Union, Joseph C. Gibbs, *History of the Catholic Total Abstinence Union of America*, p. 7. And on the conformity of the C.T.A.U. to "the point of view of respectable, Protestant America," see Joan Bland, *The Hibernian Crusade*, p. 267.

less biblical than that of the German Lutherans. It was largely a pragmatic reaction conditioned by the perception that the public schools were
"Protestant" and anti-Catholic. To preserve and perpetuate their faith,
Catholics created their own school system. For non–English-speaking
Catholics the parochial schools became as well agencies for maintaining the language. Yet whether connected with the preservation of faith
through language or not, Catholics regarded the correct education of
their children as one of those "supernatural" rights with which earthly
governments might not interfere.

Salvationist pietists were intensely antiritualistic, puritanical, and
anti-Catholic. They urged on their practitioners a severe and relatively
precise code of personal morality. That code included Sabbath observance and temperance, but it did not require the salvationist to seek out
and act on the connection between his morality and his politics. These
were separate spheres of life. Eventually, of course, these groups were
involved in the societywide drive to dry up the nation, but they did not
accept legal prohibition as quickly and unambiguously as their northern
counterparts. The Southern Baptist Convention passed no memorial or
petition on prohibition until after 1900; and only in the late 1880s did
the southern Methodists declare the manufacture and sale of intoxicants
an act of immorality.[116] Denominations whose belief systems set the
secular apart from the supernatural and that saw no necessary connection
between man's actions in the two spheres came only haltingly, equivocally, and with considerable internal discord to "political" pressure-
group activity.

Late nineteenth-century American parties can meaningfully be
thought of as political churches. They were that, not in the sense of
European mass parties of the left or the religious-clientele parties in pre-
1933 Germany—parties that involved an all-embracing world view as
well as a total, invariant, and lifelong commitment—but they embodied
a typically American form of political confessionalism.[117] Differences
in religious outlooks underlay contending definitions of what was, or
was not, sin; and religiously rooted differences in conceptions of the
nature of man and of the world produced incompatible views of the relations of society and politics. At stake were not simply distinctions

116. Rufus B. Spain, *At Ease in Zion*, p. 188; Hunter Dickinson Farish, *The
Circuit Rider Dismounts*, pp. 312–14. On the Southern Presbyterians whose General
Assembly as late as 1897 rejected explicit resolutions linking temperance and political
action, see Ernest Trice Thompson, *Presbyterians in the South*, 3:225–49. Also see
George D. Kelsey, *Social Ethics among Southern Baptists, 1917–1969*, pp. 131–51.

117. William N. McPhee and Jack Ferguson, "Political Immunization," pp. 155–
79; Walter Dean Burnham, "Political Immunization and Political Confessionalism,"
pp. 1–30; Walter Dean Burnham, "Theory and Voting Research," pp. 1021–22.

between life-styles, but ones integrally connected with irreconcilable religious values. That these differences structured party oppositions meant that parties became the secular analogues of churches. Each party represented, not a single denomination, but a loosely structured set of denominations sharing a collective central tendency. As Republican to evangelical pietists symbolized right behavior and a socially transforming morality, Democracy meant to ritualists right belief and a defense of laissez faire hedonism. This dispositional consonance between religious outlooks and party characters produced a late nineteenth-century electoral universe characterized by extraordinarily high levels of voter participation and by long-term stability.

6

The Politics of Cultural Pluralism: Demographic Change and Partisan Response

Unsaved millions of foreigners are coming to our shores, forcing upon us one of the greatest missionary questions of modern evangelism, *viz.*:—shall America be unamericanized, or shall the millions of our North American citizens be brought into sympathy with our Christian institutions through the church of Jesus Christ?

Minutes of the Maine Annual Conference of the Methodist Episcopal Church, 1891

The continuing influx of the "unsaved" posed a missionary challenge, not only to religious groups, but to political parties as well. The size, sources, and skewed geographic settlement of the immigration impacted the ongoing process of party building. It combined with differential rates of growth among the subgroups of the nation's pre-1860 inhabitants to change the demographic quality of the electorate. And as the character of the electorate changed, clientele-conscious parties were forced to respond to new demographic realities.

Demographic Change

Virtually every dimension of the nation's demographic structure changed materially over the second half of the nineteenth century. Between 1860 and 1890 total population increased from thirty-one million to sixty-one million, an increase of 98.5 percent; twenty-three million of that increase, or 77.4 percentage points of the total, occurred between 1870 and 1890.[1] And as the total population increased, its sectional distribu-

1. The rate of increase from 1870 to 1890 was 62.4 percent. The data on population used here and throughout this chapter have been taken from the relevant volumes of the decennial census of the United States. Where estimates have been calculated, unless

tion changed. The population of each geographic section was greater in 1890 than it had been in 1860. Yet the proportion of the nation's total population living in the South, New England, the Middle Atlantic states, and East North Central states declined, and that in the West and West North Central states increased. Population growth west of the Mississippi produced the organization and admission of seven new states between 1876 and 1892: Colorado was admitted to the Union on 1 August 1876, and Idaho, Montana, North and South Dakota, Washington, and Wyoming were given statehood between 1889 and 1892. As the country's population shifted westward, it also shifted from rural to urban places and occupations. Between 1870 and 1890 the proportion of the nation's population living in urban places increased from 25.7 percent to 35.1 percent, and the proportion of the work force engaged in agriculture declined from 51.4 percent to 40.6 percent.

None of these demographic characteristics, nor their rates of change, were spread evenly across the country. The New England and Middle Atlantic areas were more heavily urban and industrial than the other sections, and the South and West North Central states remained in 1890, as they had been in 1860 and 1870, the least urban and industrial. However, the 1870 and 1890 rates of both urbanization and growth of the proportion of the work force engaged in nonagricultural activities were greater for the Western and East North Central regions than for either of the older urban-industrial areas of the country.[2]

Natural population increase and continuing immigration each contributed to late nineteenth-century population growth. For present purposes it is not necessary to disentangle the relative contributions of each of these factors; it is adequate to examine the resulting structures of population at specific times.[3] And it is useful to begin by inquiring more fully into the flow of immigration, especially into its timing and geographic sources. The data in Table 6.1 offer the necessary overview.[4]

Of the total 1846–92 immigrants 69.6 percent came after the Civil War. Except for the Irish the size of the postwar immigration from each

otherwise indicated, they involved straightforward arithmetic computations using the raw data reported therein.

2. For the data on the labor force, see Harvey S. Perloff et al., *Regions, Resources, and Economic Growth*, Appendix Table A-6, p. 632; and for the data on people living in incorporated places of 2,500 or more, see U.S., Bureau of the Census, *1970 Census of Population*, Table 18, pp. 1-62–1-71.

3. For an assessment of the relative contributions of each, see Simon Kuznets and Dorothy Swaine Thomas, gen. eds., *Population Redistribution and Economic Growth, United States, 1870–1950*, vol. 3, *Demographic Analyses and Interpretations*, by Hope T. Eldridge and Dorothy Swaine Thomas, pp. 32–130 and Appendix Tables A 1.1–A 1.33, pp. 240–89.

4. I have reaggregated these data from the yearly reports in U.S., Bureau of the Census, *Historical Statistics of the United States, Colonial Times to 1957*, pp. 56–59.

TABLE 6.1   *Characteristics of Immigration, 1846–1892*

	% of Total 1846–92 Group Immigration by Time Periods		% of Total Immigrants by Country of Origin	
	1846–60	1866–92	1846–60	1866–92
Britain	22.9	67.8	15.9	17.0
Ireland	47.9	45.7	38.8	13.4
Germany	28.6	66.1	33.0	27.6
Scandinavia	2.8	95.6	0.8	10.6
Canada	8.7	87.8	2.3	8.3
Total	25.2	69.6	90.8	76.9

of the designated countries was considerably larger than its prewar influx. Although that was most dramatically the case with Canadian and Scandinavian immigration, postwar German immigration was more than twice as large as its prewar size, and British immigration nearly three times greater. The changes in the geographic sources of immigration stand out more clearly when we examine the percentage of the total immigrants supplied by each country during each of the two periods.

We can begin with the least obvious fact, which these data only imply: the beginnings of the post-1900 floodtide of immigration from southern and central Europe. Prior to 1860, 95.6 percent of the total immigration had been from northwestern Europe and Canada; between 1866 and 1892 that proportion fell to 81.0 percent, and the proportion from southern and central Europe (excluding Germany) rose from 0.5 percent to 17.7 percent. Between 1866 and 1892 this "new" immigration amounted to only 1.6 million people, compared to 8.6 million from northwestern Europe and Canada. Most of this new immigration came at the very end of the period; 65.6 percent arrived between 1886 and 1892, and fully 29.6 percent in the final two years of the third electoral era. Hence, it was likely that in most locales these recent arrivals were not yet socialized into active political participation. Whether that was invariably the case or not, however, the other shifts in the sources of immigration are of primary concern here because they involved larger groups.

The most obvious of these was the sharp decline (25.4 percentage points) in the relative size of Irish immigration during the two time segments. And that decline reflected a drop in the absolute number of Irish immigrants. Partially offsetting that was an increase in the relative contribution of Canadian and Scandinavian immigration—an increase from a combined 3.1 percent to 18.9 percent of the total immigration. Although the relative size of the German immigration fell off by 5.4 percentage points, that reflected a different set of conditions than the Irish case. It resulted, not from a decline in the absolute number of German immigrants, but from the fact that total immigration increased at an even faster rate than German immigration.[5]

These prewar-to-postwar shifts in the geographic sources of immigration seem minor when compared to the change that became starkly apparent after 1900. Yet even such comparatively mild changes were of considerable partisan significance. The drop in Irish immigration meant fewer potential Democratic recruits, and the increase in Scandinavian, English Canadian, and British immigration created reservoirs of new Republican voting strength. The French Canadian immigrants, especially in New England, were the Catholic group least likely to offer disproportionate Democratic voting support. Counterbalancing these trends somewhat was a shift within the German stream of immigration: postwar German immigration was about 6.0 percentage points more heavily Catholic than it had been prior to 1860.[6] If we lay aside for the moment the large postwar non-Catholic German immigration (which was disproportionately Lutheran), it appears that these changes in the geographic sources of immigration were marginally beneficial to the Republicans.

Continued immigration was only one source of new population and new voters; natural population increase was another. By the 1870s and 1880s the sons of the prewar immigrants were coming of voting age. Their movement into the electorate was significant due to the nature of the prewar immigration and to the way in which their attainment of civil maturity changed the structure of the voting population. The prewar stream of immigration had come mainly from Ireland and Germany. It had been heavily Catholic and confessional Lutheran. Those groups probably composed well over 55.0 percent of the total 1841–60 immigration. And the Catholic component of that immigration apparently implanted a fertility time bomb that exploded by the 1870s. That decade marked an immensely significant turning point in the sources of the continuing growth of the country's Catholic population. Catholic immigration continued after 1870, of course; in fact, it was numerically

5. Irish immigration from 1846 to 1860 totaled 1.5 million, compared to 1.4 million between 1866 and 1892; German immigration during each of the two time segments was 1.2 million and 2.9 million, respectively.
6. The raw data underlying the comparisons are in Gerald Shaughnessy, *Has the Immigrant Kept the Faith?* pp. 123, 131, 140, 149, 159, 165, 169.

greater in the decade between 1881 and 1890 than in any other decade between 1831 and 1900. Yet despite that, and in sharp contrast to the pre-1870 era, most of the total increase in the size of the Catholic population after 1870 was due to natural increase in the population. From 1841 through 1870 only 34.1 percent of the increased size of the Catholic population was attributable to natural increase in population, and 63.5 percent to immigration; but from 1871 through 1890 natural increase in population contributed 54.3 percent and immigration only 42.0 percent of the total net increase.[7]

The rate of natural increase in population among Catholics probably outstripped that of the confessional Lutherans, but both groups continued to grow in size and their adult males continued to move into the electorate. Although the data available do not make it feasible to sort out the distinguishable voting components of each politically significant subgroup, we can begin to assess the impact of these types of trends by examining the nativity structure of the potential electorate (see Table 6.2).[8]

Not only did the potential electorate during these two decades expand at a faster rate than the population as a whole—81.5 percent compared to 62.4 percent—but that growth was accompanied by a compositional change of great importance. The balance between foreign and native-stock white voters outside of the South shifted dramatically. A 12.3 percentage point difference in 1870 was reduced to a slim 2.1 percentage point native-stock lead by 1890. And in the heavily populated Middle Atlantic and East North Central regions, which together accounted for 44.4 percent of the country's 1890 potential electorate, the foreign-stock voters held a minuscule margin. However, this changed balance was not simply the result of a large increase in the number and proportion of foreign-born voters. That component of the electorate did

7. Shaughnessy, *Has the Immigrant Kept the Faith?* data on pp. 134, 145, 153, 161, 166, 172. In both time segments the remaining proportion was due to conversions—2.3 percent from 1841 to 1870 and 3.5 percent from 1871 to 1890. In his discussions of the sources of Catholic population growth (but not in his tabular presentations), Shaughnessy includes conversions with natural increase in population. The estimate that over 55.0 percent of the prewar immigration was Catholic and confessional Lutheran is also based on the data in Shaughnessy. It is a quite conservative estimate since it assumes that 10.0 percent of the German immigration was neither Catholic nor Lutheran.

8. The nativity breakdown of males of voting age is reported in U.S., Census Office, *Compendium of the Eleventh Census: 1890*, pt. 1, Table 25, p. 764. For 1870 it has been estimated from the data on age, sex, and nativity reported in U.S., Census Office, Ninth Census, *Statistics of the Population of the United States*. Excluding black males twenty-one and over in both years does not materially change the percentages, since blacks were 10.9 percent of the potential voting group in 1870 and 10.2 percent in 1890.

TABLE 6.2 *Nativity Structure of the White Electorate, 1870 and 1890*

	1870		1890	
	Foreign Stock	Native Stock	Foreign Stock	Native Stock
New England	34.4	65.5	45.2	54.7
Midatlantic	46.9	53.0	51.8	48.1
East N. Cent.	42.9	56.9	49.0	50.9
West N. Cent.	42.7	57.2	46.1	53.8
West	61.7	38.2	50.7	49.2
Total, 5 Regions	43.8	56.1	48.9	51.0
Midatl. & E.N.C.	44.9	55.0	50.4	49.5
Total U.S.	37.0	62.9	42.0	57.9

grow at a rate of 3.6 percent per year over the two decades, but in 1890 it constituted only 33.2 percent of the total white electorate compared to about 34.7 percent in 1870. The most dramatic growth, at a rate of 10.5 percent per year, was among the native-born of foreign-born parents, who by 1890 made up 15.7 percent of the white electorate of the five regions.[9] Immigration combined with natural growth of the population to produce an 1890 white, nonsouthern electorate that was considerably more "foreign" than it had been twenty years earlier.

When native pietistic religious groups lamented the arrival of those "unsaved millions" and the consequent growth of an "immigrant voting power" that had "wrought a radical change upon many of the sections of the United States," they referred implicitly to this changed nativity structure of the electorate.[10] They were never reluctant, however, to identify explicitly the referents of their growing apprehension. The increased number and voting power of those who brought with them "infidelity," who were without the "pure gospel," who were "formalists in religion," who were Catholics and Lutherans aroused their fears

9. By 1890 only 9.3 percent of the fourteen-state southern electorate was of foreign stock, and 31.7 percent was black.

10. For the quotations and more extensive exposition of the complaints, see *Annual Report of the American Baptist Home Mission Society, 1880*, pp. 23–25; ibid., *1892*, p. 63.

and reenergized their commitment.[11] And their perception of a changing religious balance among the population was not without factual basis.

Estimating the distribution of the population by religious groups always involves making use of soft data. No dimension of the nation's demography has been as underreported and underresearched as its religious structure. Federal census publications, for example, did not begin reporting the number of members or communicants until 1890; prior to that they had enumerated only the number of sittings reported by each denomination. We can estimate the pre-1890 membership by making use of a wide range of denominational reports and histories and filling in the gaps by assuming that the 1890 ratio of members to sittings was a reasonable approximation of the earlier ratio. However, formal membership is a very restrictive measure, especially for those denominations that required a conversion experience. It was generally true in the nineteenth century, as it is even now, that the number of people who had a preference for a religious denomination, or a sense of affiliation, was greater than the number who were formally members. That accounts for the fact, often remarked on in the reports and journals of the religious conferences, that church attendance was considerably greater than formal membership. The problem, then, is to estimate the number who affiliated with each denomination, rather than merely those who were formally members. Fortunately, that was a problem to which nineteenth-century religious denominations were alerted and to which they gave some statistical attention. For example, in 1886 Vermont's Congregationalists undertook a detailed inquiry into the religious condition of some forty-four towns in five counties of that state.[12] One useful by-product of that inquiry was a tabular report summarizing for each denomination both the size of its membership and that of its average church attendance. We can use the ratios derived from that report to estimate for all the New England states the number who affiliated with each denomination. Beyond that region, and because they square well with other but more limited denominational studies, I have applied the ratios derived by Richard Jensen from his analysis of the 1895 Iowa census of religious preferences.[13]

Ultimately, however, the concern is not with the size of the religious

11. *Minutes of the Central Ohio Annual Conference of the Methodist Episcopal Church, 1892*, pp. 81–82; *Minutes of the Session of the New England Southern Annual Conference of the Methodist Episcopal Church, 1881*, p. 39; *Annual Report of the American Baptist Home Mission Society, 1888*, p. 12; ibid., *1885*, p. 16.

12. For a discussion of the coverage and the relevant statistical data, see *Supplement to the Minutes of the Ninety-First Annual Meeting of the General Convention of the Congregational Ministers and Churches of Vermont, 1886*, pp. 1–3.

13. Richard J. Jensen, *The Winning of the Midwest*, pp. 85–87.

population by separate denominations but with a broader categorization distinguishing between pietists and ritualists. To accomplish that, we need to estimate the proportion of each group that might be so categorized. Admittedly, that involves hazarding a set of guesses, informed by inquiry into each denomination's historical evolution. Generally, Jensen's estimates of the relative strength of the two factions within each denomination provide an acceptable guide. And with two exceptions I have utilized his estimates. In the East there was probably a lower proportion of ritualists among the Presbyterians and a slightly higher proportion among the German Reformed than was the case in the Midwest. Therefore, my calculations assume that 35.0 percent of the Presbyterians and 60.0 percent of the Reformed in those geographical areas can be classified as ritualists.[14] The results of these calculations are presented in Table 6.3.

TABLE 6.3   *Estimated Distribution of Religious Groups, 1860 and 1890*

	1860			1890		
	Pietist	Non-professed	Ritualist	Pietist	Non-professed	Ritualist
New England	57.2	15.5	27.1	38.9	24.8	36.1
Midatlantic	47.3	19.1	33.4	34.0	24.7	41.2
East N. Cent.	50.1	20.8	28.9	41.7	27.0	32.1
West N. Cent.	50.0	30.7	19.2	44.1	23.9	30.8
West	40.8	27.6	31.5	44.9	21.0	34.0
Total, 5 Regions	50.2	20.4	29.3	40.0	24.5	35.4

As the data make clear, the pietists' frequently proclaimed fears were well grounded. Their relative strength had declined, from a lead of 20.9 percentage points in 1860 to one of 4.6 percentage points by 1890. The size of the group had increased at a rate of 2.4 percent per year over the three decades, and some subgroups had done even better—the Presbyterians and Methodists had grown at rates of 5.3 percent and 3.6 percent per year. Yet the growth of the pietistic group had been surpassed

14. Jensen, *Winning the Midwest*, p. 87. For the Midwest Jensen estimates that 50.0 percent of both the Presbyterians and Reformed were ritualists. In any event, as Jensen points out, variation of the proportions in the doubtful cases makes only an insignificant difference in the general pattern.

by the ritualistic rate of 5.3 percent per year; that, in turn, had been spearheaded by a Catholic annual rate of growth of 6.2 percent. Not only was the country's population becoming more "foreign," it was increasingly dominated by those who had yet to be brought "under the transforming power of the gospel."[15]

What was true of the country at large was even more so of its cities. Anticity attitudes have been powerful and persistent in American society. One critical source of those attitudes in the nineteenth century lay in the perception by native pietists that "the city is the stronghold of the enemy."[16] As seen through their mental eyes, cities had become cesspools of crime, vice, and unspeakable perdition. They had become "a serious menace to our civilization" because in them were "focalized" the triune dangers that imperiled it: immigrants, Romanists, and saloons.[17]

The pietistic demographic perception was wholly accurate: urban populations were disproportionately foreign stock and nonpietistic (see Table 6.4).[18] Moreover, their political role was expanding. By 1890 these twenty-five cities held 19.6 percent of the nonsouthern electorate; and perhaps more ominously, between 1870 and 1890 the size of this urban electorate had increased by 5.6 percent per year, compared to an annual rate of 3.8 percent for the nonurban electorate. Growth of this magnitude, coupled with a sense of its political implications, impressed contemporaries and led many of them to refocus and express antiimmigrant and especially anti-Catholic attitudes as more general antiurban values, for in the city immigrants settled and became "the balance of

15. *Minutes of the Annual Meeting of the General Conference of the Congregational Churches in Maine, 1873*, p. 117. The Presbyterian and Methodist growth rates were calculated from data in Bureau of the Census, *Historical Statistics*, pp. 228–29; and the Catholic rate from data in Shaughnessy, *Has the Immigrant Kept the Faith?* pp. 153, 161, 166. For other studies that point to analogous changes in specified states, see Paul Kleppner, *The Cross of Culture*, pp. 96–100; Samuel T. McSeveney, *The Politics of Depression*, pp. 8–10; Albert Charles Edward Parker, "Empire Stalemate," pp. 67–75.

16. *Minutes of the Central Ohio Annual Conference of the Methodist Episcopal Church, 1895*, p. 629; also see Anselm L. Strauss, *Images of the American City*, pp. 175–83.

17. The quotation and sentiment is from Josiah Strong, *Our Country*, pp. 172–73; also see John Todd, *The Moral Influence, Dangers and Duties, Connected with Great Cities*, pp. 19, 61–68, 209.

18. For the 1860 nativity data, see U.S., Census Office, Eighth Census, *Population of the United States in 1860*, pp. xxxi–xxxii; the 1890 nativity data are in U.S., Census Office, *Eleventh Census: 1890. Report on Population of the United States*, pt. 1, cxxvi–cxxvii, Table 19, pp. 451–85. For the religious data see U.S., Census Office, *Report on Statistics of the Churches in the United States at the Eleventh Census: 1890*, pp. 94–115.

TABLE 6.4   *Urban Population Characteristics*

Population Size (*N*)	% Foreign		% Religious Group, 1890		
	1860	1890	Pietist	Nonprofes	Ritualist
Over 500,000 (4)	40.3	72.8	20.1	26.5	52.1
100,000 to 500,000 (21)	40.5	68.1	25.7	21.5	52.7
Both Categories	40.4	70.7	22.7	24.8	52.4
U.S. Noncity*	14.5	39.4	41.6	24.9	33.4

*Excludes the 14 states in the Confederate and border areas.

power in politics, or . . . the actual majority." And this accounted for "the growing political power of rum and Romanism."[19]

Nineteenth-century political parties had to deal with this regionally and locationally skewed distribution of the population and with changes in that distribution over time. That required developing electoral coalitions that differed from one region to another, and it required maintaining psychological rapport with long-standing support groups while integrating new elements of the population. These were not simple tasks under any circumstances, especially when irreconcilable conflict existed among electorally significant subgroups. How to bridge, mute, or rechannel that conflict became a critical element of party strategies, especially Republican strategy, during the equilibrium phase of the third party system.

Partisan Response

The overriding goal of a political party is to elect its candidates to office. Attaining whatever other goals it may have, whether distribution of patronage or implementation of policy, manifestly depends on its success in achieving this electoral goal. Mobilizing at least a winning plurality

19. *Annual Report of the American Baptist Home Mission Society, 1882*, p. 59; *Minutes of the Iowa Annual Conference of the Methodist Episcopal Church, 1890*, p. 159. Such sentiments, especially with explicit reference to Catholics, were common in the conference journals of these and similar denominations. For an excellent analysis of the immigrant migration to cities, see David Ward, *Cities and Immigrants*, pp. 51–84, 105–24.

of the electorate, then, is a sine qua non for whatever else a party may seek to accomplish. Striving after that goal in a nation characterized by a heterogeneous and uneven distribution of population has significantly shaped the character of American political parties and of the political system. It has produced political parties that are essentially constituent entities preoccupied with the tasks of integrating subgroups to the virtual exclusion of integrating or articulating policies. And it has produced a national political system that has not been structured around any single and durable cleavage line.[20]

American political parties have been organized geographically—at the levels of ward, city, township, county, state, and nation. The appearance of a hierarchical or pyramidal organization has always been wholly illusory, for it has never been a hierarchy in which the flow of authority has been from the top downward, as in a corporation. Instead, the party as organization has consisted of roughly coequal layers, and the most important task, getting out the vote, has been performed in the wards (precincts) and townships. At that level each party's electoral coalition was built and was developed. And at that level each party's mobilizers pursued success by showing voters the consonance between the party's character and their own concerns, by showing them how the party represented them.

Representing a successful coalition of voters in the nineteenth-century South involved a different enterprise than building a winning coalition in New England or in the West North Central States. Only 10.2 percent of the nation's 1890 potential electorate was black, but over 50.0 percent of the electorate of the states of Mississippi and South Carolina; over 40.0 percent of the voters of Alabama, Georgia, and Louisiana; and 35.7 percent of the voting-age males of the former Confederacy as a whole were black. This helps to explain both the racial orientation of politics in that section and its absence elsewhere. By 1890 most of the nation's Irish (61.9 percent) lived in the New England and Middle Atlantic states, and the Germans (58.4 percent), Norwegians (91.6 percent) and Swedes (73.6 percent) in the East North Central and West North Central areas.[21] This points to some of the broad regional distinctions in population that confronted party builders, as do the obvious regional variations in the balances between pietistic and ritualis-

20. Walter Dean Burnham, "The United States," pp. 654–55.
21. These are percentages of the total number of Irish, Germans, etc., in the United States who lived in each of the designated combination of regions. The proportions include those who were native born but whose parents were from the specified country. The proportions were calculated from data in U.S., Census Office, *Compendium of the Eleventh Census: 1890*, pt. 3, Tables 9, 10, 11, 13.

tic groups (see Table 6.3) and the fact that 48.1 percent of the country's Catholic population, but only 15.2 percent of its Methodists, lived in cities with populations of twenty-five thousand or more. And there were similar sorts of distinctions between states within regions and between counties within the same state. For example, consider the different tasks involved in developing an electoral coalition in Barnstable and Suffolk counties, Massachusetts. The population of Barnstable County (Cape Cod) in 1890 was heavily native stock (79.7 percent) and its religious membership largely Methodist and Congregationalist (56.2 percent); but Suffolk County (Boston) was strongly foreign stock (67.0 percent) and its church membership dominated by Roman Catholics (80.9 percent).

To attempt to win elections or to increase the size of their voting clienteles, parties in most states had to integrate varied subgroups of the population. Socially, then, each party's electoral coalition was a loosely structured alliance of subgroups or subcoalitions functionally related to each other for the purpose of winning elections. Since subgroups of the population were asymmetrically distributed across the nation, the exact mixture of each party's social coalition varied from locale to locale. However, along with its voting support each subgroup brought to the party its own set of demands, or "preference orderings"; that is, each subgroup supported the party as a means of implementing its own values. And therein lay the potential for internal tension and coalition-destroying ruptures.

Some subgroup demands were incompatible with the preference orderings of other subgroups within the coalition, but party builders never attempted to resolve or mediate such intergroup conflict. To have opted for one subgroup's demands to the exclusion of another's would simply have alienated potential supporters. Clientele-conscious parties aimed at increasing voting support, not constricting it. Therefore, party builders sought to avoid, to manage, or to channel such conflict—to bargain, to compromise, to develop "a 'joint preference ordering' of organizational objectives." In short, they sought to integrate potentially (or actually) conflicting subgroups into the party in the electorate by subordinating intergroup tensions to the party's objectives. However, that was possible only if an important condition were first satisfied. The subgroups in question had to value highly the party as party; that is, they ultimately had to be willing to subordinate their particularistic demands to the party's electoral success. They had to yield to the requirements of party discipline, to that much-maligned "whip of the party drill master." In turn, that type of subordination would be forthcoming only if the involved subgroups saw their conflicting demands as negotiable ones, only if their subgroup characters involved an ethic of political, rather than ultimate, responsibility.[22]

Within this framework we can analytically locate the efforts of late nineteenth-century party builders to come to terms with the changing demographic world about them. Not only native pietists but party strategists as well perceived these changes and their political implications. And because the relative size of their normal support groups was declining—especially in the New England, Middle Atlantic, and East North Central sections, states that collectively accounted for 55.0 percent of the 1880 electorate and 51.0 percent of the congressional apportionment —Republican party builders were pressed to respond.[23]

The activities and demands of their core pietistic support groups, and especially the Yankee pietists, compounded this dimension of the Republican party's coalitional dilemma. By the late 1860s and throughout the 1870s and 1880s, these groups were alarmed by the growing immorality that they saw in their society. Their definition of sin and their demands for its eradication threatened pragmatic party builders' efforts to integrate new subgroups.

Pietists did not devise a new catalog of sinful activity to meet the conditions of the 1870s and 1880s. The evils to which they stridently drew attention were the old evils; the solutions that they demanded were the old prescriptions. Their litany of evils included "attempts to prostitute the Holy Sabbath." To counter this "incoming flood of Sabbath desecration," they demanded a return to "a scriptural observance of the Sabbath." It was time for "all the friends of the Sabbath to unite in one grand effort to be continued until the Lord's Day shall be rescued from all impending dangers by which it is so seriously threatened."[24] The

22. For the quotations and conceptions in this and the following paragraph, see Samuel J. Eldersveld, *Political Parties*, pp. 1–13, 73–97; also see Richard M. Cyert and James G. March, "A Behavioral Theory of Organizational Objectives," pp. 76–89; Kleppner, *Cross of Culture*, pp. 93–95. For the conception underlying the distinction between political and ultimate responsibility, see Max Weber, "Politics as a Vocation," pp. 115–22.

23. By 1890 these three areas accounted for 52.8 percent of the electorate and 49.9 percent of the congressional apportionment. The importance of these areas to the Republicans is even clearer in light of the fact that the greater South (border and Confederate states) held 28.4 percent of the 1880 electorate and 31.9 percent of the congressional apportionment; and the respective figures for the fourteen states in 1890 were 26.1 percent and 31.0 percent. The shift in the pietist-ritualist balance was greater in the West North Central area than it was in the East North Central states (-17.5 compared to -11.6 percentage points); but in the former the pietist lead by 1890 was still 13.3 percentage points. And the West North Central area held only 12.4 percent of the 1880 electorate and 14.5 percent of the 1890 males of voting age.

24. Respectively, the quotations are from *Minutes of the Annual Session of the Northwest Iowa Conference of the Methodist Episcopal Church, 1880*, pp. 16–17; *Minutes of the Ohio Annual Conference of the Methodist Episcopal Church, 1892*, pp.

threats came in diverse guises. They included pleasure-seeking activities: baseball playing, social visiting, secular reading, and excursions on steamboats and railroads. They also encompassed commercial and governmental activities: the buying of groceries, the publication of Sunday newspapers, the Sabbath operation of cheese factories, Army regulations providing for the Sunday inspection of soldiers, and the running of mail trains on Sunday. To discourage these and other breaches of God's commandment, pietists cooperated with each other in a varied array of interdenominational agencies, such as the New England Sabbath Protective League, the International Sabbath Association, the American Sabbath Union and its state-level counterparts. They petitioned state legislatures, and by the mid-1880s the national Congress, for laws to eradicate these sins. And they pledged themselves to vote only for candidates opposed to the desecration of the Lord's day, to choose "for our rulers, 'out of all the people, able men, such as fear God, men of truth, hating covetousness.'"[25]

Although pietists condemned Sabbath breaking as a sin that undermined "the maintenance of sound morals and piety in our land," they directed even more of their verbal fire and organizational energy at "the dominant and dominating curse of our time—*The Liquor System.*" Demon rum became to the postwar pietists what slavery had been to their prewar counterparts: "the crime of crimes"—a *symbol*, as well as a tangible cause, of the impediments along society's path to Christian perfection. For the individual drinker alcohol was a poison that impaired his physical and mental capacities and contributed to his moral debasement. Because liquor was injurious to both soul and body, the liquor traffic was an enemy of society. It bred crime, wrecked homes, fostered anarchy, and corrupted politics. And those engaged in the traffic were "uniformly obstructive and recklessly defiant" of all "practical efforts" to solve "the drink problem." Moreover, they were organized and growing in economic and political power. By 1888 the drys calculated that the proprietors and employees of liquor establishments along with their dependents constituted nearly 12.0 percent of the nation's electorate. In the face of this soul-destroying threat, this peril to the moral and material progress of the nation, it was "impious to be calm." They exhorted Christians to put on "the King's armor," arm themselves "with the

---

36–37; *Minutes of the General Assembly of the Cumberland Presbyterian Church, 1886,* p. 45; *Annual Report of the American Baptists Home Mission Society, 1879,* p. 17.

25. *Minutes of the [Presbyterian] Synod of Cleveland, 1877,* p. 30; the connection with Sabbath breaking was explicit. All of these matters can be followed in the denominational conference journals.

King's weapons," and "conquer in the King's name." The war's objective was simple: prohibit the drink traffic and thereby extirpate the sin.[26]

These attitudes were not novel. Pietists had long declaimed against Sabbath desecration and King Alcohol. It was not even new that they associated the increasing incidence of these sins with the floodtide of immigration that had deposited on American shores what they often described as the Sabbath-breaking, rum-drinking refuse of European countries, for even in the 1850s they had singled out the Irish and Germans as avowed enemies of their standards of righteous behavior. By the mid-1870s these attitudes were articulated with a heightened and sustained sense of urgency, a righteous unwillingness to compromise, and they were linked even more explicitly with injunctions to political behavior.

The "rum power's" visible organization and lobbying activities, its increasing prosperity, its growing size, and especially its ever-expanding voting power impelled pietists to action. The failure of earlier efforts to abolish the evil through high-license and local-option schemes fueled their moral conviction that any compromise was as sinful as the evil itself, for they believed that moral wrongs simply "should not be tolerated by any government. We may regulate right things, but wrong things should be suppressed."[27] To labor to suppress that evil was God's command to the saved, and it was one that must inform all dimensions of behavior. It was not enough to be "a Christian on Sunday and anything else but a Christian on election day," for every true Christian "is

26. For the quotations see *Minutes of the National Council of the Congregational Churches of the United States of America: Annual Session, 1871*, p. 58; *Minutes of the Session of the New Hampshire Annual Conference of the Methodist Episcopal Church, 1890*, p. 117, emphasis in original; *The Cyclopaedia of Temperance and Prohibition*, pp. 371–89, with the quotation on p. 387; *Minutes of the Session of the New England Annual Conference of the Methodist Episcopal Church, 1886*, p. 45; and *Minutes of the Anniversary of the Philadelphia Baptist Association, 1885*, pp. 32–33. The description of the drink traffic was common; see, for examples, *Minutes of the Annual Meeting of the Maine Baptist Missionary Convention, 1875*, pp. 41–42; *Minutes of the Vermont Annual Conference of the Methodist Episcopal Church, 1879*, pp. 47–48. For a synthesis of the dry ideology, see Jensen, *Winning the Midwest*, pp. 70–73.

27. *Minutes of the Session of the New Hampshire Annual Conference of the Methodist Episcopal Church, 1890*, p. 119. For expressions of similar attitudes, see *Minutes of the Central Pennsylvania Annual Conference of the Methodist Episcopal Church, 1889*, pp. 43–45; *Minutes of the Session of the Missouri Annual Conference of the Methodist Episcopal Church, 1890*, pp. 68–69; *Minutes of the General Assembly of the Cumberland Presbyterian Church, 1888*, p. 37; *Minutes of the Annual Meeting of the Maine Baptist Missionary Convention, 1880*, p. 63; *Minutes of the Annual Meeting of the Dane [Wisconsin] Association of Baptist Churches, 1880*, p. 10. Where they could do no better, however, pietists still accepted local option "as the best available means" for suppressing the liquor traffic; for example, see *Minutes of the New Jersey Annual Conference of the Methodist Episcopal Church, 1873*, pp. 22–23; ibid., *1880*, pp. 38–39.

obligated before God to vote as he prays, and a man who does not vote as he prays is answerable for his conduct." A man's vote was "a holy vow before God, . . . a solemn act, and never to be separated from religion." The Christian should vote "for good men only, and men pledged on the side of temperance," for "*every* good man's vote should be . . . a vote for *righteousness.*" He should not allow his vote to be "controlled by party organizations that are managed in the interests of the liquor traffic . . . or controlled . . . by the policy of non-interference" with it. The "duty of Christian men" was to refuse their voting support to "any party or person who is not thoroughly and unequivocally committed to the principle and practice of prohibition." To ignore this duty, to fail to recognize this question "*as paramount to all party considerations,*" was to cast "a vote contrary to *righteousness.*"[28]

The fulsome zeal of the pietists, their commitment to an ethic of ultimate responsibility, and the antiparty values that that engendered collided with the party builders' ethic of political responsibility.[29] Pietists insisted on pristine purity—that the acts, speeches, and postures of Republican officeholders and activists unambiguously represent their "preference orderings." This insistence conflicted with the more pragmatic efforts to integrate new subgroups into the party's voting coalition. Republicans were ever willing to condemn sin in general, but they discovered a growing political danger in alluding to its concrete mani-

28. For the quotations see respectively the address of Rev. Dr. Nevin, a Presbyterian minister, in *Proceedings of the Ninth National Temperance Convention, 1881*, p. 92; *Minutes of the Annual Meeting of the General Association of the Congregational Churches of Massachusetts, 1891*, p. 22; *Minutes of the New Jersey Annual Conference of the Methodist Episcopal Church, 1878*, p. 34; *Minutes of the Central Pennsylvania Annual Conference of the Methodist Episcopal Church, 1886*, p. 63; *Minutes of the Maine Annual Conference of the Methodist Episcopal Church, 1888*, pp. 28–29; *Minutes of the Annual Session of the West Wisconsin Conference of the Methodist Episcopal Church, 1884*, pp. 79–80; ibid., *1892*, pp. 29–30. All emphases in the original. Although there is no doubt that the Methodists were in the vanguard of prohibition rhetoric, for similar views by other denominations see *Minutes of the Anniversary of the Philadelphia Baptist Association, 1886*, p. 31; *Proceedings of the Annual Baptist Autumnal Conference for the Discussion of Current Questions, 1888*, p. 53; *Minutes of the Anniversary of the Wooster [Ohio] Baptist Association, 1883*, pp. 9–10; *Minutes of the [Presbyterian] Synod of Cleveland, 1878*, p. 66; *Minutes of the General Assembly of the Cumberland Presbyterian Church, 1886*, pp. 40–41; *Minutes of the National Council of the Congregational Churches of the United States of America: Annual Session, 1892*, p. 30.

29. For examples of the latter, see Diary of Rutherford B. Hayes, 12 October 1881, 6 November 1889, and Hayes to Miss F. E. Willard, 13 October 1888, in Charles R. Williams, ed., *Diary and Letters of Rutherford Birchard Hayes*, 4:46, 522, 127–28; the description of Matthew Stanley Quay's attitude toward politics, in A[lexander] K. McClure, *Old Times Notes of Pennsylvania*, 2:572–73; and the statement in the Massachusetts Republican platform for 1876, in *Appletons' Annual Cyclopaedia and Register of Important Events of the Year 1876*, p. 512.

festations, Sabbath desecration and the liquor traffic: too many of those "unsaved millions of foreigners" had acquired the vote; their relative electoral strength was continuing to increase. Some Republican leaders had long been aware of the partisan implications of these demographic trends; the lesson was brought home to still others by the electoral consequences of the resurgent crusade for temperance of the early 1870s.[30]

The precise nature of the problem that faced Republican party builders who tried to integrate new subgroups varied somewhat across the regions of the North. In all areas the size of the Catholic subgroup was growing, and with only a single and regional exception it was a strongly Democratic group. When Catholic votes were joined with a strong majority of German Lutheran votes in the Midwest, Republican electoral success was in grave jeopardy, as the elections of the 1870s demonstrated. Continuing German immigration steadily swelled the size of the German Lutheran component of the electorate. The Republicans at least had to inhibit the movement of these voters into the Democratic lists, to prevent a voting union of Catholics and German Lutherans arrayed in solid partisan phalanx. In New England, where there were relatively few German Lutherans, the Republicans had to balance growing Catholic voting strength by attracting greater support from native ethnoreligious groups that had only marginally swung to the Republicans—especially the more Calvinistic of the Baptists and Presbyterians. The Middle Atlantic states posed a more mixed problem, something of a combination of the other two. There the German Lutherans were generally less confessional than in the Midwest, and some of the more pietistic among them were already in motion to Republicanism. The party needed to deepen and accelerate that swing and combine it with the regular levels of support among its core groups.

Specifying, even in this very general way, the task of integrating subgroups that confronted the Republicans bares the party's tactical, rhetorical, and behavioral dilemma. How could the Republican party represent subgroups in whose political characters were imbedded irreconcilable dispositions toward the major sins of the day? How could their mutually exclusive "preference orderings" be developed into a "joint preference ordering" of party objectives? Throughout the 1870s and 1880s the solution involved reactivating latent partisan loyalties by emphasizing the party's persistent antisouthernism and stressing its standing aura as "the party of great moral ideas." Even more significantly, however, it also involved assuaging, or rechanneling, the poten-

30. Kleppner, *Cross of Culture*, pp. 110–19; Fred Emory Haynes, *James Baird Weaver*, pp. 80–82; Richard A. Hebert, *Modern Maine*, 1:236–37; for the role of the temperance crusade elsewhere, see Chapter 4.

tial conflict among subgroups over prohibition and Sabbath-keeping by representing their shared concern with an even greater contemporary evil, the sin of popery.

When Republican strategists in the 1870s cranked up their anti-Catholic themes, they were not embarking on some new political departure. Antipopery had been characteristic of Republicanism since the 1850s. Nor were they attempting by their rhetoric to *create* social-group antipathy. The mutual and deeply felt antagonism predated its partisan exposition. Indeed, the causal flow was in the other direction: Republican rhetoricians articulated antipopery themes precisely because they perceived that the groups at which they directed them were *already* imbued with anti-Catholic values. Twisting "the Pope's big toe" was a way of reminding those groups of the psychological rapport between their dispositions and the party's political character.[31]

Both immigrant and native pietists harbored and articulated powerful anti-Catholic attitudes. The anti-Catholicism of immigrant pietists —e.g., the British, Canadian Protestants, Dutch, Irish Protestants, Norwegians, and Swedes—was reminiscent of group conflict in Europe. It reflected lingering and living memories of "Romish persecution which always strengthens prejudice." Those memories also sustained active political predispositions to oppose the pope's legions in the New World.[32] To native pietists the principle of papal supremacy provided evidence that the Catholic church was an un-American growth on the society. Since American Catholics were in "vassalage to the man of sin" they "already imperil our free institutions." The native pietists' conception of the political character of the Catholic subgroup (probably shared by most immigrant pietists) reinforced that conclusion and heightened the resulting fear. Because Catholics did not think for themselves but rendered blind obedience to their priests, they readily became "the purblind tools of political demagogues in league with Jesuits and traitors." Catholicism, then, was at once both a moral and a political enemy

---

31. The quoted expression is from William H. Smith, Philadelphia, to James M. Comly, 26 August 1876, James M. Comly MSS, Ohio State Historical Society. My phrasing throughout employs terms used in the nineteenth century in a pejorative way— e.g., Romanists, papists, popery. My use of the terms does not imply an acceptance of such values but is only an attempt to recreate the argument in the terms used by contemporaries.

32. The quotation is from James I. Good, *History of the Reformed Church in the United States*, pp. 295–96. For expressions of similar attitudes, see Rasmus B. Anderson, *Life Story*, p. 17; Axel P. Johnson, *Smuggled into Paradise*, p. 26; Sam Rönnegard, *Prairie Shepherd* p. 255; Henry Jacob Ryskamp, "The Dutch in Western Michigan," p. 67. For analysis see Jensen, *Winning the Midwest*, pp. 232–33, 235, 252–55; Kleppner, *Cross of Culture*, pp. 87–88.

of "the advance of religious liberty."[33] To combat "the arrogant pretensions, the avowed purposes" of popery, it was necessary to "arouse the whole Protestant population in united and determined effort to withstand the Man of Sin." And for that united effort pietists bridged denominational distinctions and cooperated in the American and Foreign Christian Union and, later, the National League for the Protection of American Institutions.[34]

For the most part, the anti-Catholicism of these groups had already been translated into a Republican voting habit, but other groups that were not regularly or strongly Republican shared these fears of the growing influence of Catholicism. Protestant Episcopalians, for example, persistently warned that the allegiance that American Catholics owed to the pope would be used to further Rome's grand design "of extending the influence and power of the Papal See"; as a consequence, "the conflict between Rome and [American] national independence [was] irrepressible." German Evangelicals, many of whom supported Democracy as a safe haven from the "Know-Nothing" Republicans, voiced similar apprehension. And they combined these expressions with frequent denunciations of the unbiblical character of popery.[35] It was even more significant, however, that German Lutherans were predisposed to antipopery. They too called attention to Rome's aggressions, to its efforts to regain its lost power, and they proclaimed their creedal confessions the "mightiest bulwark, . . . the principles on which alone Romanism can be successfully resisted." Irrespective of their degree of

33. *Minutes of the Annual Meeting of the General Conference of the Congregational Churches in Maine, 1871*, p. 113; *Minutes of the Providence Annual Conference of the Methodist Episcopal Church, 1879*, p. 38; *Minutes of the Anniversary of the Philadelphia Baptist Association, 1875*, p. 22. Also see *Minutes of the General Assembly of the United Presbyterian Church of North America, 1870*, pp. 163–65; Lawrence B. Davis, *Immigrants, Baptists, and the Protestant Mind in America*, pp. 66–67. For the persistence of the views connecting Catholic dogmatism and political character, see Kenneth Underwood, *Protestant and Catholic*, pp. 84–85; Michael Parenti, "Political Values and Religious Cultures," pp. 259–69.

34. *Minutes of the Providence Annual Conference of the Methodist Episcopal Church, 1871*, p. 16. On the purpose of the American and Foreign Christian Union, see *Minutes of the Central Pennsylvania Annual Conference of the Methodist Episcopal Church, 1870*, p. 40; *Minutes of the Vermont Annual Conference of the Methodist Episcopal Church, 1871*, p. 52. For the National League for the Protection of American Institutions, see *Minutes of the Maine Annual Conference of the Methodist Episcopal Church, 1891*, p. 51; John Higham, *Strangers in the Land*, p. 60.

35. For examples of Episcopalian attitudes, see *The Churchman* (New York), 11 November 1876, 16 January 1886; *The True Catholic* (Baltimore), May 1851. For the German Evangelicals, see *Proceedings of the General Conference of the United Brethren Church in Christ, 1869*, p. 8; ibid., *1873*, p. 84–85; Paul F. Douglass, *The Story of German Methodism*, pp. 65–67; William H. Watson, *History of the Michigan Conference of the Evangelical Church*, p. 12; A. W. Drury, "Romanism in the United States: The Proper Attitude toward It," pp. 1–23.

confessionalism, German Lutherans regarded the papacy as Antichrist incarnate, and they lamented what they (inaccurately) perceived as a tendency by Protestants to tone down denunciations of Catholicism:

Is there necessarily bitterness and uncharitableness in pronouncing condemnation on Satan and all his crew and work, and in warning against his craft and cunning which seeks the destruction of souls? . . . The danger is not imaginary; it is terribly real and frightfully imminent. . . . The papacy has not changed since our ancestors raised their voices against it. If it ceased to be the Antichristian usurpation it is, it would cease to be the papacy. . . . Let those who love the Lord Jesus Christ and sincerely seek the salvation of souls through His precious name, beware of Rome.[36]

Among these groups, as well as among significant minorities of the more Calvinistic Baptists and Presbyterians, anti-Catholic temperaments had not uniformly produced a Republican voting response. Other character traits had been more salient to their group partisanship, but the events of the 1870s and 1880s interacted with these ingrained anti-Catholic dispositions, heightened their partisan salience, and produced yet another wave of political antipopery. The claims and assertions of the Catholic hierarchy, the acts and rhetoric of Republican officeholders and activists, and the voting behavior of the Catholic subgroup combined in the perceptions of non-Catholics, not to create a new partisan fault line, but to deepen and extend an older one, one that pitted a "Christian party" (the Republicans) against the "Catholic party."

The specific referents of anti-Catholic attitudes covered a wide spectrum. Native and immigrant pietists saw Catholics as Sabbath breakers, drinkers, and exponents of an antibiblical religion. They perceived, too, the role that Catholic voters played in blocking attainment of their cherished political goals. As groups commanded by the Lord to "teach all nations," they were resolved to do no less than bring the "uplifting power" of gospel religion to these multitudes who were "in the bonds of a fatal religious formalism." True believers that they were, they could never bring themselves to abandon all hope that their evangelization would transform even the hearts of the papists. Those efforts, of course, did not go well. In the 1870s and 1880s the home mission and church

36. Respectively the quotations are from *Minutes of the Annual Convention of the General Council of the Evangelical Lutheran Church in America, 1869*, pp. 14–16; "The Papal Antichrist," pp. 239–44. For similar expressions see *Proceedings of the Convention of the General Synod of the Evangelical Lutheran Church in the United States, 1864*, p. 40; John G. Morris, *Life Reminiscences of an Old Lutheran Minister*, pp. 128–29; "The Army of Antichrist," p. 21. Lutherans continue to be concerned about the growth of Catholic power in America; see the data in Lawrence L. Kersten, *The Lutheran Ethic*, pp. 85–87.

extension reports of the denominational conferences spoke repeatedly of the "growing danger," of the "ever-flowing, never ebbing tide" of Catholic immigration, of the hierarchy's "extreme efforts . . . to use them [Catholic immigrants] as a force in politics to accomplish their objectives." To avert this dire calamity, even more effort had to be devoted to reaching "Catholics with the truth, leading them to Christ, Americanizing them," for "we must take care of them or they will take care of us." Yet the reports spoke as well, in tones of anguish and desperation, of "the most disheartening difficulties," the "slow progress" that characterized the work. The combination of fear and exasperation produced an increasing reliance on other methods to "take care" of the Catholic menace. Over the last decades of the nineteenth century, pietistic groups depended even more heavily than earlier on solutions that entailed legal coercion and, eventually, immigration restriction.[37]

As pietists explicitly recognized the growth of the Catholic population and the consequent "proportionate diminution in the comparative numbers" of their own forces, they articulated these sentiments with an even greater sense of urgency.[38] That, in turn, imparted renewed vitality to their anti-Catholic temperaments. However, it was not simply these older referents, nor a generalized fear of Catholicism, nor even a specific recognition of its growing relative size that tapped these dispositions and channeled them in partisan directions. And for nonpietistic groups

37. The quotations are from the *Annual Report of the American Baptist Home Mission Society, 1880*, p. 34; *Minutes of the Maine Annual Conference of the Methodist Episcopal Church, 1884*, p. 31; *Annual Report of the American Baptist Home Mission Society, 1889*, pp. 49–51; ibid., *1883*, p. 13; ibid., *1879*, p. 19; *Minutes of the Annual Meeting of the Dane [Wisconsin] Association of Baptist Churches, 1885*, p. 4. For other examples of these attitudes, see *Minutes of the Session of the New Hampshire Annual Conference of the Methodist Episcopal Church, 1871*, p. 21; ibid., *1892*, pp. 314–16; *Minutes of the Annual Session of the West Wisconsin Annual Conference of the Methodist Episcopal Church, 1883*, pp. 259–60; *Minutes of the Central Pennsylvania Annual Conference of the Methodist Episcopal Church, 1884*, p. 59; *Report of the American Home Missionary Society, 1885*, pp. 52–53; ibid., *1887*, pp. 58–64; *Minutes of the National Council of the Congregational Churches of the United States of America: Annual Session, 1886*, pp. 120–21; *Minutes of the Annual Meeting of the General Conference of the Congregational Churches in Maine, 1880*, p. 138; *Minutes of the Rhode Island Congregational Conference, 1884*, pp. 33–37. For an overview of attitudes toward immigration restriction, see Davis, *Immigrants, Baptists*, pp. 63–96.

38. *Minutes of the Annual Meeting of the General Association of the Congregational Churches of Massachusetts, 1892*, p. 24. Also see the statistical analysis in *Minutes of the Session of the New England Annual Conference of the Methodist Episcopal Church, 1868*, pp. 36–42; the comments in *Minutes of the Session of the New Hampshire Annual Conference of the Methodist Episcopal Church, 1871*, p. 24; *Minutes of the Session of the New England Southern Annual Conference of the Methodist Episcopal Church, 1886*, pp. 36–37; *Minutes of the Providence Annual Conference of the Methodist Episcopal Church, 1872*, p. 30; *Annual Report of the American Baptist Home Mission Society, 1880*, p. 34; ibid., *1882*, p. 18; *Minutes of the General Association [of Congregational Churches] of New York, 1873*, p. 29.

such as the German Lutherans, it was certainly not Catholic Sabbath breaking and fondness for demon rum that worked to that end. Instead, a series of specific events in the 1870s and 1880s interacted with these underlying predispositions to achieve that effect. These events brought into focus what both types of groups perceived as the growing aggressiveness and *political* power of popery. They provided a set of immediate and concrete referents that gave partisan energy to a sometimes latent anti-Catholicism and enabled Republican party builders to unite that with a rechanneled pietist zeal.[39]

Three categories of developments were significant. First, there were several highly noticeable and symbolically significant manifestations of Catholic voting power. Even before the mid-1870s some Catholics had been nominated and elected to office in areas where they composed a large element of the electorate. In the early 1870s pietistic groups had complained that New York City was "no longer ruled by Americans, but by the subjects of a foreign power" and had called Roman Catholicism "the established religion" of that city.[40] However, not until the early 1880s were Catholics elected to the mayoralties of major cities. New York City's first Catholic mayor was elected in 1880, and Boston's in 1884. That "the Catholics have taken the city of New York"—and Boston, Lawrence, and Lowell—seemed a terrifying portent for the future, for Catholics in positions of executive power were still servants of the pope and always "ready to do priestly bidding." In the cities that they controlled they would surely create a "politico-ecclesiastical despotism" in which Protestants would be stripped of their liberty of conscience and freedom of worship.[41]

Second, beginning in the early 1870s, the Catholic clergy initiated a series of "freedom-of-worship" struggles. These entailed questions of the equality in law of Catholic with non-Catholic clergy. Specifically, they involved standing legal prohibitions on the right of Catholic clergy

39. This does not mean to imply that Republican efforts to sublimate concerns over prohibition and Sabbath desecration to anti-Catholicism were everywhere attempted or that they were everywhere and always successful.
40. *Minutes of the Session of the New Hampshire Annual Conference of the Methodist Episcopal Church, 1871*, p. 24; *Minutes of the Annual Meeting of the General Conference of the Congregational Churches in Maine, 1871*, p. 113. And see the earlier comments concerning Catholic influence in Boston and New York City in the *Minutes of the Providence Annual Conference of the Methodist Episcopal Church, 1869*, p. 17. The references were to the election of Catholics to city councils and boards of aldermen.
41. *Proceedings of the Annual Baptist Autumnal Conference for the Discussion of Current Questions, 1888*, pp. 107–23; *Minutes of the Session of the New England Southern Annual Conference of the Methodist Episcopal Church, 1888*, pp. 64–65; Elijah H. Pilcher, *Protestantism in Michigan*, pp. 59–67. For insight into the religious lines of political conflict in Boston, see *Boston Daily Advertiser*, 7 November 1876; *Boston Post*, 23, 28 November 1883, 14 December 1883, 10 December 1884.

to minister to their coreligionists who were inmates of publicly supported charitable, reformatory, and penal institutions. In some states that right was explicitly conveyed by existing statute to non-Catholic clergy, and Catholic inmates were required to attend those exercises. In others, only nonsectarian services were permitted. However, in none were Catholic priests legally authorized to celebrate mass and administer the sacraments to Catholic inmates. And when Catholics, in reaction, established their own parallel institutions—orphanages, hospitals, homes for wayward children—they received no public funds to support them.[42]

The exact nature of the Catholic challenge varied from one state to another, because state laws and practices differed, but in every state they agitated for legislation ending the requirement that Catholic inmates attend non-Catholic religious services, and they sought state support to extend Catholic services to Catholic inmates. In some states they pushed for equal legal status with the non-Catholic ministers; in others they called for public funds to support their own parallel institutions. Whatever the precise nature of the Catholic claims, however, they evoked a furious outpouring of non-Catholic ire. Non-Catholic groups saw in these efforts further evidence of papal aggressions. They were perceived as efforts to destroy "the principle of absolute 'liberty in all religious concernments,' " attempts to transform publicly financed institutions "into instruments for sectarian coercion and oppression, wholly contrary to the spirit of American institutions."[43] Legislative efforts to respond to Catholic demands produced protracted, public, and acrimonious battles in states such as Kentucky, Maine, Massachusetts, Michigan, New Jersey, New York, Ohio, Pennsylvania, Rhode Island, and elsewhere. These battles and the emotional fervor they aroused contributed to the increased partisan salience of antipopery.[44]

The election of Catholics to executive offices and the clergy's demands for freedom of worship in state-supported custodial institutions increased the fear and aroused the wrath of non-Catholic groups. How-

42. For some of the state-level differences, the Catholic challenges, and the partisan effects, see Herbert J. Bass, *"I Am a Democrat,"* pp. 21–23; Robert H. Lord, John E. Sexton, and Edward T. Harrington, *History of the Archdiocese of Boston*, 3:68–74; Rudolph J. Vecoli, *The Peoples of New Jersey*, pp. 145–48.

43. *Minutes of the Anniversary of the Philadelphia Baptist Association, 1873*, p. 26; *Minutes of the New Jersey Annual Conference of the Methodist Episcopal Church, 1875*, p. 27. For examples of similar expressions, see *The Churchman* (New York), 23 January 1886; *Minutes of the New York Annual Conference of the Methodist Episcopal Church, 1891*, p. 75; *Minutes of the Iowa Annual Conference of the Methodist Episcopal Church, 1892*, pp. 33–34.

44. *Appletons' Annual Cyclopaedia, 1875*, p. 605; William Leo Lucey, *The Catholic Church in Maine*, pp. 238–40; George Paré, *The Catholic Church in Detroit, 1701–1888*, pp. 536–38; and Frederick J. Zwierlein, *The Life and Letters of Bishop McQuaid*, 3:286–302, 311–17.

ever, the third set of developments produced a maelstrom of fury and drove antipopery to new heights of frenzy. The Catholic clergy assaulted the public school. The paroxysm of political antipopery that marked the 1870s and 1880s owed more to the "school question" than to any other single factor. That question was multifaceted and of symbolic as well as substantive significance. As non-Catholic groups saw it, the Catholic assault took several forms. First, the Catholic clergy attempted to transform the common school into a "Godless" institution by demanding that it be purged of Bible reading and any form of devotional practice. Second, in some localities they also demanded that the schools' hiring practices be changed so that Catholic applicants for teaching positions would no longer be discriminated against. Third, they objected to the anti-Catholic content of textbooks and diatribes against their religion by non-Catholic teachers. Fourth, the hierarchy threatened to undermine the public schools by extending its own parochial-school system. And fifth, they revived their earlier demands that a share of the public-school fund be diverted to support their church schools. To non-Catholic groups these varied avenues only led to a common result, the subversion of the vital role of the public-school system.

To appreciate the intensity that the school question aroused, and the fierceness with which both sides waged the battle, it is necessary to understand how the combatants perceived the role of education. We cannot do that by bringing to bear our own late twentieth-century perspectives. Those views concentrate too exclusively on the functional or instrumental role of education—better job opportunities, enhanced career earning power, or upward social mobility. Nineteenth-century rationales were singularly devoid of such instrumental referents. They focused instead on education's role as a transmitter of values, especially moral values. And that Catholics as well as non-Catholics had in mind quite specific and mutually antagonistic values made conflict inevitable and compromise impossible.

To native religious groups, pietists and ritualists alike, education as imparted by the common school was nothing less than "a handmaid to religion and the teacher . . . one of our best missionaries." Public schools, "pervaded with the spirit of Christian morality," reinforced and strengthened the principles inculcated by both familiy and church. They were the bulwarks of the Christian religion and of American institutions, "the basis of our social fabric . . . to be cherished and promulgated by the agencies of the church as well as by those of the state." They were the only "fit training ground for a morally responsible citizenship."[45]

45. Respectively, the quotations are from *Minutes of the Minnesota Annual Con-*

Why were these groups effusive in their praise of the common school, boundless in their support of it? They viewed the public school as an agency for mass evangelization and the consequent homogenization of the society. It was to them an agency of social control. These groups rejected notions of cultural pluralism; their conception of sin and their religious enthusiasm required that. They aimed instead "to unify and make homogeneous the society." Through the common school and the Gospel of Christ they sought to produce "a morally and politically homogeneous people."[46]

When they spoke of the common schools as agencies of evangelization, they were not alluding to some possibility of propagating denominationalism. When they spoke of "moral education," they had in mind the principles of morality shared in common by the adherents of gospel religion, for in the public school *all* children, even those whose parents were enslaved by "Lutheran formalism or Romish superstition," would be exposed to the Bible. That alone was cause for righteous optimism, for they believed the Bible to be "*the* agent in *converting* the soul," "the volume that makes human beings *men*." Bible reading, of course, was supplemented by textbooks and teaching grounded in that "holiness of heart and life" that was the essence of Christianity.[47] Lest any inattentive pupil miss one of its cardinal guides to righteous conduct, zealous prohibitionists by the mid-1870s began urging and work-

ference of the Methodist Episcopal Church, 1885, p. 45; *Minutes of the National Council of the Congregational Churches of the United States of America: Annual Session, 1877*, pp. 24–25; *Minutes of the Session of the Missouri Annual Conference of the Methodist Episcopal Church, 1879*, pp. 93–94; *Minutes of the New York Annual Conference of the Methodist Episcopal Church, 1890*, pp. 82–83. Also see *Minutes of the New Hampshire Baptist Anniversaries, 1875*, p. 41.

46. For the quotations see *Minutes of the National Council of the Congregational Churches of the United States of America: Annual Session, 1889*, pp. 44–45; *Annual Report of the American Baptist Home Mission Society, 1886*, p. 30. Also see *Minutes of the Session of the New Hampshire Annual Conference of the Methodist Episcopal Church, 1871*, p. 16; *Minutes of the Vermont Annual Conference of the Methodist Episcopal Church, 1888*, p. 58. For a more general discussion of conformity to Anglo-Protestant norms, see Milton M. Gordon, *Assimilation in American Life*, pp. 84–114. For analyses of the role of cultural conflict in shaping attitudes toward public education, see David B. Tyack, *The One Best System*, pp. 80–88, 104–109; William A. Bullough, *Cities and Schools in the Gilded Age*, pp. 3–14, 61–78; Selwyn K. Troen, *The Public and the Schools*, pp. 31–78.

47. The quotations are in *Minutes of the Vermont Annual Conference of the Methodist Episcopal Church, 1875*, p. 44; *Minutes of the Annual Session of the East Maine Conference of the Methodist Episcopal Church, 1881*, p. 25; *Minutes of the Session of the New Hampshire Annual Conference of the Methodist Episcopal Church, 1861*, pp. 21–22, emphasis in the original. Also see *Minutes of the Annual Meeting of the Maine Baptist Missionary Convention, 1875*, p. 25; *Minutes of the Annual Session of the Wisconsin Baptist State Convention, 1885*, pp. 18–19.

ing for instruction in temperance as part of the public-school curriculum. A series of such laws was enacted by the states in the 1880s and 1890s; by 1901 every state mandated some form of instruction in temperance.[48]

Moreover, in addition to these moral benefits, all instruction in the public school was conducted in the English language. By teaching English to the children of non–English-speaking parents, the public schools were vital agencies for "absorbing, assimilating, and digesting these foreign elements": "We are a nation of remnants, ravellings from the Old World. . . . The public school is one of the remedial agencies which work in our society to diminish this . . . and to hasten the compacting of these heterogeneous materials into a solid nature."[49] The problem, in short, was heterogeneity, cultural pluralism; and the public school was one of the problem-solving agencies.

By the 1880s it was more than *one* of those agencies; it had become, for practical purposes, the most important of them. As the immigrant generation resisted their evangelizing overtures, native religious groups concentrated more heavily on "saving" the next generations. However, they could not rely on cultural osmosis, for left without correct education "the children and grand-children of foreign-born parents are as foreign in their sympathies and loyalty to the churches of their fathers, as their parents were." However, put the child in the public school, where he would be exposed to biblical morality and would associate with other children reared in true Christian families, and both that loyalty and its underlying foreignism would be eroded. There was an "almost infinite gain in laying hold of child life, to make it what it ought

48. *Proceedings of the Eighth National Temperance Convention, 1875*, p. 39; *Minutes of the National Council of the Congregational Churches of the United States of America: Annual Session, 1889*, pp. 38–39; *Minutes of the Session of the New England Annual Conference of the Methodist Episcopal Church, 1885*, pp. 50–52; *Minutes of the Minnesota Annual Conference of the Methodist Episcopal Church, 1884*, pp. 46–47; *Minutes of the Central Ohio Annual Conference of the Methodist Episcopal Church, 1885*, pp. 183–84; *Sixty-First Annual Meeting of the American Institute of Instruction, Journal of Proceedings, 1890*, p. xxxv. Less pietistic native religious groups—e.g., the Episcopalians— shared the view of public schools as transmitters of moral and patriotic values, but the tone of their pronouncements was more pragmatic and less evangelistic; see, for examples, *The Churchman* (New York), 2 January 1886, 15 October 1892. On the state laws requiring temperance instruction in the public schools, see Tyack, *One Best System*, p. 105.

49. The quotations are from the *Proceedings of the Annual Baptist Autumnal Conference for the Discussion of Current Questions, 1888*, pp. 77–78; *Minutes of the Session of the New England Annual Conference of the Methodist Episcopal Church, 1889*, p. 85. For complementary views of the homogenizing role of the public schools, see Richard Edwards, "How Much Culture Shall Be Imparted in Our Free Schools?" pp. 56–57; Ada M. Laughlin, "The Moral Value of Art Education," pp. 141–49; John S. Brubacher, ed., *The Public School and Spiritual Values*, pp. 1–3, 58, 75, 83–84.

to be.'' It ought to be above all Christian and American; as the child internalized such values the society would become more homogeneous and godly: ''America [would] be Saved Through the Children.''[50]

Most immigrant pietists shared the essentials of this outlook. Although they never totally accepted the cultural-homogenization perspective, they did acknowledge the connection between education and transmitting moral values. Some, of course, complained that the public schools were not religious enough and within most groups, even among the Swedes, small minorities insisted on their own church schools. Others among them were concerned with maintaining and fostering the use of their native languages. For the most part, however, they relied on their fraternal and benevolent organizations, church societies, and newspapers for maintaining the language and on their churches and Sunday schools for denominational instruction. For the practical and morally reinforcing education of their children, they looked to the public schools; they were as convinced as the native groups that on the success of those schools depended ''the social equilibrium of the country.''[51]

The groups that rejected the public-school system and opted for their own schools, particularly Catholics and confessional German Lutherans, did so precisely because they, too, recognized that education inculcated moral values. From their points of view, the public school transmitted the *wrong* values. Both Catholics and confessional Lutherans viewed their own parochial schools as indispensable for transmitting their creedal beliefs to the coming generations. And non–English-speaking Catholics shared the German Lutheran commitment to those schools as agencies for maintaining their language. However, unlike the Catholic temperament, confessional Lutheran political culture involved a powerful antistatist disposition: government was of this world and therefore profane and corrupting; lest it debase the religious realm, it must be wholly separated from it. Consequently, German Lutherans never proposed a division of the public-school fund to support their parochial schools. And although they ridiculed a public-school system that pro-

50. Respectively, the quotations are from *Minutes of the Annual Meeting of the General Association of the Congregational Churches of Massachusetts, 1892*, pp. 24–25; *Minutes of the Vermont Annual Conference of the Methodist Episcopal Church, 1880*, p. 48; *Our Church Work* (Madison, Wis.), 17 July 1890.

51. *Minutes of the Sandusky Annual Conference, United Brethren in Christ, 1872*, p. 10. For information on the specific groups, see *Proceedings of the General Conference of the United Brethren in Christ, 1877*, pp. 44–48; Ryskamp, ''Dutch in Western Michigan,'' pp. 58, 72–75; Albert Hyma, *Albertus C. Van Raalte and His Dutch Settlements in the United States*, pp. 186, 225–26; E. Clifford Nelson and Eugene L. Fevold, *The Lutheran Church Among Norwegian-Americans*, 1:184–85, 294–99; Ulf Beijbom, *Swedes in Chicago*, pp. 256–58; Emmer Engberg, ed., *Centennial Essays*, pp. 76–77; Sture Lindmark, *Swedish America, 1914–1932*, pp. 191–218.

duced only "'rationalists and Pharisees,'" they never organized a movement to bar Bible reading from those schools.[52] Where Lutheran schools were numerous, native religious groups assessed their effect as being analogous to the Catholic schools, but they were not all that numerous. In 1890, for example, they enrolled 142,963 students nationwide, or only 18.5 percent of all the students enrolled in parochial schools. Geographically, they were concentrated in the East North Central and West North Central states; 86.5 percent of all the students in Lutheran parochial schools lived in these two areas.[53] Yet even in those regions the majority of parochial-school students were in Catholic schools. Catholics had the larger parochial-school system: they enrolled a majority of the parochial-school students in every area of the country, and they were the more visible and assertive both in defense of their own church schools and in attack on the public school. These factors combined with a potent and generalized anti-Catholicism to focus the school question much more sharply on Catholic than on Lutheran schools.

To most of the Catholic clergy, the parochial school was necessary for the future preservation of the faith: "It will be useless to build churches that, in one or two generations hence, will be vacant, because children or grandchildren of European parents no longer follow the religion of their ancestors. If the Church in the United States has already lost so many of her children, it is due, in large degree, to the want of Catholic schools." Only in such schools could the young be "instructed in their faith, and trained to the practices" of its rituals. "Right education" required a school in which the pupil would "be surrounded by an atmosphere of religion" and in which "the religious truths imparted to the child" would be "linked in the closest relationship to truths of the natural order."[54] The public school was obviously not adequate to that task. Yet the Catholic hierarchy normally did not cite scripture and

52. The quotation is from an 1889 statement of the Kansas District Synod and is in Heinrich H. Maurer, "Studies in the Sociology of Religion," p. 52. For the Lutheran attitudes see D. H. Steffens, *Doctor Carl Ferdinand Wilhelm Walther*, pp. 189–201; August C. Stellhorn, *Schools of the Lutheran Church–Missouri Synod*, pp. 71–80, 110–17, 170–72, 235–47; Walter H. Beck, *Lutheran Elementary Schools in the United States*, pp. 104–11.

53. The data are in U.S., Census Office, *Compendium of the Eleventh Census: 1890*, pt. 2, pp. 214, 241–43. In 1895 the pupils enrolled in the parochial schools of the highly ritualistic Synodical Conference (the Synods of Missouri, Wisconsin, Minnesota, and Michigan) composed 70.5 percent of all German Lutheran parochial-school students; calculated from data in Beck, *Lutheran Elementary Schools*, p. 224.

54. The quotations are from Archbishop McQuaid to Pope Leo XIII [1892], in Zwierlein, *Life and Letters of McQuaid*, 3:193; Pastoral Letter of Bishop Stephen Vincent Ryan, 27 February 1881, in Thomas Donohue, *History of the Diocese of Buffalo*, pp. 114–15; James A. Burns, *The Catholic School System in the United States*, pp. 28–29, 21. For similar views see J[ames] R[oosevelt] Bayley, *A Brief Sketch of the*

theological canons to justify their school system, as the confessional Lutherans regularly did, for when the Catholic clergy spoke of "saving the faith" through the instrumentality of the parochial school, they had in mind more than transmitting doctrine and proper ritual practice. They referred as well to rescuing Catholic children from the religiously unwholesome and dangerous atmosphere of the "Protestant" public schools.

Native pietists could only have applauded Archbishop McQuaid's assessment that the public schools in Rochester were conducted in the interests "of the Evangelicals . . . and in utter disregard of the rights of the minority." There, as elsewhere, the King James Bible was used; daily prayer was non-Catholic; Protestant hymns were sung; and textbooks, and sometimes teachers, ridiculed popery. As Catholics perceived it, the atmosphere in such schools was not neutral; it was distinctly anti-Catholic. That hostile atmosphere imperiled the faith of the malleable child.[55] To enable the young to escape that peril and to provide them with "right education," Catholics established their own school system.

From their inception Catholic parochial schools aroused the concern and righteous anger of non-Catholic groups. If the public schools were to mold the heterogeneous remnants of European society into a homogeneous American community, then the children of the immigrants must attend the public schools. An alternative school system literally subverted that objective. It perpetuated cultural pluralism by training succeeding generations to be as foreign and as Catholic as their parents. Catholic education did not produce a Bible-reading, Sabbath-observing, drink-abstaining, Christian American: "not an independent citizen of the American Republic, [but] a subject of the Pope." Such schools deprived Catholic children "of the education needed to enable them to act their part in American society." Their objective was to exacerbate religious animosities, to set neighbor against neighbor, and thus "to

History of the Catholic Church on the Island of New York, pp. 131–32; [James Joseph Thompson], *The Archdiocese of Chicago*, pp. 62–64; Joseph L. J. Kirlin, *Catholicity in Philadelphia*, pp. 409–10; Harry H. Heming, *The Catholic Church in Wisconsin*, pp. 292–93.

55. McQuaid made the statement in a public lecture on 15 March 1872, quoted in Zwierlein, *Life and Letters of McQuaid*, 2:128–29. The "Evangelicals" did not literally applaud McQuaid; his primary argument was for public funds to support Catholic schools. Also see, Thomas F. Cullen, *The Catholic Church in Rhode Island*, pp. 117–18; Michael J. Hynes, *History of the Diocese of Cleveland*, p. 78; Robert F. McNamara, *The Diocese of Rochester, 1868–1968*, pp. 168–69; John J. O'Shea, *The Two Kenricks*, p. 178; Paré, *Catholic Church in Detroit*, pp. 458–59; John K. Sharp, *History of the Diocese of Brooklyn, 1853–1953*, pp. 182–85; John Gilmary Shea, *History of the Catholic Church in the United States*, p. 208.

break up and destroy homogeneity." With such Catholic attitudes "there [could] be no reconciliation."[56]

The irreconcilable enemies joined battle early and often. The tempo of conflict accelerated as the pietistic hope for evangelizing the immigrant faded and as the size of the Catholic population increased. It attained the proportions of an Armageddon when the Catholic clergy determined to extend and expand the parochial-school system. In November 1875 the Vatican's Sacred Congregation of the Propaganda issued an "Instruction to the Bishops of the United States concerning the Public Schools." The "Instruction" itemized the dangers that public-school education posed to the faith and morals of Catholic children. The remedy lay in "the establishment of Catholic schools in every place." The hierarchy were mandated to build such schools; Catholic parents were commanded to send their children to them. For parents who willfully neglected this command, the sanction was explicit: "that such parents, if obstinate, cannot be absolved, is evident from the moral teaching of the Church."[57] The Instruction of 1875 was the basis for the American clergy's pronouncement at the Third Plenary Council of Baltimore in 1884: "We not only exhort Catholic parents . . . but *command* them . . . to send [their children] to Catholic, and especially parochial schools."[58] In the nine years between the "Instruction" and the plenary council, most Catholic bishops had taken their mandate to heart; they had increased their efforts to construct parochial schools and had denied the sacraments to willfully neglectful Catholic parents.[59]

Not surprisingly, these actions led non-Catholic groups to sound

56. For the quotations see *Minutes of the Session of the New England Annual Conference of the Methodist Episcopal Church, 1891*, pp. 82–83; *Minutes of the National Council of the Congregational Churches of the United States of America: Annual Sesssion, 1877*, pp. 128–29. For similar attitudes on the part of other religious groups, see *Proceedings of the Annual Baptist Autumnal Conference for the Discussion of Current Questions, 1886*, p. 70; *Annual Report of the American Baptist Home Mission Society, 1850*, pp. 9–29; ibid., *1892*, p. 14; *The Churchman* (New York), 2 January 1886; *Minutes of the General Assembly of the United Presbyterian Church of North America, 1892*, pp. 31–33. For a useful sociological analysis, see Joshua Fishman, "Childhood Indoctrination for Minority-Group Membership," pp. 329–49.

57. The relevant sections of the "Instruction" are in J[ames] A. Burns, *The Growth and Development of the Catholic School System in the United States*, pp. 189–91. The phrase "cannot be absolved" meant that such parents could not receive absolution in the Sacrament of Penance (Confession) and, therefore, in good conscience, could not receive the other sacraments of the Catholic church.

58. The decree is in Hugh J. Nolan, ed., *Pastoral Letters of the American Hierarchy, 1792–1970*, p. 131, emphasis in the original.

59. Sr. M. Martina Hammill, *The Expansion of the Catholic Church in Pennsylvania*, p. 33; Edward Field, ed., *State of Rhode Island and Providence Plantation at the End of the Century*, 2:385; McNamara, *Diocese of Rochester*, pp. 157–66; Sharp, *Diocese of Brooklyn*, pp. 182–204.

the antipopery alarm. The worst of their earlier fears had been realized. The Catholic school system was growing; more Catholic children were being denied the spiritual uplift of public education; the society's moral progress, its homogenization, was being retarded: and all of this was in response to the dictates of a "foreign potentate." Worse yet, the Catholic hierarchy revived its antebellum claim to a share of the public-school fund. That claim, if conceded, would open the floodgates to a faster and more extensive growth of these socially divisive schools.

The renewed Catholic claim to public support arose from the simple dilemma that confronted the Catholic bishops. On the one hand, they were commanded to build Catholic schools; yet the growth of the Catholic school-aged population outstripped the available financial resources. Try as the clergy might to establish Catholic schools "in every place," they were never able to build a sufficient number to accommodate even a majority of Catholic students (see Table 6.5).[60] Even after two decades of rapid expansion, only 7.1 percent of the total nonsouthern school-aged population attended parochial schools by 1890. And even where the Catholic population was extremely large—e.g., in cities such as Brooklyn, New York, and St. Louis—the percentages were only 26.7 percent, 24.8 percent, and 20.2 percent, respectively.[61] It was true, of course, that in every area outside the South the rate of growth of parochial-school enrollments exceeded that of the public schools. However alarming such figures were to non-Catholic groups, both types of measures were less than satisfying to the Catholic hierarchy. The clergy's capacity to carry out its mandate was simply and severely limited by the financial resources at its disposal.[62] The inadequacy of those resources underlay their renewed drive to divide the public-school fund. Beginning

60. The data are from U.S., Census Office, *A Compendium of the Ninth Census (June 1, 1870)*, pp. 487–88, 493–504; U.S., Census Office, *Compendium of the Eleventh Census: 1890*, pt. 2, pp. 214, 216, 241, 243. The parochial-school data include both Catholic and Lutheran schools. Good data distinguishing the two are unavailable for 1870, but in 1890 Catholic parochial schools accounted for 81.4 percent of all the parochial-school students in the United States and 80.5 percent outside the South.

61. The data for these calculations are reported in Sharp, *Diocese of Brooklyn*, p. 204; Diane Ravitch, *The Great School Wars, New York City, 1805–1973*, p. 405; and Troen, *The Public and the Schools*, p. 34.

62. It was also limited by the fact that the "Americanizers" among the clergy opposed separate schools; see John Tracy Ellis, *The Life of James Cardinal Gibbons*, 1:658; Archbishop John Ireland, "State Schools and Parish Schools—Is Union between Them Impossible?" pp. 179–85. For some of the financial problems, see Burns, *Growth and Development of the Catholic School System*, pp. 274–93. On the drive for public funding, see Val Björnson, *The History of Minnesota*, 1:406; Wayland F. Dunaway, *A History of Pennsylvania*, pp. 442–45; Hynes, *Diocese of Cleveland*, pp. 124–25; Lord, Sexton, and Harrington, *History of the Archdiocese of Boston*, 3:69; Zwierlein, *Life and Letters of McQuaid*, 2:119–21. The non-Catholic reaction is clear in *Minutes of the Central Pennsylvania Annual Conference of the Methodist Episcopal*

TABLE 6.5   *Growth of Public and Parochial Schools, 1870 to 1890*

| | % of Total Pupils in: | | | | Annual Rate of Enrollment Growth, 1870–90, as % | |
| | Public Schools | | Parochial Schools | | | |
	1870	1890	1870	1890	Public	Parochial
New England	90.1	85.4	1.8	8.4	1.5	26.8
Midatlantic	85.7	85.5	5.4	8.4	2.4	6.4
East N. Cent.	93.2	87.6	6.6	8.3	0.8	2.7
West N. Cent.	91.2	91.2	1.7	4.6	10.2	34.3
South*	67.9	90.1	3.5	1.4	21.5	2.8
West	75.9	87.1	1.1	2.9	16.6	41.2
U.S.	86.4	88.3	4.7	5.4	5.2	6.2
U.S. minus South	89.7	87.6	4.9	7.1	2.9	6.7

*The Confederate and border regions ($N = 14$).

in the early 1870s, the Catholic clergy pressed that claim in Massachusetts, Minnesota, New Hampshire, Ohio, Pennsylvania, and seventeen other nonsouthern states. Coupled as it often was with freedom-of-worship proposals, the Catholic demand for a share of the public-school fund was seen by non-Catholic groups as further evidence of papist aggression.

They similarly perceived the Catholic assault on public-school curricula and practices. For those schools to play their evangelizing and homogenizing role, it was necessary for the children of the "religious formalists" to attend them, but the public schools also had to expose those children to a Christian and American education and environment —that is, to Bible reading, to instruction in temperance, to teachers steeped in morality and virtue, and to the English language. Since most Catholic children did not attend parochial schools, the Catholic hierarchy was also concerned about the type of education and environment that characterized the public schools. To the Catholic clergy those schools were worse than "Godless"; they were "Protestant." An integral part

Church, 1870, p. 40; *Minutes of the Vermont Annual Conference of the Methodist Episcopal Church, 1871*, p. 48; *Minutes of the National Council of the Congregational Churches of the United States of America: Annual Session, 1877*, p. 129; Joseph Calvin Evers, *The History of the Southern Illinois Conference of the Methodist Church*, p. 143.

of the clergy's concern for the education of Catholic children involved making the public schools less Protestant.

Catholic efforts to transform the public schools into religiously neutral socializing agencies entailed two critical demands. First, the clergy worked to eliminate Bible reading and associated devotional practices from the public schools. Second, they demanded that qualified Catholics be hired as teachers on an equal basis with non-Catholics. That is, they demanded the elimination of the then commonly used religious qualification for employment as a public-school teacher. Both demands, along with Catholic opposition to instruction in temperance and anti-Catholic textbooks, evoked non-Catholic furor. To non-Catholic groups Bible reading and "suitable teachers" were essential if the public schools were to uplift the "irreligious." The Catholic demands for religious neutrality struck at the essence of the role that they had assigned to public education. Their perception of public education as a means of homogenizing the society could never accommodate such "Romish aggressions." That they saw the conflict as vital and irreconcilable accounts for the superheated nature of the response: "*Resolved*, That we greatly deprecate the effort which is being made by 'Haters of Light,' and especially by an arrogant priesthood, to exclude the Bible from the Public Schools of our land; and that we will do all in our power to defeat the well defined and wicked design of this 'Mother of Harlots.' ''[63]

Bible reading, devotional ceremonies, and hiring practices were matters to be resolved by local school boards. And they were questions that in the 1870s and 1880s entailed a strong Catholic versus non-Catholic dimension. Another question—bilingualism—involved, but also cut across, that line of religious cleavage. Non–English-speaking groups often looked to the public schools to instruct their children in the language of their parents. For some groups instruction in the language was connected with their religious values; for others it was exclusively an effort at cultural maintenance. Both the religious and the irreligious joined forces in numerous states and localities to create a legal framework that permitted bilingual instruction in the public schools. By the end of the 1880s, such a framework had been created in Colorado, Illinois, Indiana, Iowa, Kansas, Minnesota, Ohio, and Wisconsin; separate bilingual statutes covered cities such as Baltimore, Cincinnati, Day-

---

63. *Minutes of the New Jersey Annual Conference of the Methodist Episcopal Church, 1870*, p. 24. For other examples of the reaction to both Catholic demands, see *Minutes of the Central Pennsylvania Annual Conference of the Methodist Episcopal Church, 1875*, p. 47; *Minutes of the Maine Annual Conference of the Methodist Episcopal Church, 1887*, p. 33; *Minutes of the New York Annual Conference of the Methodist Episcopal Church, 1880*, p. 27; *Minutes of the Annual Meeting of the Congregational Convention of Wisconsin, 1890*, p. 45; Strong, *Our Country*, pp. 89–106.

ton, Indianapolis, Louisville, St. Louis, and St. Paul. The details of the statutes varied, but in general they provided that some instruction be conducted in the German language. Typically, however, none (except Cincinnati's and Dayton's) went as far as Oregon's 1872 statute, which authorized monolingual German public schools. Native groups, of course, objected to use of the public schools to perpetuate any degree of foreignism, but they objected even more strenuously to an evolving de facto monolingualism. In many public-school districts where there was a large German-speaking population, especially in the Midwest, there was an ''irresistible temptation'' to hire German-speaking teachers and to conduct the school exclusively in German, regardless of the statutory provisions. In such districts students were not exposed at all to one of the crucial agents of homogenization, the English language.[64] The German-language question cut across Catholic–non-Catholic lines, and whenever and wherever it became a focal point (as it did especially by the late 1880s), it muted the partisan salience of the antipopery dispositions of the German Lutherans.

Overt manifestations of perceived Catholic political aggressiveness —their voting power, freedom-of-worship demands, and especially the multifaceted school question—interacted with long-standing anti-Catholic dispositions to heighten the political salience of antipopery. That in most locales throughout the North *Republican* had a standing aura of opposition to Romanism and *Democracy* an image as the Catholic party guaranteed its partisanization. To insure that effect, Republican officeholders and activists labored assiduously in the 1870s and 1880s to represent antipopery.

The objectives and actions of the Catholic clergy, not the acts and rhetoric of Republicans, initially projected a revived Catholic question into the public consciousness in the early 1870s. Most of the Catholic demands called for some action by public decision makers—e.g., state legislators, school boards, city councils. Proposals to satisfy these claims were usually presented to the relevant decision-making body as petitions signed by thousands of Catholic laymen. That action invariably generated acrimonious public debate and a flood of counterpetitions. The Catholic petition campaigns were not directed exclusively at any single level of government, but they evoked positive responses only from local governments. And even they were confined to places in

64. Joshua Fishman, *Language Loyalty in the United States*, pp. 92–126, 225, 233–36; Troen, *The Public and the Schools*, pp. 55–78; Tyack, *One Best System*, pp. 106–109. To a major extent the question involved the German language, but in some locales the same developments occurred with other non–English-speaking groups; see, for an example, Laurence M. Larson, *The Log Book of a Young Immigrant*, p. 100.

which Catholics composed a large segment of the electorate. For example, in 1874 the board of directors of Boston's penal and charitable institutions authorized the celebration of Sunday Mass for Catholic inmates, and in 1875 Rochester's Board of Education prohibited all religious exercises in that city's public schools.[65]

When Catholic pressure-group activity was reinforced by a mobilizable mass base of voting support, public decision makers tended to respond favorably to the petitions, although even then the response typically was slow and only partial. Yet that limited succcess did not escape the ever-watchful eyes of religious pietists. Their reaction followed a variety of political paths. They mobilized to present their own petitions and to defeat pro-Catholic decision makers in their reelection bids, though in some cities and localities the latter was a reasonably futile effort. Of greater significance was their tendency to shift the focus of action upward in the governmental hierarchy—to call for legislation at the state level. The pietistic conferences directed their pressure-group activity at the state level to overturn the pro-Catholic decisions that had been made (or were likely to be made) in the cities and towns, to counter Catholic pressure-group activity at the state level, to obviate any possibility of its success, and to imbed their own position into the organic law of the state. Thus, in twenty-two northern states they advocated a constitutional amendment to prohibit the expenditure of public funds in support of sectarian schools and custodial institutions, which the legislatures debated and usually approved. The ensuing referenda on ratification of the amendments transformed the Catholic question from primarily an object of pressure-group activity into a direct object of mass cognitions. Indeed, that occurred even where there was no referendum, for the involved pressure groups inquired into and publicized candidate and party stances on the Catholic question.[66]

No penetrating probe was necessary; everywhere, and at all levels of government, it was clear that Republican officeholders and activists —by their *acts*, speeches, and postures—represented anti-Catholic dispositions. In the state legislative battles Republicans cohesively opposed Catholic proposals and supported the antiaid amendments. The party's most visible public spokesman, President Grant, in September 1875 announced his position: "Encourage free schools, and resolve that not one dollar appropriated for their support shall be appropriated to the support of any sectarian schools." To implement that sentiment, James G.

65. Lord, Sexton, and Harrington, *History of the Archdiocese of Boston*, 3:71–72; Zwierlein, *Life and Letters of McQuaid*, 2:142.

66. For examples of both processes, see Charles B. Kinney, Jr., *Church and State*, pp. 137–38; Vecoli, *Peoples of New Jersey*, pp. 146–47.

Blaine introduced into the Congress a constitutional amendment to prohibit the expenditure of public funds for support of schools "under the
control of any religious sect." And Republican senators voted in consonance with their party's articulated position: on the two roll calls during
the Forty-fourth Congress, the Republicans unanimously favored, and
the Democrats unanimously opposed, a reworded version of the Blaine
amendment.[67]

Generally, Republican party builders were not reluctant either to
assume such postures or to project anti-Catholic images to their party. In
fact, most probably shared the anti-Catholic dispositions of their support
groups. But not all Republican leaders agreed that antiliquor should be
subordinated to antipopery. Some Republican leaders shared a pietistic
commitment to an ethic of ultimate responsibility and believed that the
party must publicly declare and work for the right. Such men could not
be reconciled to a mere joint preference ordering; they demanded "instead of the tyranny of the bosses . . . the free and conscientious exercise of private judgment in political affairs." Their responsiveness to the
temperance and sabbatarian demands of the party's pietistic constituency
underlay much of the factionalism that rent the officeholding and activist
segments of the late nineteenth-century Republican party, for other Republican leaders were aware of the changing demography and sought to
integrate new subgroups into the party's coalition.[68] These men perceived the coalition-developing possibilities that the Catholic question
provided. By following Rutherford Hayes's rule on the question of tem-

67. For an example of the state legislative alignment, see Forrest W. Clonts, "The
Political Campaign of 1875 in Ohio," pp. 66–68. The Grant quotation and the text of
the Blaine amendment are in *Appletons' Annual Cyclopaedia, 1875*, pp. 744, 79–80,
respectively. The Senate roll calls were conveniently published in *The Tribune Almanac
and Political Register for 1877*, pp. 22–23. In the House another wording of the Blaine
amendment was approved by a vote of 180 to 7, and the seven in opposition were all
Democrats (as were 116 of those who voted in favor). The wording of the two versions
differed substantively; it was not reconciled in conference. Garfield, in accepting the
Republican presidential nomination in 1880, reiterated the sentiment of Grant's exhortation; see Benton John Lossing, *A Biography of James A. Garfield*, p. 584. For the
intensity of the religious conflict in the 1880 election campaign, see Herbert J. Clancy,
The Presidential Election of 1880, pp. 168, 173–75, 201, 214.

68. The quotation is from the 1883 platform of Pennsylvania's Independent Republicans, in McClure, *Old Time Notes*, 2:534–35; see his discussion of the Independent
movement, ibid., pp. 531–48. For similar attitudes and their relation to Republican
factionalism elsewhere, see [Neal Dow], *Reminiscences of Neal Dow, Recollections of
Eighty Years*, p. 150; Thomas J. McCormack, ed., *Memoirs of Gustave Koerner,
1809–1896*, 2:577; Kleppner, *Cross of Culture*, pp. 124–26, 146, 161–64. The tensions produced an open rupture in the form of a group of Anti-Saloon Republicans in
1886; see *Appletons' Annual Cyclopaedia, 1886*, pp. 435, 645–46. For indications that
secular antiparty attitudes played an analogous role, see Carl Schurz to Charles Francis
Adams, 9 July 1876, in Frederic Bancroft, ed., *Speeches, Correspondence, and Political Papers of Carl Schurz*, 3:258–59.

perance—"Silence is the only safety"—and concentrating instead on "the subserviency of the Democratic party to Catholic designs," these Republican strategists hoped to enlist normally non-Republican voters while maintaining the support of their core pietistic groups. The touchstone of the joint preference ordering that they envisioned was antipopery. Although some other matters may have "appealed to the heads of citizens," the "Church Question" "went straight to their hearts."[69]

Those rekindled emotions did not die quickly. As Catholics continued to press their claims throughout the 1870s and 1880s, antipapist dispositions remained strongly salient to partisanship. In their national, and particularly their state, rhetoric, Republicans continued to remind the public of their persisting opposition to "Catholic designs" and especially of their soundness on the "school question." To voter groups fearful that the country was being converted into "the home of the Popes," the late nineteenth-century Republican party persistently presented itself as the natural and active agent of opposition to the "Catholic-Democratic Party."[70]

On their surface the electoral effects of this Republican strategy were hardly spectacular. Between 1876 and 1888, in a string of forty-three German counties from Pennsylvania through Illinois and Indiana, to Iowa, Minnesota, and Wisconsin, the Republicans cut the Democratic mean lead by 2.9 percentage points. More important, the party gained over thirty thousand new voters, and the size of the Republican vote in these counties was 26.2 percent larger than it had been in 1876.[71] And among the strongly confessional German Lutheran voters of Minnesota, Missouri, New Jersey, and Wisconsin, the Republicans increased their two-party share of the vote by 5.1 percentage points, from 35.3 percent

69. Hayes to W. Dean Howells, 24 August 1876, in Leo P. Coyle, ed., "Howells' Campaign Biography of Rutherford B. Hayes," pp. 398–99; Hayes to Major W. D. Bickham, 8 June 1875, in Williams, ed., *Diary and Letters of Hayes*, 3:276; *Cleveland Herald*, 13 October 1875, quoted in Clifford H. Moore, "Ohio in National Politics, 1865–1896," p. 300.

70. The quoted expressions in the final sentence are from an 1880 campaign document, *Pope or President?* pp. 6, 2. For the national Republican platforms see Kirk H. Porter and Donald Bruce Johnson, comps., *National Party Platforms, 1840–1968*, especially the Republican declarations on the school question, pp. 54, 61, 81. The 1874–88 state platforms can most conveniently be followed in *Appletons' Annual Cyclopaedia*.

71. In the southern-stock counties of Illinois and Indiana, whose voters were also likely to be moved by antipopery, the Republicans cut the Democratic partisan lead by 6.9 percentage points and increased the size of their vote by 46.1 percent. In both the German and southern-stock areas the increase in the size of the Democratic vote was well below that of the Republicans. In the Scandinavian counties the Republicans lost percentage strength but gained more new votes than the Democrats, and in the Yankee counties they lost percentage strength and gained fewer new votes than the Democrats.

in 1876 to 40.4 percent by 1888.[72] Political antipopery obviously did not produce surging Republican majorities, but it did enable the party to make at least marginal gains among a normally Democratic voter group. And even such small increments contributed materially to maintaining the tight partisan balance.

The Democracy, of course, resisted the appellation of "Catholic party." To have been reduced to Catholic voting support alone would have too narrowly constricted the party's mass base and would have guaranteed it a permanent minority. Yet without doubt, most Catholic voters were Democrats; and the acts, speeches, and postures of Democratic officeholders and activists represented popery as surely, but not as exclusively, as those of their Republican counterparts represented antipopery. To mobilize Catholic voters, anti-Catholic German Lutherans and minorities of Calvinist Baptists and Presbyterians, as well as southern-stock salvationist pietists, the Democracy could not simply portray itself as the party of Catholics; nor could it project a simple anti-Catholic image to its opposition. Of course, that it could not and did not is strong evidence that Democratic strategists perceived the latent anti-Catholic dispositions among some of the party's support groups, and aimed at keeping those proclivities latent rather than active and partisan. To assure the disparate social groups that composed the Democratic party in the electorate of the continuing rapport between their political characters and the party's, Democratic strategists emphasized opposition to sumptuary legislation, supported Catholic freedom-of-worship claims as means of securing equal rights to all citizens, and pledged their support to the common school system.[73] The joint preference ordering envisioned by Democratic party builders was summed and symbolized in their often repeated defense of personal liberty.

To Democratic rhetoricians *personal liberty* was a phrase that emotionally expressed the party's political character. It succinctly summarized the essence of the psychological rapport that existed among the party's officeholders, activists, and voters. It was at once one of those common symbols with which all three levels of the party identified and an articulation of a political norm that guided their respective behaviors. Linked with the party's regular denunciations of temperance and sabbatarian legislation, *personal liberty* resonated emotionally with the political character of German Lutheran (as well as Catholic) groups.

72. The Republican percentages for each year are weighted sums of regression estimates calculated separately for each of these states.

73. For the Democratic national statements see Porter and Johnson, comps., *National Party Platforms*, especially the statements on the school question, pp. 51, 56, 67. The state platforms are in *Appletons' Annual Cyclopaedia*.

It reminded them of the Democracy's continuing commitment to the proposition "that it is not the legitimate province of government to control the habits, tastes, appetites, and liberties of the people." Linked with the actions of the party's officeholders in supporting freedom-of-worship measures and opposing antiparochial-school proposals, *personal liberty* struck an emotionally responsive chord among Catholic voters. It reminded them that "all laws intended to restrain . . . a full and free exercise by any citizen of his own religious and political opinion . . . are anti-Democratic and hostile to the principles and traditions of the party." Linked with the party's rhetorical and behavioral defense of a division of governmental powers and opposition to increased centralization of power in the federal government, *personal liberty* expressed values and emotions central to the political characters of its southern constituency. It reminded them that Democracy's "unswerving maintenance" of the principle guaranteed the "purity of elections, and their absolute freedom from all interferences by the officers of the Federal Government."[74]

These are simple and wholly mechanical illustrations of linkages rooted in far more complex and subtle psychological processes. Yet even such inadequate examples focus the contrast between the joint preference orderings and political characters of the major parties. The essence of that contrast lay in their dispositions toward cultural pluralism, in their irreconcilable views both of the nature of society and of the role that government should play to mold that society to those perceptions. *Democracy* symbolized a commitment to cultural diversity and to that type of inactive, restricted government that would guarantee "the largest liberty consistent with public welfare."[75] At its mass base it enrolled subgroups whose political characters disposed them to value laissez faire ethics. On the other hand, *Republican* seemingly exhibited something of a split personality. Its two spirits, pietistic homogenization and a tactical but limited pluralism, contended with each other. Yet we should not overdraw the ostensibly schizoid character of the late nineteenth-century Republican party. At its heart, in its mass base, it remained what it had been since its inception: an agency for pietistic

74. Respectively, the quotations are from the Democratic platforms in Illinois 1882, California 1882, and Alabama 1880; in *Appletons' Annual Cyclopaedia, 1882*, pp. 385, 80; ibid., *1880*, p. 14. The sentiments, but not the precise phrasing, recurred frequently, though with the anticipated regional variations. In some places—e.g., Maine and Vermont—the Democrats were slow to attack prohibition, a fact that reminds that they retained a good deal of native-stock support in such areas. Also see the insightful discussion of "Personal Liberty," in the *Cyclopaedia of Temperance*, pp. 471–74.

75. Ohio Democratic platform 1882, in *Appletons' Annual Cyclopaedia, 1882*, p. 659.

reformation—a party that symbolized, more than Democracy, a religiously grounded animus to cultural pluralism. In the 1870s and 1880s that antipathy was directed against popery, because a variety of social groups had become alarmed by their perceptions of the increasing aggressiveness and political power of Catholics, but among the party's core support groups, that focus reflected a deeper and broader hostility to cultural diversity.

Conflicting and mutually exclusive dispositions toward cultural pluralism among subgroups structured partisan combat and gave psychological meaning to party identifications in the late nineteenth century. Party battles did not reflect a broad consensus over fundamentals but an irreconcilable conflict over the very nature of the society. Electoral contests were not simply struggles to control the distribution of patronage, nor to tinker with the tariff schedules; but as one contemporary expressed it, they involved "as great a conflict of moral and social ideas as I ever knew in this country."[76]

76. L. White Busbey, *Uncle Joe Cannon*, pp. 118–19; also see the observations on the revival of "the old spirit of Know-Nothingism" in the *Boston Post*, 8 September 1876.

7

The Politics of Political Pluralism: Minor Parties and the Third Electoral System

American conditions involve very great and peculiar difficulties for a steady development of a workers' party. . . . [I]mmigration . . . divides the workers into two groups: the native-born and the foreigners, and the latter in turn into (1) the Irish, (2) the Germans, (3) the many small groups, each of which understands only itself: Czechs, Poles, Italians, Scandinavians, etc. And then the Negroes. To form a single party out of these requires quite unusually powerful incentives.

Friedrich Engels (1893)

That time has come when party fealty must be a matter of secondary importance. The liquor traffic is dominant, . . . therefore, we must reconstruct our party affiliations. A vote cast for a party today does not mean the same as it did twenty years ago. In this matter we must heed the Divine command: "Come out from among them, and be ye separate, saith the Lord."

*Minutes of the New Jersey Annual Conference
of the Methodist Episcopal Church, 1892*

Although Engels and New Jersey's Methodist ministers had little else in common, each perceptively itemized a behavioral barrier to minor-party voting. As Engels saw it, in the absence of "quite unusually powerful incentives," ethnocultural antagonisms inhibited the development of a transethnic workers' party. The Methodist ministers pointed unmistakably to a recognition of party identification as a powerful constraint on minor-party support.

In fact, these separate obstacles were interrelated, for ethnic and religious conflict had shaped the lines of partisan combat and antagonistic political subcultures had generated party oppositions. Among most social groups partisanship had become inextricably connected with subcultural values, and through habituated partisan responses party as an institution had become a positive reference group. Thus, the individual's sense of self as "Democrat"—or "Republican"—was anchored in and expressive of group political culture. That complex psychological identification then served as a kind of "self-steering mechanism" that guided and shaped voters' responses to new political stimuli. By doing that, it also constrained most voting within the bounds of the major-party system.[1]

Yet despite formidable psychological as well as organizational obstacles, minor parties did appear during the stable phase of the third electoral era. Their emergence was at once a reflection and a contributing cause of the tight competitiveness that existed between the major parties. The role they played in contributing to the era's close partisan balance is evident from a number of simple indicators. The mean vote cast for minor parties in both the 1876–88 and the 1876–92 sequences of biennial elections exceeded the major-party mean partisan lead in the Midatlantic, the East North Central, the West North Central, and the Western regions of the country, as well as in the United States as a whole. Second, in three of the seven congressional elections between 1876 and 1888 (and four of the nine between 1876 and 1892), the percentage of the total vote cast for all minor parties was greater than the difference between the major parties' percentages. Perhaps it most directly and succinctly summarizes the growing prominence of minor parties to observe that although in 1876 they received only 1.2 percent of the total vote cast, they garnered 3.6 percent in 1888, 6.3 percent in 1890, and 11.0 percent in 1892.[2] By attracting actual or potential supporters from the major parties, by mobilizing voters beyond the psychological confines of the two-party system, minor parties helped to shape the close competitive structure of the third party system. As their leaders were fond of remarking, they held "the balance of power."

1. The phrasing is borrowed from William G. Shade et al., "Partisanship in the United States Senate," p. 188, n. 8; Angus Campbell et al., *The American Voter*, pp. 327–31. Although the analysis in this chapter concentrates on the behavioral constraints on minor-party voting, that should not be construed to mean that I assume legal-institutional constraints to have been nonexistent. For an excellent analysis of these, see Daniel A. Mazmanian, *Third Parties in Presidential Elections*, pp. 89–114. However, there are strong reasons to believe that such constraints had less impact in the nineteenth century than later. With neither an official ballot nor legal prerequisites for position on the ballot, it was easier for minor parties to field candidates and to contest elections. Much of the policy focus of nineteenth-century minor parties called for state and local action, and the calculus of forming coalitions at those levels differed in kind from that that later served as a powerful impediment to sustained development of a minor party of national scope.

2. The data are from Walter Dean Burnham, "The United States," p. 676. In both 1876 and 1892 the Democratic lead over the Republicans was 3.0 percentage points; of

If that aspect of their significance is reasonably clear, *why* they were able to attract an increasing number of supporters is much less so. In very general terms, we can explain such electoral mobilization as the result of emerging social tensions, and consequent social-group demands, that could not be adequately aggregated and accommodated by the existing parties. Under such conditions the involved groups, or some portions of them, might have had recourse to minor-party voting. However, to understand the dynamics underlying minor-party support during the late nineteenth century, we need to explore the general formulation in concrete social settings. We need to identify the tensions, the involved social groups, and the parties that became their vehicles for political expression.

We can begin that examination by distinguishing between the longest-lived minor party in American politics, the Prohibition party, and a series of more evanescent and variously labeled parties of "Farmer-Labor" protest.[3]

"Come Out . . . and be ye separate"

The Prohibition party was one of the more enduring by-products of the spasm of temperance activity that characterized the late 1860s and early 1870s. Disturbed by what they saw as a growing incidence of intemperance, alarmed by the national government's implicit sanctioning of the liquor traffic and state-legislative or court emasculation of prohibitory statutes, challenged by the organizational efforts of the "liquor forces" and their explicit commitment to political action, and, above all, disillusioned by the Republican party's seeming abandonment of principle,

---

the other years enumerated, only in 1890 was the Democratic margin (10.1 percentage points) greater than the size of the total third-party vote. The high point of third-party voting was 16.2 percent in 1878, but that included instances of major-party fusion and was rather clearly an atypical case. Moreover, my observation in the text refers to persisting minor-party strength and to its trend.

3. The term *Farmer-Labor* is used here, and throughout, simply as a convenient labeling device. It includes the variously named "Farmer" or "Granger" parties that arose in the Midwest in the 1870s; the Greenback party of the mid-1870s and later, as well as the various other labels under which that party contested for office (e.g., Greenback-Labor, National, Independent); the variety of "labor" parties, some only local or statewide, that appeared in the 1880s under labels such as Workingmen's, Union Labor, United Labor, Socialist Labor; and the Farmers' Alliance, Independent, Populist or People's parties that appeared in 1890 and 1892. The use of a single term to designate these does not imply an assumed continuity; it only avoids a lengthy listing of separate party labels. At appropriate points I shall discuss particular parties or clusters of parties and shall there make use of the specific labels or more precise generic surrogates.

some who had long been active in the "cold-water" cause decided on "independent political action."

New Hampshire's State Temperance Convention in 1866 called for the nomination of independent candidates whenever the nominees of the major parties were unacceptable, and Pennsylvania's State Temperance Convention in 1867 reiterated that declaration. In July 1868 the Sixth National Temperance Convention exhorted "the friends of temperance, by every practicable method in their several localities, to secure righteous political action for the advancement of the cause." One month later the Michigan State Temperance Convention, interpreting that exhortation to involve "the organization of a separate political party, comprising in its platform of principles the effective prohibition of the liquor traffic," issued a call for a state convention to establish such a party. That convention met in Jackson, Michigan, in January 1869, formed a state party, and adopted a state platform. Yet Michigan lost the "honor" of having had the first state Prohibition party, for in December 1868 the Illinois State Temperance Convention formed a Prohibition party, nominated a slate of state candidates, and adopted the first state declaration of principles. Revealingly, that platform opened with the declaration, "We acknowledge our dependence on God, and in His Name we set up our banners in the cause of temperance." Ohio's advocates of prohibition unfurled their party's banners and placed a state ticket in the field in July 1869. And in the same year "Independent" candidates publicly pledged to the prohibitory cause contested the gubernatorial elections in Maine and Minnesota.[4]

This early state-level activity was uncoordinated. Emerging from the state temperance conventions and temperance societies, it was intended primarily as a corrective response to particularistic grievances. Most of these early state organizers aimed more at pressuring the Republicans into firmer and less equivocal postures and actions than they did at party building. However, other prohibitionists were more resolutely committed to "independent political action" of a more encompassing scope. Through the Grand Lodge of Good Templars, they initiated the call for the formation of a national Prohibition party. That call went forth to the "Friends of Temperance, Law, and Order" on 27 May 1869, and

4. *Proceedings of the Sixth National Temperance Convention, 1868*, pp. 65–66; the rest of the quotations in this and the following paragraph are from D. Leigh Colvin, *Prohibition in the United States*, pp. 60–67. For more extensive information on the roots of the Prohibition party, see Paul Kleppner, "The Greenback and Prohibition Parties," 2:1566–71. In addition to these sources, the factual information in this and subsequent paragraphs can be followed in Ernest Hurst Cherrington, ed., *Standard Encyclopedia of the Alcohol Problem*; *The Cyclopaedia of Temperance and Prohibition*.

it invited them to meet in Chicago on 1 September "for the purpose of organizing for distinct political action for temperance." On that day some five hundred delegates—representing the Good Templars, the Sons of Temperance, the state and local temperance societies, and the conferences of the pietistic churches—assembled in Farwell Hall to begin in earnest their partisan crusade for God and cold water.

Of course, not all, nor even most, of the country's temperance zealots concurred with the decision to turn to distinctly partisan activity. In 1869 and throughout its existence, the Prohibition party was plagued by persisting tensions between those who wanted a separate political party and those who favored more broadly based nonpartisan, but still political, action. In the 1870s that tension erupted in conflicts over whether or not to support "dry" major-party candidates; in the 1880s it focused on whether to concentrate exclusively on securing adoption of prohibitory amendments to state constitutions or to combine that concern with advancing the fortunes of the Prohibition party. By the 1890s, and thereafter, it was reflected in the often acrimonious rivalry between the Prohibition party and the Anti-Saloon League. Whatever concrete form such tension took, it diluted mass support for the Prohibition party and complicated the task of party building.

The last thing that Prohibition party builders needed to face was conflict among the "saints"; the other obstacles in their path were formidable enough to dissuade any but the most righteous. Although in 1869 they had proclaimed the existence of a national party and had committed themselves to state party building, their organizational efforts lagged behind their rhetorical accomplishments. Despite being able to build on existing state temperance societies and conventions, as well as the dry fraternal orders, the Prohibition party grew slowly and sporadically throughout the 1870s and early 1880s. The party fielded tickets in only six states in 1870; Minnesota and Pennsylvania were added to the list in 1871. Yet in all but two of these, Massachusetts and New York, the formation of the state party had preceded that of the national organization. Prohibition was an organized party in only eighteen (of thirty-eight) states in 1876; that number fell to eight in 1878, bounced back to sixteen in 1880, and dropped again to thirteen in 1882. With the extension of party-building efforts into the former Confederacy, Prohibition was organized in thirty-four states in 1884, twenty-nine in 1886, thirty-seven in 1888, and thirty-two in 1890.[5]

There was a peculiar rhythm to these organizational efforts. It was

5. In 1892 there were forty-four states in the Union, and the Prohibition party fielded slates of electors in forty-one of these. It did not contest for the electoral votes of Louisiana, South Carolina, and South Dakota.

not at all unusual for the party to organize and contest one election, fade from the scene by the next, and then reappear at some subsequent point. This sporadic application of organizational energy only touches the surface of a larger set of irregularities attendant upon building the Prohibition party. Even when the party had organized a state central (or executive) committee, it did not always offer a slate of candidates. In some places—as in Rhode Island in 1875, 1876, and 1880—it fused with "Independent Republicans" to nominate a common state ticket. In other places, as in Iowa in 1882, it calculatedly shunned congressional nominations and concentrated attention on that year's prohibitory referendum. In many states it nominated presidential electors, but not state candidates, and in even more it fielded only partial slates of state and congressional nominees.

Partially, these hesitant and uneven efforts at building the party as an organization were an outgrowth of the partisan-nonpartisan tension that perennially infected the crusaders for prohibition. In part, too, they arose from the ambivalent relations between the Republican party and the prohibitory cause. Yet even in isolating these factors as contributing causes of the tardy and sporadic nature of Prohibition party building, we gain insight into the character of that party. To fuse with dry Republicans, to postpone organization and defer nominating candidates in the face of "acceptable" major-party stances and candidates were acts indicative of the party builders' preoccupation, not with the party as organization, but with the *cause*.

If building the Prohibition party as an organization was a slow and uneven exercise, developing the party in the electorate was even more so. The Prohibition party, through 1892 at least, never enlisted the support of large numbers or proportions of voters (see Table 7.1). Yet the party did fare somewhat better after 1882 than it had earlier. However, the importance of the mid-1880s as a period of transition for the Prohibitionists did not lie primarily in the obvious difference between the mean percentages but in the fact that only after 1882 did Prohibition begin to emerge as a party in the electorate.

Those who attach themselves to any political party have a sense of being "of" that party; the party label becomes for them "a symbol that provides cues and order to the political cosmos."[6] At the very least we expect that the party name becomes an object of habitual loyalty and guides their voting selections. And we should expect to be able to discover the existence of such a party in the electorate, a corps of habituated party supporters, by examining the distributions of party strength

6. Frank J. Sorauf, "Political Parties and Political Analysis," pp. 36–38.

TABLE 7.1   *Prohibition Party Strength: Percentage of Total Vote by Regions*

	Means by Time Segments			
	1886	1876–82	1884–92	1876–92
New England	3.5	0.3	2.7	1.6
Midatlantic	4.7	0.6	2.8	1.8
East N. Cent.	4.1	0.7	3.2	1.8
West N. Cent.	2.0	0.1	1.6	0.9
Confederacy	1.5	0.0	0.8	0.1
Border	1.8	0.3	1.6	0.8
West	4.2	0.5	2.6	1.6
U.S.	3.3	0.4	2.3	1.4

across offices in the same election and across elections in different years. In the case of a major party, for instance, correlations of its interoffice and interyear distributions are typically positive and quite high. That at least points to a persisting geographic base of partisan support. However, applying the same surrogate test to Prohibition distributions yields a quite different pattern.

Through 1882 the shape and geographic distribution of Prohibition voting support fluctuated quite widely, not only from one election to the next, but from one office to another in the same election year. As the data in Table 7.2 illustrate, *Prohibition* only slowly became a guide to voting behavior. Only in and after 1884 did its percentage distributions exhibit the empirical properties that we minimally require of a party in the electorate.[7] In the years prior to 1884, *Prohibition* was less a rallying symbol than it was a body of partisan activists who had failed to develop any regular voting constituency among the mass electorate. In view of the decades of agitation for temperance and the plethora of well-organized and hyperactive grass-roots temperance societies, that failure was especially striking. Even agreement on a principle important to their religious-value systems could not deflect most supporters of pro-

7. Gubernatorial data have been used for nonpresidential offices for Massachusetts and Maine, and congressional data from Ohio. The data given are only illustrative of the pattern that characterized most other states as well. And that pattern persisted regardless of which elections or offices were used. The only caveat of note is that in a few states the Prohibition distributions did not stabilize as early as 1884; e.g., in Missouri the interoffice correlation in 1884 President/Governor, $r = .410$; and 1888 President/Governor, $r = .944$.

hibition from their old party identifications. They worked actively and energetically for the cold-water cause, but only a small minority of them ever abandoned fealty to their old parties.

Who were these dedicated diehards who supported Prohibition? What, in other words, were the partisan and social sources of the party's electoral coalition? There are ample clues to the partisan sources of both the party's leaders and voters. First, most of the party's prominent leaders acknowledged their former connections with the Republican party. For example, when Wendell Phillips accepted the 1870 gubernatorial nomination of the Prohibition and Labor Reform parties of Massachusetts, he explicitly described the former party affiliations that his fellow advocates of temperance had held: "As temperance men you were bound to quit the Republican party, since it has deceived you more than once." And his was no lonely voice in the wilderness. Prohibition party leaders frequently spoke of their former associations with the Republican party and of that party's earlier commitment to principle. They found dedication to morality lacking in the party's character, and that perceived void impelled their exodus. *Republican* no longer rallied their support, be-

TABLE 7.2   *Prohibition Party Distributions: Interoffice and Interyear Coefficients of Determination (r^2)*

	Massachusetts	Maine	Ohio
Interoffice			
1880	.483	.312	.003
1884	.931	.652	.552
1888	.994	.929	.925
1892	.986	.960	.774
Interyear			
President			
1880/1884	.001	.023	.439
1884/1888	.822	.815	.619
1888/1892	.893	.819	.767
Non-President			
1880/1884	.178	.033	.017
1884/1888	.802	.546	.292
1888/1892	.896	.630	.553

cause it no longer grappled with their "present living difficulties . . . the dangers of intemperance."[8]

Second, when Prohibition party leaders crafted their public rhetoric, when they set out to mobilize voter support, they addressed themselves primarily to Republican voters. Repeatedly, their state platforms accused the Republicans of having betrayed the holy cause. The Massachusetts Prohibitionists in 1875 denounced Republican pandering for "the liquor vote" and declared that "the safety of the Republican party and of the cause of prohibition, depends upon the amputation of the liquor wing of the party, making the party a unit for the right." Republican refusal to support a prohibitory amendment was condemned by the Illinois Prohibitionists in 1882 as nothing less than a "betrayal of the people." And New Hampshire's Prohibitionists in 1888 affirmed "that the Republican party . . . is guilty of the evils of the liquor traffic in this state."[9]

Of course, Prohibition's declarations also condemned the Democrats, but their attitude toward them was revealingly distinct. The Democrats were simply the party of the "liquor traffic," the "saloon party," the "Rumocracy." "Nowhere" had that party "stood for progressive temperance action, by legislation or any other means." "Everywhere the Democrats have . . . favored the liquor traffic."[10] Given this Prohibitionist perception of the political character of Democracy, it anticipated little support from voters who had an internalized sense that they were of that party. The case was different with the Republican party and its identifiers. That party had regularly provided legislative and platform support for temperance. And that party, at least more than Democracy, continued to provide legislative votes for the local-option and prohibitory amendments of the 1870s and 1880s.[11] Yet Prohibitionists reserved

8. Both quotations are from Phillips's letter accepting the gubernatorial nominations; the text of the letter is in *Cyclopaedia of Temperance*, p. 477. Also see the revealing discussion of the involvement of Prohibition party leaders in the antebellum crusade against slavery, in ibid., under the heading "Anti-Slavery Parallel," pp. 30–33; Colvin, *Prohibition in the United States*, pp. 59–60.

9. *Appletons' Annual Cyclopaedia and Register of Important Events of the Year 1875*, p. 479; ibid., *1882*, p. 385; ibid., *1888*, p. 594. These are only isolated examples of what was a very clear preoccupation in Prohibition state platforms.

10. The descriptive references were common in Prohibition platforms and in statements of the party's leaders. The summary of the Democracy's attitudes and actions on prohibition was given as an editorial remark following a cataloging of the 1888 state platform pronouncements of that party; *The Political Prohibitionist for 1889*, p. 39. Also see the similar evaluative summary given in ibid., *1887*, p. 29; ibid., *1888*, p. 143.

11. For examples of continuing Republican legislative support for such measures, see [Neal Dow], *The Reminiscences of Neal Dow, Recollections of Eighty Years*, pp. 564–65; Hobart Pillsbury, *New Hampshire*, 2:621; D. W. Lusk, *Eighty Years of Illinois*, pp. 322, 412; Joseph Benson Foraker, *Notes of a Busy Life*, 1:224–25; *Appletons' Annual Cyclopaedia, 1886*, p. 646.

their most astringent epithets for the Republicans. The Republican party was guilty of "treason," "betrayal," "fraud," "deception"; and, worst of all, it was "afraid" to apply "Christian principles to politics."[12] Such rhetoric implied a Prohibitionist perception that numerous supporters of temperance identified with *Republican* because they viewed that party as a partisan agent through which to dry up their society. The harshness, frequency, and extensiveness of anti-Republican references were aimed at converting these Republicans for temperance into Prohibition voters.

A final qualitative clue to the partisan origins of the Prohibition party's voters can be found in assessments by contemporary politicians. Republican political leaders were acutely sensitive to the advent of the Prohibition party. They realized that the Prohibitionists attracted voting support from among normally Republican voters. In 1884, for instance, Rutherford Hayes estimated that ten to fifteen thousand Republican voters in Ohio would give their ballots to the Prohibition candidates, and Benjamin Harrison counted on a loss of four thousand Republican voters to Indiana's Prohibition party. Although we may assume that such estimates were imprecise at best, they do indicate a concern among Republican leaders. In turn, that concern attests to their perception that the political character of Prohibition would appeal to some among their normal support groups.[13]

Contemporary estimates or perceptions may have been wholly or partially inaccurate. However, we need not rely on qualitative evidence alone. The data in Table 7.3 (Panel A) point to the fact that in most states (outside the Confederacy) the rise of the Prohibition party steeply and negatively impacted Republican strength.[14] In Wisconsin, for example, the Republicans lost 0.73 percentage points for every 1.0 percentage point polled by the Prohibitionists. Only New Jersey seems anomalous

12. For examples of the epithets, see the summaries and characterizations of Republican attitudes on temperance in *Political Prohibitionist for 1887*, pp. 17–27; ibid., *1888*, pp. 139–44; ibid., *1889*, pp. 30–37. The reference to "Christian principles in politics" is in the Maine Prohibition party platform, in *Appletons' Annual Cyclopaedia, 1886*, p. 522.

13. Diary of Rutherford B. Hayes, 14 October 1884, in Charles R. Williams, ed., *Diary and Letters of Rutherford Birchard Hayes*, 4:167; Harrison's estimate is quoted in Harry J. Sievers, *Benjamin Harrison*, p. 270. For additional contemporary observations that point in the same direction, see Pillsbury, *New Hampshire*, 2:563, 575, 578; H. B. Payne to J. R. Doolittle, 14 August 1884, in Duane Mowry, ed., "Letters of Senator H. B. Payne of Ohio," p. 547; Foraker, *Notes*, 1:429; John Sherman, *Recollections of Forty Years*, 2:1002–1003; [Dow], *Reminiscences*, pp. 149–50.

14. Except for Maine, the measures in Panel A were calculated by counties; those for Maine and those in Panel B were executed by minor civil divisions within counties. Partisan strength used for the regressions in Panel A was the mean for all contested offices over the 1884–92 sequence of elections. The New York data, however, are from Albert Charles Edward Parker, "Empire Stalemate," n. 15, p. 375, and involve the Republican 1880–88 losses with Prohibition strength in 1888.

TABLE 7.3   *Partisan Sources of Prohibition Support*

A. *Change in Republican 1876–92 Vote for Every 1.0% Increase in Prohibition Strength*

	Change (%)	r^2
Maine	−1.09	.353
Minnesota	−1.99	.559
Missouri	−1.25	.165
New Jersey	− .13	.024
New York	− .82	.224
Wisconsin	− .73	.302

B. *Partisan Composition of 1886 New Jersey Prohibition Vote*

County	Dem	Repub	1886 Prohib Mean
Cape May	23.9	76.0	15.4
Cumberland	37.8	62.1	20.8
Hudson	13.1	86.8	3.3
Hunterdon	62.4	37.5	12.9

and inconsistent with the brunt of contemporary testimony. There the Republican decline was relatively mild, and unlike any of the other states, the Democratic vote also declined as Prohibitionist strength increased.[15] In other words, in New Jersey the Prohibitionists cut noticeably into the strength of both major parties; this bipartisan recruitment to the cold-water coalition can best be observed by examining the relevant data at the minor civil-division level (see Panel B, Table 7.3).[16] The contrast is apparent. In heavily urban and foreign-stock Hudson County (Hoboken and Jersey City) the pattern was quite typical of the northern states: over 80.0 percent of the Prohibitionist voters had migrated to that party from their old Republican home. In the rural southern and especially the northwestern counties of New Jersey, the Prohibitionist coalition was composed of larger proportions of former Democrats than in Hudson.

15. The 1876–92 Democratic strength declined by −.05 percentage points for every 1.0 percentage point increase in Prohibition strength, and $r^2 = .004$.

16. The data are regression estimates involving the 1884–86 Democratic and Republican first differences and the 1886 Prohibition strength. A similar analysis by minor civil divisions within other states did not reveal variation as strong as in New Jersey.

The New Jersey case draws attention to the nature of Democratic-to-Prohibition voter movement. There was still some lingering old-stock support for the Democracy, and among such voters there was inducement to jump aboard the Prohibitionist water wagon. Hunterdon County in northwestern New Jersey was an extreme instance of that. It was a heavily native-stock county (87.4 percent in 1890) with a relatively low proportion of Catholics and Lutherans among its churchgoing population.[17] Given only a knowledge of its demography, one would have expected it to return large Republican majorities. Instead, it was one of those "deviant cases," a lingering remnant of the second party system—a native-stock, Protestant county that was normally and strongly Democratic. In the thirteen biennial elections between 1860 and 1884, Hunterdon's mean Democratic strength was 57.2 percent.[18] However, in 1886 the Prohibition party made inroads among the county's dry Democrats that were as sizable as those among the dry Republicans of Cape May and Cumberland counties: 62.4 percent of Hunterdon's 1886 Prohibition voters had earlier been Democrats.

Hunterdon County was an extreme, but not a unique, instance. The small Democratic-to-Prohibition voter movement in New York occurred largely among the Penn-Jerseyites, and in Ohio it was also confined to native-stock Democrats.[19] These were voters socialized into Democratic identifications that had been forged initially in an earlier electoral era. However, with the passage of time, their own and the party's political characters had become increasingly discordant. Yet they were also voters whose sense of "being a Democrat" included antipathy to *Republican*. They were, accordingly, prime recruits for a party other than Republican whose character was more nearly consonant with their own value systems. Prohibition was one such party.

That the Prohibition vote was composed largely of former Republicans, augmented by smaller numbers of native-stock Democrats, suggests the nature of its social base. The data in Table 7.4 make that

17. In 1890 only 21.2 percent of the religiously affiliated were Catholics or Lutherans; 26.3 percent were Methodists; 24.8 percent were Presbyterians; and 12.5 percent were Baptists.

18. Walter Dean Burnham, *Presidential Ballots, 1836–1892*, p. 203, errs in assigning the county to the Republicans from the 1864 through 1892 presidential elections. However, his voting data for the county (pp. 630–31) are correct and show a mean Democratic percentage for the 1868–92 presidential elections of 57.4 percent. For more on the county's dry proclivity, see Samuel T. McSeveney, *The Politics of Depression*, p. 22.

19. For insights into the social base of Prohibition voting in New York, see Parker, "Empire Stalemate," Tables XIII-2, XIII-3, XIII-4, pp. 378, 382, 384; for New York and Ohio see John Lockwood Hammond, Jr., "The Revivalist Political Ethos," pp. 234–35, 262–65.

suggestion explicit. Prohibitionist candidates ran best in areas of Republican strength, in the Yankee and Scandinavian counties, and poorest in southern-stock and German units.[20] In eastern states, such as New Jersey, the party drew support among native Baptist, Methodist, and Presbyterian voters. New York's Prohibitionists drew an average of 5.3 percent of the vote in Baptist towns, 4.3 percent in Methodist communities, and 4.0 percent in Presbyterian/Congregational units. In that state the party also polled 4.9 percent of the vote in New British towns and 6.0 percent in New Dutch towns.[21] To the west, in states like Minnesota and Wisconsin, Prohibition's mass coalition was more heavily immigrant. In those states it received its strongest support from Swedish and Norwegian Lutherans. Iowa's Prohibitionists secured little voter support from any group. The party's rise and development there were retarded by periodic Republican flirtation with the cause. What little mass strength Prohibitionists polled came from native and immigrant pietistic groups. In Missouri and Maryland the Prohibitionist social coalition was nearly exclusively native stock. In Missouri it drew support from the normally Republican northern Methodists and Presbyterians, and in Maryland from among these groups as well as from normally Democratic southern Baptists and Methodists. Prohibition's recruitment of former Democrats in Maryland was especially strong in a number of heavily white voting districts on the eastern shore—particularly in Somerset, Wicomico, and Worcester counties.[22] In such places Prohibition support and votes for local-option laws were reflections of the black-white polarities that long had characterized the political and social behaviors of the involved groups. Voting dry, whether for the party or the local laws, was simply one dimension of the broader white effort to control the social behavior of blacks.

Apart from some racially motivated support among two groups of salvationist pietists in Maryland, a common dimension underlay Prohibition voting support. Ballots for that party came disproportionately from among religious groups whose value systems mandated the sanctification of their society.[23] Among minorities within such groups, the

20. Even its low percentage in the German counties probably came from non-Germans. Regression estimates of German support for Prohibition, not surprisingly, are consistently negative. Some of the regression estimates used to calculate the means presented in Table 7.4 are unstable since the number of counties (and therefore cases) is less than thirty for Maryland and New Jersey.

21. The New York data are the 1884–92 mean Prohibition percentages cast in such units and are from Parker, "Empire Stalemate," Tables XIII-2, XIII-4, pp. 378, 384.

22. The Prohibition party also ran better in the white districts of the southwestern-shore counties than it did in more strongly black units there or among whites in western Maryland.

23. Probably most of the former Democrats who cast ballots for Prohibition candi-

TABLE 7.4   *Social Sources of Prohibition Support*

A. *Mean Prohibition Percentages by Types of Counties*

	Yankee (N = 71)	Southern Stock (N = 18)	German (N = 43)	Scandinavian (N = 33)
$\overline{M}$ 1876–82	1.3	0.0	0.3	0.4
$\overline{M}$ 1884–92	4.3	1.4	1.3	5.0
$\overline{M}$ 1876–92	2.8	0.7	0.8	2.7

B. *Mean 1886–92 Estimates of Prohibition Voting*

	Iowa	Minn	Wis	New Jersey
Swedish Luth	2.9	12.0	15.4	N.C.
Norwegian Luth	0.6	8.0	14.7	N.C.
Baptist	1.5	3.7	2.2	7.5
Methodist	2.4	1.0	2.0	4.1
Presby/Cong'l	2.1	N.C.	1.5	6.3

	Maryland	Missouri
Meth-North	4.3	2.2
Meth-South	4.2	0.5
Presby-North	5.4	5.1
Presby-South	0.0	0.7
Baptist-South	5.2	0.8

(N.C. indicates that the estimates were not calculated.)

cold-water party was seen as the best partisan hope for carrying out God's will. Yet only minorities of such groups, and relatively small ones at that, ever broke away from their normal Republican moorings to cast Prohibition votes. It is tempting to speculate that those minorities

dates in other states also constituted a minor exception. To the extent that these came from the more Calvinistic of the Baptist and Presbyterian groups, the movement was not impelled by a pietistic imperative but more likely was motivated by antiforeign and anti-Catholic values, coupled with the perception that Democracy in their states had come to represent foreigners and Catholics more so than it did their own values.

comprised the most ardent, most zealous, most pietistic within each of the larger groups, but in the absence of systematic individual data, that must remain unconfirmed speculation. What need not remain speculative, however, is the nature of the appeal that Prohibition held for evangelical pietists. It could rally voting support from among these groups because its political character was consonant with theirs. And no trait of Prohibition better summed and symbolized that shared psychological rapport than its powerful animus to party.

The small band of zealots who assembled in Chicago in 1869 to fashion an agency for "independent political action" did not see theirs as a political party in the conventional sense. Surely, they bowed to prevailing usage, employed the term *party*, and applied it to themselves. Yet when they did, they also made clear that theirs was not a party in the same way as the Democrats and Republicans, for the old parties were bereft of principle, and Prohibition was first and foremost an agent of morality. It had been called forth by the exigencies of the era, by the growing incidence of intemperance and the moral destruction wrought by the "rum power," and by the failure of conventional parties to contend for the right. Its aim was to arouse the public conscience, to alert it to the grave moral dangers that beset the nation, and to guide it to righteous action. That required engaging in the customary party practices, issuing platforms and addresses, nominating candidates, and conducting campaigns for office. However, the objective was the principle, the cause, not the building of a permanent organization that would itself become an object and symbol of habituated loyalty. That sort of habituated loyalty implied a bondage to party that was akin to "the bondage of strong drink."[24] It prevented men from seeing the right and acting on the dictates of their consciences. Party was an obstacle to righteousness, a perverting intermediary between God's commands and man's free will. And men should always be free to follow their consciences, "not bound by . . . party, bound only by the law of right."[25]

The Prohibition party's first "Address to the People of the United States" made this thinking about party explicit. Bondage to party was an ally of the liquor forces. It prevented a union of the antirum voters and allowed the rum power to dominate politics. That this should have come about was no coincidence but an inevitable consequence of having permanent political parties:

A very lamentable evil is the education of the people into the belief that a permanent political party is a great good. . . . But a permanent political party

24. The quoted phrases are from an 1882 resolution of the New Hampshire State Temperance Union, in *Appletons' Annual Cyclopaedia, 1882*, pp. 593–94.
25. August F. Fehlandt, *A Century of Drink Reform in the United States*, p. 386.

with the constant tendency of any such party to destruction is a heavy curse, for it plants itself with great, and too frequently with invincible, power in the way of all progress, and clings for its own existence to the wrongs with which it is identified. No other but temporary political parties are justifiable—no other but as occasions call for. . . . Right was it in Americans to form an anti-slavery party, and right is it now for them to pass on from the overthrow of slavery to an anti-dramshop party.

Parties, in other words, should arise in response to great moral questions, channel mass opinion on them, and then dissolve. The party organization should not become an end in itself, nor the party label an enduring symbol of mindless voter loyalty. Neither should the party tailor its acts and postures to win votes, to expand its electoral coalition; rather, it should always maintain "a brave and uncompromising regard for the right." The path of righteousness might not be the road to electoral victories, and the party might not succeed in eliminating the liquor traffic. That, however, would not be cause for despair, for "even though we shall have utterly failed in our object . . . a great success will nevertheless be ours—the great success of having done our duty."[26]

Party founders who distrusted party, who valued effort as highly as success, and who were more concerned with righteousness than with the size of their total vote lacked the dispositions to build a pragmatic, subgroup-integrating partisan vehicle. Indeed, they found precisely such traits in the old parties, particularly in the Republican party, morally obnoxious. By design, then, theirs was to be the antithesis of what the old parties had become. Theirs was to be an antiparty party.

The antiparty rhetoric that permeated Prohibitionist pronouncements, especially in its early years, reflected the evangelical pietists' persisting antipathy to any encumbrance on the operation of man's free will to do right. That disposition underlay the party builders' tardy, sporadic, and often reluctant organizational efforts, as well as the party's slowness to develop as a rallying symbol.

Yet in time even Prohibition acquired its own urge to survive. The party's merger with the Woman's Christian Temperance Union in 1882, the reconstitution of its national committee, the emergence of new leadership that had not been involved in the antebellum moral crusades, and

26. First "Address to the People of the United States," 1869, in Colvin, *Prohibition in the United States*, pp. 75–81; the quotations, respectively, are on pp. 78, 80, 81. The "Address" was written by the old New York Abolitionist Gerrit Smith. He had wanted to name the party the Anti-Dramshop Party, believing that that name would fasten upon its political opponents the label *Dramshop Party*. Also see the lengthier exposition of the Prohibition conceptions of the political process and political parties in Fehlandt, *Century of Drink Reform*, pp. 385–405.

experience in mobilizing mass support for the prohibitory referenda of the 1880s produced a distinctly greater emphasis on building the party apparatus and a commitment to its permanence. From the mid-1880s Prohibition party builders, although never enthusiastic, at least resignedly tended to accept party as a necessary evil: "So long as legislatures are made and courts created by political parties, unorganized public opinion upon any political question is of but little value. Even prohibition in the Constitution will avail but little without an efficient party honestly and earnestly committed to its enforcement."²⁷ As a consequence, much of the antiparty rhetoric of the later 1880s was probably more tactical than evangelical in its design. Even so, a religiously rooted suspicion of party was barely below the surface, and on occasion it broke through. For example, New York's Prohibition *party* in 1882 publicly resolved, "We do not identify ourselves with any partisan movement"; they identified themselves instead as representatives of the "Christian churches . . . seek[ing] such legislation as shall free our noble State from the power of rum." In 1884 Indiana's Prohibitionists prefaced their dispirited acceptance of party organization with a stirring denunciation of party practices as "subversive of public morals." And the December 1889 "Address to the People" by the National Executive Committee of the Prohibition party declaimed against an "intensity of party zeal."²⁸

Whether the purport of such rhetoric was evangelical or tactical, the effect was similar. *Prohibition* became a symbol of all-or-nothing righteousness, of unswerving commitment to God's will. It symbolized opposition to the accommodating, pragmatic, and therefore morally degenerative, customary practices of political parties. In that way it represented members of social groups whose political characters embodied antiparty values. A shared commitment to an ethic of ultimate responsibility was the essence of that affinity, and antiparty, linked with opposition to the rum power, its rhetorical linchpin.

Of course, among strongly pietistic groups ultimate commitments and antiparty values had long been rife. Religious groups such as the

27. Indiana Prohibition platform, 1884, in Colvin, *Prohibition in the United States*, p. 151. For examples of similar pronouncements, see the text of the Ohio Prohibition platform, 1889, in Colvin, *Prohibition in the United States*, pp. 184–85; Pennsylvania Prohibition platform, 1886, in *Appletons' Annual Cyclopaedia, 1886*, pp. 749–50; New Jersey Prohibition platform, 1890, in *Manual of the Legislature of New Jersey for 1891*, pp. 149–50. For details on the developments in the 1880s, see Kleppner, "Greenback and Prohibition Parties," 2:1574–77.

28. New York's Prohibitionists nominated a candidate for governor. The quotations, respectively, are in *Appletons' Annual Cyclopaedia, 1882*, p. 608; Colvin, *Prohibition in the United States*, pp. 151, 239–40; see ibid., pp. 152–54, for the 1884 convention address delivered by John Russell.

Episcopalians and Catholics urged personal abstinence from liquor but were indifferent or hostile to statutory or constitutional prohibition.[29] Confessional German Lutherans not only denounced prohibition but condemned as sinful involvement in organizations where membership was contingent on abstinence from intoxicating beverages. Even that form of voluntary obligation "would militate against Christian liberty."[30] The native and immigrant pietistic conferences had condemned any use of liquor as a sin and had resolved: "no compromise." These groups were energetically involved in the nonpartisan aspects of the crusade, the church, and local and state temperance societies and unions.[31] From among these groups Prohibition recruited political activists; from among them, too, it recruited its voters.

Most pietists were Republicans, and being of that party was for them a secular expression of religious values. To be a Republican was to be of the "party of morality." However, immorality was again on a rampage, and its resurgence was the inevitable consequence of the liquor traffic. To stamp out immorality in all of its forms, guises, and manifestations was the divine mandate of the "saved." Accordingly, some pietists viewed attitudes on prohibition as a litmus test of moral purity. To combat the rum power, they turned, as they had earlier in their battle against the "slave power," to their own partisan engine of moral reform, the Republican party, but that party compromised; it refused to stand unequivocally for the right. Thus the pietistic conferences in the 1870s and 1880s spoke of "betrayal" and declaimed against the spirit of party. Their conference resolutions warned churchmen not to be "managed" or "controlled by party" but to hold "an independent atti-

29. See the categorization of Catholic and Protestant-Episcopal temperance organizations in the *Political Prohibitionist for 1889*, p. 79. The attitudes of these and other denominations can conveniently be followed under the appropriate listings in *Cyclopaedia of Temperance*; and Cherrington, ed., *Standard Encyclopedia of Alcohol*.

30. C. F. W. Walther to the Rev. J. A. Ottesen, 5 January 1886, in Carl S. Meyer, ed., *Letters of C. F. W. Walther*, pp. 106–107. The more pietistic of the German Lutherans did endorse prohibition, but never with the uncompromising ardor nor the antiparty references that typically characterized the pietistic groups; see, for examples, *Proceedings of the Convention of the General Synod of the Evangelical Lutheran Church in the United States, 1881*, pp. 65–66; ibid., *1883*, pp. 45–46; ibid., *1887*, pp. 61–62; *Minutes of the Annual Convention of the Wittenberg Synod of the Evangelical Lutheran Church [of Ohio], 1882*, p. 27; ibid., *1883*, p. 29.

31. The discussion that follows concentrates on native-stock groups, but the fact that the Norwegians and Swedes shared analogous value systems and political dispositions is unmistakable. For more extended discussion of that, see Paul Kleppner, *The Cross of Culture*, pp. 84–88. For further contemporary evidence see Arlow W. Andersen, *The Salt of the Earth*, p. 155; Laurence M. Larson, *The Log Book of a Young Immigrant*, pp. 55, 112; N[iles] N[ilsen] Rønning, *Fifty Years in America*, p. 80; Emmer Engberg, ed., *Centennial Essays*, p. 144; A[lvin] D. Mattson, *Polity of the Augustana Lutheran Church*, p. 447; Sam Rönnegard, *Prairie Shepherd*, pp. 19–20.

tude" toward political parties, for "reform, . . . the interests of temperance and good government . . . should be independent" of parties. Whatever God condemned as sin could not be tolerated; it must be abolished. "Partisan fellowship" with organizations that countenance sin was "treason against the authority of the Son of God and antagonistic to the Gospel Church and its saving work." The choice was clearly between holiness and sin, between Christ and party: "The supreme allegiance of the Christian is due to Jesus Christ, and not to political parties."[32]

Only small minorities of pietists ever equated duty to Christ with Prohibition party voting. Most pietists remained Republicans, because to them *Republican* continued to symbolize morality; their sense of being a Republican was too strong, too habituated, to yield defection or abandonment. For other pietists morality was more exclusively linked with the cold-water cause. Both had earlier found psychological expression in their identification with *Republican*. These men abandoned their old political church reluctantly, slowly, and only when they began to perceive that its aura of "morality in general" masked a lack of righteous dedication to "morality in particular." The "party of great moral ideas" had become pragmatic; its character no longer resonated with theirs; the acts, speeches, and postures of its leaders no longer represented their hyperzealous sense of ultimate responsibility. Those who had internalized that ethic and had linked it with the prohibitory cause were responsive to the antirum, antiparty pronouncements of their religious conferences. And in Prohibition—in its antirum, antiparty aura—they found an overt cue to their voting behavior. They became converts, not

32. Respectively, the quotations are from *Minutes of the New York Annual Conference of the Methodist Episcopal Church, 1887*, p. 76; *Minutes of the Session of the New England Annual Conference of the Methodist Episcopal Church, 1887*, pp. 45–46; *Minutes of the Ohio Annual Conference of the Methodist Episcopal Church, 1888*, pp. 37–38; *Minutes of the Maine Annual Conference of the Methodist Episcopal Church, 1891*, pp. 48–49; *Minutes of the Session of the Missouri Annual Conference of the Methodist Episcopal Church, 1892*, p. 184. There was no doubt that the northern Methodists were the most explicit about connecting the twin evils of party spirit and the rum power; I suspect that Methodist ministers were the most numerous of the denominational leaders among Prohibition party activists. However, for examples of analogous, though sometimes less explicit, linkages by other denominations, see *Minutes of the Annual Meeting of the Dane [Wisconsin] Association of Baptist Churches, 1876*, p. 6; *Minutes of the Annual Meeting of the Maine Baptist Missionary Convention, 1890*, p. 56; *Minutes of the Anniversary of the Philadelphia Baptist Association, 1873*, pp. 29–30; *Minutes of the National Council of the Congregational Churches of the United States of America: Annual Session, 1880*, p. 32; *Minutes of the Annual Meeting of the General Association of the Congregational Churches of Massachusetts, 1889*, pp. 17–23; *Minutes of the General Assembly of the Cumberland Presbyterian Church, 1890*, p. 43; ibid., *1891*, p. 34; ibid., *1892*, pp. 43–44; the resolutions quoted under the appropriate denominational headings in the *Cyclopaedia of Temperance*.

because they had arrived at some new understanding of morality, but because they perceived their old political church to be permeated by moral decay and because they saw Prohibition as a pristine agent through which the "saved" would make holy their world.

The Republican and Prohibition parties competed for votes among the same social types, native and immigrant pietists. The Prohibition party's aura of righteousness enabled it to cut into Republican voting strength and thus further jeopardize that party's electoral chances, but the Prohibition party was only one of a variety of late nineteenth-century minor parties. Each of these had an impact on the electoral coalitions and strategies of the major parties.

"Quite unusually powerful incentives"

Engels was right. American conditions did involve "great and peculiar difficulties" for the development of a workers' party. He called explicit attention to the role of ethnocultural divisiveness among subgroups of workers, but he could have itemized other obstacles as well.[33] The vastness of the country and the consequent problems of communication, the geographically uneven distribution of economic activities and social groups, the mass perception of opportunities for horizontal and vertical mobility, and the prevailing pattern of partisan identifications were some impediments to "a steady development" of a political party exclusively expressive of lower-status interests.

Yet despite these "great and peculiar difficulties," there were efforts to develop such parties in the late nineteenth century. And the social strains and tensions set in motion by the process of industrialization created potential support for them. Laborers in manufacturing and mining activities worked under conditions over which, without organization, they had no control. The terms of labor—especially the pace of work, hours, and wages—were set by entrepreneurs and often were adjusted arbitrarily either in response to changing conditions in the market or simply to enhance their profit margins. Laboring men did not

33. He did in fact do that; he pointed to the nature of the two-party system as well as to the fact that American workers "have been exposed to a prosperity no trace of which has been seen here in Europe for years now." His comment on immigrant groups was the second of the three factors to which he referred, but he seems to have regarded it as the "more especially" important one. The comments are in a letter from Engels to Friedrich A. Sorge, 4 December 1893, in Lewis S. Feuer, ed., *Marx and Engels*, pp. 457–58. For an analytically useful discussion of the general problem of group cohesiveness see Lee Benson, "Group Cohesion and Social and Ideological Conflict," pp. 741–67.

passively accept such adjustments but turned increasingly to organization as a means of actively resisting them. Agricultural producers faced different genera of problems, but their responses evidenced no less awareness. The expansion of transportation and communications integrated agricultural producers into a price and market structure that was becoming increasingly international in its scope. That subjected them to fluctuations in price and income whose causes lay beyond their experiences, but whose impact impelled them to organize resistance.

For late nineteenth-century contemporaries *industrialization* was more than a catchword. It was an experience in which they were daily and directly involved. It touched their lives; it altered their patterned expectations and self-conceptions; it required them to redefine their roles and to work out new sets of structured relations. Despite the magnitude, quality, and pervasiveness of these types of changes, they were not in themselves adequate to sustain "a steady development" of a permanent and broadly based workers' party. As Engels accurately judged, the "quite unusually powerful incentives" required for that were not a persistent part of American conditions.[34]

Just what those incentives might have been remains something of an analytical enigma. Most research has been directed toward reconstructing and explicating the ideologies of radical elites, and far less attention has been focused on their following in the electorate.[35] As a consequence, we suffer an embarrassing absence of concrete information describing the social bases of voting support for particular Farmer-Labor parties. Yet knowing which social groups cast ballots for them is requisite to understanding their characters, to inquiring into the motivations of their supporters, and to specifying sets of conditions conducive to Farmer-Labor voting. These are broad analytical tasks that can be approached here only in a delimited way. Specifically, it is useful pres-

34. There is considerable irony in the fact that Engels's comments were made in December 1893, when the United States was in the midst of a severe urban-industrial depression. Perceived economic crisis is clearly one of the conditions that typically has increased levels of voting support for workers' parties. Of course, Engels implied a distinction between "steady development" and sporadic outbursts of support for workers' parties. He concluded his observation on ethnocultural divisiveness by noting, "Often there is a sudden violent *élan*, but the bourgeois need only wait passively and the dissimilar elements of the working class fall apart again"; in Feuer, ed., *Marx and Engels*, p. 458.

35. That imbalance mirrors the relative indifference that political historians have always displayed toward analyzing mass voting behavior. For recent and valuable correctives to the imbalance for the socialists in the twentieth century, see Michael H. Ebner, "Socialism and Progressive Political Reform," pp. 116–40; Sally M. Miller, "Milwaukee," pp. 41–71; William C. Pratt, " 'Jimmie Higgins' and the Reading Socialist Community," pp. 141–56; Bruce M. Stave, "The Great Depression and Urban Political Continuity," pp. 157–83.

ently to concentrate on describing their strength in the late nineteenth century and inquiring into the continuity of that support and its social composition.[36]

Support for Farmer-Labor parties was striking neither in its magnitude nor in its consistency (see Table 7.5). At its high point in 1878, it amounted to less than one-fifth of the vote cast and only slightly more than one-quarter of the vote in its region of greatest strength.[37] Moreover, a comparison of the Greenback and Populist peak years with the relevant longitudinal means evidences the surgelike quality of the vote: it tended to emerge, peak, and then decline sharply. For example, at the national level the mean Greenback vote in the three biennial elections after 1878 was only 3.0 percent. From presidential to off-year elections, the rhythm of the vote was exactly the opposite of that of the major parties. That is, the size of the major-party vote tended to decline in off years, but that of the Farmer-Labor parties was higher in those years than in presidential elections.[38] Since we expect partisanship to be more salient in presidential campaigns than in off years, that asymmetrical rhythm points to an internalized sense of party identification as a powerful constraint on Farmer-Labor voting.

Finally, the measures of central tendency point to the sectional forces underlying the small 1876 Greenback vote and the much larger 1890 and 1892 Populist votes. As is well known, Greenback support originated in the Midwest and only later spread beyond that region. The sharp reduction in both the 1878 variance and coefficients of variability reflect the party's capacity to enlist voting support beyond the region of its genesis.[39] As Greenback support began to evaporate after 1878, its distribution once again reflected a strong sectional imbalance, with its

36. The analysis that follows forms a minor portion of a larger, ongoing study that will deal with the social- and political-structural preconditions of minor-party voting, and its social sources, over the second through the fifth party systems.

37. Even that exaggerates Farmer-Labor support somewhat, since it includes all instances of fusion with major parties. Formally, the Populist or People's party contested elections for the first time in 1892; the 1890 vote reported here is for the forerunners of that party, i.e., the variously named Farmers' Alliance and Independent parties that appeared in the 1890 elections.

38. In some states of the West and West North Central areas, the vote for the Populists in 1892 was higher than it had been for the Farmers' Alliance or Independent candidates in 1890 or 1891. In those states, and in some of the former Confederate states, the 1892 Populists constituted an exception to the generalization. That exception offers strong evidence of the Populist role in shaping the post-1892 realignment. It is also important to notice that sustained Populist voting support was anchored in an organizational infrastructure, the Alliance and especially its cooperative crusade, that provided "a schoolroom for political interpretation, self-identity, and self-confidence." See Lawrence Goodwyn, *Democratic Promise*, pp. 110–53, 213–72, 307–50, 387–555; ibid., p. 629, n. 18, for the quotation.

39. The same picture emerges from an examination of the Greenback distribution

TABLE 7.5   *Farmer-Labor Voting Strength: Percentage of Total Vote by Regions*

	Greenback		Populist		Means	
	1876	1878	1890	1892	1876–88	1876–92
U.S.	1.1	13.8	2.8	8.5	3.8	4.2
New England	1.9	19.2	0.3	0.7	4.0	3.2
Midatlantic	0.3	10.5	0.1	0.9	2.4	2.0
East N. Cent.	1.9	11.8	1.2	2.8	3.6	3.2
West N. Cent.	2.5	25.3	16.8	20.3	7.5	9.9
Confederacy	0.0	10.1	0.0	15.8	3.5	4.5
Border	0.3	11.7	0.0	3.9	2.5	2.4
West	0.2	20.1	1.2	25.4	3.5	5.7
Measures of Central Tendency (by Regions)						
$\overline{M}$	1.0	15.5	2.8	10.0		
σ^2	0.9	30.4	32.8	90.6		
V (as %)	94.1	35.4	203.8	95.1		

strength reduced and concentrated in the West North Central and Confederate states. The Populists, of course, as the data make abundantly clear, were a sectional party. When they emerged as a fully organized party in 1892, their support was almost exclusively in the West, West North Central, and Confederate regions. The shape of the Populist distribution rather starkly mirrored the colonial-metropole antagonisms that partially underlay the breakup of the third party system and imparted structure to the "System of 1896."

The changing size and shape of these regional distributions alone suggests that in most parts of the country there was relatively little continuity between Greenback and Populist support. They suggest instead a

---

by states. The 1876 coefficient of variability was 156.09 percent, but in 1878 it was 86.95 percent. The coefficient of variability (V) is a measure of relative dispersion. It is obtained by dividing the standard deviation of the distribution by its mean and multiplying that quotient by one hundred to convert it to a percent. The measure is useful when the means of the distributions being compared are of enormously different magnitudes; e.g., the 1878 Greenback mean is better than fifteen times the size of the 1876 mean. In such cases one might expect a comparison of the standard deviations (σ) or variances (σ^2) to be somewhat misleading. In all other relevant instances in this study in which I have presented variances, I have also calculated and compared the coefficients of variability.

series of political organizations that may have had greater rhetorical and elite continuity with each other than they had among the mass electorate. The notion of "agrarian radicalism," on the other hand, implies the opposite; it implies a core of economically discontented voters who rather self-consciously pursued their political objectives.[40] The assumption of continuity from the Farmer parties of the early 1870s to the Greenbackers in the later 1870s to the Populists in the 1890s derives from the implications of that notion. And a reasonable elaboration of the notion has also produced an assumption of continuity between the Populists and the variously titled Labor parties that appeared in the late 1880s.

The assumption of voter-group continuity depends at the very least on a demonstration of geographic continuity. Political organizations that drew their support from fundamentally distinct geographic areas could not be assumed to have been mobilizing the same electorate.[41] Can we speak with reasonable assurance of the existence of a Farmer-Labor party in the electorate? That is, first, did each of these parties provide a cue to voting behavior across offices at each election? If so, we would expect to find relatively high levels of interoffice correlations. Second, despite the changes in party names from Greenback to Labor to Populist, did they provide an ongoing cue to the voting behavior of some geographically constant groups in the electorate? If so, we would expect the interyear correlations to be reasonably high. Table 7.6 provides relevant data.[42]

Each of these political entities, even in its initial incarnation, provided its supporters with a strong guide to their voting behavior. That contrasts sharply with the Prohibitionists (compare with Table 7.2),

40. It implies much more; see Ronald P. Formisano and William G. Shade, "The Concept of Agrarian Radicalism," pp. 3–30.

41. Two caveats need to be made explicit. First, areal discontinuity would not erase the possibility that a core group of voters remained loyal across time and that their numbers were augmented from election to election by other, but shifting, groups of voters. Second, geographic continuity is only a surrogate for continuity among voters. Technically, the better procedure might seem to be the use of regression estimates. However, regression estimates assume a closed population, and executing such estimates between two points as distant in time as 1874 and 1884, or 1892, would produce little more than statistical artifacts. And it is precisely this long-term continuity that is the focus of inquiry here. However, I have executed such interyear regression estimates. For whatever they are worth under existential conditions that violate the assumptions of the procedure, the pattern of the relevant regression estimates is consistent with the one that emerges from an examination of the coefficients of determination.

42. What is presented in the table is the mean r^2 for each involved pair of elections. Panel A makes use of data for presidential, congressional, and gubernatorial races for three elections for the Greenbackers and one each for the other parties. Panel B indicates the strength of association between, for example, the distribution of the Illinois "Independent Reform" congressional vote in 1874 with all 1876–84 Greenback distributions.

TABLE 7.6   *Farmer-Labor Party Distributions: Interoffice and Interyear Coefficients of Determination (r²)*

	Ill	Iowa	Minn	Mo	Wis
A. *Interoffice (Mean r²)*					
Greenback (1876–84)	.848	.746	.526	.987	.785
Labor (1888)	.702	.646	N.C.	.874	.893
Populist (1892)	.815	.942	.779	.993	.843
B. *Interyear (Mean r²)*					
1873 Farmer/Greenback†	.025*	.052	.022	N.C.	.031*
1873 Farmer/Labor	.010	.107	N.C.	N.C.	.022
1873 Farmer/Populist	.007*	.014	.349*	N.C.	.083*
1873 Farmer/All F-L	.017*	.052	.101*	N.C.	.036*
Greenb/Labor	.061	.269	.105	.212	.067
Greenb/Populist	.045	.244	.024	.194	.057
Labor/Populist	.179	.355	.333	.497	.051

*More than 50.0% of the zero-order *r*'s are negative.
†For Illinois the 1874 Farmer vote was used, and the 1873 Anti-Monopoly vote for Iowa.

whose early electoral efforts were marked by a distinctly weak capacity to cue behavior across offices. Whatever factors were involved in the Greenback, Labor, and Populist cases, they clearly were strong and unidirectional. In each election those labels served as rallying symbols to a group of voters whose electoral behavior was not simply specific to a candidate or an office.

However, the difference between a party label's guiding behavior in a single election and its becoming a positive reference symbol, a habituated object of loyalty and a voting cue, is one of *kind* and not merely of degree. It involves the contrast between what Engels described as "a sudden violent *élan*" and "a steady development." And the data in Panel B (Table 7.6) suggest more élan than development; they point to the considerable geographic discontinuity among the various Farmer-Labor parties. The geographic base of the Farmer parties of 1873–74 in Illinois, Iowa, Minnesota, and Wisconsin was clearly distinct from even that of the Greenback party in the later 1870s. Nor, on the whole, did the Greenback and Labor, or the Greenback and Populist, distributions display much more impressive levels of geographic continuity. Except for Wisconsin, however, the Labor and Populist distributions evidenced higher levels of association, though perhaps lower than one might normally expect given the short time between 1886 and 1892.[43] Obviously, even though each of these parties was able to cue the behavior of its supporters in a single election, it was not able to sustain that support and to transfer it to another ostensibly like-minded party. The transition from Farmer to Greenback to Labor to Populist did not entail a simple exchange of geographic bases of mass support.

The manifest discontinuity should come as no great surprise. Even excluding for the moment the 1877–79 Greenback surge, the percentage strength and distributional shape of both the Greenback and pre-1890 Labor parties fluctuated rather widely from one election to the next. In the case of the Greenbackers, that fluctuation settled down somewhat in and after 1880. From that point through 1884, excluding instances of major-party fusion and their aftereffects, the size and shape of the Greenback percentages stabilized, and the coefficients of determination between the subsequent adjacent pairs of elections were correspondingly higher than earlier. Typically, however, that stabilization meant lower, and generally quite small, levels of Greenback voting.[44] Between 1886 and 1890 the Farmer-Labor field was dominated by variously titled Labor parties. The size and shape of their distributions differed considerably from the earlier Greenbackers. And often they differed more among themselves from one election to the next than elite continuity and rhetorical similarity would otherwise lead one to expect. Nor were they consistently able to transfer their geographic bases of support intact to their presumed successors, the Populists. This evident discontinuity in the geographic bases of Farmer-Labor support reflected the fact that distinct behavioral forces were involved and that each elicited different responses among the mass electorate.

When developments occur close together, there is nearly an irresistible tendency to link them in a causal fashion. The emergence and

43. For the sake of comparability across states, I have not in this table used the 1890 Farmers' Alliance vote in Minnesota as a Populist vote. If that were included in the Populist category, the mean r^2 between the Populist and Greenback distributions would be .031 (with over 50.0 percent of the zero-order r's being negative) and .313 between Populist and Labor.

44. Nationally, the Greenbackers polled 3.2 percent in 1880; 4.1 percent in 1882; and 1.7 percent in 1884. The following illustrate the type of distributional stabilization referred to: Illinois, Greenback 1876/1880, $r^2 = .077$, but 1880/1884, $r^2 = .648$, and 1876/1884, $r^2 = .001$; Massachusetts, Greenback 1876/1880, $r^2 = .170$, but 1880/1884, $r^2 = .381$, and 1876/1884, $r^2 = .119$.

spread of the Patrons of Husbandry, or Grange, a farm organization with social and economic objectives; the enactment of state laws regulating railroad and warehousing practices; the rise of independent Farmer parties and the later Greenbackers nearly coincided in time. Of course connections existed among them, but the assumption of similarity has obscured significant distinctions.

The movement for state-legislative regulation of railroad rates and practices originated well before the Grange became popular. Its birth was not among farm groups but among groups of urban businessmen and merchants. In Illinois the grain traders dominating the Chicago Board of Trade spearheaded the movement to restrict rates; in Iowa the impetus came from merchants in the river towns; and Minnesota's anti-monopoly sentiment was organized by Rochester's merchants and businessmen against the practices of the Winona and St. Peter Railroad.[45] The enactment of the misnamed "Granger Laws" in these states was largely a response to the demands of such groups. The pattern of state-legislative support for such laws was also revealing. Votes for restrictive legislation came disproportionately from legislators representing districts that were already serviced by railroads; votes against restricting rates came from legislators representing the less-developed, poorer agricultural regions of each state.

This does not imply that farmers were unconcerned about railroads in general, or restriction of rates in particular. They were concerned, but their response was by no means unanimous. In these states farmers who lived in areas already serviced by railroads very probably supported rate restriction. Those were areas that had been settled longer and had higher average farm-product values and lower proportions of unimproved farm land. They were the areas that generally were characterized by contemporaries as being "imbued with the spirit of 'go-aheaditiviness.'"[46] Opposition to restricting rates typically was concentrated in those rural areas that were less developed and less well off. Farmers in those areas apparently still looked to the coming of the railroad as something of a panacea that would boost their lagging economic condition.

The grass-roots, rural dimension of the movement to organize Farmer parties also began in the more-developed and more prosperous agricultural areas. In Illinois, for instance, it began in the spring of 1873

45. Harold D. Woodman, "Chicago Businessmen and the 'Granger' Laws," pp. 16–24; George H. Miller, *Railroads and the Granger Laws*, pp. 59–139, passim.

46. *Alton Tri-Weekly Telegraph*, 20 November 1851, quoted in Formisano and Shade, "Agrarian Radicalism," p. 29; see ibid., pp. 28–29, for contrasts in the sources of rural support and opposition to restricting rates. For the same type of contrasts elsewhere, see Mildred Throne, "The Anti-Monopoly Party in Iowa, 1873–74," p. 313; Miller, *Railroads and Granger Laws*.

in heavily Yankee-stock Livingston county, to the southwest of Chicago; it spread from there across the Yankee belt of northern Illinois counties. Its roots were in the local farmers' clubs—which formally were independent of the Granges but which, in fact, were probably their political auxiliaries.[47] In any event, both the Grange and the local farmers' clubs shared a common Yankee character. And so did the nascent Farmer party. The unmistakable hallmarks of that character permeated the 1873 "Farmers' Declaration of Independence." In that document the leaders of the farmers' clubs declared themselves "absolutely free and independent of all past political connections," and for the success of their movement, they proclaimed "a firm reliance upon divine Providence." The character of the movement was equally clear from its very choice of name, "Independent Reform."[48] These were code words, phrases, and symbols long in usage among Yankees and clearly expressive of their values.

Although the Farmers acknowledged their reliance on "divine Providence," they resorted as well to mundane and pragmatic tactics. In 1873 they organized local conventions to nominate candidates for county offices, and in 1874 they effected a state-level organization and nominating convention. In the latter enterprise they found an ally less ethereal than "divine Providence," the Democratic party. Demoralized by the 1872 debacle, Democratic party builders desperately sought new stances and new voters. In the Farmers' movement they hoped to find both. And they did, at least in the Yankee counties of Illinois. In the race for superintendent of public instruction, in which the Democrats and Farmers had nominated the same candidate, their choice polled 35.5 percent of the vote in the Yankee counties, but the straight Democratic candidate for state treasurer polled only 28.5 percent in the same areas.[49]

47. The Grange formally disallowed political discussions at its meetings. For information on the organization of the Illinois Farmer party and those in other states, see Solon Justus Buck, *The Granger Movement*, pp. 80–102. Buck refers to the avowedly political Illinois farmers' clubs as being "more or less independent" of the Granges (p. 82).

48. The text of the 1873 declaration is in *The Prairie Farmer* (Chicago), 12 July 1873. The name *Independent Reform* was used in the 1874 "declaration of principles" adopted at the farmers' convention to nominate candidates for state offices. Significantly, that convention refused to call the declaration a party platform. For the text see *Appletons' Annual Cyclopaedia, 1874*, pp. 402–403; also see the powerful antiparty references by Indiana's Independent party, p. 413. For insight into the social composition of the Grange, especially prior to 1886, see Gerald L. Prescott, "Wisconsin Farm Leaders in the Gilded Age," pp. 188–89; for figures on the Grange membership, see Robert L. Tontz, "Membership of General Farmers' Organizations, United States, 1874–1960," pp. 147–15

49. In 1870 the Democrats had received 25.7 percent of the vote in these counties. Interestingly, but revealingly, *Appletons'* identified the farmers' candidates as "Independent Republicans"; *Appletons' Annual Cyclopaedia, 1874*, p. 404. For a more

What occurred in Illinois was reasonably typical of the sequence in other parts of the Midwest. Grange organization in the better-developed and more prosperous areas seems to have spawned political activity. Anti-Monopoly or Independent parties emerged from these local organizations of farmers or from the Grange itself, entered into cooperative arrangements with a demoralized Democracy, and contested the 1873 and 1874 elections.[50] The pattern of mass support for these parties thus involved two distinct streams of voters. They captured nearly intact the old Democratic geographic base, and they augmented that with recruits from the Republican party. That recruitment, however, was disproportionately concentrated in those counties that were already serviced by railroads. In Minnesota's "serviced" counties, for example, Anti-Monopoly in 1873 ran 14.8 percentage points above the 1868 Democratic vote; the similarly named party was 8.4 percentage points stronger in Iowa's railroad counties.[51] That limited recruitment produced sets of Farmer distributions that clearly crosscut the standing partisan lines. Indeed, it seemed to some contemporaries, including President Grant, that "political partisanship has almost ceased to exist, especially in the agricultural regions."[52]

Grant need not have worried. The party battle lines were restored by 1876. The depression that had begun in late 1873 combined with the normal reactivation of latent party identifications in a presidential campaign to end the distinctly partisan dimension of the Farmers' movement. That was assured when the Democrats, reinvigorated by their gains in the 1874 state and congressional elections, terminated the fu-

---

intensive analysis of Yankee and non-Yankee behavior in DeKalb County, Illinois, based on township and individual data, see Robert L. Schroeder, "Political Issues and Elections in DeKalb County, 1874–1896."

50. There were no fusion arrangements in Indiana, where Democratic organizational energy seems not to have lagged. The Independent party in Indiana endorsed prohibition, and the Democrats condemned the Baxter temperance law and called for a more liberal licensing measure; see party platforms in *Appletons' Annual Cyclopaedia, 1874*, pp. 413–15.

51. In those Minnesota counties without railroads, Anti-Monopoly ran only 5.8 percentage points above the 1868 Democratic strength, and in Iowa −10.7 percentage points below the 1868 level. Wisconsin was wholly anomalous in 1873, with the Reform party there gaining 9.9 percentage points in the railroad counties and 10.3 in the nonrailroad counties. That reflected, of course, the impact of the Graham Liquor Law uproar. Antirailroad agitation played a greater role in 1874; in that year Reform's strength was 7.3 percentage points above the 1868 Democratic level in the "serviced" counties and only 1.1 percentage points stronger in the other counties. For maps showing the railroad lines in each state, see Miller, *Railroads and Granger Laws*, pp. 98, 118, 141.

52. Grant's fifth annual message to Congress, 1 December 1873, is quoted in Buck, *Granger Movement*, p. 81.

sions. And some rural spokesmen had already caught the tail of the new rising star, the greenback panacea.

The Greenback, or National Independent party, was formally organized at a convention in Cleveland, Ohio, in March 1875; it nominated its first national ticket at its Indianapolis convention in May 1876. Its platform was direct and unequivocal; it demanded repeal of the Specie Resumption Act of 1875 and called for the issuance of United States legal-tender notes, or greenbacks. The origins of the movement lay in the complex, and sometimes nearly bewildering, cross-currents and debates over governmental monetary policy.[53] Throughout the late 1860s and early 1870s the attack on that policy, and support for greenbacks, had come primarily from labor groups and entrepreneurial elites. Leaders of agricultural opinion were relatively late converts to the cause of expanding the currency, but by early 1874 many of them had come into the fold. And the Indiana Independents in August 1874 issued the call for the creation of the new national party.

The initial foray of the Greenbackers into electoral politics was not replete with auspicious portents. Its vote was small and regionally imbalanced. Its strength lay largely in heavily Republican states of the Midwest. And it was not able to translate Farmer voting support into Greenback ballots. Statistical discontinuity, however, concealed important elements of commonality. Although the Greenback percentages in 1876 were much lower than the earlier Farmer strength, the currency inflators generally polled their strongest levels of support in the same counties and among the same groups as the Farmers had. And in rural areas the Greenbackers, as the Farmers had before them, drew organizational strength from the local Granges and their allied farmers' clubs. Indeed, the 1875–76 organization of local Greenback clubs probably built on these existing structures. Initially, of course, neither the local Granges nor most of the 1873–74 Farmer parties had espoused currency inflation. The deepening impact of the depression changed their focus and led an appreciable number of the involved opinion leaders to declare for that cause.[54] That propagandistic and organizational support probably accounted for the fact that in most of the states of the Midwest the

53. For lucid clarification of these matters, see Walter T. K. Nugent, *Money and American Society, 1865–1880*; Irwin Unger, *The Greenback Era*. For information on the organizational background and development, as well as on the electoral support, of the Greenback party, see Kleppner, "Greenback and Prohibition parties," 2:1551–66.

54. The Indiana Independents had earlier supported greenbackism, and the Illinois group had done so somewhat more equivocally and with more of an internal struggle. On agrarian greenbackism see Buck, *Granger Movement*, pp. 81, 94–95, 114–15; Unger, *Greenback Era*, pp. 206–209, 228–29, 293. Grass-roots pressure from the local Granges changed the position of the National Grange on currency. In 1875 the National

Greenback percentages were stronger in rural than in urban-industrial areas. In eastern states like Pennsylvania, where greenbackism had roots in labor-reform activities, the party's strength was weaker in rural areas than in coal-mining communities.

After 1876 Greenback strength surged. Its rising strength was apparent in those states that held elections in 1877, and it peaked in the congressional and state elections of the following year. Apart from its size, Greenback strength in 1877–79 was remarkable for its discontinuity with the party's 1876 base of support. New pressures and forces touched the lives of large numbers of voters, many of whom responded by defecting from their old parties and casting a Greenback ballot. The labor strikes and riots of 1877 created the requisite conditions for Greenback recruitment. The major disturbances of that year began among railroad workers. The managers' order for a 10.0 percent reduction in wages was the immediate cause, and the strike began with the walkout of the Baltimore & Ohio workers on 14 July. Thereafter, it spread rapidly over almost all of the northern roads; at its peak over 100,000 men were on strike, and strikers controlled six to seven thousand miles of railroad track, including the four major trunk lines—the New York Central, the Erie system, the Pennsylvania Railroad, and the Baltimore & Ohio.[55]

The railroad managers wanted to do more than slash wages; they aimed at destroying labor organization. Their fears had been aroused by the successful strike in 1876 by the Brotherhood of Locomotive Engineers against the New Jersey Central. When that labor union struck the Boston & Maine in February 1877, the railroad managers successfully lobbied the Massachusetts legislature for a law declaring it a penal offense for strikers to commit any act endangering commercial interests. Similar legislation was enacted in Delaware, Maryland, Missouri, New Jersey, and Pennsylvania. Faced by an extensive strike that had more of the character of a spontaneous uprising than of a union-organized walkout, the railroad managers determined to crush it, to reassert total

---

Grange leaders simply tabled all resolutions on currency by a vote of 18 to 13; in 1877, by a vote of 30 to 18, they refused to postpone indefinitely a resolution opposing specie resumption and then adopted it by a vote of 30 to 14. See *Proceedings of the Ninth Session of the National Grange of the Patrons of Husbandry, 1875*, pp. 176–177; *Proceedings of the Eleventh Session of the National Grange of the Patrons of Husbandry, 1877*, pp. 69–84.

55. The summary in this and the following paragraphs draws on Kleppner, "Greenback and Prohibition Parties," 2:1559–60; the description of "Labor Strikes," in *Appletons' Annual Cyclopaedia, 1877*, pp. 423–32, and in U.S., Commissioner of Labor, *Third Annual Report of the Commissioner of Labor, 1887*, pp. 1067–79. The events are vividly described by Robert V. Bruce, *1877*.

control, and thereby to free themselves of the future specter of union organization among the railroad workers.

The strike by forty brakemen and firemen on the Baltimore & Ohio triggered the nationwide series of walkouts. Most of these mixed protests against cuts in wages with complaints about local and arbitrary changes in work rules or conditions. As more and more railroad workers walked out and prevented the running of through trains, state militia and then federal troops had to be used to keep the trains running. Confrontations between strikers and militia and extensive violence characterized those attempts in the railroad centers of West Virginia and western Maryland, Pittsburgh, Philadelphia, Baltimore, St. Louis, Cleveland, Chicago, Columbus, Toledo, Louisville, Indianapolis, Fort Wayne, San Francisco, Buffalo, and in a plethora of smaller-sized cities and towns.

It was not only the railroad workers who struck. Workers in other industries expressed their smoldering dissatisfaction with cuts in wages and depression conditions through strikes or public demonstrations. Industrial warfare raged especially in the coal regions of Pennsylvania, Illinois, and Maryland, where cuts in wages were compounded by the companies' paternalism and high prices charged by the companies' stores. In the coal-mining communities the strike enlisted the active support of nonmining elements of the population: "The people generally were on the side of the strikers. Farmers and tradesmen contributed to their support. Whole plantings of potatoes were abandoned to their use, and . . . helped to provide the miners' families with the necessities of life."[56] To combat such solidarity in the community, the owners resorted to legalized violence, the use of outside militia. The introduction of the militia evoked a correspondingly violent response from the strikers and their supporters.

With a nationwide series of railroad strikes and riots, with violence raging in the coal fields, with almost daily demonstrations and "bread strikes" among workers in other manufacturing industries, it appeared to some that "the flame of insurrection" had been ignited. That surely exaggerated the case, but the social and psychological impact of the upheavals created conditions favorable to a Farmer-Labor party's mobilizing voters. Those conditions included a protracted depression, widespread and overt expressions of labor discontent, major political parties that did not aggregate labor-group demands, and a minor party whose character represented the discontented. As numerous voters made the requisite linkages among these separate factors, "the political striker

56. *Appletons' Annual Cyclopaedia, 1877*, p. 431. The tone of the article is generally hostile to strikes and strikers; so the admission is particularly significant.

[took] the place of the railroad striker.''[57] And the levels of Greenback voting soared.

Both the size and shape of the 1877–78 Greenback distributions displayed drastic contrasts with their 1876 characteristics. The party's regional imbalance yielded to a more even distribution of strength. That resulted from its capacity to recruit new voting strength in all areas of the country. In the old Confederate states that ability probably resulted from its serving as a viable political alternative to the Democratic party. It attracted support there from among normal Republicans, but it also recruited among normally Democratic poor-white voters who were repulsed by the Republican symbol with its overtones of Yankeeism and black enfranchisement but whose economic discontent could be mobilized and channeled politically by a neutrally labeled partisan agency whose character represented their concerns.[58] Beyond the region of the "Lost Cause," new Greenback voting strength was not simply the product of wider and stronger support among the groups that had been rallied by its label in 1876. That occurred, of course; but even more striking was the drastic change in the locational distribution of Greenback voting support. The data in Table 7.7 provide an overview of that change in several typical states, as well as a longitudinal view of the locational distribution of later Farmer-Labor voting.[59]

The 1877–79 Greenback surge involved cross-cutting recruitment of two distinct types. First, even more clearly than in 1876, Greenback voting cut across the distributions of both major parties. In Missouri, for example, the small 1876 Greenback vote had come almost exclusively from former Republican voters. In Iowa and Minnesota Greenback voting in 1876 had been larger than in Missouri, and it had borne at least minimal traces of bipartisan recruitment. During their surge, however,

57. *New York Tribune*, 9 May 1878, quoted in Denis Tilden Lynch, *The Wild Seventies*, 2:500; *Martinsburg Independent* (West Virginia), 18 August 1877, quoted in Bruce, *1877*, p. 317.

58. For suggestions along these lines, see J. Morgan Kousser, *The Shaping of Southern Politics*, pp. 25–27, 34–35, 198–99.

59. In constructing the table, the following units were used in the urban-industrial category. For Illinois I have used data for Cook County (Chicago) and for five coal-mining counties: Bureau, Grundy, LaSalle, Macoupin, and St. Clair. For urban areas in Iowa, I have used data for Burlington, Dubuque, Polk, and Scott counties; for Missouri, Buchanan and Jackson counties and St. Louis City; and for Wisconsin, city data for Eau Claire, Milwaukee, Oshkosh, and LaCrosse. For Ohio, I have used city data for Cincinnati, Cleveland, Sandusky, Toledo, and Youngstown and minor civil-division data for the mining units in Athens, Belmont, Hocking, Jackson, Perry, Stark, and Tuscarawas counties. For Pennsylvania the city data used were for Pittsburgh, Allegheny, Reading, Johnstown, Erie, Scranton, Wilkesbarre, and Philadelphia; data for mining units were in Clearfield, Fayette, Lakawanna, Luzerne, Northumberland, Schuylkill, and Westmoreland counties.

TABLE 7.7 *Farmer-Labor Percentage of Total Vote*

	Urban-Industrial			Outstate	Total State
	Coal	Urban	Both		
Illinois					
1876	2.6	0.3	1.1	3.6	3.1
1878	19.2	8.9	12.9	14.8	14.4
1880	3.9	1.1	2.0	4.9	4.6
1886	4.2	25.9	19.5	1.8	6.0
1892	2.2	0.6	0.8	4.1	2.9
Iowa					
1876		1.9		3.2	3.1
1877		13.0		14.0	13.9
1880		5.8		10.5	10.1
1888		1.5		2.3	2.2
1892		2.4		4.8	4.6
Missouri					
1876		1.0		1.7	1.0
1878		14.5		18.5	17.8
1880		2.9		10.1	8.8
1886		9.6		1.7	2.9
1890		1.1		6.3	5.4
1892		1.9		9.1	7.6
Ohio					
1876	0.8	0.8	0.8	0.3	0.5
1877	4.5	22.7	15.6	2.6	5.2
1878	7.0	12.4	10.3	5.5	6.5
1880	1.9	0.7	1.1	0.8	0.8
1886	0.5	0.1	0.2	0.3	0.2
1892	2.2	1.5	1.8	1.7	1.7
Pennsylvania					
1876	2.5	0.1	0.9	0.2	0.9
1877	33.0	9.8	16.3	5.1	9.6
1878	26.2	6.6	13.1	10.7	11.6
1880	4.7	0.2	1.6	2.8	2.3
1886	1.8	0.1	0.6	0.5	0.5
1892	0.4	0.1	0.3	1.3	0.8
Wisconsin					
1877		12.6		15.2	14.9
1879		4.4		6.6	6.4
1880		0.5		3.2	2.9
1886		31.4		4.2	7.4
1888		9.9		1.4	2.5
1892		3.7		2.5	2.6

the level of Greenback popularity and its partisan-recruitment ratios changed considerably. Missouri's Greenbackers in 1878 recruited two former Democratic ballots for every eight Republican ones they attracted; and in their 1879 gubernatorial races in Iowa and Minnesota, the Greenback party recruited in ratios of about six to four, with Iowa's Democrats and Minnesota's Republicans being the heavier donors. Second, Greenback recruitment in these elections crosscut urban-rural lines. Indeed, as the data in Table 7.7 indicate, only with the post-1876 surge did the party develop appreciable levels of urban-industrial support. And in states like Illinois and Pennsylvania, it ran stronger among coal miners than among farmers.[60]

If the sudden 1877–79 blossoming of the Greenbackers as a party attractive to voters in urban-industrial areas was impressive, even more so was the rapid pace at which that base eroded. As early as 1880 in most states, Greenback voting was stronger in rural than in urban-industrial areas.[61] Pennsylvania in 1880, with its tradition of labor-reform activity and organization and its strife-torn coal fields, was something of an exception. By 1884, however, even that state took its place in the pattern, and the Greenback rural vote was 1.1 percentage points stronger than its urban-industrial level. Even where Greenback voting was most persistent, among the coal miners of Schuylkill County, its levels of support fell off sharply after 1878. In that year 76.4 percent of the ballots cast for the Greenbackers came from the county's mining units, and the party polled 39.1 percent of the total vote cast in those units. By 1884 the Greenback vote remained heavily concentrated in the mining units, but its size had shrunk to only 8.0 percent of the total vote.[62]

The depression, strikes, and industrial violence created a "crisis" for large numbers of laboring men. That atmosphere was clearly one in which their shared economic identifications became more salient to their partisan selections than they had been earlier. Under those conditions they opted to support the party whose political character resonated with and represented their own immediate concerns. The long tradition of inflated-currency ideas and rhetoric among, at least, labor-opinion leaders; the formal amalgamation in 1878 of the old labor-reform elements into the Greenback party; and that party's self-conscious efforts, especially

60. The same pattern of 1876–78 shift characterized other states as well; e.g., Maryland, Michigan, Minnesota. The ratios to which I referred derive from the relevant regression estimates of 1876–78 (or 1879) voter movement.

61. Or it was so small, as in Ohio, that the differences were trivial.

62. Greenback support was more persistent in Schuylkill than in other Pennsylvania, Maryland, Illinois, Ohio, or West Virginia mining communities. Schuylkill County was the "home" of the Molly Maguires; see Wayne G. Broehl, Jr., *The Molly Maguires.*

at the local level, to broaden its base of support by addressing itself to the raging labor strife helped to channel the heightened salience of labor-group economic identifications into voting support for the Green-backers.[63] However, as the crisis abated and as their underlying sense of being a Democrat—or a Republican—was reactivated during the 1880 presidential campaign, most of labor's Greenback supporters returned to their old party moorings. Élan was not readily transformed into "steady development."

The mid-1880s, especially 1886 in the Midwest, saw another outburst of political cohesion among workers. The precipitating conditions, though less dramatic and less extensive, were similar to those of 1877–78. Against the backdrop of an economic downturn that had begun in 1883, the Knights of Labor launched another drive for the eight-hour day. That drive produced hundreds of strikes and culminated in a large-scale work stoppage on 1 May 1886. Three days later in Chicago, a bomb was thrown at police who were attempting to break up an anarchist rally in Haymarket Square. When the smoke from the bomb and the ensuing gunfire had cleared, ten people lay dead and fifty wounded.

The Haymarket riot was immensely important in both a substantive and a symbolic way to labor groups as well as to their opponents. However, its symbolic importance lay not only in the violence itself, nor even simply in the involvement of "foreign" anarchists, but in its use as a stereotype of a larger category of events. In 1886 there were 1,432 strikes involving 10,053 establishments and 508,044 workers. Both the number of strikes and workers involved were twice as great as they had been in 1885. And some of these strikes, such as the one of Polish workers at the Bay View ironworks in Milwaukee, involved violence of a scale that was merely less dramatic than at Haymarket Square.[64]

63. For details on the organizational arrangements and the greater role played by the Labor Reform elements at the 1878 Greenback national convention in Toledo, as well as on the persisting conflict between the agrarian and labor elements among the leaders of the party, see Kleppner, "Greenback and Prohibition Parties," 2:1560–63; for competition and conflict between Greenbackers and Socialists, see Bruce, *1877*, pp. 317–18. Unger, *Greenback Era*, pp. 376–78, underestimates the role of labor-reform elements and the labor tone of the 1878 pronouncements. The 1878 platform is in *Appletons' Annual Cyclopaedia, 1878*, p. 807; also see the Central Executive Committee's December 1878 "Address to the People," in ibid., p. 808; the state platforms can be followed in the same source. For earlier soft-money attitudes among the labor leaders, see David Montgomery, *Beyond Equality*, especially pp. 425–47. Two additional observations are relevant and should be made explicit concerning the 1878–79 Greenback support. First, Greenbackers rarely received a majority of the votes cast among laboring groups: even in the coalfields they were opposed by more miners than supported them. Second, in many locales the Greenbackers still projected temperance, anticity, and even anti-Catholic auras; yet in "crises" these elements of Greenback political character were less important than they had been earlier and would be later.

64. The strike data are in U.S., Commissioner of Labor, *Tenth Annual Report of*

To antilabor contemporaries and labor groups as well, *Haymarket* became a symbol of this accelerating industrial conflict. Among the former it evoked fear, and among some of them it provided yet another concrete referent for their antiimmigrant attitudes. Among most labor groups it symbolized their oppression, their unequal access to the levers of power, and the hostility with which politicians greeted their legitimate and mild demands. The prevailing parties were not vehicles through which labor's demands could be aggregated and transformed into policy. From these perceptions and the self-conscious party-building activities of labor organizers, a series of independent and variously named labor parties emerged in 1886.[65]

Labor parties collectively polled only 1.2 percent of the 1886 vote, and they ran above that level (at 2.6 percent) only in the East North Central region, where Labor strength was confined to Illinois and Wisconsin.[66] In these states and in Missouri as well, Labor support in 1886 was even more disproportionately urban-industrial than Greenback voting had been in 1878. The core of that support in Illinois was in Chicago, not in the coal-mining counties where 1878 Greenback strength had been. Wisconsin's Labor entry carried Milwaukee with 38.8 percent in a four-way race and ran especially well—80.9 percent—among the Poles on the city's South side. However, as early as 1888 in Chicago, Milwaukee, and other cities, Labor parties' vote totals and proportions were considerably reduced from their 1886 peaks.[67]

The transition from the Labor parties of the mid- and late 1880s to the Populists of the early 1890s was not a case of linear progression. In the first place, the Populists were considerably stronger nationally and polled higher vote totals and percentages than the Labor entities. Sec-

---

the *Commissioner of Labor, 1894*, 1:16; there were 1,436 strikes, involving 379,676 workers, in 1887. The number of lockouts also increased sharply; from 183, involving 15,424 workers, in 1885 to 1,509 and 101,980 workers in 1886; ibid., pp. 20–21. On the Bay View strike see Thomas W. Gavett, *Development of the Labor Movement in Milwaukee*, pp. 49–65.

65. Selig Perlman, "Upheaval and Reorganization," 2:461–62; Nathan Fine, *Labor and Farmer Parties in the United States, 1828–1928*, pp. 35–55. In some states, such as Missouri, they ran under the old Greenback label or a hyphenated version such as Greenback-Labor.

66. In addition to the states itemized in Table 7.7, labor parties polled 2.2 percent of Connecticut's vote, 2.7 percent of the New Jersey vote, and not as much as 1.0 percent in any other state.

67. Wisconsin's Labor party in 1886 bore the label *People's*, but it should not be confused with the later Populist or People's party. In 1888 Milwaukee's Poles voted 14.0 percent for the Labor candidate for president and 1.2 percent for the Populist in 1892. In Milwaukee as a whole, the Union Labor candidate in 1888 polled 11.6 percent; in 1890, when ethnoreligious conflict again raged in the city and the state, that fell to 2.9 percent.

ond, the Populists were unmistakably and powerfully a sectional party. Third, although the labor parties were distinctly urban, the Populists were not. Whatever behavioral influences impelled voters to cast Populist ballots, they had different sectional and locational valences from those that underlay Labor voting in the 1880s.

Rapid, uneven, and uncontrolled socioeconomic change in a nation of continental proportions induced structural dislocations of an enormous magnitude. Those dislocations, in turn, underlay the economic tensions and conflict that were rife in late nineteenth-century society. That society was not bereft of leaders who perceived the nature and causes of these dislocations, who publicly articulated an explanation of them, and who sought to mobilize mass electoral support to ameliorate their effects. The question, however, is not *whether* such economically induced conflict existed, nor even whether it attained high levels (it did!), but rather whether it generated *party* oppositions. That effect it did not accomplish.

The existence of social antagonism in itself has never been a sufficient condition for the rise of *party* oppositions. Some social conflict has been irrelevant to the political system, because the involved groups never sought to shape public decision making. Other conflicts have generated demands on the political system through channels alternative to electoral politics (e.g., through interest groups). And even when social conflict has been expressed through party activities, we need to distinguish between sporadic mobilization and *party* oppositions.

Developing new electoral cleavages among the mass public required demobilizing a potential support clientele from attachments to its old party and developing and sustaining those requisite bonds of psychological rapport between party builders and their supporters in the electorate. These conditions were more likely to be satisfied when the emergent tensions and social cleavages overlapped and reinforced, rather than crosscut and counterbalanced, each other. Yet many of the tensions and social cleavages induced by the dynamics of socioeconomic change in the late nineteenth century were of the latter types. Some groups of farmers and merchants, for example, could band together in shared antagonism to the railroads, but other groups of farmers, those who hoped that the coming of the railroads would accelerate the economic growth of their communities, joined the railroad owners and managers in persistent opposition to that goal. And when eastern farmers, and in the 1880s even midwestern farmers, became more generally opposed to the rate-setting practices of the railroads, their complaints tended to focus on *cheap* transportation, on *low* long-haul rates, as the cause of that "unfair" competition between their own agricultural products and those of "the fertile prairies of the West."[68] Labor groups may have resisted the work-discipline requirements imposed by the factory system and, even more commonly, the wage-cutting practices of the capitalists, but they were also consumers of food and not natural allies of movements to raise farm prices. A classic consumer-producer antagonism was one of the underlying factors inhibiting development of Farmer parties that mobilized and sustained urban support or labor parties with persisting rural support.[69]

The critical point, however, is that none of these genera of economic group demands were accommodated by the prevailing party system. The roots of that system lay in earlier and still powerfully relevant forms of ethnocultural cleavage. The continuing salience of that type of cleavage inhibited a sustained partisan demobilization of voters and their subsequent remobilization along new *party* lines. That internalized sense of being a Democrat or a Republican, linked as it was with deeply felt ethnoreligious values, proved too potent psychologically among the mass electorate for the builders of Farmer-Labor parties to overcome. Sporadically, of course, economic tensions reached a flash point, erupted, and temporarily distended party lines. Marginally, that was the case with the Farmer parties in the Old Northwest in the early 1870s. Even more clearly it was the case with the Greenback party in 1877 and 1878 and with the Labor parties in some urban areas of the East North Central states in 1886. Crises heightened the salience of economic identifications, produced a specifically focused sense of solidarity within economic groups, and diffused more widely a perception that the old parties did not aggregate the crisis-created interests. The result was relatively large-scale defection of a sort that crosscut the prevailing partisan distributions. However, in each instance, and for most of the involved voters, it was temporary defection and not "steady development," for the most arresting feature of the postcrisis elections was the rapid and extensive reassertion of party loyalty.[70]

68. *Annual Report of the Secretary of the Maine Board of Agriculture, 1873,* p. 339. For additional evidence of eastern antagonism to midwestern farmers, and later the antagonism of the midwestern farm groups to western producers, see *Annual Report of the Secretary of the Massachusetts Board of Agriculture, 1881,* p. 8; *Annual Report of the New Jersey State Board of Agriculture, 1890–91,* p. 10; *Annual Report of the Pennsylvania Board of Agriculture, 1880,* pp. 8–9; ibid., *1890,* p. 270; Lee Benson, *Merchants, Farmers, and Railroads*; Kleppner, *Cross of Culture,* pp. 307–10.

69. For insights into the nature of this and allied problems, see Chester McArthur Destler, "Consummation of a Labor-Populist Alliance in Illinois, 1894," pp. 589–602; Unger, *Greenback Era,* pp. 94–114, 181–90; Kleppner, *Cross of Culture,* pp. 301–306.

70. For a brilliant insight into the nature of third-party voting, see Walter Dean Burnham, *Critical Elections and the Mainsprings of American Politics,* pp. 27–30. The omission of any reference to the Populists in the paragraph is a conscious one. The

If this analysis explains Farmer-Labor discontinuity over time, it perhaps does not fully account for the relatively higher levels of geographic and statistical continuity that appeared in Iowa and Missouri and that lurked below the surface of the 1890–92 county data in Minnesota (refer to Table 7.6). In Missouri the original Greenback vote had been recruited from Republican sources; the party's 1878 surge had somewhat more bipartisan drawing power. After that, however, persisting Greenbackery reverted to its 1876 base, augmented by some of the Republican voters who had moved to the party only in 1878. To some anti-Democrats, whose own party was a distinct minority within the state, Greenback voting was a viable political alternative. That plus *Republican*'s evoking negative emotions among so many normal Democrats that it could not rally their support were the factors underlying the fusion of the Republican and Greenback parties in 1884. Fusion built on the normal Republican base, enlisted most of the persisting Greenback voters, attracted Democratic crossovers, and narrowed the political distance between that party and its opposition. In 1880 Democratic strength was 13.9 percentage points higher than Republican at the presidential level and 13.6 percentage points higher in the gubernatorial race; in 1884 the Democratic-Fusion differences were, respectively, 7.5 and 2.5 percentage points.[71]

The Republican-Greenback fusion was short-lived, however; in 1886 the Greenbackers and labor elements were in tandem, and in 1888 and 1890 Labor tickets preempted the protest field. Electoral support

---

emergence of that party in the South and in the western states presaged and played a behaviorally important role in producing the breakup of the third party system that occurred after 1892. Although Populism in both of these geographic areas shared at least that much in common, it is important to notice the distinguishing features of the movement in the South. First, its genesis there lay in that region's unique crop-lien system and the resulting "humiliating conditions of life which penetrated into every farm and hamlet of the South." Second the rise of a political party expressive of agrarian discontent in the South became entangled with the question of black voting. On these matters, see Goodwyn, *Democratic Promise*, pp. 25–50, 276–306, with the quotation on p. 25; Kousser, *Shaping of Southern Politics*, pp. 2–44, and the data on pp. 137, 145, 174, 183, 199, 215; Michael Schwartz, *Radical Protest and Social Structure*.

71. At the gubernatorial and congressional levels the average Democrat to Fusion crossover was 9.6 percent, or 3.3 percentage points higher than the normal crossover in 1876–92 elections for these offices. The effects were about the same in Maine. There the Democrats fused with the Greenbackers in 1880 and 1882. The 1880 Fusion attracted 3.4 percent of the 1876 Republican presidential voters, and the Fusion gubernatorial candidate enlisted 5.9 percent of the 1876 Republican voters for governor. In 1882 the Fusion candidate for governor polled 1.6 percent of the votes that had been cast for the Republican candidate for governor in 1880. The Maine and Missouri estimates here, and the Iowa estimates that follow, are weighted sums of regression estimates calculated by minor civil divisions (or Missouri voting districts) within counties or groups of counties.

for these later slates continued to come, as it had for the Greenbackers after 1878, from normally Republican sources. In 1892 the Populists recruited nearly all the 1888 labor voters who balloted in the second contest. Since that Labor support had come from former Republican voters, it gave the Populist coalition something of a Republican coloration. Indeed, across most of Missouri, Populist voting was what persisting Greenback and Labor voting had been: a political opportunity to express opposition to the dominant Democrats by voters who normally were Republican. It was a political surrogate for the hopelessly outnumbered Republican party. However, it was more than that in several areas of the state. In the western Ozarks, the area of its greatest electoral strength, and in the cotton-growing lowlands, the Populist coalition crosscut old party lines. On the average in these areas, it attracted about 5.5 percent of the 1888 Democrats who made an electoral choice in 1892.

Iowa's pattern was similar, but the partisan balance was different. The Republicans were Iowa's dominant party. And there persisting Greenback and Labor support came disproportionately from the minority Democrats. As Missouri's Republicans had done, the Democrats in Iowa sought to rally an electoral majority in support of a neutral, non-Democratic, label; they fused with the Greenbackers in 1884 and 1886. Finally, although the Populist rise in Iowa in 1891 and 1892 was less noticeable than in Missouri, it exhibited similar crosscutting effects.[72]

In both Missouri and Iowa Farmer-Labor longitudinal continuity reflected disproportionate recruitment from the weaker of the major parties. Persisting Farmer-Labor support in these states was at least as much a protest against an entrenched and dominant party as it was against economic conditions in general. That observation points to the importance of political-structural factors, opposed to or in interactive combination with economic-structural ones, as necessary conditions of protest-party voting. It strongly suggests that minor parties whose voters come almost exclusively from a weak minority party in dominant one-party contexts may not achieve the threshold of protorealignment parties. They presage electoral realignment only when they can recruit regularly from the ranks of the majority party as well. That, in fact, was the case with Minnesota's parties of economic protest.

The Greenback party was never as strong in Minnesota as it was in Iowa or Missouri. At its peak in 1879, it polled only 4.0 percent of the total vote. And in that year, as was typical of the Greenback 1877–79

---

72. The Democrat-Greenback fusion in 1878 represented an effort similar to that in 1884 and 1886. Most of the Populist recruitment from the Democrats came through the Labor party; but Republican-to-Populist movement, though totaling only 3.9 percent in two steps between 1888 and 1892, was direct.

surge, it cut into the voting coalitions of both major parties. What little persisting Greenback support there was in Minnesota, as well as the weak Labor party voting in 1888, displayed stronger crosscutting traces than in the other states, but the proportions and numbers of voters involved in economic-protest voting after 1879 were extremely small.[73]

It was not so much the developments of the 1870s and 1880s that set Minnesota apart from Iowa and Missouri, as it was the emergence there of a strong Farmers' Alliance party in 1890. Statewide, the Alliance gubernatorial candidate polled 24.2 percent of the vote, and the party was especially strong in the wheat-producing counties of the Red River Valley in western and northwestern Minnesota (see Map 3). That is, Alliance voting was strong precisely in those areas where Anti-Monopoly and Greenback voting had been weak.[74]

Alliance voting was not confined disproportionately to former supporters of the minority Democratic party. It was more than a political alternative for those who were mired in a forlorn minority. Of course, for some Democrats it did serve that function, and the rate of Democratic crossover to the Alliance varied both with section of the state and with the party's traditional strength. Democratic crossover was greater in western, central, and northern Minnesota than in the state's southeastern and south central counties. And outside of the wheat-producing areas of the state, Democratic crossover to the Alliance depended rather clearly on political-structural conditions; its rate was typically higher in Republican counties than in Democratic bailiwicks. The Republican case differed in a critical respect. Republican voter losses were steeper and certainly more dramatic in the Red River Valley counties, but they were also considerable in the eastern portions of the state.[75] And there Republican crossover was not regularly a function of the party's county-level weakness. In fact, most of the deviant cases of extremely low Republican-to-Alliance switching occurred in strongly Democratic counties.

73. The highest level was the 2.6 percent recorded in both 1881 and 1882. Descriptions of Minnesota's voter movement in the 1870s and 1880s derive from regression estimates calculated by counties; those for 1886 and after are weighted sums of regression estimates calculated by minor civil divisions within counties or clusters of counties.

74. That is evident from the zero-order correlations: Anti-Monopoly 1873/1890 Alliance, $r = .578$; Greenback 1879/1890 Alliance, $r = -.206$. The contrast between Greenback and Alliance voting was striking in another respect. The Greenback vote, unlike the Alliance vote, was not especially rural. Greenback strength in 1879 *decreased* by .73 percentage points for every 1.0 percentage point increase in the proportion of farmers in the population; whereas, the Alliance vote *increased* by 1.7 percentage points for every 1.0 percentage point increase in the proportion of farmers.

75. Overall, about one-third of the 1888 Republican voters who cast ballots in 1890 crossed over to the Alliance, but the rate of crossover in the west and northwest was nearly twice as high as in the eastern counties.

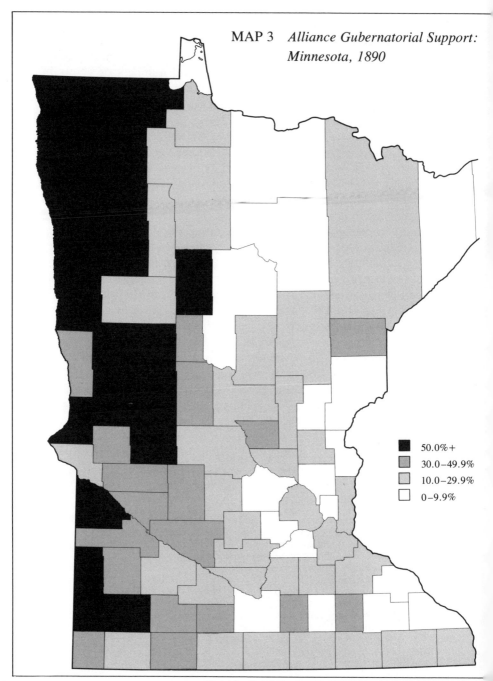

MAP 3   *Alliance Gubernatorial Support:*
         Minnesota, 1890

■ 50.0%+
▨ 30.0–49.9%
▧ 10.0–29.9%
□ 0–9.9%

By 1892 the Alliance party had been replaced in the electoral lists by the Populist (or People's) party. That substitution involved more than a new label. Given their temporal proximity to each other, one would expect to find high levels of continuity between the two parties. And there were some indicators of that. The distribution (by counties) of the Alliance vote explained 63.2 percent of the variance of the 1892 Populist vote for governor; nearly two-fifths of those who voted Alliance, and who balloted again in 1892, opted to support the Populists. Yet mixed with these indicators of continuity were unmistakable signs of discontinuity. The Populist vote for governor in 1892 was 8.7 percentage points lower than the Alliance vote in 1890, and the variance of its distribution was less than half that of the earlier vote.[76] The decline in variance suggests a decay in Farmer-Labor strength that involved something more than simply reactivating old party loyalties in a presidential election.

There are several clues to the social nature of the differences between Alliance and Populist voting. The Alliance polled 84.0 percent of its total vote outside of the state's urban areas, and it ran 12.6 percentage points stronger in rural than in urban places. The Populists polled 78.8 percent of their total vote outstate, but ran only 5.8 percentage points stronger there than in the urban centers. Although the Populists still recruited in rural areas, the association of Populist strength with the percentage of farmers in the population was only about one-third as steep as the Alliance's had been.[77] Finally, Populist recruitment from the Democrats, unlike the 1890 Alliance, was not confined to those rural areas in which the Democracy was a weak minority. Instead, the Populists were more successful than the Alliance in drawing support from among normally Democratic voter groups in urban areas.

Such clues point to sharp differences in the geographic and social sources of Alliance and Populist voting. They also suggest differences between them even within urban areas. The data in Table 7.8 starkly illustrate the extent and nature of those distinctions.[78] The data in Panel A

76. The heavy Alliance support in the wheat counties produced a variance (by counties) of 355.32; the 1892 Populist vote for governor had a variance of only 138.29. The vote for governor has been used for the Populists in 1892 since there was a partial fusion between the Democrats and Populists on the slate of presidential electors.

77. The Populist vote increased by .55 percentage points for every 1.0 percentage point increase in the proportion of farmers in the population. For the form of the association between Alliance voting and rurality, see Chapter 7, n. 74.

78. The urban estimates were calculated across the wards of the following cities: Minneapolis, St. Paul, Hastings, Red Wing, Duluth, Shakopee, St. Cloud, and Winona. The rural estimates for the Germans and Swedes are weighted sums of estimates calculated by minor civil divisions within all counties except those in which one of the cities was located. For the Norwegians the rural estimates were calculated across two sets of counties (excluding the urban counties) for each of the two religiously distinct groups of Norwegian Lutherans.

TABLE 7.8   *Farmer-Labor Social Discontinuity: Minnesota, 1890 and 1892*

A. *Correlations by Wards*

	Minneapolis		St. Paul	
	Alliance '90	People's '92	Alliance '90	People's '92
% Irish	−.299	.117	−.466	.252
% German	−.540	.003	−.264	.581
% Norwegian	.524	.718	.273	.267
% Swedish	.418	.758	.124	.083

B. *Estimates of Social Group Support*

	Alliance 1890		People's 1892	
	Urban	Rural	Urban	Rural
Irish	3.7	N.C.	19.5	N.C.
German	0.0	8.6	10.4	4.3
Norwegian	20.1	49.7	10.7	32.3
Swedish	14.1	29.1	10.7	11.6

show the changing character of Farmer-Labor voting in the state's two major cities between 1890 and 1892. In the former year the Alliance appeal in these cities was largely confined to Norwegian and Swedish voters, but by 1892 the Populists were able to mobilize a transethnic laboring-group coalition. The data in Panel B point to the rural thrust of the Alliance, to the heavy concentration of its support among rural Norwegian and Swedish voters, and to the more even rural-urban appeal of the Populists, as well as the continuing concentration of rural support for economic protest among Norwegian and Swedish voters. These differences in the locational and social sources of Farmer-Labor support reflected distinctions in political character between the Alliance and the Populists.

The Farmers' Alliance had been active in Minnesota politics since its organization there in 1881. Though racked by the customary internal debates over whether or not to resort to independent partisan action, until 1890 it had concentrated largely on pressure-group activity. And throughout the 1880s Alliance leaders had cooperated in that with laboring-group spokesmen, especially those representing the trade unions of Minneapolis and St. Paul. By 1890 these rural and urban protest leaders were ready for separate party action. The immediate impetus for that came, not from the state leaders, but from the grass roots; the local chapters of the Alliance in the wheat-producing counties petitioned the state executive committee to call a state convention. The call to the convention was in fact, as it described itself, a call "from the prairie farmer . . . from the farthest retreats of a desolate country." The St. Paul convention in July 1890 organized a party, nominated candidates for state offices, and issued a declaration of principles. In all of these actions, especially in its platform, the Alliance party evidenced its agrarian character and its appeal to an issue public aroused by prevailing agricultural conditions. Those conditions included declines in prices for wheat, an extensive incidence of mortgaged farms, higher rates of mortgage interest in the western counties than in the eastern portions of the state, drought and another locust plague that damaged the 1889–90 crops in the wheat counties, and preferential rates on shipments to terminal points in the Twin Cities. These conditions diffused the perception of a gap between expectations of the political process and its realities among an expanded proportion of the rural electorate. Immediate economic reversals interacted with smoldering rural resentments to enlarge the size of the issue public both aroused by such concerns and convinced that "politics as usual," their standing partisan identifications, were irrelevant to amelioration of the difficulties that beset them. To that issue public the Alliance party builders addressed themselves.[79]

The 1890 declaration of principles gave unequivocal evidence of the rural roots and appeal of the party. In its specifics as in its aura, the Alliance platform resonated emotionally with the concerns of a rural issue public aroused by its current economic plight. To channel that concern to Alliance voting support, the platform devoted 75.6 percent of its farmer-labor symbolism to agrarian concerns. Despite the long practice of cooperation between rural and labor opinion leaders and despite the fact that 10.4 percent of the delegates at the St. Paul convention were representatives of the trade unions of the Twin Cities, the

79. The quoted phrase is from Arthur Naftalin, "The Tradition of Protest and the Roots of the Farmer-Labor Party," p. 60. In this and the following paragraphs the factual information on Minnesota conditions and political action, but not the interpretation, has been drawn from John D. Hicks, "The People's Party in Minnesota," pp. 531–60; idem, "The Birth of the Populist Party," pp. 219–47; George B. Engberg, "The Rise of Organized Labor in Minnesota," pp. 372–94; idem, "The Knights of Labor in Minnesota," pp. 367–90; Carl H. Chrislock, "The Alliance Party and the Minnesota Legislature of 1891," pp. 297–312; idem, "Sidney M. Owen," pp. 109–26.

Alliance as a party remained preponderantly rural in its preoccupations and its base of support.[80]

The 1892 Populist party was different. Its organizational impetus came from the labor opinion leaders. Much of the organizational work of the People's party was directed by Ignatius Donnelly, who had roots in both worlds. He had been elected president of the Farmers' Alliance in Minnesota after the 1890 election; his delegation, and not that of the Alliance party, was seated at the May 1891 reform conference that created a People's party national executive committee. Some Alliance leaders later accepted Donnelly's overture to serve on the People's party state committee, but the agrarian-urban conflict at the elite level was evident in the fact that other Alliance leaders rejected that invitation, organized their own convention, adopted their own platform, and nominated their own gubernatorial candidate.[81] The Populists' concerns focused less exclusively on rural discontent than on the economic grievances of urban laboring groups. Those had been reflected in the growing membership and organizational strength of the Knights of Labor and had been expressed vividly in the 1886 strikes, especially in the street railway strike in Minneapolis. To this aroused issue public the Populists primarily addressed themselves in 1892. Only a bare majority (51.1 percent) of the party's farmer-labor platform symbolism articulated laboring-group appeals, but that contrasted markedly with the farmer-labor balance in both the 1890 and 1892 Alliance platforms. The Alliance declaration in 1892 still devoted two-thirds of its farmer-labor symbols to agrarian concerns.[82] These contrasting self-images of the

80. The Alliance leaders were even reluctant to accept the planks calling for an eight-hour day and ban on child labor, because they feared these might be applied to agriculture; see Chrislock, "Alliance Party," p. 304. However, they were not hesitant to incorporate a plank calling for the use of convict labor (which the trade union groups opposed) "to furnish the farmers of the state binding twine at cost." The platform is in the *Minnesota Legislative Manual for 1891*, pp. 486–88. For the data on the trade unionists at the founding convention, see Hicks, "People's Party," pp. 537–38.

81. The separate Alliance party effort in 1892 rapidly collapsed, however. On Donnelly's role at the 1891 convention, see John D. Hicks, *The Populist Revolt*, pp. 213–15. Donnelly was the nominee of the People's party for governor in 1892. Goodwyn, *Democratic Promise*, pp. 259–60, notes that the cooperative movement, which he regards as the linchpin of Populism, had never flourished there and that "the Minnesota Alliance gradually, almost gracefully, fell apart in 1891." This type of conflict between the rural and urban wings of economic discontent was not unique to Minnesota; see Chester McArthur Destler, *American Radicalism, 1865–1901*, pp. 164–211, 222–54.

82. The platforms are in *Minnesota Legislative Manual for 1893*, pp. 371–73. The exact distribution for the 1892 Alliance platform was 67.0 percent to rural and 32.9 percent to laboring-group symbols. Each platform, of course, contained symbols that were not unambiguously related to farmer or laboring-group concerns per se. For instance, in the 1890 Alliance platform 18.1 percent of *all* symbols dealt with other matters: an attack on the Supreme Court's original-package decision, which was a current focal point of prohibitionist ire; a call for submission of constitutional amend-

two parties had their behavioral counterparts in the distinctly different locations and social sources of their electoral coalitions.

Minnesota's Populist party did not sweep to victory among laboring-group voters in 1892. In fact, the strength of economic-protest voting throughout the state fell from its 1890 level, but the decline in urban areas of 8.9 percentage points was smaller than the 12.9 percentage-point shift in rural units. The party's capacity in urban areas to mobilize support across ethnoreligious groupings was behaviorally more significant. To enlist electoral support from among Irish and German voters —as well as from among their long-standing religious and political enemies, the Norwegians and Swedes—was an accomplishment of no small significance. To be sure, one cannot speak of a groundswell of labor-group support for the party, for only small minorities among these groups voted Populist, and the overwhelming majorities within each cast their ballots for their traditional parties. Yet even these faint traces of a socially crosscutting coalition, of a transethnic base of support, were more than Farmer-Labor parties had normally mobilized in Minnesota or elsewhere.

Building an electoral coalition that crosscut partisan and ethnoreligious boundaries was the formidable task confronting late nineteenth-century Farmer-Labor party builders. Except for crises, and even then only unevenly, their efforts were not rewarded with much success. The data in Table 7.9 provide a longitudinal overview of social-group support for these parties.[83] The penetrative capability of Farmer-Labor parties was socially quite uneven. The Greenbackers ran strongest in Yankee areas and mustered minimal support in German units. Even in the 1877–79 surge, Greenback support in German areas was conspicuously low; its peak was 2.3 percent in the German counties in 1878.[84] In the Midwest the party drew about equal levels of support in the

---

ments to popular referenda, which in the Minnesota context was unmistakably related to the question of a referendum on a prohibitory amendment. The term *farmer-labor symbolism* excludes such planks from the base for the percentages.

83. For Minnesota the estimates in Panel B are weighted sums of separate estimates made for two groups of counties; for the Norwegian Lutherans in both Minnesota and Iowa, they are weighted sums of separate estimates made for the Haugean and non-Haugean groups.

84. Most of that support was concentrated in Wisconsin's German counties. For the atypical elements involved in that state's Granger movement and Greenback efforts, see Kleppner, *Cross of Culture*, pp. 120–24, especially nn. 30, 33, pp. 121, 123. The data in Table 7.9 (Panel A) include the surge elections in the calculation of the 1876–84 means, but even if they had been excluded, the pattern would remain the same. Typically, German opposition to soft-money schemes has been explained in terms of the group's "conservatism." That is not, however, an explanation; it simply applies a stereotype to the group. And that stereotype originated with contemporary Yankees, who used it in a strongly pejorative fashion.

TABLE 7.9   *Social Sources of Farmer-Labor Support*

A. *Mean Farmer-Labor Percentages by Types of Counties*

	Yankee	Southern Stock	German	Scandinavian
$\overline{M}$ 1876–84	5.1	3.5	1.0	3.5
$\overline{M}$ 1886–92	0.9	2.6	1.4	8.2
Populist 1892	2.4	4.2	2.0	11.2

B. *Mean 1888–92 of Farmer-Labor Voting*

	Iowa	Minnesota	Missouri
Baptist-North	2.9	2.8	N.C.
South	N.C.	N.C.	2.8
Meth- North	1.8	5.7	3.5
South	N.C.	N.C.	4.7
Presby-North	2.7	4.4	5.1
South	N.C.	N.C.	2.1
Norwegian Luth	2.9	27.9	N.C.
Swedish Luth	3.9	14.4	N.C.
Catholic	0.5	4.7	0.0
German Luth	0.5	6.8	1.6

Scandinavian and southern-stock counties. Significantly, however, but excluding the surge elections and their after shocks, persisting Greenback recruitment in most places drew more heavily from the ranks of the weaker of the major parties. Though even where these apparently requisite political-structural conditions prevailed, Greenbackery was unable consistently to attract many German or Catholic voters.[85] As a

85. There were local exceptions, of course. For example, there was some lingering Greenback support among the Irish Catholic miners in Schuylkill County, Pennsylvania; in 1884 Boston's Irish wards gave the Greenback ticket a mean vote of 10.7 percent, and the native-stock wards 3.1 percent; labor strife elicited higher-than-normal levels of Greenback and Workingmen's support and Irish votes in Troy, New York. Such cases point to the necessity of examining the local *character* of the party. However, in describing the central tendency of Greenback voting support, such cases become notice- able precisely because they were such glaring exceptions. On the appeal to the Irish of Benjamin Butler, who headed the Greenback ticket in 1884, see Richard P. Harmond, "Tradition and Change in the Gilded Age," pp. 42–127; on Troy, New York, see Daniel Jay Walkowitz, "Working Class Culture in the Gilded Age," pp. 214–15, 257, 266.

consequence, its regular coalition bore the unmistakable impress of pietism, especially in rural areas. In most areas of the East and Midwest, it was native-stock pietism; in states like Iowa, Minnesota, and Wisconsin, immigrant pietists, especially Norwegians and Swedes, joined the coalition.

Of course, the more distinctly urban-oriented Labor parties in 1886 ran better among German and Catholic voters than the Greenbackers had, but their penetrative capability was locationally constricted and largely evanescent. Their more enduring successors, the variously titled Farmer-Labor parties that contested the 1888–92 elections, continued to provide a greater attraction for pietistic than for nonpietistic voter groups. That was the case where they were relatively weak, as in Iowa; even where they were stronger, as in Minnesota, their percentages among Catholic and German Lutheran voters ran behind those polled from Norwegian and Swedish pietists and were not even consistently stronger than the levels registered among the presumably higher-status, native-stock Methodists and Presbyterians.[86]

This character trait of the Farmer-Labor electoral coalition was not unique to a handful of states. It was an extensive and persisting phenomenon. In New York State the Greenbackers drew their small levels of strength from among Yankees and Penn-Jerseyites; so their percentages were higher in Universalist, Baptist, and Methodist towns than they were in German Lutheran or Catholic ones. The party's electoral coalition was disproportionately native-stock in Illinois, Indiana, and Michigan; in Ohio it mixed support from southern-stock Baptists and Disciples with that from northern Methodists and British and Welsh miners. In Kansas, Greenback voting in 1880 and 1884 associated positively with Methodism and with support for the state's 1880 prohibitory referendum. And to the west, in Colorado, the party ran best in the northern-state native and Protestant-immigrant counties and poorest among the Germans. Even in the mining camps the native Protestants gave more support than the Catholic miners.[87]

86. As the labels indicate, the German Lutheran category in Table 7.9 is not the same as the German category in Table 7.8. The 1888–92 mean for the latter category was 4.7 percent. The counties used for the data in Table 7.9, Panel A, were located in eight states: Illinois, Indiana, Iowa, Minnesota, New York, Ohio, Pennsylvania, and Wisconsin.

87. Parker, "Empire Stalemate," Table XIV-11, p. 147, and Chapter 14, passim, for data and discussion of the later Socialist Labor and Populist support; Richard M. Doolen, "The Greenback Party in the Great Lakes Middlewest," Table 4, pp. 137–39; Kleppner, *Cross of Culture*, pp. 122–23; Louise E. Rickard, "The Impact of Populism on Electoral Patterns in Kansas, 1880–1900," Tables 8, 13, pp. 35, 48; James Edward Wright, *The Politics of Populism*, pp. 104–106; for weak German support for parties of economic protest prior to 1890 in Nebraska, see Frederick C. Luebke, *Immigrants and Politics*, pp. 126–27, 133.

Though the size and regional shape of the later Populist support was quite different, its electoral coalition evidenced an analogous social valence. New York's Populist vote in 1892 was quite small, heavily rural, and strongest in Universalist, Baptist, Evangelical Synod, and Methodist towns. The same type of social pattern marked Populist support in other eastern states. New Jersey's small Populist coalition was overwhelmingly a native-stock enterprise and a nearly even mixture of Baptists, Methodists, and Presbyterians. Maryland's Populists were nearly as weak and just as strongly native stock as New Jersey's. What little support the party had came from southern Baptists and northern Methodists and Presbyterians. There was considerably more popular support for the Populists in Kansas, Nebraska, and Colorado than there was in New York, New Jersey, and Maryland. Yet even in these regions of its greatest strength, the Independent and Populist candidates in 1890 and 1892, except in instances of fusion with the Democrats, ran better among pietistic voting groups than among the nonpietists.[88]

Farmer-Labor party builders did not purposely intend to create ethnoreligiously exclusive parties. They aimed at creating transethnic, class parties. They intended to cut across the bounds of ethnoreligious-group distinctions and to mobilize a coalition that shared common economic identifications. Although the data are spotty and sometimes inconclusive, it does seem that support for Farmer-Labor parties displayed traces of economic motivation, at least more than did major-party voting. Greenback support in Michigan and Minnesota, for example, was associated with mortgage indebtedness; in Indiana it came from the relatively poor and underdeveloped rural areas, and in Illinois from the relatively prosperous northern counties whose agriculture was changing from wheat production to dairying.[89]

88. For New York, in addition to Parker, "Empire Stalemate," see Hammond, "Revivalist Political Ethos," pp. 235–36. On Nebraska see David S. Trask, "The Nebraska Populist Party," pp. 107, 112–15, 134, 141, 153; idem, "Formation and Failure," pp. 281–301; Stanley B. Parsons, *The Populist Context*, pp. 118, 131; Luebke, *Immigrants and Politics*, pp. 148, 151–56. On Kansas see Rickard, "Impact of Populism," Tables 21, 29, pp. 79, 99; Peter H. Argersinger, *Populism and Politics*, pp. 70–75. On Colorado see Wright, *Politics of Populism*, pp. 123, 153–55. On the Scandinavian, and non-German and non-Catholic, character of Populist support in North and South Dakota, see Michael Paul Rogin, *The Intellectuals and McCarthy*, pp. 110–12, 140, 175–76. Further to the west, for California, see Rogin and John L. Shover, *Political Change in California*, p. 13; R. Hal Williams, *The Democratic Party and California Politics, 1880–1896*, pp. 137–38, 163–64.

89. Doolen, "Greenback Party," pp. 152–55; Schroeder, "Political Issues and Elections." My view that these party builders purposely intended to create class parties is an assumption but one consistent with the preponderance of qualitative evidence. For useful insights see Montgomery, *Beyond Equality*, pp. 335–47; Unger, *Greenback Era*, pp. 294–305; Norman Pollack, ed., *The Populist Mind*; and Goodwyn, *Democratic Promise*.

The economic underpinnings of Populist voting in 1890 and 1892 were even more varied and complex. Drought and crop failures in the farming areas of the West and West North Central regions heightened and gave a sense of immediacy to long-standing agrarian complaints. Mortgage indebtedness, perhaps a sign of expansive optimism in "good times," likely became more onerous in the face of persistently declining prices and low crop yields. The agricultural depression also probably increased the levels of tension between village and city businessmen and their rural clients and made the latter even more sensitive than usual to the operation of warehousing, grading, and pricing practices that were controlled by organizations of "urban" businessmen. The relative weights of these and other factors varied from place to place, but their operation, the agricultural depression, and the perception of a party system that could not accommodate their immediate economic concerns interacted to create distinct and mobilizable issue publics. In Colorado, for example, Independent voting in 1890 showed a strong relationship with the relative incidence of mortgaged farms. In Kansas 1890 protest voting was strongest in areas with large proportions of mortgaged farms and low values of farmland and farm products. Populist support in Nebraska in the same year was greatest in the counties that were experiencing the most severe economic crisis. In North and South Dakota Populist strength was concentrated in the wheat-belt counties among cash-crop farmers subjected to the fluctuations of an international price and market system, but significantly, the party was weakest in the richest wheat-producing counties.[90] Iowa's weak levels of Populist voting in 1891 showed their steepest levels of association with the proportion of mortgaged farms and the 1870 to 1890 declines in the value of farm products. In Minnesota in 1890 and Missouri in 1892, the interactive effect of extensive mortgages and high mortgage values was steeply associated with protest voting.[91] Of course in other places, and even at other times in these states, Populist voting displayed traces of different

90. This summary is based on data that are uneven, but in my judgment the composite picture of an association between Populist voting and perceived economic and political grievances is plausible. For the original data see Wright, *Politics of Populism*, p. 124; Rickard, "Impact of Populism," Tables 22, 26, pp. 99, 122; Parsons, *Populist Context*, pp. 126–27; Rogin, *McCarthy and the Intellectuals*, pp. 113–15, 140–43, n. 9, p. 308.

91. The Iowa, Minnesota, and Missouri observations are based on multiplicative regression models. For Iowa in 1891 the partial beta for percentage of mortgaged farms was .594; and for the changing value of farm products, .299. In Minnesota the beta for the interactive term was .625, and in Missouri .378. Although beta weights in separate multiple-regression equations involving different sets of independent variables are not directly comparable, it is relevant to point out that the unstandardized slopes in these instances were statistically significant (using a *t*-test) at the .01 level. And it is also relevant to observe that in each equation the slope for at least one ethnoreligious variable

types of economic motivation. The Minnesota shift from agrarian discontent to higher levels of laboring-group support for the Populists was not wholly unusual. A similar type of transformation seems to have occurred in Colorado and Montana between 1890 and 1892.[92]

Farmer-Labor party builders intended to develop transethnic class-oriented coalitions. And their parties in the electorate did show traces of a capacity to mobilize specified segments of those issue publics aroused by perceived economic grievances. Yet these penetrative capabilities were markedly circumscribed. The type of coalition that they envisioned and the one that emerged were different species of electoral reality. Their appeal was not evenly diffused across all subcategories of the economically discontented. It was strongest among those oriented to economic issues who also shared a pietistic political disposition. And it evoked a persistently less positive response among economically aggrieved voter groups with ritualistic political characters. That is, economic discontent among groups with pietistic political characters was more likely to produce Farmer-Labor voting than similar economic discontent among groups with antipietistic political characters.[93] The explanation of this phenomenon does not lie in some claim that Greenbackers, Laborites, Alliance men, and/or Populists were xenophobes, nativists, or bigoted anti-Catholics. Some may have been; others clearly were not. And whatever their private sentiments, it was not to those but to the public auras of their parties that voters reacted.[94] In those auras, in the political characters of their parties, the explanation lay.

---

was also significant at that level. The relevant betas for these variables for each equation were Iowa, native-stock voters, beta = .529; Minnesota, Norwegian Lutherans, beta = .603; and Missouri, Northern Methodists, beta = .416. For the use of multiplicative models, and their behavioral implications compared with additive models, see Walter Dean Burnham and John Sprague, "Additive and Multiplicative Models of the Voting Universe," pp. 471–90.

92. For Colorado compare the data in Wright, *Politics of Populism*, Tables 7, 8, pp. 123–24, with Tables 9, 10, pp. 154–55, and see his discussion of these matters in Chapters 4, 5. The Montana case is much less clear, but see the wholly qualitative discussion in Thomas A. Clinch, *Urban Populism and Free Silver in Montana*, pp. 21–68. For indications of a shift of another sort in a western state, see the discussion of the conflict between large ranchers and settler-rustlers that flared in the 1892 "Johnson County War" and that created a new issue public mobilizable by the Democratic-Populist fusion; Lewis L. Gould, *Wyoming*, pp. 137–73. For the economic and racial currents that flowed into southern Populism, see Kousser, *Shaping of Southern Politics*, pp. 42, 137, 145, 174, 183, 199, 215.

93. Even then, only under those conditions—e.g., economic crisis and perceived political-structural dysfunctionalism—in which ethnoreligious identifications were less salient than economic ones. It is relevant as well to notice that, except in the West and West North Central regions during the early 1890s, in most instances only minorities of economically disaffected pietists supported Farmer-Labor parties.

94. The values of political elites have bearing, of course, on the characters of their

It has been both long recognized and well documented that the late nineteenth-century parties of economic protest had about them auras of religious movements. The Greenback party was less an amalgamation of economic pressure groups than an ad hoc coalition of "True Believers," "ideologues," who launched their party as a "quasi-religious" movement that bore the indelible hallmark of "a transfiguring faith." To their party activities they brought their internalized commitments to an ethic of ultimate responsibility, for they perceived their activity, not as involvement in mere partisanship, but as a "mighty movement," one that was nothing less than "the religion of the Master in motion among men." And the later Populists, no less than their dispositional forerunners, spoke in the idiom of the religious enthusiast. Their 1890 contest in Kansas, for example, they described not as "a political campaign," but as "a religious revival, a crusade, a pentecost of politics in which a tongue of flame sat upon every man, and each spake as the spirit gave him utterance. . . . The farmers, the country merchants, the cattle-herders . . . had . . . heard the word and could preach the gospel of Populism."[95]

Not all Farmer-Labor elites were religious zealots. The noncompromising spirit of religious enthusiasm characterized some much more than others. And in particular locales party builders worked pragmatically to restrain that ardor and to minimize public declarations reflective of its spirit. Yet on the whole the public images of Greenbackery and Populism in most locales evidenced the religious dispositions probably shared by most of their officeholders and activists and certainly by the bulk of their electoral coalitions.

The pietistic character of Greenbackery owed much to its organizational roots and recruitment of activists from Grange circles. The Grange was an avowedly nonpartisan organization whose ostensible objective was to increase social communication among farmers. However, the

---

parties, but the point here is that development of a nonritualist political character need not necessarily be construed as a conscious commitment to nativistic bigotry. For an analysis of the nativist claim among Kansas Populists, see Walter T. K. Nugent, *The Tolerant Populists*.

95. The quoted phrases applied to the Greenbackers are Unger's, in *Greenback Era*, p. 306. James B. Weaver, *A Call to Action*, p. 440, offered the religious description of the "character" (his term) of the economic protest movement. The description of the 1890 Kansas uprising was given by Elizabeth N. Barr and was quoted in Hicks, *Populist Revolt*, p. 159; also see Peter H. Argersinger, "Pentecostal Politics in Kansas," pp. 24–35. And see Goodwyn, *Democratic Promise*, pp. 666–67, n. 35, for the *purposive* intent behind the use of religious metaphors in Populist rhetoric. Moreover, given Goodwyn's description (pp. 309–10) of the disproportionately Anglo-Protestant character of the Alliance and Populist party organizers, it is understandable that they failed to perceive the unintended negative effects of such usage on particular voter groups.

Grange's popularity did not spread evenly in all types of social areas. Among some religious groups Grange rituals and oaths marked it as just another secret society, and all such societies were "anti-Christian and destructive of . . . the individual soul." The conferences of Norwegian and Swedish Lutherans and the German Lutheran and sectarian groups had long condemned secret societies; it was no coincidence that they increased the frequency and sharpened the tone of their denunciations in the 1870s. Although religious opposition certainly slowed recruitment to the Grange among these groups, it was not slowed among Yankees, and the early movement in the Midwest was especially concentrated in areas of their settlement.[96]

Yankee dominance makes understandable the relative quickness with which the Grange espoused the moral causes that had long enlisted the energies of the group, for the Grange became another Yankee instrument of moral reformation. It characterized itself as being permeated by a "Christian spirit"; consistent with that spirit, it denounced the great evil of the day, demon rum. It cooperated with temperance societies, especially the W.C.T.U., and urged its members to withhold their ballots from those who were sympathetic to the liquor traffic. And by the 1880s the Grange declared for immigration restriction, "to the end that our institutions may be better protected against the influence and dictation of foreign voters."[97]

96. The quotation is from Mattson, *Polity of the Augustana Lutheran Church*, pp. 277–78; for a general discussion see Fritiof Ander, "The Immigrant Church and the Patrons of Husbandry," pp. 155–68. For examples of contemporary declarations against secret societies, see *Minutes of the Annual Convention of the German Evangelical Lutheran Ministerium of Pennsylvania and Adjacent States, 1881*, p. 12; *Minutes of the Annual Convention of the General Council of the Evangelical Lutheran Church in America, 1880*, p. 47; "The Religion of Secret Societies," pp. 90–102; *Proceedings of the General Conference of the United Brethren Church in Christ, 1873*, pp. 40–43. Also see Henry Jacob Ryskamp, "The Dutch in Western Michigan," pp. 33–34. This renewed flurry of antisecrecy underlay the creation of a new (and still existing) "Anti-Masonic" organization in 1876, the National Christian Association. The focus was secret societies in general and Masonry in particular.

97. The quotations are from the *Proceedings of the Seventh Session of the National Grange of the Patrons of Husbandry, 1874*, p. 7; *Journal of Proceedings. Twenty-Third Session of the National Grange . . . 1889*, p. 108. For temperance attitudes see *Proceedings of the Twelfth Session of the National Grange . . . 1878*, pp. 105–106; and *Journal of Proceedings. Twenty-Fourth Session of the National Grange . . . 1890*, pp. 40, 79–81. For illustrative examples of local Grange action, see *Proceedings of the Tenth Annual Session of the Indiana State Grange, Patrons of Husbandry*, 1880, pp. 30–31; *Journal of the Proceedings, Eighteenth Session of the Illinois State Grange, Patrons of Husbandry, 1889*, p. 64; Leonard L. Allen, *History of the New York State Grange*, p. 52. Also see the reports of prohibitory resolutions adopted by local Granges in New York, Iowa, Missouri, Massachusetts, and Pennsylvania and reported in *Rural New-Yorker* (New York City), 13 February, 24 April, 29 May 1875, 1 January 1876; and in *The Prairie Farmer* (Chicago), 12 January 1884.

The dispositions that characterized the Grange's activists were carried with them into Greenbackery. The public aura that that party projected was expressive of the value systems of pietistic groups. One salient dimension of that image was its antipartyism. Much of Greenback antiparty rhetoric was probably tactical in its design, but it sometimes went beyond tactics to assaults on party practices as such and on the social divisiveness that *party* implied. Greenbackery depicted itself, on the other hand, not as a normal party, but as a movement "of the whole people."[98] Such visions of organic wholeness of the community had long been Yankee hallmarks. Rhetoric exalting them, decrying party practices, as well as the perfidy of the old parties, resonated emotionally with their pietistic political character; so, too, did Greenbackery's common use of *Independent* as part of its party designation. That term connoted then much more than it does currently. It had long implied a freedom from the dictates of party, a morally based opposition to organizational loyalties that restrained men from doing right. In that sense, *Independent* symbolically represented groups whose values apotheosized the free will to do right.[99]

In some locales the Greenback aura of moral reform had even more concrete referents. Often their platforms dealt with measures that were then focal points of pietistic-ritualistic conflict. And almost invariably, the Greenbackers endorsed the pietistic stance: support for prohibition, advocacy of compulsory education, and opposition to aid to sectarian institutions.[100]

98. The quotation is from the 1878 Rhode Island Greenback platform, in *Appletons' Annual Cyclopaedia, 1878*, p. 731. Greenback antiparty statements were common and appeared in virtually every state declaration; for additional examples in 1878, see ibid., pp. 236–37, 674. Because it was so atypical, see also the 1878 Indiana Greenback platform—which called, although somewhat obliquely, for a class party—ibid., p. 422. It may have been significant that Indiana's Greenback officeholders included no New York-New England natives, in contrast to the rather strong New York-New England component among the Michigan and Wisconsin Greenbackers; see Doolen, "Greenback Party," Tables 10, 13, pp. 183, 192. For additional indications of this Greenback trait and the Greenback-Grange connections, see A[lexander] K. McClure, *Old Time Notes of Pennsylvania*, 2:423–27, 548, 575–77; Herman Clarence Nixon, "The Populist Movement in Iowa," pp. 29–30. The religiously based attack on Greenbackism by pietist leaders was implicit recognition by them of the appeal of the idea among some segments of their audiences; for the attacks see Unger, *Greenback Era*, pp. 123–31.

99. On the symbolic meaning of the term, see Ronald P. Formisano, *The Birth of Mass Political Parties*, pp. 247–53. In some places Greenbackers ran simply as "Independent"; in others that was combined, as in "Independent Greenback" or "Independent National." It may have been significant that they tended to drop the "Independent" tag where there were close connections between the Greenback party and the labor-reform groups, as in Pennsylvania. The details of these matters can be followed in *Appletons' Annual Cyclopaedia, 1876–84*.

100. In some elections the Greenbackers worked out forms of fusion with the Prohibition party. For examples of these matters, see McClure, *Old Time Notes*, 2:492;

That their parties displayed character traits that were expressive of pietistic, especially Yankee pietistic, values did not mean that Greenback party builders were self-conscious nativists, but it did mean that Greenback political character failed to represent symbolically the political dispositions of antipietistic groups. German Lutherans, for example, who were repelled by temperance zeal, would find nothing in Greenback political character that was congenial with their own political temperament. Neither would the visible involvement of Grange activists resonate positively among voters in whose belief systems secretiveness had been linked with Know-Nothingism. Nor did the aura of reform attract voters whose past experiences had led them to link that with pietistic assaults on their religious values. Voter groups whose religious values predisposed them to personal liberty and laissez faire ethics found no psychological consonance in Greenbackism with its commitment to positive government and its aura of pietistic morality. Not to these types of voters, but primarily to pietists among the economically discontented did Greenback political character appeal.

There was a similar symbiotic relation between pietistic political character and the later Alliance-Populist mobilizing efforts. The tone of religious enthusiasm, the extensive and evangelical antiparty rhetoric, the symbolic use of the Independent label, and the rhetorical and sometimes organizational connections with prohibition made Populist voting less appealing to ritualistic voter groups than to native and immigrant pietists.

North Dakota's Alliance men were atypical only in their degree of forthrightness. They declared unequivocally, ''Ours is not a political party—it is more, for in it are crystallized sentiments and measures for the benefit of the whole people.'' Most state pronouncements were less direct, but typically, in both 1890 and 1892 (outside the South), they included declamations against the old parties and condemnation of party practices in general. Even in the lyrics of their campaign songs, Alliance party builders used the expression *party man* as a pejorative epithet and extolled the virtue of ''the true and independent man.'' And in Colorado, Nebraska, and South Dakota, they used the label *Independent* to rally their supporters.[101]

Benjamin F. Gue, *History of Iowa from the Earliest Times to the Beginning of the Twentieth Century*, 3:97, 126–27; *Appletons' Annual Cyclopaedia, 1877*, pp. 399–400, 489, 553, 620, 635–36; ibid., *1878*, pp. 432, 451, 577, 622–23; ibid., *1882*, pp. 385–86, 556. It will require a series of microcosmic studies to pinpoint the extent, location, and nature of county-level organizational and activist cooperation between the Greenbackers and Prohibitionists, as well as between the later Populists and Prohibitionists.

101. Warren A. Henke, comp., *Prairie Politics*, p. 7; other 1890 and 1892 state

The use of such symbols and code words both indicates the anti-party bent of the activists who crafted the rhetoric and gives insight into the nature of the shared continuum of values that they perceived to exist between themselves and their supporters in the electorate. However, ritualistic religious groups did not share those values; they had, in fact, long associated them with their pietistic political enemies. That such values were linked with Alliance-Populist political character helps explain the lagging capacity of those parties to develop support among ritualistic groups.[102]

Perhaps ritualists could perceive only vaguely that the "pietistic enemy" lurked beneath antiparty code words and Independent or People's symbols. Postures on prohibition provided them with a less ambiguous indicator of the movement's political character. The connections between Populism and the cold-water cause were substantive as well as symbolic. The prohibition crusaders recognized the farmers' organizations, especially the Grange and the Alliance, as allies in a common cause: "Indeed, the farmers' organizations rank with the churches and the special temperance societies as supporters of the Prohibition cause."[103] Grange and Alliance men brought their cold-water dispositions with them to third-party action. Where those elements could shape the party's public declarations and control its organizational activities—as in Michigan, Minnesota, North Dakota, Ohio, Oregon, and South Dakota —the Populists either declared unequivocally for prohibition or entered into varied forms of fusion with the Prohibition party. And even elsewhere, where principle yielded to pragmatism and probably as well to the demands of the urban labor leaders within the party, there were still

platforms can be found in *Appletons' Annual Cyclopaedia* and *The Tribune Almanac and Political Register* for the relevant years. "The Independent Man" was an Alliance campaign song; for its lyric and other observations and examples of antiparty sentiment, see Hicks, *Populist Revolt* pp. 167–70, with the quotation on p. 168. For the spirit of independence in Missouri, see Walter B. Stevens, *Centennial History of Missouri*, 1:648; the details of party organization there can be followed in Martin Gerald Towey, "The People's Party in Missouri." It is worth noticing that their animus to party has been one behaviorally critical way in which these American "left" parties have differed from their European analogues.

102. Nor had there yet been developed among those urban laboring-group voters who were ritualists an extensive organizational infrastructure comparable to the one that sustained Populist support among some farm groups; see Goodwyn, *Democratic Promise*, pp. 307–11, 690, n. 34. Given the then prevailing social bases of partisan cleavage, the existence of such an infrastructure, involvement in it, and the consequent development of a shared sense of economic-group consciousness very likely was a requisite precondition for the emergence of a transethnic voting coalition.

103. *Cyclopaedia of Temperance*, p. 170, and see the Grange and Alliance prohibitory resolutions of 1888–90, quoted on pp. 170–71; also see *Ohio Practical Farmer* (Cleveland), 23 August 1890, 30 January 1892.

indicators of the Populist temperance disposition. For example, in 1890 Nebraska's Independents opted for silence in their platform on the pending referendum on prohibition, but the W.C.T.U. continued to publish a weekly column in the major organ of the movement, *The Alliance*. The party's gubernatorial candidate was a leading prohibitionist, and many of the Populist county newspapers endorsed the holy cause. In Kansas Prohibitionists played roles as Alliance party activists, and the party's 1890 electoral coalition drew support from among former Prohibition party voters. And Alliance or Populist voting also appealed to former Prohibition party voters in Iowa and Minnesota.[104] Indeed, as a comparison of the social bases of support for the Prohibition and Farmer-Labor parties suggests (see Tables 7.4 and 7.9), the two types of parties competed for votes among social groups of similar political character.

The psychological rapport between the mass supporters of prohibition and of Populism was not evidence that economic protest involved reactionary, nativistic elements. No guilt by association should be inferred. Neither, of course, should it lead to ingenuous reinterpretations of the Prohibition party and the broader movement for prohibition as "radical" ones. They bore no consistent traces of a left *tendance*, even in the restricted American sense of that disposition.[105] Rather, there was considerable Populist support among prohibitionists because Populist political character, especially its tone of evangelical righteousness and antipartyism, represented their own.

104. Luebke, *Immigrants and Politics*, p. 144; Trask, "Nebraska Populist Party," p. 73; Parsons, *Populist Context*, p. 106; Argersinger, *Populism and Politics*, pp. 39, 49, 73; Rickard, "Impact of Populism," pp. 53–54, 97–98. The observations pertinent to Minnesota and Iowa are based on regression estimates (by minor civil divisions) of the Prohibition-to-Populist crossover rates. The internal Populist debates over fusion often mirrored the conflicts between leaders committed to an ethic of ultimate responsibility and those whose internalized sense of political responsibility led them to a more pragmatic and accommodating position.

105. Rogin, *McCarthy and the Intellectuals*, pp. 181–82, argues that Prohibition party platforms were "generally radical." Although that represents a somewhat strained reading of the platforms (even in the 1890s), it overlooks the fact that the itemized planks were tactical in design and, more importantly, were very clearly subordinate to the holy cause of cold water. James M. Youngdale, *Populism*, p. 32, argues that it may have been a "short step" from fighting the liquor monopoly to a struggle against monopoly in general. That short step combined with the Haugean tradition in Norway of "peasant political activism," he uses to account for Haugean support of Populism and prohibition (pp. 95–98). Although his hypothesis contains some interesting notions, unfortunately for Minnesota's Alliance party it is counterfactual. That party in 1890 drew heavier support (16.2 percentage points) from among members of the more traditional Norwegian Church in America than from the more pietistic Hauge's Synod and United Norwegians. And in Iowa and Wisconsin Populism drew more support among Swedes than Norwegians, but Youngdale's notion of "culture as a prism" predicts precisely the opposite. Finally, James R. Green, "The 'Salesmen-Soldiers' of the 'Appeal' Army," p. 29, explains activist movement from Prohibition to Socialist support as

In an electoral era whose basic cleavages had been structured by underlying ethnoreligious conflict, the development of a partisan cross-cutting, transethnic coalition involved transcending that conflict. It involved the electoral integration of economic subgroups irrespective of ethnoreligious identifications. That ritualistic religious groups in the late 1880s and the early 1890s perceived the powerful and still current importance of ethnocultural conflict and the continuing relevance of their partisan identifications to the defense of their threatened religious values was one side of Populism's failure to develop a more socially extensive penetrative capability. The other side was the character of Populism's own self-image. A party whose political temperament resonated with pietistic values in general, and prohibitionist ones in particular, was not likely to evoke an equally positive response among social groups to whom those values were anathema. The same perceptions of dispositional consonance that led pietistic groups to support Populism led anti-pietistic groups to be wary and frequently hostile. Except sporadically, and even then only in the face of "quite unusually powerful incentives," ethnoreligious-group consciousness remained more salient to partisanship than did shared economic identifications.

In the final years of the third electoral era, depression in the agricultural and mining areas of the West and West North Central regions created an atmosphere of economic crisis that shook the old partisan structure, but at the same time events in the Northeast and large portions of the Midwest raised the levels of ethnoreligious tension and produced surging Democratic majorities. To these latter events we can now turn our attention.

---

suggestive of "a hidden tradition of working-class self-reform." That tradition seems to have been rather well hidden; Green's only support is a reference to a study of antebellum Lynn, Massachusetts: Paul Gustaf Faler, "Workingmen, Mechanics, and Social Change," pp. 98–105. However, Faler's explanation concerning the temperance movement was not demonstrated but asserted. The credibility of his whole argument depends on an a priori assumption that the values he describes were uniquely working-class values. Yet his research design does not allow him even to address that matter, let alone systematically demonstrate it. Given his description of Lynn as "a center for Methodism," and one where Anti-Masonry had been strong (p. 474; also see pp. 440–41), one should not be surprised that support for temperance existed. Methodists in other locales and occupations, whether working class or not, supported temperance.

8

The Politics of Righteousness: Political Dynamics of the Third Electoral System

Iowa will go Democratic when hell goes Methodist.

Jonathan P. Dolliver (1883)

It is safe to assume that the Methodists never polled a majority among Satan's minions, but the Democrats captured a plurality of Iowa's vote in 1889. When Iowa fell to the Democracy, it was part of a large voter shift that extended eastward to the Atlantic. However, geographically separate streams of behavioral forces convulsed the electoral universe in the early 1890s. While the third party system's cleavage lines were being repaired and sharpened in Iowa and eastward, the unmistakable symptoms of systemic breakup were visible to the west. This admixture of reinstatement and disintegration underlay the large partisan shifts in mass political behavior between 1888 and 1892.

The Democratic Surge

The tight partisan balance that had typified most of the stable phase of the third party system gave way in 1890 to a surging Democratic majority. The Democrats polled 51.9 percent of the total vote cast, elected 70.7 percent of the members of the Fifty-second House. won nine of fifteen nonsouthern gubernatorial races, and gained percentage strength (compared with 1888) in twenty-one of the twenty-six states beyond the Confederacy.[1] Both the size and amplitude of the Democratic victory were impressive (see Table 8.1).

1. The Democrats lost strength only in Delaware, California, Kansas, Minnesota, and Nebraska, and in the latter three states both major parties lost strength. The Democ-

TABLE 8.1   *Partisan Strength by Regions, 1876–1892*

A. *Percent Democratic of Total Vote*

	New Eng	Midatl	ENC	WNC	West	South*	U.S.
1876	43.3	50.4	47.8	44.3	48.6	59.3	50.9
1884	41.5	46.7	47.1	44.6	45.1	57.8	48.5
1886	44.5	47.1	45.0	47.5	47.4	61.5	50.2
1888	43.2	47.1	46.0	42.3	45.3	58.4	48.6
1890	46.8	50.9	48.4	41.5	38.4	65.2	51.9
1892	44.8	47.7	47.3	31.7	29.1	56.5	46.0

B. *Partisan Lead*

	New Eng	Midatl	ENC	WNC	West	South*	U.S.
1876	12.9R	1.5D	2.4R	8.5R	2.5R	18.9D	3.0D
1884	10.2R	2.9R	2.6R	8.1R	7.7R	16.6D	0.2D
1886	6.9R	0.6R	3.2R	1.7R	0.8R	26.5D	5.0D
1888	10.9R	3.2R	3.5R	8.9R	6.9R	19.0D	0.8D
1890	2.6R	4.8D	2.2D	0.9D	11.0R	32.8D	10.1D
1892	7.2R	0.2R	0.7D	14.3R	13.9R	27.0D	3.0D

*Confederate and border states ($N = 14$).

Between 1876 and 1888 the Democrats outpolled the Republicans in three of the four presidential elections and elected their candidate, Grover Cleveland, to the presidency in 1884. With the exception of 1876, the popular-vote margins in these contests were extremely narrow; neither party commanded as much as a 1.0 percentage point lead over its major opposition. At the congressional level the Democrats fared better. They elected a majority of the members of the House of Representatives in five of the seven congressional elections between 1876 and 1888 and averaged 52.4 percent of the House membership over those congresses. With the exception of the Forty-eighth Congress (elected in 1882), the party's strength in the House was due to the overwhelmingly Democratic delegations returned by the Confederate and border states. Together, these two areas accounted for slightly more than three-tenths of the total House membership, and their 1876–88 delega-

---

racy also gained in ten of the eleven ex-Confederate states, losing percentage strength only in South Carolina. This description and the data in Table 8.1 exclude the six states that had not been admitted until after 1888: North and South Dakota, Idaho, Montana, Washington, and Wyoming.

tions averaged 88.2 percent Democratic.[2] This type of disproportionate Democratic strength in the "greater South" enabled the party to secure at least a plurality of the total national vote cast in every congressional election between 1876 and 1888. Over that sequence of congressional elections, the Democrats polled a mean of 49.3 percent of the total national vote and enjoyed an average 3.8 percentage point national lead over the Republicans. That relatively narrow national margin, in turn, was constructed from an average 24.1 percentage point Democratic lead in the greater South, which was only partially counterbalanced by regular, though narrower and declining, Republican leads in other parts of the country.[3]

The 1890 election results shattered this relatively close partisan balance. The size of the Democratic victory was virtually without precedent during the third electoral era. The Democrats opened a national lead of 10.1 percentage points, almost double the size of the largest margin they had previously held.[4] That lead translated into a commanding majority in the Fifty-second House; the Republicans were reduced to eighty-eight seats, their lowest total since the birth of the party. The Democracy's congressional victories extended from New England through the eastern portion of the West North Central states. In every region except the West (the Pacific and Mountain states), the Democrats elected a majority of the congressional delegation: 55.2 percent of the congressmen elected from the Northeast, 66.6 percent from the Midwest, and 95.4 percent from the greater South. Underlying these congressional victories were gains (over 1888) in every region of the country, except the West and parts of the West North Central states. The gains came in states where the Democrats regularly had run strong races, as well as in traditionally Republican bailiwicks. In normally Republican Massachusetts, Michigan, Nebraska, Oregon, Pennsylvania, and Wisconsin, the Democrats elected their 1890 nominees to the governorship. In Illinois

2. The economic downturn of the early 1880s yielded Democratic majorities of the vote cast and of the congressional delegations from the Midatlantic and West; their plurality of the vote in the East North Central region had translated into a majority of the House members from that area. From 1878 to 1888, Democratic congressmen from the Confederate and border states constituted a majority of all Democratic congressmen in every House but the Fifty-second; and over the full seven-House sequence, they averaged 53.3 percent of all Democratic congressmen.

3. The Republicans held the partisan lead in every 1876–88 election in New England; all but two in the Midatlantic area; and all but one in the East North Central, West North Central, and Western regions.

4. The largest Democratic lead prior to 1890 had been 5.4 percentage points in the 1882 congressional elections. The Republicans had captured over 70.0 percent of the House seats in the 1864, 1866, and 1868 elections, and their 1864 national lead had been at least as large as the 1890 Democratic lead. However, these large Republican leads were forged before the end of Reconstruction.

they won their first statewide race—for treasurer—since 1876; in Indiana, Maryland, and New Jersey, the Democratic partisan lead was wider than at anytime since the 1876–78 election sequence. Even Yankee Vermont took part in the swing toward the Democrats. The party remained a hopeless minority there; it polled only 35.5 percent of the vote, but that represented a gain of 9.1 percentage points over 1888 and was the highest level of strength the Democrats had registered since at least 1848.

At first glance, these indicators of size and amplitude may suggest similarities between the 1888–90 swing and the earlier 1872–74 or 1880–82 partisan shifts. Yet even if the wholly asymmetrical behavior of the Confederate and border regions are excluded from consideration, these earlier changes had quite different shapes from the one that occurred between the 1888 and 1890 elections. Calculated across regions, the 1872–74 and 1880–82 swings had larger means and much smaller variances than the 1888–90 shift. Both of the earlier shifts were at least partially produced by economic downturns whose impact cut across the nonsouthern regions of the country and yielded Democratic gains in each of them. The size of those gains averaged 5.6 percentage points between 1872 and 1874 and 4.7 percentage points between 1880 and 1882. And their relatively even distribution across regions can be seen in their low variances: the 1872–74 variance was 2.87; the 1880–82 gains, 0.54. In contrast, the mean 1888–90 regional gain for the Democrats was only 0.4 percentage points, but its variance was 16.10.[5] The extraordinarily skewed distribution of the 1888–90 swing reflected the declining level of Democratic support in the West and West North Central regions. The ostensibly anomalous behavior of these areas draws attention to the two separate sets of forces that underlay both the 1888–90 and 1890–92 partisan shifts.[6]

Although the Democrats scored impressive gains throughout most of the Northeast and the eastern portions of the Midwest, in the West and the western states of the West North Central region, the outcomes were mixed and displayed ominous portents for the future of two-party hegemony. In the West the Democrats elected a governor for the first time since 1876 in Oregon and registered an impressive 10.7 percentage point gain. They gained 4.7 percentage points in Nevada but lost strength

5. Even if the Confederate and border states are excluded, the difference between the 1880–82 and 1888–90 swings stand out: 1880–82, $\bar{M}$ = 3.2 percent, with σ^2 = 5.85; but 1888–90, $\bar{M}$ = 2.0 percent, with σ^2 = 18.89.

6. In fact, it would be plausible to argue that there were *three* distinct sets of forces operating. The third pertained in the former Confederate states and involved the intersection of the racial orientation of that region's political patterns with the Populist uprising.

(−0.8) in California; they were held to a minuscule 0.2 percentage point gain in Colorado. And the future was best foretold by the rise of Colorado's Independent party and the 6.1 percent of the vote that it polled. In the West North Central area the Democrats gained in Iowa and Missouri but lost strength in Kansas, Minnesota, and Nebraska.[7] Farmers' Alliance, or Independent, parties emerged in each of these states and cut into the vote of both major parties. This rise of potent, crosscutting minor parties was the most significant development of the 1890 contest in these states.

Two separate currents flowed into the nonsouthern electoral universe in 1890. The first, to the east of the Missouri River, had a reinstating effect.[8] During the 1870s and 1880s in some locales, shifts in population, the movement of new voters into the electorate, and at least a limited Republican ability to mute some culturally divisive questions collectively blurred particular aspects of the ethnoreligious cleavage that had structured party oppositions during the third electoral era. The 1888–90 shifts in these locales sharpened those cleavages and brought them once again into stark relief. At the same time, a second stream roared into the electoral universe to the west of the Missouri. There it initiated the disintegration of the third party system and began the process of shaping new bases of party oppositions.

Throughout most of the country, the 1890–92 shifts were not nearly as dramatic as those between 1888 and 1890. In the New England, the Midatlantic, and the East North Central areas, the Republicans bounced back. Yet their rebound did not offset all of the Democratic gains between 1888 and 1890, and the Democracy remained stronger in each of these areas than it had been in 1888. It was in the trans-Missouri West that systemic disintegration continued and accelerated.

There in 1892 *Democrat* ceased to function as a rallying symbol for its party in the electorate in Colorado, Idaho, Kansas, North Dakota, and Wyoming. In these states the Democrats fused with the newly created People's party. That fusion was only the first indicator of the Democracy's enfeebled condition. Its low levels of mass support even where the party label was used was the second. The Democrats made their best showing in Montana; they carried four of that state's sixteen counties, polling 39.6 percent of the presidential vote and 41.0 percent of the congressional vote. Elsewhere the party did even more poorly. In Nebraska the Democrats managed only 12.4 percent of the presidential

7. In Nebraska's three-way gubernatorial contest, the Democrats elected their candidate with 33.3 percent of the total vote.

8. Though compared to 1888, the 1892 election was a deviating one; see Walter Dean Burnham, "The United States," p. 666.

vote, in South Dakota 12.8 percent, and in Nevada a meager 6.5 percent.[9] Of the total vote cast in this nine-state area of the trans-Missouri West, the Democrats secured only 6.3 percent. And they carried only five counties, or 1.2 percent of the total.[10]

The Populists were the rising political star in the West. They received 46.0 percent of the total presidential vote cast in the four western states of the West North Central region and carried Kansas and North Dakota.[11] In the five-state Mountain region the Populists polled a plurality of the total vote, 47.1 percent, and they carried Colorado, Idaho, and Nevada. The extensiveness of Populist support was evident from their carrying 47.2 percent of the counties in the western areas of the Midwest and 66.1 percent of the counties in the Mountain region.

Agrarian depression and discontent among silver miners and mine owners created issue publics conscious of their own economic plight and aware as well, at least in an amorphous or inchoate way, of the linkage between that and regional development. Economic roles tended to become linked in mass belief systems with a brand of western regional self-consciousness. As more and more voters made those linkages, many also began to perceive that the prevailing party system could not accommodate their concerns. These conditions in combination created a potential voting clientele for a party that represented the political dispositions of such issue publics. Populist political character mobilized that clientele; it represented the demands of a semicolonial area of the country, the trans-Missouri West, against its urban-industrial imperium, the Northeast and eastern Midwest. And as the 1892 Populist tidal wave swept across these states, it cut into the Republican vote, decimated the Democracy, and presaged the breakup of the third party system.

As evidence of the disintegration of the third party system abounded on the wide prairies and in the mining camps west of the Missouri, its cleavage lines sharpened in the east. The electoral battles there in the early 1890s were not waged over silver, agrarian distress, or urban-industrial imperialism. They involved another concerted but multifaceted onslaught by ethnoreligious imperialists. The zeal of the pietists burst forth once again, and their reenergized crusade for cultural homogeniza-

9. At the nonpresidential level the Democrats did slightly better in Nebraska (22.3 percent for governor) and South Dakota (19.8 percent for governor) but poorer in Nevada (3.5 percent for Congress). On the impact of the 1892 and 1896 elections in the Mountain states and in the western part of the West North Central region, see Walter Dean Burnham, *Presidential Ballots, 1836–1892*, pp. 145–56.

10. For the data on the number of counties carried by each of the parties, see ibid., pp. 237–43.

11. In contrast, the Populists polled only 7.3 percent of the vote in the eastern tier of the West North Central states—Iowa, Minnesota, and Missouri.

tion escalated the levels of ethnoreligious tension. The data in Table 8.2 point to the broad contours of the political effect of these crusades for righteousness.

In the German counties the impact of the 1890 swings to the Democrats were most noticeable. And those counties exhibited the strongest carryover effect to the 1892 election. The 1890 shifts reversed the small secular drift away from the Democrats in the German counties and pushed their levels of Democratic voting even above those of 1876. The Democratic lead in these counties soared to a new high in 1890, and even in 1892 it was above its 1876 margin.[12]

Preoccupation with national politics has often deflected attention from developments that were not explicitly national in their immediate focus. This same concentration on "politics at the top" has produced explanations of election outcomes that presume a nationalization of electoral responses. It is disarmingly convenient, for example, to observe the shifts in 1890, point to the enactment of the McKinley Tariff in that year, notice the party-oriented voting on the measure in Congress, and conclude that attitudes toward the tariff structured party oppositions among the electorate. Within this framework casting a Democratic ballot became the way in which mass voters, or at least the portion that shifted, responded negatively to the impending increase in tariff rates.[13] That explanation assumes that such voters made the requisite connections be-

12. The second largest Democratic lead in the German counties was 15.0 percentage points in 1882. The 1892 level was larger than in any election except 1882 and 1890. The decline in the Republican lead in the Scandinavian areas reflected Populist and Prohibition voting. And the decline in the Yankee counties predated the 1890 shifts. However, that decline owed more to changes in the composition of the voting population and minor-party voting than it did to drift to the Democrats. The Democratic rebound in the southern-stock counties was also strong in 1890 but not as strong as in the German counties. Higher levels of Democratic voting in the southern-stock areas reflected the increased salience of Republican antisouthern identifications, this time in the form of support for the "Force Bill," an effort to supervise federal elections in the former Confederate states.

13. For such an explanation, see H. Wayne Morgan, *From Hayes to McKinley*, pp. 352–56; for his larger argument that the tariff issue was central to the shaping of party oppositions in the 1880s, see ibid., pp. 116–21, 165–70, 309–19, 541. Morgan makes two critical and unsupported assumptions. First, he assumes that divisions among legislators were projected from that arena to the mass public. Second, he assumes that party divisions in the legislature were unique to the tariff issue. In fact, party did shape legislative voting responses to the tariff—e.g., in the Fifty-first House 92.8 percent of the twenty-eight roll calls on the tariff saw at least 80.0 percent of the Democrats voting in opposition to at least 80.0 percent of the Republicans. The mean index of party dissimilarity was 90.7 (where 100.0 indicates total dissimilarity), but party voting was neither unique to the Fifty-first House nor confined to roll calls on the tariff. High levels of party voting typified both the House and the Senate during the 1870s and 1880s; see Walter Dean Burnham, "Insulation and Responsiveness in Congressional Elections," p. 427, Table 5; and William G. Shade et al., "Partisanship in the United States Senate," pp. 185–206.

TABLE 8.2   *Partisan Strength by Types of Counties, 1876–1892*

A. *Percent Democratic of Total Vote*

	Yankee (N = 71)	Southern Stock (N = 18)	German (N = 43)	Scandinavian (N = 33)
1876	39.8	53.3	55.8	26.5
1884	39.0	52.2	54.4	31.3
1886	38.2	50.9	53.7	32.7
1888	41.5	51.5	53.6	30.5
1890	41.6	52.9	56.4	29.8
1892	41.1	50.2	55.0	29.7

B. *Partisan Lead*

	Yankee	Southern Stock	German	Scandinavian
1876	18.9R	12.4D	12.4D	43.4R
1884	17.1R	6.5D	10.3D	33.8R
1886	16.5R	5.6D	10.1D	27.5R
1888	13.1R	5.5D	9.5D	30.6R
1890	11.8R	11.1D	16.7D	15.1R
1892	13.1R	6.4D	13.9D	23.5R

tween increases in tariff rates and increases in their own cost of living—that is, they perceived how the increase in tariff was personally relevant to them. It further assumes that that link, above all others, motivated their behavior and that its imputed behavioral effects were diffused rather broadly and evenly across most areas of the country.

There is no doubt, of course, that most voting decisions were motivated by a sense of personal relevance. The matters that touched the voter's daily life and affected his values and life-style were more likely than others to arouse his concern and evoke a voting response—especially when he perceived a link between voting and whatever he judged to be important. Yet there is no reason to assume that what mattered—what was important—was exclusively, or even primarily, what transpired at the top of the political pyramid.

The credibility of that assumption is particularly suspect in the case of the Democratic success in 1890, for the shifts to the Democrats began *before* the passage of the McKinley Tariff. The Democrats registered gains in six of the seven states that held elections for major state offices in 1889. They gained strength in Massachusetts, Rhode Island, New Jersey, New York, Ohio, and Iowa. And in four of these states—Rhode Island, New Jersey, Ohio, and Iowa—Democratic percentages declined between 1889 and 1890. Only Pennsylvania deviated from the pattern. There the Democrats were weaker in 1889 than they had been in 1888, but they gained strength in 1890. Yet even Pennsylvania's behavior showed traces of voter movement that paralleled that of the other states. Only the German counties in Pennsylvania moved toward the Democrats (by 2.2 percentage points) in 1889.

We can pursue these clues to the social nature of the post-1888 swing to the Democrats by examining Iowa in finer detail. The developments in that state draw attention to the nature of the political and social factors associated with the Democratic surge. Moreover, an analysis of the process through which the Democracy captured Iowa's governorship in 1889 affords even larger insight. First, it focuses on the types of intraparty tensions that persistently beset the late nineteenth-century Republican party there and elsewhere. Second, it highlights the types of social questions that aroused the mass electorate. We can use Iowa, then, as a case through which to structure an inquiry into the social and political dynamics of the third electoral era.

"Republicanism means . . . no saloon in the valley"

Republicanism held sway in nineteenth-century Iowa. Over the full course of the third party system, the state was normally, regularly, and rather strongly Republican. From the realignment of the 1850s through 1892, the Republicans elected a majority of the state's delegation to Congress at every biennial election except 1890, controlled both houses of the state legislature at every session, and won every gubernatorial election until 1889.[14]

As was typical with most nonsouthern states, however, Republican strength in Iowa was lower during the system's stable phase than it had been during the realigning sequence. From 1856 through 1872, the Re-

14. The Republican mean partisan lead was 14.6 percentage points. The Republicans also lost the 1891 gubernatorial election. Data on congressional elections and the partisan composition of the state legislature can be followed in *The Tribune Almanac and Political Register*. The margin of state-legislative control was typically a wide one. The exception was the Fifteenth General Assembly, in which the Democrats and Independents (Anti-Monopoly) together fell one seat short of the Republican total in the House, though in the Senate the Republicans held an eighteen-seat margin. In the Sixteenth General Assembly the Republican margin in the House was forty seats. The first statewide contest the Democrats won after 1854 was the election of a railroad commissioner in 1888.

publican biennial mean was 59.7 percent; but it was only 53.0 percent from 1874 through 1892. These two phases of the Republican time series were statistically distinct, as were the corresponding phases of the Democratic time series.[15] Yet although these longer time segments displayed comparable discontinuities, there were important differences in timing. To observe those, we can calculate the partisan mean across five biennial elections and compare that with the mean across the next five elections. If we repeat those calculations for each party for every possible set of five-election sequences between 1856 and 1892, we can pinpoint the timing of the breaks more precisely.

Sharp and statistically significant breaks occurred in the Republican series during the 1870s, and the peak break was at midpoint 1877, separating the 1868–76 sequence from the 1878–86 elections.[16] Yet although Republican longitudinal strength was disrupted during the 1870s, the Democratic series displayed no statistically significant break associated with the elections of that decade. The rise of minor parties—and some exchange of voters among three, and occasionally four parties—underlay the evident Republican discontinuity. The political effects of the depression of the 1870s in Iowa, unlike those in most other nonsouthern states, did not produce a persisting upturn in Democratic strength, but in Iowa the effects of the depression were not compounded by a Republican-identified renewal of agitation for temperance. That did not come until the early 1880s. And when it did, both the Republican *and the Democratic* series exhibited statistically significant breaks.[17]

The persistence and acceleration of the crusade for prohibition heightened ethnoreligious tensions, and the acts, speeches, and postures of Iowa's Republicans and Democrats channeled those tensions into party oppositions. That did not occur suddenly. Extending across a series

15. Using a *t*-test to evaluate the differences between means, the difference between the 1856–72 and 1874–92 Republican means, as well as that between the two Democratic means, was statistically significant at the .005 level, using a one-tailed test. Regression on time and calculation of discontinuity coefficients produced analogous results.

16. The values of *t* for the Republican series are statistically significant at the .01 level for a one-tailed test at midpoints 1873, 1875, and 1877. The Democratic time series exhibits *no* statistically significant breaks in the 1870s, even if one lowers the requirement to the .10 level.

17. The Republican break (*t* = 3.006) at midpoint 1881 was significant at the .01 level. The peak Democratic break (*t* = 2.424) was milder and lagged behind somewhat; it occurred at midpoint 1883 and was significant at the .025 level. The time lag was due to the Democrats' fusing with Greenbackers in some congressional districts in 1882; that restrained their gains in percentage strength, especially among German voters. However, the Democratic *t* value (1.825) associated with midpoint 1881 was significant at the .05 level.

of elections, it culminated in the Democracy's capture of the governorship in 1889.

Temperance agitation had long roots in the fertile soil of the Hawkeye State. As early as 1847, the cold-water crusaders had secured enactment of a local-option law, under which every county in the state, except Keokuk, had voted "no license."[18] However, that law, as many subsequent dry statutes, was neither effective nor permanent. In the winter of 1850–51, the temperance crusaders embarked on a concerted petition crusade for a stringent antiliquor law. By 1853 they were advocating a prohibitory law patterned after the famous Maine Law. And to secure their objective, they did not depend exclusively on pressure-group politics. They organized Maine Law Leagues in communities throughout the state, and their State Temperance Convention declared attitudes toward prohibition to be the litmus test of voting support. Prohibition was right and godly; and "if the political organizations of the day turn a deaf ear to our petitions and remonstrances, . . . we will, relying on the justice of our cause, rally round the standard of truth, and do battle for the right, in a separate and distinct organization."[19]

It was not necessary for the prohibition zealots to form a "separate and distinct organization"; the Whigs responded positively to their demands by endorsing the passage of a Maine Law. And the Whig candidates in 1854 enjoyed the public support of the leaders of the prohibition movement, swept to victory and shepherded a prohibitory law through the 1855 legislature. In moving from pressure-group to electoral politics, the temperance crusaders had made prohibition an object of mass cognitions. The 1855 referendum on prohibition extended and strengthened the psychological linkages between attitudes toward prohibition and party. To a large degree, this sort of transformation contributed to the disintegration of the old partisan coalitions in Iowa and the displacement of Whiggery by the new Republican party as the state's major anti-Democratic opposition.

Iowa's Republican party builders, however, were more pragmatic and socially accommodating than the earlier Whigs. They were willing to provide antiprohibition communities with a way to avoid going dry. In 1857 Iowa's legislature enacted a local-option measure that permitted a liquor-license referendum to be held on petition of a majority of the

18. The factual matters enumerated here and in subsequent paragraphs are drawn from Dan Elbert Clark, "The History of Liquor Legislation in Iowa, 1846–1908," pp. 55–87, 339–74, 503–608; *The Cyclopaedia of Temperance and Prohibition*; Richard J. Jensen, *The Winning of the Midwest*, pp. 89–121.

19. Resolution of the 1853 Iowa State Temperance Convention, quoted in Clark, "Liquor Legislation," p. 68.

legal voters of a town. If a majority voted for license, then the operation of the prohibitory law was suspended in that town and the board of county commissioners was allowed to grant a liquor license. When the 1857 licensing act was held unconstitutional by Iowa's Supreme Court, the Republican legislature amended the 1855 law to permit the manufacture and sale of beer. This appeased the irate Germans. Moreover, enforcement of the 1855 act depended on cooperation by the local peace officers. In antiprohibition counties these locally elected officials were less than zealous in seeking out violations of the law. Nor did the Republican legislature increase their zeal or provide enforcement by a state constabulary, despite the demands of the prohibitionists.

The Republicans did placate some prohibitionist demands in the 1860s. They supported legislation to increase the civil penalties for violations of the law, to make the seller liable for civil damages caused by an intoxicated person, and to make it easier for local peace officers to obtain search warrants pursuant to alleged violations. However, these positive responses were more than offset by Republican refusal to yield to the entreaties of the prohibitionists and provide unequivocal support for the cause in the party's platform. Typically, in fact, the Republicans ignored the question while the Democrats in 1858, 1868, and 1869 denounced the prohibitory law.[20]

Republican equivocation once more prompted some prohibitionists to urge establishment of a ''separate and distinct organization.'' The attitude of Republican party builders toward prohibition, one that the party's leading organ described as a disposition of ''prudence . . . and common sense,'' was not satisfactory to the religious enthusiasts. They were even less satisfied when the Republican state convention in 1869 rejected their petition for a platform favoring prohibition. The State Temperance Convention responded to that rejection by voting down a resolution endorsing the Republican ticket and adopting instead one pledging support ''only to such candidates as will squarely stand on temperance principles.'' However, the temperance zealots rejected a third-party state ticket but fielded separate legislative candidates in several counties.[21]

The spasm of organizational energy that typified the temperance movement in other states in the early 1870s was also manifest in Iowa. The membership rolls of the Sons of Temperance and the Good Templars

20. Herbert S. Fairall, ed., *Fairall's Manual of Iowa Politics, 1883*, pp. 57–58, contains a summary of the 1854–82 platform statements on prohibition.
21. The quotations are from the weekly *Iowa State Register* (Des Moines), 12 May 1869, and *Des Moines Daily Bulletin*, 11 June 1869, both quoted in Clark, ''Liquor Legislation,'' pp. 348–49; see ibid., pp. 350–51 for the other information.

expanded, a Woman's Christian Temperance Union sprang up, and the pietistic preachers spewed forth their hellfire and damnation on the liquor traffic. And these combined legions of the righteous continued to call on the "party of morality" to stand foursquare for the right—and cold water.

The 1875 State Temperance Convention almost plaintively declared that the Republican party "owes it to . . . the moral sentiment of the State" to stand for the principle of prohibition. And the temperance forces worked arduously at the Republican state convention to secure that forthright declaration of principle. They soon discovered that the Republican party owed less to "the moral sentiment" of Iowa than it owed to the state's German voters. Pragmatic subgroup integration remained the ethic of Iowa's Republican party builders. The Republican convention followed the lead of a delegate from heavily German Scott County who argued that "the questions involved in the suppression and regulation of the liquor traffic have never been a test of Republicanism." The convention voted to table the question of prohibition.[22]

The irate temperance activists reconvened their State Temperance Convention, adopted a resolution establishing a separate party, and nominated a candidate for governor. Yet no tidal wave of temperance rolled across Iowa's prairies in 1875; the Prohibition candidate polled only 787 votes, or 0.3 percent of the total cast. Since the Republicans still commanded a 14.5 percentage point lead over the Democrats in 1875, the appearance of Prohibition in the political lists was no immediate threat to their control. Developments occurred swiftly, however, and altered that Republican perception.

One of the more important of those developments was the establishment of the Iowa State Temperance Alliance in September 1876. The Temperance Alliance was an umbrella that encompassed the wide range of already-existing temperance associations. It played a coordinating role and provided focus to the otherwise discrete activities of the temperance forces. It also provided a permanent headquarters and a source of funds for the agitation. It marked the first, although rudimentary, stage in the professionalization of temperance activity.

This reactivated temperance activity of the late 1860s and early 1870s prompted the Republican party in the legislature to toughen the licensing and local-option laws through a series of enactments in 1868, 1870, 1872, 1873, and 1874. Yet while providing legislative support for some of the prohibitionist demands, the Republicans avoided presenting

---

22. Quoted in Clark, "Liquor Legislation," pp. 360–61. Davenport is in Scott County.

themselves to the electorate as the dry party. That aura might rally the "moral sentiment" of the state, but it would repel its German Lutheran and Catholic voters. Besides, as long as the treason-stained Democrats were the opposition, the moral sentiment would continue to be rallied by the Republican label. It simply had no viable political alternative.[23]

The creation of a separate Prohibition organization in 1875 was a highly unsuccessful attempt to provide such a political alternative. The emergence of the Greenbackers in 1876 posed a more serious problem. Officially, Iowa's Greenback party in 1876 designated itself the "Independent" party. The long-standing connotations of that label, the party's self-constructed aura of morality, the presence among its highly visible activists of publicly recognized Republicans who favored prohibition, and its commitment to the cause combined to make it appealing to those groups whose political characters were permeated by moral sentiment.[24] The 3.0 percent of the total vote that the Iowa Independents polled in 1876 created no jeopardy to Republican hegemony, but the persistence of the party did, as did the persistence of the Prohibitionists.

Although the State Temperance Alliance avowedly eschewed separate party action, at its May 1877 state convention it established a state central committee and empowered it to call a Prohibition nominating convention in the event that the Republicans refused again to stand for the right. The position adopted by the Republican state convention in June failed to satisfy the temperance zealots. The official platform called for the election to the legislature of "men who will represent . . . the best sentiment of the people and who will labor earnestly for the enactment of such laws as the best interests of society, temperance, and good order shall demand." After the convention Republican newspapers, at least those in counties favoring prohibition referred to an unofficial "eleventh plank," which committed the party to work for "rigid enforcement" of the prohibitory law and the passage of whatever amendments were necessary to make it "more effective in the suppression of intemperance."[25] Yet tacit understandings, especially when accompa-

23. Especially since the Democrats in 1868, 1869, and 1875 had explicitly called for repeal of the prohibitory law and the enactment of a licensing measure; see *Fairall's Manual, 1883*, p. 58; John D. Denison, *Iowa Democracy*, 1:252–54.

24. For suggestions concerning the character of the Greenback party in Iowa in 1876 and 1877, see Fred Emory Haynes, *Third Party Movements since the Civil War with Special Reference to Iowa*, pp. 153–58.

25. The platform given in *Appletons' Annual Cyclopaedia and Register of Important Events of the Year 1877*, pp. 398–99, contains no eleventh plank. *Fairall's Manual, 1883*, p. 57, gives the wording of the eleventh plank; but Clark, "Liquor Legislation," n. 66, p. 369, notes that this plank was not contained in the Republican platform printed in an earlier version of *Fairall's Manual*. Clark also observes that it was commonly referred to by contemporary Republican newspapers. Also see Benjamin F.

nied by the nomination of a gubernatorial candidate who was anathema to the prohibition activists, were not enough to prevent third-party organization. The Prohibitionists entered the battle and polled 4.3 percent of the total vote. With the Greenbackers, who also championed the cold-water cause, garnering 13.9 percent, the Republicans for the first time since 1856 received less than an absolute majority.[26] A union of the anti-Republicans, however unlikely that might seem, could overthrow Republican hegemony.

The two largest anti-Republican elements, the Democrats and the Greenbackers, did fuse in 1878. And the Republicans responded with an official endorsement of temperance: "The practical popular movement now active throughout the State for promotion of temperance has our most profound respect, sympathy, and approval." In 1879, in the hope "that the entire question of prohibition may be settled in a non-partisan manner," the Republican state platform endorsed the proposals of the W.C.T.U. and State Temperance Alliance that a prohibitory constitutional amendment be submitted to the people "at a special election."[27]

Republican party builders had not rushed forth anxiously to grab hold of the prohibition banner. They were nudged into a public endorsement of the holy effort only slowly and agonizingly and only because they were unable to prevent prohibitionist zeal from bursting into the partisan arena. As the votes of Republican legislators indicated, there was always more support for the cause among that party's officeholders than among the Democrats. The temperance leaders recognized that, and they also recognized that large groups among the Republican party in the electorate were responsive to the appeal of prohibition. Yet until that grass-roots groundswell was effectively aggregated, especially through the State Temperance Alliance, and its voting potential was demonstrated, Republican leaders clung to the middle ground. When compromise and equivocation were no longer tolerated by the religious enthusiasts and when their electoral hegemony was potentially threatened, Republican leaders tried to reactivate the loyalties of the "moral

Gue, *History of Iowa from the Earliest Times to the Beginning of the Twentieth Century*, 3:87–90.

26. In 1877 the Republicans polled 49.4 percent, and their margin over the Democrats was still a wide 17.2 percentage points; but the Democratic vote was 9.0 percentage points below the 1876 vote for Congress and 6.1 percentage points below the 1876 vote for president. The Republican strength was 9.3 percentage points lower than the party's 1876 vote for Congress, and 9.1 below the vote for president. In 1877 the Democrats again called for repeal of the prohibitory law but only after a convention fight; see Denison, *Iowa Democracy*, 1:265.

27. *Appletons' Annual Cyclopaedia, 1878*, p. 452; *Fairall's Manual, 1883*, p. 57. For an excellent statement of the pragmatic attitude that motivated Democratic party builders to fuse with the Greenbackers, see *Iowa State Leader*, 29 September 1878.

sentiment of the State.'' And especially they acted to prevent the entry of separate Prohibition slates in the 1878 and 1879 state elections.[28]

With the voting support of Republican legislators, the prohibitory amendment passed both houses of the Eighteenth and Nineteenth General Assemblies; it was presented to the people in a special election on 27 June 1882. The prohibition crusaders mobilized their grass-roots legions, and the amendment carried with 55.3 percent of the total vote (see Map 4). Ostensibly at least, Iowa went dry. The friends of prohibition rejoiced, the saloon keepers and liquor dealers wailed, the Democrats thundered against violations of ''personal liberty,'' and perspicacious Republicans who analyzed the voting patterns probably wondered why their party had abandoned its earlier course of ''prudence . . . and common sense.'' Returns from the referendum gave ample evidence of the coalition-destroying potential that prohibition held for the Republicans. The Democrats had lined up solidly against prohibition; 90.7 percent of the 1881 Democrats who cast a ballot in the referendum voted ''No.'' The 1881 Republican voters were less cohesive; 73.8 percent voted ''Yes,'' but 26.1 percent voted ''No.'' And the latter constituted a reservoir of potential recruits for Democracy.[29]

The pragmatic, subgroup-integrating disposition that generally had characterized Iowa's Republican party builders through the 1860s and 1870s had enabled the party to build considerable support among voter groups whose political characters involved antiprohibition attitudes. Despite the Democracy's persistent opposition to prohibition, its efforts to win support among such groups were stymied by its aura of treason, and probably as well by its image as the Catholic party. Yet when the temperance zealots again shifted from pressure-group politics to mass mobilization, prohibition became an object of mass cognitions. The standing aura of Democracy as the opponent of cold-water fanaticism

28. The Prohibitionists ran no slate in 1878, and the Republican margin over ''fusion'' was 3.6 percentage points. In 1879, by a vote of 41 to 32, the Prohibition state convention rejected the proposal for a separate state ticket; but a rump group bolted the convention and nominated a candidate who polled 1.1 percent of the total vote. See Clark, ''Liquor Legislation,'' pp. 507–508; *Cyclopaedia of Temperance*, p. 566. There was no Democratic-Greenback fusion in 1879. For examples of the noncompromising attitude of the pietists, see the temperance resolutions in the *Minutes of the Annual Session of the Northwest Iowa Conference of the Methodist Episcopal Church, 1880*, pp. 13–14; ibid., *1881*, p. 8; *Minutes of the Iowa Annual Conference of the Methodist Episcopal Church, 1880*, pp. 34–35, 99.

29. For examples of the grass-roots mobilization, see *History of Butler and Bremer Counties, Iowa*, pp. 720, 1164–65. The partisan proportions are weighted sums of regression estimates calculated by minor civil divisions within counties. Among the 1881 Greenback voters, 71.8 percent cast a ballot for prohibition. As would be expected, regression estimates calculated across counties indicate virtually unanimous opposition to the referendum on prohibition by the Germans and Irish.

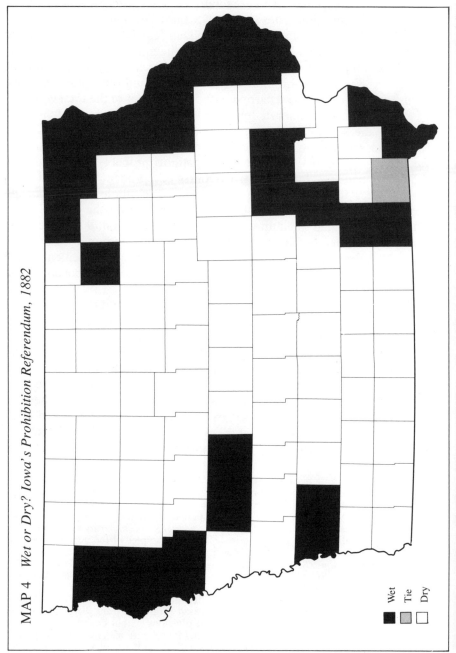

MAP 4 *Wet or Dry? Iowa's Prohibition Referendum, 1882*

Wet

Tie

Dry

combined with the new Republican posture as its defender to endow antiprohibition attitudes with partisan salience. The results were evident in the 1882 general election. Prohibition agitation produced sudden and severe swings to the Democrats, especially in German Lutheran units (see Table 8.3). As the data make clear, Democratic gains in 1882 were not confined to German Lutheran areas. In already Democratic Catholic units the revived prohibition agitation simply increased the party's strength. And the gains in most of the Scandinavian units came from disproportionate Republican drop-off, rather than an increased number of Democratic voters. Particularly in the German Lutheran units did higher Democratic percentage strength reflect new voting support that had earlier been Republican.[30]

The 1882 battle over prohibition did not immediately alter the partisan balance in Iowa. Many native-stock former Democrats continued to vote for the Greenbackers, and the Democrats fused with the Green-

TABLE 8.3   *Prohibition and Partisan Shifts: Iowa, 1881 and 1882*

	(N)	% Dem 1881	% Dem 1882	% Against Prohib 1882
Catholic Units				
Bohemian	(7)	65.7	78.7	78.3
German	(8)	79.2	87.9	88.8
Irish	(13)	70.1	75.9	71.9
Mixed Ethnic	(9)	59.1	71.6	75.2
German Lutheran				
Confessional	(13)	45.2	75.5	83.4
Less Confess	(7)	31.1	53.7	70.1
All	(20)	39.9	67.9	78.8
Scandinavian				
Danish	(3)	40.5	62.5	54.1
Norwegian	(26)	4.9	15.3	12.1
Swedish	(7)	10.0	16.8	19.4
Dutch Reformed	(3)	31.7	43.7	84.8

30. The Democrats did gain new voters in some of the more ritualistic Norwegian Lutheran areas; see Jensen, *Winning the Midwest*, p. 81. And for a discussion of the Dutch Reformed, see Chapter 5, above. The Catholic gains also involved new voting support, but not as much as in the German Lutheran areas. In German counties the Republican-to-Democrat crossover rate averaged 14.6 percentage points higher than in other counties.

backers in the third congressional district and worked out similar county-ticket arrangements in several additional counties. Although the party gained 7.2 percentage points over its 1881 level, it still lagged 12.6 percentage points behind the Republicans.

Transformation of the character of political combat in Iowa only began in 1882. It continued thereafter throughout the 1880s and into the early 1890s. The process through which Iowa's Democracy was rejuvenated occurred, then, not all at once, but in distinct stages. The first stage involved the struggle over the prohibitory amendment and culminated in the referendum and election of 1882. The second stage involved the post-1882 temperance agitation and peaked with the Democracy's statewide victories in 1889 and 1891.

Republican party leaders and prohibition zealots alike had hoped that the referendum would resolve the question. The dry crusaders hoped for a resolution that would make the state a bastion of righteousness. Pragmatic Republican leaders hoped for a resolution that would remove the emotional and culturally divisive question from electoral politics. Coalition building required subgroup integration. That, in turn, meant managing, or avoiding, conflict among the party's support groups; it meant developing a joint preference ordering of party objectives. It was easier, and certainly safer, to articulate such a preference ordering by concentrating the party's rhetoric on questions, such as regulation of railroads and tariffs, that did not evoke powerful and irreconcilable emotions. And, besides, there were issue publics that might respond positively to such appeals. To restore their pre-1882 coalition, Republican party builders had to return to that disposition of "prudence . . . and common sense" that had marked their earlier efforts at party development.

They did not do that immediately, however. And there were several reasons why they did not. First, Republican leaders seem to have misread the longer-term significance imbedded in the 1882 results. The amendment, after all, had secured majority support, and the Republicans had carried the state by a comfortable margin in the fall election. Even some Republican leaders who later exhibited a compromising attitude on the question initially urged the party to continue to stand for the right. Congressman David Henderson, for example, urged the delegates at the 1883 Republican convention not to backslide:

It is zeal that writes "Elcelsior!" [*sic*] on the mountain tops. It is honest zeal that wins victories for armies; and where that zeal has its foundation on principle the result is inevitable success. Why should the Republican party meet with defeat in this election? Has it ever lowered its flag? Not for a moment and not an inch! Has it ever faltered in the face of duty? Never! . . .

And now, my friends, the wife and child of the "drunkard" are raising their hands to you for aid. Their appeal will not be unheard. No, my fellow citizens, the heart, the brain, and the soul of the people of Iowa have declared that the evils of intemperance must be suppressed—"and that hour has come." I say to you that there is not a man in the Republican party to-day but is heart and soul in favor of that idea.[31]

Crusading for God and cold water had not defeated Iowa's Republicans. And as long as the Greenbackers were in the field to threaten the Republicans with their own uncompromising commitment to prohibition and to drain off native-stock Democratic support, there seemed little reason as yet for Republicans to strike the flag. Second, the prohibition crusaders would have nothing of compromise. They were religious enthusiasts to whom principle was as important as victory. Theirs was an internalized ethic of ultimate responsibility, not one of political pragmatism.[32] Finally, the referendum on the amendment had not resolved the matter. There were frequent violations of the law in antiprohibition communities, and some cleverly designed ways to circumvent it openly. However, the crushing blow to the hopes of the prohibitionists came in January 1883. The Iowa Supreme Court upheld the decision of Judge Walter I. Hayes of the Scott County District Court and declared that since the amendment had not been adopted in the manner stipulated by the state's constitution, it was therefore invalid.

The prohibition forces had battled for God and the right, but his will was frustrated by ungodly court decisions. The party of morality was again called upon to represent the moral sentiment of Iowa. It did not falter. And the tone of the Republican commitment resonated emotionally with the enthusiastic spirit that permeated pietistic political character. In accepting the Republican nomination for lieutenant governor, Orlando H. Manning both articulated that spirit and provided the party with its 1883 campaign slogan: "The Republican party to-day . . . is about to pass to upper and higher ground, and there firmly place its standards. We need no augury of victory. The grand constituency behind us knows what Republicanism means. It means . . . a school house on every hill, and no saloon in the valley."[33]

31. The proceedings of the 1883 party conventions are in *Fairall's Manual, 1883*, and the quotation is on p. 43.

32. For a good statement of that ethic and its antiparty consequences, see Frank Haddock, *The Life of Rev. George C. Haddock*, pp. 325–26. Also see the *Minutes of the Iowa Annual Conference of the Methodist Episcopal Church, 1883*, p. 227.

33. *Fairall's Manual, 1883*, p. 44; and the editorial insert after this remark:"Uproarious, long-continued and renewed applause." For the use of the final sentence as a campaign slogan in Iowa and elsewhere, see Clark, "Liquor Legislation," pp. 536–37. Clark incorrectly identifies the nominee for lieutenant governor as Calvin Manning.

The pronouncement in the Republican platform was less colorful. It reminded the temperance forces that the Republicans had kept their 1879 pledge to submit a prohibitory amendment to the people, and it drew attention to the fact that a majority had voted for the amendment. The party committed itself to "accept the result of that election" and to "recognize the moral and political obligation" to enact legislation to secure prohibition in Iowa, but the Republicans also expressed the hope that their commitment to prohibition would not be construed as "any new test of party fealty."[34]

Wishful thinking fathered that thought. Throughout the 1880s the acts, speeches, and postures of Republican officeholders and activists represented prohibition. In 1884 the Republican legislature redeemed the party's platform pledge. It enacted a series of laws that repealed the beer and wine exemption of 1858, closed the loopholes in existing statutes, and made Iowa—on the statute books at least—a dry state. In response to the urging of the Republican governor, William Larrabee, the 1886 and 1888 General Assemblies enacted further legislation to strengthen prohibition.[35] Larrabee's strident pronouncements embodied the uncompromising, with-us-or-against-us moralism of the religious enthusiasts. The question, as he described it in his January 1886 inaugural address, was not between prohibition and license "but whether law or lawlessness shall rule." And he left no doubt that he stood on the side of law—the prohibitory law. In May 1886 he issued a morally toned ultimatum warning violators of the law that they would "hereafter have no claim on executive clemency" and calling on "the moral forces of the State . . . [to] be painstaking and persistent in enforcing the law, both in letter and spirit." Republican state platforms continued to proclaim their endorsement of the holy cause, though typically they also averred that the dry law was not a party measure but a "nonpartisan" response to the will of the majority of Iowa's voters.[36]

34. *Fairall's Manual, 1883*, p. 45.
35. There were clear-cut, strong, and persistent party differences evident on roll calls dealing with the liquor question in the Iowa house from its 1886 through its 1894 sessions. For the relevant empirical data and excellent analysis, see Ballard C. Campbell, Jr., "Political Parties, Cultural Groups and Contested Issues," pp. 62–63, 111, 133–35, 138–41, 178, 213, 224–25. Campbell's exhaustive and perceptive analysis of the legislative sessions in these three states is immensely significant. It shows clearly the dominant role of party in shaping legislative voting coalitions and the unmistakable sociocultural nature of the shared-value continuum that linked together the party in the legislature and the party in the electorate: "The parties [in the legislature] responded to expectations among subcultures within the electorate in order to sustain the public's generalized social image of the parties" (p. 257).
36. For the 1884 law, the partisan vote on passage, and the resolutions of the State Temperance Alliance and the W.C.T.U., see *Appletons' Annual Cyclopaedia, 1884*, pp.

Most of Iowa's prohibition zealots knew who their party friends were. A die-hard band of professional Prohibitionists resumed the practice of fielding a separate state ticket in 1885, but through 1890 they never polled as much as 1.0 percent of the total vote. Ardent prohibitionists did not need to look to a separate party; they could find solace in the Republican ranks. In 1884 the Northwest Iowa Conference of the Methodist Episcopal Church commended the party for its public endorsement of prohibition, praised the "excellent laws" that the Republicans had enacted, and resolved that "we will stand by the nominees for state offices of that party." In the following year the Iowa Methodist Episcopal Conference assaulted the Prohibition party's effort to run its own candidates: "We greatly deprecate any attempt at this stage of the Temperance Reform to organize a third party in Iowa."[37]

The Methodist ministers and most other leaders of temperance opinion were reluctant to divide the voting power of the prohibition forces because they recognized their enemies as well as their friends. Democracy was the foremost of those enemies. As *Republican* over the course of the 1880s increasingly represented prohibition, *Democrat* resonated with antiprohibition political character.

The campaign for the 1882 prohibitory amendment expanded the size of the Democratic party's voting clientele. And when the party's activists gathered for their 1883 nominating convention, the assemblage was marked by none of the gloomy air of impending defeat that normally had permeated those proceedings. As the convention's keynoter declared, "We do not come up here to-day to go through the customary act of setting up a lot of candidates to be knocked down next fall, but all around us is cheering evidence of strong success this year." The source of that success lay in the "graver question of temperance." To make clear the party's position, the convention declared its opposition to constitutional prohibition and supported "practical temperance" through a well-regulated license act. And it nominated as a supreme-court candi-

---

410–12. For the quotations from Larrabee's statements, see Clark, "Liquor Legislation," pp. 551, 555, 539–68 (for details on the developments and references to the 1885 and 1887 state party platforms). For the Republican pronouncements in 1886 and 1888, see *Appletons' Annual Cyclopaedia, 1886*, p. 448; ibid., *1888*, p. 446.

37. The quotations are from the *Minutes of the Annual Session of the Northwest Iowa Conference of the Methodist Episcopal Church, 1884*, pp. 32–33; *Minutes of the Iowa Annual Conference of the Methodist Episcopal Church, 1885*, pp. 42–43. For other resolutions in which these groups explicitly committed themselves to the Republicans on the prohibition question see *Minutes of the Annual Session of the Northwest Iowa Conference of the Methodist Episcopal Church, 1883*, p. 8; ibid., *1885*, p. 25; *Minutes of the Iowa Annual Conference of the Methodist Episcopal Church, 1883*, p. 226.

date Walter I. Hayes, the Scott County judge who had first held the prohibitory amendment to be invalid.[38]

The convention's enthusiasm was not matched by the party's polling power. The Democrats lost the 1883 gubernatorial election, but they cut the Republican lead to 7.7 percentage points; and Judge Hayes ran nearly two thousand votes ahead of the ticket. Many native-stock Democrats continued to vote for the prohibitionist Greenbackers, and that party polled 7.0 percent of the Iowa vote. To restore the prodigal natives to the Democratic fold, the party builders fused with the Greenbackers in 1884, 1885, and 1886. Those efforts increased Democratic voting support among its old-stock adherents but somewhat dampened the loyalties of German Lutheran and Catholic voters. Fusion with the dry Greenbackers only deflected Democracy's onward march to consolidating and strengthening its antiprohibition coalition. The party's state platforms continued to denounce the prohibitory laws. In antiprohibition areas Democratic local peace officers tolerated, and sometimes abetted, violations of the law. And in the strongly antiprohibitionist second congressional district, the party harnessed that sentiment to partisan ends; it nominated and elected Judge Hayes to Congress in 1886, 1888, 1890, and 1892.[39]

The persistence of sin and the continuing unenforcement of the law in some localities stirred the righteous wrath and reinvigorated the political energies of the prohibition crusaders. Violations were especially flagrant in the cities along the Mississippi and Missouri rivers—cities such as Davenport, Keokuk, and Sioux City. There "holes in the wall" and "blind pigs" flourished, and "boot-leggers" became a profit-making entrepreneurial group. To stamp out sin wherever it existed, regardless of local sentiment, the prohibitionists urged more stringent and uniform enforcement of the law. Iowa's Republican governor responded to their renewed outcry. Admitting that in a "few counties and places . . . but little regard" had been paid to the prohibitory laws, Governor Larrabee urged the 1888 General Assembly to adopt "some measures . . . to quicken the consciences of the [local] officials, who neglect or refuse to perform their sworn duty." The Republican party in the legislature followed Larrabee's lead. As another stage in their continuing battle "for

38. The keynote speaker was Edward Campbell of Jefferson County. His reference was to temperance's being a "graver" question than the protective tariff. The speech, proceedings of the convention, and platform are in *Fairall's Manual, 1883*, pp. 32–40. Also see the description of the enthusiasm and optimism of the Democratic activists in the *Iowa State Leader*, 6 June 1883.

39. For the complaints concerning local Democratic peace officers, see Clark, "Liquor Legislation," pp. 569–70. The Democratic platforms can be followed in *Appletons' Annual Cyclopaedia*; also see Denison, *Iowa Democracy*, 1:336–95.

the right against established wrong," they moved to tighten the provisions of the law. The Republican-sponsored laws enacted in 1888 did not extirpate the evil, but they did help "to quicken" the electoral response of the antiprohibitionists.[40]

The religious enthusiasm of the pietists did the rest. Determined especially to impose their version of God's will on those whom they judged to be mired in sin, they turned out their grass-roots legions, dominated the Republican local caucuses and county conventions, and thus guaranteed a state convention that would stand unequivocally for the right. Perhaps even more than other Republican state conventions since the late 1870s, the gathering in 1889 was controlled by crusading enthusiasts spurred on by their shared commitment to an ethic of moral responsibility. They would neither compromise nor equivocate; "Prohibition," they declared, "has become the settled policy of the State" and "there should be no backward step. We stand for the complete enforcement of the law." To assure that enforcement over the next two years, they nominated Joseph Hutchinson, an ardent dry, for governor.[41]

To the all-or-nothing moralism of the Republicans, the Democrats responded with compromising pragmatism. Local option coupled with a high licensing tax was their chosen route to promote "the interest of true temperance." And for governor they nominated Horace Boies—a former Republican, a teetotaler, a Good Templar, and an antiprohibitionist.[42]

Iowa's 1889 gubernatorial contest revolved around the liquor question, but that contest was more than a conflict over life-styles, or even over liquor. It was a struggle between contending and religiously rooted value systems, between irreconcilable visions of the nature of the society. And involved contemporaries recognized it for what it was. Baptists, Methodists, Presbyterians, the Grange, and Boies's own Good Templars lined up for God and cold water and against Boies, the De-

40. The quotations are from Governor Larrabee's message to the legislature, 11 January 1888, quoted in Clark, "Liquor Legislation," pp. 564–65; and from John Hall, a Republican legislator, who used the quoted phrase to defend the prohibitory law during the House debates, quoted in Campbell, "Political Parties, Cultural Groups and Contested Issues," p. 252. For the conditions in the river cities, see *Cyclopaedia of Temperance*, pp. 517–18.

41. The Iowa Republican 1889 platform is in the *Tribune Almanac, 1890*, p. 21. Jensen's description of the moral enthusiasm of the delegates is excellent, but that should not be viewed exclusively as a distinction between amateurs and professionals; see *Winning the Midwest*, pp. 105–106.

42. The Democratic platform for 1889 is in the *Tribune Almanac, 1890*, pp. 21–22. For information on Boies and the background to his nomination, see Jensen, *Winning the Midwest*, pp. 104–105; for an informative discussion of the Democratic developments over the 1889–92 elections, see Denison, *Iowa Democracy*, 2:407–59.

mocracy, high license, and sin. The character of the partisan alternatives was clear. Boies and the Democracy represented cultural pluralism, that accommodating disposition that accepted a "wide difference" in social habits among individuals. Such differences did not involve immutable moral standards but depended "largely upon the customs of their fathers, the influence of education and the surroundings in which they live." Such social practices were not matters of right-or-wrong morality and therefore not proper subjects for governmental action.[43] As Democracy's temperament resonated positively with the political characters of ritualistic religious groups, Republican political character expressed Yankee pietistic values. Through "the American leaven," the leading Republican organ argued, the society would be made homogeneous and holy; but where "it has not had time to accomplish its task . . . the Democrats . . . offer the temptation of the saloon."[44]

As the pietists perceived the result, Iowa fell to Lucifer's legions in 1889: the Democrats carried the state. When they did, new voting support among the state's confessional Lutherans and its Catholic voters turned the tide. Levels of Democratic voting strength among ritualistic voting groups increased by stages in late nineteenth-century Iowa, and prohibition agitation was the crucial catalyst, the dynamic impelling that process. Table 8.4 presents a set of estimates of Democratic strength by social groups across the relevant time segments.[45] The data reveal the clear pattern of change in Democratic support. Both Lutheran groups had swung sharply Democratic in 1882, when "being a Republican" implied support for prohibition. Thereafter, as the Democrats fused with the native-stock and dry Greenbackers, Lutheran (but not Catholic and Irish) support waned somewhat. In the later 1880s, as the Republicans moved to tighten the prohibitory laws and as the dry crusade became the focal point of mass political cognitions, Democratic support among the Catholic, Irish, and confessional Lutheran groups rose to levels even higher than those of the early 1880s.

43. The quotations from Boies are in Jensen, *Winning the Midwest*, p. 108; and his January 1890 inaugural address, in Clark, "Liquor Legislation," pp. 576–77. For the resolutions of the pietistic religious groups, see Jensen, *Winning the Midwest*, pp. 106–107, 187.

44. *Iowa State Register*, 6 October 1889, quoted in Jensen, *Winning the Midwest*, p. 108; also see the *Minutes of the Iowa Annual Conference of the Methodist Episcopal Church, 1888*, p. 40, for the group's attitude toward cultural diversity.

45. These are means of regression estimates calculated for every election and office within the specified periods of time. The minor civil-division estimates within counties show somewhat wider variation than one would suppose from the county-level data. However, the latter have been used here because the voting returns were available for a larger number of elections at that level and because the weighted sums of the available minor civil-division estimates were consistent (but not identical) in their contours and relative magnitudes with those of the county-level data.

TABLE 8.4   *Estimates of Democratic Support by Social Groups: Iowa,*
1876–1892

% Dem	Confessional Lutheran	Less Confessional Lutheran	Irish	Catholic
$\overline{M}$ 1876–80	38.2	36.5	72.8	65.1
$\overline{M}$ 1882–88	68.1	52.1	76.8	70.6
$\overline{M}$ 1889–92	79.9	53.9	87.1	87.4

The prohibitionists inaccurately assessed the Democracy's 1889 gubernatorial victory as a prelude to an era of free-flowing liquor in Iowa. They dug in to defend the right. The outgoing Republican governor admonished his fellow party members in the legislature not to retreat but to stand firm, to persist as the North had during the Civil War: "As millions of happy people now bless those sturdy defenders of the Union, so will in days to come when the saloon is completely banished from our fair state, every hearth-stone invoke blessings upon those who now remain true to their convictions of right and the obligations of their trust." The prohibitionists flooded the legislature with petitions opposing any modification of the dry laws. And the stalwart band of Republicans who still controlled the legislature—by a five-seat margin in the House and by eight in the Senate—responded to these entreaties *as a party*. Though probably acting with somewhat lower levels of cohesion than in earlier sessions, and less cohesively than the Democrats supported antiprohibitory measures in the 1890 session, the Republican party in the legislature stood firmly for the right. In return for their partisan defense of prohibition against "the enemies of righteousness," the Republican legislators received both an expression of gratitude from Iowa's Methodists and their pledge "to vote . . . with that party which, in Iowa, stands as the fearless friend of the home and the uncompromising enemy of the saloon."[46]

46. In the 1888 General Assembly the Republicans held a thirty-one seat margin in the House and seventeen in the Senate. The margins here are differences between the Republicans and Democrats and exclude the few Independents and the lone Union Labor member in each body in 1890. The observations on the comparative levels of cohesion are my inferences drawn from data in Campbell, "Political Parties, Cultural Groups and Contested Issues," pp. 111, 122, 124, 132, 178, 211, 216; for the quotation from Larrabee's last biennial message to the legislature in January 1890, see Clark, "Liquor Legislation," pp. 576–79. For the Methodists' comments, see *Minutes of the Iowa Annual Conference of the Methodist Episcopal Church, 1890*, pp. 161, 232; ibid., *1891*, pp. 229–30, for their strident demand that legislation be enacted restricting the

The Democrats did not turn Iowa into a wet state, but neither did the Boies administration zealously enforce the prohibitory laws. As the saloons returned to Sioux City and other antiprohibition communities, those Iowans who had "been taught from infancy to believe that the moderate use of malt and vinous liquors . . . is not criminal, but . . . is actually beneficial" could once again enjoy their "personal liberty." Local option became the practice, if not the law.[47] And Democratic support among antiprohibitionist ritualistic religious groups remained strong during the 1890, 1891, and 1892 elections. In 1890 the Democrats lost the race for secretary of state by 0.8 of a percentage point, but elected six of the state's eleven congressmen. The next year, as the Republicans again pledged their fealty to cold-water righteousness, the Democracy reelected Boies with 49.3 percent of the total vote and a victory margin of 1.8 percentage points. However, in 1892, with the Populists polling 4.6 percent of the total vote and with a more compromising attitude on prohibition, the Republicans polled 49.6 percent and carried the state by 5.3 percentage points over the Democracy.

Among Iowa's Republicans the ethic of ultimate responsibility that had animated the religious enthusiasts yielded again only slowly to the ethic of political responsibility that had underlain the party's earlier efforts at subgroup integration. Some Republican elites—even Congressman Henderson, who had applauded the zeal of the enthusiasts in 1883—became increasingly wary of the impact of the prohibition question during the later 1880s. That concern turned to alarm when Iowa fell to the Democrats in 1889. Although the more pragmatic leaders were not able to rescue the party from the pietistic enthusiasts in 1891, they began to orchestrate the redemption shortly after the party's defeat in that year's general election. Iowa had not gone Democratic, they claimed, but antiprohibitionist; when the fight had been fought, "the sovereign voice of the people said we do not want prohibition."[48] They averred

---

immigration of those who "will not make good citizens" and their condemnation of an "imperious ecclesiasticism."

47. The quotation is from Governor Boies's inaugural address; for that and for a discussion of the Boies administration and enforcement of the prohibitory laws, see Clark, "Liquor Legislation," pp. 576–77, 583. Also see Jensen, *Winning the Midwest*, pp. 113–14.

48. *Iowa State Register*, 13 November 1891, quoted in Clark, "Liquor Legislation," p. 587; see ibid., pp. 587–96 for the details on the redemption movement through 1893. On these same matters, see Jensen, *Winning the Midwest*, pp. 200–204. Jensen argues that the tension within the GOP in Iowa (and elsewhere) was one between amateurs and professionals. Although in context his use of these terms is reasonably clear, the terms are never explicitly specified. The clearest delineation is his reference (p. 114) to "the politically less experienced dry element." It may have been that some (or all) of the dry element were party novices, though Campbell's data on the Iowa,

that the Republican party should heed the will of the majority. Late in November 1891 the Republican activists of northwestern Iowa assembled in saloon-polluted Sioux City, and there they made known their sentiment that the prohibitory laws should be repealed. And Republican leaders in other parts of the state were called on to give public testimony of their conversion to local option, which was to be published in the party's major newspaper. Some erosion of Republican support for prohibition in the 1892 session of the Senate resulted in passage of a local-option measure, but it was indefinitely postponed in the House. The State Temperance Alliance saw the danger, warned against any government that surrendered "its God-appointed place" as the champion of the right, and menacingly suggested that passage of any local-option bill would be evidence of Republican perfidy and cause for the organization of a separate party.[49]

By 1892 the Republican pragmatists had become convinced that there were more German Lutherans than Prohibitionists in the state. They did not respond positively to the thinly veiled threat of the Temperance Alliance. That may have offered them more occasion for relief than cause for apprehension. It would do the party no harm among German voters to be attacked by the Prohibition fanatics. The Republicans, instead, began their return to that old-time stance of "prudence . . . and common sense"; they adopted a state platform that ignored the liquor question and concentrated on safe and unemotional national questions. Stripped of their aura of prohibition zeal, and assisted ably by the Populists, the Republicans carried the state for the presidential ticket in 1892. They did not restore their pre-1889 levels of support among German Lutheran voters, but at least they were on their way toward eradicating the stigma of representing prohibition.[50]

Illinois, and Wisconsin parties in the legislature indicate that "amateurism" was extensive and characteristic of both parties; see Campbell, "Political Parties, Cultural Groups and Contested Issues," pp. 72–78. My own preliminary analysis of participation in Massachusetts Democratic and Republican state conventions and in Suffolk County and Boston conventions suggests a similar finding, as does the analysis of service in the Massachusetts General Court during the 1880s in Richard P. Harmond, "Tradition and Change in the Gilded Age," pp. 9–10. In any case, the amateur-professional and moral responsibility–political responsibility distinctions are not necessarily mutually exclusive ones; it may even have been likely that amateurs more than professionals had political dispositions reflective of a commitment to moral responsibility. Yet the amateur-professional distinction by itself does not seem adequate to account for the fact that Republican "amateurs," and not Democratic ones, were ardent dry crusaders.

49. For the 3 March 1892 convention of the State Temperance Alliance, the resolution quoted, and the debate over the Republican attitude toward the prohibitory laws, see *Appletons' Annual Cyclopaedia, 1892*, p. 358. Also see Gue, *History of Iowa*, 3:165–66.

50. The intraparty battle was not over in 1892; for the details on the bitter struggle

Iowa's cold-water crusade and the fact that Republicanism had come to mean "no saloon in the valley"—or anywhere else—had produced a subrealignment in the state.[51] The crusade for constitutional prohibition in 1882, followed by seven years of continuing agitation and capped by the efforts in the late 1880s to secure more effective and uniform enforcement of the law, produced a two-staged shift of ritualistic religious groups to the Democrats. The importance of attitudes toward prohibition in interpreting the electoral behavior of these groups is evident from the data in Table 8.5.[52]

Several dimensions of the data require underscoring. First, viewed over time, the four variables explain a higher proportion of the total variance of the Democratic vote during the 1889–92 sequence than earlier. That longitudinal view also draws attention to the anomalous quality of the Democratic vote when the party fused with the Greenbackers in 1886. Second, a comparison of the zero-order correlations with the partial betas shows that much of the statistical effect of the association of the demographic variables with the Democratic vote was due to their mutual relationships with the attitude toward prohibition. That is, *Prohibition Attitude* served as a powerful intervening variable; in causal modeling terms it served as an intermediate link between the demographic variables and Democratic voting.[53] Finally, the data also show the persistence of positive independent effects between the demographic variables and Democratic voting, even after Prohibition Attitude has been controlled. And when viewed over time, the increasingly steep association of the German Lutheran variable with Democratic voting becomes apparent.

----

at the 1893 Republican state convention, see Jensen, *Winning the Midwest*, pp. 201–203.

51. The third-order partial correlation shows the absence of a "homing" tendency. The Democratic autocorrelation 1876/1892, controlling for 1880, 1884, and 1888, is −.062; and the 1856/1892 correlation, controlling for all 1860–88 presidential elections (an eighth-order partial) is −.507. It is important to notice that Iowa's subrealignment merely brought that state's German Lutheran voters into line, so to speak, with the behavior of the group in states like Wisconsin, Pennsylvania, and Minnesota.

52. The correlations and regression equations have been executed by counties. The F value for each of the regression equations is significant at the .01 level. The partial F's for the unstandardized partial regression slopes show the statistical significance at the .01 level of Prohibition Attitude in all four equations; Catholic in 1882; Irish in 1882 and 1886; and German Lutheran in 1889 and 1892. It is also relevant to observe that if the unstandardized slopes are statistically significant, so are the beta weights; see H. E. Anderson, "Regression, Discriminant Analysis, and a Standard Notation for Basic Statistics," p. 164. I have executed the model for all elections from 1882 through 1892; the four elections presented here are typical of those that occurred during the designated sequences.

53. For the logical and empirical distinctions between this type of relationship and

TABLE 8.5   *Prohibition, Social Groups, and Democratic Partisanship: Iowa, 1882–1892*

	1882	1886*	1889	1892
Zero-order r's				
Catholic	.594	.433	.558	.553
German Lutheran	.518	.408	.589	.677
Irish	.539	.423	.526	.507
Prohibition attitude†	.746	.525	.825	.800
Partial Betas				
Catholic	.186	.098	.139	.160
German Lutheran	.126	.148	.196	.273
Irish	.125	.155	.113	.101
Prohibition attitude†	.528	.327	.659	.612
R^2	.638	.341	.751	.750

* Democrat-Greenback fusion.
† Prohibition attitude is percent "No" on 1882 referendum.

Iowa, of course, was not the electoral universe. Indeed, it was interesting precisely because it experienced a lag in the development of party oppositions whose social boundaries approximated those of most other nonsouthern states during the third party system. The insights derived from an examination of that process, however, have broader

cases of spurious relationships, see Hubert M. Blalock, Jr., *Causal Inferences in Non-experimental Research*, pp. 83–87; Hayward R. Alker, Jr., *Mathematics and Politics*, pp. 116–26. Technically, the data in Table 8.5 only point in the direction of Prohibition Attitude as an intervening variable. The conclusion in the text derives from a more extensive path analysis of the data, which entailed using the partial betas from a set of recursive equations. For the logical implications of the use of simultaneous equations, see Blalock, *Causal Inferences*, pp. 52–60; for an overview of the technical details of path analysis, see Fred N. Kerlinger and Elazar J. Pedhazur, *Multiple Regression in Behavioral Research*, pp. 305–31. I have also developed more elaborate regression models that include sets of economic-structural variables. For example, I have tested for the effects of measures of workers engaged in manufacturing industries, farmers who rented for shares, farmers who rented for cash, average value of farm products, as well as for interactive effects between several types of economic-structural variables and between economic and ethnoreligious variables. In every instance the effects of economic-structural variables proved spurious when controlled for the effects of religious and/or ethnic variables.

applicability. Taken in combination, several aspects of the experience in Iowa help us to understand both the underlying social and political dynamics of the third electoral era and the systemic reinstatement that marked the 1889–92 sequence. We can illustrate that by exploring analogous developments in other locales.

The Politics of " 'Amens' and 'Hallelujahs' "

Not only in Iowa did pietistic energy again burst into electoral politics. That commonly recurred throughout the 1880s in the Northeast and Midwest. As pietists' demands escalated, so did the levels of ethnoreligious tension. That brought the coalition-building dilemma that confronted Republican party builders into sharp focus.

The Republican party was above all else the party of morality. As one of its early preacher-supporters had informed his Congregational flock, it was "the *party* of God, the *party* of Jesus Christ, and [it stood] *against* the party of iniquity." To that minister, as to most Yankee pietists, *Republican* came to mean a crusading moral movement through which they would make their society holy. And they never doubted success, for to them the Republican ethos was founded on the fundamental truth that "righteousness alone can exalt a nation."[54] *As a political party*, Republican also acquired an urge for survival, and when it did, righteousness collided with the pragmatic requirements of subgroup integration.

The internal tensions produced by that collision were never wholly resolved, of course. Party builders never seek to resolve contention among subgroups but to manage it, to restrain it, to develop a joint preference ordering of party objectives. In the 1860s that had been done by concentrating on no-party-but-country themes and presenting Republicans as the patriotic alternative to the party of treason. In the 1870s, temperance zeal had been rechanneled by reminding pietists that Republican stood for righteousness through its opposition to the political encroachments of popery. By developing and articulating such joint preference orderings, Republican party builders sought to reactivate the latent loyalties of their core pietistic supporters while enlarging the

54. The quotations, respectively, are from the Reverend Mr. Nathaniel Hall, First Congregational-Unitarian parish, Dorchester, in *Boston Post*, 4 November 1856, emphasis in original; and *Centerville Weekly Citizen* (Iowa), 31 August 1872, quoted in Mildred Throne, "The Liberal Republican Party in Iowa, 1872," p. 145. Throughout the nineteenth century Republican spokesmen frequently made such claims, and the Democrats just as frequently ridiculed them for doing so. I am indebted to Professor Peter R. Knights, York University, for the full identification of the Reverend Mr. Hall.

party's voting clientele. Integrating some new subgroups, such as the Norwegians and Swedes, posed no major problems. For the most part, native and immigrant pietists recognized the mutual consonance of their religious value systems and coalesced electorally to oppose the party of "Rum, Romanism, and Rebellion." And the "Romanism" component of that symbolic triad held even broader emotional significance. It resonated with the political dispositions of some nonpietists and channeled their preexisting anti-Catholic attitudes into a Republican voting disposition.

Tactical success, however, often further complicated the problem. As the party's coalition became more heterogeneous, and especially as it began to include non-Catholic German voters, its overt commitment to righteousness seemed to wane. Increasingly in the 1870s and 1880s native and immigrant pietists criticized the party for laying claim to the mantle of morality while appealing for the votes of the Sabbath desecrators and liquor drinkers. Yet in some locales, particularly in the large cities, those voters constituted a majority. And over the final three decades of the late nineteenth century, the relative electoral importance of pietists declined in most nonsouthern areas. The imperatives of organizational vitality and demographic reality pointed the party in the direction of social accommodation and subgroup integration. However, the zeal, the religious enthusiasm, the all-or-nothing moralism of its pietistic support groups decreed otherwise. The ensuing battle was for the heart of the Republican party. It involved a contest over whether the party's character should entail a commitment to an ethic of political responsibility or to one of moral responsibility.

No political party has ever wholly conformed to historical descriptions of it. And no political party has ever been attitudinally homogeneous internally, or even wholly so within any of its distinguishable sectors. Instead, parties have always involved mixtures of competing and often conflicting forms, practices, and attitudes. The balance of ingredients in that mixture may vary enormously when the party is viewed across space, and it may change considerably over time even in a single geographic context. Moreover, a party's officeholders and activists presumably develop a norm of loyalty to the party as organization that differs in kind from the loyalty that binds together the party in the electorate. And both the degree and quality of the bonds of psychological rapport linking the three sectors of party may well differ across both space and time. All of these factors, combined with an absence of studies of the professionalization of parties and of the reciprocal relations between organizational practices and party character, make analysis difficult and generalization tenuous. Yet with these caveats in mind, it is useful to draw attention to two "impressions" of some potential analytical importance concerning the late nineteenth-century Republican party.[55]

First, there were sharp distinctions in the responsiveness of Republican leaders to pietists' demands. Whether reflective of differences in internalized values, practical political experiences, or the cumulative effect of both, some Republican leaders were more willing than others to tone down righteousness for the sake of electoral success. To men such as Rutherford B. Hayes, who himself worked for temperance, "all resorts to political parties and methods are appeals to the majority. Success if it comes, must be by reason of popularity." Moral reform, on the other hand, was to be advanced "by example, by education, by religion." The field for moral reform was "a wide one. But it is not the political caucus or the criminal court." Since success in electoral politics depended on fashioning majorities, to Hayes it was simply "useless" for politicians "to spend time on causes." To the pietists' insistence that elections were moral crusades, Hayes responded by explicitly rejecting the imputed linkage between religion and politics: "It makes white black and black white. It makes saints of sinners and sinners of saints." Although Hayes rejected uncompromising moralism as the distinguishing character trait of Republicanism, his fellow Ohioan Joseph Foraker picked up the banner of the pietistic cause. In his campaigns for governor of Ohio, he preached the old-time righteousness that resonated with the prohibitionist temperaments of the party's pietistic support groups.[56]

Similar contention rent the fabric of Republican elite unity in other states. Pennsylvania's Republicans in the early 1880s endured a bitter struggle between their moralist and pragmatic wings. The former ostensibly championed the cause of "honest" government, but in reality they aimed at more; "they expected" a government that would "rise above

55. To be explicit, these are "impressions" derived from reasonably wide reading in the relevant primary and secondary sources. Whether subsequent and more systematic research confirms their credibility or not is less important than that the research be undertaken.

56. Respectively, the quotations are from Hayes's diary entries of 14 June 1884, 6 November 1889, 12 October 1881, and 3 January 1892, in Charles R. Williams, ed., *Diary and Letters of Rutherford Birchard Hayes*, 4:153–54, 522, 46, 5:44. For Foraker's views see *Joint Debates, between Hon. George Hoadly and Hon. Jos. B. Foraker, 1885*. For the pragmatic approach of John Sherman, see his *Recollections of Forty Years*, 2:121–22, 741, 846–47, 859–61. And for more details on this type of tension among party leaders in the Midwest, see Paul Kleppner, *The Cross of Culture*, pp. 124–29; Jensen, *Winning the Midwest*, pp. 178–208. However, it should be noticed that although Jensen and I agree on the existence of such intraparty tension and on the moralism-vs.-pragmatism that was its underpinning, we disagree on the final interpretive point, viz., whether that underpinning, in turn, arose from a conflict between amateurs and professionals or from commitments to irreconcilable political ethics.

mere partisan influence." In 1882, because the regular state convention "would send the Republican party on a mission not of principles, but of spoils," they withdrew, nominated their own candidate for governor, and set about to redeem the party from its condition "of vassalage, of bondage." They were antiparty crusaders who resented and resisted the party-building and subgroup-integrating practices of the more urban-oriented, pragmatic Republicans. And especially they focused their rhetorical ire on the state's most prominent Republican pragmatist, Matthew Stanley Quay, who "had learned the lesson that when elections were to be won, as a rule, religious services and religious methods were not among the most effective."[57]

Although the specifics differed from state to state, nearly everywhere there were fire storms of pietistic protest directed at any efforts by Republican party builders to accommodate nonpietistic social groups or to develop measures fostering loyalty to the party as an organization. Pietistic righteousness would neither be stilled nor whipped into line by "the lash of the party drill master." And that some party leaders responded positively to these pietistic effusions helps to account for what otherwise appears to have been a peculiar rhythm characteristic of Republican party development. Frequently, and sometimes even after years of successful social accommodation, state (and local) Republican parties turned again to their pietistic bases, through their acts and postures stressed their pristine moral purity, and by doing so, repelled social groups that earlier they had worked to integrate into the party's voting clientele.

The responsiveness of some Republican leaders to pietists' demands only partially explains the phenomenon, for even when and where pragmatic party builders seemed to be in control, the party often publicly committed itself to pietistic goals. Such seemingly inexplicable rushes to electoral disaster draw attention to the second important "impression" concerning the late nineteenth-century Republican party. There was a reciprocal relation between the character of the party's constituent groups and the patterned ways that were developed to conduct party activities; in turn, the resulting customary practices facilitated penetration and control of the party apparatus by well-organized grass-roots groups. As a consequence, party leaders, far from being able to implement some

57. The quotations are from A[lexander] K. McClure, *Old Time Notes of Pennsylvania*, 2:545, 538, 572. McClure was a leader of the Independent movement. The lines describing, the moral lapse of the regular Republicans in 1882 were from the acceptance speech of John Stewart, the Independent nominee for governor. For further information suggestive of this type of conflict between the wings of the party and its background, see Howard Frank Gillette, "Corrupt and Contented," pp. 50–57, 71–72, 74–75, 96–109, 133–36, 142–44, 148–62, 222, 224–29, 234–43, 248–57.

"iron law of oligarchy," were frequently swept aside by grass-roots sentiment.

Antiparty values had long inhibited the institutionalization of measures that might have enhanced the capacity of the party's leaders to direct and shape such outcomes as the periodic enunciation of the party's principles (its platform) and the nomination of its candidates.[58] Typically, both were the work of party conventions.

The politics of party conventions remains one of those critical but unresearched areas of partisan activities. The subject extends far more broadly than to elite machinations at national nominating conventions. Indeed, the national convention was simply the final stage of a series of conventions. Town and ward caucuses selected delegates to city, county, and congressional-district conventions. County conventions elected delegates to the state convention, the governing body of the state party. The state convention wrote the party platform, nominated the state ticket, and selected a state central committee to serve as the executive arm of the convention in the interim between its annual or biennial convocations. Congressional-district conventions were composed of delegates elected at town and ward caucuses, or by intervening county conventions if the congressional district encompassed several counties. In both the Democratic and Republican parties the congressional-district conventions selected nominees for Congress and adopted platforms, but the Republican congressional-district conventions also directly selected the bulk of the delegates who attended the national nominating convention; the separate state conventions held in presidential years picked only a relatively small number of at-large delegates.[59] In addition, separate town, precinct, and ward caucuses were held to choose delegates to the city and county conventions that selected nominees for offices at those levels. However labyrinthian the process appears in its descriptive outline, at its core were the local (town or ward) caucuses, for at that level the delegates to the other conventions were selected.

Admission to the local caucuses did not depend on some party-administered test of past partisan loyalty. Legal status as a voter and

58. The emphasis must be on the word *institutionalize*. Certainly, there were instances in which party leaders through ad hoc arrangements and personal followings were able to control affairs, but given the structure of the Republican organization, and without institutionalized patterns of control, these could be swept aside by grass-roots groundswells. Obviously, as the discussion below indicates, the same type of reciprocal relation existed within the Democratic party.

59. For the importance that Republicans attached to the selection of delegates by the congressional-district conventions, see the debate on the matter at the 1880 national convention, especially the discussion of the Illinois case; *Proceedings of the [1880] Republican National Convention*, pp. 46–151.

sufficient interest to participate were the only prerequisites. And Republicans, much more than Democrats, were loathe to impose any more stringent requirements for eligibility. In Boston, for example, the Democratic party reorganized itself in the mid-1870s and through a series of actions changed its nominating procedures. It abolished the mass convention and authorized the Democratic City Committee to convene itself as a nominating convention. Elections to the City Committee were still to be conducted by the ward caucuses, but eligibility for election was restricted to those who had supported the party's candidates in the two preceding elections. The City Committee, in short, was to be composed of avowed party men who would have the sole power of bestowing the party's nominations. Boston's Republicans viewed these changes with disdain and overt contempt. They ridiculed the Democrats for talk of party "reform" and argued that the changes exalted "party prejudice" and made "fidelity to party the first and indispensable requisite" for election to public office.[60] To avoid the snares of party, the Republicans continued to make their nominations through conventions, and in Boston those explicitly took on the form of gatherings of "citizens" rather than of "Republicans." In criticizing the Republican failure to tighten and improve their party organization, the Democratic *Boston Post* revealingly charged that the Republicans sought to elect candidates who, once in office, were to be *"relieved of the restraints of party responsibility."* To the Republicans that charge was no criticism at all; they had repeatedly boasted that their party nominating process was wholly nonpartisan.[61]

These developments bring into focus the contrasting conceptions that Boston's Democrats and Republicans held of the role of party and the resulting differences in the character of their respective practices. The Democrats were willing to give the party organization control over the nominating process and to insulate both that organization and the

60. The Democratic reorganization extended over the 1874–79 period, but the core changes to which I refer were made between 1874 and 1876; see *Boston Post*, 4 April, 13 June 1874, 28 November 1876. For an example of the Republican reaction, see *Boston Daily Advertiser*, 3 November 1876. One of the Democratic changes made in 1879 was to designate the governing arm of the party as the City Committee, rather than the more awkwardly titled Ward and City Committee; see *Boston Post*, 24 April 1879.

61. *Boston Post*, 8 December 1876, emphasis in original; on the nature of the Republican municipal conventions, see *Boston Daily Advertiser*, 28 November, 2, 8, 9 December 1876. It is important here not to confuse two different and then current applications of the word *citizen*. For several years in the mid-1870s, the Boston Republicans used the umbrella of a Citizens' Movement to battle the Democracy. The use of the term in that context must be distinguished from its use in the calls for citizens to assemble in the ward rooms to select delegates to the Republican county and congressional-district conventions. The latter usage is of significance here.

nominating process from penetration by groups outside the party. The Republicans resisted such moves and glorified instead a process involving ward caucuses composed of interested "citizens," not necessarily Republicans, who elected delegates to the municipal nominating convention.

Of course, Boston was not the world. Not all Republican party builders elsewhere were as persistently deprecatory of the role of party. And most local Democratic parties did not follow the lead of the Boston Democracy by as self-consciously enhancing the role of the party organization. Yet everywhere it does seem that Democrats, at least more than their local Republican counterparts, assigned a positive value to the role of the party as organization. And everywhere Republican town and ward caucuses remained open to interested and involved "citizens."

That unwillingness to apply any test of past affiliation and resistance to delegating the nominating power to any designated corps of party managers mirrored the strong antiparty values that permeated Republican constituencies. At the same time, it left the nominating process as well as the party organization vulnerable to penetration and control by well-organized "interest" groups.[62] The consequences of that vulnerability became starkly evident in the 1880s.

In that decade pragmatic Republican party builders found themselves increasingly unable to contain or rechannel pietistic enthusiasm. Several concerns energized pietistic zeal, but the most pervasive was prohibition righteousness. In some locales, as in Massachusetts, that became entangled with a recrudescent antipopery. In other places, as in Illinois and Wisconsin in 1890 through 1892, even cold-water fanaticism took a temporary backseat to an assault on Catholic *and* German Lutheran parochial schools. And in all locales the pietists were aroused by examples of Sabbath desecration, by the plans to keep the 1893 Columbian Exposition (the World's Fair) open on Sundays, and by the 1888 and 1890 original-package decisions of the United States Supreme Court, which threatened the enforcement of prohibitory statutes.[63]

---

62. I am using the term *interest* here in its generic sense and in a conscious effort to underscore the obvious fact that interests and interest groups were not exclusively economic in character. See Ronald P. Formisano, "Toward a Reorientation of Jacksonian Politics," pp. 61–62.

63. The best-known of the original-package decisions is the 1890 case of *Leisy* v. *Hardin*; but the pietists were alerted to what they feared was coming by the 1888 decision in the case of *Bowman* v. *Railway Company*. The court held in that case that Iowa, despite its prohibitory law, could not exclude liquor shipped into the state from Illinois. In the 1890 case, the court held that Iowa authorities could not arrest persons disposing of liquor shipped into the state as long as that liquor remained in its unbroken, original parcels. See *Cyclopaedia of Temperance*, pp. 645–46; *Appletons' Annual Cyclopaedia, 1890*, pp. 700–701.

Historians of late nineteenth-century politics have commonly viewed prohibition as an unimportant, ephemeral, and "local" question. On but one count, and even then for the wrong reasons, the description contains a bare element of credibility. Literally and technically, it was true that prohibition was a "local" question. In most states the authority to grant liquor licenses was vested in county (and sometimes city) officers, but the conditions and terms under which local officials might grant such licenses were fixed by state statutes. From at least the 1850s, the dry forces had focused on state enactments as means of achieving their ends. Their persistent agitation resulted in a long series of separate state laws and even wholesale recodification in some instances. The general thrust of that legislation made it more difficult for applicants to obtain liquor licenses. There was almost no limit on the number of ways that effect could be accomplished. Raising the licensing fees, increasing the number of signatures of "citizens of good character" required to support the application for a license, and requiring affidavits attesting to that good character were only a few of the more commonly employed possibilities. The result was a veritable thicket of legislation, all of which depended on local authorities for enforcement. The stringency of the legislation varied from one state to another, and dependence on local officials meant considerable unevenness in the application of the law even within a single state.

For all of the ambiguity, unevenness, and complexity of this jumble of legislation, cold-water crusaders offered an unequivocal, uniform, and simple solution: prohibit the liquor traffic. They were not concerned with efficiency or rationality; they were preoccupied instead with sin and were righteously determined to make no bargain with the purveyors of evil. Their assaults were aimed, of course, at state legislatures and state constitutions, because there in the first instance lay the power to eliminate the sinful activity, but they were not oblivious to the possibilities of national action. Even in the early 1880s there were scattered calls for a federal prohibitory amendment.[64] Although that remedy remained a distant glimmer, whenever immediate peril threatened they readily

64. *Minutes of the Vermont Annual Conference of the Methodist Episcopal Church, 1883*, p. 44; *Minutes of the Session of the New Hampshire Annual Conference of the Methodist Episcopal Church, 1885*, p. 31; *Minutes of the Session of the New England Annual Conference of the Methodist Episcopal Church, 1888*, pp. 53–55; resolution of the Nebraska Temperance Convention, 1882, in *Appletons' Annual Cyclopaedia, 1882*, p. 586. To the complaints by contemporary (and usually Republican) politicians that prohibition was a "local" question that should not be injected into election campaigns for federal offices, Michigan's Methodists offered a succinct response: "Slavery was sectional, rum is almost universal." See the full discussion in the *Minutes of the Michigan Annual Conference of the Methodist Episcopal Church, 1890*, pp. 363–65.

brought their pressure-group tactics to bear on the national Congress and secured the passage of legislation reversing the impact of the Supreme Court's original-package decisions.[65]

The calls for a national prohibitory amendment and lobbying in the national legislature did not transform the prohibition crusade into something other than a peculiarly "local," and therefore nonrecurring, phenomenon. Other developments accomplished that. The national conferences and conventions of the church organizations and secular temperance societies provided both rudimentary coordination for the broader movement and opportunities for grass-roots enthusiasts to come together, mutually reinforce each other's dedication, and quite probably map out common tactics.[66]

Although detailing the network of communications and pinning down the flow of information within it are not presently possible undertakings, they are also for current purposes not necessary ones. We can derive an adequate sense of the translocal extensiveness of the agitation by noticing concrete developments in a variety of locales.

It was quite likely more than temporal coincidence that fifteen (of thirty) nonsouthern states held referenda on constitutional prohibition between 1880 and 1890. Kansas led the way in 1880; it was followed over the next seven years by Iowa, Ohio, Maine, Rhode Island, Michigan, and Oregon. Then came the heated end-of-the-decade climax: Connecticut, Massachusetts, New Hampshire, North Dakota, Pennsylvania, Rhode Island, South Dakota, and Washington held referenda in 1889,

65. In the Fifty-first House there were six roll calls on S. 398, the measure to subject imported liquors to state laws. The mean index of party dissimilarity was 78.0; the mean index of Democratic cohesion was 86.0, and the corresponding Republican measure was 70.0. These data, and other relevant measures of association, make clear the party nature of the vote. What is more significant presently is to notice that Republican cohesion was considerably lower than Democratic cohesion. On each of two roll calls, one to open a broad loophole in the bill and the other to table a motion to reconsider the vote on passage of S. 398, 34.9 percent of the Republicans voted against the strongest prohibition stance, but only 6.1 percent of the Democrats voted for that stance. That same pattern of higher levels of Democratic cohesion in opposition to prohibition than of Republican cohesion in support of it recurred in state legislatures. That provides further indication of the fact that although the roll-call voting responses followed party lines, the question was much more divisive of Republican parties in the legislature than of Democratic blocs there.

66. Any reading of the late nineteenth-century denominational journals makes clear the extent to which these groups were in communication with each other and worked to keep themselves informed of developments in other locales. Typically, the conferences received and published detailed reports on the "progress of the temperance cause" from their own and other denominations in a wide variety of locales, sent local delegates to state and national conventions of temperance groups, and often freely and without attribution borrowed from each other the precise phrasing of temperance resolutions.

and Nebraska in 1890.⁶⁷ And the referenda were only the most visible tip of the iceberg. Other state legislatures in the 1880s responded to pietists' demands by authorizing varied forms of town- or county-option or licensing elections. Some of these laws were preludes to referenda on constitutional prohibition, others represented a vain effort to placate pietistic ire after the wet majority had voted against enforced holiness, and still others were futile attempts to forestall the movement for constitutional prohibition. Some of the laws mandated that local-option elections be held at specified intervals; others authorized holding such elections after being petitioned by a designated proportion of voters. From 1881 through 1921, Massachusetts required annual town and city licensing elections; in the later 1880s Connecticut and Rhode Island authorized similar local contests. Montana in 1887 and Michigan in 1889 authorized county-option elections, and in 1890 Ohio followed suit with township option. In 1887 Missouri authorized county-option elections every four years but excluded the state's urban counties. In New Jersey a county-option law was enacted in 1888 but was repealed when the Democrats took control of the 1889 legislature.⁶⁸

The pietistic conferences and secular temperance societies played interest-group politics to secure both the prohibitory referenda and the option statutes. Where the cold-water forces worked for local-option laws, they did not view these as final and compromise solutions but only as halting steps toward their ultimate end, the absolute destruction of "Satan's ally." To hasten the triumph of righteousness, they bombarded state legislatures with petitions, sent spokesmen to testify before legislative committees, and threatened recalcitrant politicians with electoral

---

67. Only Kansas, Iowa, Maine, Rhode Island (in 1886), and the Dakotas voted dry. In 1889 Rhode Island reversed the 1886 decision; South Dakota Territory had voted dry as early as 1885. Of the fourteen states of the greater South, Tennessee and Texas (1887) and West Virginia (1888) held referenda on prohibition and voted wet. If all of these referenda are taken together, 45.9 percent of the total vote cast was for prohibition. The details and votes are conveniently given in *Cyclopaedia of Temperance*, p. 102; for Nebraska, see *Tribune Almanac, 1891*, p. 298. D. Leigh Colvin, *Prohibition in the United States*, pp. 166–73, 202–27, argues that the Prohibition party played the central role in coordinating these activities. That overstates the case, but it does draw attention to one aspect of the translocal character of the movement.

68. The term *local option* is used here to cover both town-option and county-option schemes. The geographic unit to be covered by the election was a critical consideration to the dry forces. Often county-option was a means of drying up some sinful area, usually a city, within an otherwise holy county. For the legal details of the statutes discussed here, see *Cyclopaedia of Temperance*, pp. 276–360. In the greater South some form of option election was authorized by Florida (1886), Georgia (1884), Kentucky (1887), Maryland (1888), North Carolina (1883), South Carolina (1882), Texas (1888), and Virginia (1887); Arkansas from 1879 mandated biennial county-license elections.

retribution.[69] Their pressure-group tactics often won the battle, the submission of the prohibitory amendments and the passage of laws authorizing or requiring periodic option or licensing elections. However, the outcome of the war against evil was decided in the arena of mass opinion. The constitutional referenda and the option and licensing elections made the holy cause a central object of mass cognitions, activated standing dispositions, and polarized mass opinion. And try though they did, pragmatic Republican party builders were utterly unable to contain pietistic enthusiasm or prevent its contagion from spreading to the party's caucuses and conventions and ultimately disrupting its electoral coalition.

Religious zeal cascaded into the political universe in the 1880s and left in its wake a battered Republican party. Pietists found a variety of outlets for the expression of their enthusiasm, and each redounded to the political disadvantage of the Republicans. Some marched in the ranks of the Prohibition party, which by the mid-1880s was siphoning off more and more voters from the Republicans. Conscious of Prohibition's attractiveness to large segments of their own voting clienteles, those Republican leaders who were temperamentally predisposed to respond to the pietists' demands worked within the party's councils to refurbish and purify its image.[70] Their efforts were spurred on by the grass-roots prohibition crusaders.

Most cold-water zealots never found solace in partisan Prohibition; they looked, as they always had, to *their* party, the Republicans, for righteous relief from the pernicious sin of the liquor traffic. They thought that surely, in the face of demon rum's "challenge to civilization's existence," the "party of morality" would neither be silent nor equivocal. And to be sure that it walked in the ways of the Lord, the tightly

69. For some examples of these types of activities, see *Minutes of the Session of the Baltimore Annual Conference of the Methodist Episcopal Church, 1886*, pp. 78–79; *Minutes of the Annual Meeting of the General Association of the Congregational Churches of Massachusetts, 1892*, pp. 10–11; *Minutes of the Annual Meeting of the General Conference of the Congregational Churches in Maine, 1884*, pp. 27–28; ibid., *1891*, pp. 23–24; *Minutes of the Session of the Missouri Annual Conference of the Methodist Episcopal Church, 1887*, pp. 121–22; *Minutes of the New Jersey Annual Conference of the Methodist Episcopal Church, 1884*, p. 40; *Minutes of the New York Annual Conference of the Methodist Episcopal Church, 1885*, pp. 61–62; and *Minutes of the Annual Session of the West Wisconsin Conference of the Methodist Episcopal Church, 1885*, pp. 77–78.

70. For indications that some Republican leaders consciously sought to respond to the Prohibition challenge in this way, see [Neal Dow], *Reminiscences of Neal Dow, Recollections of Eighty Years*, p. 150; John Fitzgibbon, "King Alcohol," pp. 756–57; Ralph G. Plumb, *Badger Politics, 1836–1930*, pp. 79–80; Green B. Raum, *History of Illinois Republicanism*, pp. 190, 219; Samuel T. McSeveney, *The Politics of Depression*, pp. 22–25.

knit church organizations and temperance societies mobilized their legions, turned them out to dominate local Republican caucuses and conventions, and thereby altered the character of both the party's public pronouncements and its nominees. Leaders imbued with an ethic of political responsibility and committed to tactical social accommodation were unable to withstand these onslaughts of grass-roots religious enthusiasm. Bargaining, compromising, and developing joint preference orderings were not part of pietistic political character. Instead, those dispositions yielded to an ethic of moral responsibility, to a politics of " 'amens' and 'hallelujahs' " that imparted to Republican caucuses and conventions "a Methodist camp meeting tinge."[71]

Pietists' efforts to recapture the heart of their Grand Old Party produced few overnight victories, but their ardor combined with their numbers to nudge the party slowly but perceptibly ever closer to holiness. In 1880 only the Republican parties in Kansas and Maine committed themselves to the prohibitory cause. Two years later New Hampshire's Republicans renewed their earlier cold-water pledge, and the party's platforms in Connecticut, Indiana, Michigan, and New York endorsed referenda on constitutional prohibition. By 1886 Vermont's Republicans reaffirmed their dry loyalties, and the party's declarations in Massachusetts, Missouri, Nebraska, New Jersey, and Pennsylvania either called for more restrictive laws or endorsed referenda on prohibition. To be sure, some of these endorsements were tepid. New York's Republicans in 1882, for example, expressly admitted that "there are varying opinions on the sale of liquors" and argued that the expressed will of the majority ought to decide the matter. Yet equivocal or not, they contrasted both to the Republican party's extensive silence in 1880 and to the Democrats' linking a referendum on prohibition (as in Indiana in 1882) with an unambiguous denunciation of "all sumptuary legislation." Elsewhere the Democrats typically denounced prohibition, defended "personal liberty," and left no doubt that they—better than their Republican counterparts—represented wet dispositions. Even the Democracy in Yankee Vermont, whose state convention in 1880 had voted down a

71. The quotations, respectively, are from the *Minutes of the Michigan Annual Conference of the Methodist Episcopal Church, 1891*, p. 517; *Boston Post*, 2 December 1892. For other indications of mobilization of the pietists, see *Minutes of the Ohio Annual Conference of the Methodist Episcopal Church, 1883*, p. 9; *Minutes of the Annual Session of the West Wisconsin Conference of the Methodist Episcopal Church, 1882*, p. 165; *Minutes of the Maine Annual Conference of the Methodist Episcopal Church, 1884*, p. 29; *Minutes of the Minnesota Annual Conference of the Methodist Episcopal Church, 1886*, p. 53; see the discussion in Jensen, *Winning the Midwest*, pp. 189–98, 204–205.

resolution denouncing that state's prohibitory law, in 1886 articulated an opposition to "sumptuary laws."[72]

Neither Republican postures nor the nomination of dry candidates, nor even votes by Republican legislators in support of prohibitory referenda satisfied the professional Prohibitionists. Nor did such Republican acts and postures usher in a dry millennium. In some states the pragmatists were able to regroup rather quickly and back away from the vote-losing posture. Besides, the national party had not yet declared for morality. Perceptions of backsliding and entrenched recalcitrance gave rise to a short-lived Anti-Saloon Republican movement in 1886. The small band (187 delegates) that assembled in Chicago in September of that year issued a demand "that the Republican party, to which we belong, and whose welfare we cherish, take a firm and decided stand as the friend of home and the enemy of the saloon." The Anti-Saloon Republicans, unlike the Prohibitionists, were not interested in organizing a separate party. They were Republicans and wanted to work within that party to restore its old-time righteousness. To secure that objective, they enlisted the active cooperation of "all temperance men and all friends of humanity, of whatever party or name."[73]

Two years later, at its 1888 convention, the national party did take its stand. Undaunted by their failure to secure approval for a temperance pledge from the Committee on Resolutions, Republicans for prohibition fought on the convention floor. Charles A. Boutelle of Maine moved to suspend the rules, amend the platform, and publicly commit the party to the "virtue and sobriety" that results from "all wise and well directed efforts for the promotion of temperance and morality." The grass-roots pietists had done their work thoroughly. The introduction of the resolution stampeded the delegates; by a final vote of 828 to 1, the Republican party again stood before the country as "the champion of moral reform."[74]

72. For the New York and Indiana platforms, see *Appletons' Annual Cyclopaedia, 1882*, pp. 606, 422. For Vermont, see ibid., *1880*, p. 707; ibid., *1886*, p. 834. In Indiana in 1882 the Republicans called for holding the referendum on prohibition at a special election "so that there may be an intelligent decision thereon, uninfluenced by partisan issues." Significantly, the Democrats favored holding the referendum at the same time as the general election. The other state platforms to which I refer can also be followed in *Appletons' Annual Cyclopaedia*.

73. The quotations are from the national platform of the Anti-Saloon Republicans, in *Appletons' Annual Cyclopaedia, 1886*, p. 435; also see the discussion of the Anti-Saloon Republican movement in New York State, ibid., pp. 645–46. There the Republican party managers had avoided a declaration on a referendum on prohibition by refusing to call a state convention.

74. The first two quoted phrases are from the resolution; the third was used by Boutelle in his brief remarks urging its adoption. A Pennsylvania delegate tried valiantly

We need not assume that voters responded directly to pronouncements in state and national platforms. Those enunciations have importance for other reasons. When analyzed systematically and compared with the results of a similar analysis of opposing pronouncements, platforms provide a view of party character at a particular and specified official level. Moreover, the contents of the platforms provide insight into the nature of conflict within the party and the balance between the contending forces. Such analyses of partisan pronouncements during the 1880s yield two important findings.

First, in most nonsouthern locales the Republican party, through its official postures, began more and more to represent those social groups whose dispositions included inclinations toward prohibition. Some local, and even state, parties successfully withstood the righteous assault or once burned, organized a countercharge and abandoned the rhetorical high ground of moral purity. Yet even where the party builders were able to arrest the spread of prohibition's contagion—for example, in Wisconsin and New York (after 1882)—the legislative votes of the party's officeholders and the nomination of dry candidates visibly indicated the party's character.[75] None of this ever wholly satisfied the uncompromising zealots, but it was adequate to alarm antiprohibitionists.

Second, the prohibition question caused considerably greater furor within the Republican party than it did within the Democracy. Dry elements surely existed within the nonsouthern Democratic parties. In states such as Kansas, Maine, and Vermont, where party tacticians assessed preponderant sentiment to favor prohibition, the Democrats were not anxious to condemn the holy cause. Yet in the late 1880s even in those states, the party's activists took stands for "personal liberty" and

---

but vainly to prevent the introduction of the resolution. For the details see *Official Proceedings of the Republican National Convention, 1888*, pp. 236–41. The Democrats in 1880, 1884, 1892 explicitly condemned "sumptuary laws" but said nothing on the subject of temperance in 1888; the platforms are in Kirk H. Porter and Donald Bruce Johnson, comps., *National Party Platforms, 1840–1968*, pp. 56, 67, 76–78, 89.

75. For a state-level example, see McSeveney's discussion of the efforts by Republican pragmatists to assuage the prohibition zealots in New York, in *Politics of Depression*, p. 24. Notice that New York's Republican legislators became more cohesive in support of prohibition over time. In the 1886 Assembly the Republicans divided 60 to 12 in favor of submitting a prohibitory amendment, and the Democrats voted 44 to 1 against submission. By 1889 the Republicans voted 67 to 1 for submission, and Democrats 50 to 1 against. The roll-call data are reported in *Appletons' Annual Cyclopaedia, 1886*, p. 646; *Tribune Almanac, 1889*, p. 118. The efforts by James Clarkson, who was the 1889–90 chief of Republican national patronage and the 1891–92 Republican national chairman, to expand the local Republican clubs was probably an attempt to counter grass-roots temperance organization. For information on the Republican clubs in 1888, see Jensen, *Winning the Midwest*, p. 172; John Edgar McDaniel, Jr., "The Presidential Election of 1888," p. 152.

against prohibition. And everywhere the Democracy's internal debates over the question seem to have been resolved more quickly, less ambiguously, and certainly with less heat and fury than marked the internal struggles among Republican activists. Nor did prohibition produce bolts by Democratic activists such as those by the Anti-Saloon Republicans in 1886 or the Kansas Resubmission Republicans in 1889.[76] The question was agitated more strenuously within the Republican party because the concerns of the pietists were aroused, because they perceived the matter to be one of right-vs.-wrong and therefore not amenable to compromise, because they perceived the Republican party to be the "natural" defender of moral causes, and because pragmatic Republican party builders perceived the electoral danger that the question held for the party.

The pragmatists were right. Once prohibition was driven into the electoral arena by its grass-roots supporters, once it again became an object of mass cognitions, the long-standing aura of Republican moralism, even in the absence of explicit contemporary pronouncements, was probably enough to repel antiprohibitionists. And if that were not adequate in itself, Democracy's standing and current image of opposition to sumptuary laws and defense of "personal liberty" resonated emotionally and positively with the political character of antiprohibitionists. The activities of the religious enthusiasts aroused emotions, increased the salience of attitudes toward prohibition, and heightened the levels of ethnoreligious tension. The standing images of the major parties—often reinforced by their current acts, speeches, and postures—represented these polarized dispositions and channeled them into partisan alternatives. And wherever that occurred, the partisan outcome was analogous in its contours, though not in its specifics, to the developments in Iowa.

From the coast of Maine through the flatlands of Kansas and Nebraska, prohibition agitation opened fissures in the Republican electoral coalition and created new recruits for the "party of personal liberty." It partially underlay the declining Republican strength in Kansas and Iowa in the early 1880s, cost the Republicans the governorship of Ohio in 1883, and contributed to the party's declining lead over the Democracy in Maine and Michigan in the mid-1880s. And continued agitation —combined with even more referenda, licensing and option elections in the later 1880s—largely underlay the severe post-1888 electoral

76. The Resubmission Republicans opposed prohibition and called for resubmitting the Kansas prohibitory amendment to another referendum. They organized Resubmission Republican Clubs in the cities and larger towns of the state; the movement's stronghold was in Wichita. In 1890 they fused with the Democrats. For the details see *Appletons' Annual Cyclopaedia, 1890*, p. 470; for the text of the Resubmission platform, see *Tribune Almanac, 1891*, p. 55.

swings.[77] The data in Table 8.6 offer an initial clue to understanding the involved dynamics.

In each of these states, conflicting attitudes toward prohibition clearly paralleled preexisting party lines. In Massachusetts, for example, 95.5 percent of those who had voted for the Democrats in the three elections preceding the 1889 referendum opposed prohibition.[78] More important, except for the unique case in Rhode Island, the data point (as they did in Iowa) to greater cohesion among the Democratic party in the

TABLE 8.6   *Prohibition Referenda and Partisanship: Massachusetts, New Hampshire, and Rhode Island*

	Year of Referendum	% Dem Against	% Repub For
Massachusetts	1889	95.5	73.2
New Hampshire	1889	84.7	77.2
Rhode Island	1886	63.3	100.0*

*The estimate exceeds the logical boundary of 100.0%.

electorate in opposition to prohibition than existed among the Republicans in support of it. Tactical pragmatism in the Northeast, as in Iowa, won voting support for the Republicans from nonpietists and antiprohibitionists. Throughout the states of the midatlantic and midwestern areas, the Republicans registered small gains, especially among non-Catholic German voters. In New England they made inroads among some of the more Calvinistic native-stock groups and among the Catholic French Canadians. The pietistic crusade for prohibition helped reverse those gains.

77. The observations are based on comparisons of the longitudinal partisan leads. For information on these and other instances of the impact of prohibition on the Republicans, see Jensen, *Winning the Midwest*, pp. 115–20; Kleppner, *Cross of Culture*, pp. 125–28. For contemporary observations see A. D. P. Van Buren, "Our Temperance Conflict," pp. 388–407; *Detroit Tribune*, 9, 10 November 1887, 31 October and 5, 6, 7 November 1889; *Cleveland Leader*, 3 April 1889; *Boston Post*, 3 October, 16 November 1882, 23 and 28 November, 14 December 1883, 3 July 1886; *Providence Journal*, 8 April 1886; *Chicago Tribune*, 3 April 1889. Especially see Gustave Koerner's description of the significance of the Democracy's aura of "personal liberty" to German voters, in Thomas J. McCormack, ed., *Memoirs of Gustave Koerner, 1809–1896*, 2:731–32.

78. The data in Table 8.6 are weighted sums of regression estimates calculated by minor civil divisions. The measure of partisan strength was the mean across offices for the three elections preceding the referendum.

In New Jersey the Republicans in 1888 were instrumental in securing passage of a county-option and high-license act. Over the remainder
of the year, six of the state's rural, old-stock counties voted against
"Satan's ally," but the Irish and German voters in the state's urban
counties voted differently. The Democracy scored impressive gains in
the cities, won control of the 1889 legislature, replaced the obnoxious
county-option law with a local-option measure, and thus assured the
urban voters that they would not be subjected to a reign of coerced
holiness. To avoid arousing the party's old-stock following, the Democrats retained the high-license provisions of the 1888 statute and avoided
a direct attack on county option in their platform in either 1888 or the
following year's gubernatorial contest. In the urban areas the Democracy's standing image as the defender of "personal liberty," reinforced
by the votes of Democratic legislators against county option, was sufficient for antiprohibitionists. As the 1889 Republican platform observed,
"The attitude of the two parties on this question [the liquor power]
is so clearly marked that no intelligent voter can be deceived by any
omission of either, to make a declaration on this subject." To make sure
of that, the Republicans announced their stand "for purity, for temperance and the preservation of the home."[79]

As the regression analysis presented in Table 8.7 makes clear, the
state's German voters were not deceived in 1888 or in succeeding elections. In the urban counties generally, and in Hudson County in particular, they increased their levels of support for the Democracy.[80] As
enthusiasm for prohibition percolated through Republican caucuses and
conventions and reinvigorated its aura of morality, the party lost voting
support among social groups whose political characters predisposed
them to personal liberty rather than legalized righteousness.

79. The quotations are from the 1889 Republican platform, in the *Manual of the
Legislature of New Jersey, 1891*, pp. 146–48; see ibid., pp. 144–46 for the 1889
Democratic platform. The Republicans also declared for compulsory education, another
negative code word for German Lutheran voters, in 1889 and 1890. For the 1888
platforms see *Appletons' Annual Cyclopaedia, 1888*, p. 598. For discussion of these
developments and their partisan impact, see McSeveney, *Politics of Depression*, pp.
22–24; see ibid., n. 47, p. 254, for the partisan breakdown of the legislative vote on the
1888 measure. The Republicans voted 29 to 5 for county option, and the Democrats 21
to 2 against it.

80. The New Jersey regression equations have been executed by minor civil divisions. Similar types of regression analyses for Illinois, Minnesota, Ohio, Pennsylvania,
and Wisconsin show an increasingly steep form of association between Democratic
voting and Catholic and German Lutheran variables beginning in 1889 or 1890 and
persisting through 1892. Neither serial nor sequential control by economic-structural
variables attenuates the relationship. In Michigan, where party images were temporarily
reversed in 1890, only the Catholic relationship becomes steeper in that year, and the
German Lutheran one by 1892. For discussion of Michigan, see Kleppner, *Cross of
Culture*, pp. 171–77.

TABLE 8.7   *Social Groups and Democratic Partisanship: New Jersey,*
1884–1892

| | Partial Betas | | | |
| | Hudson County | | Five Urban Counties* | |
	German	Irish	German	Irish
1884	.475	.640	.367	.555
1888	.460	.645	.374	.550
1890	.520	.644	.387	.545
1892	.523	.625	.400	.517

*Bergen, Essex, Hudson, Passaic, and Union counties.

Dispositions toward prohibition, however, were not the only important traits of political character in the late 1880s. The struggle over extending the franchise in Rhode Island; a resurgent wave of antipopery in Massachusetts; and legislative assaults on the parochial schools in Illinois and Wisconsin, as well as threats of ''compulsory education'' elsewhere, energized preexisting dispositions and contributed to the anti-Republican swing that marked the final years of the third electoral era. The dispositions thus tapped did not flow separately into the electoral universe but converged and reinforced each other and interacted as well with attitudes toward prohibition.

Rhode Island's battle to broaden the franchise was a long and bitter one. It produced an insurrection in 1841 and a new constitution that broadened the franchise among the native born and legally relegated naturalized Americans to second-class citizenship. The constitution adopted in 1842 opened two routes to the voting franchise for native-born citizens. They could acquire the right to vote if their total property holdings had a value of $134, but if their combined real and personal property had a lower value, the native born could still qualify to vote by paying a $1.00 registry tax. Naturalized citizens, however, were not given the second option; they qualified as voters only after acquiring a freehold valued at $134 or more.[81] From at least the 1840s to 1928,

81. Chilton Williamson, ''Rhode Island Suffrage since the Dorr War,'' pp. 34–50, provides the details on these developments and the requirements for suffrage. On the Dorr War see Edward Field, ed., *State of Rhode Island and Providence Plantation at the End of the Century*, 1:342–52; Kirk H. Porter, *A History of Suffrage in the United States*, pp. 93–102.

when the final vestiges of the property-owning restriction were eliminated, group dispositions toward an expanded franchise played prominent roles in Rhode Island politics. And those dispositions also acquired partisan bearings.

Even before the Dorr Rebellion the Democrats had become identified with the movement to broaden the franchise. In the 1830s and 1840s *franchise extension* meant eliminating the tax-paying requirement that disfranchised large numbers of native-born artisans and laborers. After 1843 the phrase meant opening political participation to the large and increasing numbers of mostly Catholic immigrants who flocked to the state. Even the Democracy's ardor for the cause waned somewhat in the face of that possibility. Yet by the late 1880s, despite equivocation and internal tensions, Democratic acts and postures represented a more liberal franchise requirement for naturalized citizens.

Extension of the franchise and attitudes toward prohibition intersected and created coalitional problems for both parties. Despite the constitutional obstacle, naturalized citizens, especially the Irish, were moving into the electorate and into party activities; so, too, were their sons, who were native-born citizens and were not subject to the freehold restriction.[82] As their numbers grew, so did both the size of the voting clientele supporting an enlarged franchise and the Democracy's boldness in representing that clientele. Faced with a changing electorate, pragmatic Republican leaders sought accommodation. They did not rush headlong to the defense of extending the franchise, but they sought to minimize the salience of overlapping and reinforcing dispositions. They declared for elimination of the registry-tax burden on the native born, and more importantly, they sought to quell the clamor over prohibition. Accommodation on prohibition, however, antagonized the zealots and led them to new heights of holy rage in their denunciations of the party of morality. And they did more than denounce; they voted for partisan Prohibition.

Separate Prohibition organization and political activity had been a perennial feature of Rhode Island politics since 1875. In that year, as well as in 1876 and 1880, Prohibition gubernatorial candidates polled

82. For useful information on Irish political involvement as officeholders and activists, see Leo E. Carroll, "Irish and Italians in Providence, Rhode Island, 1880–1960," pp. 67–72, especially the data in Table 2, p. 71; Elmer E. Cornwell, "Party Absorption of Ethnic Groups," pp. 205–10, especially Table 1, p. 207. It is important to notice that although both of these studies show Irish political involvement, they also show the strongly Yankee character of both parties. For example, Cornwell indicates that as late as 1888 in Providence, 61 percent of the Democratic ward committeemen were Yankees, and 35 percent were Irish; among the Republicans, 95 percent were Yankees.

better than 30.0 percent of the vote. These periodic demonstrations of the electoral popularity of the cold-water cause pressured the Republicans into righteous declarations. That renewed Republican commitment produced fusion with the Prohibitionists in 1877, 1878, and 1879; and although the Prohibitionists continued to field their own tickets after the 1880 rupture, the size of their poll shrank considerably. By the mid-1880s, as the character of the electorate continued to change, Republican ardor for enforcement of prohibition waned. That underlay the demand for a constitutional amendment. In turn, the campaign for an amendment increased the salience of dispositions toward prohibition, as well as the size of the vote cast for the Prohibition party. The Prohibition gubernatorial candidate polled 9.6 percent of the vote in 1886, and the amendment secured the support of 62.1 percent of participating electorate. At the same time 92.7 percent of the voters approved an amendment, supported by both parties, that permitted naturalized Civil War veterans to qualify as voters on the same terms as the native born.[83]

The increased salience of attitudes toward prohibition, the standing image of Republican as the supporter of cold-water righteousness, and a limited expansion of the franchise combined to defeat the Republicans in 1887. The renewed Republican pledge to the holy cause did cut the Prohibition poll to 5.3 percent, but extension of the franchise nearly doubled the absolute size of the Democratic vote.[84] The 1888 approval of the Bourn Amendment, eliminating the freehold requirement for all but city-council elections and tax referenda, increased the number of naturalized voters. That, in turn, prompted Republicans to back away from their 1888 attempt to represent native-born citizens, to vote in the legislature to resubmit the 1886 prohibitory amendment, and to attempt to make inroads among the newly enfranchised adopted citizens. As it had earlier, a compromising Republican posture in 1889 produced another split in the party. A group of Law Enforcement Republicans ran their own gubernatorial candidate and polled 8.3 percent of the total vote, and the separate Prohibition candidate attracted the ballots of another 3.1 percent of the voters. The state's expanded electorate voted 73.9 percent against the prohibitory amendment in 1889.

83. From 1881 through 1884, the Prohibition high had been 2.8 percent in 1884. The votes on both amendments are in the *Tribune Almanac, 1887*, p. 79; for the bipartisan nature of the suffrage amendment, see Williamson, "Rhode Island Suffrage," p. 42.

84. In 1886 the Democrats polled 9,944 votes (37.0 percent); in 1887 they received 18,095 (51.4 percent), and the Republican vote total increased by about 800 votes. The 1887 Democratic vote was 5,704 higher than the party's total vote in the 1884 presidential contest. For the Republican pledge on prohibition, see the 1887 platform in the *Tribune Almanac, 1888*, p. 26.

No doubt opposition to prohibition and support for expanding the franchise cost the Democrats votes among their traditional native-stock supporters. That the party did not unequivocally endorse the elimination of the freehold requirement until 1887, *after* a limited expansion of the franchise had been put into effect, attests to the nature of the tensions within the Democracy. And the relatively high proportion of Democrats who supported the referendum on prohibition in 1886 points to an overlapping source of internal conflict. To these native-stock Democrats the Republicans appealed in 1888 by calling for abolition of the registry tax for the native born.[85] Yet the native-stock voters the Democracy lost were more than offset by the larger numbers of naturalized voters that the party gained from expansion of the franchise. To that change the Democrats owed the increased levels of voting support that they received from 1889 through 1892. Over that series of annual elections, compared with the 1880 through 1888 sequence, the Democrats gained 3.1 percentage points among Irish voters and 27.8 percentage points among French Canadian voters. Democracy's representing both enlargement of the franchise and opposition to prohibition enabled it to mute, at least temporarily, the hostility between the Irish and the French Canadians. The result was an electoral coalition that was heavily immigrant, heavily Catholic, and—more than in any other New England state—reflective of the way in which ethnoreligious *and* status-group polarities reinforced each other to shape party oppositions.[86]

In Massachusetts the confluence of antipopery and prohibition battered the Republicans. From at least the mid-1880s, pragmatic Republican party builders recognized that an electoral union of French Canadians and Irish votes could jeopardize Republican control in the state. To "break the compact foreign vote" was thereafter a tactical goal of the Republicans.[87] That could not be attained, however, if the party's acts and postures exclusively represented pietistic groups. And therein lay

85. Compare the statements made by each party on the Bourn Amendment in 1888, in *Appletons' Annual Cyclopaedia, 1888*, pp. 715–16. Both party platforms were adopted prior to the April 1888 referendum.

86. The comparisons are between means of regression estimates (by minor civil divisions) for each of the designated election sequences and are given as proportions of the two-party vote. In Rhode Island over the 1880 through 1892 elections, the Democratic vote declined by a mean of $-.9$ percentage points for every \$100 increase in per capita wealth, and the mean $r^2 = .129$. By way of contrast, over the same sequence of elections in Massachusetts, the Democratic vote increased by $+.03$ percentage points for every \$100 increase in per capita wealth, and the mean $r^2 = .010$. Obviously, in neither state was the relationship especially strong, but in Rhode Island the form of the association was reasonably steep and in the direction that one would predict from a knowledge of the struggle to extend the franchise.

87. The comment was made by George F. Hoar to Henry Cabot Lodge, 18 March 1883, quoted in Harmond, "Tradition and Change in the Gilded Age," pp. 121–22; for

the Republican dilemma. The prohibition zealots readily penetrated and controlled the party's outstate caucuses and conventions, and from 1886 through 1890, they secured the adoption of party platforms supporting their goals. In its official postures the Republican party stood for "the most strict enforcement of the laws enacted to suppress this enormous evil" of the liquor traffic, supported the submission of a prohibitory amendment, and urged all who opposed the saloon power "to unite with the Republican party" to elect state legislators dedicated to the righteous principle.[88]

Even more repugnant to French Canadian political character was the parallel assault on the parochial-school system. The resurgent anti-popery of the 1880s was another phase of the protracted and acrimonious religious strife that was central to shaping the political culture of the Bay State. In the 1880s energies of the antipapists were concentrated on securing passage of legislation that modified the compulsory education statute of 1873. The 1873 act required parents to send their children to a public school for twenty weeks each year and provided a fine for non-compliance, but it excepted cases in which the child either was sent to a private school approved by the local school committee or was "otherwise furnished for a like period of time with the means of education." The "otherwise furnished" clause provided Catholic parents with the legal option of sending their children to parochial schools that had not been approved by local school committees. The objective of the legislation proposed in 1888 was to eliminate the escape clause by requiring that each private school be inspected annually by the local school committee to determine whether it satisfied the conditions for approval as a surrogate for the legally required public-school attendance. One of those conditions, mandated for the public schools by statute in 1878, was that "teaching shall be in the English language." The bill introduced in the 1889 session of the Massachusetts General Court repeated these objectives and added a fine for anyone attempting to influence parents to refuse to send their children to a public school.[89]

---

more information on the political role of the French Canadians and the fluctuations in their voting levels, see ibid., pp. 101, 127, 304, 322, 333. At scattered points throughout his study, Harmond has good information that is relevant to an understanding of party characters and party development. He has chosen, however, to view that information rather traditionally and has not provided a useful analytical integration of the material he has uncovered.

88. The quotations are from the 1886 and 1888 Republican platforms, in *Appletons' Annual Cyclopaedia, 1886*, p. 530; ibid., *1888*, p. 521. The Democrats opposed the prohibitory law "as violating the cardinal democratic doctrine of personal liberty"; see *Appletons' Annual Cyclopaedia, 1888*, p. 521.

89. The provisions of the 1873 and 1878 acts are given in Robert H. Lord, John E.

While the legislature debated the 1888 bill, developments in Boston fanned the antipopery fires. In early May Father Theodore Metcalf, a South Boston pastor, brought to the attention of the Boston School Committee the case against Charles B. Travis. Travis taught history in English High School, and some of Metcalf's parishioners charged that he taught a distinctly anti-Catholic version of the past. Travis responded to the charges by pointing out that his description of the nature of indulgences, the specific remarks to which the Catholics had objected, was essentially similar to that given in the textbook approved for the course by the school committee. That defense merely broadened the conflict. The Catholic complainants demanded that the school committee censure Travis, transfer him to teaching the less sensitive subject of English, and drop the objectionable textbook. On 19 June the Boston School Committee announced its acquiescence. That decision unleashed the rage of the antipapists. The British-American clubs; the battalions of Protestant ministers, or at least those who were not shepherds to upper-class congregations; the Loyal Women of American Liberty; the W.C.T.U.; the National Women's League; and the League of Independent Women Voters all joined forces to demand that only Protestants be elected to the school committee.[90]

The school-committee struggle convulsed the city's politics for the next several years. And the Boston groups that battled to preserve the city's public schools from domination by popery were united in outlook and through organizational connections with the broader statewide movement aimed at the parochial schools. They brought to both efforts the righteous conviction that had long been the hallmark of antipopery. They spoke often and frantically of Rome's efforts to control the country and of the need to defend American institutions. The best hope for the future lay in the proper training of the children, and that required preventing ''sectarian'' control over the public schools so that they might

Sexton, and Edward T. Harrington, *History of the Archdiocese of Boston*, 3:112–13; see ibid., pp. 101–39 for a full discussion of this and related anti-Catholic public questions and activities. The most detailed account of the legislative hearings on the 1888 and 1889 ''school inspection bills'' is in Katherine E. Conway and Mabel Ward Cameron, *Charles Francis Donnelly*. Donnelly was legal counsel representing the Archbishop of Boston at the legislative hearings.

90. The textbook in question was William Swinton, *Outlines of the World's History*, and the objectionable references were on pp. 319–20. Since 1879 women had exercised the franchise for school elections in Boston, and their groups played prominent roles in the anti-Catholic agitation. When he urged a fusion ticket of Democrats and Republicans for the school committee election in 1888, the president of the Democratic City Committee gave as a prime advantage: ''Neither party would then be obliged to call out the women, who, I think, have household duties that demand their attention.'' Thomas J. Barry, quoted in *Boston Post*, 10 November 1888.

function as agencies to homogenize the society. They perceived grave danger in the fact that so many children of immigrants attended parochial schools: "These cannot give them the training necessary to make American citizens. The parochial schools and the grog shop training is [*sic*] bad for this country."[91]

Antipopery and prohibition attitudes neatly dovetailed, as did their corresponding partisan alternatives, for the Massachusetts state Republican party was not only the party of righteousness concerning prohibition but the party that represented Yankee homogenization against "Romish" assaults.[92] That was clear from the party's profession of "unalterable devotion to the cause of the public schools, which must be preserved in their integrity." In the unlikely event that anyone missed the emotional significance of the code words, the 1891 Republican gubernatorial nominee made their meaning explicit: "The public school is needed to Americanize our youth. It is the great digestive apparatus by which the many nationalities in our State will become assimilated. . . . The commingling . . . in the [public] schools tends to eliminate differences and to make the population of a community one in their interests, tastes and sympathies." And those who shared that vision of a homogeneous society knew which party represented their perspective: "Isn't it worth your while to consider what power controls the Democratic party in this State? What way it has led it, or attempted to lead it, . . . where they have full control? What policy it is like to dictate even upon the public school question?"[93]

As *Republican* resonated with prohibition and antipopery dispositions, the Democrats through their acts, postures, and resulting electoral coalition became even more strongly the Catholic party. In the 1889–92

91. The quotation is from the speech of Mrs. Mary A. Livermore, at a "Women's Rally" in Tremont Temple, Boston, and the text is in the *Boston Post*, 16 September 1890. Not surprisingly, Mrs. Livermore recommended that her listeners read Josiah Strong's *Our Country*. For other evidence of the same attitudes, see the reports on various citizens' meetings in *Boston Post*, 26 and 30 November 1888, 3 December 1890; *Boston Globe*, 29 May 1889; *Boston Herald*, 8 July 1889.

92. The religious enthusiasm that was the hallmark of the antipopery crusade in Boston was not part of the political character of the city's Brahmin Republicans. By 1889 they had worked out an arrangement for partial fusion with the Democrats for that year's school committee elections; in 1891 they spearheaded the Public School Union's bipartisan school-committee ticket; see *Boston Post*, 27 and 30 November, 2 December 1889. For the Prohibition endorsement of antipopery on the state level, see the party's platforms in *Appletons' Annual Cyclopaedia, 1888*, p. 521; ibid., *1890*, p. 524; ibid., *1892*, p. 438; the 1890 letter of acceptance by the Prohibition gubernatorial nominee, *Boston Post*, 16 September 1890; and the acceptance letter of the 1890 Prohibition nominee for mayor, *Boston Post*, 4 December 1890. The latter claimed that the public school "is our only hope for the future of Boston."

93. The quotations are from the 1890 Republican state platform, in *Appletons' Annual Cyclopaedia, 1890*, p. 524; and the speech of Charles H. Allen, delivered at

sequence of annual elections, compared with the 1876–88 series, the Democrats increased their two-party strength among the Irish by 2.7 percentage points, and by 24.3 percentage points among the French Canadians. To defend their schools and their language from Yankee cultural imperialism, the French Canadians were willing even to support the "Irish party." And as pragmatic Republicans had long feared, the electoral union of both of the state's major Catholic groups produced Democratic gubernatorial victories in 1890, 1891, and 1892.[94]

The Massachusetts agitation over the "school question" involved a distinct Catholic-vs.-Protestant polarity, and its partisan consequence was to mute Irish–French Canadian antagonisms in the face of what each perceived to be a threat to their religion. In the Midwest agitation over "compulsory education" united German Lutherans and Catholics in opposition to Republican "paternalism." The innocuously titled acts "Concerning the Education and Employment of Children" that were written into the statute books of Illinois and Wisconsin in 1889 proved to be time bombs whose explosions shattered the Republican electoral coalitions in both states. Both the Bennett Law in Wisconsin and the Edwards Law in Illinois mandated the compulsory attendance of children at "some public or private day school," but they also restricted the definition of a legally qualified school to those institutions in which instruction was provided in the English language.[95]

German Lutherans and Catholics saw the danger that such legislation posed to their parochial schools. Instruction in those schools was

---

Norwood and quoted in *Boston Post*, 26 September 1891. Compare Allen's comments with similar sentiments expressed in "What Will Our State Become?" *Our Church Work* (Madison, Wis.), 15 May 1890; "What Roman Catholic Education Is," *The Churchman* (New York), 1 October 1892; *Minutes of the National Council of the Congregational Churches of the United States of America: Annual Session, 1892*, p. 41; *Minutes of the Maine Annual Conference of the Methodist Episcopal Church, 1891*, p. 40; ibid., *1892*, p. 64; *Minutes of the General Association [of Congregational Churches] of New York, 1891*, p. 10; *Minutes of the Session of the New England Annual Conference of the Methodist Episcopal Church, 1889*, pp. 84–86; ibid., *1890*, pp. 101–104; *Proceedings of the Annual Baptist Autumnal Conference for the Discussion of Current Questions, 1888*, pp. 15–36.

94. The 1890 results were also abetted by temporary and much smaller levels of defection among native-stock groups in rural areas; see Harmond, "Tradition and Change in the Gilded Age," pp. 318–20, for a discussion of the potential importance of both the McKinley Tariff and the defeat of an oleomargarine bill in the General Court in producing that defection. It is important to notice that the Democrats continued to nominate old-stock Yankees for the chief state offices and even for the Boston mayoralty. The second-order partial between percent Democratic and percent Catholic, controlling for percent rural and percent engaged in manufacturing activities, is .833 for 1888, .877 for 1890, and .815 for 1892.

95. The text of the laws is in the *Chicago Daily News Almanac for 1891*, p. 66. For more extensive discussion see Jensen, *Winning the Midwest*, pp. 122–48; Kleppner, *Cross of Culture*, pp. 158–71.

in the native tongue of the congregation. And in the confessional German Lutheran belief—even more than in those of German, Polish, Bohemian, and Belgian Catholics—language and faith were inextricably linked. To prohibit the use of the German language in the parochial schools was to jeopardize the transmission of the faith to the young. Quickly, unambiguously, and heatedly, these groups reacted in defense of their schools, their language, and their faith. The conferences of Lutheran ministers and even individual Lutheran congregations passed resolutions denouncing the laws, the Catholic bishops issued protests and pastoral letters condemning the effort "to destroy the parochial school system," conventions of Lutheran and Catholic laymen expressed their opposition, and in Wisconsin local Anti-Bennett Law Clubs harnessed that sentiment and channeled it into the political arena.[96]

The compulsory-education statutes had their defenders, of course. The growing corps of "professional" educators pointed to the role that the public schools played in perpetuating "free institutions" and concluded that the proper training of the young was too vital "to be left to the chance of private venture or sectarian zeal." The pietistic conferences thundered against what they saw as the efforts by Catholics and German Lutherans to "maintain foreign ideas, customs and languages to the exclusion of what is distinctly American." To eliminate those vestiges of foreignism, it was necessary "to require every citizen . . . to attain an education in English." Other church groups, especially the Episcopalians, saw the furor as another manifestation of "Romish" aggression and ominously warned "of the voting power of the Roman Catholic Church." The Grangers of Illinois and Wisconsin, borrowing freely from the phrasing of the resolutions of their pietistic religious conferences, defended the laws and warned that any "political party that dares to repeal said law . . . is unworthy of support of any American citizen, and should be buried under an avalanche of ballots by an indignant people." The organizations and press of the anticlerical Germans in Wisconsin and the Prohibition and Union Labor parties of both states offered their endorsements of compulsory education in the English language.[97]

96. Some sense of the enormous quantity of organizational and rhetorical activity that the laws elicited can be gleaned from the material in Robert J. Ulrich, "The Bennett Law of 1889," pp. 173–78, 182, 228, 236, 243, 259, 318–25, 336–40. The full text of the 1890 protest by Wisconsin's Catholic bishops is in Harry H. Heming, *The Catholic Church in Wisconsin*, pp. 283–86; the text of the pastoral letter issued by the Archbishop and Bishops of the Province of Chicago is in the *Chicago Tribune*, 12 September 1892. The pastoral was read in all of the Catholic churches in Illinois, and the *Chicago Tribune*, 17 September 1892, described it as "a strong Democratic campaign document."

97. The quotations, respectively, are from the address of Oscar H. Cooper, "Com-

With such an array of friends, compulsory education needed few enemies. The public and vocal support provided the legislation by the long-time opponents and critics of their faith could only have intensified the Catholic and German Lutheran opposition. That aroused emotion quickly flowed into partisan channels, because relief required legislative action and because the acts and postures of the major parties provided clear-cut alternatives.

Despite the pleas and efforts by pragmatic Republican leaders to mute the agitation against the parochial schools, the religious enthusiasts who dominated the party's caucuses and conventions in both states would tolerate no compromise. They would instead " 'stand by the little red schoolhouse' " and do battle for the right. Suggestions that the party straddle the issue in its platform evoked responses of righteous conviction: "To the true patriot, any compromise in this matter is impossible; compromise is no less defeat than surrender." It was better to "fall on the platform . . . for compulsory education in the English language in the schools, than to have abandoned that principle for the purposes of securing an election."[98]

The official postures of neither the Illinois nor the Wisconsin Republicans lacked principled conviction in 1890. Both declared their "devotion to the common school" and their continuing support for their state's compulsory-education law. And both implicitly admitted the electoral danger by adding that they did not intend "any arbitrary interference with the right of parents or guardians to educate their children."[99]

---

pulsory Laws and Their Enforcement," p. 186; *Minutes of the Wisconsin Annual Conference of the Methodist Episcopal Church, 1890*, pp. 56–57; *The Churchman* (New York), 15 October 1892; *Journal of Proceedings, Annual Session of the Illinois State Grange, Patrons of Husbandry, 1892*, p. 37. For the platforms see Wisconsin, Secretary of State, *Wisconsin Blue Book, 1891*, pp. 396–98; *Tribune Almanac, 1891*, pp. 84–87. For similar expressions of sentiment, see *Proceedings of the Annual Session of the Wisconsin State Grange, Patrons of Husbandry, 1891*, pp. 6, 30–31; ibid., *1892*, pp. 9–10; *Milwaukee Advance*, 4, 11, 25 October 1890; *Our Church Work* (Madison), 15 May, 11 September 1890; *Minutes of the Annual Session of the West Wisconsin Conference of the Methodist Episcopal Church, 1891*, p. 42; ibid., *1892*, p. 24; Ulrich, "The Bennett Law," pp. 241–43, 390.

98. *The Wisconsin State Journal* (Madison), 18 January 1890, coined that state's Republican campaign slogan. The remaining quotations, respectively, are from the *Milwaukee Sentinel*, 3 April 1890; Dr. Richard Edwards, the Illinois Republican candidate for superintendent of public instruction, *Chicago Tribune*, 7 November 1890. For efforts by the pragmatic Republicans to manage the aroused emotions, see the report on the Milwaukee Republican city convention, *Milwaukee Journal*, 29 March 1890; Ulrich, "The Bennett Law," pp. 214–15; Kleppner, *Cross of Culture*, pp. 161–63.

99. The quotations are from the Wisconsin Republican platform for 1890, in *Wisconsin Blue Book, 1891*, p. 390; and the Illinois Republican platform for 1890, *Tribune Almanac, 1891*, pp. 47–48. The phrasing differed slightly in each platform, but both contained the same sentiments.

It was precisely that interference with parental rights that the German Lutheran conferences, congregations, and conventions had condemned. The Democracy's official posture expressed that concern by recognizing "the natural right of the parent . . . to . . . direct the education of the child" and by attacking the " 'underlying principles' " of the compulsory-education laws as "needless interference with parental rights and liberty of conscience." Those laws were local manifestations "of the settled republican policy of paternalism."[100]

As *Democracy* symbolized parental rights and personal liberty, *Republican* represented righteous principle and the little red schoolhouse. Social groups whose values inclined them to resist public interference in the private and religious affairs of men were attracted by Democracy's political character. Democratic voting support became the partisan means through which they could defend their schools, their language, and their faith. The result was a sharp Democratic gain among ritualistic voter groups, especially among confessional German Lutherans. In Wisconsin Democratic voting in the 1890 and 1892 elections among German Lutherans averaged 13.9 percentage points higher than it had been over the 1876–88 series of elections. Chicago's German Lutheran wards, which had given the Democrats 49.2 percent of their vote in 1888, averaged 60.7 percent in 1890 and 1892. And in Illinois confessional German Lutheran support for the Democrats in those elections was 16.7 percentage points stronger than it had averaged over the 1876–88 period.[101]

The "amens" and "hallelujahs" that rang out in the Republican caucuses and conventions in the 1880s were sounds of pietistic joy over having redeemed *their* party. They brought to their party activities an energy born of conviction, and through its application the party experienced a rebirth of religious enthusiasm and righteous dedication. However, clientele-conscious Republican party builders shouted no "hallelujahs" when they saw the vote totals, for as pietistic zeal burst

100. The quotations are from the Illinois Democratic platform for 1890, in *Tribune Almanac*, 1891, pp. 48–49; the Wisconsin Democratic platform for 1890, in *Wisconsin Blue Book, 1891*, p. 394. On the linkages with Republican paternalism by the Illinois Democrats, see the lengthy editorial in the *Chicago Times*, 10 September 1892.

101. The Illinois and Wisconsin figures reflect the differences in two-party strength between the mean 1876–88 regression estimates and the mean 1890–92 estimates. Democratic voting among Catholics increased by 6.0 percentage points in Wisconsin and by 12.1 percentage points in Illinois. In Wisconsin the Democratic percentage among the more ritualistic Norwegian Lutherans also increased (due to disproportionate Republican drop-off) but by only 4.8 percentage points. For evidence of Norwegian Synod Lutheran concern over the Bennett Law, see Ulrich, "The Bennett Law," pp. 76–78, 502; Jensen, *Winning the Midwest*, pp. 135–37. For indications of similar cultural conflict and the Norwegian Lutheran reaction to it in Illinois, see *DeKalb Chronicle*, 27 September, 1 November 1890; *Sycamore True Republican*, 29 October 1892.

into mass politics with renewed fury, it escalated the levels of religious tension, activated standing dispositions, heightened their partisan salience, and fragmented the Republican electoral coalition. The result was not a new structure of social-group partisanship but a sharpened fault line of ethnoreligious cleavage that had initially shaped the party oppositions of the third electoral era. In the 1850s, crusading moralism had produced Republican majorities throughout most of the North. Nearly four decades later, in the context of a much-enlarged and qualitatively different electorate, the politics of righteousness produced a virtual Democratic landslide. Righteousness might exalt a nation, but it was surely not the route to Republican electoral victory.

9

Beyond the Third Electoral System

The materialist conception of history has a lot of [friends] nowadays, to whom it serves as an excuse for *not* studying history. Just as Marx used to say, commenting on the French "Marxists" of the late seventies: "All I know is that I am not a Marxist."

Friedrich Engels (1890)

We need not push the literal phrasing of these demurrers too hard. Marx disclaimed interest-group economic determinism, the "vulgar" notion that shared economic characteristics axiomatically generated social groups that behaved cohesively. Engels ridiculed the use of dogma as a substitute for the study of observable behaviors: "Too many . . . simply make use of the phrase 'historical materialism' (and *everything* can be turned into a phrase) only in order to get their own relatively scanty historical knowledge . . . constructed into a neat system as quickly as possible."[1]

Marx and Engels aimed their reproaches at those "Marxists" whom they judged not to have assimilated correctly the main principles of their theory of historical materialism. However, as much of Marxian social analysis, both of these strictures contain insights of broader and continuing relevance. Applied more generally, they alert us to the inadequacies of monistic and monolithic explanations of complex phenomena. They warn as well of the tendency to transmute analytical constructs into vacuous slogans and to employ the latter as virtually all-encompassing "explanations."

We can use these insights to deal with two general areas of controversy concerning both the substantive findings and the analytical significance of that genre of political history denoted by the phrase *voting-behavior studies*.[2] The first of these controversies involves a con-

1. Both of the observations by Engels are in his letter to Conrad Schmidt, 5 August 1890, in Lewis S. Feuer, ed., *Marx and Engels*, pp. 396–97, all emphasis in the original.
2. I do *not* mean to designate by that term all of the works that have made use of quantitative voting data. Some of these are progeny of a star-crossed marriage between

ceptual transmutation analogous to that that Engels scorned. Its nature is most parsimoniously designated by reference to the commonly used phrase *the ethnocultural interpretation of voting*. The second proceeds from the first and can be posed directly: if mass voting behavior was rooted in ethnic and religious identifications, then what had it to do with the shape of policy? Addressing these two areas of controversy can also provide a broader context within which to locate the findings of the present analysis of the social bases of party oppositions during the third electoral era.

Recent studies of the electoral subsystem, including this one, have assigned important roles to ethnoreligious identifications as determinants of mass partisan attachments. Typically, these studies have focused, not on explaining the outcome of a single election, but on describing and analyzing the durable bases of party oppositions among the mass electorate. That has entailed, first, offering statements describing the central tendencies of the voting behavior of a variety of groups over some specified electoral sequence and, second, constructing explanations of those observed behaviors. The descriptive findings and consequent analytical constructs of these studies have prompted some observers to speak of an "ethnocultural school" of American political history.[3] The standard description of the curriculum of that school is one in which "economic man" has been replaced by "ethnocultural man," issue-oriented politics by symbolic politics, and the allocation of tangible resources by the experiences of psychological gratification.

In creating an ethnocultural school and endowing it with a mono-

---

statistical complexity and traditional conceptual frameworks, and they manage to reflect the worst of both worlds. My use of the term here is restricted to a relatively small number of studies that have self-consciously and primarily aimed at analyses of the attitudinal bases of party oppositions. That should be recognized as a delimited and arbitrary application of the label. However, the studies to which I refer are also those regularly cited by commentators as prime examples of the misnamed "ethnocultural school." To be specific, under the label *voting-behavior studies* I include Lee Benson, *The Concept of Jacksonian Democracy*; Ronald P. Formisano, *The Birth of Mass Political Parties*; Richard Jensen, *The Winning of the Midwest*; and Paul Kleppner, *The Cross of Culture*. In addition to these monographs I also include two conceptually influential essays by Samuel P. Hays: "New Possibilities for American Political History," pp. 181–227, and "The Social Analysis of American Political History, 1880–1920," pp. 373–94. Other works might also have been included under the rubric; but in my judgment these items collectively constitute the core studies of the so-called ethnocultural interpretation of political history.

3. See Richard L. McCormick, "Ethno-cultural Interpretations of American Voting Behavior," pp. 353–55, 356–77 passim for a conceptually imprecise discussion of many of the matters addressed here. For a different level of misreading, see James Edward Wright, "The Ethnocultural Model of Voting," pp. 35–56. And for a still different approach that operates within the ethnocultural-interpretation framework, see Robert P. Swierenga, "Ethnocultural Political Analysis," pp. 59–79.

lithic analytical emphasis, observers have perpetuated in the literature a figment of their own imaginations. By abstracting from the logic of these studies and focusing too narrowly and rigidly on their descriptions and analyses of central tendencies, they have transmuted complex conceptions into vacuous labels. As a result they have created a pejorative stereotype, the "ethnocultural model," in which older species of economic determinism are portrayed as having been replaced by newer varieties of ethnic and religious determinism. That stereotype should be recognized for what it is—the creation of its critics. To my knowledge, *none* of the alleged practitioners of the school has ever argued for an *exclusively* "ethnocultural interpretation" of mass political behavior.[4]

That the findings of these studies have been pushed and shoved into a monolithic ethnocultural interpretation is due, in my judgment, to the fact that many analysts, despite their explicit disclaimers to the contrary, are still impelled to seek out monistic, always-and-everywhere explanations. Simple, easy-to-phrase generalizations readily lend themselves to graceful narrative accounts in the tradition of "grand synthesis"; whereas, extensive caveats, qualifiers, and statements of the conditions-under-which produce a historical literature that, to borrow a phrase, has about it the "smell of the lamp." And it is upsetting to the process of constructing the grand synthesis to discover, for example, that the same specified set of social attributes produced different partisan identifications in distinctive contexts. Such ostensibly anomalous findings cannot be integrated into a monolithic ethnocultural interpretation. Typically, commentators have used examples of such behaviors simply as rebuttal data, as excuses "for *not* studying history." Instead, they should be seen at once as evidence of the richness and variety of the past human experience and as opportunities "to test assumptions about complex relationships among social groups in a culturally heterogeneous society."[5] Only analytical exploration of varying contexts and conditions, and not the pursuit of simple monisms, holds potential for enhancing our understanding of the dynamics of human behavior.

In erecting their ethnocultural model, those commentators have missed that point. Even worse, they have obfuscated it. They have not simply erred; they have compounded confusion by deflecting attention away from the central aim of these studies—an understanding of the ways in which and the conditions under which different types of social attributes influenced behavior. To achieve that end, voting-behavior

4. For explicit statements to the contrary, see Benson, *Concept of Jacksonian Democracy*, pp. 270–87, especially pp. 286–87; Kleppner, *Cross of Culture*, pp. 100–101.

5. Ronald P. Formisano, "Toward a Reorientation of Jacksonian Politics," p. 59.

analysts have remained sensitive, not only to ethnic and religious attributes, but to economic ones as well. They have not implicitly assumed that *culture* could be reduced to a superstructural reflection of underlying economic distinctions but have treated each genre of attributes independently in order to determine whether, when, and how they overlapped and interacted with each other.[6] And they have explored the relations between social attributes and partisan behavior in a wide variety of contexts and under diverse conditions. The results have not been series of always-and-everywhere statements of invariable relations but delimited statements of particular relations operating under specified conditions.

To penetrate the analytical fog that has been produced by a sustained misreading of the voting-behavior studies, it is useful to focus on several relevant dimensions of their findings. We can begin that overview with a consideration of the *only* dimension that seems to have been noticed by some commentators—the summary statements of central tendencies.

Beginning in the late 1950s, political historians began to compare variations in partisan percentages across large numbers of socially distinct voting units. Those comparisons alerted historical researchers to what had long been common wisdom among journalists and politicians: ethnic and religious attributes, and not only socioeconomic ones, mattered politically. These initial efforts to reconstruct the demographic profiles of partisan coalitions stimulated a series of discretely conceived studies of nineteenth-century voting behavior. Taken collectively, these studies have provided support for the proposition that "ethnic and religious differences have tended to be *relatively* the most important sources of political differences."[7] That is, under *most* conditions and in *most* contexts, ethnic and religious aggregates have tended *more often* than have economic aggregates to behave politically as social groups.

Statements describing the *comparative* partisan salience of social attributes are more circumscribed than their critics have noticed. Specifically, such statements do not subsume two claims that some

---

6. The a priori substructural-superstructural assumption underlies the "working-class–culture" notion. For expositions of that notion that illustrate the ways in which implicit assumptions derived from ideological axioms serve as the bases for deducing both research designs *and* conclusions, see Herbert G. Gutman, "Work, Culture, and Society in Industrializing America, 1815–1919," pp. 531–88; Alan Dawley and Paul Faler, "Working-Class Culture and Politics in the Industrial Revolution," pp. 466–80. For a sophisticated analysis of the preconditions of working-group consciousness and cohesion, see William H. Form, *Blue-Collar Stratification*.

7. Benson, *Concept of Jacksonian Democracy*, p. 165, emphasis in the original; see ibid., Chapter 8, "Outline for a Theory of American Voting Behavior," for his explicitly multivariate approach.

commentators have regularly and incorrectly imputed to the so-called ethnocultural school. First, they do not imply that ethnic and religious identifications were invariably the *exclusive* determinants of partisan distinctions. Second, they do not imply that ethnic and religious identifications had the *same* partisan effect under all conditions and in all contexts.

The notion that the misnamed ethnocultural interpretation involves an exclusive preoccupation with ethnic and religious attributes is simply incorrect. It reflects a misreading of the relevant studies. First, those commentators have construed relative and conditional statements as absolute and invariable ones. Second, they have looked only at the summary statements of central tendencies and have ignored the logic of the research design that underpins them. Often, for example, critics have claimed that the posited relations between ethnoreligious and political variables are spurious ones, that they will disappear when economic attributes are examined. They allege, in short, that "ethnocultural historians" have discovered such relations because they have searched for no others. That claim simply ignores the fact that voting-behavior analysts have been concerned with and have explored the possible relations between voting choices and occupation, wealth, and status. Voting studies have evidenced that concern through exhaustive surveys of voting units, or cross-tabulations of data for individuals, classified by economic as well as ethnoreligious attributes.[8] Although the conclusions derived from these operations have pointed overwhelmingly in one direction, the research designs underlying them were not deterministic ones.

Surely, there are more direct and parsimonious routes to the required demonstration than were used in the early voting studies. To illustrate one more approach, Table 9.1 presents data that indicate the relative contributions of sets of economic and ethnoreligious predictors for four of the states discussed in some detail in this study.[9] The data for

8. Ibid., pp. 142–65; Formisano, *Birth of Mass Political Parties*, pp. 47–55; Jensen, *Winning the Midwest*, pp. 309–15; Kleppner, *Cross of Culture*, pp. 17–34.

9. The equations for all four states included these economic variables: percent manufacturing laborers; percent farm renters; percent farm sharecroppers; and average cash value of farm products. The ethnoreligious predictors varied across states. Included for Iowa were the percentages Catholic, Confessional Lutheran, German, Irish, and vote against the prohibitory referendum in 1882; for Minnesota, Catholic, German, and Irish; for Missouri, Catholic, Southern Baptist, Southern Methodist, Southern Presbyterian; and for Wisconsin, Catholic, Confessional Lutheran, and German. None of the economic predictors had statistically significant (at the .05 level) partial standardized regression slopes when controlled for ethnoreligious effects, but when the control was reversed, most of the partial standardized regression slopes for the ethnoreligious predictors remained statistically significant (at the .01 level). I have also employed a number of other simple economic indicators, indices of economic development, and

TABLE 9.1   *Economic or Ethnoreligious Variables? A Comparative*
            Assessment of Effects on Democratic Voting, 1888

A. *Effects of Economic Variables on Democratic Voting with Ethnoreligious*
   Variables Controlled

	Iowa	Minn	Missouri	Wisconsin
% variance due to ethnoreligious variables	.716	.589	.558	.638
% incremental variance due to economic variables	.011	.014	.058	.102
% Total variance	.727	.603	.616	.740

B. *Effects of Ethnoreligious Variables with Economic Variables Controlled*

	Iowa	Minn	Missouri	Wisconsin
% variance due to economic variables	.340	.090	.217	.207
% incremental variance due to ethnoreligious variables	.387	.513	.399	.533
% Total variance	.727	.603	.616	.740

1888 have been used since they make the *weakest* case for the impact of
the ethnoreligious variables. Yet even when their statistical contribution
is at its nadir, the ethnoreligious predictors remain *comparatively* more
important than the economic predictors in explaining the variance of the
Democratic vote.

To make that claim, however, is *not* simultaneously to claim that
ethnoreligious identifications had the *same* partisan effect in *all* contexts
and under *all* conditions. Voting-behavior analysts have not assumed
that some kind of immutable social and political symmetry pervaded
American life. They have not assumed a condition of cultural homogeneity capable of producing exactly the same response among all people
who shared a particular attribute or set of attributes. Any social attribute
may have different meaning and effect on different people depending on
historical and contextual conditions. Moreover, most people were in-

tests for interactive effects between economic and ethnoreligious predictors. The results
of all of these types of tests were substantially the same as the ones reported here.

fluenced by multiple reference groups. At times these overlapped and reinforced each other; but at other times, and at the same time in other places, they had crosscutting and counterbalancing effects.[10] Aspects of this variegated behavior have been explored and delineated by voting-behavior analysts, but these distinctions have been blurred by the attempts of commentators to reshape them into a monolithic ethnocultural interpretation. We can escape that mental straitjacket by drawing into focus *both* the summary description and some of the relevant behavioral variety that characterized the third electoral era.

Among the nonsouthern electorate the primary cleavage line of party oppositions during the second half of the nineteenth century pitted evangelical pietistic against ritualistic religious groups.[11] The differences between the two clusters of groups were frequently expressed in attitudes toward matters such as prohibition, Sunday closing laws, and the role of parochial schools. However, the conflicts did not involve merely distinctions between life-styles, nor can they be explained as simple reflections of ethnic and religious prejudices. To suggest, for example, that a particular group supported the Democrats because its members opposed prohibition or that some other group opposed the Democracy because its members shared anti-Catholic prejudices is *not* to offer an explanation of the bases of that group's behavior. In fact it evades that explanation precisely because it leaves the important questions unasked. Why did some groups regard any consumption of alcoholic beverages as sinful, and others see no moral evil in that same practice? Why did members of some groups share anti-Catholic dispositions? Surely, and at least in the sense that academicians commonly assign to the word, such people were "prejudiced." Yet simply to invoke and apply the term *prejudice* is not to offer an adequate explanation of group behaviors. We need to inquire into the involved psycho-

10. For discussion of these matters and a multivariate demonstration that ethnoreligious attachments continue in the 1970s to be relatively more important than socioeconomic ones as determinants of mass voting behavior, see Kevin Clancy and Lee Benson, "America the Fragmented." And for additional multivariate evidence of the persisting link between ethnoreligious identifications and partisanship, see David Knoke, *Change and Continuity in American Politics*, pp. 18–37.

11. Since my purpose in this and the following paragraphs is illustrative, the synopsis is designedly terse and eclectic. The detailed discussion has been presented earlier, especially in Chapters 5 and 8. For an excellent discussion of the ways in which status, nativity, religion, and political contexts interacted with each other in the case of early twentieth-century metropolitan elites, see Richard J. Jensen, "Quantitative Collective Biography," pp. 389–405. Moreover, Jensen's age-cohort analysis suggests both the importance of political-generational experiences and the possibility that these may have had entirely divergent partisan effects when specified by social and political contexts. For a useful age-cohort analysis of later twentieth-century data, see Paul R. Abramson, *Generational Change in American Politics*.

logical processes; we need to ask *why* the members of a group shared that disposition. Questions of that order penetrate the use of empty slogans and catchwords and bring into focus the cleavages between belief systems that underlay the distinctions in overt behaviors.[12] And in the political universe of the late nineteenth century, fundamental and irreconcilable belief system differences between distinguishable clusters of ethnoreligious groups *primarily* structured partisan cleavage among the mass electorate.

The operative word, of course, is *primarily*. And that word should not be construed to imply either *exclusively* or *invariably*, for other social attributes also played roles. Contexts and historical experiences mattered politically. After all, most citizens lived their lives and formed their reference-group orientations within specific environments. And just as American society was composed of a kaleidoscopic mix of contexts and experiences, so it reflected no monolithic uniformity in the ways in which, nor the relative weights with which, social determinants combined to shape mass partisan identifications.

In some contexts, as in Rhode Island, status-group distinctions interacted with and reinforced ethnoreligious cleavages. In other contexts and among groups such as Norwegians and Swedes, anti-Yankee attitudes—that is, perceived and articulated status-group subordinance —were crosscut and offset by shared religious dispositions and commitments to common canons of right behavior. Yet even then, and especially in older Norwegian settlements, there were still lingering partisan traces of Norwegian-vs.-Yankee conflicts over culture and status. Understanding immigrant Dutch and native Yorker voting behavior required analysis of the ways in which the combinations of determinants dynamically changed over time. For both groups the partisan salience of their earlier anti-Yankee attitudes waned as Democrat increasingly began to represent popery and its allied sins. As they perceived that Democracy's political character had become increasingly discordant with their own, the older partisan attachments of both groups were eroded. And among the more pietistic of the subgroups of the Dutch and the Yorkers, religious values interacted with and reinforced ethnocultural

12. Milton Rokeach, *The Open and Closed Mind*, pp. 109–31; for the ways in which people build up "mental maps" of religions, which then influence their everyday behavior, see idem, *Beliefs, Attitudes, and Values*, pp. 189–96. The same line of reasoning that pertains to the insufficiency of "prejudice" as an explanation also pertains to the use of the negative reference-group concept. If used only as a label, or slogan, the term is of little explanatory value. It is necessary to inquire *why* a particular group took another particular group as a negative referent. What underlay the involved belief-system conflict between the groups? McCormick's effort to deal with these matters ignores that necessity; see McCormick, "Ethno-cultural Interpretations," pp. 358–71.

dispositions to accelerate and deepen that swing. Still, in some contexts —the Pella community in Iowa, for example—where Dutch immigrants had linked support for prohibition with antiimmigrant attitudes, Dutch pietists clung tenaciously to their older Democratic partisanship. The political-generational experiences of subgroups of the German Lutherans, as well as their respective degrees of confessionalism, were both independently important in explaining variations in their patterns of partisanship. Yet so, too, were social and political contexts, for where German Lutherans perceived Democracy as the "Catholic party," they reacted negatively. And even among Catholic voter groups revealing distinctions appeared when the relation between religion and voting was specified by nativity. The religious perspectives of native-stock Catholics often came into conflict with their antiimmigrant dispositions. The effect was to cross-pressure the former and to reduce both the group's overt cohesiveness and its degree of Democratic partisanship. The same type of phenomenon recurred, though with a revealing regional variation, among French Canadian Catholics. In New England, where group-conscious French Canadians perceived Democracy as the "Irish Catholic party," they were more resistant to its partisan overtures than in the Midwest, where Irish domination was both less visible and less pervasive.

The impact of ethnic and religious identifications was no more contextually invariable for native-stock groups than it was for adopted citizens. Yankees, for example, exhibited higher levels of political cohesiveness in the Midwest than they did in New England. In the midwestern "wilderness" the sense of "being a New England man" was sharpened by contact and conflict with antagonistic subcultures. There Yankee ethnocultural and religious identifications interacted and reinforced each other. However, in those New England locales not marked by large numbers of immigrants (especially Irish Catholics), lingering religious antagonisms conflicted with ethnocultural self-consciousness and reduced the levels of Yankee political cohesiveness. The voting responses of southern-stock salvationist pietists in Maryland and Missouri gave evidence of the intertwined and reinforcing effects of regional self-consciousness, antiblack attitudes, and a resistance to northern *evangelical* pietism. And even among subgroups of the northern evangelicals in these states, in contexts marked by relatively large numbers of black voters, antiblack attitudes counterbalanced religious dispositions and underlay their swing to the "white man's party," the Democracy.

Not only did sociopolitical contexts and historical experiences matter, however; so, too, did *particular conditions*. One of the most frequently ignored dimensions of the voting-behavior studies has been their effort to begin the task of delineating sets of conditions under which economic attributes apparently attained greater partisan salience than ethnocultural ones. Insistence on always-and-everywhere class interpretations of mass political behavior has been one of the prime contributors to our currently glaring lack of knowledge concerning the requisite preconditions of class cohesiveness. It is enormously paradoxical that those who pursue such interpretations usually yearn for a politics reflective of class polarities. Yet by failing explicitly to recognize other potential bases of group cohesiveness and by failing to specify the conditions under which one set of social attributes rather than some other might have been expected to be determinative, their interpretations inhibit understanding *why* electoral cleavages have not mirrored class distinctions. In turn, that understanding is indispensable to any serious efforts aimed at developing and sustaining a "workers' party."

Under what conditions did economic attributes become more salient to mass voting behavior? What conditions stimulated economic aggregates to behave with higher-than-usual levels of group cohesiveness? At least two such conditions seem to have been important. First, in times of economic hardship—the depressions of the 1870s and 1890s, for example—shared economic identifications seemed to have crosscut and weakened the partisan salience of other social attributes. As a sense of "hard times" was broadly diffused among the mass public, voter groups responded both to that generalized perception and to its concrete referents. The effect of that response, however, was not to *polarize* mass political behavior along class lines but to induce a general movement of all voter groups in the same partisan direction.[13] That unidirectional movement narrowed, rather than increased, the voting distance between social classes. Second, other types of economic crises, especially strikes, also increased the partisan salience of shared economic identifications. That was apparent not only in the 1870s when depression *and* strikes overlapped and reinforced each other, but in the mid-1880s as well. Strikes heightened the salience of shared economic identifications, muted the impact of other social attributes, and produced stronger-than-usual levels of labor-group cohesiveness.[14] In con-

13. On the 1870s see the relevant sections of Chapters 4 and 6. On the 1890s see Jensen, *Winning the Midwest*, pp. 209–68; Kleppner, *Cross of Culture*, pp. 179–268; Samuel T. McSeveney, *The Politics of Depression*, pp. 32–162. Although the initial partisan effect of the depression of the 1930s was similar to that of the 1890s, the long-term consequence of the depression *and* the New Deal was to redefine the context for mass political behavior.

14. This is not to claim that these were the necessary *and* sufficient conditions for that cohesiveness, nor that they were at all times and in all contexts even the necessary ones. As yet we simply know too little about the involved behavioral dynamics to allow development of generally applicable propositions.

texts in which labor-group demands were not adequately articulated by the major parties, the increased salience of shared economic identifications produced surging levels of Farmer-Labor voting. Quite obviously, those surges magnified, rather than narrowed, the voting distance between social classes.

Specific circumstances that heightened voters' awareness of their economic roles, when coupled with perceptions of a gap between their economic expectations and "politics as usual," seem to have produced unusually high levels of behavioral cohesiveness among economic groupings. When those conditions were diffused through all social strata, they elicited voting responses whose aggregate shape was precisely the opposite of the one that a class-polarization model would predict. Yet when the conditions overlapped and interacted with conflicting social-class demands, they produced voting patterns, and even political parties, reflective of class polarities.[15] Even then, these conditions by themselves were not adequate to bring about an enduring transformation in the shape of party oppositions and to align mass constituencies along some left-conservative political economy axis. Quite to the contrary: as the crises faded, standing party attachments were rapidly reasserted and Farmer-Labor support was correspondingly eroded.

The patterned surge and collapse that characterized popular support for Farmer-Labor parties in the late nineteenth century is of considerable behavioral significance. The evanescent quality of that support stands in stark contrast to the stable character of partisan selections rooted in ethnoreligious attributes. That was true even in those contexts in which Farmer-Labor party builders actively and self-consciously sought to develop and sustain a permanent class-based party. The rapid collapse of popular support for such parties testifies, of course, to the psychological strength of major-party identifications, but in doing that, it inferentially points to a major difference in the ways in which these distinctive types of party attachments were anchored and reinforced.

Major-party identifications were rooted primarily in ethnoreligious group conflicts. For most social groups partisanship had become a means of expressing and defending subcultural values, and through habituated partisan responses party itself had become a positive reference symbol. Thus, the group member's self-identification as "Democrat" or "Republican" was both anchored in and expressive of the group's political culture. And, in turn, it was reinforced by continuing involvement and

15. Those reflections were uneven contextually and across social groups, and they were mild compared with those imbedded in some European party oppositions. However, even such muted manifestations of class polarities stand out for their uniqueness in the American political context.

interaction with other members of the group. The high levels of residential clustering by ethnoreligious groups in both urban and rural environments and the high rates of religiously endogamous marriages suggest daily lives that were not randomly limited in their range of contacts and relations.[16] So, too, does the proliferation of a host of ethnoreligiously exclusive secondary institutions: churches, church societies, parochial schools, ethnic clubs and benevolent societies, and so forth.[17] And within some of these, especially the churches and church-based organizations, the communication of group norms was direct and unequivocal. Quite probably and for most late nineteenth-century Americans, their involvement in this type of ethnoreligious infrastructure reinforced their sense of identity with the group and their commitment to its political-cultural expectations, especially when questions bearing directly on the group's beliefs continued to rage in the public arena.[18]

16. For useful insights into the nature and importance of these matters, see the discussions of the relevant topics in Stanley Lieberson, *Ethnic Patterns in American Cities*; Josef J. Barton, *Peasants and Strangers*; Dean R. Esslinger, *Immigrants and the City*; Harold J. Abramson, "Inter-Ethnic Marriage among Catholic Americans and Changes in Religious Behavior," pp. 31–44; Ruby Jo Reeves Kennedy, "Single or Triple Melting Pot? Intermarriage Trends in New Haven, 1870–1940," pp. 331–39; idem, "Single or Triple Melting Pot? Intermarriage Trends in New Haven, 1870–1950," pp. 56–59; Lowry Nelson, "Intermarriage among Nationality Groups in a Rural Area of Minnesota," pp. 585–92.

17. The details on these can best be gleaned from ethnic, parish, and local histories. For some indications of their extensiveness and importance, see Jay Dolan, *The Immigrant Church*; Silvano Tomasi, *Piety and Power*. On the social role of a neglected institution, the saloon, see Jon M. Kingsdale, "The 'Poor Man's Club,'" pp. 472–89; E. E. LeMasters, *Blue-Collar Aristocrats*; Perry R. Duis, "The Saloon and the Public City." We should also realize that another channel of information, the daily newspaper, was typically not politically neutral in the late nineteenth century. In 1868, for example, 79 percent of the nation's 497 daily newspapers had a declared partisan affiliation; see Peter R. Knights, "'Competition' in the U.S. Daily Newspaper Industry, 1865–68," pp. 473–80.

18. I am aware of the fact that analysts of population mobility have described high rates of out-movement from communities and of movement from place to place within those communities. The most thorough of these studies is Peter R. Knights, *The Plain People of Boston, 1830–1860*; also see Stephen Thernstrom and Peter R. Knights, "Men in Motion," pp. 7–35. The implications of such findings for analysis of political culture are not as direct as they might appear on their surface. We simply need to know a great deal more about geographic mobility before we can even speculate about its political-system implications. As a minimum, we need to inquire into at least three broad areas. First, how much geographic mobility was *group* movement? Analysts have simply assumed geographic mobility to have been an individual phenomenon and have not even inquired into this dimension. Yet histories of the settlement of midwestern communities, for example, are replete with instances of group movement. Second, we need to inquire into whether population turnover changed the predominant social character of communities. Third, for those who changed residences within a city, we need to know whether that move was accompanied by a severing of connections with their former friends, churches, schools, clubs, and so forth.

The emergence of Farmer-Labor parties, on the other hand, was not accompanied by the development of a parallel class-oriented infrastructure of secondary institutions, or at least not by one whose scope was as encompassing and whose impact as pervasive as that of the ethnoreligious infrastructure.[19] As a result, the decision to vote for the candidates of a Farmer-Labor party was not one that normally was reinforced by daily involvement with other group members who had made similar decisions. It seems likely that this absence of *ongoing* social-group reinforcement largely accounted for the surgelike quality of Farmer-Labor support.[20]

Explanations of mass voting behavior require sensitivity to sociopolitical contexts, specific conditions, and historical experiences—as well as economic, ethnic, and religious identifications. They necessitate consideration of the ways in which social identifications at times overlapped, and at other times collided, in their effects. They also mandate awareness of the ways in which contexts, conditions, and experiences shaped social and political outlooks. I have itemized these requisite dimensions not only to draw attention to the complexity of human behavior but to underscore the fact that voting-behavior analysts have self-consciously addressed that complexity. Recognition of that fact

19. Although the focus and conceptual framework in Lawrence Goodwyn, *Democratic Promise*, are quite different from those underlying this analysis of Farmer-Labor voting, the essence of his argument is complementary to that advanced here. For example, Goodwyn argues (p. 241) that for a voter to abandon his old party "required a new kind of individual autonomy and self-respect, as well as a knowledge that one was not alone, that one was participating in a new kind of collective self-confidence." That is, of course, simply another way of pointing to the importance of group memberships in producing, and later reinforcing, voting decisions. And although Goodwyn prefers terms such as "movement culture of political hope" and "political consciousness" (pp. 185, 314), in fact he is referring to active involvement in Alliance activities. Thus his argument and his description of the varying success of the Populist party in 1892 (pp. 313–30) can be reformulated in group-oriented, rather than exclusively ideological, terms: the common experiences of involvement in Alliance activities heightened awareness of shared economic identifications and the salience of these identifications to partisan selections. Thus, where the Alliance and its cooperative crusade flourished, so did Populist voting; those voting decisions were shaped and reinforced by involvement in secondary groups. Where the Alliance organizational infrastructure was nonexistent or weak, or where it did not develop patterned interaction among its members based on cooperative ventures, Populist support failed to materialize or subsequently displayed the evanescent quality typically associated with minor-party voting.

20. Although it only roughly parallels the argument here, it is instructive to notice that working-class support for Democratic candidates in the late twentieth century was stronger among those who were union members than among those who were not, and at least among UAW workers in Detroit, it was stronger still among those who expressed a great deal of interest in the union and regularly attended its meetings. For the relevant data and discussion see Angus Campbell et al., *The American Voter*, pp. 302, 305–306, 314–16; Arthur Kornhauser, Albert J. Mayer, and Harold L. Sheppard, *When Labor Votes*, pp. 29–75, 201–60.

should at least inter, with an appropriately solemn requiem, the notion of a monolithic ethnocultural interpretation. It can also serve as an opportunity to make explicit two elementary considerations of some importance to the logic of research design.

First, social attributes take on behavioral bearings only within specific contexts. Therefore, research designs that do not permit contextual explorations run the grave risk of blurring distinctive types of effects and consequently misestimating the relationships between social characteristics and partisan behavior. Computer technology and the availability of more sophisticated software packages now make it feasible to manipulate massively sized files of data. It is technically possible, for example, to estimate relations between some set of social characteristics and partisan choices across all of the counties of the nation, but to do that implicitly assumes the existence of cultural and behavioral uniformities. It assumes, for example, that "being a Baptist" or "being a laborer" had the same psychological meaning in all contexts; that intervening experiences of the group, prevailing political-structural conditions, differences in social-structural milieux, and variations in party characters had no salience to partisanship.[21] Common sense, to say nothing of historical knowledge, renders such assumptions counterfactual.

Second, a group's voting behavior must be explained historically. Therefore, research designs that do not permit descriptions of a group's voting behavior over time are most likely to produce inadequate understanding of the current bases of partisanship.[22] What does it *mean*, for example, to say that across a specified sequence of elections some group, in a particular context, voted 55.0 percent Democratic? That descriptive statement has one implication if earlier the group had been 90.0 percent Republican, but it has an entirely different implication if the group previously had been 90.0 percent Democratic. Research designs that are insensitive to the changes in the levels of a group's political cohesiveness over time, and even over electoral eras, will be unable to isolate the potential causes that changed the relative weights

21. For examples of studies predicated on such implicit assumptions, see Allan J. Lichtman, "Critical Election Theory and the Reality of American Presidential Politics, 1916–40," pp. 317–51; Ross J. Cameron, "Political Realignment in the Late Antebellum North." For suggestive overviews of some historically conditioned contextual distinctions in mass political culture that are relevant to political behavior, see two studies by Daniel J. Elazar, *Cities of the Prairie* and *American Federalism*.

22. It seems indisputable to me that analysis over time, and by definition of terms, is indispensable to *historical* study. Yet that judgment on my part should be weighed against the contrasting view that time-series analysis "is a favorite gambit of the behavioralists: presumably any phenomenon, if studied 'over time,' will reduce itself to insignificance"; James R. Green, "Behavioralism and Class Analysis," p. 101.

of the combination of determinants that shaped the group's voting behavior.

Granted the unmourned passing of a stereotyped ethnocultural model of mass voting behavior, the central finding of the voting studies still remains: although they did not operate in precisely the same ways and to exactly the same partisan effect in all contexts and under all conditions, attachments to ethnoreligious groups were *relatively* more important as determinants of nineteenth-century social-group cohesiveness and party oppositions than were economic attributes or social status. That finding, in turn, has generated new questions concerning the relation between the electoral subsystem and the more inclusive political system. Those questions bear on larger and systemically significant problems concerning the ways in which group interests were articulated, aggregated, and transformed into policy. Although it oversimplifies considerably, it is useful to pose the pertinent question directly, as more than one commentator has: what, if anything, had mobilizing voters to do with making policies?[23]

The voting-behavior studies have been widely faulted because they have not overtly addressed themselves to that question. Studies of the realignment of the 1850s, for example, have been faulted because they have not untangled the complexities of Civil War causation. Analyses of postbellum voting behavior have been criticized because they have not dealt with the shaping of tariff policy and thus have neglected matters such as the "private motives of elites, as well as long-range patterns of social and economic development."[24] The specifics of the attack could readily be extended, but that is not necessary. For the appropriate response to such charges is to admit their superficial accuracy, enter a plea of nolo contendere, and proceed to the task of attempting to clarify the thinking that underpins them.

The voting studies have not addressed and resolved these weighty problems precisely because they have not been designed to do so. It is naive to think that research designs constructed to explain the attitudinal bases of mass voting behavior could simultaneously explain the formulation of policy. Analyzing mass voting behavior involves particular types of research operations; analyzing policymaking involves other distinctive sets of research operations. Only when both have been com-

23. This is a slight paraphrase of McCormick, "Ethno-cultural Interpretations," p. 377; see ibid., pp. 371–77 for his longer discussion of the matter. For a similar series of comments, see Edward Pessen, "Some Timeless Standards for the Modern Historian," p. 247.

24. McCormick, "Ethno-cultural Interpretations," p. 375; Eric Foner, "The Causes of the American Civil War," pp. 199–201. The McCormick argument is not narrowly confined to tariff policy.

pleted can we meaningfully begin to deal with the systematic interrelations between the two. That some commentators have not recognized the enormous differences in research-design requirements imposed by each distinctive type of inquiry testifies both to their imprecise conceptualization and to their failure to treat explicitly the logic of research design.

Why, then, has this failure to indulge in illogical generalization been highlighted as a *deficiency* of the voting studies? Partially because the subject matter involved, policymaking and its consequences, is both intuitively and substantively compelling, but in larger part because that mode of generalization, at least as applied within this particular context, has become a norm of historical practice. That is, historians are accustomed to assuming that elite and mass behaviors were only separate sides of the same coin and that both could be explained in terms of some shared agreement on policy. Given that assumption, party rhetoric can be interpreted literally and construed as an indicator of sets of policy preferences simultaneously shared by both elites and masses. That enables analysts to posit a series of simple and unified inferences, ones that have "the advantage of giving coherence to the electoral and policy-making processes."[25]

That "advantage" has always been wholly illusory, of course. And the price paid for it has been too steep. The promise of simple and easy-to-phrase bases for political-system "coherence" has about it a tantalizing attractiveness, but it is better to resist its seductive simplicities and to recognize that complex relations and dynamic processes cannot be adequately accounted for by monolithic and counterfactual "explanations." And especially they cannot be accounted for by offering inferences derived from one type of research design as explanations of phenomena whose investigation mandates wholly different research strategies.

Because historians have traditionally used the manifest content of partisan rhetoric as a guide to shared policy preferences they have misunderstood the dissimilar use that the voting studies have made of the same types of evidence.[26] Voting-behavior analysts have plumbed party rhetoric, not only for its manifest content, but as well for its code words and emotionally denotative symbols. The rationale of that approach is as incontrovertible as it is direct: words, slogans, phrases, and even acts

25. McCormick, "Ethno-cultural Interpretations," p. 376.
26. Ibid., pp. 372–74; Pessen, "Some Timeless Standards," p. 247. For a discussion of manifest content and code words, see Walter Dean Burnham, "Rejoinder to 'Comments' by Philip Converse and Jerrold Rusk," p. 1053; Kleppner, *Cross of Culture*, pp. 147–57, 171, 175–77, 257–68, 356–58, 362–65.

may mean different things to different people. To penetrate beyond the ostensible meanings is to attempt to delineate the emotions that were being tapped and to perceive how analytically distinguishable ideas often were interwoven emotionally and symbolically. Such efforts require a conceptual framework sensitive to potential differences in modes of perception. To explain how and why group dispositions became salient to partisanship requires that analysts search, not only for identifiable issue publics, but also for more inclusive political subcultures; not only for indicators of congruence on issues among the sectors of party, but also for elements of psychological consonance between party character and social-group character. Only through such operations can historians discern the extent to which, and the ways in which, party *acts*, speeches, and postures interacted with and reinforced each other; how party symbolically represented social-group characters; and, thus, in time, how party functioned as a positive reference symbol for its habituated supporters.

In pursuing this approach, however, voting-behavior analysts have not made claims incongruent with their research designs. They have not claimed that such an approach explains all aspects of party behavior but have limited their inferences to the attitudinal bases of mass partisanship. Thus, none of the voting studies has ever claimed that party could be understood solely through its public pronouncements. Of course, party actions involve more than the symbolic content of campaign documents. And in analyzing the ways in which party acts and postures often reinforced each other and resonated emotionally with the political characters of party support groups, the voting studies have done much more to suggest a basis of political-system coherence than some commentators have noticed.

As means of providing insight into the attitudinal bases of mass partisanship, concepts such as *symbolic representation, social-group and party characters*, and *psychological rapport* lack the simplicity and concreteness conveyed by older notions of conscious economic self-interest. They also lack another property of the older notions: obvious, direct, and simple connections between mass voting and policymaking. The absence of obvious relations, however, should not lead to the conclusion that mass voting behavior was irrelevant to the formulation of policy. It should instead lead to research designs exploring the nature of the relation. Developing such research designs will necessarily entail frontal assaults on immense problems of concept clarification, operationalization, measurement, description, and analysis. It is neither possible nor appropriate here to discuss these problems at length, but it is useful to clarify some of the relevant lines of inquiry and to sketch at least a broad framework within which one can begin to understand the interrelations between mass voting and policymaking in the late nineteenth century.

If research is to deal with public policymaking, then initially we must indicate specifically what is designated by that term.[27] At least two subsidiary questions need to be posed and answered. First, at which jurisdictional level of government were the decisions made? Second, what type of rulemaking institution was involved?

It matters considerably whether we mean to inquire into policy made by national, state, metropolitan, county, town, or city governments. The nature of the decision-making process and the relative weights of its determinants should not be assumed to be precisely the same at all jurisdictional levels. Nor can the problem be evaded by assuming that the really important decisions, those that directly touched the daily lives of most citizens, were always made at the national level. Acceptance of a static view of the persisting dominance of national decision making has inhibited description and analysis of one of the most important dimensions of change in the political system—the longitudinal tendency for more and more decisions, affecting the lives of more and more citizens, to be shifted upward in a local-to-national hierarchy of territorial jurisdictions.[28]

Just as we cannot meaningfully deal with "government in general," so we cannot research "decision making in general." The decision-making process varies from one type of legitimized rulemaking institution to another. Thus, it is necessary to be specific about whether the decisions in question were made by a legislature, an executive, a court,

27. Two observations pertinent to my focus should be made explicit here. First, throughout my concern is with what Lee Benson has designated as "authoritative public decisions," i.e., decision making by governments. Therefore, I shall leave aside matters concerning authoritative *private* decision making—e.g., decisions made by corporations, banks, and so forth. Although most commentators have not explicitly distinguished between authoritative public and authoritative private decisions, I think a reasonable reading of their arguments indicates an exclusive concern with the relation between mass voting and decisions made by governments. Second, I am not attempting here to sketch out all the problems of logic and research design involved in dealing with the public decision-making process. My concern is explicitly limited to those aspects that seem to have clearest relevance to the linkage problem. For a more comprehensive view of the involved research strategy, see Lee Benson, "Political Power and Political Elites," pp. 281–310.

28. For evidence of lingering differences in citizen orientations to distinct levels of government, see the data and discussion in Donald J. Devine, *The Political Culture of the United States*, pp. 167–72; for what such differences may imply concerning the quality of citizens' involvement, see J. P. Nettl, *Political Mobilization*, p. 324. For a useful framework within which to locate and analyze the shifts in decision making both across types of rulemaking bodies and levels of government, see Samuel P. Hays, "Political Parties and the Community-Society Continuum," pp. 152–81.

or an administrative agency. Since each of these institutions is related to its social environment in different ways, the formal and regularized channels for organized mass influence differ considerably across types of institutions. The potential for organized mass influence on decision making by elected legislative bodies, for example, differs considerably from that on appointed administrative agencies or courts. Knowing which decisions are made by which legitimized institutions, therefore, is a question of critical concern for researchers.

There are at least two reasons why that is so. First, even citizens' inchoate awareness of the distinctions between degrees of potential influence may shape their internalized expectations of the electoral process. Some public questions, even those about which large numbers of people feel strongly, may never spill into the electoral arena precisely because citizens perceive only tenuous and indirect links between those policies and the electoral process. Under such conditions involved issue publics may seek to influence decision making through other channels, e.g., lobbying activities.

Second, once we face the fact that the concrete institutions available for the articulation of mass interests differ from one decision-making body to another, we will be better able to assess the systemic and behavioral significance of shifts in the locus of decision-making authority. At the very least such changes involve altering the balance of inputs that impinge on the decision-making process. Frequently, they have entailed calculated efforts to remove important clusters of decisions from the "caprices of party politics" and to entrust them instead to appointed "experts." The effect is to insulate the decision-making process from organized mass opinion by severing the direct link between party and decision makers. The longitudinal tendency for more and more decisions, affecting larger and larger numbers of people, to be made by "insulated" decision makers is one of the centrally important, and virtually unresearched, dimensions of change in the political system. It has played an important causal role in reshaping mass orientations toward government and toward politics in general. In turn, these "movements in men's minds" signaled profound and still reverberating shifts in political culture.[29]

However, commentators have not been concerned with this full range of jurisdictional levels and policymaking institutions. Although

29. I am freely borrowing and adapting from Ronald P. Formisano, "Deferential-Participant Politics," p. 487. For other useful formulations, see Moshe M. Czudnowski, "A Salience Dimension of Politics for the Study of Political Culture," pp. 878–88; M. Kent Jennings and Harmon Zeigler, "The Salience of American State Politics," pp. 523–35.

none has ever been explicit, it seems reasonable to infer that their concern has been limited to decision making by popularly elected legislatures, especially by the U.S. Congress. Yet some have been explicit about another highly revealing limitation. Inquiries into the relation between mass voting and policymaking have not been addressed to all types of policy, but almost exclusively to economic policy. As one of the frequently quoted commentators has put it, the acid test of whether or not "ethno-cultural historians have transcended a rational, goal-oriented view of politics" is the extent to which "they have faced the question of the relation between mobilizing voters and making *economic* policies."[30]

Of course, there is no reason to thrust economic policies and no others to the forefront of research concern. Nor is there any reason to assume that pursuit of economic policy was "rational, goal-oriented" and that the pursuit of noneconomic policy was, by implication at least, nonrational and not goal-oriented.[31] Those implications reveal a great deal about the analyst's a priori assumptions, but they shed no light on past human behavior.

In fact, by imposing on past behavior a rigid dichotomy reflecting only the analyst's values, the approach prevents meaningful reconstruction of the linkage between mass opinion and the actions of decision makers, for to understand what those actions meant to the involved contemporaries, we must recreate *their* perceptual worlds and not impose ours on them. Yet forcing past thought and behavior into rigid, artificial, and mutually exclusive categories only denudes them a priori of those sometimes subtle and complex linkages through which analytically distinguishable clusters of issues may have been related to each other in real life and thought.[32] It precludes, too, perceiving whether analogous linkages existed *in the votes* of legislators. Yet exploration of this nature is crucial to understanding what mobilizing voters had to do with making policies.

In practical terms, what does that exploration entail? It requires analyzing the central tendencies of party cleavage in the mass electorate, of the central tendencies of party divergence in the legislature, and *then*, of the relations between them. Examining those relations makes it possible to describe the degree of congruence between *party* oppositions in

30. McCormick, "Ethno-cultural Interpretations," p. 372, emphasis added.

31. For a useful discussion see M. Brewster Smith, "Personality in Politics," pp. 77–101.

32. Formisano, "Toward a Reorientation of Jacksonian Politics," pp. 60–61, 64. Commentators have phrased the dichotomy in a variety of ways: national-local, real-unreal, economic-cultural, and so forth.

the legislature and party oppositions among the mass public, to specify sets of conditions substantially altering that congruence, and to analyze its dispositional underpinning. Ultimately the answer to the question of whether or not parties aggregated and articulated popular interests and translated them into policy should not depend on some analyst's conception of what interests ought to have been involved, nor on an a priori narrowing of the range of possible relations. It should instead *proceed from* systematic description and analysis of *all relevant* past behaviors. Once we abandon simplistic dualisms and admit the heterogeneity of "interests," then we can begin the search for those "modal sets of interests and attitudes" that served as an "inarticulate ideology" reciprocally linking voter mobilization with legislative decision making.[33]

Implicit antiparty biases, an unwillingness to treat specifically and precisely the distinguishable sectors of party activity, and the imposition of rigid and artificial dualisms have combined to inhibit *historical* analysis of the role of party as an intermediary between mass voting behavior and policymaking by popularly elected legislatures. The failure to analyze the late nineteenth-century development of partisan linkages underlies the incapacity to understand either their behavioral or systemic significance. In turn, that incapacity has given rise to enormously distorted interpretations of the consequences of party actions, of the contemporary attacks on party linkages, and of the subsequent decay of those linkages.[34]

It understates the case to observe that our knowledge of how party shaped policy in the late nineteenth century is greatly underdeveloped. And it is especially meager once we move beyond the U.S. Congress to the state and local levels, but the work that has been done points to party as the single most important correlate of legislative-voting behavior.[35]

33. Frank J. Sorauf, *Party Politics in America*, pp. 351, 372–95.

34. Pessen, "Some Timeless Standards," p. 247, argues that parties can be "better understood by their actions and the consequences of their actions than by the types of voters" who supported them. That argument ignores the fact that consequences and purposive intentions are related, both logically and in the real world. It also reflects a failure to distinguish between the *logical* requirements of description and explanation.

35. The phrasing here distinguishes between a correlate and a determinant of behavior. For a review of historical studies of roll-call voting, see Robert P. Swierenga, ed., *Quantification in American History*, pp. 127–30. For longitudinal overviews of party voting in the U.S. House of Representatives, see Walter Dean Burnham, "Insulation and Responsiveness in Congressional Elections," p. 427; Jerome M. Clubb and Santa Traugott, "Partisan Cleavage and Cohesion in the House of Representatives, 1861–1974," pp. 375–402. For a similar time series for the late nineteenth-century U.S. Senate, see William Gerald Shade et al., "Partisanship in the United States Senate," pp. 185–205, especially Appendix A, p. 205; for varied data at the state legislative level, see Malcolm E. Jewell and Samuel C. Patterson, *The Legislative Process in the United States*.

Typically, however, these analyses have not addressed the question of *how* party induced roll-call voting cohesion. In some instances party voting may have been a response to overt efforts by caucuses, leaders, whips, and policy committees to exert party discipline. In other instances it may have represented a reaction to pressure by the party organization or by the party electorate. And "party," in its symbolic sense, also operated " 'within' the legislator as a series of internalized loyalties and frameworks for organizing his legislative decisions."[36] These are not, of course, mutually exclusive possibilities. Although each alternative, and each combination of them, has distinct substantive and theoretical implications and although the precise alternative always needs to be specified, the fact that party did operate to shape legislative voting is both clear and important.

Even gross indicators of the impact of party on voting in the U.S. House of Representatives vividly illustrate the differences between then and now (see Table 9.2).[37] In the late nineteenth century, in contrast to the 1960s and 1970s, roll-call voting regularly (but not invariably) reflected *party oppositions*. Party shaped congressmen's choices, and it did so across clusters of issues. Whether on tariff questions or measures to restrict the liquor traffic, currency issues or immigration restriction, civil-service reform or Mormon polygamy, regulation of private corporations or closing the Columbian Exposition on the Sabbath, *party*, more than section or shifting ad hoc issue coalitions, shaped congressional decisions.[38]

Although comparable longitudinal arrays are unavailable for each state, the limited evidence that has been gathered points—in Illinois, Iowa, and Wisconsin, at least—to analogously high and pervasive levels of *party* conflict. In these legislatures and whether on issues pertaining explicitly to ethnocultural questions or on those relating to state revenues or to the role of private enterprise, party oppositions structured policy.[39]

36. Sorauf, *Party Politics in America*, p. 339.

37. The calculations are based on data in Clubb and Traugott, "Partisan Cleavage and Cohesion," Table 1, pp. 382–83. They have used the term "party unlikeness" rather than "dissimilarity"; their "party vote" is defined as one on which at least a simple majority of the voting members of one party was opposed by a majority of the other party.

38. The observation derives from my analysis of all House roll calls, classified by subject areas, over the Forty-fifth through Fifty-first Congresses. For that purpose I have calculated indices of agreement both within subject areas and across all roll calls for all possible pairs of congressmen, as well as the types of aggregate measures of party voting reported by Clubb and Traugott, "Partisan Cleavage and Cohesion," pp. 382–84, 393–94. On indices of agreement, see Lee F. Anderson, Meredith W. Watts, Jr., and Allen R. Wilcox, *Legislative Roll-Call Analysis*, pp. 59–75.

39. Ballard C. Campbell, Jr., "Political Parties, Cultural Groups and Contested Issues." For a more limited view of his rich findings, and one that also takes into

TABLE 9.2 *Longitudinal Measures of Party Voting:*
U.S. House of Representatives

Years (Congress)	Mean Party Dissimilarity	Mean % Party Votes
1861–1893 (37th–52d Cong)	54.7	69.6
1861–1869 (37th–40th Cong)	57.2	73.5
1869–1893 (41st–52d Cong)	53.9	68.4
1965–1974 (89th–93d Cong)	24.8	36.0

"Economic" and "noneconomic" questions were not only inter-woven symbolically in party rhetoric, they were tied together as well in the voting responses of party legislators. The nature and significance of those linkages have been obscured by research designs that impose arti-ficial dualisms on past behavior. The resulting research strategies have been unable to deal with the ways in which policy bore simultaneously on the allocation of tangible resources and on the social-group values that would predominate in the society. To resolve the traditional "who gets what how?" problem, it is necessary to reconstruct the full range of those values; to recognize that ethnoreligious subcultures fostered the development of norms relevant to all dimensions of group life, including the economic; and to perceive how party may have represented social groups, not only in symbolic ways, but in tangible ones as well.[40]

Yet party's capacity to structure policy has never been invariable. At least in the U.S. House, party voting has exhibited a revealing rhythm. Within the context of a long-term secular decline, party voting there has shown a distinctive cyclical pattern whose peaks of intensity have neatly coincided with the realigning phases of electoral systems.[41]

account the backgrounds of the legislators, see idem, "Ethnicity and the 1893 Wiscon-sin Assembly," pp. 74–94. For a brilliant analysis of the interrelations among party, subcultural oppositions, and policy making in antebellum America, see William Gerald Shade, *Banks or No Banks*.

40. My formulation here is freely adapted from Shade's extremely important mono-graph, *Banks or No Banks*, especially pp. 16–19.

41. See Table 9.2 for the two phases of the third party system; for the argument and

It appears that whatever matters energized voters during realigning sequences, and however the separate elements were constrained in human belief systems, they imparted structure to the newly created party oppositions both in the electorate and in the legislature. The same seismic shocks that produced durable change in the shape of the electoral universe also transformed the general contours of legislative policy.

How did electoral realignments work such wondrous deeds? Not in mysterious, but in concrete, ways. Critical realignments, by definition, involve large and durable shifts in the competitive balance between parties. Altered election outcomes produced durable shifts in partisan control over policymaking institutions. The electoral change of the 1850s and early 1860s, for example, terminated an earlier period of divided partisan control over the federal government and inaugurated one of unified Republican control that lasted through the Forty-third Congress (elected in 1872). At the state level unified Republican control over the policymaking institutions of 62.5 percent of the nonsouthern states had been achieved by the end of 1859.[42] If we accept the unqualified aphorism that "elites make policy," then we cannot ignore these effects of critical realignments on partisan control over policymaking institutions and institutionalized elites. By altering the partisan balance in a relatively large number of legislative districts, realigning sequences accelerated partisan turnover among elites, altered the processes of elite recruitment, changed the size and shape of legislative coalitions, and thus created the conditions requisite to a change in the general contours of legislative outputs.[43]

The statement that late nineteenth-century parties served as intermediaries between mass voting and policymaking by popularly elected legislatures should not be construed, however, as an open invitation to construct some sort of monistic and monolithic "party model."[44] In-

---

more supporting evidence, see Clubb and Traugott, "Partisan Cleavage and Cohesion," pp. 386–93.

42. For the data and development of the argument, see Walter Dean Burnham, Jerome M. Clubb, and William H. Flanigan, "Partisan Realignment."

43. Michael R. King and Lester G. Seligman, "Critical Elections, Congressional Recruitment, and Public Policy," pp. 263–99. For insights that neatly dovetail with those of King and Seligman, see David W. Brady and Philip Althoff, "Party Voting in the U.S. House of Representatives, 1890–1910," pp. 753–75; David Brady, "Congressional Policy Responses to Issue[s] and Elections"; Benjamin Ginsberg, "Critical Elections and the Substance of Party Conflict," pp. 603–25.

44. Especially it should not be forced into the traditional "responsible party" model. That model, as applied, looks for party to shape outcomes in particular; whereas, the formulation here can best be thought of as focusing on outcomes in general. For the distinctions and further discussion see Theodore J. Lowi, "Party, Policy, and Constitution in America," pp. 238–76; Walter Dean Burnham, *Critical Elections and the Mainsprings of American Politics*, pp. 9–10.

stead, we should expect and look for patterned differences in the relation dependent on jurisdictional levels of government, the degree of legislative institutionalization, and the nature and strength of the connection between party in the legislature and party as organization. Too much research, especially on the state and local levels, remains still to be done before we can develop useful generalizations and move forward toward the desired goal, a dynamic theory of American politics. Although too much should not be read into the statement, it is presently useful for what it brings into focus and how that reorients our understanding.

First, it centers attention on the complexities of party and on the varied dimensions of the interrelations among party, political system, and social environment, for party was at once a positive reference symbol to mass voters, an agency of elite recruitment and socialization, and a guide to legislative voting behavior. Thus, although not all political conflict has been party conflict, that that has become such has been characterized by far-ranging and long-enduring systemic implications. Only within that context can we assess the consequences of measures and processes that cumulatively eroded the capacity of party to organize and link mass opinion with policymaking. Changes in the functions that party performed—whether brought about by civil service "reform," direct primaries, or personal-registration laws—impacted party's role as an intermediary between citizens and policymakers. So, as well, did the upward shift in decision making across jurisdictional levels of government and the "insulation" of decision making from party influences. This progressive departisanization of conflict, enormous shifts in partisan balance, and temporally coinciding changes in the rules of the electoral game contributed to the early twentieth-century demobilization of the mass electorate.[45] That demobilization, in turn, constituted one of the necessary conditions that enabled lobbying groups subsequently to play increasingly influential roles in determining the direction and shape of policy.

Second, and to return to the starting point, the statement of party's intermediary role between mass voting and legislative decision making provides a context within which to suggest the nature of the "inarticulate ideologies" that were the properties of late nineteenth-century parties. At their base those parties reflected powerful and enduring social-group conflicts. The resulting party polarities involved irreconcilable differ-

45. For useful insights concerning these matters, see Burnham, *Critical Elections*, pp. 74–90; idem, "Theory and Voting Research," pp. 1002–1023. Quite likely the effects were especially marked among voters who became eligible to participate only after 1896. Systematic exploration of these and related questions constitutes the core of work now in progress, which I have tentatively entitled "Social Predictors of Partisanship and Participation: The Fourth Party System, 1893–1933."

ences arising from ethnoreligious-group attachments and values. Matters of life-style served as manifest indicators of primordial differences in conceptions of the nature of society, of the role of the individual in society, and of the relation of government both to society and to the individual. Social-group conflict rooted in these distinctive conceptions shaped the central tendencies of party oppositions among the mass electorate. The structure of those oppositions, in turn, successively shaped patterns of elite recruitment and the general outlines of policy. To phrase it in overly simple fashion, laissez faire attitudes toward social ethics and laissez faire attitudes on matters of political economy were twin dimensions of a shared dispositional consonance that permeated all sectors of Democracy. Arrayed in *party* opposition was a broadly holistic conception of society, one that called for its moral as well as its economic integration. Party postures *and party actions* concerning the extensiveness and uses of government power were expressions of these distinctive conceptions.

However anachronistic the resulting late nineteenth-century party battles may now appear when refracted through the lenses of our late twentieth-century eyes, it is well to remember that what was at stake was neither unreal nor trivial to contemporaries. Neither were those party battles bereft of issues, ideologies, or policy consequences. Nor did they reflect a universally shared consensus concerning the relation of government to society and of government to the individual. Rather, those party battles involved nothing less than locating the boundary between the political system and the larger society.

Bibliography

Voting-behavior analysis necessarily involves the use of a wide range of both quantitative and letristic evidence. The former make possible descriptions of the social composition and partisan behavior of states, counties, and subcounty voting units. And the latter are indispensable to efforts aimed at delineating party characters and group political cultures. Only when these two broadly demarcated categories of evidence are analytically integrated can historical studies move beyond description to more complex matters of human motivation.

The bibliographical listing that follows should provide a general sense of the relevant types of both categories of evidence necessary for analysis of mass voting behavior. This listing does not itemize all of the works consulted, but it does include references to all items cited in the notes. And it is more comprehensive than that in identifying the sources used to describe the social composition and partisan behavior of voting units.

Both manuscript and published demographic materials have been used to establish the social composition of voting units. County-level data from the six decennial federal censuses between 1850 and 1900 were obtained in machine-readable form from the Inter-University Consortium for Political and Social Research. State-census data at the county level were then used where possible to supplement the federal data. Separate characterizations were made for each year in which census data were reported, and linear interpolations were executed for the intervening years. The original published sources of these federal and state data are listed in the Government Documents section of the bibliography.

The state compilations listed in that section were also valuable for descriptions of the social composition of subcounty units. Collection and reporting varied considerably from one state to another, and even from one census to another within a single state. And, of course, some states conducted no census. For one or all of these reasons, the subcounty descriptions also made use of retabulations of the manuscript population schedules for the 1870 and 1880 federal censuses and the manuscripts of the social statistics schedules for the 1860 and 1870 federal censuses. In addition, and because they contained data not reported as usefully in the published returns, the manuscript schedules of two Iowa state censuses, a unique retabulation of a Wisconsin state census, and the manuscript returns for the statistics of religion for the 1890 federal census were also used. All of these materials are itemized in the section of the bibliography that lists Manuscript Sources; their dates indicate the years for which separate descriptions were made.

Census data are indispensable but not by themselves wholly sufficient for describing the social composition of areal units. Censuses simply did not always include reports on some of the social characteristics that historians are interested in examining. Religious data are an obvious case in point, and one that required that the limited census data available be supplemented by use of a wide range of denominational and conference

statistical reports. The yearbooks, almanacs, registers, and minutes of the annual meetings of these groups contain a plethora of useful statistical data, as well as statements of
group postures on public questions. These sources are itemized under Denominational
and Conference Documents in the bibliography.

The need to supplement manuscript and published census information does not per-
tain exclusively to religious data. Nor is it simply a response to one or another species of
measurement error. It derives more generally from the fact that in some critical respects
census labels cannot be construed as definitive guides but only as preliminary clues to
the social characters of voting units.

The point can perhaps most readily be illustrated through the use of a single
hypothetical example. Suppose the manuscript census returns (for 1880) reveal that the
voting-age population of some county in the western Ozarks of Missouri, or of some
voting district within that county, was composed exclusively of citizens who had been
born in Missouri of native-born parents. Such a unit would surely merit the label *native
stock*, but so would another county, or voting district, in, say, northeastern Missouri if
that unit's population were also exclusively composed of citizens born in Missouri of
native-born parents. If we construed these census-based labels as definitive indicators,
we would assume that we had in hand two units of the same nativity composition. We
might then examine the voting patterns of these and similarly classified units; or, more
simply perhaps, use the proportion of native stock across all units as an independent
variable. Granted, such operations have some descriptive use, but that utility lies principally in their serving as guides to further exploration and not as the final products of the
descriptive process.

Even a superficial knowledge of the history of settlement in Missouri would alert
the historian to the fact that the original streams of population that flowed into the
northeastern and southwestern parts of that state came from quite different geographic
sources. By 1880 (and even earlier) most of the descendants of each reported their
nativity as Missouri-born of native-born parents. Combining such subgroups into a
single composite and using that as the final and sole operational measure runs the risk of
obscuring precisely the socially and politically important distinctions that are the objects
of analysis.

In some instances a technical solution to difficulties of this genre may turn out to be
simple enough. One tactic involves partitioning the data set for the state into subsets,
where each subset encompasses a geographic area of distinctive population-group settlement. Then, the appropriate statistical measures can be reexecuted for each of the
subsets. This tactic will prove feasible technically only when the number of cases in
each of the subsets remains large enough to generate meaningful statistical measures.
However, when the total number of cases involved is small to begin with, or when
partitioning the full data set creates one or more subsets with a small number of cases,
even this approach falters. And that is most likely to happen, of course, when the
research design has depended exclusively on the use of county-level data. That fact
points to another, although narrowly technical, advantage in pursuing demographic
descriptions to the subcounty level.

However, these technical dimensions are not of primary interest at the moment.
Rather, the point to be emphasized is that knowledge of the history of the settlement of
the state, of the histories of the population groupings within the state and even within
counties, is essential to the historian. The importance of that knowledge at the interpretive stage is self-explanatory, unless one assumes that past experiences are wholly
irrelevant to current perceptions and behaviors, but its importance at the operational
stage of research design may be overlooked. Without it at that stage, researchers may

create meaningless composites and use these under the assumption that they have operationalized analytically significant independent variables. They may, for example, be content to combine Missouri Synod and General Synod German Lutherans into a single category, or treat both the Mission and Anti-Mission Baptists simply as a ''Baptist'' grouping, or lump together in a single composite both the United Brethren who moved to the Midwest directly from Pennsylvania and those who migrated there from Pennsylvania after an intervening period of residency in Virginia or the Carolinas. Knowledge of the past experiences of each of these subgroups would caution the researcher to avoid facile combinations without first testing for potential differences in behavior. Of course, it may turn out that some (or all) of these types of distinctions had no persisting behavioral significance, but that can be known only if the distinctions are operationalized and tested in the first place. And they can be operationalized only if the historian behaves, not exclusively as a data processor, but as a historian who brings to the research a knowledge of the histories of the groups and contexts that are being studied. That requires reading widely in state, county, and local histories; in the histories of ethnic and religious groups; and in the autobiographies, biographies, journals, letters, and memoirs of contemporary members of the groups. These types of sources, which are itemized in the appropriate sections of the following bibliography, are rich in information pertaining to settlement history and the experiences of population groups.

Voting studies also require the use of sources that provide political information. The county-level voting data for president, Congress, and governor that have been used for this study were obtained in machine-readable form from the Inter-University Consortium for Political and Social Research. State-level data and returns at the county level for other offices and for referenda are from the newspaper almanacs and voting compilations listed in the bibliography. Subcounty data were recovered from the state manuals listed under Government Documents. And for a few states—Maine, New Hampshire, New Jersey, and Vermont—subcounty returns were available in the commercially published state registers listed under Other Printed Sources.

Voting data, however, are only one category of political information. Since party characters varied across space and time, it was also important to examine their public pronouncements across both dimensions. For that purpose state and national party platforms were useful. These are conveniently available for most of the nineteenth century in the newspaper almanacs, cyclopaedia, and platform compilations listed under Other Printed Sources. The course of political campaigns, and the public statements of party spokesmen made during them, were followed in contemporary newspapers. And those also served as sources of much additional information concerning party organizational practices and tactics. Finally, the published diaries, letters, memoirs, and recollections of political figures provided insight into leaders' perceptions and tactics. These are listed under Autobiographies, Memoirs, and Collections.

A. Manuscript Sources

Annapolis, Md. Maryland State Library. U.S. Census (1860). Schedule 6 (Social Statistics).
———. U.S. Census (1870). Schedule 5 (Social Statistics).
Augusta, Maine. Maine Division of Archives. U.S. Census (1860). Schedule 6 (Social Statistics).
———. U.S. Census (1870). Schedule 5 (Social Statistics).

Boston, Mass. Commonwealth of Massachusetts State Library. U.S. Census (1860). Schedule 6 (Social Statistics).

———. U.S. Census (1870). Schedule 5 (Social Statistics).

Columbus, Ohio. Ohio State Historical Society. James M. Comly MSS.

Concord, N.H. New Hampshire State Library. U.S. Census (1860). Schedule 6 (Social Statistics).

———. U.S. Census (1870). Schedule 5 (Social Statistics).

Des Moines, Iowa. Department of History and Archives. Schedules of the Iowa State Census of 1885. 142 vols.

———. Schedules of the Iowa State Census of 1895. 133 vols.

Madison, Wis. Department of Rural Sociology, University of Wisconsin. "Cultural-Ethnic Backgrounds in Wisconsin: A Retabulation of Population Schedules from the Wisconsin State Census of 1905." 11 vols. (Typescript.)

———. State Historical Society of Wisconsin, United Brethren in Christ. Wisconsin Annual Conference. Records, 1858–1893. 2 vols. (Microfilm.)

Montpelier, Vt. Vermont State Library. U.S. Census (1860). Schedule 6 (Social Statistics).

———. U.S. Census (1870). Schedule 5 (Social Statistics).

St. Louis, Mo. Missouri Historical Society. U.S. Census (1870). Schedule 5 (Social Statistics).

St. Paul, Minn. Minnesota Historical Society. U.S. Census (1860). Schedule 6 (Social Statistics). (Microfilm.)

———. U.S. Census (1870). Schedule 5 (Social Statistics).

Trenton, N.J. Archives and History Bureau, State Library. U.S. Census (1860). Schedule 6 (Social Statistics).

———. U.S. Census (1870). Schedule 5 (Social Statistics).

Washington, D.C. National Archives. U.S. Census (1870). Schedule 1 (Population), Connecticut, Illinois, Indiana, Iowa, Maine, Maryland, Michigan, Minnesota, Missouri, New Hampshire, New Jersey, Ohio, Pennsylvania, Vermont. (Microfilm.)

———. U.S. Census (1880). Schedule 1 (Population), Connecticut, Illinois, Indiana, Iowa, Maine, Maryland, Michigan, Minnesota, Missouri, New Hampshire, New Jersey, Ohio, Pennsylvania, Vermont. (Microfilm.)

———. U.S. Census (1860). Schedule 6 (Social Statistics), Pennsylvania. (Microfilm).

———. U.S. Census (1890). Statistics of Religion. 2 vols.

B. Government Documents

Iowa. Executive Council. *The Census of Iowa, as Returned in the Year 1873*. Des Moines, 1874.

———. Executive Council. *Thirteenth State Census. The Census of Iowa, as Returned in the Year 1875*. Des Moines, 1875.

———. Secretary of State. *Census of Iowa for 1880*. Des Moines, 1883.

———. Secretary of State. *Census of Iowa for the Year 1885*. Des Moines, 1885.

———. Secretary of State. *Census of Iowa for the Year 1895*. Des Moines, 1896.

———. Secretary of State. *Iowa Official Register*. Des Moines, 1886–94.

———. State Agricultural Society. *Report of the Iowa State Agricultural Society*. Des Moines, 1873–1881.

Maine. Board of Agriculture. *Annual Report of the Secretary of the Maine Board of Agriculture*. Augusta, Maine, 1873–89.

Massachusetts. Board of Agriculture. *Annual Report of the Secretary of the Massachusetts Board of Agriculture*. Boston, 1873–92.

————. Bureau of Statistics of Labor. *The Census of Massachusetts: 1875*. 3 vols. Boston, 1876–77.

————. Bureau of Statistics of Labor. *The Census of Massachusetts: 1880*. Boston, 1883.

————. Bureau of Statistics of Labor. *The Census of Massachusetts: 1885*. 3 vols. in 4. Boston, 1887–88.

————. Bureau of Statistics of Labor. *Census of the Commonwealth of Massachusetts: 1895*. 7 vols. Boston, 1896–1900.

————. *Manual of the General Court*. Boston, 1869–93.

————. Secretary of the Commonwealth. *Abstract of the Census of Massachusetts, 1865*. Boston, 1867

Michigan. Secretary of State. *Michigan Manual*. Lansing, 1877–94.

Minnesota. Secretary of State. *Census of the State of Minnesota, by Counties, Towns, Cities, and Wards, as Taken by Authority of the State, May 1st, 1875*. St. Paul, 1875.

————. Secretary of State. *Census of the State of Minnesota: By Counties, Towns, Cities, and Wards. As Taken by Authority of the State, May 1, 1885*. St. Paul, 1885.

————. Secretary of State. *Fourth Decennial Census of the State of Minnesota by Counties, Towns, Cities, and Wards. As Taken by Authority of the State, June 1, 1895*. St. Paul, 1895.

————. Secretary of State. *The Legislative Manual of the State of Minnesota*. St. Paul, 1885–94.

————. State Agricultural Society. *Annual Report of the State Agricultural Society*. St. Paul, 1887–93.

Missouri. Board of Agriculture. *Annual Report of the State Board of Agriculture with an Abstract of the Proceedings of the County Agricultural Societies*. Jefferson City, 1871–93.

————. Secretary of State. *Official Manual of the State of Missouri*. Jefferson City, 1880–94.

New Hampshire. *Manual for the General Court*. Place varies, 1887–93.

New Jersey. Board of Agriculture. *Annual Report of the New Jersey State Board of Agriculture*. Trenton, 1874–93.

————. Department of State. *Abstract of the Census of the State of New Jersey, for the Year 1875*. Trenton, 1876.

————. Department of State. *Census of 1885, with a Recapitulation of the Census of 1875*. Trenton, 1886.

————. Department of State. *Census of 1895, with a Recapitulation of the Census of 1885*. Sommerville, 1896.

————. Department of State. *Census of 1905, with a Recapitulation of the Censuses of New Jersey since 1790*. Trenton, 1905.

New York. Secretary of State. *Census of the State of New York for 1875*. Albany, 1877.

————. Secretary of State. *Exhibits Showing the Enumeration of the State by Counties, Cities, Towns, and Election Districts for the Year 1892*. Albany, 1892.

Ohio. Secretary of State. *Ohio Statistics*. Springfield, Ohio, 1869–94.

Pennsylvania. Board of Agriculture. *Annual Report of the Pennsylvania Board of Agriculture*. Harrisburg, 1881–93.

————. *Smull's Legislative Handbook and Manual of the State of Pennsylvania.* Harrisburg, 1869–93.

————. State Agricultural Society. *Report of the Transactions of the Pennsylvania State Agricultural Society.* Harrisburg, 1875–91.

Rhode Island. Census Board. *Census of Rhode Island, 1895.* Providence, 1898.

————. Census Board. *Report upon the Census of Rhode Island, 1875.* Providence, 1877.

————. Census Board. *Rhode Island State Census, 1885.* Providence, 1887.

————. Office of Commissioner of Labor. *Church Statistics and Religious Preference, 1905.* Providence, 1907.

————. Secretary of State. *Report upon the Census of Rhode Island, 1865.* Providence, 1865.

————. Secretary of State. *Rhode Island Manual.* Providence, 1881–94.

U.S. Bureau of the Census. *1970 Census of Population: Number of Inhabitants (Final Report PC[1]-A1, United States Summary).* Washington, 1971.

————. Bureau of the Census. *Historical Statistics of the United States: Colonial Times to 1957.* Washington, 1960.

————. Bureau of the Census. *Religious Bodies: 1906.* Washington, 1910.

————. Census Office. *The Seventh Census of the United States: 1850.* Washington, 1853.

————. Census Office. *Statistical View of the United States . . . Being a Compendium of the Seventh Census.* Washington, 1854.

————. Census Office. Eighth Census, 1860. *Agriculture of the Untied States in 1860: Compiled from the Original Returns of the Eighth Census.* Washington, 1864.

————. Census Office. Eighth Census, 1860. *Manufactures of the United States in 1860: Compiled from the Original Returns of the Eighth Census.* Washington, 1865.

————. Census Office. Eighth Census, 1860. *Agriculture of the United States in 1860: Compiled from the Original Returns of the Eighth Census.* Washington, 1864.

————. Census Office. *Preliminary Report on the Eighth Census, 1860.* Washington, 1862.

————. Census Office. Eighth Census, 1860. *Statistics of the United States (Including Mortality, Property &c. in 1860): Compiled from the Original Returns and Being the Final Exhibit of the Eighth Census.* Washington, 1866.

————. Census Office. *[Census Reports] Compiled from the Original Returns of the Ninth Census (June 1, 1870).* 3 vols. Washington, 1872.

————. Census Office. *A Compendium of the Ninth Census (June 1, 1870).* Washington, 1872.

————. Census Office. *[Census Reports] Tenth Census: June 1, 1880.* 22 vols. Washington, 1883–88.

————. Census Office. *Compendium of the Tenth Census (June 1, 1880).* 2 vols. Washington, 1883.

————. Census Office. *[Census Reports] Eleventh Census: 1890.* 15 vols. in 25. Washington, 1892–97.

————. Census Office. *Compendium of the Eleventh Census: 1890.* 3 pts. Washington, 1892–97.

————. Census Office. *Census Reports . . . Twelfth Census of the United States, Taken in the Year 1900.* 10 vols. Washington, 1901–1902.

————. Census Office. *Abstract of the Twelfth Census of the United States, 1900.* Washington, 1902.

———. Commissioner of Agriculture. *Report of the Commissioner of Agriculture.* Washington, 1871–93.

———. Commissioner of Labor. *First Annual Report of the Commissioner of Labor, 1886: Industrial Depressions.* Washington, 1886.

———. Commissioner of Labor. *Third Annual Report of the Commissioner of Labor, 1887: Strikes and Lockouts.* Washington, 1888.

———. Commissioner of Labor. *Tenth Annual Report of the Commissioner of Labor, 1894: Strikes and Lockouts.* 2 vols. Washington, 1896.

Wisconsin. Department of State. *Tabular Statement of the Census Enumeration [of 1885].* Madison, 1886.

———. Department of State. *Tabular Statement of the Census Enumeration and the Agricultural, Mineral, and Manufacturing Interests of the State of Wisconsin [1895].* 2 vols. Madison, 1896.

———. Secretary of State. *Wisconsin Blue Book.* Place varies, 1863–93.

C. Newspapers

Boston Daily Advertiser. 1844–64.
Boston Evening Transcript. 1850–92.
Boston Globe. 1888–92.
Boston Herald. 1880–92.
Boston Post. 1848–92.
Chicago Times. 1880–92.
Chicago Tribune. 1880–92.
The Churchman (New York). 1876–92.
The Church Times (Delavan, Wis.). 1896.
Cleveland Leader. 1880–92.
DeKalb (Ill.) *Chronicle.* 1880–92.
Detroit Tribune. 1886–92.
Dubuque Herald. 1873–78.
Milwaukee Advance. 1890–92.
Milwaukee Journal. 1886–92.
Milwaukee Sentinel. 1886–92.

National Labor Tribune (Pittsburgh). 1874.
Ohio Practical Farmer (Cleveland). 1890–92.
Our Church Work (Madison, Wis.). 1890.
The Prairie Farmer (Chicago). 1873–92.
Printers' Labor Tribune (Pittsburgh). 1873.
Providence Journal. 1886–92.
Rural New-Yorker (New York City). 1875–77.
Sycamore (Ill.) *True Republican.* 1888–92.
The True Catholic (Baltimore). 1851–52.
The Western Rural (Chicago). 1883–85.
Wisconsin State Journal (Madison). 1886–92.

D. Autobiographies, Memoirs, Collections

Anderson, Rasmus B. *Life Story.* Madison, Wis., 1915.

Arden, G. Everett, ed. *The Journals of Eric Norelius: A Swedish Missionary on the American Frontier.* Philadelphia, 1967.

Bancroft, Frederic, ed. *Speeches, Correspondence, and Political Papers of Carl Schurz.* 6 vols. New York, 1913.

Beecher, Charles, ed. *Autobiography, Correspondence, Etc., of Lyman Beecher.* 2 vols. New York, 1865.

Blaine, James G. *Twenty Years of Congress.* 2 vols. Norwich, Ct., 1884.

Blegen, Theodore C., ed. *Land of Their Choice: The Immigrants Write Home.* Minneapolis, 1955.

Conway, Alan, ed. *The Welsh in America: Letters from the Immigrants*. Minneapolis, 1961.

Coyle, Leo P., ed. "Howells' Campaign Biography of Rutherford B. Hayes: A Series of Letters." *Ohio Historical Quarterly* 66 (October 1957): 391–406.

Creighton, Joseph H. *Life and Times of Joseph H. Creighton, A.M. of the Ohio Conference*. Cincinnati, 1899.

[Dow, Neal.] *The Reminiscences of Neal Dow, Recollections of Eighty Years*. Portland, Maine, 1898.

Foraker, Joseph Benson. *Notes of a Busy Life*. 2 vols. Cincinnati, 1916.

Furness, Marion Ramsey. "Childhood Recollections of Old St. Paul." *Minnesota History* 29 (June 1948): 114–29.

Hunt, Gaillard, comp. *Israel, Elihu, and Cadwallader Washburn: A Chapter in American Biography*. New York, 1925.

Larson, Laurence M. *The Log Book of a Young Immigrant*. Northfield, Minn., 1939.

Lucas, Henry S., ed. *Dutch Immigrant Memoirs and Related Writings*. 2 vols. Seattle, 1955.

Lusk, D. W. *Eighty Years of Illinois: Politics and Politicians*. 3d ed. Springfield, Ill., 1889.

McClure, A[lexander] K. *Old Time Notes of Pennsylvania*. 2 vols. Philadelphia, 1905.

McCormack, Thomas J., ed. *Memoirs of Gustave Koerner, 1809–1896*. 2 vols. Cedar Rapids, Iowa, 1909.

Meyer, Carl S., ed. *Letters of C. F. W. Walther: A Selection*. Philadelphia, 1969.

Morris, John G. *Life Reminiscences of an Old Lutheran Minister*. Philadelphia, [1896].

Mowry, Duane, ed. "Letters of Senator H. B. Payne of Ohio." *Ohio Archaeological and Historical Quarterly* 22 (October 1913): 543–48.

Nevins, Allan, ed. *Letters of Grover Cleveland, 1850–1908*. Boston, 1933.

Rønning, N[iles] N[ilsen]. *Fifty Years in America*. Minneapolis, 1938.

Sherman, John. *Recollections of Forty Years*. 2 vols. Chicago, 1895.

Thorndike, Rachael Sherman, ed. *The Sherman Letters: Correspondence between General and Senator Sherman from 1837 to 1891*. New York, 1894.

Tourscher, Francis E., ed. *Diary and Visitation Record of the Rt. Rev. Francis Patrick Kenrick, 1830–1851*. Lancaster, Pa., 1916.

Williams, Charles R., ed. *Diary and Letters of Rutherford Birchard Hayes*. 5 vols. Columbus, Ohio, 1922–26.

E. Denominational and Conference Documents

American Baptist Home Mission Society. *Annual Report of the American Baptist Home Mission Society*. New York, 1846–92.

American Congregational Union. *American Congregational Year-Book*. New York, 1852–58.

Baptist Church. *American Baptist Register*. Philadelphia, 1852–93.

———. *Proceedings of the Annual Baptist Autumnal Conference for the Discussion of Current Questions*. Boston and New York, 1883–93.

Congregational Home Missionary Society. *Annual Report of the American Home Missionary Society*. New York, 1856–91.

Connecticut. Congregational Church. *Minutes of the General Association of Connecticut*. New Haven and Hartford, 1857–90.

Cumberland Presbyterian Church. *Minutes of the General Assembly of the Cumberland Presbyterian Church.* Memphis and Nashville, 1868–92.

Evangelical Lutheran Synod of Missouri, Ohio, and Other States. *Statistches Jahrbuch der Deutscher Evang.-Lutherischen Synode von Missouri, Ohio und andern Staaten.* St. Louis, 1884–93.

The Freewill Baptist Register. Dover, N.H., 1880–91.

General Council of the Evangelical Lutheran Church. *Minutes of the Annual Convention of the General Council of the Evangelical Lutheran Church in America.* Pittsburgh and Toledo, 1867–92.

General Synod of the Evangelical Lutheran Church. *The Lutheran Almanac.* Philadelphia, 1870–92.

————. *Proceedings of the Annual Convention of the General Synod of the Evangelical Lutheran Church in the United States.* Gettysburg and Philadelphia, 1850–93.

Illinois. Congregational Church. *Minutes of the General Association of Illinois.* Ottawa and Quincy, Ill., 1859–92.

Iowa. Methodist Episcopal Church. *Minutes of the Annual Session of the Northwest Iowa Conference of the Methodist Episcopal Church.* Sioux City, Iowa, and Rockford, Ill., 1879–93.

————. Methodist Episcopal Church. *Minutes of the Iowa Annual Conference of the Methodist Episcopal Church.* Burlington and Muscatine, Iowa, 1880–93.

————. Methodist Episcopal Church. *Official Record. Minutes of the Iowa Conference of the Methodist Episcopal Church. Annual Sessions 1844, 1845, 1846, 1847, 1848, 1849, 1850, 1851, 1852, 1853.* Burlington, Iowa, 1916.

Maine. Baptist Church. *Minutes of the Annual Meeting of the Maine Baptist Convention.* Portland and Bangor, Maine, 1855–66.

————. Baptist Church. *Minutes of the Annual Meeting of the Maine Baptist Missionary Convention.* Bangor and Portland, Maine, 1867–92.

————. Baptist Church. *Proceedings of the Maine Free Baptist Association at Their Annual Meeting.* Augusta, Maine, 1891–92.

————. Congregational Church. *Minutes of the General Conference of the Congregational Churches in Maine.* Portland and Bangor, Maine, 1848–92.

————. Methodist Episcopal Church. *Minutes of the Annual Session of the East Maine Conference of the Methodist Episcopal Church.* Place varies, 1879–92.

————. Methodist Episcopal Church. *Minutes of the Maine Annual Conference of the Methodist Episcopal Church.* Place varies, 1847–92.

Maryland. Baptist Church. *Minutes of the Annual Meeting of the Maryland Baptist Union Association.* Baltimore, 1850–92.

————. Methodist Episcopal Church. *Minutes of the Session of Baltimore Annual Conference of the Methodist Episcopal Church.* Baltimore, 1859–92.

————. Presbyterian Church. *Minutes of the Synod of Baltimore.* Baltimore and Washington, D.C., 1863–92.

————. Protestant Episcopal Church. *Journal of the Annual Convention of the Protestant Episcopal Church in Maryland.* Baltimore, 1848–92.

Massachusetts. Baptist Church. *The Annual Anniversary of the Boston North Baptist Association.* Boston, 1865–85.

————. Congregational Church. *Annual Reports of the Hampden Conference of Congregational Churches.* Springfield, Mass., 1870–87.

————. Congregational Church. *Minutes of the Annual Meeting of the General Association of the Congregational Churches of Massachusetts.* Boston, 1854–92.

————. Protestant Episcopal Church. *Journal of the Proceedings of the Annual Convention of the Diocese of Massachusetts*. Boston, 1858–90.

Methodist Episcopal Church. *The Methodist Almanac*. New York, 1859–91.

————. *Minutes of the Session of the New England Annual Conference of the Methodist Episcopal Church*. Boston, 1855–93.

————. *Minutes of the Session of the New England Southern Annual Conference of the Methodist Episcopal Church*. Boston and Providence, 1881–93.

Michigan. Methodist Episcopal Church. *Minutes of the Michigan Annual Conference of the Methodist Episcopal Church*. Grand Rapids and Kalamazoo, Mich., 1889–92.

Minnesota. Evangelical Lutheran Synod. *Minutes. English Evangelical Lutheran Synod of the Northwest*. Milwaukee, 1891–92.

————. Methodist Episcopal Church. *Minutes of the Minnesota Annual Conference of the Methodist Episcopal Church*. St. Paul and Minneapolis, 1868–93.

Missouri. Methodist Episcopal Church. *Minutes of the Annual Session of the Central Missouri Conference of the Methodist Episcopal Church*. Sedalia and Marshall, Mo., 1888–92.

————. Methodist Episcopal Church. *Minutes of the Session of the Missouri Annual Conference of the Methodist Episcopal Church*. Hannibal, Kirksville, and St. Joseph, Mo., 1879–93.

National Council of Congregational Churches. *The Congregational Year-Book*. New York, 1879–90.

————. *Minutes of the National Council of the Congregational Churches of the United States of America. Annual Session*. Boston, 1871–93.

New Hampshire. Baptist Church. *Minutes of the New Hampshire Baptist Anniversaries*. Manchester and Concord, 1867–92.

————. Congregational Church. *Minutes of the Annual Meeting of the General Association of New Hampshire*. Portsmouth, Concord, and Bristol, N.H., 1845–92.

————. Freewill Baptist Church. *Minutes of the New Hampshire Yearly Meeting of Freewill Baptists*. Concord, 1869–92.

————. Methodist Episcopal Church. *Minutes of the Session of the New Hampshire Annual Conference of the Methodist Episcopal Church*. Place varies, 1850–93.

New Jersey. Methodist Episcopal Church. *Minutes of the New Jersey Annual Conference of the Methodist Episcopal Church*. Place varies, 1844–93.

New York. Baptist Church. *Minutes of the Anniversary of the Cortland Baptist Association*. Homer, N.Y., 1877–85.

————. Congregational Church. *Minutes of the General Association of New York*. Place varies, 1848–92.

————. Evangelical Lutheran Church (General Synod). *Minutes of the Annual Session of the Evangelical Lutheran Ministerium of the State of New York*. Albany, 1851–91.

————. Methodist Episcopal Church. *Minutes of the New York Conference of the Methodist Episcopal Church. Annual Session*. New York, 1880–92.

Ohio. Baptist Church. *Minutes of the Anniversary of the Ohio Baptist Convention*. Place varies, 1848–91.

————. Baptist Church. *Minutes of the Anniversary of the Wooster Baptist Association*. Wooster and New Waterford, Ohio, 1883–91.

————. Baptist Church. *Minutes of the Annual Session of the Ashtabula Baptist Association*. Cincinnati, 1870–86.

————. Baptist Church. *Minutes of the Annual Session of the Cleveland Baptist Association*. Cleveland, 1880–92.

————. Evangelical Lutheran Church (General Council). *Minutes of the Annual Convention of the Evangelical Lutheran District Synod of Ohio.* Lima and Zanesville, Ohio, 1890, 1893.

————. Evangelical Lutheran Church (General Synod). *Minutes of the Annual Convention of the Wittenberg Synod of the Evangelical Lutheran Church.* Philadelphia, 1880–92.

————. Evangelical Lutheran Church (Synodical Conference). *Biennial Convention of the Evangelical Lutheran Joint Synod of Ohio and Other States.* Columbus, 1890, 1892.

————. Methodist Episcopal Church. *Minutes of the Central Ohio Annual Conference of the Methodist Episcopal Church.* Cincinnati and Cleveland, 1860–92.

————. Methodist Episcopal Church. *Minutes of the Cincinnati Annual Conference of the Methodist Episcopal Church.* Cincinnati, 1852–90.

————. Methodist Episcopal Church. *Minutes of the Ohio Annual Conference of the Methodist Episcopal Church.* Cincinnati and Columbus, 1856–93.

————. Presbyterian Church. *Minutes of the Synod of Cleveland.* Cleveland, 1871–90.

————. Presbyterian Church. *Minutes of the Synod of Ohio.* Zanesville, Ohio, 1865, 1866.

————. United Brethren Church. *Minutes of the Sandusky Conference of the United Brethren in Christ.* Dayton, Ohio, 1866–93.

Pennsylvania. Baptist Church. *Minutes of the Anniversary of the Philadelphia Baptist Association.* Philadelphia, 1850–92.

————. Evangelical Lutheran Church (General Council). *Minutes of the Annual Convention of the German Evangelical Lutheran Ministerium of Pennsylvania and Adjacent States.* Place varies, 1866–92.

————. Evangelical Lutheran Church (General Synod). *Documentary History of the Evangelical Lutheran Ministerium of Pennsylvania and Adjacent States: Proceedings of the Annual Conventions from 1748 to 1821.* Philadelphia, 1898.

————. Evangelical Lutheran Church (General Synod). *History of the Evangelical Lutheran Synod of East Pennsylvania, with Brief Sketches of its Congregations. 1842–1892.* Philadelphia, [1893].

————. Evangelical Lutheran Church (General Synod). *Minutes of the Annual Convention of the German Evangelical Lutheran Ministerium of Pennsylvania and Adjacent States.* Place varies, 1848–64.

————. Evangelical Lutheran Church (General Synod). *Minutes of the Annual Meeting of the Evangelical Lutheran Synod of East Pennsylvania.* Place varies, 1848–68.

————. Methodist Episcopal Church. *Minutes of the Central Pennsylvania Annual Conference of the Methodist Episcopal Church.* Philadelphia and Harrisburg, 1870–92.

————. Presbyterian Church. *Minutes of the Annual Session of the Synod of Pennsylvania.* N.p., 1861–64.

————. Presbyterian Church. *Minutes of the Synod of Philadelphia.* N.p., 1843–46.

Presbyterian Church. *Annual Report of the Board of Domestic Missions of the General Assembly of the Presbyterian Church in the United States of America.* Philadelphia, 1850–70.

————. *Annual Report of the Board of Home Missions of the Presbyterian Church in the United States of America.* New York, 1875–92.

————. *Minutes of the General Assembly of the Presbyterian Church in the United States of America.* New York, 1866–92.

————. *Minutes of the General Assembly of the Presbyterian Church [New School] in the United States of America.* New York, 1851–64.

_____. *Minutes of the General Assembly of the Presbyterian Church [Old School] in the United States of America*. Philadelphia, 1848–64.
Protestant Episcopal Church. *The Church Almanac*. New York, 1851–90.
_____. *Journal of the Proceedings of the Bishops, Clergy and Laity of the Protestant Episcopal Church in the United States of America, Assembled in a General Convention*. Boston, 1862–92.
Rhode Island. Baptist Church. *Proceedings of the Anniversary of the Rhode Island Baptist State Convention*. Providence and Pawtucket, 1850–92.
_____. Congregational Church. *Minutes of the Rhode Island Congregational Conference*. Providence, 1872–93.
_____. Methodist Episcopal Church. *Minutes of the Providence Annual Conference of the Methodist Episcopal Church*. Providence and Boston, 1848–80.
Sadliers' Catholic Directory Almanac and Ordo. New York, 1870–92.
United Brethren Church. *Proceedings of the General Conference of the United Brethren Church in Christ*. Dayton, Ohio, 1866–93.
United Presbyterian Church. *Minutes of the General Assembly of the United Presbyterian Church of North America*. Place varies, 1863–92.
Vermont. Congregational Church. *Minutes of the General Convention of Congregational Ministers and Churches in Vermont*. Windsor and Montpelier, 1847–91.
_____. Congregational Church. *Supplement to the Minutes of the Ninety-First Annual Meeting of the General Convention of the Congregational Ministers and Churches of Vermont, 1886*. Montpelier, Vt., 1887.
_____. Methodist Episcopal Church. *Minutes of the Vermont Annual Conference of the Methodist Episcopal Church*. Montpelier, 1861–93.
Wisconsin. Baptist Church. *Minutes of the Anniversary of the Dodge Association of Baptist Churches*. Place varies, 1856–92.
_____. Baptist Church. *Minutes of the Annual Meeting of the Dane Association of Baptist Churches*. Place varies, 1850–92.
_____. Baptist Church. *Minutes of the Annual Session of the Wisconsin Baptist State Convention*. Place varies, 1850–92.
_____. Congregational Church. *Minutes of the Annual Meeting of the Congregational Convention of Wisconsin*. Madison, 1887–93.
_____. Methodist Episcopal Church. *Minutes of the Annual Session of the West Wisconsin Conference of the Methodist Episcopal Church*. Place varies, 1880–92.
_____. Methodist Episcopal Church. *Minutes of the Wisconsin Annual Conference of the Methodist Episcopal Church*. Place varies, 1850–93.
_____. Presbyterian Church. *Minutes of the Presbyterian and Congregational Convention of Wisconsin*. Milwaukee and Fond du Lac, 1854–72.
_____. Presbyterian Church. *Minutes of the Synod of Wisconsin*. Milwaukee and Madison, 1872–93.
_____. Protestant Episcopal Church. *Journal of the Annual Council of the Diocese of Milwaukee*. Milwaukee, 1853–92.

F. Other Printed Sources

Appletons' Annual Cyclopaedia and Register of Important Events of the Year. . . . New York, 1862–93.
Armitage, Rt. Rev. W. E., "The German Sunday." *Transactions of the Wisconsin Academy of Sciences, Arts, and Letters* 1 (1870–72): 62–71.

"The Army of Antichrist." *Lutheran Witness* 5 (June 1886): 21.
The Baltimore Sun Almanac. Baltimore, 1876–93.
Beecher, Lyman. *A Plea for the West*. Cincinnati, 1833.
Burnham, Walter Dean. *Presidential Ballots, 1836–1892*. Baltimore, 1955.
Cherrington, Ernest Hurst, ed. *Standard Encyclopedia of the Alcohol Problem*. 6 vols.
    Westerville, Ohio, 1925–30.
Chicago Daily News Almanac. Chicago, 1885–92.
Cooper, Oscar H. "Compulsory Laws and Their Enforcement." In *The Addresses and
    Journal of Proceedings of the National Education Association, Session for the Year
    1890*. Topeka, 1890.
*The Cyclopaedia of Temperance and Prohibition: A Reference Book of Facts, Statistics,
    and General Information on All Phases of the Drink Question, the Temperance
    Movement, and the Prohibition Agitation*. New York, 1891.
Drury, A. W. "Romanism in the United States: The Proper Attitude toward It." *Quar-
    terly Review of the United Brethren in Christ* 5 (January 1894): 1–23.
Edwards, Richard. "How Much Culture Shall Be Imparted in Our Free Schools?" In
    *The Addresses and Journal of Proceedings of the National Education Association,
    Session for the Year, 1873*. Peoria, Ill., 1873.
Fairall, Herbert S., ed. *Fairall's Manual of Iowa Politics, 1883*. Iowa City, 1883.
Feuer, Lewis S., ed. *Marx and Engels: Basic Writings on Politics and Philosophy*. Gar-
    den City, N.Y., 1959.
Finney, Charles Grandison. *Lectures on Revivals of Religion*. Edited by William G.
    McLoughlin. 1835. Reprint. Cambridge, 1960.
———. *Sermons on Important Subjects*. 3d ed. New York, 1836.
Henke, Warren A., comp. *Prairie Politics: Parties and Platforms in North Dakota,
    1889–1914*. N.p., 1974.
Illinois State Grange. Patrons of Husbandry. *Journal of Proceedings of the Annual Ses-
    sion of the Illinois State Grange, Patrons of Husbandry*. Peoria, Ill., 1886–93.
Indiana State Grange. Patrons of Husbandry. *Proceedings of the Annual Session of the
    Indiana State Grange, Patrons of Husbandry*. Indianapolis and South Bend,
    1880–93.
Ireland, Archbishop John. "State Schools and Parish Schools: Is Union between Them
    Impossible?" In *The Addresses and Journal of Proceedings of the National Educa-
    tion Association, Session for the Year 1890*. Topeka, 1890.
Joint Debates, between Hon. George Hoadly and Hon. Jos. B. Foraker, 1885. Colum-
    bus, 1887.
Kuznets, Simon, and Thomas, Dorothy Swaine, gen. eds. *Population Redistribution
    and Economic Growth, United States, 1870–1950*. 3 vols. Philadelphia, 1957–
    1964. Vol. 3, *Demographic Analyses and Interpretations* by Hope T. Eldridge and
    Dorothy Swaine Thomas, 1964.
Laughlin, Ada M. "The Moral Value of Art Education." In *The Addresses and Journal
    of Proceedings of the National Education Association, Session for the Year 1890*.
    Topeka, 1890.
Maine Register. Augusta and Portland, 1856–94.
Manual of the Legislature of New Jersey. Trenton, 1890–93.
National Grange. Patrons of Husbandry. *Proceedings of the Annual Session of the Na-
    tional Grange of the Patrons of Husbandry*. Place varies, 1873–92.
National Temperance Society. *Proceedings of the National Temperance Convention*.
    New York, 1865–92.
The New Hampshire Annual Register. Concord, N.H., 1849–90.

No Party Now But All for Our Country. New York, 1863.

Nolan, Hugh J., ed. *Pastoral Letters of the American Hierarchy, 1792–1970*. Huntington, Ind., 1971.

Official Proceedings of the Republican National Convention, 1888. Minneapolis, 1903.

Ohio Platforms of the Republican and Democratic Parties from 1855 to 1881, Inclusive. N.p., n.d.

"The Papal Antichrist." *Columbus Theological Magazine* 12 (August 1892): 239–44.

Parker, Nathan H. *The Missouri Hand-Book*. St. Louis, 1865.

The Political Prohibitionist. New York, 1887–89.

Pollack, Norman, ed. *The Populist Mind*. Indianapolis, 1967.

Pope or President? [New York,] 1880.

Porter, Kirk H., and Johnson, Donald Bruce, comps. *National Party Platforms, 1840–1968*. 4th ed. Urbana, Ill., 1972.

Proceedings of the [1880] Republican National Convention. Chicago, 1881.

"The Religion of Secret Societies." *Columbus Theological Magazine* 10 (April 1890): 90–102.

Robertson, George. *The American Party: Its Principles, Its Objects, and Its Hopes*. Frankfort, Ky., 1855.

Strong, Josiah. *Our Country*. Rev. ed. 1891. Reprint. Cambridge, 1963.

Swinton, William. *Outline of the World's History: Ancient, Mediaeval, and Modern*. New York, 1874.

Todd, John . *The Moral Influence, Dangers, and Duties, Connected with Great Cities*. Northampton, Mass., 1841.

The Tribune [Whig] Almanac and Political Register. New York, 1855–94.

Vermont Register. Montpelier or Rutland, 1848–90.

Voters and Tax-Payers of DeKalb County, Illinois. Chicago, 1876.

Weaver, James B. *A Call to Action: An Interpretation of the Great Uprising, Its Sources and Causes*. Des Moines, Iowa, 1892.

The Whig Charge of Intolerance against the New Hampshire Democracy and Gen. Franklin Pierce. Boston, 1852.

Wisconsin State Grange. Patrons of Husbandry. *Proceedings of the Annual Session of the Wisconsin State Grange, Patrons of Husbandry*. Place varies, 1890–92.

G. Books, Essays, and Articles

Abramson, Harold J. *Ethnic Diversity in Catholic America*. New York, 1973.

———. "Inter-Ethnic Marriage among Catholic Americans and Changes in Religious Behavior." *Sociological Analysis* 32 (Spring 1971): 31–44.

Abramson, Paul R. *Generational Change in American Politics*. Lexington, Mass., 1975.

Alexander, DeAlva Stanwood. *A Political History of the State of New York*. 4 vols. New York, 1906–13.

Alexander, Thomas B.; Elmore, Peggy Duckworth; Lawrey, Frank M.; and Skinner, May Jane Pickens. "The Basis for Alabama's Ante-Bellum Two Party System." *Alabama Review* 19 (October 1966): 243–76.

Alker, Hayward R., Jr. *Mathematics and Politics*. New York, 1965.

Allen, Leonard L. *History of the New York State Grange*. Watertown, N.Y., 1934.

Almond, Gabriel A., and Powell, G. Bingham, Jr. *Comparative Politics: A Developmental Approach*. Boston, 1966.

Ander, Fritiof. "The Immigrant Church and the Patrons of Husbandry." *Agricultural History* 8 (October 1934): 155–68.

Andersen, Arlow W. *The Salt of the Earth: A History of Norwegian-Danish Methodism in America*. Nashville, 1962.

Anderson, H. E. "Regression, Discriminant Analysis, and a Standard Notation for Basic Statistics." In *Handbook of Multivariate Experimental Psychology*, edited by R. B. Cattell. Skokie, Ill., 1966.

Anderson, Lee F.; Watts, Meredith W., Jr.; and Wilcox, Allen R. *Legislative Roll-Call Analysis*. Evanston, Ill., 1966.

Andrews, Matthew Page. *Tercentenary History of Maryland*. 4 vols. Chicago, 1925.

Apter, David E. *The Politics of Modernization*. Chicago, 1965.

Argersinger, Peter H. "Pentecostal Politics in Kansas: Religion, the Farmers' Alliance, and the Gospel of Populism." *Kansas Quarterly* 1 (Fall 1969): 24–35.

————. *Populism and Politics: William Alfred Peffer and the People's Party*. Lexington, Ky., 1974.

Baird, Robert. *Religion in America*. New York, 1856.

Baker, Jean H. *The Politics of Continuity: Maryland Political Parties from 1858 to 1870*. Baltimore, 1973.

Barney, William. *The Road to Secession: A New Perspective on the Old South*. New York, 1972.

Barr, Alwyn. *Reconstruction to Reform: Texas Politics, 1876–1906*. Austin, 1971.

Barry, Colman J. *The Catholic Church and German Americans*. Milwaukee, 1953.

Barton, Josef J. *Peasants and Strangers: Italians, Rumanians, and Slovaks in an American City, 1890–1950*. Cambridge, Mass., 1975.

Bass, Herbert J. *"I Am a Democrat": The Political Career of David Bennett Hill*. Syracuse, N.Y., 1961.

Bayley, J[ames] R[oosevelt]. *A Brief Sketch of the History of the Catholic Church on the Island of New York*. New York, 1853.

Beard, Charles A. *The American Party Battle*. New York, 1928.

————, and Beard, Mary R. *The Rise of American Civilization*. 2 vols. New York, 1927.

Beck, Walter H. *Lutheran Elementary Schools in the United States*. 2d ed. St. Louis, 1965.

Beets, Henry. *The Christian Reformed Church*. Grand Rapids, Mich., 1946.

Beijbom, Ulf. *Swedes in Chicago: A Demographic and Social Study of the 1846–1880 Immigration*. Uppsala, Sweden, 1971.

Benson, Lee. *The Concept of Jacksonian Democracy: New York as a Test Case*. New York, 1963.

————. "Group Cohesion and Social and Ideological Conflict: A Critique of Some Marxian and Tocquevillian Theories." *American Behavioral Scientist* 16 (May–June 1973): 741–67.

————. *Merchants, Farmers, and Railroads: Railroad Regulation and New York Politics, 1850–1887*. Cambridge, Mass., 1955.

————. "Political Power and Political Elites." In *American Political Behavior: Historical Essays and Readings*, edited by Lee Benson, Allan G. Bogue, J. Rogers Hollingsworth, Thomas J. Pressly, and Joel H. Silbey. New York, 1974.

————. "Research Problems in American Political Historiography." In *Common Frontiers of the Social Sciences*, edited by Mirra Komarovsky. Glencoe, Ill., 1957.

————. *Turner and Beard: American Historical Writing Reconsidered*. Glencoe, Ill., 1960.

Berger, Peter L. *Invitation to Sociology*. Garden City, N.Y.: Anchor Books, 1963.

Berthoff, Rowland T. *British Immigrants in Industrial America, 1790–1950*. Cambridge, Mass., 1953.

Billington, Ray Allen. *The Protestant Crusade, 1800–1860*. Chicago, 1964.

Björnson, Val. *The History of Minnesota*. 3 vols. West Palm Beach, Fla., 1969.

Blaikie, Alexander. *A History of Presbyterianism in New England*. Boston, 1881.

Blalock, Hubert M., Jr. *Causal Inferences in Nonexperimental Research*. Chapel Hill, N.C., 1961.

Bland, Joan. *The Hibernian Crusade: The Story of the Catholic Total Abstinence Union of America*. Washington, 1951.

Blau, Joseph L. "The Christian Party in Politics," *Review of Religion* 11 (November 1946): 18–35.

Blodgett, Geoffrey. *The Gentle Reformers: Massachusetts Democrats in the Cleveland Era*. Cambridge, Mass., 1966.

Blum, John M.; Catton, Bruce; Morgan, Edmund S.; Schlesinger, Arthur M., Jr.; Stampp, Kenneth M.; and Woodward, C. Vann. *The National Experience: A History of the United States*. 2d ed. New York, 1968.

Bowers, Douglas. "Ideology and Political Parties in Maryland, 1851–1856." *Maryland Historical Magazine* 64 (Fall 1969): 197–217.

Brady, David W., and Althoff, Philip. "Party Voting in the U.S. House of Representatives, 1890–1910: Elements of a Responsible Party System." *Journal of Politics* 36 (1974): 753–75.

Brand, Edward P. *Illinois Baptists: A History*. Bloomington, Ind., 1930.

Broehl, Wayne G., Jr. *The Molly Maguires*. Cambridge, Mass., 1964.

Brubacher, John S., ed. *The Public School and Spiritual Values*. Seventh Yearbook of the John Dewey Society. New York, 1944.

Bruce, Dickson D., Jr. *And They All Sang Hallelujah: Plain-Folk Camp-Meeting Religion, 1800–1845*. Knoxville, 1974.

Bruce, Robert V. *1877: Year of Violence*. Indianapolis, 1959.

Bruncken, Ernest. "How Germans Became Americans." *Proceedings of the State Historical Society of Wisconsin* (1897): 190–211.

Bryce, James. *The American Commonwealth*. 3d ed. 1894. 2 vols. Reprint. New York, 1960.

Bryden, James A. "The Scots in Wisconsin." *Proceedings of the State Historical Society of Wisconsin* (1902): 153–58.

Buck, Paul. *Road to Reunion*. Boston, 1937.

Buck, Solon Justus. *The Granger Movement: A Study of Agricultural Organization and Its Political, Economic, and Social Manifestations, 1870–1880*. 1913. Reprint. Lincoln, Neb.: Bison Books, n.d.

Bullough, William A. *Cities and Schools in the Gilded Age: The Evolution of an Urban Institution*. Port Washington, N.Y., 1974.

Burgess, Ellis B. *History of the Pittsburgh Synod of the General Synod of the Evangelical Lutheran Church*. Philadelphia, 1904.

Burnham, Walter Dean. "The Changing Shape of the American Political Universe." *American Political Science Review* 59 (March 1965): 7–28.

———. *Critical Elections and the Mainsprings of American Politics*. New York, 1970.

———. "Insulation and Responsiveness in Congressional Elections." *Political Science Quarterly* 90 (Fall 1975): 411–36.

———. "Party Systems and the Political Process." In *The American Party Systems:*

Stages of Political Development, edited by William Nisbet Chambers and Walter Dean Burnham. New York, 1967.

———. "Political Immunization and Political Confessionalism: The United States and Weimar Germany." *Journal of Interdisciplinary History* 3 (Summer 1972): 1–30.

———. "Rejoinder to 'Comments' by Philip Converse and Jerrold Rusk." *American Political Science Review* 68 (September 1974): 1050–57.

———. *Sources of Historical Election Data: A Preliminary Bibliography*. East Lansing, Mich., 1963.

———. "Theory and Voting Research: Some Reflections on Converse's 'Change in the American Electorate.'" *American Political Science Review* 68 (September 1974): 1002–1023.

———. "The United States: The Politics of Heterogeneity." In *Electoral Behavior: A Comparative Handbook*, edited by Richard Rose. New York, 1974.

———, and Sprague, John. "Additive and Multiplicative Models of the Voting Universe: The Case of Pennsylvania: 1960–1968." *American Political Science Review* 64 (June 1970): 471–90.

Burns, Arthur F., and Mitchell, Wesley C. *Measuring Business Cycles*. New York, 1946.

Burns, James A. *The Catholic School System in the United States: Its Principles, Origin, and Establishment*. New York, 1908.

———. *The Growth and Development of the Catholic School System in the United States*. New York, 1912.

Busbey, L. White. *Uncle Joe Cannon; the Story of a Pioneer American as Told to L. W. Busbey, for 20 Years His Private Secretary*. New York, 1927.

Callcott, Margaret Law. *The Negro in Maryland Politics, 1870–1912*. Baltimore, 1969.

Campbell, Angus; Converse, Philip E.; Miller, Warren E.; and Stokes, Donald E. *The American Voter*. New York, 1960.

Campbell, Ballard C., Jr. "Ethnicity and the 1893 Wisconsin Assembly." *Journal of American History* 62 (June 1975): 74–94.

Carroll, H[enry] K. *The Religious Forces of the United States*. The American Church History Series. New York, 1893.

Carroll, Leo E. "Irish and Italians in Providence, Rhode Island, 1880–1960." *Rhode Island History* 28 (Summer 1969): 67–74.

Chrislock, Carl H. "The Alliance Party and the Minnesota Legislature of 1891." *Minnesota History* 36 (September 1957): 297–312.

———. "Sidney M. Owen: An Editor in Politics." *Minnesota History* 35 (December 1958): 109–26.

Christensen, Thomas P. "Danish Settlements in Minnesota." *Minnesota History* (December 1927): 363–85.

Church, Charles A. *History of the Republican Party in Illinois, 1854–1912*. Rockford, Ill., 1912.

Clancy, Herbert J. *The Presidential Election of 1880*. Chicago, 1958.

Clark, Charles B. "Politics in Maryland during the Civil War." *Maryland Historical Magazine* 37 (December 1942): 378–99.

Clark, Dan Elbert. "The History of Liquor Legislation in Iowa, 1846–1908." *Iowa Journal of History* 6 (1908): 55–87, 339–74, 503–608.

Clinch, Thomas A. *Urban Populism and Free Silver in Montana*. N.p., 1970.

Clonts, Forrest W. "The Political Campaign of 1875 in Ohio." *Ohio Archaeological and Historical Quarterly* 31 (January 1922): 38–97.

Clubb, Jerome M., and Traugott, Santa. "Partisan Cleavage and Cohesion in the House of Representatives, 1861–1974." *Journal of Interdisciplinary History* 8 (Winter 1977): 375–402.

Cochran, Thomas C. "The 'Presidential Synthesis' in American History." In *Sociology and History: Methods*, edited by Seymour Martin Lipset and Richard Hofstadter. New York, 1968.

Cole, Arthur Charles. *The Era of the Civil War in Illinois*. Chicago, 1922.

Cole, Donald B. *Immigrant City: Lawrence, Massachusetts, 1845–1921*. Chapel Hill, N.C., 1963.

Colvin, D. Leigh. *Prohibition in the United States: A History of the Prohibition Party and of the Prohibition Movement*. New York, 1926.

Connelly, James F. *The Visit of Archbishop Gaetano Bedini to the United States of America*. Rome, 1960.

Converse, Philip E. "The Concept of a Normal Vote." In *Elections and the Political Order*, edited by Angus Campbell, Philip E. Converse, Warren E. Miller, and Donald E. Stokes. New York, 1967.

————. "The Nature of Belief Systems in Mass Publics." In *Ideology and Discontent*, edited by David E. Apter. New York, 1964.

————. "Religion and Politics: The 1960 Election." In *Elections and the Political Order*, edited by Angus Campbell, Philip E. Converse, Warren E. Miller, and Donald E. Stokes. New York, 1967.

————. "Survey Research and the Decoding of Patterns in Ecological Data." In *Quantitative Ecological Analysis in the Social Sciences*, edited by Mattei Dogan and Stein Rokkan. Cambridge, Mass., 1969.

Conway, Katherine E., and Cameron, Mabel Ward. *Charles Francis Donnelly: A Memoir*. New York, 1909.

Cook, Adrian. *The Armies of the Streets: The New York City Draft Riots of 1863*. [Lexington, Ky.,] 1974.

Cornwell, Elmer E. "Party Absorption of Ethnic Groups: The Case of Providence, Rhode Island." *Social Forces* 38 (March 1960): 205–10.

Cox, John H., and Cox, LaWanda. "Negro Suffrage and Republican Politics: The Problem of Motivation in Reconstruction Historiography." *Journal of Southern History* 33 (August 1967): 303–30.

Crocker, Henry. *History of the Baptists in Vermont*. Bellows Falls, Vt., 1913.

Crockett, Walter Hill. *Vermont: The Green Mountain State*. 5 vols. New York, 1921.

Cross, Jasper W. "The Civil War Comes to 'Egypt'" *Journal of the Illinois State Historical Society* 44 (Summer 1951): 160–69.

Cross, Whitney R. *The Burned-Over District: The Social and Intellectual History of Enthusiastic Religion in Western New York, 1800–1850*. New York, 1965.

Cullen, Thomas F. *The Catholic Church in Rhode Island*. [North Providence, R.I.,] 1936.

Cyert, Richard M., and March, James G. "A Behavioral Theory of Organizational Objectives." In *Modern Organizational Theory*, edited by Mason Hare. New York, 1959.

Czudnowski, Moshe M. "A Salience Dimension of Politics for the Study of Political Culture." *American Political Science Review* 62 (September 1968): 878–88.

Davidson, James D. "Religious Belief as a Dependent Variable." *Sociological Analysis* 33 (Summer 1972): 81–94.

Davis, Lawrence B. *Immigrants, Baptists, and the Protestant Mind in America*. Urbana, Ill., 1973.

Dawley, Alan, and Faler, Paul. "Working-Class Culture and Politics in the Industrial Revolution: Sources of Loyalism and Rebellion." *Journal of Social History* 9 (June 1976): 466–80.

Demerath, N. J., III. *Social Class in American Protestantism.* Chicago, 1965.

Denison, John D. *Iowa Democracy: A History of Politics and Personalities of the Democratic Party, 1846–1938.* 4 vols. N.p., 1939.

De Santis, Vincent P. *Republicans Face the Southern Question: The New Departure Years, 1877–1897.* Baltimore, 1959.

Desmond, Humphrey J. *The Know-Nothing Party.* Washington, D.C., 1905.

Destler, Chester McArthur. *American Radicalism, 1865–1901.* Chicago, 1966.

────. "Consummation of a Labor-Populist Alliance in Illinois, 1894." *Mississippi Valley Historical Review* 27 (March 1941): 589–602.

Devine, Donald J. *The Political Culture of the United States: The Influence of Member Values on Regime Maintenance.* Boston, 1972.

Dillon, Merton L. *The Abolitionists: The Growth of a Dissenting Minority.* DeKalb, Ill., 1974.

Dobbert, G. A. "German-Americans Between New and Old Fatherland, 1870–1914." *American Quarterly* 19 (Winter 1967): 663–80.

Dobson, John M. *Politics in the Gilded Age: A New Perspective on Reform.* New York, 1972.

Doherty, Robert W. *The Hicksite Separation: A Sociological Analysis of Religious Schism in Early Nineteenth Century America.* New Brunswick, N.J., 1967.

Dolan, Jay. *The Immigrant Church: New York's Irish and German Catholics, 1815–1865.* Baltimore, 1975.

────. "Immigrants in the City: New York's Irish and German Catholics." *Church History* 41 (September 1972): 354–68.

Donald, David. "The Republican Party, 1864–1876." In *History of U.S. Political Parties*, edited by Arthur M. Schlesinger, Jr., vol. 2, pp. 1281–1407. 4 vols. New York, 1973.

Donohue, Thomas. *History of the Diocese of Buffalo.* Buffalo, 1929.

Douglass, Paul F. *The Story of German Methodism: Biography of an Immigrant Soul.* New York, 1939.

Downs, Lynwood G. "The Soldier Vote and Minnesota Politics, 1862–65." *Minnesota History* 26 (September 1945): 187–210.

Ducharme, Jacques. *The Shadows of the Trees: The Story of French-Canadians in New England.* New York, 1943.

Dunaway, Wayland F. *A History of Pennsylvania.* 2d ed. New York, 1948.

Dunbar, Willis F., and Shade, William G. "The Black Man Gains the Vote: The Centennial of 'Impartial Suffrage' in Michigan." *Michigan History* 56 (Spring 1972): 42–57.

Dykstra, Robert R., and Hahn, Harlan. "Northern Voters and Negro Suffrage: The Case of Iowa, 1868." *Public Opinion Quarterly* 32 (Summer 1968): 205–12.

Eaton, The Rev. W. H. *Historical Sketch of the Massachusetts Baptist Missionary Society and Convention, 1802–1902.* Boston, [1903].

Ebner, Michael H. "Socialism and Progressive Political Reform: The 1911 Change-of-Government in Passaic." In *Socialism and the Cities*, edited by Bruce M. Stave. Port Washington, N.Y., 1975.

Eckstein, Harry. "A Perspective on Comparative Politics, Past and Present." In *Comparative Politics: A Reader*, edited by Harry Eckstein and David E. Apter. New York, 1963.

Edelman, Murray. *The Symbolic Uses of Politics.* Urbana, Ill., 1964.
Elazar, Daniel J. *American Federalism: A View from the States.* 2d ed. New York, 1972.
———. *Cities of the Prairie: The Metropolitan Frontier and American Politics.* New York, 1970.
Eldersveld, Samuel J. *Political Parties: A Behavioral Analysis.* Chicago, 1964.
Ellis, James Fernando. *The Influence of Environment on the Settlement of Missouri.* St. Louis, 1929.
Ellis, John Tracy. *The Life of James Cardinal Gibbons.* 2 vols. Milwaukee, 1952.
Engberg, Emmer, ed. *Centennial Essays: Augustana Lutheran Church, 1860–1960.* Rock Island, Ill., 1960.
Engberg, George B. "The Knights of Labor in Minnesota." *Minnesota History* 22 (December 1941): 367–90.
———. "The Rise of Organized Labor in Minnesota." *Minnesota History* 21 (December 1940): 372–94.
Esslinger, Dean R. *Immigrants and the City: Ethnicity and Mobility in a Nineteenth-Century Midwestern Community.* Port Washington, N.Y., 1975.
Evers, Joseph Calvin. *The History of the Southern Illinois Conference of the Methodist Church.* Nashville, 1964.
Falge, Louis, ed. *History of Manitowoc County, Wisconsin.* 2 vols. Chicago, 1912.
Farish, Hunter Dickinson. *The Circuit Rider Dismounts: A Social History of Southern Methodism, 1865–1900.* Richmond, Va., 1938.
Feder, Leah Hannah. *Unemployment Relief in Periods of Depression.* New York, 1936.
Fehlandt, August F. *A Century of Drink Reform in the United States.* Cincinnati, 1904.
Fels, Rendig. "American Business Cycles, 1865–79." *American Economic Review* 41 (June 1951): 325–49.
Fenton, John H. *Midwest Politics.* New York, 1966.
———. *Politics in the Border States.* New Orleans, 1957.
Fiedler, George. *Mineral Point: A History.* Berwyn, Ill., 1962.
Field, Edward, ed. *State of Rhode Island and Providence Plantation at the End of the Century: A History.* 3 vols. Boston, 1902.
Field, Phyllis F. "Republicans and Black Suffrage in New York State: The Grass Roots Response." *Civil War History* 22 (June 1975): 136–47.
Fine, Nathan. *Labor and Farmer Parties in the United States, 1828–1928.* New York, 1928.
Fisher, James. "Michigan's Cornish People." *Michigan History* 27 (July–September 1945): 377–85.
Fishman, Joshua. "Childhood Indoctrination for Minority-Group Membership." *Daedalus* 90 (Spring 1961): 329–49.
———. *Language Loyalty in the United States: The Maintenance and Perpetuation of Non-English Mother Tongues by American Ethnic and Religious Groups.* The Hague, 1966.
Fitzgibbon, John. "King Alcohol: His Rise, Reign and Fall in Michigan." *Michigan History* 2 (October 1918): 737–80.
Foner, Eric. "The Causes of the Civil War: Recent Interpretations and New Directions." *Civil War History* 20 (September 1974): 197–214.
———. *Free Soil, Free Labor, Free Men.* New York, 1970.
Ford, Henry Jones. *The Rise and Growth of American Politics: A Sketch of Constitutional Development.* New York, 1898.
Form, William H. *Blue-Collar Stratification: Autoworkers in Four Countries.* Princeton, N.J., 1970.

Formisano, Ronald P. *The Birth of Mass Political Parties: Michigan, 1827–1861*. Princeton, N.J., 1971.

———. "Deferential-Participant Politics: The Early Republic's Political Culture, 1789–1840." *American Political Science Review* 68 (June 1974): 473–87.

———. "The Edge of Caste: Colored Suffrage in Michigan, 1827–1861." *Michigan History* 56 (Spring 1972): 19–41.

———. "Political Character, Antipartyism, and the Second Party System." *American Quarterly* 21 (Winter 1969): 683–709.

———. "To the Editor." *Civil War History* 22 (June 1975): 185–89.

———. "Toward a Reorientation of Jacksonian Politics: A Review of the Literature, 1959–1975." *Journal of American History* 63 (June 1976): 42–65.

———, and Shade, William G. "The Concept of Agrarian Radicalism." *Mid-America* 52 (January 1970): 3–30.

Forster, Walter O. *Zion on the Mississippi: The Settlement of the Saxon Lutherans in Missouri, 1839–1841*. St. Louis, 1953.

Foster, Charles I. *An Errand of Mercy: The Evangelical United Front, 1790–1837*. Chapel Hill, N.C., 1960.

Garraty, John A. *The New Commonwealth, 1877–1890*. New York, 1968.

Gavett, Thomas W. *Development of the Labor Movement in Milwaukee*. Madison, Wis., 1965.

Geertz, Clifford. "Religion as a Cultural System." In *Anthropological Approaches to the Study of Religion*, edited by Michael Banton. London, 1966.

Gerberding, G. H. *Life and Letters of W. A. Passavant, D.D.* Greenville, Pa., 1906.

Gibbs, Joseph C. *History of the Catholic Total Abstinence Union of America*. Philadelphia, 1907.

Gillette, William. *The Right to Vote: Politics and the Passage of the Fifteenth Amendment*. Baltimore, 1965.

Ginsberg, Benjamin. "Critical Elections and the Substance of Party Conflict: 1844–1968." *Midwest Journal of Political Science* 16 (November 1972): 603–25.

Gleason, Philip. *The Conservative Reformers: German-American Catholics and the Social Order*. Notre Dame, Ind., 1968.

Glock, Charles Y., and Stark, Rodney. *Religion and Society in Tension*. Chicago, 1965.

Good, James I. *History of the Reformed Church in the United States*. Reading, Pa., 1899.

Goodman, Leo A. "Some Alternatives to Ecological Correlation." *American Journal of Sociology* 65 (May 1959): 610–25.

Goodwyn, Lawrence. *Democratic Promise: The Populist Movement in America*. New York, 1976.

Gordon, Milton M. *Assimilation in American Life: The Role of Race, Religion, and National Origins*. New York, 1964.

Gould, Lewis L. *Wyoming: A Political History, 1868–1896*. New Haven, Ct., 1968.

Greeley, Andrew M. *The Denominational Society: A Sociological Approach to Religion in America*. Glenview, Ill., 1972.

———. *Ethnicity in the United States: A Preliminary Reconnaissance*. New York, 1974.

Green, James R. "Behavioralism and Class Analysis: A Review Essay on Methodology and Ideology." *Labor History* 13 (Winter 1972): 89–106.

———. "The 'Salesmen-Soldiers' of the 'Appeal' Army: A Profile of Rank-and-File Socialist Agitators." In *Socialism and the Cities*, edited by Bruce M. Stave. Port Washington, N. Y., 1975.

Greene, Victor R. "For God and Country: The Origins of Slavic Catholic Self-Consciousness in America." *Church History* 35 (December 1966): 446–60.

Griffin, Clifford S. *Their Brothers' Keepers: Moral Stewardship in the United States, 1800–1865*. New Brunswick, N.J., 1960.

Gue, Benjamin F. *History of Iowa from the Earliest Times to the Beginning of the Twentieth Century*. 4 vols. New York, 1903.

Gutman, Herbert G. "Work, Culture, and Society in Industrial America, 1815–1919." *American Historical Review* 78 (June 1973): 531–88.

Hadden, Jeffrey K. *The Gathering Storm in the Churches*. Garden City, N.Y., 1969.

Haddock, Frank. *The Life of Rev. George C. Haddock*. New York, 1887.

Hammill, Sr. M. Martina. *The Expansion of the Catholic Church in Pennsylvania*. [Pittsburgh,] 1960.

Hammond, John L. "Revival Religion and Anti-Slavery Politics." *American Sociological Review* 39 (April 1974): 175–86.

Hanushek, Eric A.; Jackson, John E.; and Kain, John F. "Model Specification, Use of Aggregate Data, and the Ecological Correlation Fallacy." *Political Methodology* 1 (Winter 1974): 87–107.

Harrell, David Edwin, Jr. "The Sectional Origins of the Churches of Christ." *Journal of Southern History* 30 (Fall 1964): 261–77.

Hart, Albert Bushnell, ed. *Commonwealth History of Massachusetts*. 6 vols. 1930. Reprint. New York, 1966.

Hartmann, Edward George. *Americans from Wales*. Boston, 1967.

Haugen, Einar. "A Norwegian-American Pioneer Ballad." *Norwegian-American Studies and Records* 15 (1949): 1–19.

Haynes, Fred Emory. *James Baird Weaver*. Iowa City, Iowa, 1919.

———. *Social Politics in the United States*. Boston and New York, 1924.

———. *Third Party Movements since the Civil War with Special Reference to Iowa: A Study in Social Politics*. 1916. Reprint. New York, 1966.

Hays, Samuel P. "New Possibilities for American Political History: The Social Analysis of Political Life." In *Sociology and History: Methods*, edited by Seymour Martin Lipset and Richard Hofstadter. New York, 1968.

———. "Political Parties and the Community-Society Continuum." In *The American Party Systems: Stages of Political Development*, edited by William Nisbet Chambers and Walter Dean Burnham. New York, 1967.

———. "The Social Analysis of American Political History, 1880–1920." *Political Science Quarterly* 80 (September 1965): 373–94.

Hebert, Richard A. *Modern Maine: Its Historic Background, People, and Resources*. 4 vols. New York, 1951.

Helfman, Harold M. "The Cincinnati 'Bible War,' 1869–70." *Ohio State Archaeological and Historical Quarterly* 60 (October 1951): 369–86.

Heming, Harry H. *The Catholic Church in Wisconsin*. Milwaukee, 1896.

Hicks, John D. "The Birth of the Populist Party." *Minnesota History* 9 (September 1928): 219–47.

———. "The People's Party in Minnnesota." *Minnesota History* 5 (November 1924): 531–60.

———. *The Populist Revolt: A History of the Farmers' Alliance and the People's Party*. 1931. Reprint. Lincoln, Neb., 1961.

Higham, John. *Strangers in the Land: Patterns of American Nativism, 1860–1925*. New York, 1970.

Hill, Samuel S., Jr. *Southern Churches in Crisis.* New York, 1966.
History of Butler and Bremer Counties, Iowa. Springfield, Ill., 1883.
History of Green County, Wisconsin. Springfield, Ill., 1884.
Holt, Michael Fitzgibbon. *Forging a Majority: The Formation of the Republican Party in Pittsburgh, 1848–1860.* New Haven, Ct., 1969.
———. "The Politics of Impatience: The Origins of Know Nothingism." *Journal of American History* 60 (September 1973): 309–31.
Honigsheim, Paul. "Religion and Assimilation of the Dutch in Michigan." *Michigan History* 26 (Winter 1942): 54–66.
Howard, Perry H. *Political Tendencies in Louisiana.* Rev. ed. Baton Rouge, La., 1971.
Hughes, Kathleen. *The Church in Early Irish Society.* London, 1966.
Hyma, Albert. *Albertus C. Van Raalte and His Dutch Settlements in the United States.* Grand Rapids, Mich., 1947.
Hynes, Michael J. *History of the Diocese of Cleveland.* Cleveland, Ohio, 1953.
Jackson, William Rufus. *Missouri Democracy: A History of the Party and Its Representative Members–Past and Present.* 3 vols. Chicago, 1935.
Jahnige, Thomas P. "Critical Elections and Social Change: Towards a Dynamic Explanation of National Party Competition in the United States." *Polity* 3 (September 1971): 465–500.
Jennings, M. Kent, and Zeigler, Harmon. "The Salience of American State Politics." *American Political Science Review* 64 (June 1970): 523–35.
Jensen, John M. *The United Evangelical Lutheran Church: An Interpretation.* Minneapolis, Minn., 1964.
Jensen, Richard J. "Quantitative Collective Biography: An Application to Metropolitan Elites." In *Quantification in American History: Theory and Research,* edited by Robert P. Swierenga. New York, 1970.
———. *The Winning of the Midwest: Social and Political Conflict, 1888–96.* Chicago, 1971.
Jewell, Malcolm E., and Patterson, Samuel C. *The Legislative Process in the United States.* New York, 1966.
Johnson, Axel P. *Smuggled into Paradise: Saga of an Immigrant Youth.* Philadelphia, 1958.
Jones, E. Terrence. "Using Ecological Regression." *Journal of Interdisciplinary History* 4 (Spring 1974): 593–96.
Josephson, Matthew. *The Politicos, 1865–1896.* 1938. Reprint. New York, [1963].
———. *The Robber Barons: The Great American Capitalists, 1861–1891.* 1934. Reprint. New York, [1962].
Kaplan, Berton H. *Blue Ridge: An Appalachian Community in Transition.* Morgantown, W. Va., 1971.
Kelsey, George D. *Social Ethics among Southern Baptists, 1917–1969.* Metuchen, N.J., 1973.
Kennedy, Ruby Jo Reeves. "Single or Triple Melting Pot? Intermarriage Trends in New Haven, 1870–1940." *American Journal of Sociology* 49 (June 1944): 331–39.
———. "Single or Triple Melting Pot? Intermarriage Trends in New Haven, 1870–1950." *American Journal of Sociology* 58 (July 1952): 56–59.
Kerlinger, Fred N., and Pedhazur, Elazar J. *Multiple Regression in Behavioral Research.* New York, 1973.
Kersten, Lawrence L. *The Lutheran Ethic: The Impact of Religion on Laymen and Clergy.* Detroit, 1970.
Key, V. O., Jr. *American State Politics: An Introduction.* New York, 1956.

———. *Public Opinion and American Democracy.* New York, 1961.

———. "Secular Realignment and the Party System." *Journal of Politics* 21 (May 1959): 198–210.

———. *Southern Politics in State and Nation.* New York, 1949.

———. "A Theory of Critical Elections." *Journal of Politics* 17 (February 1955): 1–18.

King, Michael R., and Seligman, Lester G. "Critical Elections, Congressional Recruitment, and Public Policy." In *Elite Recruitment in Democratic Polities: Comparative Studies across Nations,* edited by Heinz Eulau and Moshe M. Czudnowski. New York, 1976.

Kingsdale, Jon M. "The 'Poor Man's Club': Social Functions of the Urban Working-Class Saloon." *American Quarterly* 25 (October 1973): 472–89.

Kinney, Charles B. *Church and State: The Struggle for Separation in New Hampshire, 1630–1900.* New York, 1955.

Kirlin, Joseph L. J. *Catholicity in Philadelphia.* Philadelphia, 1909.

Kleppner, Paul. *The Cross of Culture: A Social Analysis of Midwestern Politics, 1850–1900.* New York, 1970.

———. *Ethnocultural Studies and Local History: A Preliminary Overview.* The Newberry Papers in Family and Community History. Chicago, 1976.

———. "The Greenback and Prohibition Parties." In *History of U.S. Political Parties,* edited by Arthur M. Schlesinger, Jr., vol. 2, pp. 1549–1696. 4 vols. New York, 1973.

———. "Lincoln and the Immigrant Vote: A Case of Religious Polarization." *Mid-America* 48 (July 1966): 176–95.

Knights, Peter R. " 'Competition' in the U.S. Daily Newspaper Industry, 1865–68." *Journalism Quarterly* 45 (Autumn 1968): 473–80.

———. *The Plain People of Boston, 1830–1860: A Study in City Growth.* New York, 1971.

Knoke, David. *Change and Continuity in American Politics: The Social Bases of Political Parties.* Baltimore, 1976.

Knox, Ronald. *Enthusiasm: A Chapter in the History of Religion with Special Reference to the XVII and XVIII Centuries.* Oxford, 1950.

Kornhauser, Arthur; Mayer, Albert J.; and Sheppard, Harold L. *When Labor Votes: A Study of Auto Workers.* New York, 1956.

Kousser, J. Morgan. "Post-Reconstruction Suffrage Restrictions in Tennessee: A New Look at the V. O. Key Thesis." *Political Science Quarterly* 88 (December 1973): 655–83.

———. *The Shaping of Southern Politics: Suffrage Restriction and the Establishment of the One-Party South, 1880–1910.* New Haven, Ct., 1974.

Kreider, Harry J. *History of the United Lutheran Synod of New York and New England.* Philadelphia, 1954.

Lampard, Eric E. "Two Cheers for Quantitative History: An Agnostic Forward." In *The New Urban History: Quantitative Explorations by American Historians,* edited by Leo F. Schnore and Eric E. Lampard. Princeton, N.J., 1975.

Lane, Robert E. "Political Character and Political Analysis." In *Political Behavior: A Reader in Theory and Research,* edited by Heinz Eulau, Samuel J. Eldersveld, and Morris Janowitz. Glencoe, Ill., 1956.

———. *Political Ideology: Why the American Common Man Believes What He Does.* New York, 1962.

———. *Political Life: Why and How People Get Involved in Politics.* New York, 1965.

――――. *Political Thinking and Consciousness: The Private Life of the Political Mind.* Chicago, 1969.

Larkin, Emmet. "Church and State in Ireland in the Nineteenth Century." *Church History* 31 (1962): 294–306.

Lazarsfeld, Paul F., and Henry, Neil W. *Latent Structure Analysis.* Boston, 1968.

Lazarsfeld, Paul F.; Berelson, Bernard; and Gaudet, Hazel. *The People's Choice: How the Voter Makes up His Mind in a Presidential Campaign.* 2d ed. New York, 1948.

LeMasters, E. E. *Blue-Collar Aristocrats: Life-Styles at a Working-Class Tavern.* Madison, Wis., 1975.

Lenski, Gerhard. *The Religious Factor: A Sociologist's Inquiry.* Rev. ed. Garden City, N.Y., 1963.

Levine, Edward M. *The Irish and Irish Politicians.* Notre Dame, Ind., 1966.

Lichtman, Allan J. "Correlation, Regression, and the Ecological Fallacy: A Critique." *Journal of Interdisciplinary History* 4 (Winter 1974): 417–34.

――――. "Critical Election Theory and the Reality of American Presidential Politics, 1916–40." *American Historical Review* 81 (April 1976): 317–51.

Lieberson, Stanley. *Ethnic Patterns in American Cities.* New York, 1963.

――――. *Language and Ethnic Relations in Canada.* New York, 1970.

Linder, Oliver A. "The Story of Illinois and the Swedish People within Its Borders." In *The Swedish Element in America,* edited by Erik G. Westman. 4 vols. Chicago, 1931.

Lindmark, Sture. *Swedish America, 1914–1932: Studies in Ethnicity with Emphasis on Illinois and Minnesota.* Uppsala, Sweden, 1971.

Lippman, Walter. *Public Opinion.* 1922. Reprint. New York, 1965.

Lord, Robert H.; Sexton, John E.; and Harrington, Edward T. *History of the Archdiocese of Boston.* 3 vols. New York, 1944.

Lossing, Benton John. *A Biography of James A. Garfield.* New York, 1882.

Lowi, Theodore J. "Party, Policy, and Constitution in America." In *The American Party Systems: Stages of Political Development,* edited by William Nisbet Chambers and Walter Dean Burnham. New York, 1967.

Lucas, Henry S. "The Beginnings of Dutch Immigration to Western Michigan, 1846." *Michigan History* 6 (1922): 642–73.

Lucey, William Leo. *The Catholic Church in Maine.* Francestown, N.H., [1958].

Luebke, Frederick C. *Immigrants and Politics: The Germans of Nebraska, 1880–1900.* Lincoln, Neb., 1969.

Lynch, Denis Tilden. *The Wild Seventies.* 1941. 2 vols. Reprint. Port Washington, N.Y., 1971.

Marcus, Robert D. *Grand Old Party: Political Structure in the Gilded Age, 1880–1896.* New York, 1971.

Margolis, Michael. "From Confusion to Confusion: Issues and the American Voter (1956–1972)." *American Political Science Review* 71 (March 1977): 31–43.

Maring, Norman H. *The Baptists in New Jersey.* Valley Forge, Pa., 1964.

Mattson, A[lvin] D. *Polity of the Augustana Lutheran Church.* Rock Island, Ill., 1952.

Maurer, Heinrich H. "Studies in the Sociology of Religion: V. The Fellowship of a Fundamentalist Group. The Missouri Synod." *American Journal of Sociology* 31 (July 1925): 39–57.

Mayer, George H. *The Republican Party, 1854–1966.* 2d ed. New York, 1967.

Mazmanian, Daniel A. *Third Parties in Presidential Elections.* Washington, D.C., 1974.

McAvoy, Thomas T. "The Formation of the Catholic Minority in the United States, 1820–1860." *Review of Politics* 10 (January 1948): 13–34.

_____. *The Great Crisis in American Catholic History, 1895–1900*. Chicago, 1957.

McConville, Sr. Mary St. Patrick. *Political Nativism in the State of Maryland*. Washington, D.C., 1928.

McCormick, Richard L. "Ethno-cultural Interpretations of American Voting Behavior." *Political Science Quarterly* 89 (June 1974): 351–77.

McLoughlin, William G. *New England Dissent, 1630–1833: The Baptists and the Separation of Church and State*. 2 vols. Cambridge, Mass., 1971.

_____. "Pietism and the American Character." *American Quarterly* 17 (September 1965): 163–86.

McNamara, Robert F. *The Diocese of Rochester, 1868–1968*. [Rochester, N.Y.], 1968.

McPhee, William N., and Ferguson, Jack. "Political Immunization." In *Public Opinion and Congressional Elections*, edited by William N. McPhee and William A. Glaser. New York, 1962.

McSeveney, Samuel T. *The Politics of Depression: Political Behavior in the Northeast, 1893–1896*. New York, 1972.

Mering, John Vollmer. *The Whig Party in Missouri*. Columbia, Mo., 1967.

Milbraith, Lester. *Political Participation: How and Why Do People Get Involved in Politics?* Chicago, 1971.

Miller, George H. *Railroads and the Granger Laws*. Madison, Wis., 1971.

Miller, Sally M. "Milwaukee: Of Ethnicity and Labor." In *Socialism and the Cities*, edited by Bruce M. Stave. Port Washington, N.Y., 1975.

Millspaugh, Arthur C. *Party Organization and Machinery in Michigan since 1890*. Baltimore, 1917.

Montgomery, David. *Beyond Equality: Labor and the Radical Republicans, 1862–1872*. New York, 1967.

Moore, Charles. *History of Michigan*. 3 vols. Chicago, 1915.

Moore, Clifford H. "Ohio in National Politics, 1865–1896." *Ohio Archaeological and Historical Publications* 37 (1928): 220–438.

Morgan, H. Wayne. *From Hayes to McKinley: National Party Politics, 1877–1896*. Syracuse, N.Y., 1969.

Naftalin, Arthur. "The Tradition of Protest and the Roots of the Farmer-Labor Party." *Minnesota History* 35 (June 1956): 53–63.

Nelson, E. Clifford, and Fevold, Eugene L. *The Lutheran Church among Norwegian-Americans: A History of the Evangelical Lutheran Church*. 2 vols. Minneapolis, Minn., 1960.

Nelson, Lowry. "Intermarriage among Nationality Groups in a Rural Area of Minnesota." *American Journal of Sociology* 48 (March 1943): 585–92.

Nelson, O. N., ed. *History of Scandinavians and Successful Scandinavians in the United States*. 2 vols. Minneapolis, Minn., 1893–97.

Nettl, J. P. *Political Mobilization: A Sociological Analysis of Methods and Concepts*. New York, 1967.

Nie, Norman, and Andersen, Kristi. "Mass Belief Systems Revisited: Political Change and Attitude Structure." *Journal of Politics* 36 (August 1974): 540–91.

Nolan, Hugh J. *The Most Reverend Francis Patrick Kenrick Third Bishop of Philadelphia*. Philadelphia, 1948.

Noonan, Carroll John. *Nativism in Connecticut, 1829–1860*. Washington, D.C., 1938.

Nugent, Walter T. K. *Money and American Society, 1865–1880*. New York, 1968.

_____. *The Tolerant Populists: Kansas Populism and Nativism*. Chicago, 1963.

Nyholm, Paul C. *The Americanization of the Danish Lutheran Churches in America*. Copenhagen, 1963.

Orcutt, William Dana. *Burrows of Michigan and the Republican Party.* 2 vols. New York, 1917.

O'Shea, John J. *The Two Kenricks: Most Rev. Francis Patrick, Archbishop of Baltimore. Most Rev. Peter Richard, Archbishop of St. Louis.* Philadelphia, 1904.

Paré, George. *The Catholic Church in Detroit, 1701–1888.* Detroit, 1951.

Parenti, Michael. "Political Values and Religious Cultures: Jews, Catholics, and Protestants." *Journal for the Scientific Study of Religion* 6 (Fall 1967): 259–69.

Parrish, William E. *A History of Missouri. Volume III: 1860 to 1875.* Missouri Sesquicentennial History Series. Columbia, Mo., 1973.

Parsons, Stanley B. *The Populist Context: Rural versus Urban Power on a Great Plains Frontier.* Westport, Ct., 1973.

Perlman, Selig. "Upheaval and Reorganization." In *History of Labour in the United States,* edited by John R. Commons. 4 vols. New York, 1918–35.

Perloff, Harvey S.; Dunn, Edgar S., Jr.; Lampard, Eric E.; and Muth, Richard F. *Regions, Resources, and Economic Growth.* Lincoln, Neb., 1967.

Pessen, Edward. "Some Timeless Standards for the Modern Historian." *Prologue* 7 (Winter 1975): 243–48.

Pieters, Aleida J. *A Dutch Settlement in Michigan.* Grand Rapids, Mich., 1923.

Pilcher, Elijah H. *Protestantism in Michigan: Being a Special History of the Methodist Episcopal Church and Incidentally of Other Denominations.* Detroit, 1878.

Pillsbury, Hobart. *New Hampshire: Resources, Attractions, and Its People.* 7 vols. New York, 1927.

Plumb, Ralph G. *Badger Politics, 1836–1930.* Manitowoc, Wis., 1930.

Pomper, Gerald M. *Elections in America: Control and Influence in Democratic Politics.* New York, 1973.

———. "From Confusion to Clarity: Issues and American Voters, 1956–68." *American Political Science Review* 66 (June 1972): 415–28.

Pool, Ithiel de Sola; Abelson, Robert P.; and Popkin, Samuel L. *Candidates, Issues, and Strategies: A Computer Simulation of the 1960 and 1964 Presidential Elections.* Rev. ed. Cambridge, Mass., 1965.

Porter, George H. *Ohio Politics during the Civil War Period.* New York, 1911.

Porter, Kirk H. *A History of Suffrage in the United States.* Chicago, 1918.

Powell, Thomas E. *The Democratic Party of the State of Ohio.* 2 vols. N.p., 1913.

Power, Richard Lyle. *Planting Corn Belt Culture: The Impress of the Upland Southerner and Yankee in the Old Northwest.* Indianapolis, 1953.

Pratt, William C. " 'Jimmie Higgins' and the Reading Socialist Community: An Exploration of the Socialist Rank and File." In *Socialism and the Cities,* edited by Bruce M. Stave. Port Washington, N.Y., 1975.

Prescott, Gerald L. "Wisconsin Farm Leaders in the Gilded Age." *Agricultural History* 44 (April 1970): 183–99.

Pulley, Raymond H. *Old Virginia Restored: An Interpretation of the Progressive Impulse, 1870–1930.* Charlottesville, Va., 1968.

Qualey, Carlton C. "Some National Groups in Minnesota." *Minnesota History* 31 (March 1950): 18–32.

Raum, Green B. *History of Illinois Republicanism.* Chicago, 1900.

Ravitch, Diane. *The Great School Wars, New York City, 1805–1973: A History of the Public Schools as Battlefield of Social Change.* New York, 1974.

Rezneck, Samuel. "Distress, Relief, and Discontent in the United States during the Depression of 1873–78." *Journal of Political Economy* 58 (December 1950): 494–512.

Rhodes, James Ford. *History of the United States from the Compromise of 1850 to the Final Restoration of Home Rule at the South in 1877*. 7 vols. New York, 1906.
———. *History of the United States from Hayes to McKinley, 1876–1896*. New York, 1919.
Riesman, David; Glazer, Nathan; and Denny, Reuel. *The Lonely Crowd: A Study of the Changing American Character*. New Haven, Ct., 1950.
Rogin, Michael Paul. *The Intellectuals and McCarthy: The Radical Specter*. Cambridge, Mass., 1967.
———, and Shover, John L. *Political Change in California: Critical Elections and Social Movements*. Westport, Ct., 1970.
Rokeach, Milton. *Beliefs, Attitudes, and Values: A Theory of Organization and Change*. San Francisco, 1972.
———. *The Nature of Human Values*. New York, 1973.
———. *The Open and Closed Mind: Investigations into the Nature of Belief Systems and Personality Systems*. New York, 1960.
———. "Religious Values and Social Compassion." *Review of Religious Research* 11 (Fall 1969): 24–38.
———. "Value Systems in Religion." *Review of Religious Research* 11 (Fall 1969): 3–23.
Rönnegard, Sam. *Prairie Shepherd: Lars Paul Esbjörn and the Beginnings of the Augustana Lutheran Church*. Rock Island, Ill., 1952.
Rothensteiner, John. *History of the Archdiocese of St. Louis*. 2 vols. St. Louis, 1928.
Schafer, Joseph. *Four Wisconsin Counties: Prairie and Forest*. Madison, Wis., 1927.
Schmeckebier, Laurence Frederick. *History of the Know-Nothing Party in Maryland*. Baltimore, 1899.
Schoolland, Marian M. *The Story of Van Raalte*. Grand Rapids, Mich., 1951.
Schroeder, W. Widick, and Obenhaus, Victor. *Religion in American Culture: Unity and Diversity in a Midwestern County*. Glencoe, Ill., 1964.
Schwartz, Michael. *Radical Protest and Social Structure: The Southern Farmers' Alliance and Cotton Tenancy, 1880–1890*. New York, 1976.
Schwarzweller, Harry K.; Brown, James S.; and Mangalam, J. J. *Mountain Families in Transition: A Case Study of Appalachian Migration*. University Park, Pa., 1971.
Sellers, Charles. "The Equilibrium Cycle in Two-Party Politics." *Public Opinion Quarterly* 29 (Spring 1965): 16–38.
Shade, William Gerald. *Banks or No Banks: The Money Issue in Western Politics, 1832–1865*. Detroit, 1972.
———; Hopper, Stanley D.; Jacobson, David; and Moiles, Stephen E. "Partisanship in the United States Senate: 1869–1901." *Journal of Interdisciplinary History* 4 (Autumn 1973): 185–205.
Sharp, John K. *History of the Diocese of Brooklyn, 1853–1953*. New York, 1954.
Shaughnessy, Gerald. *Has the Immigrant Kept the Faith?* New York, 1925.
Shea, John Gilmary. *History of the Catholic Church in the United States*. New York, 1892.
Shibutani, Tamotsu. "Reference Groups as Perspectives." In *Readings in Reference Group Theory and Research*, edited by Herbert H. Hyman and Eleanor Singer. New York, 1968.
Shilling, David C. "Relation of Southern Ohio to the South during the Decade Preceding the Civil War." *Quarterly Publication of the Historical and Philosophical Society of Ohio* 8 (January–March 1899): 3–28.

Sievers, Harry J. *Benjamin Harrison: Hoosier Statesman, from the Civil War to the White House, 1865–1888.* New York, 1959.

Smith, Joseph P., ed. *History of the Republican Party in Ohio.* 2 vols. Chicago, 1898.

Smith, M. Brewster. "Personality in Politics: A Conceptual Map with Application to the Problem of Political Rationality." In *Political Research and Political Theory,* edited by Oliver Garceau. Cambridge, Mass., 1968.

Smith, Timothy L. *Revivalism and Social Reform: American Protestantism on the Eve of the Civil War.* New York, 1965.

Smyth, James W. *History of the Catholic Church in Woonsocket [Rhode Island] and Vicinity.* Woonsocket, R.I., 1903.

Social Science Research Council. Report of the Committee on Historiography. *The Social Sciences in Historical Study.* Bulletin 64. New York, 1954.

Sorauf, Frank J. *Party Politics in America.* Boston, 1968.

————. "Political Parties and Political Analysis." In *The American Party Systems: Stages of Political Development,* edited by William Nisbet Chambers and Walter Dean Burnham. New York, 1967.

Spain, Rufus B. *At Ease in Zion: Social History of the Southern Baptists, 1865–1900.* Nashville, 1961.

Sproat, John G. *"The Best Men": Liberal Reformers in the Gilded Age.* New York, 1968.

Squires, James Duane. *The Granite State of the United States: A History of New Hampshire from 1623 to the Present.* 4 vols. New York, 1956.

Stark, Rodney, and Glock, Charles Y. *American Piety: The Nature of Religious Commitment.* Berkeley, 1968.

Stave, Bruce M. "The Great Depression and Urban Political Continuity: Bridgeport Chooses Socialism." In *Socialism and the Cities,* edited by Bruce M. Stave. Port Washington, N.Y., 1975.

Steffens, D. H. *Doctor Carl Ferdinand Wilhelm Walther.* Philadelphia, 1907.

Stellhorn, August C. *Schools of the Lutheran Church–Missouri Synod.* St. Louis, 1963.

Stephenson, George M. "Sidelights on the History of the Swedes in the St. Croix Valley." *Minnesota History* 17 (December 1936): 396–405.

Stevens, Walter B. *Centennial History of Missouri, 1820–1921.* 3 vols. St. Louis and Chicago, 1921.

Stickney, Charles. *Know-Nothingism in Rhode Island.* Providence, R.I., 1894.

Strand, A. E., ed. *A History of the Swedish-Americans of Minnesota.* 2 vols. Chicago, 1910.

Strauss, Anselm L. *Images of the American City.* New York, 1961.

Streiker, Lowell D., and Strober, Gerald S. *Religion and the New Majority: Billy Graham, Middle America, and the Politics of the 70s.* New York, 1972.

Stritch, Alfred G. "Political Nativism in Cincinnati, 1830–1860." *Records of the American Catholic Historical Society* 48 (September 1937): 258–64.

Strommen, Merton P.; Brekke, Milo L.; Underwager, Ralph C.; and Johnson, Arthur L. *A Study of Generations.* Minneapolis, Minn., 1972.

Sundquist, James L. *Dynamics of the Party System: Alignment and Realignment of Political Parties in the United States.* Washington, D.C., 1973.

Sweeney, Kevin. "Rum, Romanism, Representation, and Reform: Coalition Politics in Massachusetts, 1847–1853." *Civil War History* 22 (June 1976): 116–37.

Sweet, William Warren. *The Methodist Episcopal Church and the Civil War.* Cincinnati, 1912.

————. *Religion on the American Frontier: The Baptists, 1783–1830*. New York, 1931.

Swierenga, Robert P. "The Ethnic Voter and the First Lincoln Election." In *Ethnic Voters and the Election of Lincoln*, edited by Frederick C. Luebke. Lincoln, Neb., 1971.

————. "Ethnocultural Political Analysis: A New Approach to American Ethnic Studies." *Journal of American Studies* 5 (April 1971): 59–79.

————, ed. *Quantification in American History: Theory and Practice*. New York, 1970.

Thernstrom, Stephen, and Knights, Peter R. "Men in Motion: Some Data and Speculations about Urban Population Mobility in Nineteenth-Century America." *Journal of Interdisciplinary History* 1 (Autumn 1970): 7–35.

Thomas, Sr. Evangeline. *Nativism in the Old Northwest, 1850–60*. Washington, D.C., 1936.

Thompson, Ernest Trice. *Presbyterians in the South*. 3 vols. Richmond, Va., 1973.

[Thompson, James Joseph.] *The Archdiocese of Chicago: Antecedents and Developments*. Des Plaines, Ill., 1920.

Throne, Mildred. "The Anti-Monopoly Party in Iowa, 1873–74." *Iowa Journal of History* 52 (October 1954): 289–326.

————. "The Liberal Republican Party in Iowa, 1872." *Iowa Journal of History* 53 (April 1955): 121–52.

Tiryakian, Edward A. "Neither Marx nor Durkheim . . . Perhaps Weber." *American Journal of Sociology* 81 (July 1975): 1–33.

Tomasi, Silvano. *Piety and Power: The Role of Italian Parishes in the New York Metropolitan Area*. New York, 1975.

Tontz, Robert L. "Membership of General Farmers' Organizations, United States, 1874–1960." *Agricultural History* 38 (July 1964): 143–56.

Townsend, Walter A. *Illinois Democracy: A History of the Party and Its Representative Members, Past and Present*. 2 vols. Springfield, Ill., 1935.

Trask, David S. "Formation and Failure: The Populist Party in Seward County, 1890–1892." *Nebraska History* 51 (Fall 1970): 281–301.

Trefousse, Hans L. "The Republican Party, 1854–1864." In *History of U.S. Political Parties*, edited by Arthur M. Schlesinger, Jr., vol. 2, pp. 1141–1277. 4 vols. New York, 1973.

Troen, Selwyn K. *The Public and the Schools: Shaping the St. Louis System, 1838–1920*. Columbia, Mo., 1975.

Tuska, Benjamin. *Know-Nothingism in Baltimore, 1854–1860*. New York, [1930].

Tyack, David B. *The One Best System: A History of American Urban Education*. Cambridge, Mass., 1974.

Underwood, Kenneth. *Protestant and Catholic*. Boston, 1957.

Unger, Irwin. *The Greenback Era: A Social and Political History of American Finance, 1865–1879*. Princeton, N.J., 1964.

Van Buren, A. D. P. "Our Temperance Conflict." *Michigan Pioneer and Historical Collections* 13 (1888): 388–407.

Van Der Zee, Jacob. *The British in Iowa*. Iowa City, Iowa, 1922.

————. *The Hollanders of Iowa*. Iowa City, Iowa, 1912.

Vecoli, Rudolph J. *The Peoples of New Jersey*. The New Jersey Historical Series. Princeton, N.J., 1965.

Verba, Sidney, and Nie, Norman H. *Participation in America: Political Democracy and Social Equality*. New York, 1972.

Voegeli, V. Jacque. *Free But Not Equal: The Midwest and the Negro during the Civil War.* Chicago, 1967.

Wade, Mason. *The French Canadians, 1760–1967.* 2 vols. Rev. ed. Toronto, 1968.

Wagandt, Charles L. "Election by Sword and Ballot: The Emancipationist Victory of 1863." *Maryland Historical Magazine* 59 (June 1964): 143–64.

Walker, David B. *Politics and Ethnocentrism: The Case of the Franco-Americans.* Brunswick, Maine, 1961.

Wallas, Graham. *Human Nature in Politics.* 1908. Reprint. Lincoln, Neb., 1962.

Ward, David. *Cities and Immigrants: A Geography of Change in Nineteenth-Century America.* New York, 1971.

Warner, Sam B., Jr. *Streetcar Suburbs: The Process of Growth in Boston, 1870–1900.* New York, 1970.

Watson, William H. *History of the Michigan Conference of the Evangelical Church.* Harrisburg, Pa., 1942.

Weatherford, W. D., and Brewer, Earl D. C. *Life and Religion in Southern Appalachia: An Interpretation of Selected Data from the Southern Appalachian States.* New York, 1962.

Weber, Max. "Politics as a Vocation." In *From Max Weber: Essays in Sociology,* edited by H. H. Gerth and C. Wright Mills. New York, 1958.

Weisberger, Bernard A. *They Gathered at the River: The Story of the Great Revivalists and Their Impact upon Religion in America.* Chicago, 1953.

Wells, O. V. "The Depression of 1873–79." *Agricultural History* 11 (July 1937): 237–51.

Wentz, Abdel Ross. *History of the Evangelical Lutheran Synod of Maryland of the United Lutheran Church in America.* Harrisburg, Pa., 1920.

Williams, Daniel Jenkins. *One Hundred Years of Welsh Calvinistic Methodism in America.* Philadelphia, 1937.

Williams, R. Hal. *The Democratic Party and California Politics, 1880–1896.* Stanford, Calif., 1973.

Williams, T[homas] J. C., and McKinsey, Folger. *History of Frederick County, Maryland.* 2 vols. 1910. Reprint. Baltimore, 1967.

Williamson, Chilton. "Rhode Island Suffrage since the Dorr War." *New England Quarterly* 28 (March 1955): 34–50.

Williamson, Jeffrey G. *Late Nineteenth-Century American Development: A General Equilibrium History.* Cambridge, 1974.

Windsor, Justin, ed. *The Memorial History of Boston, Including Suffolk County, Massachusetts, 1630–1880.* 4 vols. Boston, 1885.

Woodman, Harold D. "Chicago Businessmen and the 'Granger' Laws." *Agricultural History* 36 (January 1962): 16–24.

Woodward, C. Vann. *Origins of the New South, 1877–1913.* Baton Rouge, La., 1966.

Wright, James Edward. "The Ethnocultural Model of Voting: A Behavioral and Historical Critique." *American Behavioral Scientist* 16 (May–June 1973): 35–56.

————. *The Politics of Populism: Dissent in Colorado.* New Haven, Ct., 1974.

Yinger, J. Milton. *The Scientific Study of Religion.* New York, 1970.

Youngdale, James M. *Populism: A Psychohistorical Perspective.* Port Washington, N.Y., 1975.

Zornow, William F. "Clement L. Vallandingham and the Democratic Party in 1864." *Bulletin of the Historical and Philosophical Society of Ohio* 19 (January 1961): 22–37.

Zwierlein, Frederick J. *The Life and Letters of Bishop McQuaid.* 3 vols. Rochester, N.Y., 1925–27.

H. Unpublished Materials

Anderson, Odin W. "The Attitudes of the Norwegian Lutheran Church towards Social and Economic Problems." Master's thesis, University of Wisconsin, 1962.

Baum, Dale. "The Political Realignment of the 1850s: Know-Nothingism and the Republican Majority in Massachusetts." Typescript. University of Minnesota, 1976.

Brady, David. "Congressional Policy Responses to Issue[s] and Elections: A Time Series Analysis." Paper presented at the annual meeting of the Social Science History Association, Philadelphia, October 1976.

Brady, Hugh. "Voting, Class, and Demography in Ante-Bellum Mississippi." Seminar paper, Northern Illinois University, 1971.

Burnham, Walter Dean; Clubb, Jerome M.; and Flanigan, William H. "Partisan Realignment: A Systemic Perspective." Paper presented at the Mathematical Social Science Board Conference on Popular Voting, Ithaca, N.Y., 1973.

Cameron, Ross J. "Political Realignment in the Late Antebellum North." Paper presented at the annual convention of the Southern Historical Association, Atlanta, November 1976.

Campbell, Ballard C., Jr. "Political Parties, Cultural Groups, and Contested Issues: Voting in the Illinois, Iowa, and Wisconsin House of Representatives, 1886–1895." Ph.D. dissertation, University of Wisconsin, 1970.

Clancy, Kevin, and Benson, Lee. "America the Fragmented: An Exploration of the Effects of Class, Ethnicity, and Religion on Political and Social Attitudes and Behavior." Paper presented at the annual meeting of the Social Science History Association, Philadelphia, October 1976.

Doolen, Richard M. "The Greenback Party in the Great Lakes Middlewest." Ph.D. dissertation, University of Michigan, 1969.

Duis, Perry R. "The Saloon and the Public City: Chicago and Boston, 1880–1920." Ph.D. dissertation, University of Chicago, 1975.

Faler, Paul Gustaf. "Workingmen, Mechanics, and Social Change: Lynn, Massachusetts, 1800–1860." Ph.D. dissertation, University of Wisconsin, 1971.

Frasier, Dudley P. "The Antecedents and Formation of the Republican Party in New Hampshire." Typescript. New Hampshire State Library, [1945].

Gillette, Howard Frank. "Corrupt and Contented: Philadelphia's Political Machine, 1865–1887." Ph.D. dissertation, Yale University, 1970.

Grossman, Lawrence. "The Democratic Party and the Negro: A Study in Northern and National Politics, 1868–1892." Ph.D. dissertation, City University of New York, 1973.

Gudelunas, William A., Jr. "Before the Molly Maguires: The Emergence of the Ethno-Religious Factor in the Politics of the Lower Anthracite Region." Ph.D. dissertation, Lehigh University, 1973.

Gutman, Herbert George. "Social and Economic Structure and Depression: American Labor in 1873 and 1874." Ph.D. dissertation, University of Wisconsin, 1959.

Hammarberg, Melvyn Alan. "The Indiana Voter: A Study in Nineteenth-Century Rural Bases of Partisanship." Ph.D. dissertation, University of Pennsylvania, 1970.

Hammond, John Lockwood, Jr. "The Revivalist Political Ethos." Ph.D. dissertation, University of Chicago, 1972.

Harmond, Richard P. "Tradition and Change in the Gilded Age: A Political History of Massachusetts, 1878–1893." Ph.D. dissertation, Columbia University, 1966.

Lambert, Kermit A. "Yankees in the Cornfields: Sycamore, Illinois, 1869–1884." Seminar paper, Northern Illinois University, 1972.

McCoy, Alexandra. "Political Affiliations of American Economic Elites: Wayne County, Michigan, 1844, 1860, As a Test Case." Ph.D. dissertation, Wayne State University, 1965.

McDaniel, John Edgar, Jr. "The Presidential Election of 1888." Ph.D. dissertation, University of Texas, 1970.

McKinney, Gordon Bartlett. "Mountain Republicanism, 1876–1900." Ph.D. dissertation, Northwestern University, 1971.

McLaughlin, Tom LeRoy. "Popular Reaction to the Idea of Negro Equality in Twelve Non-Slaveholding States, 1864–1869: A Quantitative Analysis." Ph.D. dissertation, Washington State University, 1969.

Mol, Johannis Jacob. "Theology and Americanization: The Effect of Pietism and Orthodoxy on Adjustments to a New Culture." Ph.D. dissertation, Columbia University, 1960.

Moore, Margaret M. "Voting Behavior Analysis, 1880–1892: Pennsylvania and Maryland." Seminar paper, The Smithsonian Institution, 1972.

Munger, Frank. "Two-Party Politics in the State of Indiana." Ph.D. dissertation, Harvard University, 1955.

Nixon, Herman Clarence. "The Populist Movement in Iowa." Ph.D. dissertation University of Chicago, 1925.

Otto, Luther B. "Catholic and Lutheran Political Cultures in Medium-Sized Wisconsin Cities." Master's thesis, University of Wisconsin, 1963.

Parker, Albert Charles Edward. "Empire Stalemate: Voting Behavior in New York State, 1860–1892." Ph.D. dissertation, Washington University, 1975.

Paul, William George. "The Shadow of Equality: The Negro in Baltimore, 1864–1911." Ph.D. dissertation, University of Wisconsin, 1972.

Peterson, Roger D. "The Reaction to a Heterogeneous Society: A Behavioral and Quantitative Analysis of Northern Voting Behavior 1845–1870, Pennsylvania a Test Case." Ph.D. dissertation, University of Pittsburgh, 1970.

Quay, William L. "The Philadelphia Democrats: 1880–1910." Ph.D. dissertation, Lehigh University, 1969.

Raab, Deborah. "A Study of Voting Behavior in Maryland, 1875–1890." Seminar paper, The Smithsonian Institution, 1972.

Rickard, Louise E. "The Impact of Populism on Electoral Patterns in Kansas, 1880–1900: A Quantitative Analysis." Ph.D. dissertation, University of Kansas, 1974.

Ryskamp, Henry Jacob. "The Dutch in Western Michigan." Ph.D. dissertation, University of Michigan, 1930.

Sanding, Ruth B. "The Norwegian Element in the Early History of Wisconsin." Master's thesis, University of Wisconsin, 1936.

Schroeder, Robert L. "The Challenge to Republican Supremacy in DeKalb County, 1874–1896." Seminar paper, Northern Illinois University, 1973.

————. "Political Issues and Elections in DeKalb County, 1874–1896." Seminar paper, Northern Illinois University, 1974.

Shaw, Douglas V. "The Making of an Immigrant Community: Ethnic and Cultural Conflict in Jersey City, New Jersey, 1850–1877." Ph.D. dissertation, University of Rochester, 1972.

Shortridge, Ray Myles. "Voting Patterns in the American Midwest, 1840–1872."
    Ph.D. dissertation, University of Michigan, 1974.
Silva, Philip Thomas, Jr. "The Spindle City: Labor, Politics, and Religion in Fall River,
    Massachusetts, 1870–1905." Ph.D. dissertation, Fordham University, 1973.
Smith, Rockwell C. "Church Affiliation as Social Differentiator in Rural Wisconsin."
    Ph.D. dissertation, University of Wisconsin, 1942.
Sterling, Robert E. "Civil War Draft Resistance in the Middle West." Ph.D. disserta-
    tion, Northern Illinois University, 1974.
Tomlinson, Kenneth Larry. "Indiana Republicans and the Negro Suffrage Issue, 1865–
    1867." Ed.D. dissertation, Ball State University, 1971.
Towey, Martin Gerald. "The People's Party in Missouri." Ph.D. dissertation, St. Louis
    University, 1971.
Trask, David S. "The Nebraska Populist Party: A Social and Political Analysis." Ph.D.
    dissertation, University of Nebraska, 1971.
Ulrich, Robert J. "The Bennett Law of 1889: Education and Politics in Wisconsin."
    Ph.D. dissertation, University of Wisconsin, 1965.
Walkowitz, Daniel Jay. "Working Class Culture in the Gilded Age: The Iron Workers of
    Troy, New York, and the Cotton Workers of Cohoes, New York—1855–1884."
    Ph.D. dissertation, University of Rochester, 1972.

Index

Paul Kleppner, professor of history at Northern Illinois University, is the author of *The Cross of Culture: A Social Analysis of Midwestern Politics, 1850–1900*.

Text set in Mergenthaler VIP Times Roman
Design and composition by The University
        of North Carolina Press
Printed on sixty-pound Olde Style by
        S. D. Warren Company
Bound in Roxite B 51544 Vellum by
        The Holliston Mills, Inc.
Printing and binding by Kingsport Press
Published by The University of North Carolina
        Press